W9-BSD-362

GCLS

Gloucester County
           Library System

389 Wolfert Station Road
Mullica Hill, NJ 08062
(609) 223-6000

The Macmillan
Encyclopedic Dictionary
of Numismatics

Other books by Richard G. Doty
Money of the World
Paper Money of the World
Coins of the World
Studies on Money in Early America
(with Eric P. Newman)

The Macmillan Encyclopedic Dictionary of Numismatics

Richard G. Doty

Macmillan Publishing Co., Inc.
New York

Collier Macmillan Publishers
London

For Mrs. L., and for Henry the Coin King

 Created by Media Projects Incorporated

Staff, Media Projects Incorporated
    Carter Smith: President
    Beverly Gary Kempton: Senior Editor
    Frank Nims, Ellen Coffey: Assistant Editors

Macmillan Publishing Co., Inc.
866 Third Avenue, New York, N.Y 10022
Collier Macmillan Canada, Inc.

Library of Congress Cataloging in Publication Data
Doty, Richard G.
    The Macmillan encyclopedic dictionary of numismatics.
    "A Media Projects Incorporated book."
    Bibliography: p.
    1. Numismatics—Dictionaries.   I. Title.
CJ69.D67   737'.03   81-18632
ISBN 0-02-532270-2   AACR2

10 9 8 7 6 5 4 3 2 1

Printed in the United States of America

Contents

Foreword

Numismatics as a science and coin collecting as a hobby have both made appreciable strides in recent decades. Fifty years ago, coin collecting was largely the prerogative of a leisured few. Today it is a very popular and widespread form of relaxation. The interest in numismatics, and the number of people engaged in assembling private coin collections, increased enormously after World War II. It is no exaggeration to say there are now multitudes of collectors throughout the world, as well as in the United States.

This growth has generated a demand for numismatic literature. Laymen and advanced students are hungry for books dealing with the many facets of numismatics and their historical connection. The earliest book devoted to coins, as distinct from the economic aspects of money, was Andrea Fulvio's *Illustrium Imagines,* published in Rome in 1517. During the ensuing centuries the list of publications swelled: in the late nineteenth and twentieth centuries alone thousands appeared. Most of these, however, dealt with narrow and specialized areas of highly scientific numismatics and were of use only to the advanced research student or the trained scholar. (Coins themselves were usually regarded as merely fragments of archeological evidence.) A beginning student, and particularly the new collector, found little in the available literature to guide him. Above all, few publications were concerned with anything but the Classic Greek and Roman worlds.

The considerable attention given to modern coinage, especially in recent years, has opened new fields of investigation for the reader and the potential author. Yet books encompassing ancient coinage and the numerous and multifaceted aspects of coinage since 1500 have always been in short supply. For example, the first volume to adopt a dictionary format was Carl Christian Schmieder's *Handwörterbuch der gesamten Münzkunde,* published in 1740. It was a promising beginning, but had no immediate successors. Quite probably Schmieder foresaw a market not yet recognized by his colleagues. The next attempt was made by Heinrich Halke, whose *Handwörterbuch der Münzkunde und ihrer Hilfswissenschaften* did not appear until 1909, and unfortunately did little to fill the gap. In 1915, Edoardo Martinori's dictionary, *La moneta: vocabulario generale* was published, a book somewhat limited by the author's strong Italian bias and imperfect knowledge of foreign languages.

The next most promising effort was Albert R. Frey's *Dictionary of Numismatic Names,* published in 1917 under the imprint of the American Numismatic Society in New York City. As Frey observed, "The beginner will find in it definitions of such terms as he will encounter during his perusal of numismatic works in both English and five foreign languages." He also hoped the advanced student would benefit from the citations given to the many authorities called upon in the volume's preparation. Although Frey's ambition was apt to exceed his grasp, the Society's sponsorship of a work devoted to modern numismatics and coinage was a most encouraging sign. The work was reprinted in 1973 with the addition of a glossary of numismatic terms in five languages prepared by Mark M. Salton of New York. But perhaps the best of these first dictionaries was Friedrich von Schrötter's *Wörterbuch der Münzkunde,* which was published in Berlin in 1930, and benefitted from the collaboration of several of the period's foremost numismatic scholars.

More than sixty years have elapsed since Frey's work was introduced. In that time, the world of numismatics changed beyond recognition. The explosion of public interest created a revolution and produced a clear need for a book embodying the best in modern historical and numismatic research, tailored for a greatly expanded readership. I am glad to say that Richard G. Doty's *Macmillan Encyclopedic Dictionary of Numismatics* is such a book and more than meets these requirements. The author, Curator of Modern Coins and Paper Money at the American Numismatic Society in New York, is eminently qualified for the task he set himself. His considerable knowledge of history and wide experience with coins are joined in a text distinguished for its clarity and readability.

The scope of Dr. Doty's book, which covers coinage from its beginnings to the present, is far broader than its predecessors. In addition to coins, coin denominations, and methods of coinage, he deals with the related fields of medals, tokens, decorations, and paper money. And he does not neglect the more remote topics of coin weights and primitive money, about which there is little available in English. The fascinating and difficult subject of forgeries, and the detection of them, is also given ample treatment. A brilliant range of splendid photographs fully supports the text. In short, there is no question that Doty's new encyclopedic dictionary will be the standard in the field for years to come. It is a highly recommended addition to the library of anyone interested in numismatics.

HENRY GRUNTHAL

Introduction

In numismatics, as in many other branches of human knowledge, we are currently in a period of growth and are rapidly expanding the boundaries of our knowledge. But as we do so, we become even more specialized. Those of us in the numerous branches of numismatics now find that we speak variants of the same language, and are occasionally confused by one another's terminology. Thus, a major reason for writing the *Macmillan Encyclopedic Dictionary of Numismatics* was to bring together the myriad disparate terms, and to relate them within a single book.

But the hobbyist too claimed my attention. If today's specialists are unsure of terminology, what of the collector who begins with a limited vocabulary or none at all? I thought that a general dictionary of numismatic terms, ranging from the basic to the specialized, would be of use to collectors. This book was also constructed with them in mind.

Then too there is the lamentable fact that nothing like the present book exists. Albert R. Frey's *Dictionary of Numismatic Names,* published in 1917, is the only numismatic dictionary in English readily

available to the public. However, it is hopelessly outdated and frequently in error. Furthermore, it contains no illustrations, a feature I consider essential to such a work. There is much activity in the production of numismatic lexicons in Germany—the works of Schrötter and Kroha are outstanding examples—but these books have yet to be translated into English. In short, my experience as a museum curator convinced me of the need for a volume akin to this. Unable to find one, I sat down to compile it.

As I did so, I set several goals. I wished to discuss each term in enough detail to adequately explain it to the reader. Therefore every entry begins with a brief definition, followed by a longer account of the subject. The latter traces the purpose, value, and history of the coin or other object, and describes its appearance. Entries for mechanical processes describe their subjects in the same way. Each article is complete in itself; cross-references are provided to allow further research if desired.

Upon beginning this book, I discovered almost immediately that to keep it within manageable proportions I would have to limit the number of entries. Thus, I selected topics on the basis of their importance to numismatics as a whole and to its sub-disciplines (ancient coinage, paper money, mint errors, etc.). The choices are mine alone, and are based on thirty years of collecting and working with everything from ancient coins to modern scrip. Here are the terms I have asked others to define in the course of those years, and the terms others have asked me to define. So this dictionary acquired its rationale and its form.

If it is true that no book emerges from a vacuum, but rather from need, interest, and circumstance, it is equally true that no book has a single author. It is, in fact, an aggregate of the compiler's experiences and readings. In my own case, I acknowledge the influence of many people. Some I have read; they are listed in the Bibliography. Others contributed to my knowledge through conversation; they include Henry Grunthal, Kenneth MacKenzie, the late Raymond Weil, and my fellow-Curators at the American Numismatic Society, who exhibited exemplary patience as I questioned them continuously during eight months of writing. My special thanks go also to Francis D. Campbell and Margaret R. D'Ambrosio. As Librarian and Associate Librarian, respectively, of the American Numismatic Society's collection of books and related materials—the most extensive numismatic library in the world —they were particularly helpful in the compilation of the Bibliography. Except as noted, all coins and other numismatic objects are from the Society's collection. All errors are my own.

A final word: the reader will note that dimensions are given in millimeters, while weights are in grams. In the main this was done to more accurately describe the items' sizes and weights, but it complies with numismatic practice outside the United States. For the reader unfamiliar with the system, conversions from metric to traditional measures should pose no problem if the number 25 is kept in mind: 25.4 millimeters equals one inch; 28.35 grams equals one ounce avoirdupois. Thus an ounce is slightly more than 25 grams, while an inch is almost exactly 25 millimeters.

The Macmillan
Encyclopedic Dictionary
of Numismatics

A

ABBREVIATION A shortened form of a word or series of words, ordinarily appearing as part of a coin's legend.

Abbreviations have been employed almost from the beginning of coinage, as most coins are too small to convey a great deal of information, especially if the words are spelled out. Abbreviations may appear in a coin's legend, or anywhere else—in its exergue, its field, or on its edge. Wherever their location, they convey information either about who issued the coin (a ruler, along with his titles, for example), or about the coin itself (its denomination, the percentage of precious metal it contains, where it was struck, who manufactured it, or other facts considered important by the coiners). Although both these uses of abbreviations can appear on any given coin, one usually predominates.

The use of abbreviations was common in ancient times. The Greeks adopted them in part because initially they lacked the skill to cut elaborate legends in a coin die. While their skills improved rapidly, eventually yielding some of the triumphs of Western numismatic art, Greek legends and inscriptions remained simple, with abbreviations a prominent feature.

The Romans used abbreviations on coinage more consistently than any other ancient people. While abbreviations on republican issues often named the coin's place of mintage and the magistrates responsible for it, coinage of the Roman Empire employed abbreviated obverse legends primarily on behalf of the ruler. These legends, which frequently continued on the reverse, set the tone for much of Western coinage until modern times. Facts about the coinage itself were usually contained in shorter inscriptions on the reverse—a practice which has continued to the present.

A large brass sestertius of Nero (ruled A.D. 54–68) illustrates the Roman penchant for abbreviating long statements. The obverse legend reads NEROCLAVDCAE-SARAVGGERPMTRPIMPPP, without punctuation, which translates: "Nero Claudius Caesar Augustus Germanicus, Pontifex Maximus [high priest of the Roman state religion], Tribune [originally the representative of the people in the Roman re-

Abbreviation.

Left: Roman Empire, Nero, sestertius, A.D. *64–66.*
Center: Bavaria, thaler, 1769.
Right: Durango, Mexico, 8 reales, 1862.

public], Emperor, Father of the Country." The only reference to the coin itself is a large sc on the reverse, the abbreviation for *Senatus Consulto* ("By Decree of the Senate"), meaning the coin theoretically was struck under the aegis of the old Roman legislative body, which had been rendered impotent by the new imperial regime.

A Bavarian thaler, minted some seventeen hundred years after Nero's sestertius, illustrates the continued use of abbreviations to honor a state's ruler. Here, the abbreviated legend reads D.G.MAX.IOS.U.B.D.S.R.I.A.&EL.L.L., which in translation states: "By the Grace of God, Maximilian Joseph, Duke of Both Bavarias, Arch-Chamberlain of the Holy Roman Empire, Elector and Landgrave of Leuchtenberg." The reverse of this particular coin bears a portrait of Christ with St. Mary, the patroness of Bavaria. Except for the date, no data is given concerning the coin itself, either in an abbreviated form or spelled out in full. With the Bavarian thaler, the use of abbreviated legends to extol a prince reaches its apex and clearly reflects the importance of the ruler in the eighteenth century.

This predominance ended, however, and with it went the emphasis on the ruler in numismatic abbreviations. As republican forms of government arose in the Americas and elsewhere, abbreviations said more about the nature of the coinage

itself. The shift is best seen in a Mexican peso (or eight-real piece) of the middle nineteenth century. Below a liberty cap, we read: * 8R. D°. 1862. C.P. 10 D°. 20 G°.— all of which refers to the coin. It is an eight-real issue of the Durango mint. Struck in 1862, its metallic content was checked and guaranteed by an assayer whose initials were C. P. (This was a common practice on nineteenth-century Latin American gold and silver coinage and often involved two assayers.) The assayer guaranteed that this coin had a silver fineness of 10 dineros, 20 granos, an old Spanish measurement which worked out to 90.27 percent pure silver. The other side of the coin bears the national arms and the simple legend REPUBLICA MEXICANA.

With the exception of such minor elements as mint marks and designers' initials, abbreviations are disappearing from contemporary coinage. Modern coinage emphasizes a simple, uncluttered design, without long legends or inscriptions. Not only are abbreviated renditions of long royal titles unnecessary today, but abbreviated data on the coins themselves is less essential. After all, if a modern coin is made of an inexpensive alloy, citizens are unlikely to be concerned with its nature or purity. While abbreviations still have a place on coinage, it is relatively minor.
See also MARK (MINTMASTER'S OR ASSAYER'S); PIECE OF EIGHT; SENATORIAL COINS; SESTERTIUS; THALER.

ADJUSTMENT MARKS Parallel striations on one or both sides of a coin, made by filing the planchet before striking, to reduce its weight in order to meet legal standards.

Adjustment marks are most often found on large gold or silver coins minted from the seventeenth to the early nineteenth century. A direct reflection of minting practices during that period, they are most common on coins from small mints with somewhat backward minting practices. Less frequently, adjustment marks appear on coins from larger mints where a sizable amount of bullion had to be turned into coinage in a fairly short time. Thus, we often see them on coins from the small French mint at Pau, or from the fledgling United States Mint at Philadelphia; and they are occasionally encountered on issues from the flourishing Spanish colonial facility at Mexico City.

In the minting process, the metal to be coined was rolled into a long strip by mechanical means, then punched into circular blanks by a machine working on much the same principle as a cookie cutter. Each blank planchet was weighed, and if within the legal tolerance, struck into a coin. If too light, it was remelted. But if it was too heavy, the blank was quickly filed on one or both sides until it reached the proper weight. The coining process effaced most of these filing or adjustment marks, but some remained, particularly on those areas receiving the least impression from the dies. Thus adjustment marks appear principally on the devices of a coin, rather than in its fields, and are usually near the center. Then too, they are more often found on the reverse than on the obverse, because mintmasters of the period preferred to obscure part of the shield or other elements making up the reverse design rather than to deface part of their ruler's portrait on the obverse.

Adjustment marks are easily mistaken for scratches. True adjustment marks, however, are apt to closely parallel each other, and they often lack the sharpness of a scratch. Examining the coin under a magnifying glass will usually resolve any questions.

Improved minting practices have made such marks a rarity on modern coins.

See also EMERGENCY MONEY; MILLED COIN; PLANCHET; SCREW PRESS.

Adjustment marks. France, écu, 1763.

Æ (also AE) An abbreviation—derived from the Latin *aes*, for any common metal—describing a coin containing no gold or silver.

In classical times *aes* referred mainly to copper, either in its pure state or mixed with tin or zinc, and modern specialists in ancient numismatics continue to use Æ in the same fashion. Strictly following etymology, however, Æ applies to any nonprecious metal, such as the many alloys used for modern money.

One or more numbers often immediately follow the abbreviation Æ. A numismatist, for example, may describe a Roman coin as Æ 1, 2, 3, 4,—that is, as a first, second, third, or fourth bronze, in descending order of size. This terminology is used to indicate fourth- and fifth-century bronze and copper coinage, whose actual denominations may be uncertain. Specialists in ancient Greek coins may use a one- or two-digit number after Æ to refer to the coin's size in millimeters. Thus Æ 28 signifies a copper or bronze coin with a diameter of 28 millimeters—slightly over one inch. Again, this description gives a useful idea of the coin's size, even if the denomination is unknown.

See also Æ; A'; FIRST BRONZE.

Aes grave. *Roman Republic, 240–220 B.C.*

AES GRAVE An early and cumbersome form of the Roman as, cast in bronze, the best known variety of which bears the head of Janus on the obverse, the prow of a ship on the reverse.

Aes grave means "heavy bronze" in Latin, an apt description for these coins, which at the time of their introduction were tariffed at a Roman pound each and were about 75 millimeters in diameter. (The normal Roman pound was roughly equivalent to three-quarters of a modern pound, and it was divided into twelve unciae or ounces.) A mark of value is present on one or both sides of these early coins.

Central Italy, including Rome, was affected by two numismatic currents. In Greek city-states to the south, a tradition of struck coinage in gold and silver prevailed. Under the influence of this tradition, Rome began to strike coins on the Greek model about the beginning of the third century B.C. But at the same time there was in Italy a strong native tradition of casting bronze in either round or oblong shapes for exchange and Rome issued the first *aes grave* around 300 B.C. following the Italian tradition.

Awkward in the extreme, the *aes grave* was difficult to trade, prompting the casting of subsidiary pieces: the semis, whose mark of value was an s; the triens, whose worth was expressed by four dots; and the quadrans, sextans, and uncia, whose values were expressed by three, two, and one dot respectively. Twelve unciae made up one *aes grave*.

The coin illustrated here dates from between 240 and 220 B.C. when the primitive Roman monetary system was severely strained by endemic war and concomitant inflation. This resulted in a reduction in the size and the weight of the *aes grave*. By 210 B.C., it only possessed one-twelfth its original weight, and was struck, not cast, a technique made feasible by its reduced size. Now referred to as an as, it remained an important Roman monetary unit until the third century A.D.

See also *Aes signatum;* As; BRONZE COINAGE; CAST COINAGE.

AES SIGNATUM An ancient rectangular bronze ingot, weighing approximately five Roman pounds.

The *aes signatum* preceded the *aes grave,* which was in turn a descendent of the earliest Roman money, the *aes rude,* a rough lump of cast bronze of irregular weight. The *aes signatum* bore devices on

Aes signatum. *Roman Republic, c. 300 B.C.*

either side—frequently a bull, reminding us that the word "pecuniary" derives from the Latin *pecus* ("cattle"), and that cattle were a measurement of wealth, in ancient Rome and elsewhere. Introduced before 300 B.C., the *aes signatum* gave way to the *aes grave* and its subdivisions, after a brief period during which the two monetary forms may have existed side by side.

See also *Aes grave;* As.

ALBUS   A billon coin popular in the German Rhineland and the Low Countries from the fourteenth through the seventeenth centuries.

The name, derived from the Latin word for "white," describes the pale appearance of the silver and copper mixture in the coin. Like other coins of the day, the albus was quite thin; it averaged about 25 millimeters in diameter.

Technically, the albus was a variety of a well-known German coin, the groschen. However, albi may be distinguished by their types. Frequently issued by clerical authorities, they usually bore a figure of St. Peter on the obverse, and the arms of the issuing government on the reverse. They interest numismatists in part because some of them were among the earliest coins to bear a Christian date in Roman numerals. Increased debasement was a factor in the disappearance of the albus after 1700.

See also BILLON; DATING SYSTEMS; GROSCHEN.

Albus. Palatinate, 1437.

ALLOY   A mixture of two or more metals.

Alloys can occur naturally; or they can be man-made, to produce a stronger, more durable coining material than that derived from a single metal, or to stretch a limited supply of precious metal. The Lydian stater, generally regarded as the first coin, was struck from a natural alloy of gold and silver called electrum.

It was discovered in ancient times that the addition of a small amount of copper to gold or silver, or of tin to copper, greatly increased the durability of those metals. By increasing the ratio of base to precious metal, early minters could produce more coins to pay troops in time of war, or to enlarge the money supply. Although the debasement of coinage could lead to inflation, it was a tempting recourse, and we find it resorted to throughout history.

Until the present century, a limited number of alloys were in use. For precious metals, there was gold with copper (or silver), in an approximate 90 percent–10 percent arrangement; and silver with copper, in about the same ratio. For base coinage, the relationship was usually 95 percent copper to 5 percent tin or zinc.

With the twentieth century, which has seen the virtual disappearance of precious metals from circulation as well as chronic inflation, the importance of alloys has increased immeasurably. Experiments have been conducted with dozens of cheap alloys to replace the two precious metals traditionally used for coinage. Not only must the new metallic mixtures be durable, but also pleasing to the eye—if a coin is intrinsically worthless, at least it can be attractive. Then, too, an alloy should be resistant to corrosion and discoloration, hence the use of stainless steel and nickel in modern coinage. But should nickel (or any other metal) be demanded for another purpose, a new alloy can be created. During World War II, when nickel became essential to the war effort, the United States and Canada produced non-nickel five-cent pieces.

The new alloys, however, were not very successful. The United States coin, consisting of 56 percent copper, 35 percent silver, and 9 percent manganese, proved difficult to strike and resulted in millions of coins with laminations.

See also BATH METAL; BILLON; BRASS COINAGE; BRITANNIA METAL; BRONZE COINAGE; COPPER-NICKEL COINAGE; ELECTRUM COINAGE; LAMINATION; POTIN; TOMBAC; WHITE METAL.

ALTERATION A deliberate change, made by someone in an unofficial capacity, usually in the hope of making a profit.

The term can be applied to any numismatic item, but numismatists customarily restrict its use to privately induced changes on coins or paper money. Official changes are called overstrikes or overprints.

There are two basic types of alterations. In the first, changes are made on a current coin or note to circulate the piece at an increased value. The second type of alteration is aimed at the coin collector, not the ordinary public. Here, a common numismatic item is altered to make it appear rare and desirable—and thus worth more.

The first category of alteration is uncommon on coins, but relatively common on paper, for obvious reasons. People know what their circulating coinage looks like, and any alteration is usually detected. However, there have been a few successful alterations of circulating coins for profit. The best-known example occurred in the United States in 1883, when a new five-cent piece was issued with merely a large v to indicate its value. Since the five-cent and five-dollar gold pieces were almost identical in size, someone got the notion of gold-plating the former and passing it as the latter. Such deceptions are rare, as they require the introduction of a new coin, whose value is not directly stated, and governments are ordinarily wise enough to avoid doing this.

Altered paper money is another case entirely. When paper currency became general, it was inevitable that people would set out with eraser, pen, and ink to make money by altering it, and in nineteenth-century America, numbers of them did so. Banking was a private affair then, with the country's fiscal institutions issuing their own paper money, theoretically backed by their cash reserves. Thousands of types of paper, in a bewildering variety of denominations (the so-called broken bank notes), saw circulation. It was a blessed state of affairs for a dishonest person who was handy with a pen. As notes with thousands of designs existed, no one could be certain how any given note should look. Moreover, as only a small percentage of the issuing banks were known, notes from obscure or out-of-state banks circulated at a discount, if they circulated at all.

With only pen and ink, the value of a note could be raised from $1 to $10. Or an out-of-state bank note, purchased at a discount, could be altered to seem issued from a bank closer to home. The really daring executed both alterations on the same note.

This golden age of paper alteration in the United States ended after the Civil War when the federal government took control of currency issue and immediately decreased the number of designs. (The elimination of alterations is a major reason for the year-after-year retention of the same designs and portraits on American currency.) In the United States and elsewhere, alteration of circulating paper for immediate gain is now rare, and alteration of paper money for sale to collectors has not yet become popular, although it may in the future.

However, alteration of common coins to make them seem attractive to the collector is currently a popular branch of numismatics. There is always some soul industrious enough to provide what appear to be rare and costly coins simply by changing common ones. A mint mark may

Alteration. *United States, cent, "1815" (altered from an 1845 cent).*

be carefully lifted from one coin and soldered to another to create a rarity; a date may be retooled, a digit altered. 1804 dollars have been fashioned from 1801 dollars and 1913 Liberty head five-cent pieces from 1903s, once it was discovered such coins were valuable. Even nonexistent coins are created. No cents were coined in the United States in 1815, for instance, so people altered the 4 on 1845 cents to provide collectors with this "rare" date.

See also AUTHENTICATION; BROKEN BANK NOTES; COUNTERFEIT AND FORGERY DETECTION; FANTASY; TOOLED.

ALTUN An important gold coin of the Ottoman Empire, minted for use in foreign trade, and introduced shortly after the fall of Constantinople to the Turks in 1453.

Intended to rival or displace the popular Venetian zecchino, the altun was struck in a similar size and weight (about 21 millimeters in diameter, approximately 3.5 grams in weight).

The first altun were struck only at the Constantinople mint, but as Ottoman

Altun. *Ottoman Empire, A.H. 883 (A.D. 1478–1479).*

power spread, they were eventually minted in the Near East, Africa, and eastern Europe, as well as Turkey. Adhering to strict Koranic law, early issues were devoid of types or decorations, and merely bore the title of the reigning sultan, and the place and date of mintage. Around 1700, however, a tughra, the personal monogram of the ruler, was added.

The commercial importance of the altun declined after the eighteenth century, as did its weight; the last specimens struck for circulation were issued during the reign of Mahmud II (ruled 1808–1839).

See also TRADE COINS; TUGHRA; ZECCHINO.

ALUMINUM COINAGE The striking of coins from the light, silvery-looking metal aluminum—a twentieth-century phenomenon, made possible by modern technology and necessitated by contemporary economics.

Because it was unavailable in large quantities, aluminum was not a practical metal for coinage until recently. Unlike gold, aluminum does not occur free in nature, but forms chemical compounds with a number of other elements. It was first used in the United States and elsewhere in the 1800s to produce patterns, for it takes an excellent impression from coin dies, but it was not seriously considered for regular coinage at that time.

Not until the 1880s was a method devised to economically extract metallic aluminum from its most common ore, bauxite, and produce pure aluminum in sufficient quantities for coinage.

Once the metal was readily available, however, several factors still mitigated against its use for coins. Most important, it was so light that it was difficult to persuade people it was a "real" metal. In addition, in the economically secure late nineteenth century, the employment of metals that had always been used in trade—gold, silver, and copper—continued, and there was no need of aluminum coins. The new metal was treated as a curiosity and struck into souvenirs and lucky pieces.

The first use of aluminum in a monetary function was in the production of tokens in the 1890s. This underscored the general low opinion of the metal at that time: if it had no intrinsic value, let it stand for something that did—a drink at a saloon, or merchandise, for example.

The first years of the new century saw aluminum's tentative debut as a coinage metal, struck for British East Africa and British West Africa in 1907, in low denominations (half cents and cents and tenths of a penny, respectively). Even tariffed at such modest rates, the new coins proved unpopular and were soon replaced.

In succeeding years there was a sporadic use of aluminum for coins and tokens, but the metal only became popular with governments—if not with their citizens—after World War II. Widespread inflation made it apparent to governments that if they were going to continue to strike lire, francs, or forint, they would have to use an extremely inexpensive metal. The advantages of aluminum were obvious: it was inexpensive; it took an excellent impression from coin dies under moderate pressure, which produced sharp images while prolonging the life of the dies; and it was fairly attractive. The use of aluminum for coinage spread as inflation spread, and its continued usage seems certain. Today, the metal is widely employed throughout Europe, Africa, Asia, and Latin America. The Italian five- and ten-lire pieces, for example, are solid aluminum.

See also INFLATION; LIRA; PATTERN; TOKEN.

Amulet. China, c. 1750.

AMULET   A magical charm often made of metal and frequently suspended from a chain or cord around the neck.

Amulets are of interest to numismatists because of their size, inscriptions, designs, and method of manufacture. They may bear inscriptions or designs similar to those seen on contemporary coins and medals. Religious amulets dating from the Renaissance and Reformation fall into this category and are avidly sought by collectors of the periods' coinages.

Far Eastern amulets, like the coins of the region, were often cast with a square hole in the middle, an inscription consisting of a set number of characters, and a wide border. Although the production and wearing of amulets has undergone a decline, today we see reminders of them in St. Christopher medals, and they are still produced in limited quantities in the Far East.

See also CAST COINAGE; EXONUMIA.

ANONYMOUS BRONZE   A large, distinctive copper coin of the middle Byzantine Empire, with designs and inscriptions

Aluminum coinage. Italy, 10 lire, 1950.

Anonymous Bronze. Byzantine Empire, 988–1028.

devoted to religious subjects rather than to the reigning emperor.

The typical Anonymous Bronze bears a full-face portrait of Christ on the obverse, with a religious legend and an inscription on the reverse, usually rendered in three or four lines. The reverse inscription proclaims Christ King of Kings, and to underscore the point, one or more crosses may appear. Minted in Constantinople from the 960s to the 1090s, Anonymous Bronzes are of particular interest because the full-face portraits of Christ were often expertly rendered, an indication that the coins were produced in a period when the arts flourished.

The portrayal of Christ and other religious figures was not a new feature on Byzantine coinage. Indeed, the first coin portrait of the Redeemer appeared nearly three centuries earlier on a gold solidus of Justinian II (ruled 685–695, 705–711). Christ occupied the obverse of this coin, the emperor the reverse, and this practice, partially an attempt to identify church and state in the popular mind, was common through most of the later centuries of Byzantine coinage. What is striking about the Anonymous Bronzes, however, is the total predominance of Christ in the design and inscriptions. Does this indicate the state was ultimately secondary to the church? It seems not. While Christ is supreme on the Anonymous Bronze, He shares His position with the emperor on gold and silver coinage. And it is an historical fact that, in the partnership between Byzantine church and state, the church was always the subordinate member.

Anonymous Bronzes can be dated with some degree of accuracy. Stylistic and epigraphical changes took place, but a primary way to determine their chronology is to examine the overstrikes, which were persistent on this coinage.

See also CROSS ON COINAGE; FOLLIS; OVERSTRIKE; PORTRAIT.

ANTONINIANUS   The predominant coin of the Roman Empire in the third century A.D.

It was named by modern numismatists after the emperor who introduced it, M. Aurelius Antoninus Caracalla (ruled A.D. 211–217). Distinguished from most other coins of the period by the radiate crown which adorned the head of the emperor depicted on the obverse, the antoninianus had an initial diameter of about 21 millimeters and an initial weight of about 5 grams, which decreased along with its silver content as time went on. The debasement of the antoninianus provides our best example of inflation in ancient times.

If the name of the coin is unclear, so are the reasons for its introduction, in A.D. 215. Prevalent opinion holds that it represented a double denarius, as evidenced by the use of the radiate crown. (The dupondius, or double as, had long carried such a design feature.) A second theory, however, is that the new coin directly reflected the rise in the value of gold coins relative to silver ones, an argument supported by the fact that, though the denarius of A.D. 215 weighed about 3.1 grams, the anto-

Antoninianus.
Left: Roman Empire, Caracalla, A.D. 215.
Right: Roman Empire, Tetricus I, A.D. 270–274.

ninianus weighed 5, not 6 grams, as logically it should have if intended as a double denarius. In short, it may have been introduced as a "heavy" denarius, intended to shore up the old 25-to-1 relationship to gold. At present, we do not know; further study may resolve the question.

In any case, the silver content of the antoninianus at the time of its introduction was almost exactly 50 percent. By 270 it was closer to 3 percent. Such a dramatic drop in a coin's intrinsic value in less than sixty years indicates an ailing nation. In the Roman Empire military anarchy began in A.D. 235 with the assassination of the reigning emperor, Alexander Severus, and by A.D. 284 there had been more than twenty "official" emperors, only one of whom died of natural causes.

Furthermore, the peoples surrounding the empire took advantage of Rome's domestic strife. While the Sassanians invaded Syria and Asia Minor, the Goths and Franks overran the northern imperial frontiers, leaving much of the empire in ruins and the Roman government in a quandary. To dispel invaders and quell army mutinies, an abundant money supply was needed, and taxes, though raised, were not enough to meet the demands as the empire's population declined seriously in the third century. The answer, then, was to debase the coinage.

As the antoninianus reflected political unrest, it also mirrored a degeneration in artistry. The emperor's portrait grew crude and stereotyped, and reverse designs were static. In part, the speed with which these "emergency" coins were produced is responsible for the wretched portraiture, but something of the early grandeur of Roman numismatic art disappeared, and sadly was never to return.

The antoninianus disappeared around A.D. 300, during a major currency reform undertaken by the emperor Diocletian (ruled A.D. 284–305). It is of particular interest not only as an example of the consequences of inflation but as a model for the famous series of barbarian imitations —the so-called "Barbarous Radiates"— which date from the end of the third century and prominently display a radiate crown.

See also BARBAROUS IMITATIONS; BILLON; DENARIUS; INFLATION; POTIN; PORTRAIT.

Æ The numismatic abbreviation for silver, from the metal's Latin name, *argentum.*

Technically, the term is applied only to coins with a silver content of 50 percent or more, "billon" being used when the silver content is less than 50 percent. As with Æ, Æ is occasionally coupled with numbers to describe the size of a silver coin when its precise denomination is not known. This practice is much less frequent for silver coins than for non-precious metal ones, however, since numismatists have traditionally paid more attention to the former than the latter. By custom, if historical sources yield no existing name, a convenient one is agreed upon. A good example of this practice is the "antoninianus." The abbreviation for silver can also appear as the two separate letters AR.

See also Æ; ANTONINIANUS; AV; BILLON.

ARAB-BYZANTINE COINAGE   An early Islamic coinage of brief duration, which borrowed its designs, weights, and legends from contemporary issues of the Byzantine Empire

Arab-Byzantine coinage is inextricably linked to the spread of a new religion, Islam, and is a classic example of an imitative coinage, one struck by a people suddenly forced to produce coins without any native coinage tradition. Prior to the sixth century, inhabitants of the Arabian peninsula lived either as nomads or in scattered communities on the Arabian coast. Their trade with the outside world was modest, and was carried on by barter, or by using other peoples' coinage. By the sixth century A.D., however, the peninsula was becoming overcrowded, and Arab migration to Iraq, Palestine, and Syria had begun.

With the birth of Islam, migration assumed enormous proportions. Islam's founder, Mohammed, introduced the new faith, based on monotheism, around 620. Exiled from his home, Mecca, in 622, he fled to nearby Medina, and it is this flight, or Hejira, which marks the beginning of the Moslem calendar. Hence, virtually all Islamic coins bear dates computed from that event.

What was born as a simple religious movement became a fighting one, committed to conversion and expansion into the Byzantine and Sassanian empires, which were at that time sorely weakened by decades of warfare. By Mohammed's death in 632, Mecca and perhaps a third of the Arabian peninsula had been conquered for the new faith. Within a few years the remaining two-thirds would fall—as would Syria by 634, Jerusalem in 639, Egypt in 640, and Carthage in 698. Few escaped the onslaught. Arab armies crossed the Straits of Gibraltar to conquer most of Spain. The Sassanian capital, Ctesiphon, had fallen by 637; fourteen years later, in 651, the entire empire had been destroyed. By 724, Arab armies had reached the Indus River and the gates of China. Never had the world seen anything quite like it, nor would it again.

The new lands brought new problems, and one was the necessity of striking coinage. The conquered peoples were accustomed to coinage for their day-to-day transactions, and they expected it from their new masters, who were ill acquainted with its use.

What would appear on the new coins? What standards would they have? Where would they be struck? The solution was to issue coins similar to those previously used in the conquered states. People would accept them, the coins could be struck at existing mint facilities, and the conquerors could develop their own coinage at their leisure.

Thus, the basic Byzantine denominations of follis and solidus were retained. While the Byzantines used copper and gold (and a very small amount of silver) to strike their coins, their Arab copyists used large amounts of copper, some gold, and no silver. The copper follis minted by the Byzantines was about 25 millimeters in diameter, weighing 5 grams or less by the mid-seventh century; its imitation was approximately the same size and weight. The Byzantine solidus weighed about 4.5 grams and was 20 millimeters in diameter; its Arabic equivalent weighed almost exactly the same, although its diameter varied—solidi from North African mints were small and thick, those from Syria larger and thinner.

But the designs on Arab-Byzantine coins are the most striking aspect of the series, for they closely imitate the Byzantine originals. Koranic law forbade the use of images. No matter: the Arabs, in need of a design, temporarily sacrificed religious purity to expediency and found a follis of Justin II (ruled 565–578) to be a convenient model. The original depicted the emperor and his consort seated on the obverse, with a legend giving their names. The Arabic copy showed the same seated figures, with a new legend in Greek and Arabic naming the mint responsible for the coin. The most spectacular example of such an imitation is an undated Syrian sol-

Arab-Byzantine coinage.
Top: Byzantine Empire, Heraclius, solidus, c. A.D. 639–641.
Bottom: Syria, dinar, late seventh century.

idus. Its predecessor and model was a solidus of Heraclius (ruled 610–641), which depicted the emperor and his two sons on the obverse, a cross on steps on the reverse. The Arabic imitation retained the obverse design, but an Arabic legend was substituted for the Latin one on the reverse, and the offending Christian cross was replaced with a globe on a pole, a vague gesture in the direction of Islamic orthodoxy, and familiar on Arab-Byzantine copper coinage as well.

Arab-Byzantine coinage ceased in most places shortly before 700, although in North Africa and Spain it persisted into the eighth century.

See also ARAB-SASSANIAN COINAGE; BILINGUAL MONEY; DATING SYSTEMS; DINAR; FALS; FOLLIS; HEJIRA; IMITATION; SOLIDUS.

ARAB-SASSANIAN COINAGE Seventh-century Islamic issues closely resembling those of the old Sassanian empire.

This coinage appears to date from about the same period as the Arabic mutations of Byzantine coins, and much of the information under Arab-Byzantine coinage is also relevant here. However, there are two important differences between these coinages. First, Arab-Sassanian coins are even closer to their prototype than Arab-Byzantine coins. In most cases, an Arab-Sassanian coin is distinguished from a purely Sassanian one only by the addition of a brief Arabic inscription on the lower margin of the obverse. Otherwise, the types (a king in elaborate headdress for the obverse, a fire-altar flanked by two standing figures for the reverse) are virtually identical, and major legends continued to be rendered in Pehlvi, the language of the Sassanian empire. The fabric, diameter, and weight of originals and copies are essentially the same. Like its Arabic successor, the Sassanian coin was thin and flat, about 33 millimeters across, and it weighed 4 grams or a bit more.

The other difference between the two series is in the metals used to mint them. Arab-Byzantine issues in silver are unknown; their eastern counterparts are unknown in anything else. Here, as in places farther to the west, the Arabs used what was already there, and as silver was fairly plentiful in the Sassanian Empire, where large numbers of silver drachms were struck, the Arabs merely refined a system already in use for hundreds of years.

The Arab-Byzantine and Arab-Sassanian imitations served well enough in trade, but their use of imagery, in violation of religious laws laid down in the Koran, dismayed many zealous members of the faith. Hence, in 697 and the years immediately thereafter, reforms were implemented. New coins of gold, silver, and copper were minted, and while their weights and diameters closely copied older coinages, their types did not. Portraits were dropped, and replaced with Arabic legends and inscriptions. This set Islamic style for the next several centuries and persists to the present on issues from the more orthodox Islamic countries.

See also ARAB-BYZANTINE COINAGE: BILINGUAL MONEY; DIRHEM; DRACHM; IMITATION.

Arab-Sassanian coinage.
Left: Sassanian Empire, drachm, A.D. *590–628.*
Right: Arab imitation, A.H. *58 (*A.D. *677–678).*

ARCHAIC COINAGE Coinage of a specific style and execution, particularly certain Greek coins produced between c. 620 and 480 B.C.; the term is also used for

Archaic coinage. *Athens, tetradrachm, c. 480 B.C.*

money in the same style struck after 480 B.C.

The style and execution of archaic coins indicate that artists and moneyers were unfamiliar and uncomfortable with the design and technical possibilities of a metallic currency. Designs on archaic coinage tend to be elementary and crude. There is little in the way of legends or inscriptions—in fact, many archaic coinages bear no legends at all. Then too, the range of subjects depicted is limited. Simple objects and animals are frequent, and human figures, if portrayed at all, are stiff and angular. Designs are usually restricted to the obverse, while the reverse shows only one or more indentations, indicating how the coins were made.

A bean-shaped lump of metal (the planchet) was cast. The iron or bronze die consisted of a design cut by hand in reverse into one end of a tapering metal cylinder, similar in appearance to a chisel. When striking began, the die was set in an anvil. The metal lump was placed on top, and a punch—a hammering tool—was carefully positioned on top of the lump. This punch was hit with a sledgehammer, forcing the planchet into the die. The result was a coin. What had been carved in intaglio in reverse on the die now appeared in relief on the coin. Shortly before 500 B.C., the idea of carving a design on the punch was conceived and the first "true" coin—one with a real obverse and reverse—was fashioned. Many scholars believe the widespread use of the punch to create reverse designs marks the end of the archaic period.

Archaic coinage underwent a definite evolution as time passed. On the earliest coins, renditions were uncomplicated, and the Lydians, who probably invented coinage in the mid-seventh century, depicted rudimentary lions and bulls on their staters, struck around 600 B.C. Traders soon carried the coins from the Anatolian kingdom to the adjacent Greek-speaking areas. The Ionian Greeks, in turn, took the concept to the West. As it travelled, the coiners' skills were sharpened. Designs increased in complexity; if simpler ones were preferred, they were done with greater care. When the punch began to be utilized for a reverse, the fact that it was originally nothing more than a square, tapered piece of metal was revealed by the continuing placement of reverse types within a square border.

Although archaic coinage evolved, it remains distinct from its successors. Look closely at an Athenian tetradrachm, minted around 480 B.C. The obverse pictures Athena, patroness of the city; the reverse shows an owl, sacred to the goddess. Note Athena's stylized hair and headdress, and the smile on her lips—a telltale mark on portraiture of the archaic period. Above all, look at her eye—seen in full, although her head is in profile. The owl stands stiffly within a deep square, product of the reverse punch. This is no ordinary owl, but rather the concept of an owl. Note too, the brevity of the inscription. These elements are peculiar to archaic coinage.

The Athenian tetradrachm is perhaps the best-known of all archaic coins. By the time this specimen was struck, other Greek cities had far surpassed it in artistry. But the Athenians continued to strike tetradrachms with this same archaic appearance well into the fifth century. The coins were of good silver, widely respected in international trade, and there seemed no legitimate reason to "modernize" them. As a term, archaic coinage applies to both style and time of issue, but rather more to style. Trading entrepôts such as Athens retained conservative designs long after other cities abandoned them.

See also DIE; HAMMERED COINAGE; OWL; PILE; PLANCHET; PORTRAIT; PUNCH; STATER; TETRADRACHM; TRADE COINS; TRUSSELL.

AS A word used to describe two closely related Roman coins.

The first as was a bronze issue of the Roman republic. The very heavy early cast specimens properly occasioned the name *aes grave* ("heavy bronze"). Inflation brought about a steady reduction in the coin's weight, and by 210 B.C. it was replaced by a bronze coin light enough to be struck rather than cast. It was called simply an as, and was minted in Rome until c. 85 B.C. Designs on the bronze as were most often taken from the *aes grave*, although brief inscriptions identifying moneyers were added to the reverse, as was done on the denarius of the same period. This form of the as may have been a casualty of the civil wars during the last years of the republic; for when an as coin was revived in about 23 B.C. it was quite different.

Augustus, who ruled the Roman Empire from 31 B.C. to A.D. 14, directed his attention to a restructuring of the coinage, particularly minor coinage. No bronze had been regularly issued since the mid-80s, yet such minor coinage was needed, as the overused republican asses were virtually worn smooth. Around 23 B.C., Augustus reformed Rome's non-precious metal money with the introduction of the brass sestertius, weighing about 25 grams and equal to four asses; the dupondius, also brass, and weighing roughly 12.5 grams; a copper as, around 11 grams in weight; and the small copper quadrans, weighing 3 grams, four of which equaled one as. For the next three centuries the obverse of the as usually bore a head of the reigning emperor with a legend giving his titles; the reverse bore an inscription, or more frequently a type—which could be an animal, a god or goddess, a personification, etc. Reverses could also contain legends, and if so, they were often a continuation of the obverse legend or an additional reference to the ruler. All asses carried the abbreviation SC for *Senatus Consulto* ("By Decree of the Senate").

The as proved to be a useful coin, and was produced in large quantities in Rome and elsewhere until well after A.D. 200. Its modest purchasing power made it serviceable in day-to-day transactions, while its size was ample for slogans and designs urging loyalty to the emperor and state. Coinage was a natural means of propaganda and it was not uncommon to have an emperor's prowess in war, his piety, even deserving members of his family, extolled on imperial coins such as the sestertius and the as. In time the as underwent a modest reduction in size and weight. If the as of Augustus was approximately 30 millimeters in diameter and 11 grams in weight, that of his distant successor Trajan Decius (ruled 249–251) was only 25 millimeters in diameter, and weighed a gram or so less. The fall in the size and weight of the as was minor compared to that of the antoninianus, but it too reflected the influence of war and inflation. As time went on relatively few asses were struck. The sestertius became the prime subsidiary coin, and its shrinking weight and diameter roughly paralleled decreases in the as.

After the reign of Trajan Decius, production of the as virtually ceased: some later pieces may or may not have been intended as asses, but not until the coinage reform of the 290s did another large copper coin, the follis, make its appearance in Rome.

As. Roman Empire, Vespasian, A.D. 71.

See also *Aes grave;* Antoninianus; Bronze coinage; Cast coinage; Dupondius; Follis; Senatorial coins; Sestertius

ASSAY To determine the purity of metal before it becomes a coin.

The fact that the metal has been assayed and found acceptable is often indicated on a struck coin, which may bear the assayer's initials, monograms, etc. The designs on the first Lydian and Greek coins suggest that assaying was performed, and that the governments vouched for the quality of the metal. However, indications of metallic purity have usually been confined to gold and silver coins. Although copper and other base metals are assayed before striking, their low intrinsic value has left the public relatively unconcerned about their metallic purity.

The assaying of precious metals, however, has traditionally been of consequence, as gold and silver—in the form of ingots, foreign coins, plate, etc.—contain other metals, present as alloys or trace elements, and the proportion of gold or silver needs to be established. Until fairly recently, the method used was roughly this: a piece of metal was trimmed from each ingot or mass of bullion to be tested; this was placed in a cupel, a small cup made from bone-ash. The cupel was heated by a charcoal fire until it became red-hot; as it heated, the base metals oxidized or flowed into the porous sides and bottom of the cupel. At this point the metal was weighed, as it had been before cupellation, and the difference between the old and new weights told the assayer the loss in base metal. The metal was then refined and turned into coinage. For more accurate results, modern assaying methods rely primarily on chemical precipitants rather than heat. But today the logic for assaying has lost much of its force.

See also Fineness; Mark (mintmaster's or assayer's); Seal.

ASSIGNAT A late eighteenth-century form of paper currency, the issues of which engendered the worst inflation of paper money the world had yet known.

Most numismatists restrict the term to the paper money of revolutionary France, although several nations experimented with assignats, including Poland and a number of French-supported states in Italy.

By the outbreak of the French Revolution in 1789, paper money was a fairly well-developed concept. Its first employment in Europe was in Sweden in the early 1660s. The French experimented with it during the following century and created the assignat. The difference between the assignat and preceding forms of paper

Assignat. France, 400 livres, 1792.

money lay in the nature of its guarantee. Earlier paper had been backed, however tenuously, by cash. The assignat, on the other hand, was backed by property, namely lands expropriated from the Catholic Church.

This, of course, had the advantage of weakening the Church, which had continually opposed reform. If sold, the lands would provide the government with ready income, in the form of notes issued against its value. Furthermore, paper money could always be used to pay bills and fight wars—matters of no small consideration. Even though France still had a king in 1789, monarchical Europe was rather dubious about his government and war was a distinct possibility.

The new, liberal government had failed in its attempts to raise money in more orthodox ways. Many Frenchmen distrusted the new regime, and refused to buy its bonds. As 1789 gave way to 1790, the assignat became more attractive.

In April 1790 the National Assembly authorized the first printing, and not long after assignats began to roll off the presses. Initially, notes were released in large denominations, but as the public, increasingly suspicious of the government and its money, began hoarding small- and medium-denomination coins, assignats appeared in smaller denominations. Had history developed as planned, the revolutionary government would have been more than able to redeem both small and large notes. Hard money would have come out of hiding, and tax revenues would have increased, ensuring the fiscal health of the revolutionary government. But history is given to capriciousness and in 1792 France found itself at war with most of Europe.

Conservative peasants refused to accept assignats at face value; even radicals found them unwelcome, as riots by Parisian workers attested. Gold and silver were hoarded, and assignats, no longer used to purchase land—as the government had intended—were marshalled to pay taxes.

The war dragged on, France was invaded, and the government sought yet more money for defense. Inevitably, it turned to the printing press. Assignats glutted the market, and their value fell: by July 1795 they were worth less than one percent of their stated face value. The assignat had failed, and the French monetary system was a shambles.

Early in 1796, in an effort to bring order out of chaos, the government printed a new form of paper money, the mandat territorial. Assignats were convertible into mandats at the rate of thirty to one. Within a year, it was apparent the mandat was as ill-fated as the assignat; its value too was falling and on February 14, 1797, all paper money of the French Revolution was demonetized. By then, France's military situation had improved; the young General Bonaparte was winning stunning victories in Italy, and the generous amounts of gold and silver that found their way back to France allowed it to return to an ordinary monetary system.

See also BANK NOTE; INFLATION; PAPER MONEY.

AV The numismatic abbreviation for gold, derived from *aurum*, the Latin for gold.

The use of AV and its alternate forms AU and AV is largely restricted to catalogs where a shortened description of metallic content may be necessary. Unlike Æ, it is not used with one or more numbers to describe the size of a piece except in extremely obscure coinages. Occasionally, however, it is used in this way to describe a non-monetary numismatic item (a decoration or a medal).

See also Æ; AR.

AUGUSTALE A gold coin struck in southern Italy, introduced about 1231 and abandoned later in the thirteenth century for more traditional coinage.

Augustale. *Brindisi, c. 1231.*

The augustale appears to have been minted at Messina and Brindisi, and was the product of Frederick II, Holy Roman Emperor and king of the Two Sicilies (ruled 1197–1250). Frederick took his imperial title seriously, and his augustale was directly inspired by the aureus minted by imperial Rome. On the obverse, he is seen in profile wearing a laurel wreath and drapery, features which closely parallel Roman portraiture. On the reverse is a large eagle with its head turned to the right, the treatment of which is more Germanic than classical. Legends stating Frederick's titles as Holy Roman Emperor appear on either side of the emperor and the imperial eagle. The continuation of personal titles from one side of the coin to the other may have been occasioned by space limitations, but was probably also inspired by the Roman aureus, on which the same practice had been used.

If the design of the augustale was reminiscent of the aureus, so too was its fabric. Dies were cut in a fairly deep intaglio to make the types stand out boldly, a departure from most medieval coinage, which had a very shallow relief. The augustale's diameter (20 millimeters) matched that of the old aureus, but its weight was somewhat less—5.2 grams as opposed to the aureus' 7.8 grams at the time of Augustus.

We may speculate that this evocation of ancient Rome's coinage had political motivations. By producing a coin similar to the relics of pagan Rome's golden age, might not Frederick II be telling his subjects they were in a second golden age, blessed by a new Christian Roman Emperor? In any case, the augustale was so named because its treatment of the obverse type was akin to the coinage of Augustus, Rome's first emperor.

The augustale looks like no other coin of the medieval period. Indeed, it seems born of the Renaissance, and for the next two centuries it would stand alone. However, Frederick was not anticipating the future, but returning, as the Renaissance coiners would, to ancient Rome as a source of numismatic inspiration.

See also AUREUS; PORTRAIT.

AUREUS An abbreviation of denarius aureus, or "golden denarius," the basic gold coin of the later Roman republic and the early and middle stages of the Roman empire.

Gold coins first appeared in the Roman state about 216 B.C.; known as staters, they were issued on an emergency basis to meet the fiscal demands of the Second Punic War (218–201 B.C.). These coins weighed 6.8 grams. In a second emergency issue, consisting of pieces valued at 60, 40, and 20 asses and struck in 209 B.C., the coins were smaller, the sixty-as piece weighing only 3.4 grams, and the others in proportion. The republic soon stopped the production of this second gold series, and gold was not a regular part of Roman coinage for another century and a half.

Its reintroduction was a direct result of the years of civil war that characterized the last decades of the republic, and this time its incorporation into the coinage system was permanent.

Aureus. *Roman Republic, Julius Caesar, 44 B.C.*

The man responsible for the resumption of Roman gold coinage was Sulla, a military leader who held sway through most of the 80s, and had a new coin, the aureus, struck in his name. His coins were relatively small (18 millimeters in diameter) and heavy (around 10.7 grams), and were probably struck in Athens rather than Rome. By the middle of the century, Rome was making its own aurei, albeit of lighter weight. The issues of Julius Caesar, struck in quantity between 49 and 44 B.C., weighed between 8 and 9 grams, although they were slightly broader than their predecessors (about 20 millimeters, a diameter they retained for the next three centuries).

Augustus stabilized the weight of the aureus at about 7.8 grams, as part of his general coinage reform. It was the equivalent of twenty-five denarii, each of which weighed between 3.75 and 3.8 grams. With a gold-to-silver ratio of 1 to 12, this is an early example of a bimetallic coinage system.

While the smallness of the aureus made it unsuitable for elaborate art, some notable work was nonetheless accomplished. The usual obverse type was a profile portrait of the ruler or a member of his family (the latter is quite common, perhaps because gold's intrinsic worth made it inviting for commemorative issues). The reverse was often used to depict a god or goddess important to the emperor or the state, or an allegorical figure representing one of the ruler's virtues.

The weight and fineness of the aureus remained stable for many years, and even in the disastrous third century A.D. it fared better than most Roman coins. Still, by 225 its weight had descended to some 6.3 grams and thirty years later it was frequently half of that, or even less. Unlike the antoninianus, whose precious metal content virtually disappeared, aurei seem to have been struck in good gold throughout the century.

In the 280s, the aureus increased in weight. Sixty were struck to one Roman pound, which meant each coin weighed about 5.3 grams. The reform barely outlasted Diocletian's reign, however, and around A.D. 310, a new emperor, Constantine the Great (ruled A.D. 306–337) began the replacement of the aureus with the solidus, a new and lighter gold coin. Weighing about 4.5 grams, the solidus was of major significance during the rest of the Roman Empire and through much of the ensuing Byzantine Empire.

See also COMMEMORATIVE; DENARIUS; EMERGENCY MONEY; SOLIDUS; STATER.

AUTHENTICATION Establishing the authenticity of a numismatic item.

In the last twenty years, as numismatics has grown in popularity, the need for and importance of authentication has increased dramatically. Inflation has made the acquisition of coins and paper money so attractive that numismatics now embraces several million collectors and devotees it could not claim in 1960. In addition, more leisure time and the publication of numerous clearly written and well-illustrated texts on coins, bills, and metals, have swollen the ranks of collectors—many of whom look for new coins and bills, but many more of whom are in search of older materials: United States large cents, gold coins, old paper money. It is a sad fact of life that while collectors have increased in number, the items they seek have not. Great Britain struck exactly 932 crowns in 1934, and no matter how many people covet one, the number of 1934 crowns will not increase. Hence, collectors bid against each other, and value and prices soar. So, too, does the alteration of common coins and the forgery of rare ones.

Until twenty years ago, most forgeries and alterations were crude, and readily detected by the collector with the help of a stereo microscope or even a decent magnifying glass. However, the spectacular rise in the value of coins—and later, paper —that began around 1960, had several curious effects. Speculators were drawn to numismatics; writers in the field produced better, more fully illustrated books; collectors in turn, became more sophisticated and less easily duped by a forgery or alteration.

The practitioners of these skills followed suit and systematically refined their methods. Instead of casting forgeries, they began striking them from dies faithfully copied from genuine coins to produce "coins" that in some cases look better than the originals! Improvements are most obvious in forged coinage, but advances have also been made in the alteration process. Paper money has yet to be affected, but as its value to the collector ascends, its time will come.

All of this has led to the establishment of worldwide authentication groups that can conduct tests on coins and notes beyond the range of the collector. Although visual inspection and comparison of genuine pieces with a quality microscope and a highly trained eye remain the most important tests, others include X-ray spectrography and accurate specific gravity measurement, each of which elicits particular facts about a suspect piece.

Today, the collector contemplating an expenditure of hundreds or thousands of dollars on a coin wants written assurance from a dealer or an authentication group that the coin is genuine. This is especially necessary should the collector wish to sell the coin at some future time; if it is rare, and forgeries are known, he will be unable to sell unless he can offer a guarantee of authenticity by a neutral third party. The authentication agency, then, serves both collector and dealer.

At present, the best known and most widely trusted authentication organizations are: The American Numismatic Association Certification Service (ANACS), 818 North Cascade, Colorado Springs, CO 80903; the International Numismatic Society (INS), P.O. Box 19386, Washington, D.C., 20036; and the International Bureau for the Suppression of Counterfeit Coins (IBSCC), P.O. Box 4QN, London W1A 4QN, England. In addition to authenticating coins, ANACS and the IBSCC regularly publish photographs and descriptions of new forgeries appearing on the market. As procedures for authentication vary, it is wise to write these organizations before submitting anything for consideration.

See also ALTERATION; COUNTERFEIT; COUNTERFEIT AND FORGERY DETECTION; FORGERY; SPECIFIC GRAVITY.

AXE MONEY A flat, thin copper currency used in trading by the Aztecs and other pre-Columbian Mexican tribes.

The native name seems to have been siccapili; numismatists, however, choose to call it axe money as it resembles the head of an axe. Typical specimens are some 200 millimeters long and, at their broadest point, 100 millimeters wide. They were cast, and most were probably manufactured late in the pre-Columbian period. They bear no marks of value, which has made some numismatists conclude that their purpose was ceremonial rather than economic. This seems unlikely, however, as axe money is not unlike the Chinese spade and knife pieces which, although

Axe money. Mexico, c. 1500.

fashioned after actual tools, were undeniably intended to circulate as money. In addition, the cast siccapili bore a set relationship to another form of Mexican currency, the cacao bean, one siccapili equalling 8000 cacao beans.

Axe money is also akin to a copper trade piece shaped more like a hoe. Modern Mexicans refer to both pieces as *tajaderas* ("chopping knives"); their manufacture came to an end with the Spanish conquest of Mexico in the sixteenth century.

See also BARTER; KNIFE MONEY; SPADE MONEY.

B

BADGE Any decoration meant to be worn suspended by a loop from something else.

The badge—which can be attached to a ribbon, sash, collar, or bar—has long been a striking way to display chivalric and campaign decorations, and gallantry awards.

Usually die-struck, badges may be fashioned in one metal or several. The Purple Heart, for example—a United States gallantry award—is minted in bronze, while the German Iron Cross con-sisted of iron and silver. Badges created for chivalric orders are often enamelled in several colors after striking, and may also contain precious or semi-precious stones.

Badges can be created in any shape—a cross, a star, even an animal—but the most popular shape is a circular one, especially for campaign badges. This award, which is the most familiar decoration, often resembles a coin, with obverse and reverse types, legends and/or inscriptions, and a size and thickness within the range of ordinary coinage. It may contain the name, rank, and military group of the recipient in the form of an edge engraving, or as one on the reverse of the badge. It is customary to suspend campaign and gallantry awards from a short ribbon of a distinctive color and pattern. If the recipient has been given more than one campaign or gallantry award, he or she may elect to wear the badge of the most distinguished award with bars to record the others. A bar has the same colors as those in the ribbons of the original badges.

Badge. *United States, Haitian Campaign Medal, 1915.*

See also CAMPAIGN AWARD; DECORATION; GALLANTRY AWARD; ORDER; RIBBON; SASH.

Bag marks.
Left: United States, dollar, 1902.
Center: United States, dollar, 1894.
Right: United States, dollar, 1896.

BAG MARKS Minor nicks or other surface abrasions on an uncirculated coin, an essential factor to be considered in the grading and pricing of coins.

Bag marks are caused by careless handling of the coin between the mint and its destination, and are usually found on coins of a relatively soft metal such as gold or silver, and on large, heavy coins regardless of their metallic content. For example, they are common on uncirculated Morgan dollars, struck in 90 percent silver and weighing 26.73 grams, and they are also seen on Eisenhower dollars, which weigh 24.59 grams, contain no silver and were struck from copper-nickel, a fairly hard alloy. Coins are shipped in large lots sewn in canvas bags, and if they are not packed with care they will knock against one another, causing bag marks.

Collectors consider bag marks significant because they can radically affect a coin's value. In the United States, the customary way to describe an uncirculated coin is with the abbreviation "MS" for "Mint State," followed by a number; bag marks directly affect the grading number assigned to a coin.

The three coins pictured are American silver dollars of the Morgan design. They have been chosen to illustrate the relationship between bag marks and grading. The 1902 dollar would be graded MS-60 in current terminology, the lowest grade for an uncirculated coin. Note the heavy bag mark, almost a gouge, opposite Liberty's throat, as well as lighter abrasions opposite her nose and on several parts of the legend. On the other hand, the 1894 dollar with less noticeable bag marks at the back of Liberty's cap would be MS-65. The third coin, an 1896 dollar, would probably grade close to MS-70, the highest degree of preservation to which a coin can aspire. No abrasions are seen and the uninterrupted, satiny sheen of the surfaces assures us that the coin is essentially the same as it was when it left the mint.

How does this translate into dollars and cents? While it is difficult to generalize, it would be safe to say that had all three coins been of the same year—1896 for example—a coin in MS-60 would be worth about $30, a MS-65 some $75, and a true MS-70 coin perhaps ten times that —all due to the presence or absence of bag marks.

See also GRADING SYSTEMS; MINT LUSTER; MORGAN DOLLAR.

BANK NOTE A paper certificate issued by a bank, promising payment to the bearer of a specified amount of money in the form of coinage.

The term "bank note" is best used to describe the product of a totally or partially private bank. To be entirely accurate, paper currency which is strictly governmental should be referred to by another term.

The bank note was a natural outgrowth of the expanding economic system of seventeenth- and eighteenth-century Europe. The discovery and exploitation of the Indies, the ongoing warfare between developing states, the birth of the Industrial Revolution, all called for a simplified way to handle money. The bank note was devised to meet this need.

It did not spring from a vacuum, however. Its predecessor, the bill of exchange, was a private written agreement between merchants for a set sum of money, and the bank note was simply a refinement of the concept. A bank of known fiscal probity would issue paper promissory notes in set denominations. If the bank's paper was strictly tied to its cash reserves, and the fact was well recognized, the paper was accepted at its stated value by any businessman. Transportation of large amounts of specie was no longer necessary, and commerce was made easier and safer.

The first note-issuing bank was Sweden's Stockholms Banco, organized in 1656, which printed notes for general circulation between 1661 and 1666. Both it and the more famous Bank of England (organized 1694; first paper money issued the following year) were private concerns, but they functioned under royal charters and had the blessings of their respective governments. And indeed, they had good reason to offer support, as in each case the bank lent its government money during a financial emergency.

Bank note. *Sweden, Skaraborgs Läns Enskilda Bank, 10 kronor, 1888.*

The Stockholms Banco succumbed to temptation and issued bank notes far in excess of its redemptive capacities, causing a run on its holdings which forced it to close its doors. The Bank of England, on the other hand, was more judicious and survives to this day, at least in name.

During the eighteenth century the concept of the bank note spread throughout Europe, with many of the note-issuing banks partially government owned. In the British Isles they tended to be more private affairs.

But the great age of bank notes was the early nineteenth century, by which time the idea had travelled to the United States, where rapid economic expansion necessitated large amounts of money. Hundreds of banks were incorporated, awarded state charters, and began to print paper money. Unfortunately, much of it was not supported by adequate specie reserves, and bank failures occurred with a monotonous frequency—in 1819, 1837, and 1857—as they did also in Europe. In 1825–1826 hundreds of British banks went under, their notes suddenly worthless.

The chronic instability of the private bank, and a growing notion that governments should produce paper money, led to a gradual phasing out of the private bank note after 1850. Government treasury notes or promissory certificates often replaced it. Where national banks were established, the Banque de France and the German Reichsbank for example, control was essentially vested in the government, not in the bankers, and currency was government-issued.

Today there is no purely private, note-issuing bank. Our use, or misuse, of the term "bank note" to describe any form of paper money is a throwback to the days when private issues were the rule, and our lingering fear of paper money recalls the reasons why private issues disappeared in the first place.

See also BILL OF EXCHANGE; BROKEN BANK NOTES; PAPER MONEY.

BARBAROUS IMITATIONS A term for a group of coins, produced between 400 B.C. and A.D. 400, which were imitations of Greek and Roman issues.

Those responsible for the imitations were obeying a simple economic and artistic law: lacking a native coinage tradition, they borrowed one, usually from an adjacent area.

The coin used as a model had to fulfill certain requirements: it had to be of proven utility in trade; it had to have been produced in sizable quantities, allowing barbarian minters enough specimens from which to work; and finally it had to have a visually appealing design, to catch the eyes of the unlettered peoples who would use the imitation.

As few Greek and Roman coins met all these demands, barbarous imitations are found in a small number of well-defined types. One of the most interesting was a series of imitations of the Macedonian stater of Philip II (ruled 359–336 B.C.). Philip's stater was a small gold coin—weighing 8.6 grams, and some 18 millimeters in diameter—the purity and convenient size of which made it a popular trading coin within the Greek world and beyond. By 300 B.C., Celts of the Danube basin were producing copies of it; while cruder than Philip's issues, the basic types

Barbarous imitations.
Top: Macedon, Philip II, stater, 359–336 B.C.
Bottom: Channel Islands, barbarous imitation of above, 75–50 B.C.

(a head of Apollo on the obverse, a figure in a two-horse chariot on the reverse) were still recognizable.

The Danubian imitations proved so popular in trade that they were copied in turn by less civilized tribes. Such copying of a copy occurred time and again as the "stater" moved north and west across Europe, until its original designs underwent a complete metamorphosis. When the coin reached the limits of western Europe, Apollo's head had assumed a nightmarish appearance, and all the reverse elements had degenerated into a single horse of a distinctly surrealistic mien. This total transformation of Philip's gold stater took nearly three centuries.

Two other barbarous imitations were based on Roman coins. On one, the Barbarous Radiate series produced in the fourth century (taken from Roman antoniniani of the third century) the radiate crown on the emperor's head was retained and expanded while most other design elements were dropped. If legends appeared, they were jumbled and meaningless.

Another famous barbarous copy dates from the late fourth or early fifth century and was inspired by a coin of Constantius II (ruled A.D. 337–361), which depicted the emperor on the obverse, and a Roman soldier in the act of spearing a vanquished barbarian on the reverse. The original coin circulated widely in the Roman Empire, and the adaptation of it by the very peoples who were about to overrun the empire was ironic, at the very least.

See also ANTONINIANUS; IMITATION; POTIN; STATER; TRADE COINS.

BARTER The direct exchange of one commodity for another: the first step in the development of money.

Barter has appeared at all times, in all places, and among all peoples. Although we are inclined to think of it as a practice restricted to primitive peoples, this is not so, as the temporary reversion to barter in the American South after the Civil War, or in Hungary after the Second World War, will attest.

Any trading system based on barter must sooner or later deal with two problems: first, the fluctuation of a bartered commodity's value—grain can be scarce one year, abundant the next; and second, peoples' needs at any given time. The farmer who wants to trade his cow for cloth may encounter a weaver who is disinclined to accept a cow as payment.

Basically such problems are inherent and insoluble; a society requires a stable unit of exchange that represents value. While societies have used everything from cacao beans to farm implements to feathers of rare birds, many settled on precious metal.

Gold and silver became natural units for use in barter. The metals might have been scarce, but they were still available in limited quantities to almost everyone, and their colors evoked the sun and the moon, important symbols to early civilizations. Then too, works of art could be fashioned from them, as could a variety of personal adornments. All of this served to encourage the use of gold and silver in trade.

There were uncertainties, however— the purity of the gold, the amount of silver. With time, a third party took its place between buyer and seller, refining and weighing the gold and silver, then marking each piece to indicate that it had done so. It was the government, and its product was the coin.

See also ASSAY; COMMODITY MONEY; MONEY.

BATH METAL   A soft alloy of 75 percent copper, 24.7 percent zinc, and 0.3 percent silver, named after the city in which it was developed (Bath, England).

Bath metal, also known as Wood's metal, has a distinct brassy characteristic and is a shade paler than pure copper. Its softness enables it to take an excellent

impression from coin dies with a minimum of force, but it also means that it wears very poorly.

Bath metal was used in the manufacture of Rosa Americana coins, struck under contract by William Wood in the early 1720s for the English colonies on the Atlantic Coast. The coinage, minted in twopence, pence, and halfpence denominations, was extremely unpopular with its colonial audience, due in part to its metallic content, but more to the fact that it was vastly underweight.

See also ALLOY; ROSA AMERICANA COINAGE.

BILINGUAL MONEY   Coins or bills with legends or inscriptions in two different, current languages.

Until this century, bilingual money often indicated a territory's colonial status; today it is more apt to reflect the existence of two distinct politically important ethnic groups in one country.

Examples of bilingual money in colonial areas are myriad. Indo-Scythian coins of the first century B.C. revealed obverse legends in Greek, reverse ones in Kharoshthi, the language of the conquered peoples in that north Indian state. Two thousand years later, Indian coinage was again bilingual—with the obverse legend of the silver rupee of George V (ruled 1910–1936) in English and the reverse in English and Urdu. After the nation's independence in 1947 most legends continued to be rendered in English, with subsidiary ones in Hindi. This phenomenon reflected the Indian past and the problems confronting its present. English had been the official language of British India for so long that it was a legacy of many Indians. Then too, the number and diversity of the country's local languages made the use of English on coinage expedient. Hence it is one of India's two official languages, to be used in documents, public debate as desired, and on coins (the other

Bilingual money. Canada, Bank of Canada, dollar, 1967.

is Hindi, readily understood by many Indians). Bilingual money, as India attests, can not only reflect a colonial status, but can be the result of one. Belgium and Canada, on the other hand, are examples of nations using bilingual money to represent the two distinct and influential peoples each contains.

When Belgium won independence in 1830, its population was divided almost equally between French-speaking Walloons and Flemish-speaking Flemings. With the Walloons in control of the government, French became the official language.

Angered by their exclusion, the Flemings' agitation for equality of language resulted in a curious bilingual coinage. Instead of Flemish and French appearing on a single coin, a separate but equal system was devised in 1882 with two parallel series, identical in design, but with one bearing legends in French and the other in Flemish. Paper money, on the other hand, held both languages on the same piece, one on either side.

By the late 1930s the Belgian government began striking a single series of coins with French and Flemish on the same piece, and continues to do so. But in the name of harmony, legends or inscriptions are kept brief, and as "neutral" a coinage as possible is created.

The history of Canada's bilingual money is more briefly described. As an English colony, its coinage naturally favored English, although locally produced tokens frequently carried legends in French, the language of Quebec. After Dominion status was granted in 1867, protests by the Quebecois for recognition increased, eventually leading to a cautious use of bilingual money. Canada's paper currency has had French and English inscriptions in a carefully controlled parity since 1935, and French is now beginning to appear on commemorative coinage.

BILL OF EXCHANGE A form of paper currency used in late medieval and early modern Europe, most commonly between merchants.

The bill of exchange, spawned at a time when heightened wealth and commerce required easier ways of handling large sums of money, operated much like a modern bank check. For example, Party A in York (or perhaps Virginia, as it was a significant form of English colonial currency) promised to pay a sum of money to Party B in London by or before an agreed-upon date. Assuming A's credit was good, and the fact was known in the business community, Party B could use the bill to purchase goods from Party C, pay his debts to Party D, and so forth. Eventually the bill was presented to A for payment and the note then destroyed. As with all later paper currency, the bill of exchange was only as good as the reputation of the original issuer.

And it had limitations, which contributed to its decline and demise. As it was handwritten, it could be readily counterfeited. Furthermore, it generally represented a sizable amount of money and hence was of little use to most people in

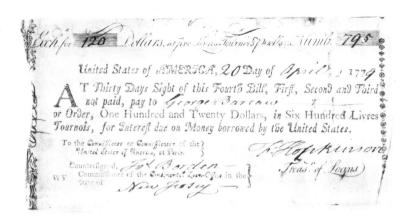

Bill of exchange. United States, bill of exchange for 120 dollars, 1779.

day-to-day transactions. Above all, the private nature of the bill of exchange (one businessman promises to pay another), restricted it to a small portion of the community. By the nineteenth century it had passed from the scene, and the public and private paper money it engendered were flourishing media of exchange.

See also BANK NOTE; CHECK; PAPER MONEY.

BILLON An alloy of silver mixed with an equal or greater proportion of a base metal, usually copper, and one of the few alloys to be dignified by a numismatic abbreviation, Bi.

Numismatists tend to spell billon in full, or, in a more candid recognition of its metallic content, to refer to it as Æ.

In an uncirculated state, a billon coin resembles a silver one, except it is less shiny and paler in color. Laminations may also be present, for the alloy is difficult to mix and the planchets can contain striations or even cracks. The alloy is brittle and cracks may be extended and laminations fall away entirely during the striking process. If a billon coin has been circulated, its high points often appear coppery or brassy. Before the planchets are minted into coins they are blanched with a weak acid which removes a portion of the copper close to the surface and leaves a porous mass of silver. When struck, this

silver is compressed, and the coin emerges with a short-lived shiny surface. Once in circulation, the thin plating of the precious metal wears off the coin's high points, revealing its base nature. The effects can be embarrassing, as Henry VIII of England (ruled 1509–1547) learned to his chagrin. In need of money, the king increased the amount of copper in the silver testoon, which bore his portrait in full-face. As fate would have it, the point where the silver plating first wore through happened to be Henry's nose. The king quickly earned the sobriquet "Old Coppernose."

Although no longer used as a coining metal, billon has a distinguished history stretching from ancient days to the twentieth century. Known to the ancient Greeks, it later formed the basis for the Roman antoninianus; the Byzantines struck coins in it, as did their conquerors, the forces of Islam. The seventeenth and eighteenth centuries, however, comprised the great age of billon coinage which then dominated central Europe. German and Austrian towns, kingdoms, and other authorities struck billon coinages in a bewildering variety of denominations. The coins were apt to be flat and thin, and many of them represented denominations which, because of inflation, could no longer be struck in good silver. It seemed of little matter, and towns went on using the metal to strike good-looking but largely valueless coins. The public, in turn, accepted them with relative calm, probably preferring coins with even a small amount of silver to coins with none at all.

After 1800 production of billon coinage dropped off rapidly; it made one of its final appearances in Europe in the scheidemünzen, produced by Prussia and other states before German unification in 1871. Its kin, however, an alloy of 10 percent silver and 90 percent copper, nickel, and zinc, was used for Mexican pesos as late as 1967. In recent years better, cheaper alloys have largely replaced billon as a coining medium.

See also Æ; ALLOY; ANTONINIANUS; GROAT; LAMINATION; PESO; POTIN; SCHEIDEMÜNZEN; TESTOON.

BIMETALLIC CURRENCY Coinage struck under a monetary system which uses two precious metals—ordinarily gold and silver—rather than one, as its base.

For a bimetallic system to function properly, the gold-silver ratio must be realistic, accurate, and above all stable. Should the ratio be out of balance, too little of one metal would be minted and too much of the other. If the supply of one metal increases, its value in relation to its partner descends and, as seen in the United States in the late nineteenth century, this can lead to grave economic and political problems. A boom in America's production of silver depressed its value in relation to gold. While Western mining interests, farmers, and debtors in general clamored for the free and unlimited production of silver coinage with an artifically high ratio of sixteen units of silver to one of gold—the legal ratio established in 1834—Eastern business interests favored replacement of bimetallism with a single monetary standard based on gold. This was achieved in 1900 with the Gold Standard Act, but not before great opposition, culminating in the presidential campaign of 1896, had been overcome.

See also GOLD STANDARD; MORGAN DOLLAR.

BIT The Spanish-American real; anything of that general size and weight, punched or cut from a Spanish-American silver coin, and usually counterstamped by local colonial authorities for use in the Caribbean Basin (also spelled bitt).

The discovery of vast silver deposits in Mexico, Peru, Bolivia, and other areas was especially important when Spain conquered the Indies in the sixteenth century and introduced its coinage system to the new lands. Mints were quickly organized, in part to satisfy local monetary needs, but also to fashion the bulky silver ore into coins, which could be more easily transported. The major coins were the Piece of Eight, weighing around 27 grams; the two-real piece, about 6.8 grams; and the real itself, with a weight of slightly under 3.4 grams. Their diameters varied greatly, due to the crudity of the minting process. By the 1730s, however, with the introduction of modern coining machinery, they were standardized at about 39, 27, and 20 millimeters, respectively.

Emboldened by Spain's conquests, other European nations attempted to establish American colonies, and some succeeded. England colonized North America's Atlantic Coast. France acquired the future Quebec. And England, France, the Netherlands, Denmark, and Sweden secured control of a number of areas in and around the Caribbean—Jamaica, the Guianas, Curaçao, and Guadeloupe, among others. Coinage was needed for local and external trade, and as silver and gold were not native to these lands, colonial authorities worked with available foreign coinage, primarily the Spanish-

Bit.
Left: Trinidad, 1811.
Right: Danish West Indies, 50 bit or 10 cents, 1905.

American reales and their multiples, which reached them through trade (most of it illegal) with the Spanish Empire. Much of it was used exactly as it entered from abroad. A real was frequently renamed a bit; but nothing was done to alter its design.

Yet there was a move to create a distinctly local coinage. To that end authorities tested the metal in an existing coin, then counterstamped it with a local seal, thus guaranteeing its worth. This was a flourishing practice in the eighteenth and early nineteenth centuries, and almost every European Caribbean colony had a local currency based on Spanish-American coins. The values of the new pieces were usually expressed in bits and their multiples.

The one-real piece was rarely used for this purpose. However the larger Spanish-American silver coins, multiples of the real, were adapted in one of two ways. In some cases, a hole was punched in the coin's center, the core removed and stamped for use as one bit. The remainder of the coin (usually a Piece of Eight) was then counterstamped for circulation as a multiple of the bit. The number of bits contained in each Piece of Eight varied from place to place. In Trinidad, for example, the core was tariffed at one bit, the rest of the coin at nine, resulting in an exchange ratio of ten Trinidadian bits to eight Spanish-American reales.

A more common method was to cut the Piece of Eight (or its four- or two-real subsidiary coins) into pie-shaped wedges, and counterstamp them with an abbreviation registering their place of issue. As the counterstamps were rather small, the coins resembled triangular pieces of silver with one curved edge, and bore what seemed to be hallmarks. The cut coinage was issued in bits and their multiples.

Cut and counterstamped coinage reached a high point in the Caribbean around 1810. By 1900, however, England, France, Holland, and Denmark were supplying their larger colonies with some form of coinage for local use, and their smaller ones with ordinary national coinage. The counterstamped bit and its equivalents were consigned to obsolescence.

Yet the name survived. When Denmark provided the Danish West Indies with coinage in 1905, it followed local custom and struck denominations expressed in bits. While the English colonies in North America never counterstamped Spanish-American coins for local use, they were as dependent upon the real and its multiples as were their Caribbean counterparts. The word "bit" for real was as familiar in New York as in Trinidad, and remained in the vernacular long after the new United States acquired its own monetary system. Although few Americans today realize it, when they refer to a quarter dollar as "two bits," they are paying tribute to the Spanish-American real.

See also COB; COUNTERSTAMP; HOLEY DOLLAR; PIECE OF EIGHT; REAL.

BLUEBACK A term conceived during the American Civil War (1861–1865), describing paper money printed by the Confederate States of America during that period, and probably inspired by greenbacks, the name then popular for federal currency issues.

Early Confederate paper money was produced in the same fashion as the so-called broken bank notes—engraved, and printed on just one side. Given the rudimentary state of nineteenth-century technology, especially in the South, only small amounts of paper money could be printed this way. The lithographic process was far speedier, and the South, chronically short of specie even before the outbreak of war, turned to it late in the summer of 1861. Unfortunately, lithography does not produce as fine a line as does printing from an engraved plate. Furthermore the danger of counterfeiting is enhanced. The Confederacy, nevertheless, chose to run the risk, one compounded by a lack of de-

cent printing inks, quality paper, and skilled lithographers.

As the war lengthened and its cost grew astronomical, paper money was the only avenue open to the South. Inflation was rampant. Prices climbed, and more money was needed when less hard cash was available, forcing the Confederacy to add to its supply of paper money and hope for the best. Inevitably, this money was lithographed, not engraved.

In an attempt to improve the quality of the lithography—somewhat to raise civilian morale, but more importantly to check counterfeiting—notes were printed with designs on both faces. Even simple reverse designs (merely the denomination in a frame, or the value expressed in words and numbers), make counterfeiting a more difficult task. The first such notes are dated December 2, 1862, and feature blue reverses for the denominations from $5 through $100. One- and two-dollar notes, on the other hand, were still printed on one side—perhaps the Confederacy assumed that no one would bother to counterfeit bills of so modest a value.

For the next two and a half years, bluebacks were printed in increasing numbers as people became less certain of victory and the value of Confederate currency. No complete financial record of blueback production exists, but the last issues, dated February 17, 1864 and released through 1865, amounted to somewhat over 525 million dollars alone; the aggregate of bluebacks printed was about 1,100 million dollars.

The fall of the Confederate capital, Richmond, in April 1865, and the surrender of Southern armies later that spring, spared the Confederacy the necessity of redeeming the paper. And a triumphant federal government rejected any notion that it should be responsible for its adversary's money. Bluebacks immediately lost what little value they had possessed, yet large numbers of them still exist, if only because so many were printed in the first place.

See also COUNTERFEIT; GREENBACK; INFLATION; LITHOGRAPHY.

Boat money. Thailand, c. 1800.

Bookmark. Japan, 5 momme, 1772.

BOAT MONEY   Bronze currency shaped like dugout canoes, used in northeastern Thailand and parts of Laos up to the middle of the nineteenth century.

The average boat piece, the design of which may have been inspired by the boats that plied the Mekong River, is a narrow oval, some 85 millimeters long by 15 wide, weighing around 40 grams. The "coins" do not bear inscriptions, and one side of the piece slopes gently inward toward the center, increasing its resemblance to a canoe. Like many Thai issues of the premodern period boat pieces were cast, and were one of several trading media that seem oddities to Western eyes, including the more famous bullet and packsaddle pieces.

See also BULLET MONEY; PACKSADDLE MONEY.

BOOKMARK   A long, narrow form of paper money issued in feudal Japan.

Typical specimens measure 155 millimeters by 35, and the majority date from the eighteenth and nineteenth centuries.

Bookmarks, whose Japanese name is hansatsu, were promises to pay set amounts, usually in silver, to the bearer. Most were printed on both sides by the woodblock method in black ink, although bicolor specimens are known. All bear one or more validation stamps.

Bookmarks reflect the period's political shifts: the power of the central government, personified in the shogun, declined, while the influence of clans and provincial governments grew. Hence, hansatsu were not produced by the shogunate, but rather by local authorities; they continued in use until the emperor restored a strong central government in 1868. In his desire to strengthen his control and modernize the country, the emperor gave Japan its first modern, centralized bank-note system, ending production of hansatsu.

See also PAPER MONEY.

BORDER   The ring-shaped outer area of a coin.

Normally the border is thicker than the surface which it surrounds. On modern coins borders tend to extend between .5 and 1.5 millimeters in from the rim. Borders serve two purposes. They protect coins from excessive damage by ensuring that the first place to receive wear is the relatively unimportant border, rather than

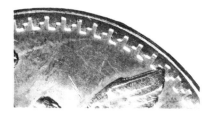

Border. Mexico, 50 pesos, 1925 (detail).

an essential portion of the design or legend. Borders also enable coins to be properly stacked. Coins without borders, for instance, would have "bulges" in their fields, as did Greek and Roman coins, and would never stack evenly, a serious drawback for modern banks and businesses. Raised borders eliminate the problem, as the surfaces where two coins meet when stacked are perfectly flat in relation to one another.

Two separate manufacturing stages are involved in applying a border. In the first, "upsetting," a flat planchet is compressed edgewise between two rollers. The upsetting machine smooths the planchet's edge, making it perfectly round, and thickens its periphery so its borders fit snugly into the periphery of the dies, thereby displacing less metal when the border is struck. In turn this means less force need be applied to the dies during the striking process. Dies last longer, an important consideration for modern coiners when mint production can run into several hundred million coins a year.

The second stage is the striking process, when the border forms part of the working die and is struck on the planchet along with the rest of the design. Borders on most contemporary coins are plain, although such ornate borders as the beaded border, dentilated border, or the fancy "step" border found on early twentieth-century Mexican coins were once in favor.

See also DENTICLES; PLANCHET; UPSET EDGE.

BRACTEATE A broad, exceptionally thin form of the silver penny, popular in Germany and surrounding areas from about 1100 to 1350.

The word "bracteate" is an eighteenth-century invention, derived from the Latin *bractea,* meaning a veneer or thin plate of metal. The outstanding characteristic of the bracteate is its appearance. Only one die was used to strike the coin, and, unlike

Bracteate. *Hersfeld, pfennig, 1201–1213.*

most other dies, it was cut in relief, not in intaglio. The result was a coin whose devices and legends were depressed on one side and raised on the other, due to the thinness of the silver planchet used for striking. The raised surface was the obverse; the intaglio surface, which received the actual strike, was the reverse.

The bracteate sprang from an attempt to increase the size of a coin but not its silver content. From the eighth century to the thirteenth, the prevalent coin of western Europe was the penny—known also as the denier, denaro, pfennig—with an average weight of a gram or slightly more, and a diameter of some 20 millimeters. Its smallness inhibited the production of an artistic coin. Limited European silver supplies, however, made a larger, heavier coin impractical.

But with the same amount of silver the penny could be enlarged if it was made thinner. By 1100 such a possibility had been recognized. Were a coin thin enough, a strike with only one die would produce designs on both its sides. It could be made large enough to incorporate designs with high relief—unknown in the West since the demise of the Roman Empire—and still use a modest amount of silver. Furthermore, a die's life would be extended and only half as many would be needed.

Large numbers of bracteates were minted in the twelfth and thirteenth centuries, primarily in German towns and bishoprics, but also in Switzerland, Hungary, Bohemia, Poland, even Scandinavia.

Although modern numismatists are not positive about the way they were struck, it is felt some issues may have been minted with dies cut from hardwood rather than metal, and at least for certain series it is suggested that a number of coins were struck at once, with the imprint's clarity gradually lessening from the top of the pile of planchets to the bottom. That several bracteates could be struck at one time is a reminder that the coins had a thickness roughly equivalent to tinfoil. Needless to say, they were fragile.

They were also beautiful. The large surface meant artists had space, and they filled it with some of the finest examples of small medieval art—churches abound, as do bishops, princes, and kings, usually seen full-face, standing or seated. Whatever was portrayed, it covered most of the coin, reducing legends to a minor role.

The bracteate's popularity began to decline in the fourteenth century. Beautiful or not, it simply was not practical. The heavier silver coins then being minted in Italy, chief among them the grosso, proved far more useful in trade than the penny, and the discovery of new silver deposits in central Europe meant Germany and other regions could strike heavier and larger silver coins of their own. Gradually these supplanted the bracteate and, ultimately, the penny itself. Production of bracteates fell off dramatically after 1350, but in some places they continued to be struck until almost 1700.

See also DENARO; DENIER; GROSSO; PENNY; PFENNIG.

BRASHER DOUBLOON A privately struck gold pattern, produced by New York goldsmith Ephraim Brasher in 1787, which is perhaps the most famous American coin.

The Brasher doubloon, of which seven specimens are known, directly reflects political events in the young United States of America. Through most of the 1780s the new republic lived under the Articles of Confederation, which established a weak central government, while vesting real powers in the states. One of these powers was the right to coin money, or award the right to a private coiner, such as Ephraim Brasher.

Like several other states, New York needed copper money to alleviate a chronic scarcity of small change. Brasher, along with several other New York metalworkers, competed for the authority to coin the state's coppers, and on February 11, 1787, he applied to the New York legislature for the right to do so.

The legislators were somewhat dubious. Brasher was a noted goldsmith, but coining copper is a different matter from working with gold. Could Brasher supply enough coppers to meet the demand, and could he do so with enough speed?

To prove his worth, Brasher minted his famous "doubloon." His actual coins would be struck in copper, of course; he used gold for his patterns by way of creating a dramatic effect. The dies were cut by hand: the obverse depicted a sun rising over mountains, with the name of the state and its motto in Latin, and Brasher's own name, presumably to indicate he personally guaranteed the coin's quality. On the reverse was a heraldic American eagle with Brasher's hallmark (the letters EB within an oval cartouche) punched on it, another Latin motto, and the year, 1787. Six of the Brasher doubloon specimens have the counterstamp on the wing, while the seventh shows it on the eagle's breast.

Brasher's efforts, alas, were for nought. As the photograph reveals, whatever skills he possessed as a goldsmith did not extend to coinage. The obverse type resembles random gougings more than mountains, while the eagle on the reverse is extremely crude, certainly not the creature of majesty fancied by the New York government. The very shallow treatment of some of the design elements—the eagle's wings and the arrows in its left talons, for example—indicate Brasher was

Brasher doubloon. United States, 1787.

not at home as a die-sinker. Finally, the lettering, done by punches, was irregularly applied. The state legislature did not grant Brasher his contract. Two years later, a new federal constitution assigned control of the coinage to the national government; a federal Mint was created in 1792 and was in operation later the same year. The day of the contract coiner had ended in America, but at least Brasher had become a part of numismatic history.

See also DOUBLOON; MINT ACT OF 1792; PATTERN; PRIVATE GOLD COINS; STATE COINAGE.

BRASS COINAGE Money struck in an alloy of zinc and copper, with the latter always the dominant element in the mixture.

Although the metal is pale-to-deep yellow when struck, and hence resembles gold, it discolors easily, turning a dark yellow-gray with use. The alloy's similarity to the precious metal when first struck led to its use in counterfeiting, and earned it an undeserved reputation for worthlessness, which is unfortunate. In fact, brass wears well, far better than copper, and can rightfully claim a distinguished part in the history of money. Indeed, technically, the United States "copper" cent, a mixture of 95 percent copper and 5 percent zinc, is a brass coin.

Brass was used for coinage from 300 B.C., sporadically by the Greeks, more regularly by the Romans, who struck their sestertii and dupondii in an alloy of 80 percent copper and 20 percent zinc, called *orichalcum*. Brass is also found in some of the "Greek Imperials," local coinages struck in Greek-speaking regions of the Roman Empire up to around A.D 300.

Although brass coinage ended in the West shortly before A.D. 300, and did not reappear for over a thousand years, it made an early debut in Chinese numismatics, and continued to play an important role there until modern times. It was frequently used in the most common Chinese coin, the ch'ien or cash, and through the centuries billions of these distinctive, square-holed coins were cast in brass. Imitating Chinese techniques, the Japanese cast many of their nami sen in brass.

In recent years brass has given way to more attractive and durable alloys, and, while still occasionally employed in coinage, its real numismatic importance is currently in the areas of medalets and tokens.

See also CASH; DUPONDIUS; JETON; MEDALET; NAMI SEN; SESTERTIUS; TOKEN.

BRITANNIA METAL A lightweight alloy composed of 90–91 percent tin, 7–8 percent antimony, and 1.4 percent copper.

The metal, which has an attractive silvery sheen when first struck, has never been used for coinage because it oxidizes rapidly and takes on an unpleasant black patina. It is also quite soft, making it unfit for coinage.

Nevertheless, in the nineteenth century it was used to a limited extent for inexpensive medals and souvenirs, which were privately minted and sold to commemorate great events (the coronation of a king, his death, etc.). The center of the practice was the British Isles, hence the name.

See also MEDAL; WHITE METAL.

BROADSTRUCK Struck outside a restraining collar, as a broadstruck coin.

Broadstruck coins are wider and thinner than usual, because of a failure in the process which should keep the metal in the planchets from spreading. Unlike the edges of ordinary coins, which are straight up-and-down, the edges of broadstruck coins often bow inward because of the outward movement of the metal planchet while under vertical pressure from the dies.

In modern coinage there are three dies, not two. Today's coining press has an upper and a lower die; the third die is in the form of a collar which acts on the planchet simultaneously with the upper and lower dies.

The modern planchet, in its final, pre-struck stage, has undergone an upsetting process, and been made slightly smaller in diameter than the upper and lower dies whose impression it will receive. It is also smaller than the collar, into which it must fit as it is struck. In the minting process, a mechanical layer-on places the planchet on the lower die, which then descends a set distance into the collar. The upper die comes down with tremendous force, causing a spread of metal into die designs and against the inside of the collar. The upper die is retracted, and the lower die rises through the collar, allowing the coin to be ejected.

The broadstruck coin is created when the collar fails to surround the planchet—because it or the lower die may not be in the proper position, or because the planchet may be too large to fit into the collar. The latter can occur if the planchet has somehow eluded the upsetting operations. In either case the blank receives its impression from the upper and lower dies in the ordinary way, but the absence of the third, collar, die causes the metal to spread far more than usual. Thus, the coin's borders —the areas struck by the peripheries of the dies—are much broader, while the uninterrupted flow of metal from the center outward makes the legend's letters blurred and spread out at the top, while remaining crisp and compact at the bottom.

The broadstruck coin is a phenomenon spawned by mechanical coining devices. One cannot describe an ancient or medieval coin as broadstruck, for, in a manner of speaking, all early coins were broadstruck. What we today consider an error was then the rule.

See also COLLAR; ERROR; MACHINE-STRUCK COINAGE; PLANCHET; UPSET EDGE.

BROCKAGE

BROCKAGE A mint error that produces a coin with two obverses or reverses, one of which is in relief, the other in intaglio and a reverse mirror image of the relief, but with less distinct legends and types.

As has been noted, a coin is minted when an upper and a lower die are brought together under pressure to strike the planchet between them. However, if the coin is not ejected from the lower die, and another planchet is inserted and struck, two mint errors are produced. While the new planchet receives an ordinary impression from the top die, as it is forced against the coin on the lower die it receives a second impression of the top die, but this time in reverse. This is the coin generally known as a brockage. The original coin, on the other hand, having been pushed yet more forcefully into the lower die, is likely to emerge with a strong impression on that side and a weak impression on the other. There is no universal agreement on terminology for this second coin. It too may be called a brockage, although it seems wise to restrict the term to those coins with clear intaglio and relief impressions. Should the second coin be struck several more times, causing its

Brockage. *United Kingdom, halfpenny, c. 1860.*

sides to flare out in a cuplike manner, the resulting error does have a special name: it is called a cupped coin.

Thus far we have described a brockage produced on the top planchet, or one with two obverses, which happens because the top die—at least in the case of the modern coining press—is the obverse die. But a brockage with two reverses occurs when for some reason the first coin adheres to the *top* die (a speck of moisture or grease can make it do so), and a new planchet is inserted into the coining mechanism.

Brockages are known on ancient coins, but they became more frequent as minting was mechanized and coins were produced with greater speed and in greater numbers. The brockage is still uncommon. Indeed, the error is so desirable that many attempts are made to forge it by forcing one coin into another with a vise or sledgehammer. However, the alteration usually reveals traces of the original design beneath the intaglio, and its die axis is likely to be off, making it fairly obvious, and not a serious threat to collectors.

See also CUPPED COIN; ERROR; FORGERY; PLANCHET.

BROKEN BANK NOTES A privately issued paper currency used in the United States between 1800 and 1865, the name of which reflects the fact that many of the issuing banks went "broke."

Not all did, however. A number of banks reorganized and ceased printing paper, while others successfully liquidated and went out of business. For this reason, "obsolete bank note" might be a more accurate term than "broken bank note," but as the latter has been used by numismatists for over a hundred years, it is used in this book.

The roots of the broken bank note rest in the eighteenth century, when a lack of precious metals made it necessary for the American colonies to print paper money rather than mint coins. Colonial paper worked fairly well much of the time, and those issues printed to aid in Britain's wars were redeemed by the Crown.

In 1775, with the outbreak of the American War for Independence, the Continental Congress authorized the printing of paper money to pay expenses; but as the war continued for the better part of a decade, the value of this Continental Currency slipped to a tiny fraction of its stated worth. The individual colonies—or states, as they began calling themselves—printed their own paper money, but this too depreciated, even more than federal issues.

The battle of Yorktown in late 1781 turned the war in America's favor, and a peace treaty was eventually signed in 1783. By 1789 the present Constitution had been ratified. It forbade states to issue paper money, and was deliberately silent on the federal government's right to do so. Undoubtedly, Hamilton and other leaders of the Federalist movement hoped to replace paper money with coins, and their Mint Act of 1792 was designed for just that purpose. However, the new Mint,

Broken bank notes. *South Carolina, Planters Bank of Fairfield, 5 dollars, 1855.*

which struck its first regular coins in 1793, was hampered by worn machinery, a modest production capacity, and a short supply of metal.

Nonetheless, Americans needed some form of money, and paper currency, though frowned upon by Hamilton and a good many average Americans, was better than no currency at all. If the federal government declined to print it, and the states could not, an alternative was the private banking house, which could be chartered by the state to print paper money against its cash reserves. Such was the genesis of the broken bank note. Private issues were introduced just before 1790, and served as a dominant form of money in the United States until the end of the Civil War.

Broken bank notes are interesting for several reasons, not the least of which is their appeal to counterfeiters. The first private bank notes, either typeset or printed from engraved copper plates, were simple and easy to imitate, impelling the legitimate printer to devise new ways to outwit his illicit colleague. Vignettes were adopted; mechanical lathes produced fancy work; watermarked paper came into use; and by the 1840s, notes in more than one color were being printed. In no case was the motivation aesthetic. Yet the notes were a delight to the eye, and many of the issues produced from the late 1830s to the early 1860s are miniature design masterpieces and lessons in history. A clear picture of how early Americans lived and what they considered beautiful emerges through their choice of vignettes and ornamentation. Farmers are here, as are merchants, sailors, factory workers, and slaves—on a note produced by a South Carolina bank.

Beautiful or not, private bank notes suffered from a tarnished reputation, which was darkened by depressions and the collapse of hundreds of banks during the panics of 1819, 1837, and 1857. Americans preferred specie, if they could get it.

During the Civil War, the private banking system proved completely incapable of producing the gigantic sums of money needed by the North and South, particularly as its issues were theoretically tied to specie reserves, however tenuously. Governments, though, could issue national currency, tied to cash reserves or not as circumstances permitted—and both governments did so. Northern greenbacks were more or less linked to specie reserves; Southern bluebacks not at all.

By the middle of the war, production of purely private bank notes began to wane in the North. In 1863 the National Banking Act created national bank notes, paper money printed by the government on behalf of banks with bonds deposited in the federal treasury. Many banks voluntarily entered the new system. A tax on private bank notes of ten percent of their face value was enacted in 1865, in an effort to persuade recalcitrant banks to buy federal bonds and enter the national banking network. The law, which went into effect in 1866, sounded the death knell of the private, note-emitting bank in the North.

Nor did it fare better in the South. The Confederacy fell in the spring of 1865, and so did its entire fiscal system. Reconstruction governments issued some paper money on a state basis shortly after the end of the war, but when the South revived economically it followed the North's example and used federal currency.

See also BANK NOTE; CONTINENTAL CURRENCY; ENGRAVING; MINT ACT OF 1792; NATIONAL BANK NOTE; PAPER MONEY; TYPESET; VIGNETTE; WATERMARK; WILDCAT NOTES.

BRONZE COINAGE Money struck or cast in an alloy of copper and tin, first used in China several centuries before the Christian era.

Traditionally, the alloy consisted of 90 percent copper and 10 percent tin, but the bronze in modern coinage frequently combines 95 parts of copper with 4 of tin and 1 of zinc. Freshly minted bronze is pale, with a copper to light-tan hue; after exposure to the air, it turns a uniform light-to-deep brown. If oxidation continues long enough, it can develop the hard or soft green or blue crust often seen on ancient bronze coins. Left unchecked, bronze disease can develop.

Barter pieces in the shapes of cowrie shells and agricultural implements were being cast in bronze in China by 1000 B.C. The use of bronze for this coinage paralleled its use for actual farming tools, for it had been found that the mixture of copper and tin was more durable than either of the metals alone. Here we see a clear evolution in the use of bronze, from tools to trade, as well as one of the few examples in early coinage of a metal chosen for practicality rather than beauty.

Bronze's immediate popularity in the East was not paralleled in the West. While coinage in the Mediterranean world began in the seventh century B.C., bronze was hardly used there until the middle of the fourth century, and was not widespread until even later. Whenever possible, the Greeks employed silver, even though it meant coins of low value were extremely small. However the practice was expedient as purses and pockets had yet to be invented and ancient Greeks frequently carried small change in their mouths. It was possible to do so with silver, but bronze coins would have had an unpleasant taste, and their oxidized surfaces might even have poisoned the bearers.

All the same, bronze coins eventually won popularity in the Greek world and were prominent not only in the Ptolemaic kingdom of Egypt, but in the eastern Mediterranean, and Greek-speaking states in southern Italy. The Romans, for their part, showed more enthusiasm for bronze than the Greeks.

Bronze coinage disappeared from the West with the Middle Ages, and was not seen again until early modern times. The medieval world, for most of its thousand-year time span, used silver for coins, with gold reemerging at the end of the period.

Late medieval and early modern monetary systems used gold for coins of high value, silver for those of moderate value, and silver or billon for those of low value. Western Europeans, like the Greeks, preferred silver coins—even tiny ones—to those of base metal.

In time, however, copper coins, followed by the more durable bronze coins, were to be found, first in Europe, then in the Americas. Even if it tarnished, a low-denomination bronze coin was less difficult to handle than a silver coin of the same value, for it was larger and easier to keep track of, an advantage reinforced by an expanding and increasingly complex economy. Bronze coinage has been used widely in modern times as inflation, one of the most vexing problems of the age, has driven precious metal coinage from circulation. Today, nearly every industrialized nation uses the bronze coin in its coinage system.

See also AES GRAVE; BRONZE DISEASE; COWRIE; FOLLIS; KNIFE MONEY; SPADE MONEY.

BRONZE DISEASE Destructive corrosion of bronze, brass, and copper coins due to oxidation.

If a coin is buried, as was the case with most ancient coins, oxidation can take several forms. It can appear as attractive, hard, green-to-black patina, through which the coin's design are clearly visible. It can also show as hard green, blue, or black spots, obscuring part of the legends and designs. Or it may form a powdery, light-green patina, in spots or in larger patches. The first two forms of oxidation are relatively benign. Should a copper or bronze coin have a hard patination, whether uniform or spotty, it is wisest to leave it alone. The third form of corrosion is more troublesome. This is bronze disease, and as it frequently acts under the visible surfaces of a coin, it is difficult to detect and almost impossible to stop. Some things may help, however.

The easiest (though by no means the most satisfactory) way to deal with bronze disease is to gently remove the surface powder with baking soda or a mild commercial preparation, and then lacquer the coin. This produces a highly artificial look, but, providing the metal is sealed against oxygen, the spread of the disease will be arrested.

A more thorough method is to soak the coin for several hours in a cleaning solution. (A liquid jewelry cleaner may be used, providing it is heavily diluted with distilled water.) The coin should be checked from time to time, and gently brushed until all traces of the green powder have disappeared. The surface will be bare and pitted, and possibly still covered with reddish-brown patches of copper oxide. If a patch is thick, an enclosed pouch of bronze disease may be present and the patch must be opened with a sharp instrument and the inside rinsed with the cleaning agent. Washing and brushing in distilled water completes the cleaning process, but the coin should be examined frequently for new outbreaks of the disease.

See also PATINA.

BULL AND HORSEMAN COINAGE

Small coins of silver or billon, struck by the Rajput rulers of India from the ninth through the twelfth centuries A.D.

Their name aptly describes them. On the obverse is a reclining humped bull with a symbol resembling a trident on its flank; on the reverse is a mounted figure, probably the king, holding a lance pointing downward. Obverse legends are in Nagari, above the bull; on the reverse, where they continue, to the right of and above the mounted figure, they are in the Bactrian language. When first introduced, late in the ninth century, the coin weighed about 3.2 grams, with a diameter of some 18 millimeters. Its silver content was reasonably good and the types and legends competently executed.

Bull and horseman coinage. *Ohind, silver coin, late ninth century.*

Later issues of the series were smaller and thicker, and their silver content steadily declined, as did the quality of their art. Early issues reveal the attempt to depict subjects in the round, but from the early tenth century on the bull and horseman were portrayed merely in outline, and in time even the outlines became more abstract. However, quantities of them were produced and collectors will find they are readily available at modest prices.

With the Mohammedan conquest of India in the late twelfth century, native bull and horseman coinage ended, although the Moslems struck imitative issues in the following century, somewhat along the lines of Arab-Byzantine issues.

See also ARAB-BYZANTINE COINAGE; IMITATION.

BULLET MONEY A distinctive, almost globular form of silver, and in rare instances, gold coinage, used in Thailand from the fourteenth through the nineteenth centuries.

Bullet money is seen in a variety of sizes; the unit silver piece in the series, called a tical or baht in Thai, weighed 15

Bullet money. *Thailand, 4 baht, 1851–1868.*

grams and was slightly less than 15 millimeters in diameter. It began as a thick, round glob of metal, the ends of which were hammered upward to form a very tight "U"; coinage was completed with one or more validating punches.

Silver issues of bullet money ranged in weight and value from ¹⁄₆₄ to four ticals; issues in gold, valued at up to sixteen ticals and weighing up to approximately 15 grams, are also known. In the 1860s, European-style money was introduced in Thailand and the minting of bullet money ceased. However, the name of the old coin was preserved and today the basic coinage unit is still called a baht.

See also BOAT MONEY; PACKSADDLE MONEY; PUNCH-MARKED COINS.

BULLION Precious metal, usually gold, in an unalloyed state and ordinarily in the form of ingots.

Bullion is the basis for most of the modern world's currencies, i.e., it is understood that paper money has the backing of gold or silver. The public cannot exchange paper money for government bullion, of course, but, if only for psychological reasons, a system of paper money and fiduciary coinage (coinage intrinsically worth less than its stated value) cannot exist indefinitely without some bullion reserve.

Bullion also refers to the intrinsic value of the precious metal in a coin. If we say a British silver crown has a bullion value of ten dollars, we mean the silver in the coin, disregarding the other metals present, is worth that amount. Unless a coin is mutilated, pierced, or worn smooth, a gold or silver coin has a collector value in excess of its intrinsic worth as bullion.

See also INGOT; PAPER MONEY.

BUNGTOWN Any of a series of counterfeit English halfpence, circulated in America in the late eighteenth century.

Bungtown. *American counterfeit or "bungtown" copy of an English halfpenny, dated 1788.*

Bungtown counterfeits tended to weigh less than 6 grams, as opposed to genuine British halfpence, which weighed over 9 grams; they were also smaller—27 millimeters in diameter, as opposed to 29. They fall into two series. Members of the first are called evasions. Produced in England and Ireland, evasions bear portraits and reverse designs similar to those on genuine coins, but their legends contain blunders or are altogether different from the originals, and they often show dates for years when no halfpence were struck —all attempts to evade British counterfeiting law. Then too, they frequently seem worn, as though from years of circulation; in reality, such pieces were gently struck from shallow dies to create just that illusion. These "coins" were imported to the new United States in the same period when Americans, desperately short of small change, began manufacturing a second series of bungtowns.

It too was lightweight, but its designs more closely matched the originals (the halfpenny of George III was the coin most often imitated), and its legends were usually identical with their genuine English counterparts. The dates, however, which were a minor part of the total design, could vary. Thus, while George III struck halfpence yearly from 1770 to 1775, American-made bungtowns carry these dates and others well into the late 1780s.

The origin of "bungtown" is unclear. Some numismatists believe it is a contraction for Birmingham, England, a noted source of counterfeit copper coins in the seventeenth and eighteenth centuries.

Others think it was originally a slang word for a real American town. If so, the town's identity has never been established. A recent and convincing argument is that "bung" derives from a pejorative term for the anus, and the bungtown meant a coin from a town which was, quite literally, a hole. Whatever its genesis the word was in use by the mid-1780s to describe counterfeit halfpence, and at one time encompassed any lightweight, counterfeit copper coin circulating in America.

See also COUNTERFEIT; EVASION.

BUSH NOTES   Twentieth-century emergency money, printed in the bush of German East Africa (now Tanzania): some of the earliest paper money printed in Africa.

In 1885, East Africa became a protectorate of Germany, which provided it with money minted in the homeland; in 1902 the system was made decimal, with 100 heller equalling one rupie. Furthermore, the colonial Deutsch-Ostafrikanische Bank (German East African Bank), was established, issuing bank notes, printed in Germany, based on the rupie and its multiples.

With the outbreak of World War I in 1914, the British blockade made it impossible to import money from Germany, leaving the colony to produce its own currency.

Coins, all dated 1916, were struck in several denominations at a makeshift mint in a railway yard at Tabora, while typeset notes were issued from a Dar-es-Salaam printing press commandeered by the German East African Bank and from another press at Tabora. In September 1916, Dar-es-Salaam and Tabora both fell to British forces and colonial minting and printing came to a halt.

The colonial government, still in need

Bush notes. German East Africa, Deutsch-Ostafrikanische Bank, 5 rupie, 1917.

of money to pay its remaining armies, scattered and regrouped. Lacking both a mint and a press, it printed paper money by hand, from rubber type. The result was the bush note. Each was dated July 1 or October 1, 1917, and carried a German imperial eagle stamped on the reverse. Although no place-name was given, they were ostensibly issued by the German East African Bank.

Notes were printed with whatever was available. Inks tended to be black or purple (stamp-pads were their probable source). Most bush notes were on white paper, though other colors were used when printers' supplies were depleted.

Bush notes were used through most of 1918 to pay the armies that remained in the field until the Armistice in November. Indeed, many of them may have been printed in 1918, but with an earlier date.

See also BANK NOTE; EMERGENCY MONEY; TYPESET.

C

CABINET FRICTION Slight surface wear on the high points of a coin or medal, caused by friction due to inclusion of the piece in a collection.

Unlike the signs of wear generated by circulation, cabinet friction takes place after a piece is removed from circulation. It is not nearly as common a malady today as it once was. Until well into this century, coins and medals were customarily displayed in wooden or metal trays, which in turn were stored in multilevel cabinets. When a tray was removed, the high points of its numismatic items could rub against the tray immediately above it. Ancient coins and large medals, both with designs in high relief, were in particular jeopardy.

Such storage systems are now largely obsolete, as modern collectors opt for ease of transportation and inexpensive protection for their coins and medals. Dozens of products, from loose-leaf binders to plastic envelopes, are on the market, and their use has significantly reduced the incidence of cabinet friction. However, some of the paper envelopes used for coins are made of rough, coarse-fiber material that can cause abrasions; these should be avoided.

A soft paper coin envelope, on the other hand, protects the coin without damaging it. It should be remembered that a paper envelope with a high percentage of sulfur can badly tarnish any silver, copper-nickel, or copper coin stored in it.

See also GRADING SYSTEMS.

CAMPAIGN AWARD A decoration which does not denote individual heroism but merely records the fact that its recipient was present and fought in a certain military action.

Unlike chivalric decorations and those for gallantry, the campaign medal is a relatively recent invention. Although the first, the Dunbar medal, was granted by Cromwell's Parliament in September 1650 to participants in a successful battle against the Scots, it was an isolated example and nearly a century and a half would pass before others were issued.

The origin of the modern campaign decoration has its roots in the Napoleonic Wars (1792–1815) when individual British commanders and public-spirited private

Campaign award. United Kingdom, India General Service Medal, 1849–1895 (with two bars for specific campaigns).

citizens bestowed medals on those who had served in various battles and campaigns. While not issued by the British government, they were nonetheless worn with its blessing. Several years after the battle of Waterloo, fought in 1815, the British government produced the first modern, collectible campaign medal, and awarded it to all British soldiers in that final battle of the Napoleonic Wars. The Waterloo Medal was well received, and Great Britain was soon awarding similar pieces for other campaigns. By the end of the nineteenth century, the campaign award had spread throughout the world.

Several elements make up campaign awards. The most obvious is the badge. Typical badges are circular, from 30 to 40 millimeters in diameter, usually of bronze or silver, and have obverse and reverse types, legends, and inscriptions arranged much as they would be on coins. A head of a real or imaginary person often adorns the obverse, and an allegorical figure the

reverse. The badge hangs from a ribbon that is itself significant, as its color or colors and their arrangement (often adapted from a nation's flag), indicate the campaign for which the medal is given. Metal bars can also be added to the ribbon.

Basically, there are three distinct types of campaign decorations. The first might be called the war medal, and is given to anyone participating for any length of time in a nation's forces when that country is at war. Large numbers of such awards were conferred by the victorious allies in both World Wars, and they are the most familiar campaign award.

The second, given more sparingly than the war medal, is for service in specific engagements, each one of which has a distinguishing badge and ribbon.

The third is actually a hybrid of the first two. Given for one or more campaigns in a war, or series of wars, it has a bar or bars across its ribbon to indicate the campaign(s) in which the recipient served. The best example is the first India General Service Medal, held by those British soldiers who fought in the dozens of campaigns in India from the 1850s to the 1890s. The campaign in which the recipient took part was inscribed on a silver bar, along with the date of the engagement. This kind of award, usually known as a general service medal, was and still is produced mainly in Britain, although from time to time a few other European states have bestowed it. Many campaign awards have the name and unit of the recipient engraved on the edge, making them particularly interesting to collect.

See also Badge; Decoration; Gallantry award; Order; Ribbon.

CARTWHEEL The name popularly adopted for the large, unwieldly British copper penny and twopenny pieces dated 1797, and used also for American silver dollars minted between 1794 and 1935.

In late eighteenth-century England

Cartwheel.
Left: England, penny, 1797.
Right: England, twopence, 1797.

small change was in short supply, with counterfeit coppers and privately manufactured tokens comprising the bulk of everyday minor change. The Royal Mint had last issued copper coins in 1775, and thereafter was disinclined to replace old copper coins with new ones.

Yet the public needed copper coins of established weight and purity; if the Royal Mint would not produce them, at least it allowed someone else to do so. In June 1797, Matthew Boulton was given royal permission to strike copper coinage at his Soho mint, and the cartwheel was born.

Boulton's establishment was a modern one. He had applied the principles of steam power, as perfected by his friend and business partner James Watt, to the production of metal buttons, machine parts, and lately, tokens. It was the excellence of these, plus the speed of their production, that won Boulton a contract to mint coins. Each token was perfectly round, of identical weight, well struck—and could be coined far more rapidly than pieces produced with a screw press. Boulton applied these methods to penny and twopenny pieces, and in this sense his were the first truly modern coins.

The cartwheel series is interesting for a number of reasons. The coins were extraordinarily large by the day's standards. To restore the public's faith in minor coinage, Boulton set out to coin a twopence which actually had an intrinsic worth of twopence in copper. The result was a coin weighing exactly two ounces (56.7 grams)

with a diameter of 41 millimeters. Boulton's penny was 36 millimeters in diameter and weighed one ounce (28.35 grams). The new coins were unusually attractive, with a bust of George III (ruled 1760–1820) on the obverse, and a seated figure of Britannia, the allegorical personification of Britain, on the reverse, along with the date and the Latin word for "Britain."

The obverse legends gave George's titles in an abbreviated form, and legends on both sides were incuse, struck in intaglio on a broad border surrounding each side, which reveals Boulton's conviction that legends would wear better thus displayed. He may also have wanted to call attention to the enormous striking power of his new steam press, which could impress such a design into thick copper as no screw press could. The wide, raised border lent credence to the term "cartwheel," for in fact it did resemble the rim of a wheel.

Boulton's coins were greeted with mixed reactions. While the penny was popular, and—judging by the vast number of highly worn specimens surviving—widely used, the twopence was another matter. It was simply too heavy and clumsy to be of much use, and so it was produced, in limited quantities, for only a short period of time. Although all specimens of the penny bear the date 1797, it was struck for a number of years.

"Cartwheel" is also a nickname for American silver dollars, particularly those of the Morgan design, which were large and heavy (38.1 millimeters in diameter, 26.7 grams in weight). Clumsy or not, they were a mainstay in the American West and remained so until the middle 1960s.

Occasionally cartwheel is used as part of the term cartwheel effect, to describe the surface appearance of uncirculated coins. As they are struck, metal is forced outward from the coins' centers to their peripheries, leaving faint striations resembling the spokes of a wheel. If the coin is rotated, these "spokes" revolve, much like a wagon wheel in motion.

See also MACHINE-STRUCK COINAGE; MOR-
GAN DOLLAR; PENNY.

CASH A Chinese base-metal coin with a square hole in its center, the Chinese name for which is ch'ien; the word "cash" seems to derive from the Portuguese *caixa* (a chest or strongbox).

The typical cash was a medium-sized round coin, 25 millimeters in diameter, weighing 4 grams. It was usually cast in brass or copper. However, cash could be larger or smaller, heavier or lighter, and could be cast in a variety of other metals, including iron. These anomalies are not surprising when it is remembered that the cash was minted in virtually the same form for almost thirteen centuries. The enormous output of cash through its very long life makes it one of the most significant coins ever produced, and probably the most common.

Each cash had four characters on the obverse, surrounding a central square hole, encircled in turn by a wide, plain border. The characters on the right and left read *t'ung pao,* or current money; those at the top and bottom gave the *nien-hao,* the name the reigning emperor chose to distinguish his administration from earlier ones. (Examples of Western equivalents of *nien-hao,* though they did not appear on money, are Franklin Roosevelt's New Deal and Lyndon Johnson's Great Society.) The reverse of the cash also had a wide border, with or without additional characters. Most cash had plain reverses until the twelfth century, from which time —until the coin's demise—reverses frequently divulged such information as the coin's place of mintage and, upon occasion, the year during which it was cast. Like its Western counterpart, the cash's reverse conveyed information considered secondary by its makers.

The cash was introduced with the birth of the T'ang Dynasty, under emperor Kao Tsu (ruled 618–627), and minted in huge quantities, as it was in the succeeding Sung, Ming, and Manchu dynasties. Large numbers of cash were not only needed to supply China's vast population, but also because a single cash had a very modest value—one thousand cash equalling one *tael,* or Chinese ounce, in silver. The Chinese ounce was heavier than its Western namesake, some 37 grams as opposed to 28.35. As a result of their low value, cash were frequently strung together in lots of a hundred or a thousand. These strings were among the most common means of exchange in pre-modern China.

The square hole in cash sprang from the minting process. Most often cash were cast in a two-piece mold; the center of each mold had a deep channel, running from the top almost to the bottom. Side channels branched out from the central one, each ending in a reverse imprint, which created one side of the coin. The two molds, usually made of clay, were carefully strapped together so channels, obverses, and reverses were directly aligned. Molten metal was poured into the mold and allowed to cool. The two halves were then unstrapped, and individual cash broken off the metal "tree."

A new cash had rough edges, particularly where it had been attached to the "tree." The square hole made it possible to string a number of cash on a square metal bar, which was turned on a hand lathe while a coiner smoothed their edges.

The gradual disappearance of cash came with Western penetration of China in the nineteenth century. By 1900, China had a new monetary system in which one thousand cash equalled one yuan or dol-

Cash. China, ch'ien or cash, 1068–1077.

lar. Single cash were produced for a few years, but soon gave way to copper multiple pieces worth five, ten, or twenty cash (twenty cash equalling two American cents). Whatever their denomination, these descendants of the traditional cash were no longer cast by hand, but struck by machines.

See also CAST COINAGE; HOLED COINAGE; *NIEN-HAO;* TAEL; YUAN.

CAST COINAGE   Coinage produced by pouring molten metal into a one- or two-piece mold.

As the casting process does not use direct pressure to achieve design impressions, these are apt to be fuzzy, and not nearly as well defined as those produced by striking. However, casting served its purpose well in the past. Without the need for pressure, it was possible to cast larger coins than could be struck by hand, which was of particular help to those pre-industrial people who relied on outsize, base-metal coins for monetary exchange. The *aes grave* of the early Romans is typical of an early cast coin.

The cast coin is easier to produce than its die-struck counterpart. No sophisticated equipment is necessary, merely one vessel in which to melt metal and another into which it can be poured. The latter, a coin mold, can be made of clay, metal, or a number of other materials. The simplicity of production has made casting attractive to coiners in emergencies, both in ancient and modern times, and a most in-

teresting cast coin was introduced in Mexico during the early phases of its Revolution (1910–1920). In June and July 1913, Rafael Buelna, a military leader, cast silver pesos in sand molds. Most were melted down when it was discovered that the silver used for their manufacture contained enough gold to make the coins worth more than their face value.

Cast coinage was consigned to obsolescence by the modern, machine-powered mint, but for hundreds of years it successfully met the monetary needs of millions of people.

See also *AES GRAVE*; CASH; EMERGENCY MONEY.

CAST COUNTERFEIT   A counterfeit coin produced by the casting process rather than being struck from dies.

Cast counterfeits have been with us from ancient days, and through the years casting has probably been used more often to fashion counterfeits than has striking. Why? Because cast counterfeits are easier to produce than die-struck ones. Moreover, since they usually employ a genuine coin for the manufacture of a mold, such fakes are likely to more closely resemble legitimate coins than those struck from dies, which must be manufactured from scratch. Although the dies used for such counterfeits simulate official dies, details are easily added or lost, making the die-struck counterfeit suspicious in appearance.

But then, cast counterfeits are not perfect either. An ordinary coin is struck under pressure, forcing metal into the minor crevices of an intaglio die. With the cast counterfeit no such pressure is necessary, nor, until recently, was it even possible. This lack of pressure results in a "coin" that does not seem as clear as the genuine coin, and perhaps is missing minor details.

The surfaces of cast counterfeits can also reveal their secret. Parts of the field

Cast coinage. Sinaloa, cast peso of General Buelna, 1913.

Cast counterfeit.
Top: Peru, a genuine gold ⅕ libra, 1920.
Bottom: A cast counterfeit of the same coin.

and designs may dish inward because of differential shrinkage when molten metal cools; pits, caused by rough molds, or bubble-marks, from excessive heating of the metal or the presence of oxygen or water in the mold, can also be seen. Although care.in casting can prevent most of these problems from occurring, it cannot completely eliminate one basic characteristic of cast counterfeits. They are ordinarily somewhat smaller in diameter than the genuine coin, a phenomenon caused by the shrinking of molten metal as it cools in a mold. This is of little assistance in detecting ancient cast counterfeits, as the real coins varied so in size, but it does help to spot counterfeits of modern coins, which are not supposed to vary in size within a given denomination.

In ancient times people cast counterfeits under primitive conditions, and this continues today. The cast counterfeit was not that familiar in medieval and early modern Europe, however—or in any region where flat, thin coinage was the norm. In such areas, die striking was the rule, as it proved more suitable for fabricating thin counterfeits.

The advent of machine-struck coinage presented fresh challenges for counterfeiters—a major reason for its introduction—and most likely the incidence of cast counterfeits declined in the seventeenth, eighteenth, and nineteenth centuries as counterfeiters tried and failed to reproduce the perfect edges, well-struck designs, and flat fields fashioned by modern mints.

In the twentieth century however, the cast counterfeit enjoyed a renaissance, for a new procedure was created which yielded truer facsimiles. It was the centrifugal casting process, and was most widely used for gold coins.

It worked as follows. Using two halves of a rubber mold, obverse and reverse impressions were taken from a genuine coin. From the mold one or more wax "models," each with wax sprigs attached, were produced, and the entire assemblage was then placed in a metal cup filled with plaster of Paris. The plaster covered the model, but not the upper parts of the sprigs. After it had hardened, the cup was heated, causing the wax to run along the chambers left by the sprigs. The fruit of this labor was a mold for a counterfeit coin.

The mold was placed on one end of the arm of a centrifuge. The other end held a vat of molten metal, connected to the mold by a duct. When the centrifuge was activated, its arm rotated, and centrifugal force pushed the hot metal along the duct into the plaster mold. The application of centrifugal force was important, as it meant a denser counterfeit with details made clearer by the pressure applied. Then the centrifuge was switched off, the mold was broken, and a remarkably persuasive counterfeit emerged.

The centrifugal or lost wax process was initially designed to cast jewelry and dental fillings, but by the 1940s, when counterfeiters realized its potential, counterfeit British sovereigns and other popular gold trade coins soon appeared. At this juncture the practitioners of the art made a telling discovery. It was more profitable to forge rare coins with the new procedure than to counterfeit common ones. (It should be noted that at the time centrifugal casting was first generally used, gold coins were traded as bullion, not as coins; the new cast fakes, containing less gold than real coins, were meant to do the same thing.) Cast forgeries and counterfeits are still being produced. But other, better, methods have been discovered for forging coins, and cast counterfeits also seem to be on the decline. The casting method is now only used for bullion coins, not circulating ones.

See also COUNTERFEIT; COUNTERFEIT AND FORGERY DETECTION; DIE-STRUCK COUNTERFEIT; FORGERY; MACHINE-STRUCK COINAGE; SOVEREIGN.

CENTENIONALIS A small and widely circulated billon or copper coin of the later Roman Empire, introduced around A.D. 320, during the reign of Constantine the Great (ruled A.D. 306–337).

When it first appeared the centenionalis weighed approximately 3 grams, had a diameter of about 20 millimeters, and seems to have been intended as a replacement for the follis, whose average weight had descended to less than 3.5 grams. Weight and size of the new coin would also diminish in the years to come. The coin's place in the Roman monetary system is uncertain, and there is no universal agreement that it was even called a centenionalis at the time of its circulation. In any event, numismatists tend to drop its cumbersome

Centenionalis. Roman Empire, Constantine I, c. A.D. 327.

name, and refer to it by the abbreviation Æ 3, for third bronze.

Like other coins of the period, the centenionalis bore mint marks in the exergue on the reverse. Obverse designs were profile portraits of the emperor or members of his family, rendered in an increasingly non-naturalistic style; reverse designs had a patriotic or propaganda intent. Homage was paid to the emperor, to the army, to Rome's importance as an enclave of civilization in a world of barbarians, and to the eternity of the Roman state. The spontaneity seen on earlier Roman coins is absent from the centenionalis and other fourth-century issues. The monotony of the types and their treatment indicate an empire in decline.

The centenionalis seems to have been demonetized in 348. After 395, the name was applied to the tiny nummus, or Æ 4.

See also Æ; FOLLIS; NUMMUS; PORTRAIT; SILIQUA.

CHECK A written order directing a bank to pay a stated sum of money.

The modern check is made of paper, and printed on one side only. The printing furnishes general directions for making payment, while blank spaces—to be filled in by the user—are left for the date, amount, the name of the payee, and the signature of the payer.

The check was born in the same climate of economic development as the bill of exchange. The first to use checks to transfer funds were probably English goldsmith-bankers, who adopted the practice around 1650. As the notion gained in popularity, the check gradually superseded the bill of exchange. To pay by check was safer and more convenient than to pay in specie. Moreover, a cancelled check was proof of payment, and could be used to settle disputes between creditors and debtors.

In recent years, check collecting has become a fast-growing branch of numismatics, due to opportunities to acquire interesting material at a relatively modest cost. While seventeenth- and eighteenth-century checks are quite rare and consequently expensive, nineteenth-century issues abound, as do those of later years. Check collectors can specialize in a variety of fields—they can concentrate on checks bearing interesting vignettes or other design features, those produced in a given area or time period, or those with signatures of famous people.

See also BILL OF EXCHANGE.

CHOGIN   A large oval cast silver or billon ingot, issued in Japan between 1601 and 1865.

The typical chogin (translated "long silver" and also rendered cho-gin) weighed around 150 grams and measured approximately 100 millimeters in length by 33 in width. The chogin's silver content varied, and could drop to 50 percent or below, the remainder being copper. Each piece had a number of weight and validation stamps on its obverse and a blank reverse, and each had one or more characters indicating the reign during which it was cast—hence chogin can be

Chogin. Japan, 1601–1614.

dated with reasonable accuracy. The chogin was a product of the Tokugawa shogunate, established in 1599. It was not a circulating. coin. Like its relative, the Chinese tael, it was a bullion piece, intended more as a convenient way of storing wealth than as an actual trading unit. The Japanese tended to rely on base-metal coins for most purchases, as did the Chinese, although they did issue small silver pieces for circulation, which the Chinese did not. The chogin, along with other numismatic products of feudal Japan, was a casualty of the Meiji restoration of 1868. The new emperor instituted reforms, and within two years of his seizing power from the last shogun, a western-style mint was producing decimal coins to replace traditional issues, including the chogin.

See also ICHIBU GIN; INGOT; KOBAN; MAMEITA GIN; PUNCH-MARKED COINS; TAEL.

CHOP MARK   A small punched indentation on a coin, applied by a Far Eastern banker to guarantee its weight and purity.

Marking coins in this manner was widely practiced from approximately 1750 to 1920, most often on heavy silver trade coins manufactured in North and South America. Examples are the American dollar, the Piece of Eight, and the Mexican peso.

Increased trade between East and West necessitated chop marks. Chinese and Japanese silks, spices, lacquers, and other goods crossed the Pacific to the Americas and thence to Europe and were paid for with coins, usually large silver pieces. When these coins reached the Orient they were treated as bullion, as most coins circulating in the Far East were of copper, bronze, or brass; gold and silver rarely circulated as coins in that part of the world.

When a Piece of Eight arrived in China, it was weighed and tested for purity by the banker who received it. If he found it of good silver and of proper

Chop mark. *Chop marks on an 1803 Mexican Piece of Eight.*

weight, he stamped a metal version of his personal seal or, chop, on it. The coin could then be stored, or used—by weight —to pay the banker's debts. If, in fact, it was paid out, another banker was likely to test it again and affix *his* chop. And so it went. Since the merchants and bankers were not a trusting lot, every coin entering into trade could receive dozens of chops before eventually being withdrawn from commerce and, once and for all, stored in a vault.

The collector value of coins with chop marks depends on several factors. If they are marked enough to distort the surfaces and obliterate the types and legends, the value of the coins is much less than if there were no chop marks. On the other hand, a few chop marks make relatively little difference to a common coin's collector value. The value of such coins is enhanced should the chop be from an area where chop marks were rarely used, or should it appear on an unusual coin, i.e., one seldom employed in Far Eastern trade. Forgeries exist in these last two categories, and collectors should be cautious; a coin with a chop mark from an area not known to have used them is probably a fantasy.

The validation of coins by chop marks fell off once machine-struck, Western-style coinage entered the East. The new coins introduced a new concept: money was accepted by denomination, not weight.

See also COUNTERSTAMP; DOLLAR; FORGERY; PESO; PIECE OF EIGHT; TRADE COINS.

CHRISTOGRAM A monogram representing Christ's name, common on coins of the late Roman and early Byzantine empires.

The Christogram—also known as a Chrismon, or a Chi-rho, the names of the two Greek letters from which it was composed—was usually rendered as ☧ on early issues, and ☧ on later ones. It could be said that the Christogram is the numismatic evidence of Christianity's growth in the late classical world. It had been gathering converts for two centuries, but under Rome's Constantine the Great (ruled A.D. 306–337) Christianity was given a mighty boost. Before a crucial battle in 312 during a civil war, he claimed to have seen a fiery cross in the sky with the words in Greek, "By this sign conquer," beneath the cross. He ordered the cross to be painted on his army's shields and won the battle. A grateful emperor granted freedom of worship to Christian and non-Christian alike, and was himself baptized at the end of his life.

Roman coinage reflected this religious change, as such Christian elements as crosses and angels began to replace the familiar pagan ones. The Christogram was among them, making an initial appearance on a centenionalis, struck around 327, over a *labarum* or banner. In time, its use was extended: a splendid example is found on a large copper coin of the usurper Magnentius (ruled A.D. 350–353), where it was set between the Greek letters alpha and omega. The symbol, displayed on a labarum would soon become a common reverse feature on gold and silver coins.

Christogram. *Roman Empire, Magnentius, large copper coin, 353.*

By the late fourth century, the second form of the Christogram was finding favor, and would be prominent not only on Roman coins until the extinction of the western empire in 476, but on the money of Byzantium, Rome's successor in the East. Its use there was abandoned in the seventh century for a simple or ornate cross, which was to remain a mainstay of Byzantine coinage for several centuries.

See also CENTENIONALIS; CROSS ON COINAGE.

Civil war tokens.
Top: A "patriotic" Civil War token, 1864.
Bottom: A "store card" (City Hotel, Fall River, Massachusetts), 1864.

CIVIL WAR TOKENS Also known as "Civil War cents," and less frequently as "copperheads," these base-metal pieces circulated as one-cent coins and were privately struck in the North during the American Civil War.

First struck in Cincinnati in late 1862 as a kind of private emergency money, Civil War tokens were born of uncertainty over the war's outcome. The South could not decisively defeat the North and win independence, but at the time remained too strong for the North to conquer.

Inflation gripped both North and South, and even minor coins grew scarce as hoarding became common. Lacking the metal and machinery to produce coins, or a substitute, the South turned to scrip—low-denomination paper issued by private merchants, banks, or towns—as a solution.

The North, on the other hand, had metal and machines. While it too used scrip, it also produced low-value metallic tokens, the Civil War tokens. It had found this answer in a roundabout way. As low-denomination coins disappeared, people used postage stamps for small change. (These stamps were the genesis of fractional currency, described elsewhere.) But they were troublesome, for they were not designed to withstand the rigors of circulation, and deteriorated quickly. In 1862 the notion of enclosing the stamp in a round, two-piece metal shell was conceived. The top half would carry a mica "window," allowing the stamp's denomination to be seen, while the lower half would be solid metal, left blank or used for advertisements. The encased postage stamp was born. It did protect the stamp, but it cost money to produce, while the stamp was still only worth a set value. In short, it did not resolve the North's dearth of small change.

But a metallic token did. If cent-sized pieces of copper were coined, the public would readily use them for change. And since ten dollars' worth of copper could be turned into more than one thousand tokens, it was possible for a coiner to make a perfectly legitimate profit. And for a merchant also; people would accept the tokens as cents even though they cost the merchant far less when he paid the coiner.

Necessity and economics gave rise to an industry that furnished thousands of different types of tokens, struck largely in copper, bronze, and brass.

Civil War tokens fall into two categories: those parading nationalistic types and slogans, dubbed "patriotic" tokens or "patriotics" by collectors; and endless varieties of advertising tokens called "Civil War store cards," or simply "store cards."

Merchants in every conceivable business, from undertaking to saloon-keeping, issued store cards, many emblazoned with the proprietor's portrait, the location of his business, and whatever advertising could fit in the remaining space. The publicity pleased the merchant; the small change pleased the public.

Over eleven thousand different kinds of Civil War tokens, including die and metal varieties, were issued between late 1862 and mid-1864. Considering that several thousand pieces could be produced from any given pair of dies, this meant that literally millions of tokens joined the federal money supply in less than two years (one author estimates their number at approximately twenty-five million), and they were likely to stay in circulation, as people hoarded real coins, not tokens.

Alarmed by such a massive infusion of tokens into Northern commerce, Congress passed a law in April 1864 forbidding private individuals to issue money, including tokens. By that time, Union armies were gaining on the Confederacy, and in the fall of 1864 ultimate success was in sight. The public, less pessimistic about the nation's future, brought its real one-cent pieces out of hiding, while the federal government showed its faith by coining a record number of cents.

The scarcity of small change ceased; however, millions of Civil War tokens survived, and many were kept as curios. Today they are readily available.

See also EMERGENCY MONEY; ENCASED POSTAGE STAMP; FRACTIONAL CURRENCY; SCRIP; STORE CARD; TOKEN.

CLAD COINAGE   Money struck on planchets composed of two or more metals, bonded together under pressure.

Clad coinage should not be confused with coinage from an alloy. For clad coinage, the planchet consists of several separate layers of metal, which are visible when the coin is viewed edge-on. In an alloy the metallic components are mixed, and lose their individual identities.

Clad coinage. *German Federal Republic, pfennig, 1966 (edge).*

Clad coinage is essentially a post-1945 phenomenon, and, like coins from new alloys, is one response to post-war inflation. In essence, it can produce a new, base-metal coin with the same general characteristics as one of precious metal, but the requirements are stringent. The weight must be roughly the same, to ensure its utility for vending machines, and its appearance must be similar if the government wants to retain established designs. While the outer layers of the clad coin must be made of a fairly durable metal, to wear well and protect the inner core, the interior and exterior layers cannot be *too* hard, or the life of the coin dies will be shortened. Finally, since the clad coin represents value, its composition must be difficult to counterfeit.

As few clad compositions can meet all these requirements, one practice has been to create coins with new designs and/or sizes, abandoning the pretense that the clad, base-metal coin represents an unbroken line of descent from earlier issues. Such is the case in the German Federal Republic, where low-denomination issues are struck in a clad composition with a steel center and outer layers of bronze or brass. Germany may also have chosen clad coinage to introduce more attractive coins than those used in Hitler's Third Reich, and thereby distinguish between the old and new regimes.

The more frequent approach, and the one adopted by the United States in 1965, retains past designs, but substitutes copper-nickel and copper for silver. In appearance and weight, the coins resemble the silver issues they are meant to replace; and they are nonmagnetic, and therefore usable in vending machines. Since their centers are copper, they require less pressure to strike than issues composed of a copper-nickel alloy; their outer shells, composed of an alloy of 75 percent copper and 25 percent nickel, are resistant to wear.

Although this particular clad coinage meets many of the requirements mentioned earlier, it does not meet them all. Clad copper-nickel coinage may prove less harsh on dies than nickel, or even copper-nickel issues, but it is still far more destructive than silver coinage. Copper and nickel in any combination makes an extremely hard metal; greater pressure is required to strike a copper-nickel clad coin than a silver one, hence dies rapidly wear out. It will never be as ideal a metal for coins as silver.

A number of methods exist to produce the clad strip of metal from which planchets are punched and the coins minted. The simplest is to simultaneously run two or more strips of metal between rollers under tremendous pressure. However, should the pressure not be sufficient, the coin may simply fall apart. With today's more sophisticated technique one sheet of metal is placed between two others, and the three fused by igniting an explosive material applied to the outer surfaces of the top and bottom sheets. The resulting three-layer sheet is then tested for thickness and stamped into coin planchets.

The difficulties in producing clad coinage as opposed to alloyed coinage render it of limited use, and in years to come its role in the world's money is likely to be limited.

See also ALLOY; COPPER-NICKEL COINAGE; INFLATION; PLANCHET.

CLASHED DIES Dies damaged by being struck directly against each other, rather than against the surfaces of a planchet.

Clashed dies. *United States, half dollar, 1813. Note clash marks at Liberty's ear.*

Each clashed die will bear a more or less extensive relief-image of the types, legends, etc. present on the other die. If the dies are subsequently used to strike coins, they too will show these images, but in intaglio and reverse.

It is axiomatic that progress exacts its price: the mechanization of coining gave us the clashed die. Once coins could be rapidly struck by machines, the minter had less time to make certain a planchet was in its place before the mechanically controlled upper and lower dies came together. Furthermore, the screw press and its steam- and electrically powered descendants could strike coins with a much greater force than could be marshalled with the traditional sledge hammer method. Indeed, that is one of the reasons such machines were adopted. But if they could strike coins more forcefully, they could do the same to dies.

The great days of clashed coinage were the eighteenth and nineteenth centuries. While imperfect coins from clashed dies were produced by small mints with poor machinery, they also came from bigger and more modern facilities. Coins struck from clashed dies are not especially rare, and in some series are so common they outnumber the perfect coins. Early American half dollars, struck with a screw press, show numerous die clashes, particularly those minted between 1807 and 1825. Clash marks are also familiar on copper-nickel three-cent pieces, struck between 1865 and 1889. Indeed they can still be found on freshly minted American coins, although to a lesser degree.

The noticeability of a clash mark depends on the nature of the design struck. If an obverse die has a larger design than its reverse, or if legends are prominent on one die and almost absent on the other, the marks will be easily seen should the dies clash.

Coins from clashed dies can be considered as errors. It is a rule of numismatics that the less grievous a coin's error, and the more often it is seen, the less worthy it is of description or collecting. Thus, the larger the clash, the more desirable the coin, a thesis not without a certain logic. Any coin with an obvious mistake is less apt to escape a mint and make its way into circulation and, ultimately, to the hands of a collector.

In most instances, an older coin with a clash mark is worth less than a newer one. Returning to early U.S. half dollars: die clashes are so recurrent on the issues of 1813 that a clashed specimen has about the same value as an ordinary coin. A 1955 half dollar with a minor clash, however, can command twice as much as its unflawed counterpart. In 1813, with mechanized coining in its infancy, clashed dies were expected. By 1955 progress had made them the exception.

See also ERROR; GHOSTING; MACHINE-STRUCK COINAGE.

CLIPPED PLANCHET A coin blank that is less than completely circular, usually with a crescent-shaped or straight edge along part of its circumference.

Clipped planchets occur early in the coining process. The metal used in coinage is first fashioned into a long, thin strip by means of heavy rollers. It is then gauged, and if of the correct thickness moves to the next step, the blanking operation, during which the strip is conveyed along a tread while circular cutters punch planchets from it. It is at this juncture that

Clipped planchet. United States, Civil War store card struck on a clipped planchet, 1863.

the error known as a clipped planchet can be made. If the strip does not advance at the prescribed speed, one punch overlaps a hole already made by another, and the resulting blank looks as though a crescent-shaped "bite" had been taken from it. This curved planchet clip is probably a more frequent error than the straight clip. Straight clips occur when a planchet is cut too far toward the end, or edge, of the strip.

Most clipped planchets are discovered and removed before they reach the coining press. Yet some do escape the inspectors' eyes, are minted and enter circulation. They are so highly prized by error collectors that attempts have been made to create them outside the mint. At first glance, it seems easy to duplicate the straight clip simply by filing down part of a coin along a straight axis. The crescent-shaped clip is reproduced in roughly the same fashion. With close inspection of the "error," however, its true nature is usually detected. While the edges of a genuine clipped planchet are rounded and tapering, those of a privately manufactured clip are sharp and at precise right angles to the sides of the coin.

Clipped planchets have been with us since the outset of machine-struck coinage in the sixteenth century, and were probably encountered more often then and during the next two centuries than they have been since. They are almost exclusively confined to base-metal coins.

See also ERROR; MACHINE-STRUCK COINAGE; PLANCHET.

CLIPPING Trimming the edge of a gold or silver coin to pilfer some of its precious metal.

Clipped coinage was a nuisance from the earliest days until shortly before 1700. The primitive state of technology made it impossible to prevent. Ancient and medieval coins of the same denomination varied in size and weight, were seldom perfect circles, and had plain edges. Such characteristics invited clipping, and if a clipper used a modicum of care, and was not excessively greedy, there was virtually no way to tell whether or not he had worked on any given coin. Governments did what they could to discourage the practice: the Greeks and Romans discovered the beaded border, and there is little doubt they meant it to deter clipping; early Islamic coins featured a simple, unbroken border, perhaps chosen for the same reason. However, surviving coins from the ancient and medieval worlds indicate these expedients worked badly, if at all, and clipping continued to be a problem until the coining process changed.

Shortly after 1500, several inventions made it possible to improve that process and hence to reduce the incidence of clipping and similar practices. Rolling machines and planchet cutters were invented, making it possible to mint coins of an identical thickness and size. If either was at variance, it could be detected.

But it took two inventions, of the sixteenth and seventeenth centuries respectively, to finally seal the fate of clipping. The first was a collar—in effect a third coin die that surrounded each coin as it was struck. It ensured the coin's roundness and, more importantly, it meant an inscription or design could be added to its edge, the area vulnerable to clipping.

The collar's drawbacks (described in the entry Collar), generated new machinery designed to put a fancy edge on a planchet *before* it was struck. The machines, introduced in London in the 1660s, were in use throughout Europe by 1700 and, along with collars, made clip-

Clipping.
Left: Massachusetts, Pine Tree shilling, c. 1670 (clipped).
Right: Massachusetts, Pine Tree shilling, c. 1670 (unclipped).

ping almost impossible—as even the smallest amount of metal removed from a coin's edge was obvious.

The purpose of the collar and other such devices was tersely stated on the edge of a 1662 English crown: DECVS ET TVTAMEN ("An ornament and a Protection"). That the new processes were needed is clearly illustrated by the two coins pictured. They are both Pine Tree shillings, struck in Massachusetts around 1670 from identical dies, with the same amount of silver and to the same initial diameter. But the coin on the left was clipped, while the coin on the right was not.

See also BORDER; COLLAR; CROWN; EDGE-MARKING MACHINERY; FILING; SWEATING.

COB A crude coinage of silver or gold, struck in various parts of the Spanish Empire from the sixteenth to the eighteenth centuries.

Cobs are instantly recognizable by their general appearance and types. They are very irregularly round, often quite thick at the centers, and progressively thin toward their edges. Their designs are equally distinctive. Early cobs usually featured a Spanish shield on the obverse, a cross with castles and lions (for Castile and Leon) on the reverse. Later issues transferred this design to the obverse, and a new type, an inscription flanked by the Pillars of Her-

Cob. *Potosí, 8 reales, 1712.*

cules, adorned the reverse. While early cobs do not bear dates, and hence are somewhat difficult to ascribe to a particular king, about 1605 dates began to appear, and our chronology thereafter should be fairly clear. That it is not can be ascribed to a final characteristic of the cob: they were so wretchedly minted that typical specimens lack essential design elements. In fact, a cob that shows complete impressions from both upper and lower dies is a distinct rarity.

This phenomenon was caused by the method used to manufacture the coins, which in turn directly reflected political and economic conditions in the Spanish Empire.

The Spanish journeyed to the Indies in search of gold. They found a good deal of it, and even more silver, both of which had to be quickly and cheaply transported to the mother country, where they could be used to aggrandize the power of the Spanish kings. The most effective means was to refine and mint the metals where they were unearthed, so Spain authorized several colonial mints, the first at Mexico City (1535). The mintmasters were charged with producing gold and silver coins rapidly and inexpensively. The result was slipshod work.

The derivation of the word "cob" is uncertain, but the accepted explanation is that its origin is *cabo de barra*, translated "end of a bar," which is a clue as to how cobs were made. A rough silver or gold bar was cast, then crudely sliced into coin-size planchets. The irregular thickness of the planchets partially accounts for the in-

complete designs on most cobs. The planchets were quickly struck with dies made locally, and only the highest points of the blanks received a decent impression. As there was no particular attempt to center the planchet when it was struck, most cobs bear legends running off the obverse and reverse surfaces, aesthetically abominable. But aesthetics were of no matter: speed was.

Early cobs, struck before 1600, show more concern for appearances than do later issues, and we can speculate that seventeenth-century Spain, in need of additional money to arrest its eroding position in Europe, encouraged quantity over quality. Cobs were minted in Spain as well as America; when gold and silver ingots arrived in Seville from the Indies, they too were rapidly made into coins, and Spanish cobs were the result.

With the end of the Hapsburg dynasty in 1700, and the ascent of the House of Borbón, which also supplied France with kings, there came the realization that no quantity of cob coins could retrieve Spain's glory. Instead, roads were built, model factories established, onerous trade restrictions eased, and Spanish-American mints refurbished. Gradually they yielded round, attractive new coins, with Mexico City's mint the first to install up-to-date machinery featuring the screw press; in 1732 it struck its first modern coins. Lima followed in 1751 and Potosí in 1767, although all three mints struck both cobs and new coins for several years.

The cob passed into oblivion, but its influence was felt for some years. Counterstamped cobs circulated in Central America and the Caribbean well into the nineteenth century, and issues from northern Argentina, Honduras, and Venezuela, all dated about 1820, closely copied the designs on early cob coins. An alternate name for the cob is macuquina.

See also BIT; COUNTERSTAMP; PIECE OF EIGHT; REAL.

COIN WEIGHTS Round or square objects, usually of brass, bronze, or copper, with the same weight as specific coins, formerly used to make certain a coin had the proper metallic content and weight.

The typical coin weight frequently resembled the coin whose validity it was meant to test, with obverse and reverse types very near the original. This was deliberate, as most people were illiterate in early times and only recognized coins by their designs, not by their inscriptions.

The operation of the coin weight was simple. With a scale consisting of two balance pans suspended from a central arm and pivot, the merchant who wished to test a florin, for example, merely dropped the coin in one pan and the weight in the other. If the two pans balanced, he knew the coin had not been clipped and its gold was good.

Coin weights are known from antiquity but were not generally used until the mid-fourth century A.D., after which they became prominent in Byzantine, Islamic, medieval Western, and early modern numismatics. Although most often made of metal, there are many examples in glass, fashioned by the Byzantines and their Islamic successors.

The coin weight was put to active use during periods of vigorous foreign trade, particularly if the coinage of the era was easy to clip, file, or counterfeit. Hence large numbers of weights appeared in the late medieval and early modern ages, but were less used after the eighteenth century when coins were struck by machines, making them harder to alter or falsify. An-

other factor abetted their demise. As long as dozens of states struck gold pieces of different weights and values, weights—principally intended to measure gold coins—were an absolute necessity. But standardization of gold coins from one country to another began to make headway in the eighteenth century, as did the use of paper money for those large transactions which had previously been dependent on coins: consequently the need to weigh coins diminished. By 1800 the coin weight had virtually disappeared in the West, although its use in certain parts of Asia continued for some time.

Today's hobbyists collect coin weights; those found in the carved boxes that originally housed them and with the balance-scales that accompanied them are especially desirable.

See also EXONUMIA.

COLLAR A ring-shaped piece of machinery, devised to restrain metal as a coin is struck, and within which the obverse and reverse dies operate.

As pressure from obverse and reverse dies forces the metal in the planchet outward, the collar ensures the metal will spread only to a certain point. The result is a perfectly round coin.

Invented in the late sixteenth century, collars were first used solely for this purpose, but soon it was recognized that the inside surface of the collar could also serve as a third die. If a design or lettering was put in the collar in reverse, as it was in the upper and lower dies, the coin's edge could carry a raised impression as well—which might, in turn, eliminate counterfeiting and clipping. A problem immediately arose: if you use a collar as a third die, how do you release the coin once it has been struck? The edge devices will fill the crevices of the edge die, in effect locking the coin into place.

Several schemes were concocted. First, if a plain, one-piece collar easily releases a

Coin weights. England, coin weight for a Portuguese dobra or 8-escudo gold coin, 1747.

coin, so does a reeded one, i.e., a collar with parallel vertical markings. Furthermore, coins with reeded edges are difficult to clip, file, or counterfeit. While such coins are widely used today, they were not popular when the collar was invented, as minters believed more ornate edges furnished greater protection. Such being the case, two more collars were fashioned.

The first, still used occasionally, is known as the segmented collar (or *virole brisée* in French). Dating from the 1570s, the segmented collar consisted of three or more sections, which joined as the coin was struck but could be separated by a mallet or, later, by a mechanical process, to release the coin. However, it had two disadvantages which have yet to be completely overcome. It slowed down the coining process—the antithesis of what machinery was supposed to do—and it required an accuracy in striking that was beyond the ability or patience of most coiners.

The scond invention enjoyed no more success. It was a ribbon made of spring steel, engraved with the desired inscription or design. Fit inside a solid collar, it could be removed from the collar and separated from the coin once it was struck. This too was a tedious method, and demanded great concentration if it was to perform correctly.

Late in the seventeenth century both devices were generally abandoned for a totally new machine, which marked a coin's edges while it was still in the planchet stage. The edge-marked planchet was then struck in an ordinary screw press, without the benefit of a collar. In effect, one of the goals of a collar, a perfectly round coin, was sacrificed in favor of a coin with an ornate edge.

In the nineteenth century, coinage with plain or reeded edges, applied by a one-piece collar, came into vogue. However, if edge lettering was needed, it was done in an incuse form while still in the planchet stage, making it possible to use the one-piece collar. Today the solid collar is almost universal, and segmented devices

are usually reserved for restrikes or commemoratives.

See also CLIPPING; EDGE-MARKING MACHINERY; LETTERED EDGE; MACHINE-STRUCK COINAGE; ORNAMENTED EDGE; REEDED EDGE.

COMMEMORATIVE A coin or note honoring a particular person or event, with a design markedly different from that of ordinary money.

While the commemorative coin has been known since classical times, the commemorative bill is a twentieth-century phenomenon.

The first makers of commemorative issues were the ancient Greeks, who found the medium ideal for celebrating important events. People inspected coins closely, and remembered their designs and inscriptions; the durability of coins meant they served to celebrate an event over a long period of time. Finally, they cost little more to issue than ordinary coins; the only additional expenditures were in the effort to achieve artistic designs and in careful striking of the coin.

One of the earliest commemoratives, an Athenian decadrachm dating from 467 B.C., celebrated Athens's defeat of the Persians, a victory for Greek civilization as well as the people of Attica. Perhaps the most beautiful commemorative ever struck is another decadrachm, dating from later in the fifth century. This one, from Syracuse, is thought by some scholars to have been struck to celebrate the defeat of an Athenian expedition to Sicily in 413 B.C. Both coins reflect fierce civic pride, and are significant in the homage they pay to an event, and a way of life, rather than to an individual.

After the brief flowering of commemorative coinage among the Greeks, it lay dormant for nearly two thousand years. Resurrected in the Renaissance, commemoratives have thrived since, with a steady growth in production which continues

Commemorative.
Top: Athens, decadrachm, 467 B.C.
Center: Syracuse, decadrachm, 413 B.C.
Bottom: United States, dollar, 1976.

today. Some of the first modern commemoratives came from Germany, and celebrated various people and events in the Protestant Reformation. By the 1870s and 1880s the practice was reasonably common throughout Europe, and was making its appearance in the Americas.

What had been a moderate rise in popularity in the sixteenth through nineteenth centuries became an explosion in the twentieth. Why? Both patriotism and profit are part of the answer. The twentieth century is an age of heightened tension and competition between nations, with each hawking its political and moral wares to the world and to its citizens. Commemorative coinage emerges as a particularly useful tool. It reminds citizenry of a noble event in the history of a nation, a

virtuous leader, a deserving party, the righteousness of goals. Small wonder then that practically all nations today issue some commemorative coins: for certain countries their release has burgeoned into a national industry.

The second key to their proliferation is the revenue to be earned by the issuing government. Commemorative coins are sold at a profit by national or designated private agencies, and are generally moderately priced—at least in today's inflated numismatic market—which attracts those collectors who find themselves priced out of the more traditional coin market. One early United States dollar in fine condition, for example, costs as much as a hundred recent large Austrian silver commemoratives. Although in some instances it could be said that the business of commemorative coinage is overextended (see Noncirculating Legal Tender), on the whole it has benefited numismatics by drawing new hobbyists to the field, and the popularity of such coins with governments and people is likely to continue.

The same is true of paper money with a commemorative intent. This is a branch of numismatics still in its infancy, but the vogue of the Philippine "Victory" overprints, and the special notes printed for the Canadian Centennial, indicate that collectors would welcome commemorative paper money.

See also Decadrachm; Medal; Noncirculating legal tender; Overprint; Presentation piece.

COMMODITY MONEY Objects of a fixed value used in commerce in the absence of coins, tokens, or paper money.

The use of commodity money should not be confused with barter. In the barter system, a trading object has value in direct relation to other objects, and this value fluctuates constantly. With commodity money, a trading object has a fixed value (which may need to be officially readjusted occasionally), *expressed in terms of real coins.* Those using commodity money know that were coins or notes available, the commodities would have a set rate of exchange, and, indeed, could be exchanged for ordinary money at a definite rate.

The use of fixed-value commodities is most often found in remote or economically retarded areas. A striking example of this practice is seen in the early English settlements of the area that was to become the United States. The first colonial communities were small, and essentially left to their own devices. They traded with each other, but without the convenience of coins; the seaboard colonies contained no precious metals with which to mint coinage, and England was disinclined to send coins to America.

The colonials had little recourse but to search for other means of exchange. Abandoning barter as inadequate for an expanding society, they evolved the notion of commodity money. A set amount of something useful in international trade—tobacco, perhaps—or of value in domestic life—such as nails—was pegged against a set amount of English money. The commodity then functioned as a coin to be used to purchase goods, pay taxes, etc. The system worked well as long as the quality and supply of the commodity remained stable and the demand for it did not fluctuate severely. But supply and demand are seldom frozen, and their rise and fall seriously threatened the entire system. Tobacco is a case in point.

First grown commercially in 1612 in Virginia, tobacco was soon the mainstay of the colony's economy. Smoking had become a habit among the English, and as the demand for tobacco rose, so did its price—at least temporarily—and its usefulness for exchange. The Virginia House of Burgesses passed a law in 1619 giving tobacco the status of money. A pound of the best-grade leaf was fixed at three English shillings, and lower-grade tobacco at a shilling and a half.

The value of this commodity money, however, could not be held firm when colonial farmers opted to grow their own money supply, generating a classic case of agricultural overproduction. Tobacco's worth slipped below the 1619 rates; the legislature, in turn, lowered the fixed official rate, and, when that too failed to keep pace with the actual rate (by 1665 the leaf was traded at one penny a pound, regardless of its official rate), it enacted laws restricting its production—again to no avail. Despite its drawbacks, tobacco continued to be used as commodity money for many years. There were, after all, few substitutes.

The system is not without other complications, some of them fairly bizarre. Virginia, for example, also used nails as commodity money. They were costly to import, and difficult to make at home, but a growing new society was in dire need of them. Hence they had value, and the larger the nails, the greater that value. By custom, nails were traded in lots of one hundred, yielding the term "tenpenny nail," which indicated that one hundred nails of a particular size were worth tenpence, not an untidy sum. Indeed nails were so attractive as commodity money that the Virginia House of Burgesses was impelled to pass a law in 1646 making it illegal to burn down abandoned houses. It seems the citizenry was turning to arson in its quest for nails.

Once an economy reaches a certain size and complexity, the use of commodity money wanes. Such was the case in the colonial United States. Shortly before 1700 paper money was invented, and in the ensuing century was widely accepted along the Eastern Seaboard as a means of exchange.

See also BARTER; MONEY; PAPER MONEY.

COMMUNION TOKEN Any of a series of round, oval, or octangular pieces, usually struck in lead, tin, or Britannia metal, and most commonly used in the Calvinist Church of Scotland.

Communion token. *Lesmahagow, Scotland, 1837.*

The communion token originated in Switzerland, where it seems to have been introduced by John Calvin in 1561. It was a time of religious intolerance, and the communion token was created as a precaution, although later much of its original meaning was to be lost. A church member who wished to take communion was given a token before the service, often on the previous night; upon entering the church he presented it to a guard, proving he belonged to the congregation. In this fashion strangers, possibly hostile government agents, were kept at bay while the faithful worshipped in safety and secrecy.

The typical communion token is octangular, perhaps 30 by 20 millimeters. One side bears the name of the church and the date; the other frequently carries a quotation from Scripture, THIS DO IN REMEMBRANCE OF ME, with the appropriate citation, FIRST CORINTHIANS XI, 24. Communion tokens emanated from hundreds of locales in Scotland, Canada, and elsewhere, and the lure of local history is drawing a number of collectors to the field. Prices of communion tokens are still low, but are not likely to remain so.

See also EXONUMIA; TOKEN.

CONDITION CENSUS A term suggested by Dr. William H. Sheldon in his book, *Early American Cents, 1793–1814* (1949).

Like many specialized hobbyists before him, Sheldon concentrated on establishing the identities of the finest known specimens of particular coins—in this case,

early American cents. He established the condition census as a rapid way to do so. The condition census is usually expressed as two numbers, separated by a hyphen. The first number, to the left of the hyphen, indicates the condition of the most perfect known specimen of the coin being described. The number to the right registers the average condition of the five next-finest specimens known. Should there be fewer than five such coins, the right-hand number gives the average condition of those specimens that *are* known. It must be emphasized that Sheldon contrived the condition census to help in the examination of die varieties of a particular series, not a complete series. In other words, he sought the finest known specimen of a particular cent die variety coined in, let us say, 1794. He was not interested in identifying the finest known *cent*, or the choicest *1794* cent. Instead, he studied the series, die variety by die variety, and while his condition census has been extended to other denominations, such as dollars and half dimes, numismatists still use it only within a series, not across it. (Sheldon's condition census fit into a method he devised to describe the condition of coins—discussed under Grading Systems.)

The condition census is a particularly American phenomenon, and collectors specializing in early United States coinage have found it of considerable service. Any rare coin within the charmed circle of the condition census provokes exceptionally keen bidding when it reaches the market. European collectors, on the other hand, have yet to embrace the concept, and their American counterparts customarily restrict it to American issues.

See also DIE VARIETY; GRADING SYSTEMS; LARGE CENT.

CONTINENTAL CURRENCY The first national paper money of the United States of America, issued to finance the American Revolution.

Continental Currency was unsupported by cash reserves, and its dramatic decline in value is a classic lesson in inflation.

In the spring of 1775, decades of friction between Britain and her colonies on the Atlantic coast of North America broke into open warfare. The future United States had almost incalculable potential wealth, but few actual assets that could be turned into specie. Nor did the land contain precious metals in any quantity—at least, so far as was known. The would-be nation, desperately short on cash, faced the wealthiest nation in the world.

The Continental Congress, the government of the insurgent colonies, turned to the only available source of money, the printing press. To pay for its war of independence it would print paper money in the form of certificates, entitling the bearer to a set amount of money in gold or silver, based on the "Spanish milled dollar," or, as it was known, the Piece of Eight. The notes would say nothing about redemption and with good reason, for the Continental Congress had no money with which to honor them. It was hoped the states would donate funds to the common cause, and anyway, if the war was quickly won, few problems would arise.

Printed by Hall & Sellers, Benjamin Franklin's successors in Philadelphia, the first Continental Currency rolled off the presses in the spring of 1775; other printings followed as needed, the last dated 1779. Most of the bills had a similar appearance—rectangular, about 95 by 75 millimeters, and typeset rather than engraved, employing a wide variety of letter fonts and slugs. The obverse of each note carried a lofty allegorical vignette (most of them suggested by Benjamin Franklin), while on the reverse of most was a "nature print," impressed by a lead plate—an anti-counterfeiting device of Franklin's invention. Each note also bore serial numbers and signatures, added by hand after the note had been printed. The issues of 1775–1778 are printed only in black; those of 1779, however, are black and red, the second color necessitated by the British habit of counterfeiting the previous notes, an early example of numismatic warfare.

Through 1775 and 1776, Continental Currency circulated roughly at par. As citizens held fast to the notion that the British would soon be driven from their shores, most saw no reason to redeem their notes for specie. But the war ground on, its outcome increasingly uncertain, and optimism languished. The Continental Congress, while now able to borrow modest sums from abroad, printed most of the additional monies it needed. Americans, realizing the government could not redeem the money, were less ready to accept Continental Currency at par, and eventually to accept it at all. The United States suffered the worst monetary depreciation in its history.

The figures are arresting. In January 1777 the Continental paper dollar was on a par with the Piece of Eight. One year later it took 1.46 paper dollars to buy a Piece of Eight; by January 1779 nearly nine paper dollars were needed, and by April 1780, this had escalated to forty. To exacerbate conditions, issues of paper money printed by the states depreciated even more sharply than did those of the federal government.

At the beginning of 1780 the Continental Congress simply stopped printing money. By that time it had issued a quarter-billion dollars, more than the combined worth of every house, farm, and factory in the country.

With the battle of Yorktown, in 1781, America won its independence and could turn its attention to the money supply. It found a shambles. Although some Continental Currency had been redeemed (at two-and-a-half cents on the dollar) much of it remained outstanding. The fiscal architects of the new state were confronted with redeeming the Continental Currency still in private hands, and determining the future of paper money in America.

As it happened, solutions to the second problem came first, since the majority of delegates to the 1787 Constitutional Convention represented groups opposed to paper money. While they did not detail the new federal government's right to print it, they specifically forbade the states to do so, in the hope that the nation would be established on a firm specie basis and thus keep faith with its citizens. That left the holders of Continental Currency, with whom it was also necessary to keep faith. There was not enough free cash to pay them at par, but—as stipulated in the Constitution—they had to be paid something. By an act of August 4, 1790 and subsequent laws, it was possible to exchange one hundred dollars of Continental Currency for one dollar in interest-bearing bonds, the last of which were paid by 1813 (when the United States was again at war with England).

From the number of surviving specimens it is clear that not all Continental Currency was turned in for redemption. Much is available to collectors today at relatively modest cost. However, over the years, numerous copies of Continental Currency have been privately made. Most are printed on paper resembling parchment, with all elements—including signatures and serial numbers—in the same color, while the originals were on thick, cream-colored paper and their signatures and serial numbers differed in color from the rest of the note.

See also COPY; INFLATION; PAPER MONEY; PIECE OF EIGHT; TYPESET.

CONTINENTAL DOLLAR The earliest pattern coin struck for the United States of America; three specimens are known in silver, about a dozen in brass, and several hundred in pewter.

The typical Continental Dollar, at least in pewter, is 39 millimeters in diameter and weighs 15 grams. Its edge is ornamented, in relief, with a simple leaf pattern. The obverse depicts a sun and sundial, with the Latin FUGIO ("I Fly") to one side and a second motto under the sundial, MIND YOUR BUSINESS; the whole has been interpreted: "Time flies, so mind your business." The legend CONTINENTAL CURRENCY 1776 surrounds the central type (on several varieties, currency is spelled with one "r"). The reverse has an outer design of thirteen conjoined links, each with the name of a colony. This suggestion of unity is reinforced by the inscription WE ARE ONE, surrounded by AMERICAN CONGRESS. It is thought that these designs were created by Benjamin Franklin, and similar ones appeared on an issue of low-value Continental Currency dated February 17, 1776. The devices for the bills were apparently cut by Elisha Gallaudet, a New York engraver who probably also cut the dies for the Continental Dollar, but the coins' actual minter is unknown.

Coinage reflects a nation's sovereignty, and it is natural that the United States

Continental Dollar.
Top: United States, 1776.
Bottom: A modern copy of the Continental Dollar.

wished to produce its own coins, yet there was a more urgent reason for doing so. An issue of specie, even a modest one, would strengthen public faith in Continental Currency. By early 1776, proposals were made to establish a national mint in Philadelphia, and, while it was admitted that a shortage in bullion might prove to be a problem, it was felt that at least some coins could be produced from privately held silver plate. While Congress debated, dies for a new coin based on the Piece of Eight were prepared, and the first Continental Dollars were struck, in silver, probably during the fall of 1776. The possibility that they were conceived as the linchpin of the American monetary system is likely when we consider that the printing of Continental Currency of the one-dollar denomination was suspended after the issue of May 9, 1776, Congress probably assuming it would be replaced by a dollar coin.

Congress had ambitious plans for the new coinage. It began with the idea, suggested by Franklin, that dies used to strike the silver Continental Dollar could also be used to strike copper coins. One hundred of the coppers would equal one Continental Dollar, and this is the genesis of the American decimal system, first discussed more than a decade before it was enacted into law. (The move to use the same dies for coins of high and low value may explain the brass versions of the Continental Dollar.)

By the end of 1776, Congress was seriously considering a national mint. The pewter specimens of the Continental Dollar, the most common variety of the pattern, seem to have been struck at this time to encourage Congressional action, which came on February 20, 1777, with the Mint Act. The Continental Dollar, introduced as a pattern, could now become a circulating coin.

Or could it? When the act was passed, the value of Continental Currency had begun its descent; a silver or copper coin tied to a depreciating paper money system would be removed from circulation as rapidly as it was struck. The mint existed in name only, and the Continental Dollar lived out its time as a pattern. Ten years later, however, its designs resurfaced, and approximations are found on the Fugio cent of 1787.

Collectors should be aware that over the years myriad copies of the Continental Dollar have been either cast or struck. Cast copies are easily detected, because they *are* cast, and hence their designs are never as clear as the originals. Moreover, while the originals had ornamented edges, cast copies do not. The low boiling points of lead and pewter make them particularly good materials for these pieces. Struck copies are also rather simple to recognize. If cast copies look too poor to be genuine, struck ones look too good; most were minted in Philadelphia in 1876 to celebrate the American Centenary. New dies were sunk to strike the replicas, skillfully fashioned by the Philadelphia Mint. Lettering is small and very precise, and the reverse links are perfectly round. However, the edges of these 1876 copies are plain, and that in itself is enough to reveal their true heritage. In addition, they were struck under modern minting conditions, and their entire fabric is that of a nineteenth-century coin, not one of a screw-press product from an earlier time.

See also CONTINENTAL CURRENCY; COPY; DECIMAL COINAGE; FUGIO CENT; PATTERN.

CONTORNIATE

A base-metal, coin-like object, with a distinctive turned-up rim, produced in the late Roman Empire.

The contorniate resembles the sestertius, a much earlier Roman coin. Typical specimens are about 36 millimeters in diameter, weigh some 23 grams, and are usually made of bronze. Some seem to have been struck, and others cast.

Little is known about contorniates. We know they were not coins, for their weights do not fit into any official category of the period, and their types do not remotely resemble those of contemporary coins. What was their purpose then? Numismatists are unsure, just as they are uncertain about the exact date of the contorniate, the reason for its turned-up rim (which gave the piece its name, from the Italian *contorno*, or ornamental border) or even who struck it.

Visually, contorniates are quite arresting. Larger than any official Roman coinage minted after about A.D. 150, the contorniate's style also sets it apart from its time. By the late fourth century, Roman numismatic art was stiff and formal. The portrait in profile was giving way to facing

Contorniate. Roman Empire, c. 400.

varieties. Reverse types were increasingly religious in nature, and there was little variation or naturalism. The contorniate, on the other hand, not only emphasized the profile portrait but was the canvas for superior artistry reminiscent of portraiture in the first and second centuries. Themes on reverse types were also more apt to be secular than sacred, with scenes from the circus and Roman games particularly favored. Indeed many numismatists have concluded that the reverse types of contorniates indicate they could have been tickets to games, especially given their large size and peculiar edge.

Yet the obverse types encourage speculation in another direction. Because emperors and other famous men of pagan years were portrayed on contorniates, and their style and size was evocative of pre-Christian days, could they have been designed as a subtle bit of anti-Christian propaganda, suggesting a return to the old ways of Rome?

We shall probably never know the whole truth about the contorniate. We can merely record it as one of the earliest types of exonumia in the Western world.

See also EXONUMIA; PORTRAIT; SESTERTIUS.

COPPER-NICKEL COINAGE

Money struck from an alloy of copper and nickel, in which copper is always dominant.

A ratio of approximately 90 percent copper to 10 percent nickel yields a pale pink, rather attractive alloy. If the percentage of nickel is increased to 25 percent of the total, the alloy will have a steely appearance.

Copper-nickel coinage is relatively recent on the numismatic scene. Nickel was not isolated until 1751, and was for many years little more than a laboratory curiosity. As it is extremely hard, it was obviously useful for coins, but its very hardness meant it would shorten the life of coin dies significantly, through breakage or attrition. Nickel, then, was dismissed as a ma-

Copper-nickel coinage. United States, cent, 1857.

terial for coinage until the middle of the nineteenth century.

The Swiss Confederation, in 1850, was the first state to experiment with a copper-nickel alloy. It had already been learned that an alloy of nickel and copper would be hard, but not as excessively so as nickel alone. Dies would wear longer, and the coins would be more durable than the standard issues of silver or copper. The alloy had still other virtues. It did not tarnish inordinately, and could be made to resemble silver and used to mint moderate-sized but low-value coins in something other than copper or bronze, both of which tarnished badly. The Swiss adopted a copper-nickel composition for their five-, ten-, and twenty-centime pieces. However, their alloy contained, in addition to copper (50–60 percent) and nickel (10 percent), zinc (25 percent) and silver (5–15 percent, depending on the denomination). Shortly thereafter, a purely copper-nickel coin would be produced in the United States.

The lowest-denomination coins in that country were cents and half cents, which had been struck from copper since their introduction in 1793. By the mid-1850s, the half cent was no longer circulating, while the large cent was proving more of an annoyance in commerce than an aid. The coinage law of February 21, 1857 introduced a smaller cent, made from an alloy of 88 parts copper and 12 parts nickel, which was used until 1864, when it was abandoned in favor of bronze. But in 1865, copper-nickel reappeared in a three-cent piece, and in 1866, in a five-cent piece, or "nickel." The alloy's proportions were 3 parts of copper to 1 of nickel, a ratio still in use.

As copper-nickel coinage spread during the latter half of the century, the majority of countries adopting it leaned to a 75–25 ratio, although several Latin American states experimented with an approximate 90–10 proportion. Employment of the alloy increased in the twentieth century, when worldwide inflation hastened the search for a suitable replacement for silver. Today, most countries mint coins with the copper-nickel alloy, having found its appearance, durability, and cheapness to be advantages far outweighing its somewhat harsh effect on coin dies. The British name for the alloy is cupro-nickel.

See also ALLOY; CLAD COINAGE; LAMINATION; SMALL CENT.

COPPER PLATE MONEY Large, flat, rectangular, or square plates of copper, used as money in Sweden in the seventeenth and eighteenth centuries; also known as kopperplatmynt or simply platmynt.

Platmynt takes the shape of a crudely hammered, thick copper plate. One side is blank; the other has five validation stamps, looking much like coins at first glance. Four of the stamps are round, appear on the four corners of the platmynt, and exhibit the crowned monogram of the ruler and the date. The fifth stamp occupies the center, and can be round, triangular, or square. It carries the denomination, and frequently the inscription SILF:MYNT— short for "silver money"—as the copper was meant to circulate at a value directly tied to that of silver. As a liberal amount of copper was needed to equal a modest amount of silver—especially in Sweden, then the world's major source for copper—the Swedes were apt to find themselves with an unreasonably cumbersome coinage, and they did. The earliest platmynt, and the largest ever struck, was a ten-daler piece dated 1644: it measured 61 by 36 centimeters and weighed 20 kilograms.

Copper plate money. Sweden, 2 daler, 1720.

Platmynt was produced from 1644 to 1759. Despite its obvious disadvantages, sheer necessity had guaranteed it a 115-year life.

Sweden aspired to the rank of a world power, particularly during the period of Charles XII (ruled 1697–1718), the "Madman of the North." Visions of dominance in the Baltic generated wars, which cost money. Hence platmynt, which had two somewhat interesting effects. First, the Russians borrowed the idea in the 1720s, and briefly experimented with platmynt of their own. Second, and of more importance, the Swedish platmynt's inordinate weight and bulk eventually impelled local bankers to fashion a more serviceable medium of exchange. About 1660 they invented and used paper money, the first people in the West to do so.

See also BANK NOTE; TOKEN.

COPY A privately made reproduction of a numismatic item, manufactured for sale to collectors at a modest price.

The word *replica* is interchangeable with copy; the words counterfeit, forgery, imitation, restrike and reprint are not. Copies are not meant to deceive either collectors or the public, while *counterfeits* and *forgeries* are intended to do just that. The word *imitation* best describes real coins which reproduce the designs of other real coins. Copies are neither struck from original dies, as *restrikes* are, nor printed from original plates, as are *reprints*. And while copies are privately produced, restrikes and reprints are ordinarily made by a mint or other official body.

Copies have existed for hundreds of years. Some of the earliest date from the Renaissance, with the so-called Paduans—reproductions of ancient Roman coins, made by Cavino and Bassiano about 1550. Unfortunately, truly splendid specimens of Roman coins, particularly the large bronzes, have never been numerous, and have always been expensive. But if a collector could not own a rare and unaffordable second-century sestertius, at least he could possess something which simulated it, and was perhaps even as beautiful. That, in short, is the theory behind copies.

The categories into which copies fall

Copy.
*Left: A struck copy of a Higley threepence token by
Bolen, c. 1860.*
*Right: A cast promotional copy of a Massachusetts
cent, c. 1960.*

reflect the range of collectors' interests. Thus, there are copies of medals, medallions, even decorations; but the major emphasis has been on coins and, in the last quarter century, on paper money. The coins and related objects most frequently copied are early American. Their manufacture began in the middle of the last century, when coin collecting reached the United States. Research on the early American series was undertaken, books were written, and collectors vied for the acquisition of genuine early coins. It was soon apparent that the supply of these could not meet the demand; initial production had been modest, and over the years many pieces had been lost.

Still, coins such as the Higley threepence, a rare Connecticut copper issue of the late 1730s, were constantly sought; indeed no collection of numismatic Americana would be considered complete without one. And when they could not be had, the American collector settled for copies, as had his Italian predecessor hundreds of years before. Hence John A. Bolen, A. S. Robinson, and other enthusiasts either made their own copies, or paid others to do so. The idea was infectious.

Early American copies, those dating perhaps from 1860 to 1910, were either struck from dies carefully reproduced from a genuine coin, or made by the electrotype process, in which two "shells"— copies of an obverse and reverse—were produced by electroplating, and then soldered together. Although both methods yielded fairly clear, faithful replicas, they fell from favor in the twentieth century with the introduction of the cast copy.

The cast replica, though simpler to make, yielded poorer results. The surfaces of cast copies tend to be buckled, their designs and legends are often indistinct, and their edges reveal a telltale seam at the point where the obverse and reverse molds join. Yet they served their purpose well enough. As time passed, however, that purpose changed. People were entering the copy market in increasing numbers, but unlike earlier generations of serious collectors, they saw copies as souvenirs. During the Boston Tercentenary of 1930, copies of the Pine Tree shilling sold briskly; reproductions of the Spanish Piece of Eight were favorites in any place linked to pirates; and so on. These inexpensive cast copies were usually made from an alloy of lead, tin, antimony, and anything else that happened to be available, and their pale gray color was frequently masked by plating with another metal. Today, most copies are produced in precisely the same fashion.

Few copies of paper money seem to have been made before 1950. Much like modern coin replicas, paper money copies are basically souvenirs. Most are reproduced by lithography or more recently, photolithography. Especially popular copies are of colonial and state notes, Continental Currency, broken bank notes, and Confederate money, and thousands of specimens are known.

Copies need not create a problem for numismatists, but they do. Too often the uninitiated can be confused by what is an original and what is not—and sadly disillusioned when the "rarity" that has been in the attic for half a century is offered for sale. The Hobby Protection Act, passed by the United States Congress late in 1973, offers some resolution by mandating that each copy or replica be clearly labeled COPY on either its obverse or reverse.

Though it does nothing about copies made before 1973, it is a helpful addition to subsequent copies.

Collectors should be aware of the abundance of copies in certain coin and paper money series, most of them American. Pay careful attention to particularly rare coins in colonial and early federal issues, and examine private and territorial gold coins, as numerous copies of rarities in that series have been manufactured since 1960.

For paper money, examine anything printed on what purports to be parchment; a plethora of replicas of colonial and Continental Currency, broken bank notes, and Confederate issues were reproduced on a yellowish paper called "vegetable parchment" in the 1960s, and have caused confusion since. Genuine early American currency is on pale paper, and its designs are clear, while the copies, reproduced by photolithography, are not.

See also Broken bank notes; Continental Currency; Continental Dollar; Counterfeit; Electrotype; Forgery; Imitation; Piece of Eight; Pine Tree shilling; Private gold coins; Restrike.

COUNTERFEIT   To create false money for private gain by immediate circulation.

Counterfeit coins and paper money are intended to deceive the public, not numismatists and collectors. Pieces designed to lure the experts into buying them for their rarity are called forgeries.

Both coins and paper money can be counterfeited. The two methods of counterfeiting coinage are described under Cast counterfeit and Die-struck counterfeit. What is examined here is the most prevalent modern counterfeit, that of paper money.

At first glance, paper money should be more difficult to counterfeit than coinage. The modern bill is replete with deterrents—detailed engraving, subtle shadings of color, intricate scrollwork, watermarked paper, paper with security threads, etc. Coins on the other hand are simply pieces of metal, and the complexity and precision of their designs are elementary in comparison to those of the note. But two points about counterfeit bills are significant.

First, as precious metal is no longer used for circulating coins, those of the late twentieth century, fabricated from alloys of low intrinsic value, are not worth counterfeiting. Bills are: as coins of high value disappeared, paper money took their place.

Second, the reason for the precision and complexity of today's bills, and the elaborate steps taken to manufacture them, is the counterfeiting of earlier and simpler notes. In effect, the modern bill is a composite of every successful anticounterfeiting device known. If late twentieth-century bills present an almost insurmountable challenge to counterfeiters, the latter have only themselves—and their predecessors—to blame.

One imagines that counterfeiters were

Counterfeit. United States, lithographed counterfeit of a 5-dollar bill, series of 1899.

attracted to paper money in the first place because the potential return on an outlay of only a few cents for paper and ink was enormous—assuming, of course, the raw materials were handled artfully. Small wonder that the first printed counterfeits appeared fast on the heels of the first real notes. And they were troublesome, as both the Chinese of the Ming dynasty and the English colonials of eighteenth-century America discovered. Although there was no way to increase the intrinsic value of the paper and ink, counterfeiting might be avoided if production required an increase in time and effort, thus making paper money too "expensive" to imitate.

Governments began to fashion more elaborate designs, more complicated printing processes, etc. For their part, counterfeiters were always one step behind, but gaining. Their tasks were made less formidable in places such as England, where very simple designs were used well into the twentieth century, or in an area such as the American South during the Civil War, where paper money was typeset or lithographed. But where money was printed from engraved plates, the labor of the counterfeiter was, and still is, onerous. Minute lines must be picked up and rendered in perfect detail; ways must be found to duplicate the intricate lathework in medallions and guilloches. Inking must be clean and tidy, and the ink's color as close to the original as possible—no small feat when governments so zealously guard their formulas. Still and all, counterfeiting persists.

The modern counterfeit is usually engraved. While lithographed counterfeits have been circulated, they do not have the same "feel" as engraved ones, nor do they allow the counterfeiter to achieve the preciseness his product must have if he hopes to market it. Generally, the imitator can enjoy greater ease if the nation whose bills he is counterfeiting seldom changes the looks of its money. If the same colors and designs are continuously used, eventually someone is bound to produce a perfect counterfeit. The United States has been greatly troubled by counterfeits over the past fifty years, in part for this very reason.

See also Cast counterfeit; Die-struck counterfeit; Engraving; Forgery; Guilloche; Lithography; Medallion; Paper money; Security thread; Watermark.

COUNTERFEIT AND FORGERY DETECTION Procedures which, if accurately employed, may reveal the fraudulent nature of a numismatic item.

The detection of modern, die-struck forgeries can usually be effected only by special authentication agencies established for that purpose. Nevertheless, there is much detection the individual collector can do on his own with a minimum of equipment.

Fakes can be found in any branch of numismatics, but the vast majority are in coins and paper money. With either of these, a distinction must be made between counterfeits and forgeries. Of the two, the counterfeit, made for circulating immediately as a genuine coin or bill, is more easily detected than the forgery, which is made for the collector. The successful counterfeit relies on the fact that most people do not look at their money very closely. If a fake coin or bill has the general characteristics of a real one, this is enough. The piece only has to be traded once (from the counterfeiter to his victim) to be successful. If the counterfeit is discovered later, the discovery is of little concern to the counterfeiter.

Should the counterfeiter decide to become a forger, however, his problems multiply, for no longer can he rely on a quick, absentminded acceptance of his product. His customer is the very person most apt to look at it closely, a collector. Forgeries, therefore, usually show more care than counterfeits, and are harder to detect.

Because of the nominal values of

today's coins, counterfeiting presents little threat, but in the days of gold and silver coinage, it was a grave problem, and counterfeits of these abound. How can one recognize a counterfeit, and indeed a forgery?

The collector's tools are visual examination and memory, in others words, *experience*. If you have inspected several thousand Pieces of Eight in books, at coin shows, in collections, you will probably be able to spot a counterfeit.

There are other tools, and some are particularly helpful in spotting cast counterfeits. Aside from the visual examination, there is the tactile one. Pick up the coin. Is the weight right (obviously, a decent scale is useful, but a simple balance scale is quite adequate), or does it feel lighter than other specimens? Does it *feel* right, or is it greasy to the touch—an indication that it was cast? Hold the coin tightly in your hand. Does it warm up rapidly? If so, it may have been cast from lead. Does it *sound* right? Balance a gold or silver coin on your finger and tap it with a pencil. It should emit a long, rich tone. Base-metal counterfeits, on the other hand, produce tones of descending quality, while lead ones barely ring at all.

The most vulnerable part of a cast counterfeit is its edge. Examine it carefully. If it is reeded, is the reeding perfect? Probably not. Unlike a genuine coin, does it have a thin line along part or all of its surface? It can, as this is where the two molds join and the line is difficult to remove without leaving evidence. If it has been completely removed, filing marks may still be visible.

Finally, a cast counterfeit will usually be slightly smaller in diameter than a genuine, struck coin. Measure it with an inexpensive, marked caliper.

It is no harder to discover a die-struck counterfeit coin than a cast counterfeit. New, unofficial dies were ordinarily used to produce such fakes, and the resulting "coins" always look slightly different—and sometimes very different—from genuine

coins minted with official dies. Again, a visual examination is important; the coin's style, lettering, and entire method of execution will appear odd and expose it as a counterfeit.

Other methods are used to detect counterfeit paper money. Most paper money is counterfeited with more skill than are coins, perhaps because the amounts of money involved are often larger, and prompt greater scrutiny by the public. But some things are obvious.

If the counterfeit is lithographed rather than engraved, even a cursory examination reveals it. The colors are flat and dull, while the fine details found on the original engraved bill are either absent or coarsened on the lithographed counterfeit. The bill feels wrong. Engraving actually deposits a minute line of ink on the surface of the paper, giving it a slightly rough texture, while lithography does not.

For these and other reasons, few lithographed counterfeits are produced today.

Counterfeit and forgery detection. Detail of a counterfeit United States 10-dollar bill, series of 1928 B. Note the crudity of the engraving.

Most fakes are engraved, but they too have telltale characteristics that can be seen with a magnifying glass. Check the paper on which the bill is printed, and compare it with that used for genuine paper money. Do they correspond? Now turn to the quality of the engraving, and examine the cross-hatching used to produce the shading effect. Is it crisp and clear? Look at the scrollwork and guilloches. Are they applied with a sure touch? If the bill has a portrait, check the eyes. Are they lifelike? Finally, consider a few other points. Bearing in mind that colors on paper money can change through circulation, misuse, or chemical action, see if the bill's colors are in the normal range. And the serial numbers—are they crisp, well-applied, and in a straight line? As with suspect coins, visual experience is a key to successful detection.

When we move into the realm of forgeries, we are on more difficult ground. As mentioned, forgeries, of necessity, tend to be more carefully done than counterfeits, and never was this so true as it is today. Fortunately, we need not be concerned with paper money forgeries—yet. But coin forgeries more than make up for that blessing.

Early forgeries were struck, and many were quite good. They were primarily aimed at a small group of wealthy collectors; in Europe they concentrated on ancient coins, and in the United States on colonial ones. The most celebrated early forger was probably Carl Wilhelm Becker (1772–1830), whose Greek and Roman products were so superior that, to this day, many are in museums as genuine coins. Becker suffered with the problem of any forger who makes his own dies, however, and some of his creations show minor stylistic elements that simply do not look "ancient" to the experienced eye.

A solution is to use an actual coin in the forgery process, and in this century two methods of doing so have emerged. One is the lost wax process (also known as a centrifugal cast) in which a wax replica is made of a genuine coin. It is embedded in plaster, and then heated. A duct allows the wax to run off, and molten metal is forced into the mold under pressure. The "coin" will be a fairly decent copy of the original —at least to the unaided eye. Although the method was originally used to produce counterfeit coins, its possibilities for forgery were discovered in the 1950s and it was widely used for that purpose in the following decade. This type of forgery is not inordinately hard to discover using magnification. Look at details, especially at the borders; they may be somewhat weak. Also, the fields will not be flat and unblemished, as they should be on a genuine coin. Pitting and bubbles may be present.

The second modern forging practice, prominent in the past fifteen years, also uses a genuine coin, and is capable of creating far more dangerous forgeries than any previous method. Called explosive impact copying, it actually makes dies for forgeries directly from a genuine coin. Obviously, the coin has to be made harder than the die blank for the transfer to work, and this is achieved with a detonating capsule that drives the die blank against the coin with an explosive force. The time between the impact of the die blank on the coin and its reception of a reverse impression *from* the coin is then measured in microseconds, and is so rapid the coin has no time to spread out to any major degree. In effect, the coin has been rendered harder than the die.

Such forgeries almost defy detection. However, there are some clues to heed. As the forgery is, in a sense, a double transferral from an original, official die, its details are somewhat weaker than are those on a genuine coin, in which a die's image is transferred only once. Moreover, there is a very slight "spreading effect" from the forgery's center to its periphery, for the original coin spreads a bit during the explosive impact process. Finally, since a genuine coin, nicks and all, acts as a die for the forgery, all forgeries struck with that die will show the same nicks in the same places. They can be removed from the forgery die, but if so, minute scratches could be left behind, and *these* will appear on the forgery.

However, these are minor points upon which to accept or reject a coin. Any suspect coin should be referred to an established authentication service for examination. Forgeries from the explosive impact copying method are particularly numerous among American gold coins of the nineteenth and twentieth centuries, and, following the shifts in collectors' interests, are now appearing in other series as well.

See also AUTHENTICATION; CAST COUNTERFEIT; COUNTERFEIT; DIE-STRUCK COUNTERFEIT; ENGRAVING; FORGERY; LITHOGRAPHY; SPECIFIC GRAVITY.

COUNTERSTAMP A punch mark or marks, officially applied to a coin or a segment of a coin to change its value and/or indicate its acceptance as legal tender in a place beyond where it was issued.

The official nature of the counterstamp distinguishes it from chop marks and advertisements, which are privately stamped on coins.

The counterstamp, like the overprint, belongs, in part, to emergency money, as it is used in areas which do enough trade to require coinage, but do not have the time, technology, or inclination to set up an ordinary mint. The islands of the Caribbean are an example. So too are the seventh-century Byzantine Empire and seventeenth-century Spain, where fiscal and political turmoil made time of the essence in preparing acceptable money.

Counterstamps can be traced to classical times. They are seen on some coins in the Greek Imperial series, where they made civic issues current in areas other than those where they had been intended to circulate. They were also used to indicate the altered value of a coin circulating within a specific Greek city. Roman coinage, too, displays counterstamps, particularly base-metal issues of the first century A.D. Although the reasons for their use are unclear, in some cases they seem to have been inspired by military necessity.

The counterstamp was largely abandoned in the Western world in the second century A.D. It revived briefly in the Byzantine Empire during the reigns of Heraclius (ruled 610–641) and Constans II (ruled 641–668), when new money was needed quickly and it was faster to revalue and revalidate old coins—the follis and its subdivisions only—than to strike fresh ones. These Byzantine issues were essentially the last counterstamped coins manufactured in the West until early modern times. During the seventeenth century the counterstamp was reintroduced in two widely separate places, and its operation in each reveals much about the nature and purpose of counterstamps.

The first area to consider is Spain, where the state of the economy necessitated the counterstamp. The reigns of Philip III (ruled 1598–1621) and Philip IV (ruled 1621–1665) were rife with inflation and economic dislocation, generated largely by Spain's attempt to retain its status as a world power. Coppers of the four-maravedí denomination were counterstamped with a VIII in 1602, doubling their value. In 1636 their worth was set at twelve maravedís, and reaffirmed in 1641, so once again the coins were counterstamped. When that rate met with resistance, the coins were given a final counterstamp in the middle and late 1650s, lowering their value to eight maravedís. Needless to say, the result was a series of coins whose original designs had long since been obscured.

In the second instance, Brazil, we see counterstamps used for political as well as economic purposes. This Portuguese colony was without a modern mint until 1695, but there were enough colonists to require some form of circulating currency, and it was logical that local authorities

Counterstamp.

Top: Spain, counterstamped 4-maravedi piece,
seventeenth century.

Bottom: Brazil, Portuguese coin counterstamped for
use in the colony in 1663 and 1688.

would turn to counterstamped coinage. The raw materials for two series of counterstamped coins were whatever Spanish-American and Portuguese coins happened into the colony. The first series, appearing in 1663, was a simple one, featuring a mark of value within a rectangular field, the whole surrounded by a device that vaguely resembled a crown. The next was produced in 1688, and was rather more complex. The Brazilians applied a crude edge-marking machine to the plain edges of the 1663 counterstamped coins. For the obverse and reverse, they then created circular counterstamp punches, roughly resembling a doughnut with a large center hole. The punches covered the entire surface of the coin, except for its center, and carried legends with the name and titles of the ruler on one side, and a religious motto on the other. Hence the peripheries of the counterstamped piece had updated legends, while its central devices remained relatively untouched, with the 1663 counterstamp of value still visible. In sum, the new counterstamp punch was so elaborate it closely resembled a coin die itself.

The celebrated days of counterstamped coinage were the late eighteenth and early nineteenth centuries, when whole and fractional Spanish-American and other coins were stamped for use in the Caribbean, a practice that continued there and in Central America longer than anywhere else. Until 1889, Costa Rica regularly counterstamped foreign silver coins with the national arms, and continued the tradition by counterstamping its own silver coins in 1923, doubling their value.

Today, counterstamping has all but disappeared. A synonym for counterstamp is countermark.

See also BIT; CHOP MARK; EMERGENCY MONEY; FOLLIS; GREEK IMPERIALS; MARAVEDÍ; OVERPRINT; OVERSTRIKE.

COWRIE A marine mollusk *(Cypraea moneta)*, found in abundance in the Indian and Pacific oceans, whose attractive shell was used as a medium of exchange in the Far East, Africa, and Oceania.

Cowries were prized for their beauty and, in certain areas, for the difficulty involved in acquiring them.

The Chinese may have been the first to use them in exchange, doing so in the second millennium B.C. The top or hump of the cowrie shell was frequently ground off before it was traded, and before 1000 B.C. replicas were created in cast bronze.

Cowries long served in trade in areas bordering the Indian and Pacific oceans. In Bengal, the cowrie had a definite value against coinage: 3,840 of them equalled one silver rupee. Gradually cowrie money

Cowrie. *China, cowrie shell and replica, 1766–*
1122 B.C.

spread from Africa's east coast to its western shores, and by 1850, it was known from Nigeria to Timbuktu. However, European colonization severely restricted its role, and by 1900 the cowrie was obsolete in all but the most remote areas. Its days of eminence are commemorated in Ghana's monetary system, in which the unit of exchange is a cedi, from the native *sedie*, meaning cowrie.

See also BARTER; I PI CH'IEN.

Cracked dies. *A cracked die used to produce an American medal in 1875.*

CRACKED DIES Dies with broken surfaces, or with parts of their surfaces missing.

This condition can be caused by overworking the dies to produce more coins from them than their metallic composition (usually steel) can handle. Cracked dies can also result from applying excessive pressure in the coining process, using particularly hard or brittle materials for coins, or even from a speck of foreign matter lodged on the lower or upper die. Then too, dies can crack if they do not harden properly and become brittle. If cracked dies are used long enough, they will shatter completely.

Cracked dies are significant because they have a direct effect on the coins they strike. Once a crevice or fissure is opened in a die, it is incorporated into the die's design, and when the die is used to strike coins, the crack appears on the finished coin—in relief, along with the types and legends. Hence coins minted from cracked dies are considered errors.

Numismatists have various terms to describe these errors. A die break is a raised, wandering line, usually heading from the coin's edge to its center, or linking such peripheral elements as the letters of the legend, or, as on the Mexican peso, the tips of the rays. A die chip, on the other hand, can appear anywhere on a coin's surface, usually as an irregular blob of metal, large or small.

By far the most spectacular sign of the cracked die is the cud. Here, a section of the die actually separates from the whole, usually at or near the die's periphery.

As with most other errors, the more obvious the anomaly, the greater its value to the collector. Cracked dies are no longer as common as they once were. Today annealing is done more scientifically, care is taken to preserve the life of coin dies, and defective ones are removed immediately. Even so, minor cracks in dies do go undiscovered, and the errors emanating from them are popular—and inexpensive—items for collectors.

See also CUD; DIE BREAK; DIE CHIP; ERROR.

CROAT A Spanish form of the gros tournois, and the first heavy silver coin struck on the Iberian Peninsula by Christians.

Originating in the time of Alfonso III, Count of Barcelona (ruled 1285–1291), this new coin, heavier than the lightweight medieval penny, was spawned in Barcelona rather than elsewhere because of the city's enviable position as a commercial entrepôt for the western Mediterranean. Larger and more valuable silver coins were in demand, and the croat soon occasioned several imitators from the inland states of the peninsula, among them the grueso of Navarre and the more famous real of Castile and Leon.

At its inception, the croat was around

Croat. Barcelona, 1285–1291.

24 millimeters in diameter, and weighed about 3.1 grams—smaller and lighter than the gros tournois, but a considerable improvement compared to the penny (or dinero, as it was known in that region); it turned out to be a highly useful coin for Barcelona's burgeoning trade.

If the size and weight of the croat suggest an economic advance, its designs suggest an artistic one. This is particularly true for the obverse. Although the ruler's titles are given clockwise from a cross at 12:00, a common medieval practice, the portrait, while crude, is in profile, a distinctly uncommon practice in medieval Europe at this time. A profile portrait allows the die-cutter to depict more individuality than a facing rendition, which leads us to assume the rulers of Barcelona took their positions seriously enough to help their subjects distinguish one count from another. In any event, this kind of portraiture on the Catalan croat indicates the area was moving out of the medieval age and into the modern one more rapidly than much of Europe.

Yet the reverse design of the croat remains medieval. A simple cross with pellets and circles in its angles dominates, while the reverse legend announces the name of the city where the coin was minted.

The croat was struck until the beginning of the eighteenth century, with only minor changes in its design. Issues minted after the death of Philip II (ruled 1556–1598), however, were more often called reales, even though their designs differed from those on other Spanish coins of that name.

See also CROSS ON COINAGE; GROSSO; GROS TOURNOIS; PENNY; PORTRAIT; REAL.

CROSS ON COINAGE   The display of Christianity's primary symbol on coins, particularly those from the Byzantine Empire and the medieval West.

The years 500–1500 are the central ones for this practice, which had its beginnings years before. The first use of the Christian cross as a numismatic type was in the Roman Empire of the fourth century, and an early example is the Christogram. The Greek letters chi and rho indicate the first two letters of Christ's name, but when placed on top of one another, they also form a type of cross. In this sense, use of the Christian cross can be traced to the 320s. By the 360s it begins to appear in a more recognizable form, first as a small element on a labarum, or banner, later in more ornate form, supported by an angel.

The cross is almost always seen as a reverse type on late Roman coinage, with the emperor's portrait on the more important obverse, a basic practice that was retained as long as the cross was a popular coinage motif. It is symbolic of the church-state relationship in the late Roman and medieval worlds, where both church and state were necessary to health and well-being, but in reality the state took precedence over the church.

The late fourth century saw the final partition of the Roman Empire. Its western half was soon occupied by barbarian states, most of which embraced at least part of the classical legacy, and in time the Christian faith. To the east, a Roman state existed for several more centuries, becoming increasingly Greek and less Latin in its cultural outlook and orientation. Historians took note of the fact by giving this new state a new name: the Byzantine Empire.

The first centuries of the Middle Ages were years of heightened anxiety for all people. It was a time of foreign and domestic turmoil, disease, and uncertainty.

Little seemed fixed and immutable; nothing could be depended upon. An exception was the Christian faith. If a man believed in its tenets, his future might be assured, even if his present was not. Thus, the harsher life became in the medieval world, the greater was the importance of the Christian faith.

It is self-evident that money reflects the human condition. In the Age of Faith, therefore, it is not surprising to discover coinage with a religious emphasis—in legends and inscriptions, in depictions of saints, angels, and Christ Himself. But most often, faith was expressed by the cross.

For the Byzantines, it dominated the reverses of tenth- and eleventh-century Anonymous Bronzes, and figured prominently in the designs on the silver hexagram and the gold solidus, many early specimens of which depict a cross on steps.

There was a parallel development in the West. The cross was most conspicuous on the post-Roman coinages of Gaul and Visigothic Spain, and a familiar reverse type for the penny or denier and its various imitations. The typical medieval penny had a full-face portrait of the ruler on its obverse, with a cross, often surrounded by pellets or other devices, on its reverse. This reverse design was carried over to the gros tournois, and its thirteenth- and fourteenth-century descendants.

In both parts of medieval Europe, the West and the Byzantine Empire, the display of the cross on a coin served two purposes. It paid homage to the true religion, and it used up space. Something had to fill a reverse die and for the coiner, the cross was not only theologically appropriate, but easy to render.

The significance of the cross underwent a change, as medieval man's concept of himself and his world changed. The years after 1000, particularly those after 1200, saw increasing prosperity and peace. Man's destiny seemed more within his reach, and God's intervention perhaps less

Cross on coinage.
Left: France, tremissis, seventh century.
Center: Florence, florin, 1256.
Right: France, écu, 1690.

necessary. Then, too, ambitious rulers emerged, and they fancied their role as a more glorious one than that of the humble vicar of Christ.

As the medieval West grew more secular, and rulers more modern, the prominence of the cross declined. It became essentially a design element, and its religious significance waned.

An early Florentine florin exemplifies the first point. Its cross, drastically reduced to one small element in the design, sits atop a scepter carried by John the Baptist, patron saint of the city. The second point is illustrated by a French écu struck by Louis XIV (ruled 1643–1715). While its cross is indeed prominent, even cursory scrutiny exposes the "cross" as merely a clever design, devoid of religious meaning. In fact, it is made up of eight L's, all standing for Louis.

Today, the use of the cross on coinage is essentially relegated to the realm of heraldry, its religious importance having ceased with the end of the Middle Ages. If a cross is part of a nation's coat of arms, or is seen on the monarch's crown, it might appear on the modern coins.

See also ANONYMOUS BRONZES; CHRISTO-GRAM; DENIER; GROS TOURNOIS; HEXA-GRAM; PENNY; SOLIDUS.

CROWN 1: A large British silver coin, struck sporadically from 1551 to 1937—its later copper-nickel equivalents were minted until 1965—and valued at one crown to five shillings. 2: A general term for any silver coin roughly the same size as the British crown; such coins frequently form the monetary units of the countries in which they are issued.

There were abortive efforts to introduce a gold crown in the 1520s and later, but when we say "crown," we are mainly thinking of a silver coin. This English silver crown could be described as an offshoot of the European thaler, a large coin introduced late in the fifteenth century, which in succeeding centuries became popular throughout most of Europe.

The first English silver crowns were minted under Edward VI (ruled 1547–1553), and were part of a general effort to improve the quality of the island's money.

The reform brought forth new coins —the threepence and sixpence, subdivisions of the testoon or shilling; and the crown, a multiple of the shilling. The crown equalled one-sixth of a "fine" sovereign (one of high gold content), or five shillings, and was significant for a number of reasons. First, at almost 42 millimeters in diameter and 31 grams in weight, it was by far the most massive coin the English had ever produced. Edward's issues were struck by hand; were the coin to be minted in quantity, machinery would have to be devised or imported. Second, the crown was a well-designed coin, more Renaissance than medieval in appearance. The obverse portrays Edward in full armor mounted on a horse; his titles in Latin make up the legend. The reverse has a strikingly simple English shield at the center of a cross, the arms of which separate the words of a pious legend, again in Latin. The modern quality of the coin is highlighted by the use of Arabic numerals to give the dates of the issues—1551, 1552, or 1553. It is the first English coin to do so; indeed, the nation would not regularly date its coins for more than another century. For many years, the crown was not an overwhelming success, or indeed

Crown. England, 1552.

much in evidence. The English were slow to adopt machinery for minting, and the next issue did not appear until 1601, near the end of the reign of Edward's half-sister, Elizabeth I (ruled 1558–1603). This crown, slightly lighter than its predecessor, but with the same diameter, depicted the queen on the obverse, facing left, while the reverse was almost identical to that on Edward VI's coin. The issues of 1601 and 1602 indicated the date on both sides, with a "1" or "2" at about 12:00; the other three digits were missing.

With the advent of Charles II (ruled 1660–1685), the crown, now valued at four to a guinea (another new coin), was struck in quantity for the first time. Several factors made it feasible, not the least of which was the adoption of the screw press in 1662, enabling a coiner to produce coins more easily. Moreover, there was an abundance of silver on hand. England's flourishing world trade brought much of it from abroad; several large silver mines were opened in western England, and in 1662, Charles II obtained 1.5 million silver écus from Louis XIV in exchange for the town of Dunkirk.

Numbers of crowns were struck until about 1750, and through the period they were fairly uniform—almost exactly 40 millimeters broad and weighing 30 grams. The obverse carried a portrait of the ruler and a legend giving his or her titles. The legend continued on the reverse, which also held the date. The reverse type was four crowned shields, each representing a royal possession. Edges were lettered by means of edge-marking machinery, as coins with plain edges were apt to be clipped or filed.

During most of the long reign of George III (ruled 1760–1820), the crown was not minted. But it reappeared at the end of his rule, with a beautiful new reverse which it would carry through much of its remaining career. It pictured the patron of England, St. George, in the act of slaying a dragon, and was executed by the Italian medallist Pistrucci.

The twentieth-century crown reflects the monetary problems of the twentieth-century world. Its silver fineness was 925 through the year 1902, after which no crowns were minted until 1927. The new issue was, and would remain, only 500 fine until after World War II, when silver was removed from all English coins including the crown. The last crown was a commemorative issue, struck in 1965 to pay homage to Winston Churchill. Three more related issues have appeared, each commemorative in nature, but they are part of England's decimal coinage system, and their denomination is expressed as twenty-five pence, not one crown.

Using the size and weight of a coin as criteria, collectors tend to refer to a broad range of coins as crowns. Any silver coin with a diameter of 33 to 50 millimeters and weighing somewhere between 20 and 30 grams qualifies, and even the large, copper-nickel coins that have replaced silver ones are sometimes referred to this way. A Mexican peso, a French five-franc piece, a Chinese yuan, are all covered by the amorphous term crown. Needless to say there would be less confusion if coins were called by their real names.

See also COLLAR; DATING SYSTEMS; EDGE-MARKING MACHINERY; MACHINE-STRUCK COINAGE; THALER.

CUD An abnormally raised area of metal at the edge of a coin, token, or medal: a

sign that the die used to strike the piece broke completely at that point.

The cud differs from the die chip and die break. The die chip can occur anywhere on the coin, and is usually only slightly raised, as is the die break: the die which produced them was still in one piece when it struck the coin.

There are several varieties of cuds. The most common has a small blob of metal on the rim of the coin, but not on its designs or fields. Although this rim cud can occur on a coin's reverse, it is generally seen on its obverse side. In either case, rim cuds are minor errors, and of no particular value to collectors.

This is not so of the retained cud, which involves part of the design surface of the die, extending to its edge; when the die breaks the errant piece remains more or less in place. When a coin is struck by such a die, metal is forced into the depression left by the die fragment, but later the metal is brought up against the fragment and receives an impression of it. If the die fragment is just barely under the surface, the impression is moderately sharp. However, the lower the fragment slips, the weaker will be the impression, as most of the force needed to mint a sharply impressed coin will have been spent. To the collector, such errors are the most desirable.

More desirable still is the cud produced once the die fragment has fallen

Cud. United States, cent, 1831. Note circular die break and prominent cud near the bottom of the coin.

away completely. In this case, the cud is a very raised, irregular, and unmarked blob of metal, with no trace of the original design. If it is large enough, it will have induced a corresponding depression on the other side of the coin.

Collecting cuds has just recently come into favor, and will probably attract enthusiasts to a growing degree. Because these coins are the same size, metal, and weight as normal ones, many leave the mint and enter circulation, where they now wait for collectors.

See also CRACKED DIES; DIE BREAK; DIE CHIP; ERROR.

CULL A worthless or inferior numismatic specimen.

An item can be described as a cull when it shows signs of excessive wear or mistreatment, such as a hole or other extensive damage. The term is most often used for a defective article discovered in a large lot and then separated from the better specimens.

The word is of some importance in buying and selling. A lot of English pennies, for example, might be advertised as: "In average circulated condition—no culls." While the term "average circulated condition" is open to dispute, at least the prospective buyer is assured that the lot does not contain worthless material.

On the other hand, auction houses also sell lots of ancient or mixed coins with only a cursory description of their condition. They might also announce: "Sold as is—no returns." In this case, the collector can be certain culls are in the lot. However, the price of the lot, or particular coins within it, can make it an attractive purchase, culls and all. It is always advisable to buy from reputable dealers, and carefully read the entire description of any lot of numismatic material offered for sale.

CUPPED COIN A spectacular error closely related to the brockage.

The cupped coin should not be confused with the cup-*shaped* coin, of which the Byzantine scyphate coinage is the best-known example. The scyphate coins and related pieces, including the ramatankas of South India, were deliberate adaptations of the cup shape, and convex and concave dies were used to achieve the effect. The cupped coin, on the other hand, is an accident, and a rather rare one at that.

The piece illustrated, an American cent minted in 1896, is an excellent example of a cupped coin. On the obverse, note the rise of the sides to form a cup; also the coin's extreme thinness, as seen by the metallic split at 3:00. On the reverse, the original design (the words ONE CENT, within a wreath, surmounted by a shield) is almost completely obliterated, and the feathers on Liberty's headdress are beginning to show through on this side, in intaglio. These are characteristic of the cupped coin, and serve as clues to the error's origins.

More often than not, the cupped coin is produced by the same chain of events that creates the brockage. The coin is struck once in the ordinary manner, receiving impressions from the upper (obverse) die and lower (reverse) one, from which it should then be ejected. If it is not, and another planchet is placed over it, the new planchet receives the customary relief impression from the top die, and an intaglio impression from the coin beneath it. This new planchet is a brockage.

But what happens to the original coin? It accepts a very sharp impression from

Cupped coin. *United States, cent, 1896.*

the bottom die, for the addition of the second planchet generates tremendous pressure, driving the coin vigorously into the die. The force can be of such strength that it causes the metal in the second coin to spread outward into the narrow boundary between the dies and the restraining collar. The cuplike appearance of the error is now beginning to take shape. The added pressure also explains the thinness of the piece, in comparison to a normal coin. If the side of the coin in contact with the lower die is very strong, its other side, which in effect serves as a die for the intaglio side of the brockage, will be very weak, and its designs will tend to spread. If the coin is not ejected at this juncture, the sides of the "cup" become more pronounced, as it receives further impressions. On one side, the die impression will be even sharper, or might show a doubling of the design, while on the other side the original design will become progressively weaker, and all but disappear.

In the case of the 1896 cent cited earlier, there was still another complication. Notice that it is the *obverse* which is sharply impressed, and the reverse which is not. This anomaly is explained by the fact that the original coin in the brockage process can adhere to the *upper* die—because of moisture or mechanical failure—as well as to the lower one. If so, the obverse of the coin receives the direct die impressions, and the reverse does not.

The cupped error (as opposed to the deliberately fashioned cup-shaped coin) emanates from modern minting, as opposed to the brockage, which is known from ancient and early modern times.

See also Brockage; Error; Scyphate coinage.

CURRENCY A general term embracing any and all money actually in circulation in a given time and place.

It is linked to the word "current," referring to those monetary items still in use. The public tends to restrict the word to paper money, as distinguished from coinage, but this is both arbitrary and inaccurate. Providing coins circulate, they are as much currency as is paper money, which is exchangeable for coinage.

See also Noncirculating legal tender.

D

DARIC A famous gold coin of the ancient world, minted by the Persian Empire between the late sixth and mid-fourth centuries B.C., and purportedly named after Darius I (ruled 522–486 B.C.), who first coined it around 515.

The daric was round or bean-shaped, about 14.5 millimeters in diameter, nearly 4 millimeters thick, and weighing around 8.3 grams. Its types were simple, in keeping with those characteristic of archaic coinage. The obverse of the daric depicted the king, invariably in a stiff military pose. He was pictured shooting with a bow and arrow, or running, holding a bow and a spear. Neither obverse nor reverse bore a legend or inscription. The reverse type was merely an oblong punch mark with no design. The daric exemplified the primitive style of the first Greek coins of the seventh and sixth centuries. But the Persians borrowed the style at a time when the Greeks were abandoning it, and steadfastly retained it for almost two hundred years. Developments to the West passed them by: the glories of Grecian coinage left the Persians unimpressed, and the crude daric and its equally graceless companion in silver, the siglos, were struck year after year in essentially unchanged form. The reverse punch was never developed into a true reverse die for the daric. The king on the obverse was never named and, as his features underwent little modification from reign to reign, it is difficult to distinguish the coins of one king from those of another. The last darics were coined under Darius III (ruled 336–330 B.C.), after which Persia was conquered by Alexander III of Macedon, who brought beauty to the region's coinage.

But it was a beauty imposed by strangers. The inhabitants of the sprawling Persian state had been content with their

Daric. Persian Empire, Darius I, c. 500 B.C.

Left: The Development of Greek Numismatic Art
Top left: *Phocaea, electrum 1/6 stater, sixth century B.C.*
Top right: *Poseidonia, stater, 550-470 B.C.*
Bottom left: *Mende, tetradrachm, later fifth century B.C.*
Bottom right: *Agrigentum, tetradrachm, 413-406 B.C.*

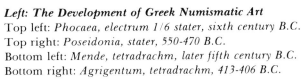

Right: A Masterpiece of Greek Coinage
Syracuse, decadrachm, 413 B.C.

Left: The Rise of Portrait Coinage
Top to bottom: *Delphi, stater, 346-339 B.C.;
Leontini, tetradrachm, 466-422 B.C.; Pontus,
tetradrachm, 120-63 B.C.*

Above: The Birth of Roman Coinage
Top: *Roman Republic, as, c. 211 B.C.*
Bottom, left to right: *denarius, c. 211 B.C.;
denarius, c. 140 B.C.; didrachm, early third
century B.C.*

Left: The Spread of the Greek Idea
Top left: *Egypt, tetradrachm, 323-285 B.C.*
Top right: *Bactria, tetradrachm, c. 200-150 B.C.*
Bottom left: *Macedon, tetradrachm, 359-336 B.C.*
Bottom right: *Elymäis, tetradrachm, c. 82 B.C.*

Money of Japan and Korea
Top: *Japan, eiraku sen, c. 1600.*
Center: *Japan, koban, 1860-1867.*
Bottom left: *Korea, 3 chon, 1882-1883.*
Bottom right: *Japan, ichibu gin, 1859-1868.*

Below: Western-Style Coinage Comes to the Orient
Left to right: *Japan, yen, 1870; Korea, 5 fun, 1895; China, yuan, 1912; Japan, 1,000 yen, 1964.*

The Early Medieval West
Top, left to right: *France, tremissis, seventh century; France, denier, 814-840; Italy, Ostrogothic Kingdom, 40 nummi, 534-536.*
Center: *England, penny, 871-899.*
Bottom: *Germany, Halberstadt, bracteate, 1149-1160.*

Byzantine Empire

Top, left to right: *Anastasius, tremissis, 491-518; Constans II, solidus, 641-668; Justinian II, solidus, 685-717.*

Bottom, left to right: *Isaac II, asperon trachy, 1185-1195; Alexius I, hyperpyron, 1081-1118; Theophilus, solidus, 829-832.*

The Rise of Islam

Top left: *Arab-Sassanian drachm, c. 650.*

Top right: *Northern Iraq, dirhem, A.H. 95 (A.D. 713-714).*

Center left: *Egypt, dinar, A.H. 362 (A.D. 972-973).*

Center right: *Ottoman Empire, altun, A.H. 886 (A.D. 1481-1482).*

Bottom: *Byzantine Empire, John V, silver coin, 1341-1391.*

The Artistry of Medieval Coinage

Top: *France, franc à cheval, 1350-1364.*

Bottom: *England, noble, 1361-1369.*

Medieval Coinage: The Revival

Top, left to right: *Venice, grosso, c. 1202; France, gros tournois, c. 1266; Castile and Leon, real, 1350-1369.*

Bottom, left to right: *Florence, florin, 1256; England, groat, 1351-1361; Germany, Meissen, groschen, 1376-1406.*

Gold Coinage of the Late Middle Ages
Top left: *Castile and Leon, dobla, 1454-1474.*
Top right: *France, écu d'or, 1380-1422.*
Center: *Cologne, riel or florin, 1437.*
Bottom left: *Scotland, lion, 1390-1406.*
Bottom right: *England, angel, 1461-1483.*

The Coinage of the Italian Renaissance
Top left: *Milan, testone, 1466-1476.*
Top right: *Milan, testone, 1535-1556.*
Center: *Ferrara, testone, 1471-1505.*
Bottom left: *Milan, testone, 1476-1481.*
Bottom right: *Mantua, testone, 1519-1540.*

Coinage of the Northern Renaissance
Left, top to bottom: *England, sovereign, c. 1504-1507; Brabant, real d'or, 1515-1555.*
Right, top to bottom: *Scotland, "bonnet-piece" or ducat, 1540; Austria, ducat, 1589; Württemberg, goldgulden, 1520.*

The Birth of the Thaler
Top: *Netherlands, Overyssel, daalder, 1584.*
Center, left to right: *Bohemia, Joachimsthaler, c. 1520; Brunswick-Wolfenbüttel, thaler, 1537; Sweden, riksdaler, 1559.*
Bottom: *Tyrol, guldengroschen, 1486.*

Coinage of the New European Nation-States
Top: *Netherlands, rijksdaalder, 1583.*
Center, left to right: *France, half franc, 1602; England, crown, 1601; Spain, 4 excelentes, 1497-1516.*
Bottom: *Sweden, riksdaler, 1632.*

The Development of Mechanized Coining, 1550-1800
Top, left to right: *France, hand-struck teston, 1552; France, machine-struck teston, 1552; England, penny, 1797.*
Bottom left: *England, crown, 1662.*
Bottom right: *Spain, 8 reales, 1586.*

The Fabric of Eighteenth-Century Coinage
Top left: *France, décime, 1799-1800.*
Top right: *England, halfpenny, 1750.*
Bottom left: *Austria, thaler, 1710.*
Bottom right: *Russia, ruble, 1742.*

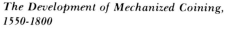

The Expansion of Europe
Top left: *Portuguese India, half cruzado, 1500-1521.*
Top right: *Mexico, 3 reales, 1536-1556.*
Center left: *Guatemala, 8 reales, 1760.*
Center right: *Brazil, 12,800 reis, 1731.*
Bottom left: *Massachusetts, Oak Tree shilling, "1652" (1660-1667).*
Bottom right: *Virginia, halfpenny, 1773.*

The First Colonial Revolt: New States in the Americas
Top, left to right: *United States, 10 dollars, 1795; Mexico, insurgents, 8 reales, 1813; Argentina, 8 reales, 1813.*
Center: *Bolivia, 8 soles, 1827.*
Bottom, left to right: *Brazil, 960 reis, 1823; Ecuador, 8 escudos, 1839; Guatemala, 8 reales, 1826.*

Tradition and Change: Coinage in Nineteenth-Century Europe
Top, left to right: *Italy, 100 lire, 1883; United Kingdom, crown, 1893; France, 100 francs, 1862.*
Bottom, left to right: *Germany, Prussia, 5 mark, 1888; Russia, platinum 12 rubles, 1833; Greece, 20 lepta, 1831.*

Numismatic Art in the United States: Apogee, 1900-1925
Top, left to right: *20 dollars, 1907; 10 dollars, 1907; half dollar, 1916.*
Center left: *5 dollars, 1908.*
Center right: *quarter dollar, 1916.*
Bottom left: *5 cents, 1913.*
Bottom right: *cent, 1909.*

The Age of Unrest: Coinage in Twentieth-Century Europe
Top left: *Italy, 100 lire, 1956.*
Top right: *Germany, 5 mark, 1934.*
Center left: *Prussia, 5 mark, 1914.*
Center right: *Italy, 100 lire, 1923.*
Bottom: *Chinese Soviet Republic, 500 cash, 1934.*

The Departure of Empire and the Second Colonial Revolt
Clockwise from top: *Ghana, shilling, 1958; Kenya, 10 cents, 1969; Egypt, 20 piastres, A.H. 1375 (A.D. 1956); Algeria, dinar, A.H. 1383 (A.D. 1964); China, 5 fen, 1976; United Kingdom, 10 new pence, 1971.*
Center: *China, yuan, 1933.*

coinage as it was; indeed its persistent sameness symbolized the stability of their monarchy and state. Furthermore, the Persians wanted a coin to be useful in *trade*. It need not be beautiful, or even round, but it had to be of good metallic content and convenient weight, and guaranteed by a widely respected issuing authority. The daric more than met the requirements. No less a personage than the king stood behind each coin, the proof emblazoned on the obverse for all to see.

A coin the size of the daric affords little room for realistic portraiture or inscriptions, and the Persians, always a commercial people, may well have decided not enough was to be gained from an artistic coinage to make the effort worthwhile. All the same, they could have enlarged the obverse portraits, thus distinguishing rulers from one another. That they did not suggests that it was the concept of monarchy the Persians revered, rather than the individual ruler. Certainly, it is known that the notion of a semi-divine monarchy, embraced by Alexander the Great and his successors in the East, sprang in part from Persian thought. The daric illustrates the fact that the link between the nature of a people and the money they evolve is not accidental.

See also ARCHAIC COINAGE; HOARD; SIGLOS; TRADE COINS.

DATE LOGOTYPE A number punch with two or more digits, formerly used to place dates on coin dies.

The date logotype was designed to speed up the production of coinage dies; its operation in the United States extended from approximately 1840 to 1900. Two- or three-digit logotypes were the rule, although at least one instance of use of a four-digit punch is known, belied by a variety of 1858 half dime with a normal date punched in over an inverted one. A number of countries employed the date logotype, but improved techniques of die

Date logotype. United States, cent, 1851 (detail). Note traces of an inverted "18" under the "51" of the last two digits; the "18" logotype was initially stamped there in error.

preparation, culminating in the complete hub produced by the Janvier lathe (invented by Frenchman Victor Janvier in the late nineteenth century), made it obsolete early in this century.

See also DIE VARIETY; HUB; JANVIER REDUCING MACHINE; PUNCH.

DATING SYSTEMS Methods employed to establish the chronology of a coin, medal, or other numismatic item, and placed on those items by the issuer.

Dating serves several purposes. Its primary one, of course, is to set a particular object in a particular time in the public mind.

A coin may be dated to celebrate a memorable event or cultural achievement of the past or present. Or a date can be added to a coin or note to call attention to the issuer (and the quality) of that particular piece of money—in which case such related information as a mint mark is often appended. Dating systems are used to distinguish one government's wares from another's—part of their purpose in ancient Rome, as we shall see. Dating systems can have a religious connotation; the Christian and Islamic systems, the two most generally used today, have such roots. Finally, a dating system is also used simply to record the passage of time in an orderly fashion.

Over the years, a substantial number of dating systems have been devised. Some are of passing interest only, but others, in use for hundreds—even thousands—of years, are significant in the story of money.

Dating coinage began in the Greek-speaking world, where it was essentially confined to the Hellenistic period of the last three centuries before Christ, and even then it was by no means universally practiced. Hellenistic systems tended to rely on eras reckoned from an important year in the relevant dynasty's history. Coins could also be dated according to the regnal year of a ruler. In short, no universal dating system applied to all Greek coinage. However, for several centuries such a system did exist with Roman coinage, at least to a degree.

The first Roman coins bore no dates. By the second century B.C., moneyers' names, in full or abbreviated form, were seen on Rome's basic republican coin, the denarius, and, assuming one can decipher the name and research it (see Bibliography), the student can often determine a particular coin's year of issue. This is not a true dating system as we understand it, however, for it is based on names, not numbers. But the transition from republic to empire generated a more orthodox dating system, which was used fairly regularly for more than three hundred years. As is logical in a state glorifying one-man rule, the Roman imperial dating system centered on the multiple offices held by that man.

When Augustus (ruled 31 B.C.–A.D. 14) established a monarchical form of government in Rome, he kept alive the fiction that he was restoring the republic, not creating an empire. The republic had had a number of important offices—those of consuls, tribunes, censors, and more—that Augustus and his successors filled themselves, or staffed with trusted lieutenants, preserving the republican form while changing its substance. Thus it was quite possible for one man to be a tribune, a *pontifex maximus* (chief priest of the state

religion), a consul, an *imperator* (originally a military leader entrusted with absolute power for a limited period of time), etc. He might hold all of these offices at once, or begin as *imperator*, acquiring other positions and their titles from time to time. Some or all of the honorary titles appeared on coins in an abbreviated form. It was incumbent upon an emperor, after all, to remind his subjects of his illustrious career. Many offices were renewed annually, and the abbreviations are often followed by the Roman numbers indicating the number of times an emperor was "elected" consul, etc.

All of this means that the modern collector, armed with a few facts (often just the date of the original bestowal of an office or a title), can accurately date Roman coins. (See especially Z. H. Klawans: *Reading and Dating Roman Imperial Coins*, cited in the Bibliography.) Unfortunately from our point of view, the Romans' system, cumbersome though it was, passed out of use about A.D. 300.

The Roman dating system, at least as used on coins, might be described as internal—that is, confined to the reign of a particular ruler. Rome's Byzantine successors employed a somewhat different internal system for their sixth- and seventh-century copper coinage, simply marking Year One with the onset of each new reign. Justinian I (ruled 527–565) first used the system on coinage in 538–539, when he struck a series of large copper folles with a reverse inscription ANNO XII, for the twelfth year of his reign. His successors continued the practice on copper (although they never extended it to other metals) to the end of the seventh century, by which time a new dating system had evolved among Byzantium's rivals.

This system was *external*, consecutively applied to coins of a number of reigns, and Islamic in derivation. Reflecting the zeal of the new faith, it was based on the flight (Hejira) of the prophet Mohammed from Mecca to Medina, in A.D. 622. This, then, is the starting point of the Islamic calendar and the dating of coins struck in accordance with it.

At first glance, deciphering Islamic dates would seem to be an easy task. (The numbers used, incorrectly called "Arabic" in the West, are given in Table I.) Unfortunately, such is not the case. First, until the fourteenth century, dates on Islamic coins were spelled out; numbers were not generally used until the fifteenth century and later. Furthermore, the base of the Moslem year is lunar, not solar, which makes it some 3 percent shorter than its Western counterpart. This can be amended with tables giving the coordinates of Christian and Islamic dates, or with the following uncomplicated formula: subtract .03 from the Moslem date and add 621. Using a coin dated 1370 as an example: determine three percent of 1370 (41.10), round it off to the nearest whole number (41), subtract that number from 1370 (1329), and add 621. The coin was struck in 1950. This formula is accurate enough for general purposes, but it should be remembered that most Moslem years fall into parts of two Christian ones. Our 1370-dated coin could have been minted at any time from October 13, 1950 to October 1, 1951.

While the Islamic dating system was spreading in the East, dating by a system based on the birth of Christ was taking hold in the West. An early cleric fixed Christ's birth in the 754th year of Rome, which became Year One in the Christian calendar. Although the system was in fairly widespread use in the West by 1000, it did not appear on coinage until much later. The explanation lies in the nature of coins in the Middle Ages, and the nature of numbers. As coins tended to be small, any date expressed would have to be in a compact form and the "Arabic" numerals which would make this possible were not in common use until late in the period. Die-sinkers, then, were faced with the problem of putting a series of *Roman* numerals on a small coin. While most did not make the attempt, a few met the challenge.

The first coin to bear a Christian date is from the Danish city of Roskilde, and its Roman numerals state, appropriately, 1234—MCCXXXIIII—and constitute the entire obverse legend. With the adoption of "Arabic" numerals, Christian dating became more popular, and the first coin to be so dated was struck in 1424 in the Swiss canton of St. Gall. Still, use of the Christian date was essentially limited to Germany and some other sections of western and central Europe through the remainder of the fifteenth century and well into the sixteenth, and was not universally employed until after 1650.

Although the Islamic and Christian dating systems are the ones most widely used today, there are others worthy of a brief description. (See Table.) More often than not, Far Eastern coinages have used systems based on individual reigns. Certain Chinese coins of the Sung dynasty bear a *nien-hao* on the obverse and one or more Chinese numerals on the reverse, indicating the year of the reign during which the coin was cast: in essence, this dating system is seen on most modern Chinese and Japanese coins. China's late imperial government used both a complex arrangement, based on a sixty-year cycle, and a simpler one, giving the year of a particular reign. The Republic of China chose to retain the latter. To find the date of a pre-1949 mainland coin, or any Tai-

Dating systems.
Left: Egypt, 25 piastres, A.H. 1380 (A.D. 1960).
Right: China, yuan, year 25 (A.D. 1936).

Table I Standard International Numeral Systems

	0	1	2	3	4	5	6	7	8	9	10	50	100	500	1000
Western	0	1	2	3	4	5	6	7	8	9	10	50	100	500	1000
Arabic-Turkish	٠	١	٢	٣	٤	٥	٦	٧	٨	٩	١٠	٥٠	١٠٠	٥٠٠	١٠٠٠
Indian (Sanskrit)	०	१	२	३	४	५	६	७	८	९	१०	५०	१००	५००	१०००
Thai-Lao	๐	๑	๒	๓	๔	๕	๖	๗	๘	๙	๑๐	๕๐	๑๐๐	๕๐๐	๑๐๐๐
Ordinary Chinese Japanese-Korean	零	一	二	三	四	五	六	七	八	九	十	五十	百	五百	千
Hebrew		ב	ג	ד	ה	ו	ז	ח	ט	י	נ	ק			

wan issue to the present, look for the first number character in the legend and read right to left. A typical coin would thus read 2–10–5 right to left, meaning it was struck in the republic's twenty-fifth year ($2 \times 10 + 5 = 25$). The base date in this instance is 1911, and the addition of 25 to 1911 informs us that the coin was struck in 1936. The Japanese follow the same system for issues struck since 1870, except that characters read from right to left until 1948, when the direction was reversed. Today Western numbers are replacing Japanese characters. Early Korean coinage used a dating system based on a regnal year; modern issues are in keeping with Western practice.

Other dating systems widely used in earlier times or currently employed include: the Samvat or Vikrama Era, dating from 58 B.C., and the Saka Era, dating from A.D. 78, both found on coinages of the Indian Subcontinent and adjacent areas; the Buddhist Era, dating from 543 B.C., and the Ratanakosind-sok Era, beginning in A.D. 1781, which have been used in Thailand; and the Jewish Era, beginning in 3761 B.C., and used on all coins of the State of Israel.

See also FOLLIS; HEJIRA; *NIEN-HAO*.

DECADRACHM A large Greek silver coin (also spelled dekadrachm), equal in value to ten drachms, and issued sparingly in the fifth and fourth centuries before Christ.

The most extensive coinage of decadrachms took place on the island of Sicily, where they were struck between 480 and 390 B.C. in Syracuse, a wealthy Greek city. Although they seem to have been intended for commemorative purposes, at least one writer believes that, late in their career, they may also have functioned as an integral part of the money supply.

Be that as it may, the majority of Syracusan decadrachms are celebratory in nature, and can be linked with historical

Decadrachm. Syracuse, c. 480 B.C.

events. The piece shown is a good example. It is one of the earliest decadrachms, dating from around 480 B.C., a year that saw the defeat of the Carthaginians, to which this large coin may refer. On the obverse is a *quadriga*, or chariot, drawn by four horses, with Nike, goddess of victory, descending from the clouds to crown the horses' heads with a wreath. The running lion in the exergue might be a reference to Carthage. The reverse carries a head of Arethusa, patroness of Syracuse, with four dolphins, representing the sea which protected the city. This is a typical decadrachm in size (some 34 millimeters in diameter) and weight (45 grams).

This early decadrachm was unsigned. Later ones, especially those issued during the height of the coin's production, were frequently signed by Eumenes, Kimon, or other outstanding artists of the day. If the addition of artists' signatures was unusual, as it was, an explanation might be found in the coins' unparalleled beauty, giving their designers every right to celebrate themselves, as well as the victories of Syracuse. It would be another two millennia before such personal touches would be seen again.

Although Syracuse was always the center of the decadrachm's minting, the Athenians struck such a coin in 467 B.C., also for commemorative purposes, and it was minted sparingly during and shortly after the reign of Alexander the Great (ruled 336–323 B.C.). As king of Macedon, Alexander conquered much of the world; thus it is not surprising that one of the last decadrachms, possibly minted about 320

B.C., was the product of an Eastern mint, perhaps that of Babylon.

See also COMMEMORATIVE; DRACHM; ENGRAVERS' MARKS.

DECIMAL COINAGE A coinage system based on the number ten, its multiples, and its subdivisions.

In modern practice, coinage consists of a unit that can be divided into halves, quarters, tenths, twentieths, and hundredths—and every coin bears a fixed relation to every other coin in the system. In the case of the United States, the unit is a dollar, in turn divided into ten dimes, each worth ten cents. At various times, other coins have been added—the five-cent piece, quarter dollar, and at one point, a fifth dollar (a short-lived denomination in the United States, but one which has enjoyed a measure of popularity elsewhere). Regardless of a coin's name, two points hold true for all decimal systems: they are based on logic rather than tradition, and have a root number of ten. The countries to adopt such systems do so because they make monetary computation less burdensome; hence, the state appears to be committed to reform.

Decimal coinage is essentially a modern phenomenon. The Greeks and Romans experimented with a ten-to-one relationship, but were by no means consistent in their efforts. Although the decadrachm, equal to ten one-drachm coins, appeared sporadically in the fifth and fourth centuries B.C., the stater and the tetradrachm remained the major silver coins of Greece's Golden Age. In Rome, the denarius was initially tariffed at ten asses, but this relationship was soon abandoned in favor of a sixteen-to-one ratio which lasted to the third century A.D., when both coins passed out of use. When the decimal system reemerged, as it did fifteen hundred years later, it was in a most unlikely place—the backward Russian Empire of Peter the Great (ruled 1682–1725).

In 1700, Peter introduced the world's first truly decimal coinage system. The arrangement would facilitate the conduct of business in Russia, and would also serve notice that under Peter, whose travels in the West had convinced him Russia must adopt Western technology and ideas, the country was committed to a course of modernization.

For the Russian decimal system, Peter relied on two coins already in existence, the kopek and the ruble. The kopek, formerly struck in silver, would be made of copper, and one hundred of them would equal one silver ruble. Other denominations were occasionally added, and most fit directly into the decimal system. (An exception was the three-kopek piece, which is still struck today.) Many of Peter the Great's coins, and those of his immediate successors, expressed their denominations both in numbers, for those who could read, and in a series of dots, for those who could not. Despite Peter's efforts and the clear logic of decimalization, the new system remained confined to Russia until the late eighteenth century. From that time forward, however, its spread was rapid. By the late nineteenth century it was current throughout most of Europe and Latin America; today its use is universal.

The fledgling United States was instrumental in the growth of the decimal system. Having debated the concept through much of the 1770s and 1780s, America

Decimal coinage.
Left: Russia, 20 kopeks, 1784.
Right: United States, cent, 1793.

made it legal with the Mint Act of 1792. The base of the country's money was an old coin, the Spanish-American Piece of Eight, which, in essence, became the new American dollar. The dollar, however, was composed of ten dimes, or one hundred cents, instead of eight reales. Most modern decimal systems are direct descendents of this early American reform. The French issued their first coins based on the decimal system in 1795, and carried the concept with them during their campaigns throughout Europe for the ensuing twenty years. By 1815 the decimal idea was well known there, even though its practice remained restricted to France. By 1880, however, most of Europe had adopted it, due, in part, to the zeal of the French-inspired Latin Monetary Union which had helped spread the reform.

By this time, decimalization was also the norm in Latin America. Except for changes in designs, the first coinages of the independent Latin American states were continuations of the Spanish and Portuguese colonial systems. By 1850, however, reform was in the wind, and the hemisphere's new governments, inspired in some ways by the spirit of the American and French Revolutions, began to tailor their money to a modern world. Change is seldom instantaneous, however: Mexico went decimal in 1863, but the peso retained its old name (eight reales) until 1898.

Decimalization reached Africa and Asia in the late nineteenth century, when European colonizers penetrated these regions, bringing their monetary systems with them. By the 1890s, decimal coinage systems existed in African areas governed by the French, Belgians, and Italians; British regions were without it, as Britain was still on a non-decimal system. In Asia, China and Japan adopted decimal coinage as part of a modernization campaign launched to resist Europe's partition of the continent. By 1900, with the exception of the British Empire, the world's coinage was based on the decimal system. And

even here there were exceptions. Canada inaugurated a decimal coinage in 1858, a reflection of its proximity to the United States, while Hong Kong and Ceylon were decimal by 1870.

Once independent, Africa's erstwhile British colonies adopted decimalization in the 1960s to underscore the end of their colonial status. During the same period, Australia, New Zealand, and South Africa decimalized their coinages. And in 1971, at long last, Britain accepted the system, making the world's monetary basis completely decimal.

See also DOLLAR; KOPEK; MINT ACT OF 1792; RUBLE.

DÉCIME A French copper or bronze coin worth one-tenth of a franc, and minted in Paris and other cities between 1795 and 1801 (and again in 1814–1815).

The décime sprang from attempts to reform France's cumbersome monetary system. Until 1795 the nation's monetary unit was the silver écu, divided, in turn, into 6 livres, 120 sols, 480 liards, and 1,440 deniers.

While there had been discussions about a rationalization of French coinage years prior to the outbreak of the Revolution, it was not until 1795 that internal and external conditions were conducive to such reforms. The worst excesses of the Reign of Terror had ceased by mid-1794, and the new government, the Directory, took its revolution abroad where French

Décime. *France, year 7 (of the French Republic), 1798–1799.*

armies conquered and assured their country's salvation.

The improved atmosphere made reforms possible, and one of the first areas examined was the French monetary system. In a series of decrees given their final form in April 1803, a new reckoning system was gradually established on the ruins of the old. Its monetary unit was the franc, five of which equalled a silver coin approximately the size of the former écu. Each franc was then divided into one hundred centimes or ten décimes.

It was several years before the system was in full operation. While the franc itself did not appear as a coin until 1802, the five-franc piece was introduced in 1795, as was the décime. The décimes of 1795–1796 were 28 millimeters in diameter, weighed 10 grams and were made of copper. A companion two-décime piece was struck during the same period, weighing exactly twice as much, with a diameter of 31 millimeters. Both pieces were quite close in size and weight to the sol and double sol of Louis XVI's final years, and this was probably deliberate.

Late in 1796 the weight of the décime was doubled, yielding a coin the same size as the early double décime. The government effected the reform by two separate methods. They overstruck two-décime coins with larger one-décime dies, hoping the undertype would be obscured (which it usually was not). They also counterstamped the word UN ("one") over the figure 2 on the reverse, a somewhat more successful practice. In either case, the government soon had a new issue of *bronze* décimes in circulation. Struck in large numbers through the remainder of the Directory (which ended in 1799) and the first years of the reign of Napoleon Bonaparte (ruled 1799–1814, 1815), down to 1801, it is the type most frequently encountered by collectors.

The designs of this décime are important. On the obverse is a legend with the name of the issuing state, and a female head, symbolizing the French Republic.

The head was designed by Augustin Dupré, also responsible for the "Hercules" design still used on French silver coins. From a numismatic viewpoint, however, the décime's reverse design is of greater significance, for here we are told about its denomination, where it was made, when, and by whom. The locale of each issue is shown by a mint mark—A for Paris, BB for Strasbourg, K for Bordeaux, etc; identification of each mint's director is given by a *différent* or privy mark, which appears near the wreath and below or to the right of the coin's date. But it is the date itself that is the most curious feature of the piece. The décime, in common with other French coins of the period, is dated by the French Revolutionary calendar, the commencement of which was September 22, 1792 (when the French Republic was proclaimed). Hence a décime dated L'AN 7 ("Year 7") might have been coined late in 1798 or through most of 1799. The new calendar, of course, was meant to signify the transcendent differentness of the new form of government, and was used on coinage through the year 1805, by which time France had become an empire. Inconsistent as this may seem, it is not nearly as contradictory as some other French coins were until the end of 1808—on their obverse was a portrait of Napoleon with the legend NAPOLEON EMPEREUR; on their reverse the country was identified as RÉPUBLIQUE FRANÇAISE.

By this time, the bronze décime had been replaced with a smaller billon piece, valued at ten centimes. It resurfaced briefly, however, in 1814–1815, when Strasbourg—which changed hands several times between the supporters of Napoleon and King Louis XVIII (ruled 1814–1815, 1815–1824)—struck décimes bearing a crowned, ornamental letter (either an N or an L) on the obverse, and the denomination, mint mark, and year enclosed in a wreath on the reverse. In 1838 the principality of Monaco resurrected the reverse design once again for its own décimes. Rendered as décimo, the denomination had some vogue in nineteenth-century Latin America, although it no longer resembled its French Revolutionary prototype.

See also ASSIGNAT; DATING SYSTEMS; DECIMAL COINAGE; DENIER; ÉCU; MARK (MINTMASTER'S OR ASSAYER'S); OVERSTRIKE.

DECORATION An award bestowed on an individual by an official (usually governmental) authority, and meant to be worn.

It is important to keep the terms medal and decoration separate, for their indiscriminate use has led to much confusion among collectors and the general public. A medal may be given as an award, but it is designed to be displayed in a case, on a wall, etc.—not to be worn.

A decoration consists of one or more (usually more) elements. It can be a badge suspended by a loop from a ribbon, or a star worn with a sash. Whatever its components, every decoration falls into one of three categories. If it is part of the paraphernalia associated with an order, it is apt to be quite elaborate. If it is given for an act of heroism, it is a gallantry award; if bestowed simply for participation in a war or military action, it is known as a campaign award.

Decorations have been with us since the days of ancient Greece and Rome, when they took the form of gold buttons or wreaths. Not until the late Middle Ages did they begin to resemble the modern decoration. The earliest decorations were those granted as tokens of membership in chivalric orders. While many medieval orders traced their origins to impossibly remote periods, the earliest confirmed national order, which is still in existence, appeared in Portugal in 1162—the Military Order of Aviz. Other, more famous orders—the English Order of the Garter, for example—came somewhat later. Regardless of its time of origin, every chivalric order in every country, be it monarchical or republican, was established for a single purpose: to bind people of importance to the state by awarding them something which could be worn, thus singling them out as worthy of the government's recognition.

The next decoration to be introduced was the gallantry award. An early form of it is the Armada Medal, accorded by England's Queen Elizabeth I (ruled 1558–1603) to leaders of the sea defense against the Spanish Armada in 1588. Later rulers, Charles I (ruled 1625–1649) for one, maintained the custom, and today such decorations as the Victoria Cross and the Croix de Guerre are equally prized by their recipients and by collectors.

The most recent decoration, and by far the most common, is the campaign award, essentially a product of the nineteenth and twentieth centuries. It could easily be argued that its rise in popularity indicated the growing influence the common man has had on society.

As decorations are so avidly sought today by so many collectors, their three basic types are listed individually in this book.

See also BADGE; CAMPAIGN AWARD; GALLANTRY AWARD; MEDAL; ORDER; RIBBON; SASH; STAR.

Decoration. *Nicaragua, Order of Grey Town (star).*

DEMAND NOTE A type of provisional paper money issued by the United States in 1861 and 1862, and the first federal paper money to see general circulation after the famous Continental Currency, printed nearly a century earlier.

That national paper money, which had disappeared after the 1770s, should reappear nearly a century later indicates a shifting society in need of drastic fiscal measures. And so it was, for the outbreak of the American Civil War came in the spring of 1861.

Within a few weeks both sides knew theirs was a conflict likely to span months, perhaps years. The vast amount of money it would cost was obvious. For the South, this was both a bane and a blessing. While it lacked hard cash to pay soldiers and purchase supplies, it also lacked stringent regulations against printing paper money. (Such regulations existed when the South was part of the Union, but once it had seceded, it saw no reason to abide by them.) The national Southern government and its member states, then, hastily printed paper currency, promising to redeem it once the war had been won.

In the North, where constitutional provisions were still in force, individual states did not have the right to print money, and indeed it had never been determined whether the federal government had such a right. Thus Congress embarked on a lengthy debate which eventually resulted in the Legal Tender Act of 1862. But to fill the gap while Congress talked, the Congressional Acts of July 17 and August 5, 1861 authorized the demand note—having sanctioned a $250 million borrowing program, against which the notes would be issued, on July 17. Demand notes were printed in denominations of five, ten, and twenty dollars, the first ones probably reaching the public on August 10, and they were issued until April 1862, to the amount of sixty million dollars. Although their faces were printed in black, their reverses were green, and they were quickly dubbed "greenbacks."

The demand note issue is interesting for a number of reasons. First, it bore neither the seal of the United States Treasury nor the signatures of the Treasurer or the Register of the Treasury. Originally it was assumed the two gentlemen would have time to sign each demand note, but this proved highly impractical. Treasury clerks signed the bills instead.

Second, the name of the note signified that payment was guaranteed "on demand." In practice, this was restricted: notes were payable only in New York City, Philadelphia, Boston, Cincinnati, and St. Louis. They were redeemable in coin (although not gold coin), which meant that their value held up fairly well as against specie. However, this was not the case with their successors, the legal tender notes, values of which fluctuated with the nation's victories and defeats during the war.

Finally, in common with several early federal notes, demand notes were privately printed by contractors hired by the

Demand note. United States, 10 dollars, 1861.
(Courtesy *The Comprehensive Catalog of U.S. Paper Money*, by Gene Hessler)

federal government, which at the beginning of the war had no machinery capable of printing money. This remained the case until the autumn of 1863, after which the first notes actually printed by the United States appeared.

On February 25, 1862, the Legal Tender bill became law, with an initial authorized currency issue of $150 million. Issues of the new currency (not redeemable in specie) were prolific through the remaining war years, casting the demand note into oblivion. Most were redeemed, and today well-preserved specimens are particularly sought by collectors. Historically, the demand note commands attention out of all proportion to the size of its issue. Circulating United States currency is now counted in the billions of dollars, but all of it actually dates back to the demand note, which was really the first modern paper money issued by the United States.

See also GREENBACK; LEGAL TENDER NOTE.

DENARIUS   The basic Roman silver coin from the late third century B.C. until the early third century A.D.

Its name derives from the Latin for "a piece of ten asses," for one denarius was originally tariffed at ten of these large bronze coins. About 145 B.C., the ratio was raised to sixteen asses to the denarius, where it stayed until the coin's demise.

The denarius was first struck around 211 B.C., partly to finance Rome's participation in the Second Punic War. However, it proved of enormous convenience in trade, and remained in active use when the Punic Wars were a mere memory. The first denarii weighed some 4.5 grams, and had a diameter of 18 to 19 millimeters. The head of Roma, patroness of the city, adorned the obverse. She wore a winged helmet, and an X, representing the coin's value, was behind her head. The reverse of the early denarii displayed two figures on horseback, Castor and Pollux, keepers

Denarius.
Top: Roman Republic, c. 211 B.C.
Bottom: Roman Empire, Nero, A.D. 66.

of Rome's well-being; beneath them was the simple inscription ROMA.

These first denarii were anonymous in the sense that a study of the coins themselves does not reveal which magistrates struck which coins. Then too, its anonymity makes it difficult to date the series with any great accuracy. However, one can see a modest decline in the coin's weight and a slight expansion in its size within a few years of its introduction. By 200 B.C. it weighed slightly under 4 grams, and was about 20 millimeters broad. By the early second century—when moneyers' initials (and later, names) begin to appear on the coins—the task of dating them becomes easier. Although Roman numismatists are not able to identify all of the moneyers and establish a thorough chronology, at least we are now moving out of darkness into twilight.

More is illuminated as the second century progresses. As mentioned, the denarius' value was raised from ten to sixteen asses in the 140s, and this fact was indicated on coins by the symbol ✳ in place of X. By the 130s the types themselves were changing; a most Roman numismatic phenomenon, self-advertising, was rearing its head, and moneyers took to celebrating themselves and their ancestors on their coinages. The types found on denarii proliferated, and literally hundreds existed during the Roman Republic's last century.

Moneyers were not alone in using the denarius to pay homage to themselves; military leaders and their supporters would soon do the same. The years 130 to 30 B.C. were not happy ones for the republic. Dictators came and went, and they began to use coins to proselytize, to convince the populace of their God-given right to rule. But the masters of self-aggrandizement came somewhat later— Gaius Julius Caesar, who, it might be said, killed the republic, and his great-nephew, Octavian (later the emperor Augustus), who gave it a decent burial.

Shortly before Caesar's assassination in 44 B.C., his portrait and titles were emblazoned on the denarius, the first time a living Roman had been so portrayed. Octavian continued, and institutionalized, this radical new departure, and though careful to observe republican forms, he exercised a regal prerogative when he placed his portrait on most of his coinage, including the denarius. Augustus's imperial successors did the same, for if self-advertising was important in a republic, it was crucial in an empire where no man ruled by divine right. While emperors could cloak themselves in all manner of honors and titles, issue coins, and build public monuments embellished with their names and images and those of protective gods and goddesses, one title escaped them—*rex*, king.

What did the early imperial denarius look like? A portrait, usually of the reigning monarch, graced its obverse, and as the denarius was fairly small, portraiture was less masterful than on larger coins such as the sestertius. Nonetheless, much of it was very good indeed, particularly in the late first century A.D. Interestingly, imperial portraits are often downright unflattering; it seems die-cutters were determined to present the ruler's visage as it was, not as he might wish it to be.

A legend, with the emperor's titles and other information in abbreviated forms, completed the obverse design. The reverse legend might give additional titles or information about the ruler, or refer to a standing or seated allegorical figure, representing an imperial virtue or success. Occasionally there was a second portrait, most often a member of the imperial family. In general, the reverse types were simpler than those on larger coins, as engravers had a restricted space in which to work.

For the most part, the weight of the denarius remained stable at slightly under 4 grams until well into the first century A.D.; however, during Nero's reign it began to depreciate.

Nero (ruled A.D. 54–68) sought vast sums of money. His sumptuous way of life was costly and then too, Rome needed rebuilding after the great fire of A.D. 64. Hence, the emperor reduced the amount of precious metal in his coinage. The aureus suffered only slightly, its weight going from around 7.7 grams to 7.3, but the weight of the denarius declined much further, from about 3.80 grams to 3.25. Perhaps of even greater importance, Nero also decreased the silver fineness of the denarius, from approximately 95 percent to 82 percent.

In the following century, the debasement of silver accelerated. War and domestic strife necessitated increased government spending during the years of the last third of the second century and the next century. Compelled to produce more money, the imperial treasury did the obvious: it debased the coinage.

Under Marcus Aurelius (ruled A.D. 161–180), the silver content of the denarius was reduced to 75 percent, and by the time of Septimius Severus (ruled A.D. 193–211), its content was around 50 percent. His son and successor, Caracalla (ruled A.D. 211–217), introduced a new coin, the antoninianus, designed to rekindle public confidence in the state's silver coinage. It did not. At its introduction in A.D. 215, the antoninianus contained about 50 percent silver, as did the denarius. But its silver content soon declined, which seems to have helped drive the denarius from circulation. The last true denarii were struck in the 240s, and attempts to reestablish the coin later in the third century met with no success.

The name survived, however, even if the coin did not. Denier, denaro, dinar, and other names for coins used throughout the world derive from the denarius, and in many areas it was used unchanged to describe the medieval silver penny.

See also ANTONINIANUS; AS; DATING SYSTEMS; INFLATION; MARK (MINTMASTER'S OR ASSAYER'S); PENNY; SESTERTIUS.

DENARO The Italian equivalent of the French denier, or penny, first introduced around A.D. 800.

The independent states into which Italy was then divided eagerly adopted this silver coin, and it played a leading role in the numismatic history of the peninsula until the thirteenth century. The introduction of the heavier silver grosso around 1200 and the resumption of gold coinage after 1250 removed the denaro from its position of eminence, but it long remained an important subsidiary coin.

The piece illustrated is an example of a very early denaro. It was minted under Sicone, duke of Beneventum (ruled 817–832): Beneventum was, in fact, where the denaro was first coined. The obverse, following French custom, uses the duke's monogram as the central type. The reverse reveals the influence of the Byzantine Empire that once controlled the area: it carries a cross on steps, a standard type on Byzantine gold and silver coinage. This denaro has a diameter of 17 millimeters, and weighs 1.26 grams. Later coins would

Denaro. Beneventum, 817–832.

be somewhat lighter and, in many instances, contain less silver. Designs continued to be quite simple There was little room for self-expression on a denaro, or on any of the period's small silver coins.

See also CROSS ON COINAGE; DENIER; GROSSO; MONOGRAM.

DENIER Most commonly, a term referring to a small French silver coin, first introduced in the middle of the eighth century and the prototype for all later pennies.

The denier had imitators throughout Europe, and the collector's term for all these early medieval silver coins is penny.

The standard denier originated in the time of Pepin the Short (ruled 751–768), when the early medieval world was recovering from the dislocations suffered under the barbarian conquest of the western Roman Empire, and trade, though limited, had resumed. A small silver coin such as the denier made sound economic sense.

It also made political sense. The Carolingian dynasty, of which Pepin was the first representative, was ambitious to establish the real power of the French throne. A uniform royally minted coinage would help to do so. France had had no such coinage for several centuries; much of what was struck was done by local and clerical authorities, and its quality varied. The tremissis was the basic gold coin of the pre-Carolingian period, while silver coinage consisted of small, rather thick pieces, imitative of Roman and/or Byzantine coins, and not struck in quantity. These coins are also known as deniers, but they bear little resemblance to what was to follow.

To supply the French economy with money, and to centralize control, the new Carolingian monarchs would make coinage a royal monopoly, and eventually establish a monometallic currency, with the silver denier as the base.

Pepin's denier weighed about 1.3

Denier. France, 793–814.

grams, significantly more than silver coins of the previous Merovingian dynasty, which generally weighed 1.1 grams or less. The new coins were also larger and thinner than the old. The designs on these first royal deniers were extremely simple, with the obverse bearing the king's initials and the reverse the name of the mint.

After Pepin's son, Charles the Great, or Charlemagne (ruled 768–814), succeeded to the throne, the denier acquired its most typical form. Its weight was raised to 1.7 grams in 793–794, and its diameter was 21 millimeters—4 millimeters more than Pepin's coin.

Its designs reveal that the era of "true" medieval coinage had been reached: the lettering, types, indeed the entire fabric of the coins are characteristic of that period. The piece illustrated has a cross as its central obverse device, with an abbreviated Latin legend proclaiming Charles as King of the Franks. The reverse carries his monogram within a beaded circle, a design element also used to surround the obverse cross. The reverse legend indicates the town where the coin was minted.

Charles's successors discontinued some designs and substituted others. Louis the Pious (ruled 814–840) had a Christian slogan and a crude image of a church on the reverse of his deniers, and a cross on the obverse. It was during his reign that France went definitively on a silver standard, where it remained for several centuries.

By the mid-ninth century, the denier or coins like it were in use over much of Europe. The English adopted it shortly before 800, the Italians slightly later; as time progressed, its popularity spread eastward.

After the mid-thirteenth century, the denier's importance in French coinage began to wane, as increased trading spawned newer, heavier silver coins. However, it remained as a denomination until the middle of the seventeenth century, even though its size and silver content had diminished. The last specimens of this originally silver coin were struck in copper.

See also CROSS ON COINAGE; GROS TOURNOIS; MONOGRAM; PENNY; TRADE COINS; TREMISSIS.

DENTICLES Rounded tooth-shaped objects used to create borders on coins, frequently found on European-style gold and silver coinage, and occasionally on base-metal coinage, minted from about 1650 to 1850.

Like all border devices, denticles were meant to protect a coin from excessive wear. They were deeply carved into obverse and reverse dies, and formed the highest point on coins struck from those dies, which meant the coins could circulate for long periods before their legends and devices received significant wear.

The denticle's elongated shape distinguished it from other border elements. The popularity of the denticle is explained by the period's technology. As most coins were struck without a collar, the metal was not arrested when it flowed outward. Any border used would have to be wide, to en-

Denticles. Colombia, 2 escudos, 1824 (detail).

sure the maximum protection of a coin. Furthermore, planchets were frequently struck off-center, again necessitating a wide border to protect the off-center coin.

Other border styles could have been created to solve such problems, but the dentilated border had a particular advantage which recommended it to minters. As coins were struck in a screw press and their metal forced out from the center, radiating flow-marks often resulted. These marks interfered with many borders, but not with the dentilated one, whose denticles also radiated out from a coin's center. Indeed, unless the flow-marks were exceptionally heavy, they were not noticeable on a coin with denticles.

With the arrival of steam-powered coining machinery in the nineteenth century, the dentilated border yielded to the plain or beaded types.

See also BORDER.

DIDRACHM A Greek, and later Roman, silver coin, equal to two drachms.

The Greek version is commonly known as a stater, and its weight and size varied with its place of mintage.

The idea of the didrachm reached the nascent Roman Republic by about 300 B.C., and the didrachm, the earliest Roman silver coin, dates from around that year or slightly later.

It manifests a strong Greek influence. First, it was struck, not cast. (Earlier Roman issues had always been cast, following in the Italian numismatic tradition.) Then too, the didrachm's size and weight (19 to 20 millimeters, and 7 grams, respectively) seem to have been based on the standard used in the Greek city-states of southern Italy. Finally, the Roman didrachm is Grecian in style, particularly the early coin. Hercules or Roma adorn the obverse, with the Roman Wolf and Twins or a personification of Victory on the reverse, but even though the subjects are Roman, their execution appears Greek.

Didrachm. Roman Republic, c. 235 B.C.

The figures are realistic and carefully drawn, a far cry from those on the denarius, a later Roman coin. The explanation is simple: dies from the didrachm were carved by Greek artists imported by the Roman government for just that purpose.

By the time the Romans began minting the didrachm, they were on their way to a collision with Carthage. The first of three wars between the rival republics started in 264 B.C., and lasted until 241. Rome needed money for its military operations, and the didrachm proved convenient. The war affected the new coin, however: tariffed at 7.00 grams around 269 B.C., by about 261 its weight had decreased to 6.55 grams, where it remained for the next forty years.

Around 235, a newly designed didrachm, the type in the illustration, was introduced. In common with the as, it had an obverse bearing a head of Janus. Its reverse is somewhat more elaborate, and shows Jupiter, hurling a thunderbolt and holding a scepter, in a quadriga or chariot drawn by four horses, and driven by a figure representing Victory. Beneath them is the word ROMA on a panel. This new reverse may be interpreted as an early example of numismatic propaganda, for not long after its debut the Roman Republic was embroiled in the Second Punic War, the greatest external threat it ever suffered.

Once again the monetary system was placed under immense strain, and this time the quadrigatus (the name generally given to the didrachm with the Janus/quadriga design) could not withstand it: standards declined as the war progressed, and around 211 B.C. it was abandoned for the denarius.

Didrachms struck after 235 revealed a distinctly Roman style. Figures were less artistic than those on earlier pieces, but they possessed an arresting vigor nevertheless. For the modern numismatist, the evolution of the Roman didrachm's style is its most salient characteristic.

See also DENARIUS; DRACHM; STATER.

DIE A piece of hard metal with a design in reverse, used for coining money.

In practice, two dies are needed to strike a coin: an upper die, which is driven into the piece of metal to be turned into money, and a lower die, into which that piece of metal is driven.

In ancient times, the lower die was the more important of the two. Originally adapted from an official seal, this lower or pile die was fixed in an anvil, hence its third name, anvil die. Metal was driven into it by hand with a sledge hammer, but the hammer did not strike the metal directly. A punch was placed between them, ensuring greater accuracy and clarity of striking. This punch was the ancestor of the second die, also called a trussell die. Its initial function was merely to help produce one clear image, but eventually it was obvious the punch could simultaneously impress two images, one on the planchet's upper side and another on the lower. This

Die.
Left: An obverse die used to strike private gold pieces in North Carolina, 1842–1852.
Right: A coin struck from such a die.

was done in time, but in contrast to modern coinage, when we refer to an obverse on an ancient coin we mean that image created by the lower die.

This gradually changed after the introduction of machine-struck coinage about 1550, and in most cases the modern coining press strikes obverses with upper dies, reverses with lower ones. There have been other changes too. In the beginning, each die was engraved by hand and dies, made of metal varying in quality, had a short life expectancy. Modern dies are hubbed, a process in which large numbers of identical dies are produced by mechanical means. And they last longer, because they are made of high-quality steel. The theory behind the die, however, remains unchanged: the transfer of a negative image from a hard piece of metal to a softer one, to create a positive imprint.

See also HUB; OBVERSE; PILE; PUNCH; REVERSE; SEAL; TRUSSELL.

DIE AXIS A term used to describe the relationship between the two sides of a coin.

This is best demonstrated by the reader's examination of a coin taken from his or her pocket. Hold the coin between thumb and forefinger with the obverse held upright and toward you. Now rotate the coin between your fingertips, so that its reverse comes into view. You will see the reverse in one of two positions: inverted or upright. If the coin's reverse is inverted in relation to its obverse, the coin has a normal die axis. In numismatic writing, this is expressed with two arrows: ↑ ↓. The first arrow stands for the obverse, which is always considered upright and to which the reverse is compared—never the other way around. The second arrow stands for the orientation of the reverse in relation to the upright obverse. Another way to describe this is to say the coin has a reverse at six o'clock.

This is the die axis for much of the

world's coinage, but other axes are possible. If your coin's reverse is upright in relation to the obverse, it has a medallic die axis (so designated because most medals are struck in this fashion). The arrow symbol is: ↑ ↑ (in words: reverse at twelve o'clock).

Ancient peoples were less concerned with die axes than we are. In many cases no attempt was made to control the relative positions of the upper and lower dies. In other instances a consistent die axis was intended, and while many coins show a rough orientation at the six o'clock or twelve o'clock positions, there were other arrangements as well. If you see a catalog reference to a die axis as ↑ → , it means that when the obverse is upright, the reverse is a quarter-turn to the right, or at three o'clock.

The die axis is primarily a researcher's tool, and is a useful way to provide information about a coin in abbreviated form.

DIE BREAK
A raised, wandering line that extends across the obverse or reverse of a coin.

A die break is the result of a cracked die, and indicates improper use or manufacture of the die. The die crack producing the break can (and probably will) grow worse the longer the die is used and can lead, in time, to a shattered die. The die might simply fall apart, or a peripheral portion might break away, leaving the rest in place for a few more impressions. Should this occur, a cud is produced.

The die break is a coining error. It is so recurrent, however, that until the present century at least, the break had to be extensive and obvious to make the coin worth more than an ordinary specimen. Until recently, dies were produced from steel of widely varying quality. If the steel was too brittle, the die could break in one or more places. The breaks, in turn, were transferred to the planchets as they were made into coins. The die break was especially common on coinage from small or

Die break. Greece, 20 lepta, 1831. Note the die breaks at the top and bottom of the coin.

makeshift mints, and logically it can be assumed that die breaks were more frequent on thick, heavy coins than on thin, light ones: the former required more striking pressure—which led to cracked dies—than the latter.

These observations are confirmed by an examination of coins. Die breaks are found on thick Greek and Roman coins, but less often on thin medieval dinars and pennies. They appear too, on the early products of the Unites States Mint, especially on coins of low value. (A cracked die used to create large cents received far less attention than one used to make ten-dollar gold pieces.) The improvement of coining machinery in the nineteenth century did not eliminate die breaks. Minters at small establishments were probably not at home with the new presses, and abused them, and coin dies, inadvertently.

The die break is still with us, although improved technology has made it less common, and a more careful inspection of coins means that any die break leaving the mint is likely to be minor. A modern coin with a major die break would be a decided rarity, and worth a tidy sum to collectors.

See also CRACKED DIES; CUD; DIE CHIP; ERROR.

DIE CHIP
A raised blob of metal, usually fairly small, which can appear anywhere on a coin's surface.

Die chip. *United States, cent, 1817 (detail). Note "mouse" in Liberty's hair.*

The die chip is simply evidence that, for some reason (usually metallic weakness or excessive use), a small part of the coin die has chipped away. Die chips often occur within a letter of a legend or within, or connected to, a type. These are the areas of the die that are weaker than the plain, unadorned portions that create the fields of the coin. Examples of die chips are found on a particular 1817 American large cent with what seems to be a mouse hiding in Liberty's hair; several Morgan dollars with the G of IN GOD WE TRUST filled in; and another United States cent, struck in 1960, with what looks like LIBIERTY for LIBERTY on the obverse inscription. None of these die chips is especially rare.

Although the die chip is a legitimate coinage error, it is usually so minor in nature it cannot command much of a collector premium. Many errors described as filled dies are actually die chips.

See also CRACKED DIES; ERROR; FILLED DIES.

DIE-STRUCK COUNTERFEIT

A spurious coin manufactured in approximately the same manner as its genuine counterpart, by being struck from dies.

The mode of manufacture distinguishes it from the cast counterfeit.

Die-struck counterfeits have never been as numerous as cast ones, for the simple reason that it is easier to make a casting mold from a genuine coin than it is to en-grave a die. At best the latter is laborious. Until very recently, it was impossible to make a coin die directly from a real coin; any die for false coinage had to be prepared one step removed from the original. The early forger had to examine a detail on the genuine coin, make a mark or sink a punch where he thought the mark or punch should go, examine another detail, duplicate that, and so on. Inevitably, there were mistakes, and the engraver could only hope the public did not closely scrutinize his wares.

With the cast counterfeit, the rendition of the counterfeit's details was correct, as the design was transferred directly from a real coin to a mold—although this meant some of the clarity of the struck coin was lost. Yet more clarity was lost in the "coining" process when metal was poured into a mold instead of forced into a die. (This lack of detail was somewhat alleviated by centrifugal casting, described elsewhere [see Cast counterfeit], but the cast counterfeit was never as finely detailed as the struck original.) The die-struck counterfeit, on the other hand, *could* reveal minor details (even if they differed slightly from those on the original).

Die-struck and cast counterfeits entered the numismatic picture early in the history of coinage. Die-struck counterfeits were common in medieval and early modern times, as the period's flat, thin coinage of simple designs could readily be copied in this fashion. Counterfeiters continued to strike from dies until this century. Vast numbers of brass, die-struck English pieces, meant to resemble the "spade" guinea of George III (ruled 1760–1820), cropped up at the beginning of the nineteenth century. Some were fashioned as jetons or gaming pieces. But others were meant to circulate as real gold guineas, and probably did in places where money changed hands rapidly. Later in the century, Spain was inundated with die-struck counterfeits of the ten-escudo gold piece of Isabella II (ruled 1833–1868), which were struck in brass and then gold plated.

Die-struck counterfeit.
Top: Genuine United States cent, 1891.
Bottom: The counterfeit cent. The counterfeit is die-struck, as is the genuine coin.

Although most counterfeiters have concentrated on precious-metal coinage, cast and die-struck counterfeits of low-value coins have also appeared. The rationale is that no one closely examines a minor coin and, assuming the copy can be made for less than its face value, the counterfeiter will turn a profit—providing, of course, he markets enough "coins."

The die-struck counterfeit in the illustration is of an American cent dated 1891, and is shown with a genuine coin for comparison. The fake illuminates the risks in die-striking a counterfeit. Examine the reverses closely: the engraver apparently lost his way, and the wreath and shield on the counterfeit coin are only rough approximations of the original.

Further, the coin's general appearance reveals a second problem with the die-struck counterfeit—it takes good equipment to strike a good fake. This counterfeiter was evidently using a small coining press, incapable of exerting enough pressure to create a clear, complete impression.

The die-struck counterfeit is no longer with us. The die-struck *forgery,* on the other hand, is alive and well. While creating good forgeries for collectors may require new, expensive equipment and sophisticated techniques, counterfeiters have discovered that the profits to be made more than compensate for the investment of money and time.

See also CAST COUNTERFEIT; COUNTERFEIT AND FORGERY DETECTION; FANTASY; FORGERY; GUINEA; JETON.

DIE VARIETY A coin, medal, or token struck from a particular pair of dies; all pieces struck with those dies will have identical characteristics.

This term is usually applied to coins produced by dies partially or completely handmade one by one. Unless an issue is minuscule, a certain number of obverse and reverse dies are needed for any given coinage series. Originally each die was cut by hand; when letter, numeral, and device punches were invented, they were still applied die by die. Inevitably, dissimilarities crept into the die-making process and appeared on the coins. One craftsman might render the hair on a portrait a bit differently from his colleagues; or one of the thirteen stars might be unusually close to Liberty's head on a particular die for an American large cent, and farther away on others.

To illustrate, let us call a given obverse die "1," a given reverse die "A." All coins with this obverse and reverse combination form a die variety, 1-A. Any coin showing the telltale marks of the two dies is a die duplicate of all other coins with the same characteristics. And 1-A would obviously be a different die variety than 2-B, which would represent new obverse and reverse dies.

It becomes more complicated, however, because obverse and reverse dies do not usually wear out at the same rate. Perhaps obverse die 1 was very finely done, while reverse die A was not. A, then, might break, and a new reverse die, B, would replace it. Now there would be two die varieties, with the same obverse but different reverses: 1-A and 1-B. The die receiving the least direct pressure lasts the longest;

this has always been the lower die, which undergoes pressure of a secondary nature (from the planchet being driven into the die from above), while the upper die sustains pressure of a primary nature (from the hammer or machinery which drives it directly against the planchet).

In ancient times, the obverse die was the lower one, and the reverse, the upper die. Thus, an ancient coin with obverse 1 might appear in combination with several reverses. With the invention of coining machines, the obverse die became the upper die: now the *reverse* die tended to last through several obverses. A good example appears in William H. Sheldon's *Early American Cents, 1793–1814* (1949), in which he describes what he called reverse X of the 1794 large cent. This reverse was found coupled with his obverses 21, 22, 23, 24, 25, and 26. It was then retired, and obverse 26 was joined to reverse die Y. Had obverse 26 eventually broken and reverse Y been paired with a new obverse die, the progression would read as follows: 26-X, 26-Y, 27-Y. This is a die linkage: two separate die varieties, 26-X and 27-Y, are connected to one another by an intermediate die combination, 26-Y. Die linkage enables numismatists to establish a relative coining chronology, and is a valuable tool. While we may not know the exact year an undated ancient coinage was introduced, through a die linkage we are able to establish which coins were struck first.

Die varieties are useful for estimating the approximate size of a coinage issue. If it is found that all known specimens in a series were produced by one obverse and two reverse dies, we can conclude the issue was very small. By the same token, a series with a large number of die varieties must have comprised a great many individual coins.

It is important to note that the term die variety refers to coins struck from an unaltered die. The die break, which can distinguish one coin from another, occurs *after* the die is finished, not during its manufacture, and is not a die variety.

Die variety. *United States, cents, 1814.*

The illustration shows two die varieties of the 1814 American cent. The reader will note slight variations in the placement of the stars, etc., but the major difference is in the 4 of 1814. One coin shows the digit with a crosslet, while the other does not.

With the nineteenth and twentieth centuries, and the development of such tools as the reducing lathe and the hub, the mass production of essentially identical dies has been universally adopted. If die varieties still exist, the differences are apt to be so minute they are of little interest to the numismatist.

See also DIE; HUB; LARGE CENT.

DINAR The most important early Islamic gold coin, the first of which were probably struck at Damascus, capital of the caliphate, and introduced by the Umaiyad caliph Abd al-Malik in A.H. 77 (A.D. 696–697).

The dinar was partly a new coin and partly an old one. Its designs were new, and will be discussed later. Its size and weight were old: at 19 millimeters in diameter and weighing 4.3 grams, it was the same size and weight as the Byzantine solidus.

To understand this old coin in a new guise, we must go back to the seventh century, and the creation of Islam. Its tenets are in the Koran, which prohibits the depiction of living objects in statuary, painting—or on coinage.

But despite the teachings of their faith,

the warriors and traders of Islam (who lacked a strong coinage tradition) found it far easier to imitate the coinage of other peoples than to design one bearing no representations of living objects. Religious doctrine yielded to expediency, at least for the time being.

The Islamic conquerors produced two parallel series of coins, both imitative. In areas bordering the Mediterranean they copied Byzantine coins, omitting the name of the emperor, but keeping his image. To the East, they borrowed from coin designs of the fallen Sassanian Empire. These too had images—of the Persian ruler on the obverse, and, with piety yielding utterly to expediency, emblems of the pre-Islamic Zoroastrian religion on the reverse. Conqueror and conquered alike needed coins for trade, and a harmony of the spiritual and temporal would have to wait.

It came shortly before 700. Historians are not completely certain of the reasons for the change, but they do know the caliphate was by then well enough established to have time for such reforms.

In A.D. 696, a new dinar appeared, and it neither borrowed from nor copied any other coinage (at least in terms of design). Containing only legends and inscriptions, it set the tone for later issues in silver and copper and, to some extent, for every Islamic coin struck from then on.

Each side of this dinar bore a central inscription in three lines. The obverse reads: "There is no god except Allah alone. He has no partner." The legend adds: "Mohammed is the Prophet of Allah whom He sent with guidance and the Religion of Truth that He may make it victorious over every other religion." The reverse inscription states: "Allah is One, Allah is the Eternal. He begets not neither is He begotten." It also gives the year the dinar was struck "In the name of Allah."

The dinar was considered an effective competitor for the Byzantine solidus and acceptable to the Islamic faith's strictest adherents. And the coin would circulate, for it was struck to a size and weight familiar to everyone.

Except for the addition of the name of the mint and that of the reigning caliph, the general appearance of a dinar in A.D. 900 was very much what it had been in 700, at least to the untrained eye. In time, however, there were changes: while the dinar's weight remained stable at 4.3 grams over a long period, its diameter was increased, bringing it more in line with its silver companion, the dirhem. Experiments within the limits allowed by Koranic law began when the Fatimids of Egypt and North Africa struck dinars with inscriptions within concentric circles late in the tenth century, while other states enclosed the central inscription in boxes. In time, the weight of the dinar was altered as well —and was descending slightly by the late twelfth century. By the thirteenth it stood at 3.7 grams in many areas, by the fifteenth at 3.4 grams. It was raised to 3.6 grams early in the following century, under the Turkish sultan Suleiman I (ruled 1520–1566). By now renamed a funduk, the erstwhile gold dinar finally passed from use in the eighteenth century; the last examples of this venerable coin were struck in Morocco around 1790. However, Algeria and several other countries have revived its name for their monetary units.

See also ARAB-BYZANTINE COINAGE; ARAB-SASSANIAN COINAGE; DIRHEM; FALS; SOLIDUS.

Dinar. Syria, A.H. 80 (A.D. 699–700).

DINERO The Spanish equivalent of the French denier.

The earliest dineros are from Aragon,

Dinero. Castile, 1073–1109.

and seem to have been struck during the reign of Sancho Ramírez (ruled 1063–1094). Their genesis there is explained by the fact that Aragon was more commercially developed than much of the rest of the peninsula, and thus found a coin based on the denier useful in trade. The Moorish conquest of the Iberian Peninsula by 718 delayed coinage advances such as the denier.

When the denier finally made its way south, it was widely embraced by the peoples of the Spanish kingdoms. The kingdom of Castile and Leon, nucleus of modern Spain and the guiding force behind the reconquest of Spain from the Moors, adopted the denier a few years after Aragon. Its first dinero, pictured here, was struck under Alfonso VI (ruled 1073–1109), and was minted at Toledo, captured by Alfonso in 1085. The obverse bears a cross, while the reverse, seen here, has a Christogram as its central device, a reflection of the religious fervor generating the reconquest. The mint's name is in the legend surrounding the Christogram. This specimen weighs slightly less than a gram and is 18 millimeters in diameter, typical measurements for the dinero. Its silver content is fairly low; at its best, the dinero was a billon coin, rather than a silver one.

By the end of the sixteenth century the dinero was merely a small copper coin, but its influence was to be lasting. The most widely used Spanish word for "money" is still *dinero.*

See also Denier; Dinheiro.

DINHEIRO   The Portuguese counterpart of the denier.

Much like the dinero, the dinheiro's transition from France to Portugal occurred rather late, due in part to the Moorish conquest. The first dinheiros (indeed, the first Portuguese coins) date from the reign of Sancho I (ruled 1185–1211), and were actually copied from the billon Spanish dinero rather than the silver French denier. Thus the Portuguese dinheiro was born debased, unlike most coins which begin at a level of relative purity.

Essentially, the dinheiro was the only coin struck by Portuguese kings for the next century and three-quarters. The coin pictured is from the reign of Ferdinand I (ruled 1367–1383), and is quite typical. Made entirely of copper, it is small (15 millimeters in diameter) and light (.75 gram). Its types are interesting for their mixture of religious motifs, which are common on medieval coinage, and expressions of nationalism, which are not. The obverse has a large cross, usually found on the reverses of medieval coins. Its reverse carries a design of five shields, each with five dots, and is said to represent the five Moorish kings defeated by Alfonso I (ruled 1128–1185) at the battle of Ourique in 1139. The shields, arranged to form a cross, are seen on Portuguese coins to the present day, and eventually were incorporated in Portugal's national arms.

By the time the illustrated piece was struck, new coins were being introduced; the dinheiro's importance declined and it disappeared shortly after the reign of Ferdinand.

See also Denier; Dinero; Milreis.

Dinheiro. Portugal, 1367–1383.

Dirhem. Islamic Spain, A.H. 156 (A.D. 772–773).

DIRHEM The most important early Islamic silver coin, and a companion to the gold dinar.

While the dirhem had a radically new look, in many respects it remained an old coin in a new guise, as did the dinar.

The dirhem was a logical outgrowth of the Sassanian drachm and its later Arabic imitations. Like the drachm, it was flat and very thin, measuring about 29 millimeters and weighing 2.9 to 3.0 grams. Its weight indicated a lowering of standards from previous issues; the Sassanian drachm weighed some 4 grams. Still, the course from the old coin, which featured imagery, to the new one, which did not, is clear: the new denomination's very name was an adaptation of drachm, the name for the Sassanian silver piece.

First struck in A.H. 79 (A.D. 698–699), the dirhem's design elements were almost identical with those of the first dinar. In the coin illustrated, the centers of the obverse and reverse carry the *Kalima*, the Islamic invocation of faith; the obverse legend gives the date of the coin and the name of the mint, while the reverse legend is another religious formula. Note the absence of imagery, reflecting its prohibition as stated in the Koran. The dirhem, like the dinar and the fals, was meant to comply with the religious beliefs of the faithful. Figures had appeared on earlier Islamic coins, but it would be several hundred years before they did so again.

The coin illustrated was struck in Spain in A.H. 156 (A.D. 772–773), and is testimony to the wealth of that part of the Islamic world at the time.

The dirhem proved successful, and was minted from Spain to the Caspian and North Africa to Iraq for hundreds of years in a fairly unchanged form. Although designs grew slightly more complex—some areas favored inscriptions within squares, others inscriptions in an eight-pointed star—the coins consistently bore pious inscriptions and, except for those of a few maverick mints, never bore images. Suffering the same fate as most other coins, the dirhem's weight was reduced and by the fourteenth century it was obsolete. However, memories of it survive in Jordan and Libya, where its name is used for today's currency.

See also Arab-Sassanian coinage; Dinar; Drachm; Fals.

DOBLA A medium-sized gold coin introduced in Spain under Alfonso XI (ruled 1312–1350).

His dobla was about 25 millimeters in diameter, and weighed around 4.6 grams; its appearance in fourteenth-century Castile and Leon suggests an increase in trade under the period's aggressive monarchs. Most early doblas were struck in Seville, the main trading entrepôt for goods from the South, which leads to the conclusion that gold for the dobla probably came from Africa.

The dobla was a handsome medieval coin. The issues of Alfonso XI featured the central type of a castle on the obverse, a lion on the reverse—punning on the two parts of the kingdom, Castile and Leon. Legends with the king's names and titles

Dobla. Castile and Leon, 1312–1350.

surround the central types. Alfonso's successor Pedro the Cruel (ruled 1350–1369) modified the dobla's design. He placed a profile portrait of himself, facing left, on the obverse, and quartered the arms of Castile and Leon on the reverse.

The coinage of the dobla continued sporadically through the fourteenth and fifteenth centuries. Pedro's early experiment with the profile portrait was largely abandoned; later doblas concentrated more on the familiar castle/lion combination, and if the monarch's likeness appeared on his coins it was generally as a seated, enthroned figure.

With the accession of Ferdinand II of Aragon and Isabella I of Castile (ruled 1479–1504)—the "Catholic Monarchs"—Spain was united. The reforms of this extraordinary pair included that of gold coinage. A 1497 ordinance (the Pragmatic of Medina del Campo) abolished Spain's previous monetary systems and initiated a new and unified coinage. That Ferdinand and Isabella were able to do so testifies to the strength of their regime, for coinage had always been a jealously guarded right among the states from which a united Spain was created. The excelente, a gold coin exactly equal to the Venetian ducat, was introduced; earlier silver coins were replaced by the real, equal to thirty-four maravedís. (One excelente equalled 375 maravedís, or about 11 reales.) With modifications, this system served Spain—and its growing overseas empire—for the next three hundred years.

The dobla did not fit into the new monetary system, and its production had ceased even before the introduction of the reforms of 1497.

DOLLAR The monetary unit of the United States and, at present, a number of other countries.

The word "dollar" derives from thaler, the generic name for a type of large silver coin first struck in Middle Europe about 1500. The dollar's general size, fineness, and weight also descend from the thaler, but even more directly from a Spanish-American coin, the Piece of Eight.

America's adoption of a Spanish rather than an English system may need to be explained. While both Spain and England prohibited clandestine trade, laws yielded to economic expediency. The Spanish colonials wanted goods from the English-Americans—fish and timber among them—and offered to pay in specie. The English colonies lacked native sources of precious metal, while the Spanish world was awash in it.

This mutually beneficial arrangement had immediate and somewhat odd results. The famous Pine Tree shillings, and other silver coins minted by Massachusetts from 1652 to the early 1680s, were actually struck in silver from Mexico, Peru, and Bolivia, not Massachusetts. The colonial government simply removed underweight Pieces of Eight and subsidiaries from circulation, melted down their silver, and fashioned new coins.

Americans, then, became accustomed to speaking in two monetary languages, an "official" one, based on pounds-shillings-pence, and an "unofficial" one, based on the Piece of Eight.

By the eighteenth century, people started calling the Piece of Eight a "dollar." No one is certain how thaler was transformed to dollar, but the Dutch were striking daalders and the Swedes dalers, both intended as equivalents of the thaler. By the late 1760s, the colony of Maryland was printing paper money with values expressed in dollars; within fifteen years the term would be almost universal, although a dollar *coin* would not emerge for another decade.

The Revolutionary War began in 1775, and when it ended eight years later many Americans were left disenchanted with all things English, including the money system. In 1775 most colonies expressed their money in terms of pounds; by 1777, however, numbers of them were seesawing—expressing their notes in pounds *and* dol-

Dollar. United States, 1794.

lars. By 1780 only a few still clung to the word "pound."

Debate was heard throughout this period about the possibility of a new national coinage and what, if any, relationship it would have to a foreign system. Gradually it became apparent that the Piece of Eight, with which Americans were familiar, was the logical monetary unit for the new republic. But Thomas Jefferson and others recommended the Piece of Eight (eight reales of thirty-four maravedís each) be made more rational, and replaced by a coin with subsidiaries related to it and to each other by tens—in short, a decimally oriented Piece of Eight.

In essence, this is what took place when the Mint Act of 1792 created a new coin based on the Piece of Eight. This coin, weighing slightly under 27 grams, of about 90 percent silver, would equal ten smaller pieces, called dimes, and each dime would consist of ten coppers, called cents. The coin and its parts would be simple to use and, because it closely approximated the size and weight of the Piece of Eight, it would be readily accepted by citizens and foreigners alike. It would be called a dollar.

The first United States dollars struck for circulation emerged from a hastily constructed federal Mint in 1794. They were of the design illustrated, and between 39 and 40 millimeters in diameter. It was hoped they would be an instant success. They were not.

Unfortunately, the dollar was not as pure as the Piece of Eight, and hence was overvalued in relation to that coin. It also contained less than a dollar's worth of gold. Nor was this all. It was discovered that dollars shipped to the West Indies could be exchanged on a one-to-one basis for Pieces of Eight, which held more silver than the dollar. These Pieces of Eight were exported to the United States, where they were eagerly turned into dollars by the Mint. A merchant could now export his "new" dollars again to the Caribbean, where they were traded for yet more Pieces of Eight—and so the process continued. Though the difference in silver content between the Piece of Eight and the dollar was minute, anyone willing to play the import-export game for a long enough time could be wealthy.

In short, the dollar was fast becoming an export commodity. In 1804 the Director of the Mint suspended the coinage of silver dollars. When it was resumed in 1840, the dollar—its weight and fineness reformed—did what it was meant to do, and circulated as a coin. The height of silver dollar production occurred in the latter half of the nineteenth century, when the American West was found to have vast deposits of silver, used to fashion big and shiny Morgan dollars. The strike, however, was of such enormity that silver glutted the market, and was grossly overvalued in relation to gold. This led to political turmoil: debtors wanted large amounts of depreciated silver dollars to be coined; creditors did not.

Dollar production dropped after 1900 and between 1904 and 1921 no silver dollars were coined at all. They were issued sporadically in the 1920s and early 1930s. The last silver dollar meant for circulation was struck in 1935. The coin was revived in 1971, but minted in a clad alloy featuring copper-nickel. The public greeted it with less than enthusiasm, as it did a newer and more convenient coin, introduced in 1979. Although the dollar is sure to continue as a monetary denomination and unit of account, its future in the United States as a coin is questionable.

However, it has been broadly accepted

(in a modified form) in numbers of other countries, including Canada, Australia, New Zealand, and several island groups in the Caribbean.

See also CLAD COINAGE; CONTINENTAL DOLLAR; DECIMAL COINAGE; MINT ACT OF 1792; MORGAN DOLLAR; PEACE DOLLAR; PIECE OF EIGHT; THALER.

Double-struck coin.
Left: Brunswick-Wolfenbüttel, thaler, 1633.
Right: France, sol, 1792.

DOUBLE-STRUCK COIN A coin which receives two or more impressions from a coin die or dies, either accidentally or by general mint practice.

Coins double-struck by accident are errors, and command high premiums. Those double-struck by intention are not errors, and command no particular premium. Indeed, a perfectly struck coin of this type is usually worth more than one marred by double striking. The line between the error and the ordinary is difficult to draw with precision, but it would not be amiss to say that while early hand-struck coins were often double-struck, modern coins made by machine should not be.

If, in ancient times, the coin being struck by hand was large and thick, or had designs in high relief, it required more than one striking to transfer the designs from dies to coin. In theory, the first hammer-blow from above caused the imprints of the dies to "take" sufficiently on the planchet so it remained correctly positioned for future strikings. The designs were then impressed even more until the coiner decided they had gained enough prominence to consider the coin finished. But in practice, slippage was frequent. The first strike might not take on one or both sides of the planchet, allowing the latter to shift or rotate between blows. Eventually it would take the designs, but the impression of that first strike might still be visible, and a double-struck coin would result.

While many coins, including modern proofs, have been struck several times, the term double-struck is used only if the coin shows evidence of more than one striking.

The coin in the first illustration, from Brunswick-Wolfenbüttel and dated 1633, is a fairly good example of a pre-mechanical, double-struck coin. The doubling effect is most readily seen in the inscription and fancy border surrounding the central type. This is often the case on double-struck coins: the explanation lies in the same circumstances that make a rotating wheel's peripheries cover more distance than its hub. In this case a round die replaces a circular wheel.

By the eighteenth century the use of coining machinery was almost universal. While numbers of machines were invented, one predominated well into the nineteenth century. This was the screw press, which literally squeezed designs into planchets with such pressure that the incidence of the double strike was substantially reduced. There was no longer a reason to strike the planchet a second time, except in the case of proofs.

Nevertheless, the double-struck coin continued to appear from time to time, and it could now be described as an error.

The second piece, a French sol of 1792, illustrates the double-struck error. Its planchet was struck once in a screw press, receiving the impression you see on the left and center. But it was not removed in time, and it received a second strike, seen on the right. The coin is worn, indicating it may have circulated, error or no.

Double strikes are rather common on French copper coinage of this period, suggesting careless, decentralized mint practices.

Two other examples of doubling are worth mention. The first, a partial doubling, is seen on Liberty's profile on some early United States large cents. It is not a double strike in the strict sense of the term, as the coin was struck only once, but rather an indication that the obverse dies on the screw presses used by the early Philadelphia Mint were loose, and "chattered" during the striking process. A second form of doubling can occur during the hubbing process used to mass-produce dies. A working die may slip as it is being hubbed, resulting in doubling on the die, which is then transferred to coins struck with that die. Again, this is not double-striking, even though it resembles it, as in the case of the 1955 "double die" American cent.

See also ERROR; HAMMERED COINAGE; HUB; SCREW PRESS.

DOUBLOON   The name given to two famous Spanish and Spanish-American gold coins of the fifteenth through nineteenth centuries.

The doubloon began as a double excelente, one of the denominations produced by the Spanish coining reforms of 1497. It then measured some 29 millimeters, and weighed 7 grams. It was intended to equal two Venetian ducats, and was struck with distinctive facing obverse portraits of Fer-

dinand and Isabella. Isabella died in 1504 and Ferdinand in 1516, but their successor, Charles I (ruled 1516–1556), continued to mint the double excelente in large quantities for another twenty years. It was this double portrait on a double ducat that eventually earned the coin its name, doubloon (in Spanish, doblón).

When Charles reformed Spanish gold coinage in 1536, coins on the excelente system, struck in pure gold, were replaced by a new issue of escudos, struck in 22-carat gold and with a shield as their obverse type. A royal decree had established a Spanish mint at Mexico City the previous year, in recognition of the Indies' importance as a source of precious metals. This new colonial mint was soon joined by others, primarily located in or near mining areas.

In time, the name "doubloon" was transferred to the eight-escudo piece struck at these mints and in Spain, and it is this doubloon most commonly thought of when the word is used.

The new doubloon was far larger than its earlier namesake, and was first coined in Spain in the period of Philip III (ruled 1598–1621), and in the Americas at the end of the seventeenth century. It weighed about 27 grams, roughly corresponding to the Spanish ounce; indeed, the coin was often dubbed an onza (short for *onza de oro*). It measured some 37 millimeters in diameter (at least when struck in a screw press; specimens struck by hand, called cobs, were smaller and thicker).

Early Spanish doubloons featured an obverse design with a shield and ornate crown, a reverse with a cross in a quatrefoil. Their American counterparts showed the cross on the obverse, with the date and the crowned Pillars of Hercules on the reverse. New designs were conceived in the 1720s. In Spain, the portrait of the monarch now adorned the obverse, while the crowned shield was relegated to the reverse. By the following decade, American mints adopted these designs, giving the

Doubloon. Chile, 8 escudos, 1751.

doubloon an appearance it retained until the early nineteenth century.

The Spanish doubloon did not survive its country's loss of her overseas provinces, and in 1820 the last Spanish eight-escudo piece was coined. The American doubloon, however, did survive. The eight-escudo denomination was retained by Mexico, Peru, and Spain's other independent successors in Latin America, and was struck until the latter half of the nineteenth century. Then it, too, fell victim to the move to decimal coinage.

See also COB; DOBLA; DUCAT; VIS-À-VIS TYPE.

DRACHM   A small silver coin which circulated widely in the Greek world and the areas adjacent to it: the basic unit of much Greek coinage.

The coin's weight averaged 4 grams or slightly above, with diameter in the neighborhood of 16 millimeters. The drachm purportedly took its name from a handful *(drax)* of six iron spits *(obeloi)*, which were formerly used as currency. This relationship of six obols to the drachm continued after the invention of coinage.

The drachm first appeared around 560 B.C. It was produced in fair numbers by Athens and neighboring states, always playing a secondary role to the larger tetradrachm (piece of four drachms), although the drachm was the basic monetary unit. Athenian drachms are essentially smaller versions of the tetradrachm; the coins' design elements are similar, at times all but identical.

Alexander the Great (ruled 336–323 B.C.) carried his ambitions and his coins to the Persian Empire, which he captured in 331 B.C. When a native dynasty, the Arsacids, ejected the Greek interlopers around 250 B.C. and created the Parthian Empire, they made no attempt to resume coinage of the old Persian variety. Borrowing instead from the Greeks, they struck quantities of silver coins, particularly drachms.

Drachm. *Parthia, 123–88 B.C.*

The coin illustrated dates from the time of Mithridates II (ruled 123–88 B.C.), and, despite a certain decline in style, it is obviously a modified Greek drachm. The Parthians struck increasingly degenerate drachms until the extinction of their house in AD. 226, by which time the drachm had also disappeared from its birthplace. Greece was now part of the Roman Empire, and used Roman coins. The Sassanians, successors to the Parthians, continued to strike coins called drachms (which now bore no resemblance to their Greek forebears) until their defeat at the hands of Islam around 650. The Arabs, in turn, paid tribute to the coin's place in history by naming their new silver coin a dirhem, a word derived from drachm.

See also ARAB-SASSANIAN COINAGE; DIRHEM; OBOL; TETRADRACHM.

DUCAT   One of the most significant gold coins of medieval and early modern times, first struck in Venice in the mid-1280s.

The coin illustrated is from the first issue, coined at the behest of the doge Giovanni Dandolo (ruled 1280–1289). Its obverse shows him kneeling before St. Mark, patron of the city, while its reverse bears Christ standing within an oval frame. The name ducat derives from the last word in the reverse legend, and eventually was applied to a number of similar Italian gold coins. The alternate name for the ducat, zecchino, stems from the Italian for mint, *zecca*. Our ducat has a diameter of 20 millimeters and a weight of 3.5 grams, and would retain the same designs, size, and weight for the next several hundred years.

Ducat. *Venice, 1284–1289.*

The Venetian ducat was conceived to compete as a trade coin with the florin and the genovino. Sizable deposits of gold had been unearthed in Hungary, inducing Venetian businessmen and traders in search of a profit to settle there as exporters and creditors; they were paid in gold, making a Venetian gold coin inevitable.

Doge after doge struck the ducat. Each coin contained the name of the reigning doge in the obverse legend; otherwise, there was no attempt to date the piece. We can date them to within a few years, as documents exist giving us the regnal years of the doges, but we cannot go beyond this approximation with any certainty.

The ducat outlasted the independent Venetian state. Venice fell to the French in 1797, and was soon ceded to Austria. The latter allowed the Venetians to continue striking ducats of the traditional design, and they did so for some years. In 1819 the coin's design was changed to conform with other coins of the Austrian Empire, and for the first time, the Venetian ducat bore a date. The redesigned ducat was struck in some quantity at the Venice mint until 1866, when the city joined the new kingdom of Italy. The Austrians, however, minted the ducat in other parts of their empire until after the outbreak of World War I.

The ducat was imitated over much of Europe—not necessarily its designs, but rather its fineness and weight. These were the elements which made it what it finally came to be: one of the most successful trade coins in history.

See also FLORIN; GENOVINO; TRADE COINS; ZECCHINO

DUCATON   A large silver coin issued in the Low Countries and elsewhere during the seventeenth and eighteenth centuries.

Typical specimens have a diameter of some 45 millimeters, and weigh around 32 grams. The ducaton was meant in part as a trading coin, and its success was vouched for when, called a ducatoon, it was adopted for trade in colonial America.

The coin originated in the Spanish possession of Milan, where it was first struck in 1605 bearing the name ducatone. Its spread was rapid: Parma struck ducatones in 1617; the following year it found its way to the future Belgium, where it was struck in fair numbers under Albert and Elizabeth (ruled 1598–1621); in 1659, it was adopted by the Dutch.

The piece illustrated is from the Dutch city of Campen, and dates from the first year of issue, 1659. It is a typical Dutch ducaton. On the obverse is an armored mounted figure—the coin is occasionally called a "silver rider"—and beneath him is a shield with the arms of the city. The obverse legend (in abbreviated Latin) reveals it is a silver coin of the city of Campen. The reverse carries a national type and legends: the central figure of a crowned lion represents all the United Provinces of the Netherlands (i.e., the Dutch nation), while the legend celebrates the amicable relationship between the area's political entities. This coupling of local and national elements is a familiar feature on Dutch coins of the period, and reflects the political condition: a confederation bound by a rather weak central government.

Ducaton. *Campen, 1659.*

In the eighteenth century the Dutch issued the ducaton for their possessions in India, and struck it for home consumption until the 1790s, by which time it had been abandoned elsewhere.

See also TRADE COINS.

DUMP   A small, unusually thick coin of any metal.

A dump may be created by removing a circular piece from a larger (usually silver) coin. The thickness of the resulting coin will be out of proportion to its modest diameter. The Caribbean bit often cut from the center of a Spanish-American Piece of Eight is one example of this type of dump; another is the fifteen-pence coin of New South Wales, companion to the Holey Dollar of 1813. In both instances the dump sprang from an emergency; governments must provide a circulating medium, and if they are unable to create their own for whatever reason, they simply make use of someone else's coinage.

Another form of dump, however, is deliberately fashioned for or by people who happen to like small, thick coins. The piece in the photograph is illustrative of this variety. It is a two-stuiver piece, minted in Ceylon by the Dutch East India Company in 1783. It was intentionally struck in a rather small (26 millimeters) but extremely thick (6 millimeters) module, as thick coins were popular among the native peoples of Ceylon and adjacent areas. The name is also used for the thick copper farthings struck in 1717 and 1718

Dump. Dutch Ceylon, 2 stuiver, 1783.

by George I of England (ruled 1714–1727).

See also BIT; EMERGENCY MONEY; HOLEY DOLLAR.

DUPONDIUS   A Roman coin worth two asses, minted sporadically in the Roman Republic, and gaining prominence in the early years of the Roman Empire.

The first emperor, Augustus (ruled 31 B.C.–A.D. 14) completely revamped coinage about 23 B.C., and adopted the dupondius as an essential part of the new system. The coin would be worth two asses as before, but was now to be struck in *orichalcum* (brass), not bronze. Its diameter would be about 28 millimeters and its weight 12.5 grams. It was a logical solution to a persistent problem of the Roman Republic in its final years: it produced little bronze, upon which its coinage was based, and thus had a disabling paucity of small change.

Augustus's coinage would now be based on gold and silver, not bronze, and the *aes* coinage would be of a fiduciary nature, not an intrinsic one. That is, copper and brass coins would have a stated value higher than their real, metallic value, just as an American clad quarter dollar does not contain twenty-five cents' worth of metal.

Augustus planned and minted four subsidiary base-metal coins. Two were made of *orichalcum*, the sestertius and the dupondius, and two of copper, the as and quadrans. A semis, tariffed at two quadrantes, was introduced later. Each Roman subsidiary coin was worth double the one below it. With the dupondius, this proved troublesome. Made of brass, it was extremely close in size and metallic appearance to the as, but worth twice as much. To alleviate the confusion, Augustus's imperial successors placed a radiate crown on the dupondius' portrait of the ruler and omitted it on the as. While this was done as early as the period of Tiberius (ruled A.D. 14–37), it was not consistent until Nero (ruled A.D. 54–68).

Dupondius. *Roman Empire, Tiberius, c.* A.D. *22.*

The first dupondii were rather simple. Early issues of Augustus carried an inscription within a wreath on the obverse, a large SC (for *Senatus Consulto,* "By Decree of the Senate") on the reverse. The SC was surrounded by a legend with the names of the magistrates responsible for the coins, Augustus's way of paying lip service to republican tradition.

Toward the end of his reign, Augustus's portrait began to appear on the dupondius as well as on other subsidiary coins, a practice retained by his successors. The coin illustrated points out some of the basic aspects of the dupondius, and indeed, of Roman coinage in general. The piece was made around A.D. 22, under Augustus's successor, Tiberius (ruled A.D. 14–37). On the obverse is Augustus's head with a radiate crown, and the legend DIVVS AVGUVSTVS PATER. The legend (and portrait) extol Augustus, and indicate the desire of a reigning emperor to identify himself with his deified predecessor. Tiberius, by issuing a coin with a description of Augustus as both a god *and* his father clearly hoped to garner good will. The reverse design, the letters SC flanking a temple, again expressed the notion of divinity seen on the obverse. The imagery is ironic; in fact, Augustus and Tiberius detested one another, and Augustus chose Tiberius only when he saw no other possibility. Basically the coin's general form remained unchanged for what was left of its life. Portraiture predominated on the obverse; pictorial representations (as opposed to long legends and inscriptions) graced the reverse. As with other Roman coins, portraiture and reverse elements reached a pinnacle of artistic expression in the first century A.D. The dupondius was of ample size to allow strong, detailed portraiture, and this denomination holds some of the finest examples of Roman numismatic art.

The Roman dupondius fell upon hard times in the late second century, along with many early imperial coins. Its weight dropped, evidence of the debasement of the Roman monetary system, and its obverse portrait and reverse elements revealed far less artistry. The coin passed into history around A.D. 250.

See also AS; BRASS COINAGE; INFLATION; SENATORIAL COINS; SESTERTIUS

E

ÉCU   A large French silver coin, struck intermittently from 1641 to 1793.

Numbers of conflicting royal edicts about the écu resulted in its diameter varying from 38 to 41 millimeters, and its weight from 23.6 to 30.6 grams. However, 29.5 grams can be safely regarded as the coin's average weight.

The écu was often referred to as the écu blanc or écu d'argent, names adopted to distinguish the piece from several gold issues, also called écus. Its name comes from the French word for shield—*écu*, applied to gold and silver coins alike because of the shield which dominated the design of both.

In the year 1640 the French monetary system was in serious trouble. Minor coinage was mostly debased, gold coinage was undervalued at its official rate and hence tended to be exported, and there was no equivalent of the useful silver thaler. Moreover, with few exceptions, French coins were still struck by hand, which meant clipping was rife.

The government of Louis XIII (ruled 1610–1643) eventually took steps to correct these problems. It counterstamped all billon coins and made them current at a reduced flat rate. Then too, it lowered the fineness of its gold coinage to keep it in circulation. And it produced a rival to the thaler: the silver écu.

As this écu was to be a large coin, and difficult to strike by hand, Louis and his ministers installed modern screw presses with which to mint it. Although the French had pioneered the use of the screw press ninety years earlier, the invention had never taken hold—furthermore, the French had not been producing coins large enough to make the machinery necessary. But now it was needed. Presses were purchased, and the distinguished Belgian medallist, Jean Varin, was engaged to superintend the coining.

Varin's écu featured a masterful portrait of the king on the obverse and a crowned shield with fleurs-de-lis on the reverse; it was this coin that served as the model for most French écus minted from that time forward. Louis XIV (ruled 1643–1715), however, experimented with other designs for the écu's reverse—which sometimes carried a cross fashioned of eight "L's," and at other times showed

Écu. France, 1709.

three crowns arranged in a triangle, as seen on the piece illustrated. By 1709, when this écu was minted, machinery was used to mark the edges of the coins, as a protection against clipping. In the early eighteenth century the reverse shield was formed into an oval and surrounded by a wreath, a final touch that endured through the reign of Louis XV (1715–1774), and most of the tenure of Louis XVI (ruled 1774–1792).

In 1789 the French Revolution began; by 1791, the king was virtually powerless, and early in 1793 he was beheaded. For much of Louis XVI's reign, the écus struck carried traditional types and legends. Those legends, as the 1709 écu shows, refer solely to the king: *his* titles are given, *his* domains are enumerated, and the French people are never mentioned.

The écus appearing in 1792, however, mirror the changes generated by the French Revolution. The king's portrait, while still gracing the obverse, is far more realistic, and by no means flattering. And its legend no longer proclaims him "King of France"; he is now "King of the French." Furthermore it is stated in French, not in Latin as before. The reverse has been completely restyled; instead of the crowned shield with yet more royal titles in Latin, it carries an angel, writing on a tablet inscribed CONSTITUTION. The legend around the figure reads REGNE DE LA LOI ("Reign of Law"—referring to the Constitution of 1791), while an inscription in the exergue tells us this is the "Fourth Year of Liberty" (counting

1789 as the first year). The edge lettering too, has been revolutionized, and now celebrates "Nation, Law, and King."

Écus of this reformed style were struck after France became a republic, and even after the king's execution, presumably because republican designs had yet to be prepared. When they were completed, in 1793, the coin was simply called a six-livre piece, but its weight and fineness remained the same. The unrestricted issue of assignats in 1793 and the following years drove the écu out of circulation, and France's entire monetary system was altered in 1795. A new, five-franc silver coin appeared that year, and proved an adequate replacement for the écu, which passed into oblivion.

See also Écu d'or; Fleur-de-lis; Machine-struck coinage; Thaler.

ÉCU D'OR An important late medieval and early modern French gold coin.

The écu d'or was first struck, on a tentative basis, under Louis IX (ruled 1226–1270). This early version was undervalued in relation to the silver coinage, and seems never to have been put into general circulation. Louis's immediate successors abandoned the écu d'or, and it was not struck again until the reign of Philip VI (ruled 1328–1350), when its reintroduction corresponds with the outbreak of the Hundred Years' War with England (1337–1453). Philip's coin weighed about 4.5 grams, was roughly 29 millimeters in diameter, and was made of pure gold. Later issues, such as the illustrated piece, weighed a bit less and were slightly alloyed.

The dominant design on the écu d'or was usually a crowned shield *(écu)*, which gave the coin its name. The original écu d'or of Louis IX had displayed a shield with fleurs-de-lis on its obverse and a legend with the king's titles. Its reverse bore a decorative cross with lilies in its angles, and a legend reading CHRISTVS VINCIT,

Écu-d'or. *France, 1380–1422.*

CHRISTVS REGNAT, CHRISTVS IMPERAT ("Christ Conquers, Rules, Commands"). These obverse and reverse types and legends remained significant on the écu d'or throughout its life.

During the fourteenth and fifteenth centuries the coin was struck in substantial numbers, and it found frequent imitators, among them the English, who occupied much of France in this period. However, its importance decreased late in the fifteenth century, even though a slightly redesigned écu d'or was introduced under Louis XI (ruled 1461–1483). Called an écu au soleil, it carried a small device representing a sun above the crowned shield. The écu d'or reached the last phase of its career in the early 1640s. By then weighing under 3.4 grams, the écu d'or's gold content was reduced from 23 to 22 carats, and it became the subsidiary of a larger and more famous coin, the louis d'or. The écu d'or was demonetized in 1679.

See also CROSS ON COINAGE; ÉCU; FLEUR-DE-LIS; LOUIS D'OR; TRADE COINS.

EDGE-MARKING MACHINERY Mechanical contrivances used to put designs on the edge of a coin before or after it has been struck, but not while it is being struck.

Edge-marking machinery is distinguished from the collar, which can act as a third die and impart a design during the striking process.

The machinery came into use in England shortly after 1660 to compensate for the deficiencies of the various forms of collars employed at the time. Something was clearly needed to create an edge design quickly, while retaining a design intricate enough to deter counterfeiting and clipping. The edge-marking machine met the requirements. Not only was it a new device in coining machinery, but it altered the coining process itself. Previously, coins' edges were marked as they were struck; now they could be marked while still in the planchet stage.

The marking machine was first used at the British Royal Mint under conditions of such secrecy that for many years the identity of its inventor was uncertain. It now seems to have been an expatriate Frenchman, Pierre Blondeau. In 1685 an improved version of the device, produced by Jean Castaing, a skilled engraver, debuted at the Paris mint. It was so successful it could mark twenty thousand planchets a day, and all edge-marking machines of the period were hence described as "Castaing machines," whether or not he was involved in their manufacture.

The illustration (taken from a unique manuscript of 1783) shows an edge-marking machine in operation. It consisted of a heavy table with a metal plate on top. Two parallel steel bars were positioned on the plate, with the distance between them slightly less than the diameter of the planchet to be marked. One of the bars was fixed, while the other could be moved forward or backward, parallel to the fixed bar, by a lever and cogwheel arrangement. A planchet set between the two bars rotated as the lever (often in the form of a "steering wheel," as in the photograph) was moved. The ornaments or inscriptions for the edge were cut on the inner sides of the two parallel bars, half on each; by making the planchet perform one complete revolution, the entire design was transferred to its edge. It was then struck in the manner of an ordinary coin.

The Austrians amended this basic machine during the eighteenth century: they found that when each bar had a slight cur-

Edge-marking machinery. *A "Castaing machine" at work.*
(From Samuel Thompson's *An Essay on Coining*, a unique manuscript of 1783. Courtesy of the Library of the American Numismatic Society, New York)

vature a better impression was produced. The simple edge-marking machine operated for two centuries, and was used to mint some of history's most important coins—the Piece of Eight, the "Levant Thaler" of Maria Theresa, and the first United States dollars, among others.

In the nineteenth century this marking technique fell into disuse when the steam-powered coining press and its descendants made the coining process ever more rapid. The hand-operated edge-marking machine, unable to match the accelerated pace, was discarded for the one-piece collar, whose artistic possibilities were limited but whose output was greater. However, in some places, the old device lingered for many years. In Mexico, for example, mints used the hand-cranked machine to mark the edges of eight-real pieces until 1897; an examination of these coins indicates their edge devices were often applied *after* the coins were struck—decidedly unusual but perfectly possible.

While the old Castaing machine has disappeared, a modern version has seen some use. It marks planchets mechanically

in an *incuse* fashion, making it possible to then strike them in an ordinary one-piece collar. Some of the edge designs will be flattened, but most will remain. Prototypes of the machine appeared in Europe early in the last century, and the technique is still used for the coinages of West Germany and Israel, among other countries. Edge designs are a significant part of commemorative coinage, but not of ordinary issues.

See also CLIPPING; COLLAR; LETTERED EDGE; MACHINE-STRUCK COINAGE; ORNAMENTED EDGE; PLANCHET; REEDED EDGE.

ELECTROTYPE A copy of a coin or medal made by an electroplating process; such copies were manufactured in large quantities in the late nineteenth and early twentieth centuries, as they produced faithful reproductions of rare coins at a modest price.

An electrotype was prepared in the following manner. A negative cast of each side of the coin to be copied was prepared from wax or plaster of Paris. Next, the casts were coated with a thin layer of graphite, to act as a conductor in the electroplating stage. The negative casts were then attached to copper leads and immersed in an electroplating bath composed of an acidic copper sulphate.

The negative casts on copper leads served as a cathode. The anode was a sheet of electrolytic copper. A weak electric current—usually amounting to one volt—was sent through the bath, causing the copper to leave the surface of the anode and reappear on the cathode. The process continued until the copper positives were fairly thick and rigid, at which point the current was switched off and the positives were removed. The negative casts were detached, and the copper "shells," or positives (each of which was a virtually perfect reproduction of one side of the original coin) were cleaned, strengthened, and soldered together. The electrotype was then finished

Electrotype. *Electrotype molds for a copy of the* Rosa Americana *twopence of 1733.*

—although if the coin to be copied was gold or silver, the electrotype still had to be plated.

The illustration shows two molds used for producing electrotypes of the extremely rare Rosa Americana twopence of 1733. They are unusual in having been made of metal, not wax.

Electrotypes are no longer created for sale to collectors; the cost of their production has risen and the tastes of collectors have changed. Such major institutions as the British Museum, however, still make them sporadically, and the method remains one of the finest ever conceived for copying rare coins.

Collectors occasionally encounter electrotypes offered, knowingly or not, as genuine coins. Should a collector come upon a doubtful piece, several tests may help to determine its nature. First, the surfaces of an electrotype are likely to be quite smooth and lack the sharpness and roughness of a genuine coin. The color of the piece might also be slightly unusual, particularly if it was plated. Also, the piece will not ring at the pitch of an authentic coin, if it rings at all. Examine the edge. A thin, light line is the telltale mark of solder, exposing the point at which the two shells were joined together. Finally, the edge on an electrotype will usually be smooth, whereas it may be reeded or ornamental on the original.

See also Copy; Counterfeit and forgery detection.

ELECTRUM COINAGE Coins made from a mixture of gold and silver that occurs naturally; electrum was the first metal used for coinage.

The earliest people to use the metal as a coinage medium were either the Lydians or surrounding Ionian Greeks, and the earliest coins appeared between 620 and 600 B.C.

While the question has yet to be definitively answered, majority opinion is that the Lydians were the first to use electrum for coinage—and therefore the first to strike coins. There is much logic to naming the Lydians the pioneers of coinage. Lydia was a small but wealthy country in western Asia Minor. The Paktolos River flowed through its capital, Sardis, and electrum formed naturally in the river's silt, from which it could be dredged—perhaps with sheepskins (a clue as to the origins of the legend of the Golden Fleece). Once melted and refined, the electrum was cast into bean-shaped planchets and struck with a simple obverse die and reverse punch. The Lydian monetary unit was the stater, weighing between 14 and 16 grams, and averaging 19 millimeters in diameter. Subsidiary issues were struck in greater numbers than the staters themselves. The illustrated piece was valued at one-third of a stater, and weighs about 4.7 grams, with a diameter of 13 millimeters.

Lydia's neighbors, the Ionian Greeks, adopted electrum coinage at about the same time, and the sixth century B.C. saw the alloy used widely. By the reign of Croesus (ruled 560–546 B.C.), there were signs of a change. The Lydians had found that natural electrum could vary enor-

Electrum coinage. *Lydia, electrum ⅓ stater, early sixth century* B.C.

mously in its relative proportion of gold to silver. There were complaints that specific coins contained too little gold and too much silver, and disputes over the quality of electrum coinage began to hinder business transactions. An obvious solution presented itself: separate the two metallic elements, and fashion coins from each. Croesus seems to be the first king to have done so, and the concept of gold and silver coins soon spread to adjacent peoples. The use of natural electrum as a coinage medium diminished.

Man-made electrum, however, was another matter. It became clear that if nature or accident could alloy gold and silver, so too could a skilled mintmaster. And if it were alloyed with care, the proportion of gold and silver could be kept stable and the problems of natural electrum coinage avoided. The man-made alloy was used in parts of the Greek-speaking world until about 250 B.C. and has seen occasional use since, although it has been employed more often in counterfeiting and debasement than in legitimate coining.

See also ALLOY; ARCHAIC COINAGE; HAMMERED COINAGE; STATER.

ELONGATED COINAGE

ELONGATED COINAGE A variety of exonumia in which an ordinary round coin is stretched into a thin oval, generally by passing the piece between two rollers.

Elongated coinage is a peculiarly American phenomenon, and dates from the latter part of the nineteenth century —when children discovered what intriguing effects could be created when a coin set on a railroad track was run over by a train. Later it was found that a hand-cranked rolling machine could produce the same, or even better, results. Furthermore, a message, advertisement, or image could be applied to the coin, simply by inscribing it on one of the rollers in reverse.

The coins most frequently used for this purpose were small cents, as only minimal pressure was needed to elongate them,

Elongated coinage. United States cent, elongated and issued by the Mid-Hudson Coin Club, 1974.

and they were of little monetary value. Elongated cents were made and sold as souvenirs at the Columbian Exposition and subsequent national and world fairs, and they still convey a holiday spirit. Although they are now in fashion among coin collectors, the public has always cherished them as inexpensive reminders of a special place and time.

See also EXONUMIA.

EMERGENCY MONEY

EMERGENCY MONEY A general term for any and all objects used as money that are produced and circulated under abnormal conditions.

The term can refer to such disparate items as siege pieces, notgeld, provisional paper money and coinage, and some private scrip and tokens. To qualify for the term, the piece in question must be produced during a period of stress, when the authorities who customarily and legitimately provide the public with ordinary currency cannot do so. These issuing bodies may be either governmental or private, as long as they are a nation's customary suppliers of money. Thus, an American broken bank note for five dollars dated 1837 does not fall into this category, for such banks customarily supplied the paper money needs of the United States at the time. But a scrip note for ten cents issued in that year would be classed as emergency money, for it replaced an officially struck coin which had disappeared from circulation during the Panic of 1837. Another term for emergency money is necessity money.

See also BUSH NOTES; CIVIL WAR TOKENS;

COUNTERSTAMP; ENCASED POSTAGE STAMP; GUTSCHEIN; HARD TIMES TOKENS; KLIPPE; NECESSITY MONEY; NOTGELD; OVERSTRIKE; SCRIP; SIEGE PIECE.

ENCASED POSTAGE STAMP A form of emergency currency featuring an official government stamp placed in a protective holder, meant to function as a coin.

While a number of countries have experimented with encased postage stamps during periods of emergency, the earliest and best-known examples of their use come from the United States and date from 1862. At that time, the initial enthusiasm with which North and South began the Civil War had all but evaporated. Doubt and uncertainty caused people to hoard specie, and while gold and silver issues were the first to be garnered, soon even base-metal coins were being removed from circulation.

Recognizing the problem, the Union government sought various solutions, and turned at last to the issue of low-value paper money. Before that, however, it authorized the use of government postage stamps for small change. The stamps proved troublesome in an unaltered state —they got stuck, wore out, blew away, and were easily misplaced. It was decided they might be easier to handle if they were kept in small envelopes, with the denomination written on the front. The back of the envelope, in the meantime, could be used for advertising.

The paper envelope, however, did not work as well as had been hoped. It was too easy for people to put a stamp-sized piece of colored paper in the envelope and pass it during rush hours. An envelope with a window displaying the stamp was the obvious solution, but such a container could not be devised until a suitable substance— thin, transparent, and sturdy—had been invented.

Late that summer John Gault, a Boston inventor, fell upon an answer. He fashioned two round, brass shells, one with a mica window to reveal the stamp and its denomination; the other blank (ready for an advertisement or other message to be stamped on it). The stamp was held between the two shells, which were crimped together, and the encased postage stamp was born.

Gault sold his idea to a number of eastern and midwestern merchants. A well-known button manufacturer, Scovill & Co., made the holders, and Gault soon found he had a brisk business. But even the encased postage stamp had its drawbacks. Were a three-cent stamp encased, it circulated at three cents—even though, with the addition of the casing, it cost about five cents to put it into circulation. The citizenry's willingness to spend money to obtain small change exemplifies the desperate condition of the American monetary system. It also meant that should a better, and cheaper solution be found, Gault would be out of business.

And there were better ideas. Cent-sized copper tokens, the famous Civil War cents, appeared in Cincinnati late in 1862. By the following year, millions were being struck. The government made its contribution by circulating fractional currency in 1862 and ensuing years. These small-sized government notes satisfied the need for small change reasonably well and consigned John Gault and his invention to oblivion.

Elsewhere, however, similar devices have been used in this century. After World War I, encased stamps functioned as small change in Germany, Austria, and

Encased postage stamp. *United States, encased 10-cent stamp, c. 1862.*

several other countries. They may reappear whenever the need for change is so acute it forces people to pay a premium for it.

See also CIVIL WAR TOKENS; FRACTIONAL CURRENCY; NOTGELD; POSTAGE STAMP MONEY.

ENGRAVERS' MARKS Names, initials, or monograms, placed on coin dies by their designers.

Coinage may be considered an art (albeit a minor one), but unlike painting and sculpture, the bulk of its creations are unsigned. Most examples of numismatic art at its finest—the outstanding Greek, Roman, and Renaissance issues—were fashioned by artists whose very names will remain forever unknown.

But such is not always the case. Engravers' marks, the numismatic equivalent of an artist's signature, may be traced to the fifth century B.C. Some of the most talented engravers of that day, men such as Kimon and Euainetos, put their names on their splendid coins. However, it was a practice largely confined to Sicily, and seems to have fallen into disuse after the fourth century B.C. Indeed, engravers' marks did not reappear until the introduction of modern coinage, money minted since 1700.

Engravers' marks can consist of one or more initials, as is common on British coins of the last century and a half, or as a monogram, the standard form on much of United States coinage. And occasionally a full name is seen on a piece: Agustin Dupré, a celebrated French engraver of the late eighteenth century, chose to sign his creations with his last name.

The photograph, illustrating the placement of engravers' marks, shows part of the obverse of a United States pattern silver dollar, designed by Christian Gobrecht in 1836. The complete type is a figure of Liberty, seated on a rock. Gobrecht placed C. GOBRECHT. F., his abbreviated reference in Latin, on the base of the rock. Origi-

Engravers' marks. United States, pattern dollar, 1836 (detail).

nally he put it in the field between the rock and the date, but the complaints of government critics forced him to find a less conspicuous spot. The tiny inscription seen here was still considered too prominent, and eventually Gobrecht had no choice but to remove his name completely. In the course of time the mint adopted his pattern with modifications, and several million Gobrecht dollars were coined between 1840 and 1873, but none revealed their designer's name.

See also ABBREVIATIONS; DECADRACHM; MONOGRAM.

ENGRAVING An intaglio, reverse image of something to be placed on a coin, token medal, or note.

For coins, medals, and tokens, the engraving takes the form of a die. (The process creating it is described under the entry Die.) For paper money, the engraving appears on a plate, and this is the work to be defined here.

An engraved plate is merely a combination of sharp grooves, inscribed so deeply that, when the plate is inked and its surface wiped clean, ink remains in its grooves. A sheet of paper then pressed against the engraving picks up ink from the grooves and a positive impression of the plate is produced. The grooves need not be as deep as those in the carving to make a coin die, but they must be sharp enough to catch and hold the printer's ink. If not, the elements of the positive print will be weak or absent in spots. This can and does happen, as collectors of paper money know; it is a signal that the engraving was too shallow, or was used so often that some of its details simply wore out. Improper inking can lead to the same end.

Historically, engraved plates for printing paper money have been shaped from one of two metals. Copper prevailed from the late seventeenth century to the early nineteenth, when steel came into fashion. Each metal has advantages and disadvantages. Copper gives a lovely impression, but its relative softness means plates made from it must be retouched every few thousand prints. Steel, on the other hand, lasts far longer, but is extremely difficult to work with because it is so hard.

Given the technology of the seventeenth and eighteenth centuries, it was logical for engravers to choose copper for their work. Yet even though it was rather easy to engrave, it held certain frustrations. At the time, it was close to impossible to manufacture a truly flat plate, although only flat plates give reliable impressions. Therefore, once a decent plate had been prepared engravers went to inordinate lengths to keep it in use, retouching, re-engraving, and re-dating it. There is a Massachusetts bill that bears fifteen such dates, ranging from 1714 to 1740, each added in an effort to keep an old plate in use.

Early engravings on copper tended to be quite plain. Each plate was done entirely by hand, and if vignettes appeared, they resembled small line drawings. By the nineteenth century, vignettes grew larger, and there were attempts to impart roundness and depth with cross-hatching and other techniques. At about the same time, it was learned that steel could be engraved as well as copper.

England, then undergoing its Industrial Revolution, provided the steel to which an American, Jacob Perkins, applied his skill and expertise. Perkins found that if specially selected soft steel was used for engraving, it could be hardened and made fit for printing. With this process, the advantages of a copper plate could be combined with those of a steel plate.

An even more important discovery was the way to transfer images from hard steel to soft. In the past, each plate had been engraved individually. Perkins invented a method of "hubbing" designs, thereby making many more plates in the same amount of time. His technique used a hard, finished, flat steel engraving. A roller of soft steel was pressed back and forth across the design, until it had picked up all its elements. The roller was then hardened; it could be employed later to transfer the design back onto soft steel plates which, also hardened, were used in the actual printing process.

It was an invention of momentous consequence. Just at the time when a burgeoning economy heightened the need for uniform paper money, the money could be produced. Small wonder that Jacob Perkins is considered the father of the modern bank note.

Other inventions made his discoveries even more useful. A geometric lathe was devised to make borders, and also medallions—the round or oval decorative frames for the denomination of a note. Still other new techniques of engraving were invented, and new inks and papers employed.

The illustration shows a plate engraved for the Nashua Bank of New Hampshire about 1862. It is interesting for a number of reasons. The central vignette of a soldier and sailor reminds us the plate was created during the American Civil War. It is also evidence of Perkins's transference process. Initially, the scene was intended for a United States three-dollar bill, to be issued in 1862. However, when the government abandoned plans for the odd denomination, the printing company simply used the vignette on a plate for this private bank. The medallions at three of the four corners show the use of a geometric lathe.

Engraving. *New Hampshire, Nashua Bank, engraved copper plate for printing 100-dollar bills, c. 1862.*

Work so intricate only became possible with the invention of this machine. Finally, this plate is made from copper, unlike most of those then in use, and it features an engraving for a single bill. As it was common practice during the period to produce four or more engravings on a single steel plate, we may surmise that this hundred-dollar bill was to be a special limited issue.

The printing and engraving processes have advanced immeasurably since this plate was engraved, with notes in a variety of colors now being printed, and fancy guilloches and the security thread widely used. But for craftsmanship, this old plate, with its pleasing combination of ornate engraving and open spaces, yields nothing to its modern relatives.

See also BANK NOTE; BROKEN BANK NOTES; DIE; GUILLOCHE; HUB; IMPRESSION; LITHOGRAPHY; MEDALLION; PAPER MONEY; SECURITY THREAD; VIGNETTE; WATERMARK.

EPIGRAPHY The study and use of inscriptions, particularly their deciphering and interpretation.

The science has some employment in numismatics, where, along with a careful examination of types and styles, it can help to establish chronologies for undated coins, determine their place of issue, and otherwise supplement the obvious information they yield.

See also INSCRIPTION; LEGEND.

ERROR Any numismatic item with evidence of a mistake made during its manufacture.

While errors occur on tokens, medals, and decorations, we will follow the interest of collectors and concentrate on those that relate to coinage and paper money, and particularly the modern errors, produced by machinery. Progress led us to mechanical coining and printing processes; in turn they enlarged the possibility of error and multiplied the number of mistakes. There are two reasons for this. First, mechanical processes added to the number of steps needed to mint money, and more steps meant more stages during which something could go wrong. Second, since mechanization accelerated the production of money and increased its output, more errors were bound to occur.

It is worthwhile to briefly discuss these processes, and the errors which can take place in their course. Coins begin as a wide, thin, strip of metal, elaborated by being drawn between two rollers. Laminations, cracks and peelings may be caused if the metal in the strip is improperly alloyed or contains impurities. The strip may be too thin or too thick. If it is too thin, and it is cut into blanks, the coins struck from it will be overly thin and probably have weak designs. An overly thick coin, on the other hand, can easily jam the counting machines used to record production, and hence be kept from circulation. The thin coin can escape detection however, as can the laminated one, and both are mint errors.

Coin blanks or planchets are cut from the strip. They may become clipped because the strip is improperly positioned during the blanking operation. The clipped planchet is also an error, whether or not it is eventually struck into a coin. Furthermore, it is at this point, clipped or not, that the planchet can be mixed accidentally with finished coins, bagged, and sent into circulation.

But assuming the blank remains in the production process, it is next upset—compressed edgewise between two rollers to give it a slightly raised edge, which will protect it from wear. Should the planchet miss this operation, and continue in the coining process, it will be too big to fit in the collar of the coining machine. This will force it to expand outward as it is struck (it will not be restrained by the collar), and a broadstruck coin will emerge.

The planchet, its edge upset, is now ready to be made into a coin. At this point, there is a danger of a number of errors. These will be the product of the two major causes of malfunction: problems with the dies, and problems with the machinery. Let us first examine die problems. A die may, although it is unlikely, be badly hubbed, with doubling taking place. If so, it will mint coins with a doubled image. It may become cracked or chipped through

excessive use, carelessness, or incorrect steel used in its manufacture, in which case all its cracks and chips will appear on the coins it strikes, in relief. A piece of the die may be ready to fall out, or part of the collar may be about to break, creating any of several varieties of cuds once coinage begins.

Now let us consider the mechanical process. Expressed in the simplest terms, a planchet is placed on a lower die, within a collar. The upper and lower dies come together, then separate. The fresh coin is then pushed out of the collar by the lower die, brushed aside by mechanical means, and dropped into a container beside the press. If the mechanical layer-on fails, allowing the two dies to come directly together, clashed dies may result. Each side of the coins struck from such dies will show part of the designs on the other side. If the planchet is improperly centered, the collar will not completely surround it, and an off-center coin is minted. Or if the mechanical device meant to remove struck coins does not operate, a brockage and/or a cupped coin may be produced. Should a bit of foreign material be caught in the die, part of the die's designs will not be transferred to the coin. This is generally known as a filled die. Occasionally, something comes between the die and the planchet, and the latter will receive an impression of both the die and the foreign matter.

There are still more possibilities for errors. The coin could be struck more than once. It might rotate in the dies after receiving the first impression and be struck a second time from a different angle; or the ejecting mechanism might function imperfectly, allowing a previously struck coin to receive a partial second strike when it is halfway out of the collar. A coin can accept two or more blows, yet show doubling on only one side. In this case the die giving the double impression rotated between strikes while the other did not. The doubling effect can even occur in a single strike, caused either by a die that is itself already doubled, or by a movement of one

Error.
Early American coinage errors, as seen on the large cent.
Left: Blank planchet, 1840–1857.
Center: Double-struck Connecticut copper, 1787.
Right: Cent of 1802, struck with a pin embedded in the planchet.

die, usually the top one, during a single strike.

Finally, beyond all other potential traps in the coining process, there is the off-metal strike. In this instance, the planchet itself was intended for another denomination or issue (or even, as happens in very large mints, for another country's coin). Should it find its way into the wrong lot and be struck, a spectacular error may be created.

The photograph shows three early American errors. The first is a blank, upset planchet, meant for a large cent. Somehow it escaped the coining process and was put into circulation. The middle coin, a Connecticut copper of 1787, was struck once in a screw press, then only partially ejected, and struck again. Notice the two clips: the coin was an error even in the planchet stage. The third coin is another United States cent, and was struck with a small nail or pin embedded in the planchet.

Paper money errors can be dealt with more briefly. Engraved plates for each of the note's sides are inked and readied for use. These plates are large, and commonly contain sixteen or thirty-two engravings of the notes. One plate is needed for the obverse, a second for the reverse. Yet a third device can be used to print serial numbers, seals, and signatures on the bills. Paper is printed wet or dry, first on one side, then on the other, or, in very modern establishments, simultaneously. The impression of

the third device is added, and the sheets are left to dry, cut into individual notes, then released to circulation.

Many errors can be made in the process. Inadequate inking may cause bills to reveal only a partial design. Or, one side may be totally without print, as are the bills with obverses but no reverses now seen in the United States. These are a good example of the mixed blessing of automated printing which, while speeding up production, increases the chance of error. Bills can also be printed off-center. They may contain gutter folds, or more spectacular mistakes of the same type. Their inks may smudge, or a design meant for one side of the note be transferred, in reverse, to its other side. Then, too, a scrap of paper can perhaps fall on the sheet and be printed along with it; should the scrap fall off later, there will be a blank space in the design. As bills are almost always printed in the same direction, an inverted error is possible if a sheet is fed to the press upside down.

Inversion can also take place in the final stage, making signatures and serial numbers appear upside down. Further, the signature and number stamp can be applied off-center, or a malfunction of the mechanical numbering device can result in mismatched serial numbers.

Even if the printed sheet escapes these pitfalls, it is not out of jeopardy. The machine that cuts it into individual notes may be incorrectly employed, causing prized errors. But by far the most sought after of all errors is the double denomination bill —a bill printed on one side, moved by mistake to a pile of half-finished notes awaiting an impression from a plate of another denomination, and then printed on its blank side. Hence, the fifteen-dollar bill, with its obverse for five dollars and its reverse for ten dollars—the coveted trophy in the popular game of collecting money errors.

See also BROADSTRUCK; BROCKAGE; CLASHED DIES; CLIPPED PLANCHET; COLLAR; CRACKED DIES; CUD; CUPPED COIN; DIE BREAK; DIE CHIP; DOUBLE-STRUCK COIN; FILLED DIES; FREAK; GHOSTING; GUTTER FOLD; HUB; LAMINATION; MISALIGNED DIES; MISMATCHED SERIAL NUMBERS; MISPRINT; MISSTRIKE; OFF-CENTER; OFF-METAL; PLANCHET; RAILROAD RIM; ROTATED DIES; TRANSFER PRINTING; UPSET EDGE.

ESSAY NOTE   A trial print made to test a new design, to examine the results of a new printing or manufacturing concept, or otherwise review the features of a note before it is officially authorized (the metallic equivalent of an essay note is a trial strike).

The term "essay note" is *not* synonymous with "specimen note." The latter is a complete example of an approved note, usually made for purposes of identification by the world's major central banks.

The illustration shows a rare, nineteenth-century essay note. Printed in New York by the American Bank Note Company, it was conceived as a trial for a new peso issue by the Banco Nacional de Chile. Charged with testing this part of the design, the printer inked his plate with black and printed on ordinary thin white paper. Once he saw the results were satisfactory, he punch-cancelled the essay. As there is neither a signature nor a date, the age of the piece is uncertain: 1865 would be reasonable, however, for the bank was organized in that year, and issued this kind of note between 1866 and 1877.

See also SPECIMEN NOTE; TRIAL STRIKE.

EVASION   A close copy of a coin with just enough deviation in design and/or legend to avoid violating counterfeit laws.

The best-known evasions appeared in the eighteenth-century British Isles. By a statute of 1742 the manufacturing of counterfeit copper carried a maximum sentence of two years' imprisonment, reflecting the influx of underweight copper halfpennies and farthings. Yet, a few years later the counterfeiters had plotted a way to get their wares into circulation and not risk jail. They would strike "coins" with designs or legends slightly dissimilar to those of the originals; should they be arrested, they could then prove their products were distinct and not counterfeits. Furthermore, people were hungry for small change, and since they were largely illiterate, altering the legends would mean little.

In 1771, Parliament enacted a law that elevated the counterfeiting of copper coin-

Essay note. Chile, Banco Nacional, cancelled 1-peso essay, probably 1865.

age from a misdemeanor to a felony. And as merchants had bought and sold the fake coppers at a discount, enabling the counterfeits to enter circulation easily, this too was made a felony. But the new law failed to include evasions, and quantities of them, all dated 1771, quickly appeared, and continued to do so through the late 1790s.

The piece in the illustration is one such evasion. It weighs 6.3 grams, and contains about two-thirds as much copper as a genuine halfpenny. The designs and inscriptions are the points of greatest interest. The obverse bears a portrait roughly corresponding to that of the king, George III (ruled 1760–1820), while the reverse features a seated figure that seems more or less correct in its execution. But consider the legends. On the obverse, there is GREGORY III. PON. instead of GEORGIVS. III. REX., and on the reverse, BRITAIN RULES rather than BRITANNIA. The counterfeiter was obviously attempting to fashion legends which looked like the originals to the unschooled eye. It should also be noted that this evasion was struck with shallow dies, to make it seem a worn but genuine coin, a favorite counterfeiters' trick at the time, but one that can be detected by the mint luster on this "worn" piece!

Some of these evasions, created by the thousands at clandestine mints in England and Ireland, found their way to America and were part of the Bungtown series.

See also BUNGTOWN; DIE-STRUCK COUNTERFEIT.

Exergue. Italy, 20 lire, 1936 (detail).

EXERGUE

EXERGUE A term designating the lower part of a coin's design, when it is separated from the rest of the design by a horizontal line.

Most often, the exergue is characteristic of the reverse, a fact we owe in part to the ancient Greeks and Romans, who frequently chose standing or seated figures for reverse designs. They set the figures off from the rest of the coin by putting a straight line where they sat or stood. Often they used this portion of the coin for a brief inscription, stating the issuing authority, mint, etc.

The exergue is still used this way, as can be seen in the illustration of a detail of a 1936 Italian twenty-lire silver coin. The designer's name, the value (L. 20), the national arms (the shield of Savoy, flanked by the fasces of Mussolini's government), and a letter "R" (for Rome, the place of mintage), could all have gone elsewhere, but Mussolini's government opted for the exergue, perhaps to emulate Roman usage.

See also MINT MARK.

Evasion. England, counterfeit halfpenny of the evasive type, dated 1771.

EXONUMIA Objects which resemble money, but are not designed to circulate as money.

The term was invented by numismatists to describe a large number of disparate items with only one point in common; they looked like money but were not. Thus exonumia embraces, among other things, wooden nickels, contorniates, some amu-

Exonumia.

Top: Ohio and Missouri sales tax receipts, c. 1935.
Bottom: Advertising handbill made to resemble a
United States note, 1869.

must meet three basic criteria: appearance, function, and intent.

The illustration shows three typical pieces of exonumia, all from the United States. Two, sales tax receipts from the states of Ohio and Missouri dating from around 1935, are of a "public" nature, and were issued by a duly constituted authority. They were never intended as money, but as indicators that money had been paid. Their vague resemblance to money qualifies them as exonumia.

The third piece which looks "official" until you begin to read it, is actually an 1869 advertising handbill extolling the virtues of a hair dye. It is a form of exonumia seldom produced today in the United States, as the government takes a dim view of printing anything with a likeness to its paper currency. Indeed, a man was recently prosecuted for marketing a bath towel with a reproduction of an American note on it, surely one of the largest (and least favorably received) items of exonumia on record.

lets, coin weights, and love tokens. On the other hand, it does *not* include counters, jetons, or spielmarken, which resemble money and, to a limited degree, actually function as such. Nor does exonumia cover medals. No reason is given for the exclusion; tradition simply prohibits it. For objects to qualify as exonumia, they

See also AMULET; COIN WEIGHTS; COMMUNION TOKEN; CONTORNIATE; ELONGATED COINAGE; LOVE TOKEN; WOODEN NICKELS.

F

FABRIC A piece's weight, workmanship, style, module—all those things which characterize it—a term more often employed for ancient and medieval coins and medals than modern ones; seldom used to describe tokens, and never applied to paper money.

The fabric of a piece is one of the things to consider when it is suspected of being a counterfeit or forgery. The visual and tactile impressions we gain from a coin's fabric can be our most important tools. Does it look and feel like other specimens? If not, can we adequately explain the variation? If we cannot, and the fabric is simply too different, the coin may very well be bad. Every numismatic dealer has tales of a colleague who can spot a forgery from several feet away. This is an exaggeration, of course, but it pays homage to the importance of fabric in counterfeit and forgery detection.

See also COUNTERFEIT AND FORGERY DETECTION.

FALS A popular Islamic copper coin, introduced around A.D. 700, and intended as part of a reform in which Islamic money would be struck in strict accordance with the Koran.

The fals was a logical outgrowth of previous Islamic experience. The name derives from "follis," a popular Byzantine copper coin which had long served as one of the basic denominations in the Byzantine Empire. When the Arabs seized great parts of the empire in the 630s and 640s, they struck imitations of the follis and changed its name to "fals." Lacking a design tradition of their own, the Arab conquerors employed designs very similar to those on Byzantine coins.

Arab-Byzantine fals were minted until about 700, when their appearance was changed. The new coin emphasized religious inscriptions (particularly the *Kalima*, or declaration of faith), and legends denoting the place and date of the coin's manufacture. Imagery, however, was generally eschewed, in accordance with Islamic doctrine.

The exact date this reformed fals appeared is unclear. It seems to have been introduced a few years after the dinar and dirhem, and the earliest specimens bear no dates. The piece illustrated is one of the first to do so: it was struck in A.H. 87

Fals. Syria, A.H. 87 (A.D. 705–706).

(A.D. 705–706), and is a typical fals, measuring 23 millimeters in diameter, with a weight slightly under 3.5 grams.

The fals was struck by various Islamic states over a period of several centuries; in general, the religious strictures of Islam were respected, and the coin did not bear images. Its final appearance was in nineteenth-century Morocco, where, renamed a "falus," it was *cast,* not struck, down to A.H. 1289 (A.D. 1872–1873).

See also ARAB-BYZANTINE COINAGE; DINAR; DIRHEM; FOLLIS.

FANTASY An imaginary coin or other numismatic item, with the general appearance of a real piece, but not issued by official authorities.

The term is largely restricted to coinage, although sometimes it is applicable in the area of decorations: self-styled potentates have occasionally awarded membership in nonexistent chivalric orders to friends and supporters. One such individual was Jacques Lebaudy, who proclaimed himself Emperor of the Sahara about the beginning of this century, then founded the Order of the Sahara. Lebaudy's "empire" came to an inglorious end, and he himself was murdered in 1919, but a few of his awards remain.

The fantasy coin is more common than the fantasy decoration, and several types are covered by the term. In America, fantasies of rare coins include the "restrikes" of the 1804 cent and 1811 half cent, privately minted from genuine but discarded United States dies. Fantasies of nonexis-

tent coins within a series are typified by the famous "1804 dollar." No dollars with that date were minted in 1804. However, eight were struck with that date about 1835 for presentation purposes, and in 1858 another seven were minted for sale to collectors. In this case we find an official authority (the United States government) looking the other way while some of its employees produced fantasies for private gain.

Another variety of fantasy purports to come from a nonexistent country, such as "Auracania-Patagonia," for which an eccentric Frenchmen struck pesos in his name (as king of the region, of course), in 1874. Or a fantasy may proclaim it is from a "real" country, coined in the name of a "real" ruler. The fantasy illustrated falls into this category.

It is a silver four-peseta piece, supposedly minted for Isabella II, who ruled Spain from 1833 to 1868. However, it was struck in 1894, nearly thirty years after she was driven from her throne. Furthermore, it displays a bust of the queen that never appeared on genuine coins; the reverse adapts a design which had been used before, but only on copper coins. Finally, it was not struck in Spain, but in London under the supervision of one Reginald Huth, and minted by the noted medalists of the period, Pinches & Co.

Why should various Britons have labored to produce a "Spanish" coin? Because there were enough coin collectors in late nineteenth-century England to make

Fantasy. A 4-peseta piece, purportedly struck on behalf of Queen Isabella II of Spain in 1894. Her reign ended in 1868.

the venture worthwhile. Huth and his friends also struck fantasies relating to the deposed queen of Hawaii, Liliuokalani, which sold briskly in the United States. On the whole, fantasies have been designed to appeal to the collector. Although the fantasy has virtually disappeared in this century, its place has been filled in part by Noncirculating legal tender coins.

See also COUNTERFEIT; NONCIRCULATING LEGAL TENDER; RESTRIKE.

FEDERAL RESERVE NOTE The only type of paper money now issued for use in the United States, with the exception of the one hundred dollar denomination, for which a few legal tender notes are still issued.

The Federal Reserve note dates from the early twentieth century, when Progressives actively struggled for reform of society's social, political and economic evils. One evil they attacked with particular vehemence was the "trust," or monopoly. In 1913 a Congressional investigating committee exposed a "money trust," in which a small number of people exercised control over the American banking system. Recognizing the threat to the economy of such practices, the Federal Reserve Act was passed in 1913. It was directed to the reform and partial decentralization of the banking system while keeping most of its operation in private hands. The nation was divided into twelve Federal Reserve districts, each with the power to issue currency. National banks in each district were required to join the system, purchasing stock of the Reserve Bank of their district and depositing their reserves therein. These reserves would form the basis for the issuance of paper money—Federal Reserve notes.

At first glance, this seems to be a minor reform. It was, in fact, a watershed in American history. For the first time in the Republic's financial career, there existed a national bank of issue and discount, similar to the national banks established in Europe at an earlier time. Ironically, the Federal Reserve Act would go far toward centralizing the American banking system, by injecting into it a new, potentially dynamic element—the federal government. Gradually it was recognized that through a Federal Reserve system the government could exert some control on the nature of the country's monetary establishment. In periods of deflation, interest rates could be lowered and the money supply increased; in times of inflation, opposite measures could be applied—a valuable tool to maintain the economy on an even keel.

Yet all of this lay years ahead. The Federal Reserve system began operation on November 16, 1914. As the issuing of paper money was one of its primary responsibilities, the first Federal Reserve notes, printed in denominations of five dollars to one hundred dollars, were released almost immediately, and belong to the series of 1914. Higher denomination notes were added later. In passing, it should be mentioned that the date on a bill is not necessarily its date of issue. It actually refers to the date a particular bill

Federal Reserve note. United States, dollar, series of 1977.

with a particular design was authorized. You may see a small letter (A, B, etc.) after the date: this indicates a change in Treasury personnel. The Federal Reserve note in the illustration bears the inscription SERIES 1977. While it could have been issued that year, it could also have been printed in 1978 or 1979. In the latter year, the United States Treasury personnel changed, and the new notes carried the inscription SERIES 1977A.

In keeping with other United States currency, Federal Reserve notes were printed on a large module until 1929, when President Hoover reduced the size of American currency.

That year also saw the stock market collapse, and the onset of the Great Depression, when the United States banking system entered another period of crisis. By 1933, it was completely paralyzed, and its restructure was the first order of business for Hoover's enegetic successor, Franklin Delano Roosevelt. But as the United States currency system was reorganized, older types of paper passed from the scene and the Federal Reserve note, a more flexible form of currency, became the dominant form of paper money. The national bank note was the first to disappear, a casualty of the banking woes of the early 1930s. Production of the silver certificate ceased in the 1960s, and essentially the legal tender note went the way of the others. Today Federal Reserve notes are in universal use and likely to remain so in the future.

See also LEGAL TENDER NOTE; NATIONAL BANK NOTE; SILVER CERTIFICATE.

FIAT MONEY   Paper currency that is not convertible into coin or specie of an equivalent face value.

In former times, fiat money was apt to indicate an emergency situation or a strong-man rule, which explains a term frequently used in relation to fiat money —"forced circulation." The phrase is a polite way of saying that if people do not accept the fiat money of an authority, the authority will make them wish they had done so. The Mexican Revolution of the 1910–1920 period produced many examples of this form of currency. Political and military groups contended for power; towns, cities, and regions changed hands almost daily; and each group of revolutionaries favored its own paper money. The bewildered inhabitants watched the form of their money change from day to day. Most of it was paper, and almost none of it was backed by or redeemable in specie. As a result, it was circulated by force. Indeed, there are recorded cases of people being shot for their refusal to accept fiat money.

The piece illustrated is a good example of money put into circulation by force; it was issued by a group calling itself the *División de Occidente* of the *Ejército Constitucionalista* (Western Division, Constitutionalist Army). This faction recognized Venustiano Carranza as Mexico's president. Carranza did eventually gain control of the entire country, but at the time of the note's issue he was only one of several contending leaders; his money had nothing to recommend it over anyone else's, and his bills and those of his subordinates had to be

Fiat money. Mexico, Ejército Constitucionalista, División de Occidente, 5 pesos, 1915.

put into circulation by force. The note you see said as much. Beyond a rather crude design, it carries the inscription ESTE BILLETE CIRCULARÁ FORZOSAMENTE DE ACUERDO CON EL DECRETO DE 20 DE ENERO DE 1915 ("This bill will circulate by force, in accordance with the decree of January 20, 1915"). The decree in question merely stated that bills would circulate by force. They were exchangeable for other Carranza notes, which, as it happened, also circulated by force.

Fiat money of this and other varieties will circulate, of course—any money is better than none, and few people have the temerity to defy a government—but it is unlikely to do so at full value. Specie is always preferable to paper money, and fiat money is ever plagued by depreciation and inflation.

Fiat money is not a thing of the past. Most current paper money is also irredeemable in specie, and in this sense it, too, is fiat money, however respectable the issuing authority may be. This is one of the major reasons for this century's persistent inflation.

See also EMERGENCY MONEY; INFLATION.

FIELD The blank space on either side of a coin, token, or medal not occupied by types, legends, inscriptions, etc.

The field is ordinarily smooth, and usually represents the highest point on the die and the lowest point on any piece struck with that die. Numismatic terminology often speaks of things such as mint or *officina* marks appearing "in field" or "in the field," indicating such marks are freestanding, and set apart from the design.

See also EXERGUE.

FILING The former practice of removing precious metal from a coin's edge by means of abrasion.

Like clipping, filing was a persistent problem during the era of hammered or hand-struck coinage; normal coins varied so widely in their diameters that a good deal of metal could be removed before a coin became demonstrably short-weight. A solution to the problem would have to wait for the invention of coining machinery.

This took place in several stages between 1500 and 1700. First, a mechanical blanking device was contrived, enabling all coins of a particular denomination to begin the same size. The real difficulty was in the coin's edge. A number of inventions appeared in the sixteenth and seventeenth centuries, each capable of imparting a design or inscription to the coin's edge. These devices (described under Collar and Edge-marking machinery) dramatically reduced the incidence of filing, as very little metal could be removed before part of the edge design was lost.

It is now safe to say that filing and clipping are of the past. Aside from the technological advances, coins are no longer produced in metals of enough intrinsic value to make filing and clipping profitable.

See also CLIPPING; COLLAR; EDGE-MARKING MACHINERY; MACHINE-STRUCK COINAGE; SWEATING.

FILLED DIES Dies which have become clogged with grease or other foreign matter in parts of their designs, leaving weak or absent impressions on the coins they strike.

In United States coinage, the 1922 "plain" cent is a filled-die coin. Cents were minted only in Denver that year, and the mint used a small D as a mark, placed directly below the date on the obverse. This mint mark is faint or altogether absent on a few 1922 cents, however, indicating that something was stuck in the tiny crevices that made up the D.

The term filled dies is also used to describe coins with similar anomalies produced by different processes. For

Filled dies. United States, 5 cents, 1937 D.

example, so-called "filled letters"—such as solid O's—are usually a consequence of chipped dies, not filled ones. This part of the die is weak, and may simply break away. A blob of metal will then enter the space formerly occupied by that part of the die, resulting in a filled letter. This is not a filled die but its opposite. Nevertheless, collectors persistently use the term for the phenomenon.

The illustration shows a second type of filled die, the famous "Three-Legged Buffalo Nickel" of 1937. Once it was generally assumed that a bit of grease had pervaded the depression representing the buffalo's fourth leg, which was absent on coins struck with that particular die. But research determined that what was thought to be a filled die was actually a clashed one. Someone allowed the coin press with this reverse die to remain in operation without a planchet between it and the obverse die, and a clash took place.

The die was quickly scrubbed with emery powder glued to the end of a stick, while it was still in the press. The press was then switched on, and coining continued. The maimed buffalo seen on this coin was the outcome.

Collectors are wise to examine any "Three-Legged Buffalo Nickel" with extreme care, as a number of ingenious fakes have been produced over the years. On genuine pieces, the motto E PLURIBUS UNUM is small and weak, for the entire die was scrubbed. In addition, faint traces of the fourth leg may be seen at the top and bottom. Finally, the coin's obverse, which

is not seen here, has severe pitting at the back of the Indian's neck.

See also CLASHED DIES; DIE CHIP; ERROR.

FILLER An inferior specimen of a coin or note, retained in a collection until a more pleasing specimen is located.

If they are coins, fillers are usually well-worn and may be holed; if they are notes, they are apt to be dirty or torn. Fillers constitute an important part of any collection, large or small, in keeping with the notion that even a bad piece is better than none at all.

See also CULL.

FINENESS The percentage of precious metal contained in a coin.

Fineness can be expressed in several ways. For example, a United States twenty-dollar gold piece may be said to be "900 fine," "90 percent fine," ".900 fine," or "composed of 90 percent gold." It is understood that the remaining percentage is a base metal.

While collectors and scholars speak of a coin's fineness, this information is rarely seen on the coin. We know of the purity of ancient coins from chance literary sources, and we have access to official coining laws for modern pieces. But the coins themselves are usually silent, with one notable exception—Latin America, where governments of the nineteenth and twentieth centuries frequently added references to fineness to their coins. Their domestic audience was accustomed to the metallically excellent issues of the Spanish Empire, and many Latin American coins circulated widely in the Far East, where merchants had to be certain the new coins were as good as the old. Hence the fineness was spelled out for all to see.

During the early and middle nineteenth century, standards were carried over unchanged from the Spanish Empire to its successor states. On the Piece of

Fineness. *Mexico, peso, 1947.*

is fading from the lexicon. Numismatists now tend to refer to these coins by their proper names, if they are known. If not, the notation Æ, followed by a two-digit number indicating the coin's diameter in millimeters, is preferred.

See also Æ; FOLLIS; SESTERTIUS.

Eight, for instance, we frequently find the abbreviated legend 10 D: 20 G:—indicating a silver fineness of 90.27 percent. As countries shifted to decimal coinage, they adopted decimal fineness as well—90 percent in most cases, 80 percent in a few, and 50 percent in still others.

The coin illustrated shows the citation of fineness on a modern Latin American coin. This 1947 Mexican peso has an inscription with the coin's total weight (14 Gr.—14 grams) and its silver fineness (0.500—50 percent). The rest of the coin is base metal, added to increase the piece's wearing powers, and also to "stretch" the silver, and thereby mint a larger coin. The decline in the Mexican peso's value, fanned by the inflation of World War II, had made it necessary to reduce the coin's intrinsic value. In Latin America, as everywhere else, gold and silver have disappeared from circulation. Today, except for a few high-value commemoratives, the reference to fineness on Latin American coins has been abandoned.

See also ABBREVIATION; ALLOY; DECIMAL COINAGE; PESO; PIECE OF EIGHT; TRADE COINS.

FIRST BRONZE A generic term for the largest and heaviest bronze, copper, or brass coin in an ancient series.

It is interchangeable with the term Æ 1, and is most frequently employed for the brass sestertius. The term is used far less often for other ancient coins, and indeed

FIRST STRIKE A coin minted from clean new dies, either for presentation or as the first piece in a normal minting run.

Such coins tend to have very shiny, mirror-like fields, while their types often look somewhat dull and "frosty." In all of this, a first strike may closely resemble a proof or specimen coin, and its appearance is often described as "proof-like."

As the die producing the first strike is used to mint more coins, its fields become less perfectly flat and shiny. The devices lose their frosted appearance as the minute pits and striations contributing to that effect wear down after the first few impressions. The die becomes an ordinary one and, while it may be good for thousands of additional coins, all of them will be normal "business strikes," without the proof-like characteristics of the first strike. The latter is special, then, either as a piece made for presentation or as an example of the highest degree of perfection attainable by a coin intended for circulation. Hence, first strikes command sizable premiums among collectors.

See also GRADING SYSTEMS; PRESENTATION PIECE; PROOF; PROOF-LIKE.

FLEUR DE COIN A French term meaning mint condition or uncirculated.

It is sometimes abbreviated FDC, and is the equivalent of the Italian *fior de conio,* the German *stempelganz,* and the Spanish *flor de cuño.*

See also GRADING SYSTEMS.

Fleur-de-lis. Two Sicilies, 10 tornesi, 1859.

FLEUR-DE-LIS A persistent medieval and modern heraldic device representing a stylized iris flower.

It is purported to have been in use as early as the sixth-century Byzantine Empire, and appeared on thirteenth-century French coinage as a symbol of the ruling line—and later of France itself. While we are apt to think of fleurs-de-lis as essentially French—the term itself is French and means "flower of a lily"—the Florentines actually used it as the obverse type on their florins before its advent in France.

Fleurs-de-lis can be seen on many English coins from the middle of the fourteenth century until the end of the eighteenth, a legacy of the Hundred Years' War, during which the kings of England claimed the crown of France. The device has also played its part on Spanish coinage from the early eighteenth century to the present, for the ruling house in that country is a junior branch of the Bourbon dynasty of France, which used fleurs-de-lis as its badge. The piece illustrated shows its employment in yet another country, the Two Sicilies, today part of Italy. Its prominence on this ten-tornesi coin indicates the kings of the Two Sicilies also traced their ancestry to the French ruling house.

During the late eighteenth and early nineteenth centuries, it was a source of some controversy in France. The French Revolution removed it from coinage as a hated reminder of the monarchy, but with the Restoration of 1814–1815, it reappeared, to vanish once and for all with the revolution of 1830.

See also FLORIN.

FLORIN An important gold coin of the later Middle Ages, introduced by the city of Florence in 1252.

The florin's development in Florence reflects the city's economic importance: with Genoa, it was the chief exporter of European products at the time. Both cities received gold as payment for goods, and each had the gold reserves necessary to mint gold coins, as well as the economic strength to make such coins desirable for internal and external use. The florin was introduced in the early 1250s, and its Genoese equivalent, the genovino, at about the same time.

The florin weighed a bit over 3.5 grams when it was introduced, and was made of pure gold. It retained these specifications for many years, as it had to, to be a successful trade coin. Like other medieval coins, it was relatively small (20 millimeters) and thin. The obverse bore a fleur-de-lis and a legend with the name of the town—FLORENTIA. The reverse featured a standing figure of St. John the

Florin.
Top: Florence, gold florin, 1256.
Bottom: United Kingdom, silver florin, 1849.

Baptist, patron of Florence, who was identified in the reverse legend. These designs and legends were to remain essentially the same for the next three centuries. Within the series, coins can be dated to a certain degree by mintmasters' marks and other minor details, but there are still chronological gaps that may never be bridged. Even though florins were struck well into the sixteenth century, they never bore dates in the orthodox sense.

At the time of the florin's introduction, Western coins were not dated—with the lonely exception of a small Danish issue in the 1230s—but by the end of the period, many coins did carry dates. Why not the florin? And why go to the trouble of putting privy or mintmasters' marks on an undated coin? We can advance two possibilities. First, the florin was primarily meant as a trade coin. Were it to be successful as such, it would be wise to change it as little as possible: the people using it might grow suspicious if its designs, legends, or the way in which they were rendered underwent a sudden change. Second, standards of purity and weight had to be maintained. Small identifying marks would help to do this, for a lightweight coin could then be traced to the person responsible for it. So the Florentines employed these marks as a way to conduct an internal bookkeeping and ensure everyone's honesty. Fortunately, we are finding enough written sources to occasionally enable us to attach a particular symbol to a particular minter—and thus arrive at a date.

The florin was extensively copied throughout Europe. The English minted it for use in France in the fourteenth century, while the French themselves produced it about the same period. Spreading into central Europe, florins were minted in Hungary and several German states. Early copies of the Florentine coin were usually fairly faithful reproductions, while later ones substituted a new, locally significant obverse for the fleur-de-lis.

By the early sixteenth century the Flor-

entine coin had vanished, but it lent its name to several later coins. The Austrians produced silver florins from the 1850s to the 1890s, while the English inaugurated a coin of the same name in 1849. This latter piece, shown here, deserves attention as an early attempt to decimalize the archaic English monetary system.

This florin was valued at one-tenth of a pound, or two shillings. It was the culmination of several years' discussion of the British system, which was based on twelve pence to the shilling, and twenty shillings to the pound, making it difficult to understand and use in trade. Other countries were undertaking decimalization at the time, and English reformers did not wish to be left behind. But the florin was the only concrete result. In 1971 the United Kingdom adopted a complete decimal system and the florin was retariffed at ten new pence, one-tenth of a pound, just what it had represented more than a century earlier.

See also DATING SYSTEMS; DECIMAL COINAGE; FLEUR-DE-LIS; GENOVINO; IMITATION; MARK (MINTMASTER'S OR ASSAYER'S); TRADE COINS.

FOLLIS A name given to two ancient copper coins, one minted during the late Roman Empire, the other in the early and middle years of the Byzantine state.

The Roman version of the coin was introduced as part of the general coinage reforms of the emperor Diocletian (ruled A.D. 284–305) and his co-emperor Maximian (ruled A.D. 286–305). Diocletian took command of an empire which was virtually in ruins. Civil war was endemic; foreign invasion and occupation were uncomfortably close to being a reality. The monetary system was a shambles. Diocletian, realizing the Roman domains were too vast for one man to rule, invited Maximian to share power. Although his reforms touched many areas of Roman life, of primary interest here are his monetary policies, for they altered the types and nature of Roman coinage.

These changes seem to have been proclaimed in 294. The standard for the gold aureus was retained at sixty to the Roman pound, each coin weighing 5.3 grams. A new silver coin, the argenteus or siliqua (the actual name is unclear), appeared in the mid-290s; it weighed about 3.2 grams, and was in a sense a revival of the old denarius. Finally, a new copper coin was introduced about the same time. This was the follis. It weighed 10 grams, measured 29 millimeters in diameter, and contained a minute amount of silver (generally between 1.5 and 4.0 percent), found as a surface plating and as a trace element in the copper itself. The presence of silver has led some numismatists to refer to the coin as a billon issue rather than a copper one, which is perhaps unnecessarily precise.

The follis marked a radical new direction in Roman coinage. Earlier issues had a general uniformity of obverse types and a broad variety of reverses. The folles of Diocletian followed a strict standardization of both obverse and reverse. So the early folles, minted in numerous facilities separated by hundreds of miles, were made to a common mold. The emperor's head appeared in profile on the obverse, rendered in the stiff, unnatural style of the period. The reverse bore a standing figure, with the legend GENIO POPVLI ROMANI ("the Guardian Spirit of the Roman People"). The coin illustrated, dating from around 300, is of this type.

The career of the Roman follis was not an especially happy one. While Diocletian had intended it and the other members of his reformed monetary system to halt the third century's terrible inflation, this did not happen. Prices rose, and in 301 the emperor made a famous attempt to standardize another aspect of Roman life with his Edict on Maximum Prices setting standard prices for every purchasable item in the empire. He also seems to have doubled the value of his copper and silver coins in relation to gold ones. This may explain a new reverse type for the follis, a statue of Moneta, the personification of money, with the legend SACRA MONETA (or variants thereof), indicating the inviolable nature of the new valuation. However, Diocletian's Edict on Maximum Prices failed. So did his revalued follis.

Diocletian stepped down from the throne in 305, and persuaded his colleague to do the same. The emperors' two junior partners became co-emperors, and the artificial system of imperial succession which Diocletian had initiated was given its first test. It too failed. Civil war erupted, and lasted for much of the next twenty years, putting the reformed monetary system under considerable stress. It proved too severe for the follis, which began to fall in weight as early as 306. During 307 it fell to some 8 grams, and subsequently to 6.5. By 313 its average weight was just over 4 grams; by 320 it was less than 3.5. As the coin's weight declined, the inventory of its types grew, largely the result of the period's political chaos.

The Roman follis disappeared about the year 320, to be replaced by a slightly lighter coin, the centenionalis. This coin weighed 3 grams, and purportedly contained more silver than the follis. As the fourth century wore on, the Romans occasionally struck larger copper coins, which may or may not have been meant as revivals of the follis; perhaps it is wiser to refer to them as Æ 1. Henceforth, when we speak of the follis, we refer to a Byzantine coin rather than a Roman one.

The emperor Anastasius (ruled A.D. 491–518) was responsible for the reintroduction of the follis in the East. In his time the lowest-value precious metal coin was the tremissis and the highest-value non-precious metal circulating coin was the nummus. The nummus, however, was of so little value that it took several thousand of them to equal one tremissis. Rome's local authorities revived the follis around 475, and gave it a value of forty nummi. This concept was officially put into practice with the Byzantine coinage

Follis.
Top: Roman Empire, Diocletian, c. A.D. 300.
Bottom: Byzantine Empire, Justinian I, A.D. 538–539.

reform of 498, and the follis was reborn as a forty-nummi piece.

The revived coin was first struck with an approximate diameter of 24 millimeters, and a weight of 8.5 grams. It showed a profile portrait of the emperor on the obverse and a large M (the Greek figure for forty), flanked by stars, on the reverse. The M was surmounted by a cross, while the exergue gave the name of the mint in an abbreviated form. Within a few years of its advent the weight of the follis was doubled, and its diameter wavered between 32 and 40 millimeters. The basic design elements, however, went unchanged until well into the sixth century, at which time the emperor Justinian I (ruled 527–565) added two new and very important elements. First, in keeping with the trend to full-face portraiture, the follis's obverse was altered (in 538) to reveal the emperor in this now fashionable pose. We may dispute the results, but evidently the Byzantines found it pleasing, for they used full-face portraiture on the follis as long as they minted it.

Justinian's second change was the dating of his folles. The system was limited, merely giving the year of the reign in which a coin was struck, but it is still useful to scholars. In part because Byzantine portraiture was so wretched, it is seldom easy to distinguish one emperor's portrait from another. The Byzantine follis seen here is from Justinian I's reign, and illustrates the use of his dating system. The piece also represents the maximum size and weight achieved by Byzantine folles—about 42 millimeters in diameter and nearly 25 grams in weight.

The follis grew smaller from the mid-sixth century on. At first, major design elements (the full-face portrait, the large M) were retained even as the coin shrank, but the M eventually disappeared from the reverse, as it was no longer needed. It had been put there originally to indicate a value of forty nummi—as against other coins with other letters (K for twenty nummi, I for ten, E for five)—but as inflation reduced the size of the follis, it also removed the subsidiary coins from circulation. By the reign of Theophilus (829–842), the forty-nummi piece was the only copper coin in circulation, and there was no need to identify it with a special mark.

For the final stage in the evolution of the follis, which took place in the tenth and eleventh centuries, see the listing Anonymous Bronze.

See also ANONYMOUS BRONZE; CENTENIONALIS; DATING SYSTEMS; INFLATION; MINT MARK; MONETA; NUMMUS; *OFFICINA* MARK; PORTRAIT; SILIQUA.

FORGERY An unauthorized copy of a genuine numismatic item, made for sale to collectors at a price based on its presumed rarity.

A counterfeit is a copy of a coin or note in current circulation. It is intended as a straightforward substitute for money. Counterfeits, to be profitable, must be of lower intrinsic value than the money they are intended to replace. In forgery, on the other hand, the intrinsic worth of a product is relatively unimportant. Forgers largely confine their operations to rare coins, which are always worth more than the intrinsic value of their metal. A forger can make considerably more from the sale of a single coin than a counterfeiter can from passing a great number of bad notes.

The methods of forgery have altered through the years. In the beginning, when there were few collectors, and entire series of coins were obscure and unknown, the forger, one might suppose, lived in a golden age. Before the invention of photography and the mass circulation of books, few collectors had seen enough of any particular coinage to differentiate the real from the forged. But with all this on the credit side (from the forger's standpoint) his ledger also had a debit column. The small number of collectors meant a limited market and low prices for his wares.

Today the forger enjoys some signal advantages over his earlier counterpart. Collectors number in the millions, and many look to numismatics as a way to evade inflation. On the other hand, they have resource tools undreamed of in previous years. Books, authentication agencies, college courses in numismatics, coin clubs, all abound. It behooves the forger to create a better product than ever.

In the days of Carl Wilhelm Becker, the famed German forger of the late eighteenth and early nineteenth century, it was merely necessary to cut a die in the general form of the original. A real coin could be used as a model, and minute differences could be ascribed to the whim of the ancient die-cutter. But today's collector, educated by books, catalogs, and color slides, is likely to know what a genuine coin should look like, and less apt to accept a deviation.

When the days of hand-cut dies for forgery production came to an end, real coins served as the bases for forged ones. At first casting methods were used; later, coins were the actual bases for creating

Forgery.
Top: Prussia, 3 mark, 1914 (genuine).
Bottom: A forgery of this coin.

dies. A process was discovered making it possible to make a coin harder than a piece of steel for a microsecond—time enough for the steel to take the coin's impression and become a die. With this improved procedure, called explosive impact copying, the forged coin has come of age.

The illustrated coins graphically underscore the excellence of modern forgery. The top photograph shows the obverse and reverse of a genuine Prussian three-mark silver coin of 1914. In the bottom photograph a forgery of the same coin is seen. Except for a *very* slight weakening of detail, so faint it does not show in the photograph, there is essentially no way to determine which coin is which. Forgeries such as these have made coin collecting dangerous as well as profitable, and the reader is strongly advised to submit any extremely expensive coin for authentication before purchasing it. If the dealer from whom you contemplate buying a piece refuses to have it authenticated, find another dealer.

One word of comfort: forgers tend to concentrate on particular areas of coinage.

At the time of writing, they seem to be exerting their main efforts on low-mintage, nineteenth- and twentieth-century gold coinage. There also seems to be some activity in rare, large silver coins of the last century or so—particularly German and Italian issues. There is relatively little forgery of ancient coinage (a blessing, for this area could be highly vulnerable), and almost none of medieval coinage.

Some forgery is occurring in other numismatic fields, such as medals or paper money, but these areas present special problems to forgers, and the potential market is still limited.

See also AUTHENTICATION; CAST COUNTERFEIT; COUNTERFEIT; COUNTERFEIT AND FORGERY DETECTION; DIE-STRUCK COUNTERFEIT.

FRACTIONAL CURRENCY

FRACTIONAL CURRENCY   A term usually applied to official United States paper money printed in denominations of less than one dollar, produced in the nineteenth century.

Fractional notes were issued from 1862 to 1876, and their initial authorization was a direct consequence of the economic disorder generated by the American Civil War.

The war began in the spring of 1861, and by the summer of the following year there was much uncertainty about its outcome and the future. Hoarding ensued, as it so often does in such instances. Not only gold and silver coins, but base-metal ones as well, were removed from circulation and hidden.

Alarmed by the situation, the government took steps to remedy it with an act of July 17, 1862, authorizing the acceptance of postage stamps as currency. The new law, however, spawned new problems—stamps were easily soiled or stuck together, and soon a run on post offices almost exhausted supplies of postage stamps for any purpose, including the original one of paying for postal deliveries.

In response, General F. E. Spinner, the Treasurer, devised a similar but apparently more workable solution: print small denomination notes which *looked* like postage stamps. The demand for small change would be satisfied, and since people were looking for money rather than stamps, the postal department could get on with selling stamps to those who needed them for postage. The idea was adopted, and the first of the small notes entered circulation on August 1, 1862. Reflecting their origins, the bills, issued in denominations of five, ten, twenty-five, and fifty cents, were called "postage currency."

Unfortunately, it so happened they were illegal, at least in their initial form. The government vowed to redeem them in United States notes as well as in stamps; but it did not have the legal power to do so. An act of March 3, 1863 amended the situation, and the diminutive notes, derisively dubbed "shinplasters," were celebrated numismatic features of the Civil War and Reconstruction periods.

In all, there were five issues of fractional currency. The first—the "postage currency"—was released between August 1862 and May 1863. The second, third, fourth, and fifth, called fractional currency, were issued between October 1863 and February 1867, December 1864 and August 1869, July 1869 and February 1875, and February 1875 and February 1876, respectively.

The piece illustrated is from the second issue, and exhibits the characteristics of that particular series: a very fine small engraving, symbolizing the wealth of the

Fractional currency. *United States, 50 cents, second issue, 1863–1867.*

country, and a head of George Washington in the center. The curious darkish oval on the obverse surrounding Washington's head is actually a gold-colored surcharge placed there by government officials, perhaps as an anti-counterfeiting device. The reverse reveals a federal shield with the bill's denomination, and additional surcharges—50 in the center and 18–63 at the lower corners.

Fractional currency continued for more than a decade after the war's end; small change was in short supply for a number of years, and the notes proved handy in trade. When the last note was printed, the government had issued $368,720,000 in this currency, and it is estimated that $2,000,000 worth of the paper is yet to be redeemed. Presumably, it is in the hands of collectors, destroyed, or simply lost.

The term fractional currency also applies to a series of Canadian subsidiary notes, dated 1870, 1900, and 1923. These notes were issued in only one denomination, that of twenty-five cents. The initial issue of 1870 was in the nature of an emergency printing, aimed at relieving a shortage of small change. People were pleased with the notes, however, and more were issued on later occasions.

See also Civil War tokens; Emergency money; Encased postage stamp; Postage stamp money; Shinplaster.

Freak. New York, copper, 1787.

FREAK Any coin or note which displays a major error, especially one so bizarre in appearance that speculation arises as to how it was produced.

The piece shown is such an error. It is a New York State copper, minted in 1787, which bears two obverses and no reverse. While there will never be complete agreement on how this error was struck, one might speculate that it was minted normally, accidentally flipped over and left on the lower die while a new planchet was placed atop it, and then struck again. This would produce a coin with two obverses, one with a somewhat weak image fashioned by its misuse as a "die" for the top planchet.

See also Error.

FROSTED PROOF A proof or specimen coin with mirrorlike fields, and devices and letters that have a dull, matte aspect.

In its look, the frosted proof is akin to a cameo, with the raised portions graphically set off from the flat areas surrounding them. The Austrian commemorative coin illustrated is an excellent example of a frosted proof.

The dies for these coins receive special treatment. Once checked for imperfections, they are etched and immersed in a weak acidic solution which gives the entire die a frosty finish. The areas representing the fields (the highest points on the dies) are then carefully polished until the matte finish is completely removed. The result is a die with a surface both shiny and dull. The popularity of the frosted proof with

Frosted proof. Austria, 50 schilling, 1974.

both mints and collectors stems from the dramatic contrasts between its devices and fields. It is the most common type of proof in current production

See also MATTE PROOF; PROOF; SANDBLAST PROOF.

Fugio cent. *United States, 1787.*

FUGIO CENT The first circulating coin issued under the authority of the United States government, late in the eighteenth century; also known as the Franklin cent.

As no federal coining establishment existed at the time, the government was unable to mint Fugio cents directly, and they were privately contracted. It was the coiner's inability to meet the terms of his agreement that helped convince the federal government a national mint was necessary.

The Fugio cent derives its name from the Latin FUGIO ("I Fly"), in the obverse legend. The central device on the obverse is a sundial with a sun about it; FUGIO is to the left, a date (1787) to the right. Beneath the sundial is the inscription MIND YOUR BUSINESS. Benjamin Franklin had suggested similar designs for Continental Currency and the Continental Dollar, and the obverse of the Fugio cent merely reworks his ideas. The reverse was also inspired by Franklin, and depicts thirteen joined rings, each representing a state, with the words WE ARE ONE surrounded by UNITED STATES (or STATES UNITED). It was Franklin's influence on the coin's design that gave it its second name, Franklin cent, although Fugio cent is preferred.

The genesis of the coin lay in the desperate scarcity of small change in the newly independent nation. Under the country's first constitution, the Articles of Confederation, the national government enjoyed the right to coin money, and so did the states. Faced with the shortage of small change, several states either made their own or hired independent contractors. State coinages were limited to copper issues, and the results were often questionable. Indeed many of the coins were so lightweight and badly struck they actually hindered trade rather than facilitating it.

In 1787 the federal government therefore decided to issue an official coin to act as a standard against which state issues could be judged. Lacking a mint, the government could not strike the coins and James Jarvis, part-owner of a firm making copper coinage for the state of Connecticut, was selected to do so. Jarvis had been recommended for the contract by Colonel William Duer, the Secretary of the Treasury, who, in exchange, was to receive a percentage of Jarvis's profits.

For there were to be profits. Jarvis agreed to strike approximately three hundred tons of Fugio coppers (we may also call them "cents," remembering that the denomination did not officially exist on a national level until 1792), each of which would contain far less than a cent's worth of copper. Even with the labor required to find the copper and turn it into coins, Jarvis's prospect of a sizable profit was good if he fulfilled his contractual obligations.

Unfortunately, he was unable to do so, and a potentially beneficial operation for coiner and government alike became a disaster. The government received only a small portion of its coins, and Jarvis came uncomfortably close to being given a jail sentence.

To be awarded the contract in the first place, Jarvis committed himself to a twenty-thousand-dollar bond, which Congress demanded as insurance that he would produce the coins (over thirty million of them). In addition to raising the bond, Jarvis had to find his own copper. Although his friend Colonel Duer located a small amount, it was not nearly enough for the task. Jarvis was left with no alternative but to try to buy the remaining copper on credit.

In November 1787 he sailed to Holland, then one of the world's major banking centers, in search of backers. Finding none, he moved on to England, where he failed to interest Matthew Boulton, the greatest private coiner of the day, in his project. He returned to the United States in mid-1788, only to learn that the federal government was voiding his contract, on the grounds that he had defaulted on his first delivery of cents, promised for the previous December. Not only did Congress refuse Jarvis's pleas for an extension, it asked for its twenty thousand dollars, as stipulated in the bond. With no money, and no way to raise it, Jarvis chose the only course left open to him. He fled the country.

Meanwhile, some Fugio cents had actually been produced. When Jarvis was in Europe his representatives in the United States managed to make a partial delivery to the Treasury in May 1788 of four hundred thousand coins—probably made from Colonel Duer's initial copper contribution. More likely than not, they were struck in New Haven, Connecticut by Samuel Broome, Jarvis's father-in-law.

It would abuse history to portray Jarvis simply as the victim of a heartless government. When Colonel Duer tapped him to strike the Fugios, Jarvis had been coining Connecticut coppers, more profitable than coining government cents. He immediately instructed his workers to use a quantity of the copper provided by Colonel Duer—actually government property—to strike the Connecticut coppers, a private

business venture. To make matters worse, Jarvis had no contract with the state of Connecticut, in effect, making his coppers illegal. The story of the Fugio cent has no heroes.

In any case, the federal government now had four hundred thousand shiny new cents to circulate, a standard against which state coppers could be measured. But the picture was less bright than it seemed. Jarvis's workers had skimped on the amount of copper they put in the Fugio cent. It was underweight by the new federal standard and could not circulate at its intended value without causing serious problems. The government opted to rid itself of the Fugio cents as best it could.

An obscure speculator, one Royal Flint, took the coins on credit, agreeing to pay the government as soon as he released them at a profit. His timing was calamitous. He attempted to dump the Fugios on the market when numbers of counterfeit British halfpennies, and other lightweight counterfeits, were circulating at a value far above their intrinsic worth, and the situation was so out of control that merchants and consumers soon refused to accept any coppers, including the Fugio cents. Flint was left with a large number of coppers he could not circulate, and an even larger bill to the government he could not pay. Being available, if not especially guilty, he went to jail for his part in the Fugio cent scandal.

Such was the course of the United States's experiment with contract coinage. Many Fugio cents were never circulated; they are the only early United States issues which can be expected to be in excellent condition as a general rule.

See also CONTINENTAL CURRENCY; CONTINENTAL DOLLAR; MINT ACT OF 1792; STATE COINAGE.

G

GALLANTRY AWARD A decoration given for singular heroism demonstrated in war or, less often, under other circumstances.

England's highest gallantry decoration, the Victoria Cross, is perhaps the most famous gallantry award and is shown here. The Victoria Cross grew out of the carnage and heroism of the Crimean War (1854–1856), and was suggested by Prince Albert, husband of Queen Victoria. The Queen announced its establishment early in 1856, and the first awards were accorded in June 1857. The cross was created from bronze taken from a gun captured during one of the campaigns of the Crimean War; initially it was issued with a blue ribbon denoting heroism at sea, or a crimson ribbon for heroism on land. The blue ribbon passed from use during World War I, and since then all Victoria Crosses have been accompanied by a crimson ribbon.

Other gallantry awards include the French Croix de Guerre, the Prussian Pour le Mérite, and the American Congressional Medal of Honor. For gallantry awards to have any significance, the number granted must be limited. Because of the resultant relative scarcity and the aura of heroism which surrounds the gallantry award, it is avidly sought by collectors.

See also BADGE; CAMPAIGN AWARD; DECORATION; ORDER; RIBBON.

Gallantry award. *United Kingdom, Victoria Cross, c. 1860.*

Gazetta. Ionian Islands (under Russia), 1801.

GAZETTA A copper coin, mainly struck by Venice for colonial use during the seventeenth and eighteenth centuries.

The typical gazetta had a diameter of 27 millimeters and weighed slightly under 5 grams. Its central obverse type was the winged lion of St. Mark, emblem of the Venetian Republic. The figure II appears in the exergue of the obverse, as the gazetta was equal to two soldi, small copper coins of the period. The reverse recorded the colonies for whose use the piece was intended. These included part of Crete, several of the Ionian islands, and much of the Dalmatian coast. Gazette were not dated; the coin seems to have been a first issued about 1632 and was phased out by the Venetians during the late eighteenth century. Little research has been done on this coin, however, particularly in regard to later issues.

The gazetta was revived in 1801 during the Russian occupation of the Ionian islands, and this is the coin shown in the illustration. It carries a date, and is also quite rare, unlike undated gazette, which are not.

The gazetta earned a measure of immortality as the source of the word "gazette," meaning "newspaper." According to one tale, the first newspaper printed in Venice cost two soldi—or one gazetta—per copy, and the coin's name was transferred, in time, to the publication.

GEM An uncirculated coin of superlative quality, exhibiting fewer than the average number of problems or blemishes expected on coins of its series.

An ancient coin in gem condition is more closely centered than usual, and shows no evidence of double striking (common on many coins of the period).

A heavy, machine-struck piece of this standard displays neither bag marks nor other minor blemishes often found on these pieces. Coin dealers frequently use the term as an adjective, referring to a particular coin as "gem B.U." ("gem brilliant uncirculated"). While somewhat redundant, the term should mean the coin is in far better condition than the average mint state specimen.

See also GRADING SYSTEMS.

GENOVINO One of the earliest gold coins of the Middle Ages, struck by the Italian city of Genoa from the 1250s until 1415.

The genovino was introduced at the same time as the florin, or perhaps slightly earlier, and was intended primarily as a trade coin, although it never reached the position enjoyed by its Florentine rival.

The diameter of the genovino was around 20 millimeters, and it weighed approximately 3.5 grams. The central obverse type was a gate—a pun referring to the city, as the word for "gate" (*janua*) and "Genoa" sounded much alike. On the reverse, the central type was a large cross. The first genovini had very simple legends, the obverse again pertaining to the gate (IANVA), while the reverse carried the name of Conrad III, the Holy Roman Emperor who granted coinage rights to the city in 1139. Later genovini, including

Genovino. Genoa, 1356–1363.

the one illustrated here, were a bit more ornate, and carried longer legends. After 1339, when the city lost its communal form of government, genovini began to feature the titles of the current ruler, or doge. Interestingly, the actual name of the ruler was not given, but merely his ordinal position in the succession. Thus the name of the first doge, Simon Boccanegra, does not appear on his coins; instead, the legend reads DUX IANVENSIUM PRIMVS ("the first Genoese doge"). We can see in this a reminder of the political rivalries endemic to Genoa throughout its history, rivalries so virulent that a ruling doge did not consider it politic to obtrude his own name on the city's coins.

See also FLORIN; TRADE COINS.

Ghosting. *United Kingdom, penny, 1918. Note ghost image of ruler's head, the type used on the other side of the coin.*

GHOSTING A mint error in design, which results in a depressed ghost image of an obverse head appearing on a coin's reverse.

In the case of a ghosted coin, neither the dies nor the coining procedure are technologically defective. In fact, the coin is a normal strike, and cannot be called an error: rather it is the dies' designs that are defective.

The piece in the illustration demonstrates the ghosting phenomenon. If you look closely at the fields surrounding the seated figure, you will see the faint outlines of a head, especially to the immediate right of the seated figure's head. This is the "ghost" of the head on the obverse—in this instance, that of George V of England (ruled 1910–1936). His pennies struck between 1912 and 1925 were defective in their design and exhibit a high incidence of ghosting.

How does ghosting come about? In part it is caused by the modern coining technique, which emphasizes the creation of coins with a single blow of the press. Since this affords only one chance for a correct strike, designs must be balanced to bring up as much relief as possible. It is never advisable to design a coin whose two sides have a great deal of relief directly opposite one another, for the single strike of the modern press does not bring up all of this relief. The metal in the planchet expands under pressure, filling most of the cavities of the dies, but in a single blow it can only fill them to a certain degree. The designs on the finished coins then, will be weak on one side or both, and may also disclose a sinking or depression on one side, as the metal shifts in an effort to fill one of the dies. This is the origin of the ghosting on the English penny: metal has moved downward to fill the dominant obverse design, and the places where it shifted (or the outlines of the king's head) are clearly exposed on the reverse.

See also BROCKAGE; CLASHED DIES; ERROR; MACHINE-STRUCK COINAGE.

GOLD STANDARD The linkage of a nation's monetary unit to a specific amount of gold.

In the United States, for example, the dollar was tied in 1934 to a standard gold dollar of $15\frac{5}{21}$ grains, 90 percent fine. The gold standard was in effect during much of the history of money, but today it has virtually disappeared from use.

See also BIMETALLIC CURRENCY.

GRADING SYSTEMS Organized rules, standards, and terminology by which the degree of preservation of a coin or other item is described.

Grading systems allow us to compare two coins and, along with rarity and demand, they establish the buying and selling prices for coins, tokens, paper money, etc.

At present, two systems are prevalent. One expresses a coin's state in words or letters, the other uses a combination of letters and numbers to do so. The first system is used throughout the world for all coinage, and can be applied to other numismatic items such as paper money. In the United States its most important terms, in ascending order, are *good* (G), *very good* (VG), *fine* (F), *very fine* (VF), *extremely fine* (EF or XF), *about uncirculated* (AU), and *uncirculated* or *mint state* (UNC or MS).

The second system is primarily applied to United States coins, especially early ones. It was conceived by Dr. William H. Sheldon, whose main collecting area was early American cents. He devised a numerical scale, on which 1 represented the worst possible condition of preservation of an unmutilated coin, while 70 was the best possible condition. Sheldon found some financial justification for his scale; a coin in condition 50 tended to be worth approximately fifty times as much as a specimen of the same die variety in condition 1. He combined his numbers with the most common abbreviations that described coins verbally, to make the Sheldon Grading System. Originally used only to grade cents, it has since been extended to other branches of American coinage, although it is rarely used in other areas of numismatics.

To see how these grading systems work, examine the coins illustrated. They are United States dimes from the 1820s, ranging in grade from *good* to *uncirculated*. The coin in *good* condition (G-4 on the Sheldon scale) is heavily worn. Its design is weak; the head and bust of Liberty are

mere silhouettes, and most of the inscription on her ribbon has worn away. The stars are faint and merge with the rim, but the date (1824) remains clear. The next coin is graded *very good* (VG-8). Here we can see most of the letters of LIBERTY on the figure's headband. The coin is flat and lacking in details, but its design is clear, and its stars stand out from the rim. This dime, too, was struck in 1824.

The next coin is an 1827 dime in *fine* condition (F-12). Nearly half of the details in Liberty's hair, drapery, and cap are visible, but little of the detail of her face remains. Next is a typical example of a coin in *very fine* (VF-20) state. This 1825 dime has moderate, even wear, but all of its major features are distinct. The word LIBERTY and the ribbon upon which it appears are fairly discernable. Most of the drapery, although worn, is quite bold, as is the hair; the figure's eye and lips are well defined.

The next coin is from 1827, and would be graded *extremely fine* (EF-40). It reveals faint traces of mint luster. There is slight wear on Liberty's hair above her eye and ear, and very slight wear on her curls. Her features are now well defined, as is the clasp on her drapery and the drapery itself. The next dime, the earliest in our series, dates from 1820. It has been chosen as a more or less typical example of an *about uncirculated* (AU-50) dime. A good deal of mint luster is present. There are faint traces of wear above the eye and over the ear. This coin was struck by a screw press, and Liberty's drapery clasp is not clearly visible; then too, her features in general are weaker than they might have been. These anomalies come from the mode of manufacture, not from actual circulation. The reverse of this coin (not seen here) is much stronger than its obverse, earning it an overall grade of *about uncirculated*. Finally, we have a coin in *uncirculated condition* or *mint state* (MS-60). It lacks full mint luster and has a few blemishes, but displays no evidence of wear.

Some additional observations about

Grading systems.
The grading of early United States dimes.
Top, left to right: G-4, VG-8, F-12.
Bottom, left to right: VF-20, EF-40, AU-50, MS-60.

grading systems are in order. Initially we discussed a 70-point maximum. What about coins with numbers above 60, and those with grades between, say, 40 and 50? According to the Sheldon system, coins graded above MS-60 can and do exist. Few if any MS-70s will be found, but MS-65s, sometimes called "choice uncirculateds," are known and, if they are in the early American series, will command much higher prices than MS-60s. Uncirculated proof-like or first-strike coins also fall in the 60-plus range. And it is perfectly possible to have coins with intermediate numbers, EF-45 or even EF-49, for instance, which put them on the borderline of AU. Such coins, which are better than average for their grade but not quite equal to the hierarchy's next grade, are an endless source of dispute. This is even more true when we move to MS-60 and above. If the piece is better than the average uncirculated coin, how much better is it? And who makes the decision? And, considering the vagaries of striking and the myriad steps involved in a coin's manufacture, what is the basis for the number decided upon?

An escape from the impasse would be to rationalize the Sheldon grading system. Retain a five-number grading spread, let us say, and then, instead of quibbling over whether a coin should be graded MS-60 or

AU-59, declare, "MS-60, but lacks mint luster and has slight edge ding"—or some such statement.

Three grading terms have not been mentioned. Two are lower grades than those most commonly used: *fair* and *poor*. Neither is ordinarily abbreviated, and they would fit into Sheldon's scheme as Fair-2 and Poor-1. In the case of a coin in fair condition, the date and more than half of the legends can be discerned, although only faintly. The coin in poor condition can be just barely identified, but nothing more, and its date may be entirely absent. Sheldon did not include mutilated coins in this category, yet most numismatists would do so.

The other grading condition is *proof*. This type of coin presents a dilemma, for its very method of manufacture makes it impossible to grade by ordinary standards. Collectors now tend to grade such coins on the same numerical scale as MS coins. Thus, a Proof-60 is an "average" proof, one in Proof-65 is "choice," and one in Proof-70 (if such a coin exists, perfectly struck and untouched since the day it left the mint) is referred to as a "perfect gem proof."

Occasionally it happens that one side of a coin is in better condition than the other. If so, the coin with a typical *fine* obverse and a typical *very good* reverse, for instance, will receive the notation F/VG or F-12/VG-8, and its price will be approximately midway between those of coins in the two grades.

The grading system applied to ancient and medieval coins, modern non-United States coins, tokens, medals, and paper money is usually simpler than that used for United States coins. It employs the terms just examined (or their abbreviations): these terms retain their essential meaning even when referring to something as totally different as paper money. Thus, we know a note advertised in "good" condition will have been circulated long enough to possibly tear, be stained, or even lose a corner—in short, that its state of preservation parallels that of a coin in the same condition.

See also FIRST STRIKE; GEM; PROOF; PROOF-LIKE.

GRAIN A unit of weight measurement, used in reference to coinage.

One grain equals .064799 gram; it thus takes about fifteen and one-half grains to constitute one gram. And 31.1035 grams equals one troy ounce. The grain was formerly used quite extensively as the basic unit for a coin's weight. It has been largely superseded by the metric gram, an invention of the late eighteenth century. Older catalogs still speak in terms of grains, however, as do some British publications.

GRAINING A technical term for the milled edge of a coin.

The word "graining" is rather indiscriminately used to describe two edges which, although similar in appearance, are produced by completely dissimilar processes. The first is the reeded edge, which is placed on a coin by a closed collar surrounding the coin as it is struck. This collar has vertical striations at measured intervals, which are transferred to the coin's edge, lending it a design and a pro-

Graining. *British Guiana, 2 guilders, 1809 (edge).*

tection against clipping. The reeded edge also allows the coin to be ejected from the collar after striking.

The second edge resembles the reeded one, but was produced in an entirely different fashion: it was added by edge-marking machinery in the planchet stage. Coins with this edge had parallel striations, but they were usually thicker than those with true reeded edges, and it became fashionable to slant them to one side. Such coins are referred to as "obliquely reeded." The illustration shows a coin with graining of this type. The term graining should actually be abandoned for a more precise one: and reeded edge should be restricted to those coins struck with a closed, striated collar.

See also COLLAR; EDGE-MARKING MACHINERY; ORNAMENTED EDGE; REEDED EDGE.

GREEK IMPERIALS A term for local issues from Greek-speaking areas during the first three centuries of the Roman Empire. "Greek Imperials" is not literally accurate (after all, these coins were struck under the *Roman* Empire, not a "Greek" one, which never existed) but the term has remained in use because it can encompass a number of disparate coins, linked primarily by language and time.

The early years of the Roman Empire were prosperous ones for the Greek-speaking East. Imperial trade (the selling of Egyptian grain to Rome, the purchase and resale of luxury goods to the same entrepôt) boomed, and so did more local commercial enterprises. This created a demand for coinage, particularly that of low value, so useful for modest transactions. The Greek Imperials went far toward meeting the demand.

We can talk of two major subdivisions within the Greek Imperial series. The first featured coins that circulated fairly extensively within an entire province: billon or silver coins, descendants of the earlier purely Greek tetradrachm, as well as some issues in copper. The best known of these provincial coins, and certainly the most common, come from Alexandria, Egypt— billon tetradrachms minted with a gradually decreasing silver content from the reign of Tiberius (ruled A.D. 14–37) to that of Diocletian (ruled A.D. 284–305). The piece illustrated dates from A.D. 66. Its diameter is about 24 millimeters, and it weighs approximately 12 grams. This type of coin seems to have been tariffed at about one denarius. Later issues were smaller, and eventually their silver content all but disappeared. The last Alexandrian tetradrachm—indeed, the last Greek Imperial coin—was struck in A.D. 295–296.

The second group embraces local issues, intended for a more limited circulation. These coins were struck in copper, *orichalcum* (brass), or bronze, and compose the majority of coins in the Greek Imperial series. Generally referred to today with the abbreviation Æ plus a number indicating their diameter, they were struck by scores of cities and towns over a long period. Their output peaked in the third century, and the Greek Imperials from that period are among the least costly of all ancient coins.

They are of two types. The first, which might be called the "imperial" series, always has an obverse portraying the emperor or a member of his family, with the reverse indicating the name of the issuing city, and sometimes the name of the magistrate responsible for the coin. The second series is a "local" one, which often

Greek Imperials.
Top: Alexandria, Nero, tetradrachm, A.D. 66.
Bottom: Emesa, Caracalla, large bronze, A.D. 211–217.

shows a local deity on the obverse and a locally significant type or scene on the reverse.

These coins are not representative of the finest in ancient numismatic art. Indeed, the relief on Greek Imperials tends to be fairly shallow, unlike that on classical Greek coinage; the portraiture is no more than adequate, and the reverse types are pedestrian or worse. Yet it must be remembered these minters were not striving for artistic mastery, but for coins that would circulate locally: and the high degree of wear often associated with the coins is indicative of their success.

It was also important to strike appealing coins, hence the depiction of local deities and scenes. And here lies the significance of Greek Imperials to the modern numismatist. The coins frequently show buildings, temples, shrines, or monuments of which an area's inhabitants were especially proud. As most of these no longer exist, their depiction on coins is often our only visual record.

The second illustration is a good example of this aspect of the Greek Imperials. The coin was struck at Emesa, home of the cult of the sun-god Elagabal. The obverse bears the head of the emperor Caracalla (ruled A.D. 211–217), and the reverse shows the temple of the sun cult, whose appearance is known only from its portrayal on a number of coins of this period.

See also BILLON; DATING SYSTEMS; POTIN; TETRADRACHM.

GREENBACK   A general term for federally issued United States paper money.

The name originated with the demand note of 1861, whose reverse was printed in a dark green ink, which has since been used to print the reverses of most United States paper money. Tradition, as might be expected, plays a part, so does the government's apparent belief that it has an ink formula which is impossible for counterfeiters to reproduce. Its faith in the ink is probably justified, as no one has ever exactly duplicated the formula. On the other hand, a number of counterfeiters have come close enough to fool the public.

See also BLUEBACK; COUNTERFEIT; DEMAND NOTE; LEGAL TENDER NOTE.

GROAT   An English silver coin worth four pennies, introduced during the 1279–1280 coinage reform of Edward I of England (ruled 1272–1307).

Prior to Edward's reform, there had been only one English coin in circulation, the penny. It was a small coin of modest value, and was proving inadequate to meet the demands of England's burgeoning foreign and domestic trade. Other countries were experimenting with larger silver coins of a higher value—the Italians had started to do so about the beginning of the thirteenth century, and the French by the 1260s. Edward's groat was introduced in part as an English competitor to these coins.

The illustration shows one of the first groats, struck about 1280. For a medieval coin, it is quite large (28 millimeters in diameter) and relatively heavy (about 5.8 grams). It reveals what a medieval coin designer could do with a larger space in which to work than the penny afforded him. We see a full-face portrait of Edward within a quatrefoil on the obverse, and a legend with the king's titles. The reverse has an ornamental cross as its central type, and two surrounding legends, the outer one proclaiming Edward lord of Ireland and duke of Aquitaine and the inner one reading CIVI LONDONIA—the city of London, where the coin was minted. None of these design elements represents a radical departure from former practice; but they look better and are more pleasingly executed than earlier coins—and for that, the groat is to be thanked.

While the first groat boasted a fortunate choice of design, it was not a success as a circulating coin: it was slightly underweight in relation to four pre-reform pennies and as a result met with considerable resistance. It was soon withdrawn, and seventy years passed before another groat made its appearance, this time under Edward III (ruled 1327–1377). This later coin was more enthusiastically greeted. It weighed about a gram less than the first groat, but by now the weight of the penny had also been reduced.

The groat entered the mainstream of English coinage, and was struck regularly over the next century and a half. Its basic obverse and reverse design elements were retained to around 1500, although its weight diminished as time went on. It began to yield to newer denominations—the testoon or shilling, and its half the six-

Groat. *England, c. 1280.*

pence—in the period of Henry VIII (ruled 1509–1547) and Edward VI (ruled 1547–1553), and after the reign of Elizabeth I (ruled 1558–1603), it was no longer coined regularly for English use.

It continued to be struck for certain purposes, however. As a fourpence, it is part of the Maundy series struck from the time of Charles II (ruled 1660–1685) to the present. And it was issued for circulation under William IV (ruled 1830–1837) and Victoria (ruled 1837–1901), for use in British Guiana and parts of the West Indies, where people were accustomed to trading with a small silver coin.

See also GROSCHEN; GROSSO; GROS TOURNOIS; MAUNDY MONEY; PENNY; TESTOON.

GROSCHEN A late medieval German and central European silver coin; the equivalent of the French gros tournois, which was first struck in the 1260s, and whose size and weight made it immediately popular as a trading coin.

The Rhineland area of Germany produced an equivalent coin (the turnosgroschen, later called a groschen) by 1300. And Bohemia, with its rich silver mines near Prague, began to strike the coin at the same time. Its Prager groschen was extensively copied in Poland, Saxony, and in other areas where large silver deposits existed. Rather quickly the groschen became one of the best-known coins in central Europe, going far toward supplanting the silver pfennig or penny.

The piece illustrated is a typical fourteenth-century German groschen, minted between 1332 and 1349 by Walram von Jülich, archbishop of Cologne. It is 26 millimeters in diameter and weighs some 3.9 grams. We see the archbishop's head on the obverse and a cross surrounded by legends on the reverse. While the cross was standard on the groschen, portraits were often replaced by heraldic devices.

The groschen was struck in large numbers during the fourteenth and fifteenth

Groschen. Archbishopric of Cologne, 1332–1349.

centuries, after which its popularity, along with its silver content, declined. In time it became a subsidiary piece, and the larger and more valuable thaler replaced it as a trading coin. An indication of its earlier importance is the retention of its name by Austria, where one hundred groschen now equal one schilling.

See also GROSSO; GROS TOURNOIS; PFENNIG; PRAGER GROSCHEN; THALER; TRADE COINS.

GROSSO Among the earliest of the large, heavy silver coins of the Middle Ages, issued by Venice in 1202.

The grosso illustrated weighs 2.2 grams and measures 21 millimeters in diameter. This was the official weight for the coin, which was tariffed at twenty-four denari. Grosso is simply the Italian for "big"—which the coin was, at least in relation to the earlier denaro.

The grosso is interesting for several reasons. First, there is the nature of its design. We are accustomed to seeing coins of this period with a distinctly "medieval" ap-

Grosso. Venice, c. 1202.

pearance. That is, they often bear crude full-face portraits on the obverse, a cross on the reverse; usually the lettering is rather large, making brief legends the rule. The grosso is different. Its obverse shows two standing figures—St. Mark (patron of Venice) presenting a banner to the doge (the city's elected ruler)—while its reverse bears a seated figure of Christ. The doge's titles are on the obverse in small, precise lettering, while the abbreviated reverse inscription refers to Christ ("Jesus Christ, King of Kings, Savior"). Nothing in contemporary western Europe was like this coin. The standing figures, the small lettering, and the generally finished appearance, are reminiscent of Byzantine coin design and reflect the centuries of commercial contact between the empire and the Venetian Republic. Ironically, the grosso was introduced in part to pay for Venice's participation in the Fourth Crusade (1202–1204), which ended in the destruction of the Byzantine Empire.

The Venetians struck the grosso regularly until the middle of the fifteenth century, when its disappearance closely coincided with that of the Byzantine Empire.

The most important aspect of the grosso was not artistic, however. Rather, it is significant as the first successful trade coin of the new, larger type. The French gros tournois would soon be patterned on it, and, in turn, this new coin would be imitated throughout Europe: groats, groschen, etc., were all, to some degree, inspired by the earlier Venetian grosso.

See also CROAT; DENARO; GROAT; GROSCHEN; GROS TOURNOIS; PRAGER GROSCHEN; TRADE COINS.

GROS TOURNOIS
A French silver coin patterned on the Venetian grosso, introduced in 1266 and struck for almost a century in an essentially unchanged form.

The gros tournois was first coined under Louis IX (ruled 1226–1270), who intended to establish royal coinage as superior to feudal issues. It symbolized his desire and that of his successors to concentrate political power in their hands rather than share it with local magnates. To effect such a policy, Louis devised the gros tournois; its size (27 millimeters) and weight (4.2 grams) made it ideal for the quickening business tempo of thirteenth-century France. The king declared its minting a royal monopoly, thereby increasing his power—at the expense of the barons—and ensuring that proper weight and fineness standards would be maintained.

At its introduction, the gros tournois was the heaviest silver coin in Europe, and adhered to a standard originally devised by the abbey of St. Martin at Tours, the city from which the coin takes its name. Like most medieval coins, it bears a cross, on the obverse in this case. A legend with the king's name (LVDOVICVS REX) surrounded the cross, while a pious religious legend flanked the king's name. On the reverse was a crude, stylized view of the castle at Tours, a legend with the city's name, and an outer border formed by a ring of fleurs-de-lis.

Louis IX's immediate successors retained these designs, and merely substituted their own names in the central obverse legend. By this time imitations of the gros tournois were spreading across northern Europe. Coins of the same name were introduced into the Low Countries prior to 1300, and were extremely close copies of the original. Later issues, such as those in Germany and Bohemia, had dif-

Gros tournois. France, c. 1266.

ferent designs and used names which, while derivative, were not the same as the French coin's. In France itself the gros tournois was discontinued after the reign of Charles V (ruled 1364–1380).

See also CROAT; CROSS ON COINAGE; DENIER; GROAT; GROSCHEN; GROSSO; TRADE COINS.

Guilloche. China, Central Bank of China, 20 cents, 1930 (detail).

GUILLOCHE An ornate pattern, usually symmetrical and multicolored, added to paper money to make it more attractive and harder to counterfeit.

Asa Spencer, an obscure nineteenth-century American inventor, perfected a way of translating ornate, precisely regular, curving designs onto a steel printing plate; to do so he created the geometrical lathe, a contrivance of major significance for the protection it gave legal issues of paper money.

Spencer's machine consisted of a gearbox containing horizontally layered, mutually eccentric discs. The discs' movements were led by gear wheels and other systems, whose purpose was to guide the movements of a small steel die against a fixed diamond or hard steel point. The system provided infinite design possibilities, from simple circles to the most ornate guilloches.

First used to make guilloches in the nineteenth century, Spencer's machine (with improvements) is still widely employed. A second guilloche style was fashioned around 1960, produced by a complicated engraving system based on the pendulum principle. This method allows for a freely swung, asymmetrical curve (and multiples thereof). Its potentials, which represent a departure from the rather hackneyed geometrical designs, are worth pursuing. Many modern notes use guilloches engraved by the pendulum method, but thus far the general results have not been completely satisfactory. Like the geometrical lathe, the pendulum engraver is only a machine (albeit a highly

complicated one), and it needs the hand of an artist behind it to create a truly beautiful design.

The illustration shows a typical guilloche, placed on a small-denomination Chinese bank note of 1930. Note the extreme fineness and complexity of the line.

See also COUNTERFEIT; ENGRAVING; MEDALLION.

GUINEA An English gold coin, the equivalent of twenty (and later twenty-one) shillings, minted between 1663 and 1813.

At the accession of Charles II (ruled 1660–1685), England's monetary system was sorely in need of overhauling. The mint had experimented with machine-struck coinage as early as the 1560s, but the new methods had encountered resistance and were quickly forsaken. By 1660 all money in circulation was of the old, hand-struck variety, and subject to clipping, filing, and forgery. Furthermore, much of it had been issued by the Commonwealth, the republican government which had executed Charles I, father of the new king.

Charles II ordered that all coinage be machine-struck, and bear royal portraits and legends, not republican ones. Dies were prepared by the day's finest engravers, machinery and technicians were imported from France, and the first new coins were struck in 1662—silver pieces, called crowns. Machine-struck gold coinage began the following year with the guinea. This had a diameter of 25 millimeters, weighed slightly under 8.4 grams, and had a fineness of .917, or 22 carats. It was valued at twenty shillings, or four crowns.

Charles had intended to use the gold coins of the erstwhile Commonwealth as a basis for striking new, royal issues. (In the 1690s all pre-1662 coins were recalled, melted, and reissued.) In the case of the guinea, however, he also used gold from the Guinea Coast of Africa, brought to England by the Africa Company, a royally chartered enterprise whose badge featured an elephant. Guinea was adopted as the coin's name, and an elephant appeared under the king's head on the obverses of many of the coins.

The guinea's relation to silver coinage varied: at first it approached thirty shillings; late in the 1690s its value was reduced, first to twenty-one shillings and six pence, and later to twenty-one shillings, where it remained for the rest of its career.

The guinea illustrated was minted late in the eighteenth century, during the reign of George III (ruled 1760–1820). This particular coin is known as a "spade" guinea, because of the peculiar shape of the shield on its reverse. In the late eighteenth and early nineteenth centuries innumerable jetons, as well as outright counterfeits, of this piece were struck from brass. However, their light weight

exposes them. Today, the spade guinea is forged in real gold for collectors, and some of these are quite impressive.

As a coin the guinea did not survive the reign of George III. Guineas with the spade reverse were minted in large numbers from 1787 to 1799. The fiscal emergency caused by the Napoleonic Wars then halted production of the coin until 1813. In that year, a limited issue of guineas with a new design was coined: these were the last to be struck. Although the sovereign, valued at twenty shillings rather than twenty-one, took its place, the use of the guinea as a unit of reckoning continued for a century and a half after the last coins of that name were struck.

See also JETON; MILLED COIN; MONEY OF ACCOUNT; SOVEREIGN.

GULDEN Originally the northern European equivalent of the Italian florin: as such, a gold trading coin of late medieval and early modern times; later, a term for certain silver coins.

The gulden was first struck in the late fourteenth century, and was clearly imitative of the florin in design, weight, and fineness. The piece illustrated here, minted in the Palatinate between 1398 and 1410, is a typical early gulden. On the obverse is the standing figure of St. John the Baptist, fashioned in a style reminiscent of that seen on the florin; on the other side, a series of shields has replaced the fleur-de-lis. This gulden is made of good gold, has a diameter of 22 millimeters, and weighs slightly under 3.5 grams—fairly close to the weight of the florin. On later gulden St. John was replaced by another standing figure: usually a local patron saint, sometimes the ruler who struck the coin.

The gulden was widely issued in western Germany and the Low Countries. With time its gold content varied from place to place, deviating from the florin's

Guinea. England, "spade" guinea, 1798.

Gulden. Kur-Pfalz, 1398–1410.

standards. For example, the kings of Hungary struck gulden with a good reputation, while rulers along the Rhine produced an unreliable series. The inconsistency of the coin's gold content led to a distinction in nomenclature. Eventually, a coin with a high gold content would be called a ducat (after the Venetian coin, not widely imitated in the north), while the term gulden was reserved for coins of lower quality. In time, this process led to the renaming of the Florentine florin as it entered northern trade. Germans now called *it* a ducat, as the word was no longer interchangeable with gulden.

The confusion was augmented by the appearance of a new heavy silver coin, also called a gulden, though it did not contain any gold. The silver gulden's genesis was unusual. Count Sigismund of the Tyrol (ruled 1439–1490), wishing to exploit the silver reserves recently discovered in his territory, struck a large silver coin with the value of a smaller gold one. This coin, the direct ancestor of the more famous thaler, was known as a guldengroschen, or simply a gulden. It was well received, and soon other large silver coins—particularly those minted in the Low Countries—took the same name.

For a time, gold and silver gulden circulated side by side: but the gold coin was in effect obsolete by the end of the seventeenth century, while its silver counterpart continued to serve southern and western Germany for another two hundred years. The Netherlands's current monetary unit is still known as a gulden—an indication of the original gulden's distinction in the area.

See also Ducat; Florin; Joachimsthaler; Thaler; Trade coins.

GUN MONEY An emergency coinage issued in Ireland by supporters of the deposed James II of England in 1689 and 1690.

The coins were effectively base-metal promises to pay, and were made from any available brass or brass-like objects that could be melted down, including cannon, the source of the name "gun money."

When James (ruled 1685–1688) arrived in Ireland, planning to use it as a base in his struggle against his successor William III (ruled 1688–1702), he was enthusiastically received. However, he discovered money was hard to come by. While Ireland possessed operable mints—at Dublin and Limerick—there was little precious metal from which to strike coins. The only solution was to use whatever metal was available to produce coins that would be redeemable in real money should James regain his throne.

The issue of sixpences, shillings, and half crowns was authorized in June 1689; we may assume that production began almost immediately. Considering the odds against the Irish coiners, they created a well-designed product. The obverses bore the head of the king, facing left, coupled with his titles; the reverses had the numbers VI, XII, or XXX (for six, twelve or thirty pence, respectively) above a crown and crossed scepters, with JR (for JACOBVS REX) flanking the crown. A most interesting fea-

Gun money. Ireland, half crown, May 1690.

ture of this coinage is that it states not only the year, but the month in which it was issued. The reason is not known, but it has recently been suggested that when James came to redeem the pieces for good coinage, the inclusion of the month would settle any potential disputes as to the order in which they should be redeemed.

James's minters quickly found that even the supply of odds and ends for base-metal coins was limited. Therefore a second issue, reduced in size, was authorized in April and June of 1690. This introduced another denomination, the crown, which had an equestrian figure of James on its obverse, and a reverse showing a cross shaped by shields representing the lands he claimed. Many specimens of this new series were simply overstruck on coins of the first series, and the haste with which this was done often shows in a strong undertype visible through the overstrike.

In the spring of 1690 William II arrived in Ireland to personally direct the campaign against his predecessor. James was defeated and withdrew to France, where he spent the remaining years of his life. His last supporters in Ireland were forced to capitulate in October 1691.

Dated issues of gun money are known through October 1690. These late pieces must have been struck in Limerick, for Dublin and its mint had fallen several months before. The same city produced a series of halfpennies and farthings, most struck over gun money, all dated 1691; they were minted during the siege of the city, and are generally included with the pieces described above in any discussion of gun money.

King James's flight and the subsequent defeat of his Irish supporters meant his emergency coinage would never be redeemed for full value. Eventually the English honored some of it, although they set its exchange value so low in relation to English money (a large half crown could be turned in for three English farthings) that one suspects them of deliberately attempting to insult an already prostrate foe.

No complete mintage figures for Irish gun money have ever been found. Estimates of the total output range from £965,000 to £1,596,000 in face value—which of course means several times that number of actual coins. Since only a small fraction were turned in for English coin, there are numbers of surviving specimens, although choice ones are distinctly difficult to find.

See also EMERGENCY MONEY; OVERSTRIKE; SIEGE PIECE.

GUTSCHEIN One of several closely related types of German emergency currency, issued during and after World War I.

The term means "voucher" in German, and tends to be used in relation to small-denomination bills printed by municipalities for local use (and not for sale to collectors) between 1917 and 1920. It was one of several kinds of emergency money, collectively known as notgeld. The French equivalent of the word gutschein is *bon*, and is found on many emergency notes issued there between 1914 and about 1923.

The piece illustrated is a typical specimen of gutschein, and comes from the town of Santomischel (now Zaniemysl, Poland). The note is small (65 by 38 millimeters) and was printed by movable type on one side only. A rubber stamp with the town's seal, applied to the blank reverse, made the note current.

Austria also printed a large quantity of small-denomination notes called gutschein, most of it in 1920. These were pro-

Gutschein. *Santomischel, Germany, 5 pfennig, 1917.*

duced partly for collectors, however, and they show closer similarities to German notgeld printed for the same purpose than to German gutschein.

See also EMERGENCY MONEY; KRIEGSGELD; NOTGELD.

GUTTER FOLD   A paper money error, resulting in a generally narrow blank area, which crosses the printed face of the note.

This white area indicates a fold in the sheet of paper used to print the bill so that that area could not receive an impression during the printing process. When the fold is not discovered until the bill has been cut from the sheet, the cut will also be jagged.

Gutter folds were more common in the past than they are today, as wet sheets of paper were used in early printing. With the primitive presses then in use, such sheets were easier to print and took clearer impressions. Moistened paper is hard to handle (and particularly *thin* moistened paper, of the kind used to print early paper money), as it tends to adhere to plates, and also to fold over very readily. Modern paper money printing frequently employs a dry printing process. This reduces the risk of gutter folds, but they can still occur.

The illustration shows a detail of a counterfeit Confederate twenty-dollar bill. The gutter fold is plainly seen, as is the typical jagged cut at the bottom of the note. This counterfeit was lithographed, but so was the original—in fact, given the limited printing facilities of the South at

Gutter fold. *Confederate States of America, 20 dollars, 1861 (counterfeit; detail).*

the time, the note looked as good as those it was meant to counterfeit. Southerners apparently thought it was real, for the blank reverse of this bill carries a validation stamp applied by authorities in Jackson, Mississippi. Actually, the evidence that it is a counterfeit is not the gutter fold, but rather the signatures. They are not those the bill should possess, which would have been added by hand after printing. Instead, they are printed directly on the bill, definite proof that it is not genuine.

See also ERROR; LITHOGRAPHY.

H

HACIENDA TOKEN A kind of token used chiefly during the eighteenth and nineteenth centuries in Latin America, to pay workers on large estates (*haciendas*).

Such tokens were ordinarily only redeemable on the hacienda where they were issued, at the *tienda de raya* (company store) or another establishment operated for that purpose.

The hacienda token was a natural outgrowth of the prevailing land and labor system of Spanish America. The original Spanish colonizers needed abundant labor to operate the large farms they were establishing. Chattel slavery, the first expedient attempted, proved impracticable for several reasons. But in the 1550s an alternate solution to the labor problem was found —debt slavery, or peonage. A landowner would loan an Indian money or goods, placing him in debt. The Indian could then work off his obligation by laboring on the hacienda: the debt, however, seemed to have no end. The Indian continued to labor, and when he died his descendants inherited the obligation. So it went, generation after generation.

Aside from working on his lord's land

for a set time, the peon might work a tiny plot of his own, or perform a special service for his landlord, for which some form of payment was needed. He could then obtain goods from his master or goods and services from his fellow peons. This was the genesis of the hacienda token.

These came in a variety of sizes, shapes, and metals. Early examples were often fashioned of copper, and cast rather than struck. They usually had a value of less than a quarter of a real. A typical early hacienda token is illustrated on the left, this one issued in Mexico by Miguel Peres

Hacienda token.
Left: Mexico, Miguel Peres, 1804.
Right: Peru, Hacienda Almendral, 40 centavos, 1878.

in 1804. Later ones were usually struck, and were frequently issued in higher denominations. The second illustration shows a copper-nickel token from Peru, dated 1878. It carried a value of forty centavos, and may have been struck outside the country.

The term hacienda token is somewhat confusing. While it should refer only to those tokens issued by haciendas for their own use, in common practice the phrase also designates certain other non-official pieces manufactured to meet an absence of small change.

See also TOKEN.

HAMMERED COINAGE Coins struck solely by the application of human force, as opposed to those minted by mechanical means.

Hammered coinage was the traditional money minted and circulated between the seventh century B.C. and the sixteenth century A.D.; in remote or backward areas, or those where mechanically produced coinage was impractical, it lingered well into the eighteenth century A.D.

The method was simplicity itself, but the results could be magnificent, as much ancient Greek coinage attests. Two dies were needed. The upper one, called the punch or trussell die, was a tapering cylinder of variable length with an engraved design cut into its under face. Its lower counterpart, the anvil or pile die, was a bar of variable length with an engraving on its upper face; it ended in a lower point, and was frequently splayed outward about halfway up, so it could be forced into a block of wood and held in position during the minting operation. Both dies were usually engraved in intaglio, which produced an impression on the coins in relief. A variant was the hinged die, wherein upper and lower dies were connected to each other by an arm running out from each cylinder, joined by a hinge. This al-lowed exact positioning of the dies in relation to one another.

Next came the planchet. In ancient times, this was cast, then weighed and checked to ensure the coin contained the correct amount of metal. For the thinner coins of medieval times, planchets were cut from a sheet of precious metal, one by one. However they were produced, the blanks were now ready to be struck into coins.

This was the simplest part of the operation. The planchet might be struck cold or hot; cold striking was the rule in the Middle Ages, hot striking earlier. In either case, the blank was placed on the lower die, while the upper die was driven into it with a sledge hammer. This forced the metal into the intaglio portions of both dies and imparted their designs to the coin's two sides. Except for quite small, thin pieces, the process usually needed more than one blow. The first blow fixed the planchet in place; subsequent ones brought up the designs. The coin frequently slipped between strikings, as seen by the number of double-struck ancient and medieval coins surviving. Once sufficient depth of design had been reached, the two dies were separated and the coin removed.

This is how coins were made during the first two millennia of their existence. That the method was primitive cannot be denied; that it served people's needs is also obvious. Had it not, it would have been discarded far sooner.

See also DIE; DOUBLE-STRUCK COIN; PILE; PLANCHET; PUNCH; SEAL; TRUSSELL.

HARD TIMES TOKENS A series of United States tokens—usually struck in copper, and patterned after the large cent —dating from the 1830s and early 1840s.

Like their Civil War counterparts, Hard Times tokens can be divided into two broad categories. One of these referred to national issues of the day. The

Hard Times token.
Top: A "national" Hard Times token, 1838.
Bottom: A Hard Times token of the store card type,
1837.

other was the "store card" variety, conceived to circulate as a business advertisement in addition to its role as small change. Unlike Civil War "patriotic" tokens, the "national" Hard Times tokens were often satirical. They twitted Andrew Jackson and his successor, Martin Van Buren, for policies considered responsible for the depression. (Jackson, noted for his stubborness, was frequently depicted as a mule.)

The national Hard Times tokens afford a panoramic view of American opinion in the late 1830s and early 1840s. Distrust of politicians is here, as is an intense nationalism. Other emotions of the body politic are also revealed: the national token illustrated discusses the slavery question. The obverse adapts a much earlier English design, and shows a kneeling slave in chains, with the legend AM I NOT A WOMAN AND A SISTER. The reverse is a close copy of a contemporary United States cent, with the inscription LIBERTY 1838 substituted for ONE CENT.

The second illustration shows a store card of the period. Its design is straightforward, with an advertisement on the ob-

verse, and a homily (referring to the business, of course) on the reverse. Most store cards in this series are quite simple, many consisting merely of inscriptions, without types. To some extent, this policy would be followed in the next generation by the minters of Civil War store cards.

Hard Times tokens were produced in large numbers for several years, and many are available to collectors at modest prices. Lyman H. Low, who published the first serious catalog of these pieces in 1899, listed 164 distinct varieties, and numismatists have been adding to his list since that time. Their coining ended in the middle 1840s. Economic conditions were improving, "real" money emerged from hiding, and the tokens, like their paper counterparts the shinplasters, were no longer needed. The circulatory life of Hard Times tokens was relatively short, a reason most pieces are in such good condition.

See also CIVIL WAR TOKENS; EMERGENCY MONEY; LARGE CENT; SHINPLASTER; STORE CARD.

HEJIRA The "flight" of Mohammed from Mecca to Medina on July 15, A.D. 622.

Because of his religious teachings, the prophet was forced to quit Mecca, and the day of his departure marks the beginning of the spread of Islam from its city of birth. The Hejira was thus considered of seminal importance: so much so that it, and not some other date (Mohammed's birth, for instance), was chosen as the basis of the Islamic dating system.

See also DATING SYSTEMS.

HELLER A small silver coin of the Middle Ages, the successor to bracteates and deniers in many German-speaking areas.

The coin was first struck by the city of Hall in Swabia (today Schwäbisch Hall, West Germany), which gave the piece its name. The first heller may have been

Heller. Hall, c. 1400.

trians used the heller as part of their monetary reform of 1892 (one hundred heller equalling one krone), and it circulated there until 1923.

See also BRACTEATE; DENIER; KREUZER; PFENNIG.

coined as early as the time of Frederick I Barbarossa (ruled 1152–1190), when Hall was a free city of the Holy Roman Empire. The coin was also known as a handheller, because its obverse type was an upraised hand. Its reverse was a cross, and the original heller carried no inscriptions. It was small (about 16 millimeters in diameter), and very thin and light, weighing under a gram. The specimen illustrated weighs 0.81 grams; examples weighing as little as 0.33 grams have been reported.

Initially the heller was struck in good silver, and there is little doubt that it was meant to replace the denier, which was becoming increasingly debased by 1200. The new coin was an instant success: Hall produced it for over three centuries with unchanged designs, while other German towns, particularly in the Rhineland and the south, eagerly adopted versions of it. Their early issues were often close copies of the Hall coin with its hand-and-cross designs, but variations crept in as time passed.

So did debasement. By the fifteenth century, many heller were minted of inferior silver; the metal then degenerated to billon, and finally to copper. The size and weight of the heller remained modest, and late copper issues had very low values, eight of them equalling a kreuzer in some areas, while in others, two heller equalled one pfennig.

However, this low-value copper heller had a long life. It was struck by the free city of Hamburg until 1865, and the denomination was later adopted for the colony of German East Africa, most of whose coinage was struck in Hamburg. The Aus-

HEXAGRAM   A Byzantine silver coin of the seventh and early eighth centuries; it was equal to one-twelfth of a gold solidus, and had a theoretical weight of six scruples (6.82 grams), hence its name.

The hexagram was first struck in 615, under the emperor Heraclius (ruled 610–641). The new coin was needed to fill a monetary gap, for Byzantine coinage at the time consisted of high-value gold coins and low-value copper ones, with nothing in between. This in fact was to be characteristic of Byzantine coinage production: an emphasis on gold and copper, with relatively little silver.

The hexagram was an effort to alter this, and for a while it succeeded. Far heavier than its predecessors, the early Roman denarius and the later siliqua, the hexagram was, in some ways, a revival of the ancient didrachm. The coin varied wildly in diameter, like copper coins of the same period, but it tended to average around 24 millimeters. The variation in size and the crudity of the planchets used to strike early hexagrams suggests they started life as an emergency issue. Certainly, the year of their introduction saw the Constantinople mint hastily overstriking earlier copper coins for the same purpose. The crisis (a consuming war with the Sassanian Empire) was overcome, but the hexagram kept its awkward "chunky" air, as though it had been struck by people with little time to spare.

Early hexagrams were cruder than later ones, but the designs of both usually paralleled those on Byzantine gold. The hexagrams of Heraclius and his immediate successors had obverses with busts or figures representing the emperor, and frequently members of the imperial family. The reverses showed a cross on steps. Coins with such basic types were struck in quantity until the end of the reign of Constans II (ruled 641–668), when their production seems to have declined. During the first part of the reign of Justinian II (ruled 685–695 and 705–711) hexagrams retained the traditional design, but in 692 the emperor's image was substituted for the cross on the reverse, while his place on the obverse was taken by a full-face bust of Christ. This new practice accorded with changes in the gold solidus, and is important in the histories of coinage and art.

Byzantine coins had always had a religious tone, as seen by their faithful use of the Christian cross. But Justinian II raised the degree of religious emphasis on coinage, and his successors (with the exception of the Iconoclast emperors, who eschewed religious imagery on coinage and elsewhere) tended to follow suit. Christ, Mary, and the saints became regular features of Byzantine coinage, and retained their hold until the fall of the empire in 1453. In the process, the inventory of types available to Byzantine minters expanded enormously, and so, in time, did the repertoire of those coiners farther west. The depiction of Christ on the hexagram and other Byzantine coins, an indication of the influence of the Christian faith during the Middle Ages, broadened the horizons of numismatic art.

The illustrated piece is from the reign of Justinian II, and is one of the first hexagrams to depict Christ. Notice the portrait: it is more lifelike than earlier Byzantine efforts, almost as though the engraver brought greater care to this subject than he would have for a mere emperor. This coin inaugurates the period of outstanding artistry on Byzantine coinage, which was to last from shortly before 700 to just after 1050.

By the time our hexagram was minted, the denomination had lost its position of eminence; those issues after the 680s were probably of a ceremonial nature and not meant for actual circulation. The denomination as such disappeared early in the eighth century, its role taken by a lighter and thinner coin, the miliaresion.

See also CROSS ON COINAGE; DIDRACHM; MILIARENSIS; SILIQUA; SOLIDUS.

HIGLEY TOKENS An extremely rare series of early American copper tokens, dating from the late 1730s.

The gentleman responsible for them was Samuel Higley (1687?–1737), owner of a copper mine near Granby, Connecticut (Granby tokens is an alternate name for the series). Higley was a man of many parts. Although he trained as a doctor, his passion was metallurgy; in 1727, he discovered a way to produce steel from American iron, the first man in British America to do so. He extracted copper from his own property, and though he exported most of it to England, he used some of it to mint tokens for the surrounding area. As a skilled blacksmith, Higley knew how to sink dies and construct a crude coinage press. And once his tokens were finished, he found they had a ready-made market, as the citizens of colonial Connecticut were desperate for metallic currency of any kind.

In those days, the colonies on the Atlantic seaboard used paper money. More often than not, incoming foreign coins returned to England to pay for goods purchased there, and native sources of precious metals had yet to be discovered.

Hexagram. Byzantine Empire, Justinian II, 692–695.

Higley tokens. Connecticut, Higley threepence token, 1737.

A token fared differently, however. It was apt to stay in America because it *was* a token, with a stated value far above its intrinsic worth; while it would not alleviate the shortage of high-value gold and silver coins, it would supplement the short supply of low-value pieces. As it happened, Higley had the skills, the audience, and the copper.

Higley tokens were quite simple in design. A deer formed the main obverse type, below which was the figure III, with a legend reading THE • VALVE [value] • OF • THREE • PENCE. The reverse bore three crowned hammers, the legend CONNEC-TICVT, and the date (1737). These first coppers were criticized as too lightweight, a difficulty Higley resolved with his usual enterprise. He replaced the old legend with a new one, VALUE • ME • AS • YOU • PLEASE—while retaining the value III below the obverse type.

In 1737 Samuel Higley died at sea, en route to England to deliver another load of copper, leaving his elder brother John to continue the coinage. John Higley is probably responsible for the piece in the illustration, which bears no date but was presumably struck later in 1737. He also produced a small series of coins dated 1739, after which the Higley mint closed, in part because of new British monetary regulations.

Higley tokens are rare, and the few that survive are often worn: the piece illustrated is in average condition, or perhaps better. Although the Higleys' long circulation indicates the colonies' dearth of small change, there is another reason for their scarcity. Since they were fashioned of pure copper, colonial metalworkers found them more useful as alloying agents than as tokens, and many, probably most, of them went into the melting pot. It is ironic that Samuel Higley, a metallurgist in spirit, should have had the achievement for which he is noted all but obliterated by his fellow metallurgists. An unofficial monument, of sorts, to Higley's work can still be seen: the pit from which he extracted his copper was later turned into a prison, and served as such for years. It is deserted now, but the hole remains.

See also TOKEN.

HOARD   a group of coins which was lost or hidden *as a group.*

Hoards reveal much useful information about the nature and circulation patterns of coins. Following Philip Grierson's lead in his *Numismatics* (London, 1975), we may list four distinct types of hoards: accidental losses, emergency hoards, savings hoards, and abandoned hoards.

The hoards called accidental losses consist of relatively few coins—those that would be contained in a lost purse or bag. Coins in accidental loss hoards normally represent the circulating currency of the time, and can be of high or low denomination. They are of value to the numismatist because they show what kind of coins circulated in a particular place and time. An early Anglo-Saxon hoard discovered in 1828, for example, contained English gold coins, as one might expect, but also Merovingian ones, and even one Byzantine piece.

The contents of the emergency hoard are usually of the same nature as those of accidental losses, for the original owner buried what he had at a given moment, without attention to the individual quality of the coins. The conscious decision to conceal something distinguishes this hoard from the first.

The emergency hoard can be private or public. An example of a private emergency hoard would be a number of coins hastily buried by an individual during a period of political unrest. An official or public hoard, on the other hand, might be a military pay-chest, hidden for safety during a war. In either case, whoever deposited the hoard was unable to retrieve it—perhaps because of death, abandonment of the site, or simple forgetfulness—and it lay untouched for hundreds, even thousands of years.

The emergency hoard's value stems from the fact that it was directly removed from coinage circulating at a certain time and place. Thus the numismatist can determine the proportion of old and new coins that circulated concurrently. It is also a valuable tool for dating both coins and events. If dated coins exist in the hoard, they may be useful for assigning time-frames to undated ones. With such hoards as evidence, a specific event, such as the sacking of a city, can be given a specific date. And if more than one emergency hoard is found, and the contents overlap, the numismatist may be able to establish a chronological order for an otherwise undated coinage series. An example is the research on the English pennies of William I (ruled 1066–1087) and William II (ruled 1087–1100). Die linkages can reinforce our conclusions here.

Other uses of the emergency hoard include the ability to track the wanderings of peoples—the barbarian raiders of the fifth century, for instance—who left no written record of their travels. Then too, emergency hoards are grim testimony to the movements of armies, for those in their path tended to bury their money.

The third category is the savings hoard, created over a number of years by amassing the heaviest or least-worn gold and silver coins in circulation. Coins of high value and quality are apt to dominate. These hoards are not as useful as the previous ones, for they do not reveal the spectrum of coins in circulation at a given moment. They have advantages, however: the ancient and medieval gold and silver coins seen in museums were very often discovered in savings hoards.

The abandoned hoard is the remaining type in the Grierson classification system. Here coins have been deliberately disposed of by people who have no intention of retrieving them. Buried hoards, in which a person is interred with his wealth as part of the funeral rite, fall into this class. The Sutton Hoo burial hoard of seventh-century Britain is such a deposit, and an unusual one, as it contains coins of high value: more often, funerary hoard coins were of a modest to low value, and obsolete when they were deposited, making it difficult to date their burial. Other examples of abandoned hoards include coins buried in building foundations, and even those thrown into ancient (and modern) wells for luck. The voluntary hoard is of little consequence in the science of numismatics, but it does offer insight to human nature.

HOLED COINAGE   Money minted with a hole, usually round or square, and often in the center of the coin (the hole must be created by the minting authority; any coin with a privately made hole is merely a mutilated coin).

Coins have had holes for a number of reasons. An established manufacturing practice can require them, as was the case of the Chinese ch'ien or cash, which had a square center hole. The hole permitted several ch'ien (rough-edged after the casting process) to be strung on a square rod, which was then spun on a hand-operated lathe, allowing the edges to be smoothed. A government may also find a hole useful for stretching the metal used to strike a coin. An example is a pattern for a United States gold dollar of 1852. The circulating gold dollar was a small coin, the diameter of which (13 millimeters) made it hard to use. Someone thought of a coin with a hole in the center; the pattern was larger, mea-

Holed coinage. Congo Free State, 10 centimes, 1887.

suring 16.5 millimeters, but its wide central hole made it resemble a washer, and the plan was discarded.

Holed coins may also be issued for the gratification or convenience of those using them: the coin in the illustration is a good example. Minted in Belgium for use in the Congo Free State (later the Belgian Congo, now Zaire), it was of low value, and numbers of coins were needed to total even a modest sum of money. How were these coins to be carried about, or kept safely when they were not being used? The hole provided the answer: they could be strung and pieces added or removed as necessary. Or, as the Chinese did, people could trade entire strings, each containing a set number of coins. The custom of stringing was a powerful inducement to providing the holed coin. And not only coins: many tokens were holed, particularly transportation ones which, when strung, were handy for conductors.

People have also enjoyed holed coins because of their distinctive mien. If a government issues two coins, similar in size and general metallic appearance but of different values, one may have a hole to readily distinguish it from its companion. France, for example, once issued silver francs *without* holes, and silvery copper-nickel twenty-five-centime pieces (virtually identical in size but worth only a quarter as much) *with* holes.

See also CASH; EMERGENCY MONEY; HOLEY DOLLAR; TOKEN; VECTURE.

HOLEY DOLLAR An emergency coin produced in New South Wales, Australia, in 1813.

The piece was simply an overstruck Spanish-American Piece of Eight from which the center had been punched; hence its name. The Holey Dollar was valued at five shillings, while the punched-out center piece, known as a "dump," was valued at fifteen pence. The Holey Dollar and the dump were the first distinctive Australian coins.

The colonization of New South Wales, nucleus of the future Australia, began in 1788. Lack of coinage was an overriding problem for the infant settlement, and the early colonists functioned as best they could, primarily by barter, rum being an important medium of exchange.

In 1791 the governor of New South Wales declared the Spanish dollar, or Piece of Eight, to be the colony's legal coinage. It was to have a fixed value of five shillings. British and other coins would also circulate at fixed rates. But these coins flowed out as fast as they flowed in, for if Australians received coins in exchange for their raw materials, they had to quickly exchange them for manufactured goods.

On November 26, 1812, the war sloop *Samarang* arrived at Port Jackson with a cargo that proved a solution: £10,000 in Pieces of Eight (about forty thousand coins). The governor of New South Wales, a Scotsman named Lachlan Macquarie,

Holey Dollar.
Left: *New South Wales, 5 shillings, 1813.*
Right: *"Dump" of 15 pence, 1813.*

had thought of a way to provide the colony with its own currency. His idea was simple: create an overvalued five-shilling piece by removing part of the Piece of Eight and using the detached part (the dump) as a circulating coin too. Since both would be overvalued, they should stay in the colony, rather than being gobbled up in foreign trade.

Macquarie directed William Hershell, a convicted forger, to cut a circular piece from the center of each coin. The obverse of the dump was stamped with the colony's name and the date surrounding a crown, and its reverse with the inscription FIFTEEN PENCE. The remainder was counterstamped NEW SOUTH WALES 1813 on the obverse, FIVE SHILLINGS on the reverse. The coins were apparently released the following year, 1814.

The Holey Dollar and its dump were quite well accepted for a number of years. Eventually, however, the authorities phased out the Holey Dollar in exchange for ordinary English coins, a process that went on until the autumn of 1829. Of the forty thousand Holey Dollars originally struck, less than two hundred are currently known, but a recent estimate of existing dumps is about one thousand. Perhaps more dumps survive because their worth was so minimal people simply forgot to exchange them.

See also DUMP; EMERGENCY MONEY; HOLED COINAGE; PIECE OF EIGHT.

HUB A positive impression in steel of a design to be reproduced in reverse on a die.

The hub is crucial in the mass production of coin dies; indeed, without hubbing, the production of coins could not hope to meet the demand.

In the hubbing process, a relief design of a coin's obverse or reverse is prepared. It is then mounted in a machine resembling a coining press, where it occupies a position analogous to that of an upper die.

Hub. *A hub used to prepare dies for Civil War patriotic tokens, c. 1863.*

A coned die blank of soft steel is centered beneath it, in the bed of the press. The hub is then driven into it. The first strike makes a slight impression on the cone, after which it must be removed and annealed—made malleable enough to receive the next strike and a correspondingly deeper impression. There are as many repetitions of this process as needed—usually three to five. Should the lower cone slip at any time, it can receive a slight secondary impression, out of line with earlier ones. This phenomenon is called "hub doubling," and it resulted in the 1955 "double die" American cent. After the die has been struck the requisite number of times, it is removed and inspected, and if its quality is adequate it is hardened, reexamined, and sent to the machine shop for final tooling.

Historically, the hub itself has been produced in two different ways. Early ones were the product of a master die, carved in intaglio by hand. This master die was then used to create the master hub, with a screw press—or, later, a steampowered one—supplying the necessary force. The designs of the hub were rarely complete; the hub illustrated—designed to prepare dies for United States Civil War tokens and dating from around 1863—is an exception for the nineteenth century.

By that time the United States and other countries were beginning to produce hubs using new methods that employed a reducing machine—actually a pantograph, which reproduced a hub of the correct size and relief from a larger-than-life original. The process allowed a design to be transferred more completely than previously, but it created some particularly mediocre coins: what seemed an attractive design when it was many centimeters across often lost its charm when drastically reduced.

The term hub is distinctly American, the English preferring punch to describe complete hubs as well as smaller elements placed on coin dies.

See also Die; Janvier reducing machine; Punch.

I

ICHIBU GIN A small, rectangular Japanese silver coin, minted between 1837 and 1869.

At its introduction, the piece weighed about 8.7 grams, measured 16 millimeters by 24, and was essentially pure silver. Later issues showed a deterioration in silver fineness, while sizes and weights remained unchanged.

Like several issues of its time, the ichibu gin was a mixture of characteristics typical of Far Eastern coins (its Japanese characters form the predominant design feature of the obverse and reverse) and others that appear Western. The coin was *struck,* not cast, displays small rosettes in border designs on obverse and reverse, and even has something of an ornamental edge—all of which are associated with Western coinage. Finally, the piece is rectangular, an odd shape for coinage East *or* West, and a quality we must simply call "Japanese." To hypothesize a bit, one could say that in its bizarre blend of the oriental and occidental the coin was symbolic of a nation in flux, moving from one culture to another.

The ichibu gin (and other pre-modern Japanese coins) were essentially products of the feudal shogunate. When the last shogun was displaced in 1868, in a revolution that made the Japanese emperor a ruler in fact as well as in name, it led to the Westernization of the country—on Japanese terms. The traditional coinage was examined and, in 1870, the first modern machine-struck coins in the Western style were released, soon displacing those of the past, including the ichibu gin.

See also CHOGIN; KOBAN; MAMEITA GIN; OBAN; TEMPO TSUHO.

Ichibu gin. Japan, 1837–1854.

IMITATION A coin that strongly and intentionally resembles another.

The term is often used as a synonym for copy, forgery, replica, or counterfeit, a confusing and incorrect practice. The words copy, forgery, and replica refer to modern-day reproductions of noncirculating coins, produced for sale to collectors. A counterfeit is a copy of a circulating issue, and by intention worth less than its legal counterpart. An imitation is completely different. It is a public or private coin deliberately fashioned after a well-known prototype, usually a trade coin. The motive is not to defraud: coiners of the imitation merely seek as wide and accepting an audience as possible for their wares, and to better their chances, they imitate a successful coin.

Such coins are no longer produced, although their career was long, beginning in ancient times and continuing well into the twentieth century. Imitations were often struck by people for whom the concept of coinage itself was fairly recent. What ordinarily took place was this: one people would come into trading contact with a less economically developed group. The more advanced group used coinage, which was exchanged in the less advanced area for raw materials or other goods. The benefits of using coins were quickly seen by this second group, and they naturally wished to strike their own. They began by copying the designs on the trade coins. The copying of designs and legends served two purposes. It made the imitators' wares more acceptable, and gave them something to put on their coins, no small consideration for people inexperienced in coin design. Absolutely faithful reproductions were not necessary, and the legends and inscriptions did not have to be literally correct. In fact, as the latter were in a foreign language, and not understood by most members of the community, a rough approximation would do perfectly well.

The weight and metallic purity of the imitative coins, however, had to approximate those of the trade coins, at least at first, for they circulated alongside the old. After the original coins had been successfully replaced, there might be a reduction in the imitations' weight and fineness.

Imitation.
Left: Netherlands, ducat, 1840.
Right: Afghani imitation of Netherlands ducat, c. 1850.

The world of imitations is extensive. Numbers were spawned in ancient times; the Macedonian stater, the Roman antoninianus, and other well-received coins of antiquity circulated among, and were imitated by, the barbarians of central and western Europe. Arab-Sassanian and Arab-Byzantine issues of the seventh century may also be classed as imitations, and imitations of later medieval coins (the denier, the gros tournois, the florin) abound. An entire series of imitative rupees was struck in Tibet in the early part of this century, with the earlier Indian rupee of Queen Victoria serving as a model.

The coins in the photograph allow us to compare an imitation and its original. The piece on the left is a Dutch trading coin, a gold ducat of 1840. The piece on the right is an imitation, fashioned in Afghanistan around 1850. Note the serious attempt to accurately reproduce the standing figure; but other elements, such as the date and the obverse legend, were given far less attention. The imitation was made in good gold and in fact weighed more than the original (3.86 versus 3.49 grams); obviously, there was no intent to defraud, but rather a desire to provide people with a coin whose design inspired trust.

See also ARAB-BYZANTINE COINAGE; ARAB-SASSANIAN COINAGE; BARBAROUS IMITATIONS; COPY; COUNTERFEIT; FORGERY; RUPEE; TRADE COINS.

IMPAIRED Damaged or mishandled: an impaired coin is one in less than perfect condition due to mishandling, rather than, or in addition to, the normal wear encountered in circulation.

The term is most frequently used in reference to proof coins, specially minted pieces for presentation or sale to collectors. The impaired proof is one that has been scratched, nicked, or otherwise abused either at the mint after it was struck or by someone on the outside. The coin remains a proof, of course, but its collector value will have diminished considerably. The exact position of such coins in the grading spectrum is somewhat problematical.

See also GRADING SYSTEMS; PROOF.

IMPRESSION A word used to describe the quality or nature of the printing on a piece of paper currency.

We may speak of a sharp impression, meaning the plate used to print the money was newly engraved, correctly inked, and carefully employed. A weak impression means a worn plate, insufficient ink, and poor printing methods. A blurred impression lacks definition, perhaps because the paper moved during the printing process. The word "impression" is usually accompanied by a qualifying adjective; its coin equivalent is strike.

The term is also—rarely—used for a reproduction taken from a coin in paper, wax, plaster, or some other substance.

See also ENGRAVING; LITHOGRAPHY.

IMPRINT The name of the printer or engraver of a piece of paper money, most commonly seen at the bottom of a note, outside the main designs (although there are exceptions).

The practice of indicating the printer's identity on the note dates back to the eighteenth century. Benjamin Franklin placed his imprint in a prominent position on the bills he printed for Pennsylvanian and other authorities. During the first two-thirds of the nineteenth century, the age

Imprint. Spain, Banco de España, 100 pesetas, 1938 (detail).

of the private bank note in America, the use of imprints was extended. While Franklin's imprint was on the reverse of his notes, forming an integral part of the design, later printers moved their imprints to the obverse, generally placing them at or near the bottom margin of the note. They were less conspicuous in that position, but their presence was still felt to be essential. Wherever it appeared, the imprint was a form of free advertising for the firm producing the bill.

The noted European printing houses were soon duplicating this American practice. While the importance of the private bank note diminished, governments were finding it easier to rely on private firms for their paper money rather than go to the expense of creating state-run establishments. The privately printed bill, whose imprint indicates its origin, is still with us, although mounting nationalism and the diffusion of printing skills have somewhat lessened its popularity. On the other hand, the number of state-run printing establishments is rising, many of which also use imprints.

The illustration shows the imprint on a hundred-peseta note issued in 1938 by the Banco de España, the fiscal arm of the Nationalist government during the Spanish Civil War (1936–1939). The Nationalist movement ultimately triumphed with the aid of several fascist regimes of the time, notably those of Germany and Italy: the imprint on this note proclaims it the product of a German firm.

See also BANK NOTE; BROKEN BANK NOTES.

INCUSE COINAGE Coins whose obverses and/or reverses are deliberately rendered in intaglio, rather than in relief.

The advantage of an incuse design is clear: the coin can stay in circulation almost indefinitely without becoming illegible. The disadvantages are equally clear: dies for incuse coins are more difficult to make, and coins struck with them are less attractive than those minted in the usual fashion.

The latter point is partially the result of conditioning, however. Such coins look strange to us because we are not accustomed to them, but other people in other times and places have found them aesthetically pleasing. The earliest and best-known examples of incuse coinage are from the Greek city-states of southern Italy. Coins of this period were minted by driving a metal planchet into an incuse die with a punch, which made an incuse mark on the planchet, and was eventually turned into a second die. In most places this die, like the lower one, was carved in intaglio, producing a coin with obverse and reverse designs in relief. But the city-states of Metapontum, Kroton, Sybaris, etc., retained the original, relief form of the punch, and carved it into a relief *die*. They left the obverse or lower die as it was, and the coins they struck were thus raised on one side, depressed on the other. In essence, the two dies had to be mirror images of one another: if they were not, maximum relief on the obverse and maximum depression on the reverse could not be achieved. For the same reason, the two dies also had to be perfectly aligned. The logical way to achieve such precision would be with hinged dies, but in the absence of surviving dies of this period we cannot be certain exactly how the striking was accomplished.

The reign of the incuse coin in southern Italy was a brief one. The piece illustrated was struck in Metapontum between 550 and 470 B.C. The latter date would mark the limit for this type of coin: the region's cities then joined the mainstream of Greek coinage.

The incuse coin has seldom been struck since. We see a hint of the method

Incuse coinage.
Left: Metapontum, stater, 550–470 B.C.
Right: United States, 5 dollars, 1914.

in Matthew Boulton's "cartwheel" coinage of 1797, which had incuse legends; the next, and last, notable attempt to strike something akin to an incuse coin occurred in the United States, early in the twentieth century. The two-and-one-half-dollar and five-dollar gold pieces (quarter and half eagles) minted between 1908 and 1929 featured designs set below the surface on both obverse and reverse. These designs were not rendered in intaglio but in relief, which means technically they cannot be described as incuse coins, even though collectors tend to do so. Although the public gave the new coins a lukewarm reception, it must be said in their behalf that they wore very well. The piece in the illustration is a sandblast half eagle proof of 1914.

See also Archaic coinage; Cartwheel; Die; Hammered coinage; Sandblast proof.

INFLATION A reduction in the purchasing power of money.

Inflation is always an indication that a society has lost faith in the agency responsible for the production of money, which, more often than not, means the government. People may suspect its coins of not containing an adequate measure of precious metal, or they may see the state as unable to honor the commitments implicit on its paper money. Economists speak of inflation as a situation in which there is too

Inflation.
Left: Westphalia, notgeld for 50,000,000 mark, 1923.
Right: Hungary, Ministry of Finance, 200,000,000,000,000,000,000,000,000 pengo, 1946.

much money for too few goods, causing a rise in the price of the goods. At bottom, however, lies the problem of trust.

It is unnecessary to detail inflation's history at this point: it has existed in ancient, medieval, and modern times. The Roman antoninianus bore its scars. So did the medieval heller. And the United States dollar bears them now.

The two pieces illustrated show inflation in the twentieth century at work. The example on the left looks like a coin, but is not. It is a piece of inflation notgeld, valued at fifty million marks, and struck in Westphalia, Germany, in 1923. It is a large token, over 44 millimeters in diameter. But the German mark, valued at 4.2 to the dollar in 1914, would be valued at a rate of 4.2 *trillion* to the dollar by the beginning of 1924. It is apparent then that this token was of little real worth, however impressive it may be in size and stated value.

German hyperinflation, which spanned the years 1921 to 1924, grew out of the nation's defeat in World War I, during which the government printed vast amounts of money to be redeemed should Germany win. It did not, and defeat on the battlefield led to the overthrow of the imperial government. The new republican regime had the task of rebuilding the nation, but many of its citizens believed the civilians in the new government were responsible for Germany's loss and humiliation. Moreover, these leaders were sadly lacking in charisma. The new regime, then, was held in contempt by a sizable portion of the population, while the rest were simply apathetic.

Germany was committed to pay vast reparations to the Allies, at the same time that the war had left goods and services in short supply. Inevitably, the republic resorted to the printing press to buy its way out of the dilemma. Just as inevitably, hyperinflation ensued. While American loans allowed the government to reestablish the mark at the pre-1914 level, its inability to solve its problems created an atmosphere of cynicism and scorn for the democratic process, the seeds that were to bear Adolf Hitler.

Germany's 1921–1924 inflation was the worst yet experienced in history; twenty years later, Hungary underwent an even more severe upheaval. The root causes were the same: a lost war, an unpopular government, privation and shortages, distrust, a resort to the printing press. Hungary's inflation lasted only one year, but it produced paper money the denominations of which defy belief. The Hungarian unit of exchange was the pengö. Prior to the outbreak of World War II in 1939, five pengö equalled about one dollar. The note illustrated, produced at the height of the inflation, purports to be worth two hundred septillion pengö (a two followed by twenty-six zeroes). The bill is crudely lithographed, for the simple reason that Hungarian authorities judged it would be worthless in a few days; if such was to be the case, there was little reason to print a better product.

This bill dates from June 1946. Later that summer, the Hungarian government obtained massive aid from the United States and the Soviet Union, abandoned the old monetary system, and created a new one on its ruins. But the damage had been done. Hyperinflation had destroyed the Hungarian middle class and bred disdain for the government, which was eventually replaced by one fashioned after Russia's form of dictatorship.

It is a sad fact that inflation will undoubtedly play as important a role in our future as it has in our past.

See also ALLOY; ANTONINIANUS; ASSIGNAT; CONTINENTAL CURRENCY; MARK; NOTGELD; PAPER MONEY.

INGOT A piece of gold, silver, or any other metal, carrying information about its weight, purity, and, frequently, its origins.

The piece shown is a typical ingot. There is an assayer's punch near the top, the notation 1.44 oz (1.44 ounces, the

Ingot. Silver City, Nevada, $2.55 ingot, 1852–1868.

weight of the ingot), and references to G.025 and S.970 with a large F, which means the ingot contains 97 percent silver, and 2.5 percent gold. Its value ($2.55) is given at the bottom. This particular ingot comes from Silver City, Nevada, and like most early pieces, does not bear a date. Research indicates, however, that it was made between 1852 and 1868. Incidentally, all information is on the "obverse"; the "reverse" is blank except for a simple border design.

The career of the ingot parallels that of the coin. Indeed, in one sense the first coins *were* ingots, for they were merely pieces of metal stamped with a seal guaranteeing their fineness. While these early coin-ingots were usually made of precious metal, the experience of the Romans with the *aes signatum* indicated that a base-metal ingot could also function as a unit of exchange. But a clear distinction between coin and ingot soon arose.

The ingot serves primarily as a measured unit of a metal. Like anything else, it is *worth* an amount of money; but it is not money itself. It can be stamped with a figure giving its worth; but that figure represents only the ingot's intrinsic value at the time it was stamped—subsequently its value will fluctuate, perhaps daily, with the value of the metal it contains.

In recent times, the world has seen a new phenomenon: a gold ingot in the shape of a coin, meant to be sold as one to investors and collectors. The South African Krugerrand is the best-known such piece: although frequently advertised as a coin, it is not. The proof is in the fact that the owner of a Krugerrand cannot spend it in a store. Were it a coin, he could. And what of other pieces bought and sold for their gold content, such as the American double eagle, the Mexican fifty-peso piece, the Russian chervonetz? Are these coins, ingots, or something in between? In such cases, one must base a definition on the original intent of the piece. Was it issued as a coin or as something else? Was it meant to circulate? This approach helps clarify matters. The United States pieces were actually designed for circulation at the time they were minted. So too, were most (but not all) of the Mexican coins. Many pieces dated 1947 are in fact restrikes, minted anywhere between 1949 and 1974, and were seen as a convenient way to dispose of a sizable quantity of gold. They could be classed as ingots with some justification. At present none of the fifty-peso pieces is used directly in commerce, just as the American double eagle no longer circulates. Here, then, are real coins that in effect have become ingots, not through a deliberate act but through the caprice of the marketplace.

The 1923 chervonetz is somewhat harder to classify. It was originally seen as a continuation of the Tsarist ten-ruble piece. Later, the Soviets disposed of the coins that had not entered circulation by selling them, partially for their bullion content, partially for their appeal to collectors. The Russian government then struck the chervonetz with current dates, and the same gold content as the issues of 1923. These pieces are definitely ingots, not coins.

See also BULLION; MARK (MINTMASTER'S OR ASSAYER'S); RESTRIKE.

INSCRIPTION   The letters or words running across the field of a coin or medal.

The term is sometimes used interchangeably with legend, but this is inaccurate. *Legends* circle the inside borders of a coin, while *inscriptions* ordinarily follow a straight, horizontal line or lines.

The illustration depicts an extreme example of the use of the inscription in numismatics. It shows the reverse of a huge quadruple thaler from the German state of Brunswick-New Wolfenbüttel. The piece is one of a series of oversize coins from that section of Germany, and measures a full 77 millimeters in diameter with a weight of nearly 115 grams. Its sheer size encouraged the coiners to strike it more than once to bring up its details, and parts

Inscription. Brunswick-New Wolfenbüttel, quadruple thaler, 1676.

of the coin's inscriptions show signs of double-striking. But its size also allowed the die-sinker enough space for a leisurely description of the life and death of August Friedrich, a member of the ruling house, whose death in 1676 this piece was designed to commemorate.

See also LEGEND.

I PI CH'IEN   A small, cast bronze Chinese "coin," dating from the fourth and third centuries B.C.

I pi ch'ien are roughly oval, tapering more at one end than the other, and all have partial or complete holes, added by the government so they could be traded in strings. The term *i pi ch'ien* means "ant-

I pi ch'ien. China, fourth–third centuries B.C.

nose money," or "ant and nose money," and seems to have been applied to these pieces as early as the twelfth century A.D. Some specimens, including the one in the illustration, have lower characters that resemble an ant, while others have characters that appear as a stylized human nose.

A logical surmise is that the i pi ch'ien grew out of the Chinese use of cowrie shells for trade. The general outline of the piece simulates a cowrie, and one can trace a line of descent from real cowrie shells through stone, bone, and ultimately metal imitations, culminating in the i pi ch'ien. The piece seems to have originated in the Ch'u state of southwestern China, and may have functioned as a subsidiary to a series of extremely rare gold pieces unearthed there.

The typical i pi ch'ien weighs between 3 and 4 grams and measures around 21 millimeters by 14. The characters are on one side only, and are sunk below the surface of the metal. The obverse is slightly convex, while the blank reverse is flat. The use of this money went out of fashion with the introduction of more orthodox round money, especially the pan liang.

See also COWRIE; PAN LIANG.

J

JANVIER REDUCING MACHINE An improved machine for cutting master hubs, invented by Victor Janvier, a French medallist of the late nineteenth and early twentieth centuries.

Janvier's machine was actually a reducing lathe, created to reproduce a small hub from a large model, using the principles of the pantograph. The process was not new, for the French had invented a *tour à réduire* (reducing machine) not long after 1800, and the English had improved on it at mid-century. What was new was the fact that Janvier's lathe could cut superior reproductions from model to hub, and could also work in different heights of relief. In effect, his machine could produce a completely perfect, ready-to-use hub, with all dates and legends present. No previous machine had ever been able to do as much, and Janvier's lathe found instant acclaim and success. It simplified the process of hub production, and enlarged the artistic possibilities of coinage itself. With modest improvements, the Janvier reducing machine is still used today.

To see how it works, we must first imagine that a large model has been prepared. The model and a metal blank are assembled in a lathe, consisting of a belt-work mechanism that rotates both the model and the blank, each of which is in close arrangement with the same long arm. They do not touch the arm, but are touched by two pointers—one records the designs on the model, the other transfers them to the blank.

The model revolves slowly, while the tracer resting on it remains stationary. The blank revolves in the same direction as the model, but its tracer—the cutter — is also rotating at a high rate of speed. Like the tracer for the model, the cutter is positioned at the center of the blank to start with, and moves downward as it cuts. As both model and blank rotate, the tracer picks up information from the model and passes it to the cutter, which then reproduces it on the blank with all details present but greatly reduced. This reduced design appears first in the blank's center, spreading outward as the process continues.

In this first step the design is reduced from, say, 30 centimeters to 10 or 12. This intermediate model is then examined, touched up as needed, and used to make the model for the final hub. The latter can be used to produce working dies, but is more likely to serve in the manufacture of a master die, with which hubs will be struck. These in turn produce the actual dies used for coinage.

See also HUB.

JETON   A counter or token used to reckon money (also spelled "jetton").

Most probably, the jeton originated in thirteenth-century France, and was intended to accelerate and simplify the prevailing system of reckoning, which proved extremely cumbersome because it used Roman numerals.

In a sense, the jeton was a refinement of the abacus. Instead of a series of wires, there was a square, looking very much like a checkerboard. And in place of beads were copper or brass discs—jetons.

Early jetons copied the coins in circulation. The piece shown is typical: dating from late fourteenth-century France, it was probably meant to represent a franc à pied, a gold coin struck under Charles V (ruled 1364–1380).

In the thirteenth and fourteenth centuries, countries throughout western Europe produced jetons; along with the écus d'or, florins, and nobles they were intended to represent, they are proof that the medieval west was experiencing an economic revitalization.

By the late fourteenth century, most jetons were made in Nuremberg, Germany. Their production became the mo-

nopoly of a few families, the Schultes and Krauwinkel families among them. Nuremberg produced jetons for purely local use, but its products also spread across Europe, and Nuremberg jetons are those most frequently encountered by collectors.

With the modern era, double-entry bookkeeping and other new skills accelerated the conduct of business, and the old-fashioned jeton, no longer needed, passed from the banking scene. It emerged in other areas, however, frequently forming the basis of the medalet. It was also transformed into a gaming counter, and used for wagering in card games: such tokens, known as spielmarken, were struck until the beginning of this century.

See also MEDALET; SPIELMARKE; TOKEN.

JOACHIMSTHALER   A large silver coin struck in Bohemia early in the sixteenth century that would lend part of its name to an extensive series of coins of the same approximate size and weight; several coins which actually antedated the Joachimsthaler are still called thalers.

The origins of the Joachimsthaler lay in the expansion of silver mining in central Europe in the fifteenth and sixteenth centuries. Greater production was leading to coins of greater proportions. While most medieval silver coins were rather small because silver itself was scarce, more abundant supplies meant bigger coins could be struck. There were technological problems, to be sure; a moderate- to large-sized coin is difficult to strike by hand. Still, the coins were needed and hence were minted. In time, machinery would be invented to fashion them more effectively.

The first of the large coins, and the direct ancestor of the Joachimsthaler, was the guldengroschen, initially struck in the Tyrol in the mid-1480s. The rulers of Saxony began to mint their own guldengroschen in 1500, after which numbers of mints issued them, paralleling the heightened mining of European silver. In

Jeton. *France, late fourteenth century.*

Joachimsthaler. Bohemia, 1525.

1516, a most promising mine, the property of the counts of Schlick or Šlik, was opened, and around it grew the town of St. Joachimsthal ("St. Joachim's Valley"). This new settlement expanded rapidly: in 1517 it had 400 inhabitants; by 1531 its population stood at 17,490.

Its overlord, Count Stefan of Schlick, was the man responsible for the development of the mine and the coining of its silver. His decision to do so was facilitated by the elevation of St. Joachimsthal into an official mining town, thereby according it special political privileges. Count Stefan immediately engaged a mintmaster to begin coining, even though this was not one of the town's rights. But protracted negotiations with the Bohemian parliament won the count such a right. Patterns for the new coins were produced in 1519, and the first coins struck in 1520. Almost immediately, they were dubbed Joachimsthalers.

The Joachimsthaler was heavy, with a weight of 29 grams and a diameter of 40 millimeters. Its silver content was 93 percent, less than other guldengroschen of the period: apparently the count hoped to realize a profit on his enterprise. The coin's obverse pictured St. Joachim, with the arms of the Schlick family. Many specimens, including the one illustrated, were dated; others were not. The obverse legend named Count Stefan and his brothers the authorities responsible for the coin. The reverse paid homage to the family overlord, the king of Bohemia—his names and titles formed the reverse legend, while the heraldic lion of Bohemia was its central type.

The coin was struck in quantities quite sizable for the period. By 1533, production of silver from the mine reached 87,000 marks. (The mark was a unit of weight which varied from place to place; at St. Joachimsthal it measured a trifle under 256 grams.) Obviously, a great many coins could be struck from such an amount of silver, but by this time the Schlicks were no longer making a profit. Stefan had perished at the battle of Mohács in 1526; the family holdings were divided, and eventually were lost. The real beneficiary of the mine turned out to be the Holy Roman Emperor Ferdinand I (ruled 1527–1564), who acquired it in 1528, and under whose ownership production reached a peak in the 1530s. Minting of Joachimsthalers continued until c. 1540, and in time the name came to designate any large silver coin with the original's general lines. The term, if not the coin, proved cumbersome, however, and was shortened to thaler.

See also GULDEN; MARK; THALER; TRADE COINS.

JUGATE The term for the depiction of two heads side by side on one face of a coin: the complete head of one of the subjects is shown, with at least the profile of the other.

Jugate portraiture has not been widely used in numismatic art, for the obvious reason that in theory it calls for two people to rule the same country at the same time

Jugate. England, 5 guineas, 1691.

—an infrequent occurrence. All the same, it has happened occasionally, and the jugate portrait has centered attention on the fact. Other ways to do so are with vis-à-vis portraiture, or the depiction of one ruler on the obverse and the other on the reverse.

The earliest use of the jugate technique took place in the Hellenistic period. A gold octadrachm of Ptolemy III of Egypt (ruled 246–221 B.C.) depicts his head along with that of his wife and co-ruler, Berenice. The piece illustrated is much later, struck during the joint reign of William and Mary of England, which lasted from 1688 until her death in 1694. The king, as can be noted, occupies a more prominent position, nearer to the viewer, for at the time he was England's effective ruler, even though he claimed the throne through his wife. The relative importance of the subjects in a jugate portrait is commonly revealed in this fashion.

In the last century the jugate portrait has been confined to commemorative coinage. Several United States half dollars of the 1920s and 1930s bore such portraits, and upon occasion they appear on commemorative issues of other countries. The technique has occasionally appeared on medals as well.

See also COMMEMORATIVE; OCTADRACHM; PORTRAIT; VIS-À-VIS TYPE.

K

KEPING Originally, a series of copper coins issued by the East India Company for use in Malaysia in the late eighteenth and early nineteenth centuries; the term more commonly refers to a large series of private copper tokens, issued mainly by merchants in Singapore during the first half of the nineteenth century.

Alternate spellings are kepang, kepeng, kapang, and kupang. The word is of Malayan origin, and means a bit, or piece.

The keping tokens were generated by the phenomenal growth of Singapore: founded in 1819, it rapidly dominated trade in the Malay Archipelago. In consequence, it soon found itself lacking small change, an absolute necessity for the normal pursuit of business.

The East India Company, which ruled the area at the time, refused to help business by providing official small change. Taking matters into their own hands, local merchants issued small copper tokens, the kepings, in the late 1820s, and continued to do so until the 1850s.

Most of the merchant tokens were rather elementary. A popular type featured a rooster on the obverse, the value and date on the reverse. Dates were expressed according to the Islamic era, and inscriptions were rendered in Malay. The exchange value of these pieces is problematical: certain sources indicate they went for four hundred to a Piece of Eight, but their actual exchange rate varied, and such extremes as eighty kepengs to the dollar and sixteen hundred to the dollar have been recorded. The total number of kepings struck is not known, but it must have been several hundred million. Most were coined in England, and imported to Singapore in casks of 100,000.

The demise of the keping finally came when the East India Company began shipping specially minted coins, valued at a quarter-cent, half-cent, and cent, to Singapore. The first such shipment arrived in May 1847; further issue of kepings was prohibited after January 1, 1848. Merchants continued to import them until 1853, as merchandise rather than as coins.

The piece illustrated is a keping from Sarawak. Its size (21.5 millimeters) and weight (2.1 grams) are correct for the entire series. Its legends are unusual, how-

Keping. Sarawak, dated 1841 but struck later.

ever, and require a bit of explanation. Sarawak was given to Sir James Brooke by the sultan of Brunei in 1841, for his help in quelling a rebellion. Brooke thus became the first of a famous line of "White Rajahs," who ruled Sarawak until 1946.

The obverse of this piece refers to Sir James. The central type is a badger, derived from the crest of the family arms. Below it are the initials J.B. (for James Brooke) and SEP! 24 1841 (the day Brooke received power). The reverse states the value of the piece (one keping) and a Hejira date (1247). This date corresponds to the Christian year 1831–1832, and is explained by the fact that the British manufacturer of the coin simply reused an old reverse die of the early 1830s. The *actual* date is unclear, but the coin was probably struck in 1842 or 1843.

See also TOKEN.

KLIPPE   A general term—probably from the Swedish *klippa*, to clip or cut with shears—for a coin struck on a square, rectangular, or lozenge-shaped planchet.

Klippe. City of Cologne, thaler, 1592.

The klippe must be distinguished from the ordinary square coin. The shape of the latter is chosen and it is commonly part of an entire series of square coins. The klippe's shape, on the other hand, is often dictated by necessity (an urgent need for coinage, insufficient time to make round planchets), and the coin is frequently the only square one in an otherwise round coinage series.

The piece shown is a good example. It is a thaler from the city of Cologne, dated 1592. The obverse displays the arms of the city, the reverse those of the Holy Roman Empire, Cologne's overlord. Except for its shape, it is identical to those struck before and after it.

Klippes are best known in Germany and the Low Countries, where they were produced during the Wars of the Reformation, which occupied much of the sixteenth and seventeenth centuries. Even at that period, not all klippes were struck simply to meet the emergency. Both the Saxons and Danes used the form for commemorative purposes; the odd shape of the coin was a vivid reminder of an event. The present century has seen the occasional appearance of another type of klippe, one produced as a pattern for a proposed coinage design. Several Polish issues of the early 1930s fall into this category.

See also COMMEMORATIVE; NECESSITY MONEY; SIEGE PIECE; SQUARE COINAGE.

KNIFE MONEY   An early form of bronze Chinese currency, cast in the shape of a knife.

There is no universal agreement as to when knife money was introduced. The piece shown was probably cast in the ninth century B.C., but the form itself may have been invented two hundred years earlier. The general Chinese name for such pieces is tao.

The tao is one of a number of objects which might be called "barter coins"; as such, it sheds light on one theory of how coinage developed. According to this notion, the evolution was in three stages. The first was barter, pure and simple, in which various objects were traded for one another. The second stage was a monetary one, in which certain objects were agreed upon as exchange media: in the case of China, these were metallic replicas of original trading items, used because of their greater durability or convenience. In the third stage, metallic trading pieces were forsaken and coins as we know them came into existence.

The curious forms of early Chinese money, then, become understandable. The bronze cowries represent real shells, but do not break as easily. The bronze knives and the contemporaneous spades are also durable, but have other advantages as well. Smaller than their prototypes, they are more conveniently transported. And since they represent farming implements, and China is a farming country, they will always be welcome in trade, either for knives or spades or other objects of equal value. Knife and spade money share two characteristics: first, they tend to decrease in size and weight through time, and second, very early knives and spades lack inscriptions, while later ones carry them.

The tao in the illustration measures 177 millimeters from end to end, and weighs nearly 49.6 grams. Later issues were smaller and thinner, weighing only a quarter or a fifth as much. The knife (and the spade along with it) finally passed from use in the third century B.C., as new, round coinage came into vogue. There was a brief move to revive it during the reign of the usurper Wang Mang (ruled A.D. 7–23), but this regression to an earlier form was dropped after his overthrow.

Virtually all forms of ancient Chinese money have been extensively forged over the past hundred years or so, and some are quite difficult to detect. These are cast (as were the originals), and frequently exhibit most convincing signs of "patina-

Knife money. *China, ninth century* B.C.

tion," either from being buried or cleverly painted. It is always wise to avoid a piece which appears grossly underpriced. It is also wise to obtain a certificate of authenticity, or written return privileges, from the seller.

See also CAST COINAGE; MONEY; SPADE MONEY.

KOBAN The best-known Japanese gold coin of the Tokugawa Shogunate (1599–1868).

Although the koban was actually introduced in the latter part of the Ashikaga era (1392–1568), few early specimens have survived. The piece was first minted in quantity in 1600. It had a face value of one ryo, and ten koban made up the largest gold coin of pre-modern Japan, the oban.

The first Tokugawa koban weighed 18 grams, and contained 84.2 percent pure gold. It had an impressive purchasing power, and could in theory be exchanged for twenty strings (165.4 pounds) of copper coins. The value of the koban in relation to silver fluctuated; in fact, it was an important characteristic of precious-metal money in the pre-modern Far East that coins were traded essentially as commodi-

Koban. Japan, 1837–1858.

ties, not as coins in the Western sense. Therefore any statement of exact ratios is at best theoretical.

The koban illustrated was made between 1837 and 1858. It is oval, and measures some 60 millimeters by 30. The koban was actually struck with a number of punches. The larger and fancier ones on the obverse give the coin's denomination and the authority under which it was issued, while those on the reverse refer to the mint and the era during which it was produced.

Significantly, this koban weighs only 11.2 grams, and its gold content is less than 60 percent. During the later years of feudal Japan there was a general downward slide in metallic content and fineness, induced by the shogunate's inept domestic policies. The last koban, minted during the Manen era (1860–1867), weighed only 3.3 grams, with a gold content of slightly under 60 percent. The koban disappeared, as did other premodern coins, with the expulsion of the last shogun and the resumption of imperial control in 1868.

See also OBAN; PUNCH.

KOPEK A Russian silver coin introduced in 1534.

The new coin equalled two silver dengas, and its name probably derives from *kopie*, Russian for "spear." The kopek's obverse bore a representation of a horseman with a spear, perhaps to distinguish it from the denga, which also pictured a rider, but one armed with a sword. Like the denga, the early kopek falls under the heading of wire money: planchets used to mint it were prepared by cutting off prescribed lengths of heavy silver wire, then hammering them into ovals. The resulting coins often lacked much of their designs, for the dies were round. A very brief obverse inscription might appear under the horseman; a longer one, arranged in several lines, served as the reverse type. These silver kopeks were extremely light, weighing between one-half and two-thirds of a gram, and at their widest measured only 15 millimeters. They were minted over a period of almost two centuries with no major changes.

In 1700, Peter the Great (ruled 1682–1725), put Russia on a decimal coinage system. His reform envisaged a special role for the kopek. One hundred kopeks would equal one silver ruble. The new kopek would be struck by machinery, as would the other coins in the decimal system. (This reforming tsar also introduced the screw press to Russia.) To make certain the coin was large enough to be pleasing in design, it would be made of copper rather than silver.

The first of these new kopeks was struck in 1704. It still bore the figure of a horseman with a spear on the obverse,

Kopek. Russia, copper kopek, 1707.

presumably to help the illiterate understand that the new coppers were the equivalent of the old silver coins. A long obverse
legend announced the tsar's titles, while a
central reverse inscription gave the denomination and date (the latter rendered
in Cyrillic letters rather than in numerals).
The copper kopek radically departed
from previous Russian coining practice,
and the man responsible for the innovation was somewhat unsure of what he had
wrought: during the years between 1704
and 1718, both copper *and* silver kopeks
were minted. Most of the silver ones were
wire money.

The designs, modules, and even metallic content of the kopek have been altered
since Peter's reign. Yet its position as a
linchpin of the Russian decimal system remains as important today as it was when it
was introduced nearly three centuries ago.

See also DECIMAL COINAGE; RUBLE; SCREW
PRESS; WIRE MONEY.

KREUZER A name applied to a number
of central European coins, which remained in use in some areas until the late
nineteenth century.

The first kreuzer was struck about
1258 at Merano, a Tyrolean town on the
Italian border. Silver had been discovered
in the Tyrol in the previous century, and
the minting of coinage was a sensible way
to dispose of the metal. By the time the
counts of Tyrol decided to strike these
coins, the grosso and similar pieces, larger
and heavier than the old denier, were particularly favored in European trade. The
kreuzer, then, would be fashioned after
them. Initially it was called a tirolino, in
deference to its origins, but the German
term kreuzer, which refers to the double
cross forming the obverse type on early
specimens, eventually replaced it.

The piece illustrated is from the time
of Count Meinhard II (ruled 1271–1295),
when the kreuzer was at the height of its
popularity. Our coin weighs 1.6 grams,

Kreuzer. Tyrol, 1271–1295.

and has a diameter of 21 millimeters. The
double cross shapes the central obverse
design, while a spread eagle is the reverse
type. A legend, starting on the obverse
and ending on the reverse, relates Meinhard's name and titles. This coin was a
splendid success in southern Germany, so
much so that the counts of Tyrol continued to strike it with identical types for
more than a century. The legends, too, remained the same and were simply updated.

In time the weight and silver content
of the piece diminished, and after 1500 it
was only struck sporadically in the Tyrol,
but by then the coin had travelled well beyond the confines of its original home. At
first struck from silver, and later from copper, the kreuzer became an indispensable
small-change piece in Austria, Hungary,
and much of southern Germany. The
Austrian Empire struck copper coins of
that name until 1891, one hundred of
them equalling one florin or gulden.

See also GROSSO.

KRIEGSGELD A term for a metallic
form of German notgeld, issued between
1917 and 1921; literally translated, the
word means "war money," as this currency
was a direct outgrowth of World War I.

As the war ground on, the morale of
German citizens declined. Uncertain
about who would be the victor and who
the vanquished, people started hoarding
anything of tangible value, and coins, of
course, were among the most coveted.
Hoarding began in border areas with the

Kriegsgeld. Warburg, Germany, 5 pfennig, 1917.

outbreak of the war and eventually spread throughout the country.

By the spring of 1917, paper notgeld, usually in denominations of less than one mark, was being issued by hundreds of cities, towns, and businesses. Soon after there came low-value *metallic* notgeld, known by a variety of names—gutschein, kleingeld, kriegsmünze, notgeld—or kriegsgeld, the name given to the entire series. A number of denominations were struck, although they were never valued at more than fifty pfennig. Most kriegsgeld were round, but some were hexagonal or, as illustrated, octagonal. This token was struck in iron; iron and zinc were the metals most frequently used for minting kriegsgeld. Results from them were indifferent, but at least their supply was plenti-

ful. The designs' quality also varied, although many kriegsgeld tokens exhibit a degree of skill, suggesting they were struck in establishments specifically set up for that purpose. This would parallel the career of paper notgeld, production of which was largely concentrated in the hands of a few printing houses by the end of the war.

Kriegsgeld was struck until 1921. The use of the word on the token declined after 1919, as the war itself had ended, and later issues tended to simply be called notgeld. This was perfectly legitimate: the latter term means "emergency money," and even if the war were over, the state of emergency was not. Thus we have notgeld struck in metal. To compound the confusion, we also have kriegsgeld printed on paper. The German people tended to use the terms indiscriminately at the time; using kriegsgeld for metallic tokens of the period and notgeld for paper is suggested as a way to avoid confusion between the two series.

See also EMERGENCY MONEY; GUTSCHEIN; NOTGELD; ZINC COINAGE.

L

LAMINATION A "peeled" area on the surface of a coin or planchet.

Laminations are caused by impurities in the metal. They may also occur because of improper alloying practice, particularly in the case of copper-nickel mixtures.

Occasionally, a non-ductile substance finds its way into that area of the mint where raw metals are refined and is mixed into an ingot, where it remains until the ingot is drawn through the rollers and made into the flat, thin strip from which planchets are stamped. As the foreign matter passes between the rollers, it is crushed, and may leave an easily detectable small hole in its place. But if the impurity runs beneath the surface, it can simply spread out, separating the metal surrounding it into layers, or laminations. When this metal is fashioned into planchets and then into coins, the pressures of these later stages may bring out major laminations. These are usually visible before the coin is released; but if the lamination is well below the surface, it may not show up during these later stages. The laminated coin can make its way into circulation, its defects being discovered only with the passage of time.

The coin in the illustration is an excellent example of a laminated error. Although the laminations cover approximately 50 percent of the obverse of this 1917 cent, it circulated nevertheless, as attested to by the wear on the high points of its design.

The second form of lamination, due to faulty alloying procedures, is prevalent on coins with a nickel content, which usually means the copper-nickel coin. Nickel is a notoriously troublesome metal from which to strike coins. It is exceedingly hard, shortens the life of dies, has a high melting point, and can be alloyed with other metals only with great difficulty. The latter two

Lamination. United States, cent, 1917.

traits mean a high incidence of laminations on coins made from alloys containing nickel.

Others can occasionally be even worse. During World War II, the United States removed nickel—a critical war material—from its five-cent piece, and substituted a mixture of copper, silver, and manganese. Nickel was saved, but the new alloy proved even harder to control than its predecessor and quantities of laminated coins were produced.

See also ALLOY; COPPER-NICKEL COINAGE; ERROR; PLANCHET.

LANDMÜNZEN German copper or base silver coins designed for circulation only in a specific *land* or province, as opposed to pieces which were current throughout an entire kingdom.

The coin shown well illustrates the operation of landmünzen. It was struck by Ernst I, who ruled the duchy of Saxe-Coburg-Saalfeld from 1806 to 1826. In the latter year, Gotha joined his holdings, and he reigned as duke of Saxe-Coburg-Gotha until his death in 1844. The landmünzen was struck for both Saalfeld and Coburg (the piece in the photograph is a six-kreuzer issue for circulation in Coburg), and subsequently for Gotha. In addition to issues for local use, there was a second issue to be circulated throughout the entire duchy. These coins were of higher value than the landmünzen, and their precious-metal content was good. The example of Saxe-Coburg-Saalfeld (or -Gotha) typifies the operation of the

Landmünze. Saxe-Coburg-Saalfeld, 6 kreuzer, 1825.

landmünze system. The rationale for it is obscure, but one supposes governments found it an inexpensive way to nurture local pride and supply essential small change at the same time.

Landmünzen seems to date from the mid-seventeenth century, when the existence of disparate districts ruled by one monarch was commonplace. It was widely produced for the next two centuries. In 1871 the creation of the German Empire, with a national currency based on the mark, assigned landmünzen to history.

See also KREUZER.

LARGE CENT A very important United States copper coin, first discussed in the 1780s, created by law in 1792, and struck in quantity from 1793 to 1857.

The Fugio cents and state coppers of the 1780s are direct ancestors of the large cent; in the latter category, the state of Massachusetts actually struck coins with the expressed denomination of a cent in 1787 and 1788. Still, while the idea of a large copper coin called a cent had existed for numbers of years, it was not until the early 1790s that the significance of the coin was assured. In 1792 the United States Congress enacted the Mint Act, establishing a decimal coinage, the unit of which would be the silver dollar, consisting of one hundred copper cents.

The original cent was supposed to weigh 264 grains (or about 17.1 grams), but the stipulated weight was reduced before the first circulating cents were struck, and the issues of 1793 to 1795 were struck to approximately 13.5 grams. The weight was again reduced later in 1795, and large cents minted from then until 1857 were slightly under 10.9 grams. As their diameters increased from 26 or 27 millimeters to 29, and they contained less metal, the use of lettered or ornamented edges seen on the first issues was suspended.

Work on a federal Mint was undertaken in 1792; a year later it struck its first coins—the large cent and the half cent. The coiners' working conditions were arduous: pay was minimal and hours were long. Located in Philadelphia, the new Mint was forced to close each summer to let its employees escape the yellow fever which plagued the city each year. (One of the large cent's early designers, Joseph Wright, failed to leave in time, and died.) Machinery had to be imported or improvised at home; whatever its source, it broke down with frustrating regularity. Metal was hard to procure. In the case of precious metals, the Mint assayed the metal and turned it into coin for free, an inducement to contribute bullion, but also a drawback, for it meant the Mint operated continually at a loss. For copper, it placed advertisements in newspapers and hoped for the best. And the Mint's woes were only exacerbated by persistent Congressional criticism, demanding the facility be closed and American coinage contracted for abroad.

The piece illustrated points to yet another of the Mint's problems: finding qualified designers. This 1793 large cent, one of the first of that denomination to be struck, was designed by Henry Voigt. His lack of expertise is sadly evident. The obverse and reverse designs are too shallow, Liberty's face is crudely interpreted, and the artist, in a gross misjudgment of the space on the reverse, found he had to abbreviate the country's name to AMERI.. The central chain device was especially unfortunate. Voigt adapted it from the earlier ring reverse seen on the Fugio cent. He converted the round rings into oval links, however, and what had been conceived as

Large cent. United States, 1793.

a symbol of solidarity was generally thought to be one of slavery, an ill omen for the new Republic. Opposition to the coin was emphatic. Voigt was fired, and a new designer employed, who produced a cent with a wreath in place of the chain. The elements of Liberty for the obverse and a wreath for the reverse would be basic fixtures for the large cent until its demise in 1857. Liberty was rendered in numerous ways (so, to a lesser extent, was the wreath) but the large cent was never to attain even the modest heights of artistry achieved on gold and silver American coins.

Large cents prior to 1816 are fairly scarce. Later issues are more common, especially those minted between the late 1830s and the middle 1850s. By the latter period, however, the large cent was becoming something of a liability. While many people objected to its size and weight as cumbersome, the government was discovering that, with the price of copper rising, it cost almost as much to mint the coin as it was worth. Several new patterns were proposed, and one of them, a copper-nickel piece with a flying eagle on the obverse, entered circulation late in 1857, the legislation implementing the small cent having been passed the previous February. In all probability, the old and new cents circulated side by side at least a few years, for many large cents of the 1850s show considerable wear.

About the time the large cent was abandoned in the United States, it was introduced in Canada. The first cent for general Canadian circulation was released in 1858, and it, too, was a "large" cent, the hundredth part of a decimal dollar (which was not struck until 1935). The government of Canada struck large bronze cents, measuring 25.4 millimeters in diameter, until 1920, when the coin fell victim to an economy campaign at the Canadian mint.

See also DECIMAL COINAGE; DOLLAR; FUGIO CENT; MINT ACT OF 1792; SMALL CENT; STATE COINAGE.

Larin. *Ceylon (Sri Lanka), sixteenth century or later.*

LARIN A silver currency used along the maritime trading route that extended from the Persian Gulf around the west coast of India as far as Ceylon.

The larin coinage was broadly employed between approximately 1500 and 1700, and was minted in two varieties. The first type, illustrated here, is generally known as a bent or fish-hook larin because of its shape. This type circulated in Ceylon and the Maldive Islands, and some, including the one in the photograph, were made in Ceylon. The second type of larin, the straight or hairpin variety, which was sometimes later fashioned into the hook shape if it came to Ceylon, comes from western India and the Persian Gulf region.

Larins usually weighed some 4.9 grams, and were made of good silver. Straightened, our specimen would measure about 43 millimeters in length, fairly typical for this series.

These pieces are coins, albeit rather unusual ones. A thin strip of silver was cut, adjusted for weight, folded over on itself, and then struck with a die on one or both sides. Since the planchet was relatively narrow, much or most of the inscription could not be transferred to the coin. These incomplete legends make it hard to attribute larins with any degree of certainty.

It is known that a series of debased larins was used on the west coast of the Persian Gulf in the eighteenth century. And the name, at least, was kept for the modern coinage of the Maldive Islands, where one hundred lari equal one rupee.

See also WIRE MONEY.

LEGAL TENDER NOTE A type of United States paper money introduced in 1862 and still circulated.

The name of these notes derives from the reverse inscription on early issues, which defined them as legal tender for all debts public and private. They are also known as "United States notes," since this inscription often appears at the upper or lower margin of the obverse.

Like its immediate predecessor, the demand note, the legal tender note was engendered by the turmoil of the American Civil War. The war effort of North against South was costly, but the period's archaic taxation system yielded no orthodox means for Abraham Lincoln's government to raise money. The Legal Tender Act, passed by Congress on February 25, 1862, was a solution. It provided for an initial issue of one hundred and fifty million dollars in legal tender notes, exchangeable for 6-percent government bonds, and redeemable in five years. A later clause broadened the exchange scope of the notes, but a basic fact remained: unlike the earlier demand note, the legal tender note was *not* immediately redeemable in coin. It was fiat money, acceptance of which was a legal obligation.

The notes did not win the public's enthusiasm and their value slipped against specie. While there had been solemn promises that the first legal tender issue would also be the last, a second one was called for on July 11, 1862, putting one hundred and fifty million dollars in new notes into circulation; a third Legal Tender Act, passed early in March 1863, authorized yet another one-hundred-fifty-million-dollars' worth of legal tender notes. All the issues were to be backed by interest-bearing bonds. However, the legal

Legal tender note. United States, dollar, 1862. (Courtesy *The Comprehensive Catalog of U.S. Paper Money,* by Gene Hessler)

tender notes authorized on March 3, 1863 were not issued during the Civil War, the government having overhauled its tax system and created elaborate machinery for internal revenue collection. The new taxes meant a solvent government, and, in the eyes of its citizens, a more credible one. No longer did it need to resort to the printing press; this and the prospect of a Northern victory raised the value of the legal tender note, which had reached its nadir of some thirty-five cents against one dollar in gold in mid-1864. By the following spring, it had virtually doubled.

With the end of the war, pressures on United States currency abated. Legal tender issues were printed under the authority of the 1863 act, over a long period of time, with series dates ranging from 1869 to 1923. Their importance diminished as the twentieth century wore on— as did that of most United States paper currency. Today the Federal Reserve note, introduced in 1914, is the dominant form of American paper, although a few hundred-dollar bills, the last representatives of the legal tender or United States note, are still produced. In this respect, the legal tender note is unique, for it is the only early American federal currency which has managed, even partially, to maintain its identity in the face of the Federal Reserve note.

See also DEMAND NOTE; FEDERAL RESERVE NOTE; FIAT MONEY; GREENBACK; NATIONAL BANK NOTE.

LEGEND The words or abbreviations, etc., surrounding the fields of a coin or medal.

Ordinarily, such pieces are round, causing the lines created by their legends to resemble circles or arcs. It is this that distinguishes the legend from the inscription, which runs across the field of a piece. The illustration shows the apotheosis of the legend. It is the reverse of an English half-penny token of 1796, and the legend in fact *is* the reverse. The token was made for an enterprising nurseryman from Gloucestershire, who must have instructed the die-sinker to see to it that a goodly amount of information fit in a restricted space. The result was this spiral legend. The proper placement of several dozen letters on a constantly moving plane taxes the ingenuity; this particular engraver met the challenge with a curving line beneath the letters, which enabled him to align them correctly. Flourishes at either end complete the design.

See also INSCRIPTION.

Legend. Newent, Gloucestershire, halfpenny token, 1796.

LEPTON A general term for a small ancient Greek copper or bronze coin; more specifically, a series of small bronze pieces struck by authorities in Judea between the late second century B.C. and the middle of the first century A.D., among the earliest coins minted by the Jews.

The first Jewish coinage was formerly dated to the time of Simon Maccabaeus, who served as Judea's high priest and civil governor between 145 and 135 B.C. In 140, Simon is said to have received permission to strike coins from his nominal overlord, Antiochus VII of Syria. Both Simon and his successor, John Hyrcanus I (ruled 135–104 B.C.), supposedly struck coins, and it was formerly said that the lepton was introduced during the latter's reign. Ya'akov Meshorer has recently argued that this chronology is highly unlikely, and that the coinage of the Jews, including the lepton, probably does not antedate the reign of John's eventual successor, Alexander Jannaeus (ruled 103–76 B.C.).

Alexander's long administration produced a large number of lepta. Considering the average circulation life of ancient coins (which seems to have been much longer than for modern ones), the widow's mites mentioned in the Bible could very well have come from this reign. This would have given them a circulatory life of about a century by the time Christ observed their use and mentioned it in a parable. The coins could also have come from the time of Herod the Great (ruled 37–4 B.C.), which is perhaps more likely.

One of Herod's coins is illustrated here. As its popular name ("mite") would suggest, it is an exceedingly small coin, measuring between 15 and 16 millimeters in diameter, and weighing a scant 1.65 grams. The designs of the coin were determined by the Bible, which forbade the use of "graven images"—Jewish coins therefore tended to rely on the depiction of inanimate objects for their designs. The obverse of this lepton bears an anchor, surrounded by a legend referring to the king; the reverse features two cornucopias, an allusion to the prosperity of the country during this king's tenure.

Herod's death in 4 B.C. triggered a chain of events culminating in Rome's command of Judea. Her procurators, the most famous of whom was Pontius Pilate (ruled A.D. 26–36), ruled Judea for most of the period between A.D. 6 and A.D. 66. Like the former kings, they too issued lepta. Although their coins were similar to earlier ones, they contained a reference to the emperor and his regnal year in Greek. Coins of the general size and weight of a lepton were struck through, but not after, the great Jewish Revolt of A.D. 66–70. One authority, incidentally, states that the lepton had a fixed value of 1/400 of a shekel. The Greek name for the coin comes from that language's word for "small" or "thin."

The Greeks themselves revived the lepton almost two thousand years later, once they were independent of the Ottoman Empire. Their new nation needed a new coinage, and they conceived one based on a decimal system, in which one hundred lepta equalled one drachma. Modern lepta were struck between 1828 and 1879, and multiples of the lepton are still minted.

See also SHEKEL; TALENT.

Lepton. Judea, 37–4 B.C.

LETTERED EDGE Incuse or relief lettering placed on the edge of a coin before or during striking.

Today lettering serves primarily as ornamentation. When it was introduced, however, its purpose was more basic—the protection of the coin against filing and falsification.

Several processes have been used to fashion the lettered edge. In one, a segmented collar with the designed lettering surrounds the coin as it is struck. The pressure of the upper and lower dies forces the metal outward, and it picks up an impression of the edge lettering. Although this method, developed in the sixteenth century, has been improved at various times, it is still apt to retard coining. Edge-marking machinery was invented in the seventeenth century, and imparted a lettered edge to the planchet before it entered the coining press. The planchet was then struck without a collar, so the edge devices would not be marred. It performed well enough for lettering edges, but made standardization of size difficult to achieve. Such machinery was generally abandoned in the nineteenth century, in favor of the segmented collar, or an altogether new method that applied *incuse* lettering to the edge during the planchet stage. The planchet was then struck in a one-piece collar. Not only was roundness assured, but it was a faster process than the one using the segmented collar. It is still widely practiced.

The photograph shows part of a typical lettered-edge coin done with a segmented collar. The coin is a French five-franc piece of 1867, and the entire edge inscription reads DIEU * PROTEGE * LA * FRANCE ***** ("May God Protect France" —a timely plea, in light of the ensuing Franco-Prussian War). Note the vertical raised "seam": it marks the dividing line between two pieces of the segmented col-

Lettered edge. Lettered edge on a French 5-franc coin, 1867.

lar. This coin is silver, and its lettered edge discouraged counterfeiting or clipping. In contemporary coinage, if the lettered edge is used at all, it is only in the name of tradition or design. Today's base-metal coins are hardly worth counterfeiting, and are definitely not worth clipping.

See also CLIPPING; COLLAR; EDGE-MARKING MACHINERY; FILING.

LION DOLLAR A large Dutch silver coin, minted from the 1570s until the end of the seventeenth century, deriving its name (Dutch leuwendaalder or leeuwendaalder) from the lion rampant on the reverse.

The lion dollar first appeared in 1575, during the Netherlands's revolt against Spain: the province of Holland was the first political entity to strike the coin, and its designs set the standard for later issues. As mentioned, a lion rampant graced the reverse. It was surrounded by a legend referring to the anti-Spanish confederation of Dutch cities and states. The obverse alluded to the local issuing authority: a standing figure supported a shield with the arms of Holland, and the legend announced this to be, in fact, a silver coin of that polity. The coin was the size of a thaler, measuring around 42 millimeters, weighing 27–28 grams. Its silver fineness was relatively low at slightly under 87 percent.

Lion dollars of this style were struck from the 1570s to the 1690s, and most are wretched creations. The silver for their manufacture seems to have been poorly mixed, and little care was taken to produce decent planchets, hence the coins' surfaces are often porous and wavy, to the obvious detriment of the designs. The coins were not struck in collars; indeed, no care was taken to ensure their roundness. They are the evidence of a busy, mercantile people, importing silver from Spain and the Americas, and rapidly turning it into trade coins. The lion dollar was the north Euro-

Lion dollar. Campen, leuwendaalder, 1684.

pean equivalent of the Spanish-American cob.

The piece in our illustration was minted in the city of Campen in 1684, and well illustrates the poor quality of the lion dollars. Actually, this in one of the *finer* specimens. Note the signs of double-striking on the obverse; while most of Europe was producing coinage with machines at this juncture, the Dutch still did so by hand. Shortly before 1700, the lion dollar (often called a "dog dollar," because of the crudity of its reverse type) was replaced by more carefully struck coins intended primarily for internal consumption rather than trade abroad. The lion dollar was necessary during the height of Dutch economic and political power; with these in decline, the need for this crude but effective trading coin also declined.

See also COB; DOUBLE-STRUCK; THALER; TRADE COINS.

LIRA The basic unit of modern Italian coinage, whose roots may be traced to the late fifteenth century.

The word lira was originally a unit of account, referring to one Roman pound's worth of silver, from which two hundred forty pennies or denari could be struck. The inflation of the late Middle Ages had lowered the amount of silver in the denaro, so two hundred forty now repre-

sented a very modest weight. Still, when Nicolò Tron, the doge of Venice between 1471 and 1473, introduced the lira as a coin, it weighed 6.5 grams and measured 27 millimeters in diameter, a sizable coin for the period—the largest European silver piece then being struck, in fact.

But it was not immediately popular. As shown in the illustration, Tron chose his own portrait for the lira, an act which imitated royal practice and was resented by the citizens of Venice whose sentiments were deeply republican. While large Venetian silver coins were welcomed eventually, no subsequent doge dared to display his likeness on them.

Experimentation with the lira would also take place in Milan. Galeazzo Maria Sforza, who ruled the duchy from 1466 to 1476, introduced his own lira. The issue was heavier than the Venetian one, and weighed nearly 10 grams. As Sforza was a duke in an area espousing royalty, he was able to put his portrait on his lira with impunity. The splendid rendition of the duke's head gave the coin a new name, the testone (from *testa*, head), which soon replaced lira for the Milanese coin. It also gave birth to an entire series of medium-sized silver coins, called testons, testoons, etc.

The lira itself was struck sporadically in Savoy and Genoa during the sixteenth, seventeenth, and eighteenth centuries, but it was at the beginning of the nineteenth that it won wide acceptance. Napoleon Bonaparte, who proclaimed himself king of a united Italy in 1805, established the lira, which was to duplicate the French franc's

Lira. Venice, 1472.

size, weight, and fineness, as the monetary unit of his realm. His Italian kingdom collapsed in 1814; but when the kings of Sardinia took over a united Italy half a century later, they too made the lira the national unit of exchange, a position it still enjoys (although it is now made of aluminum, not silver).

See also DENARO; MONEY OF ACCOUNT; TESTONE; TESTOON.

LITHOGRAPHY A method of printing on paper without the use of an engraved plate, discovered a few years prior to 1800, and employed to some extent for the printing of paper money.

In classical lithography, a flat piece of exceedingly fine-grained limestone is used in place of the engraved plate. The surface of this stone has a distinct porous quality enabling it to accept the transfer of images when applied in a greasy ink; once transferred, the images will reject water but accept ordinary ink. The blank areas, to which no image has been transferred, will reject both water *and* lithographer's ink, because of the nature of the stone. When printing begins, the ink is rolled onto the stone, then wiped off. The greasy areas hold the ink, while the untreated ones do not. A sheet of moistened paper is then placed on the stone, and pressed against it. The ink is thus transferred from stone to paper, and a lithograph emerges.

Lithography does not have the advantages of engraving, at least for the printing of paper money. While it allows for subtlety and a delicately shaded line, it is not adequate when a hard, bold line is needed, nor is it particularly effective for printing large blocks of color, unless by an expert's hand.

Worst of all, a lithographed note is far more simple to counterfeit than an engraved one. If the counterfeit seems a trifle dull and soft, so would a genuine bill. In the past, lithography was commonly used to counterfeit engraved paper money, but the absence of the raised line, the "feel" of an engraving, exposed the counterfeit. When the original is a lithograph, there is no such protection. Consequently, the lithographed bill is most often used in emergencies, as the process has one great advantage over engraving: it is easier.

The two illustrations show a Confederate twenty-dollar note of 1861. It is seen in its entirety in the first photograph, while the second shows its left-hand vignette in detail. Note the crudity in both instances. The fancywork on the right of the note was a woefully inadequate attempt to reproduce the lathework on an engraved note. The letters of the country's name are spotty, and those inscriptions which resemble handwriting are poorly executed, unclear, and incomplete. Seen in close-up, the sailor in the left vignette is crude indeed. In short, this note is simply

Lithography.
Top: Confederate States of America, 20 dollars, 1861.
Bottom: A detail of the same bill. Note crudity of the vignette.

a bad copy of an engraved bill, and, as might be expected, it was extensively counterfeited. Why was it lithographed and not engraved? Because those who issued it had little choice; the Confederacy's technology was backward. Before the onset of the Civil War, local bank notes had been printed in the North by firms in New York City and Philadelphia. Now these suppliers were cut off, and an increasingly effective Northern blockade forced the South to print its own bills. It did, using lithography for the purpose.

In fairness, it must be said the Confederacy's lithographed money improved as time went on. New inks and technicians were smuggled through the blockade, and by 1864 the South was actually producing some excellent work. It was also producing more of it, as war expenses and inflation rose.

In general, then, lithography has been used when notes of low value are contemplated (essentially, money not worth counterfeiting) or in emergencies. The Mexican Revolution, the Russian Revolution, and the Hungarian hyperinflation of 1945–1946 saw a spate of lithographed notes. Today, paper money is rarely lithographed.

See also BLUEBACK; COUNTERFEIT; EMERGENCY MONEY; ENGRAVING.

LOUIS D'OR The most important French gold coin of the seventeenth and eighteenth centuries.

The piece was first struck in 1640 under Louis XIII (ruled 1610–1643), and was tariffed at ten livres. Minted in twenty-two-carat gold, the louis d'or (which took its name from the reigning monarch) measured 24 millimeters in diameter, and weighed 6.69 grams.

The new coin was struck by machine, not by hand: the introduction of machine-struck coinage and the retirement of the old, hammered variety was the crux of Louis's reform, which saw an improved

Louis d'or. France, 1775.

coinage as an effective bulwark against clipping and counterfeiting.

The obverse of the first louis d'or bore the portrait of the king while the reverse had a cross made up of eight L's. These designs went unchanged for the rest of the reign, and through most of that of his son, Louis XIV (ruled 1643–1715).

With the accession of Louis XV (ruled 1715–1774), the weight of the louis d'or was raised to 8.16 grams and it was valued at twenty livres. An edict of 1726 fixed its value at twenty-four livres, or four écus, where it remained until its demise during the French Revolution.

Under Louis XV, the coin's design was somewhat refashioned. As before, the monarch appeared on the obverse, but the cross reverse was abandoned for a crown over the shields of France and Navarre, two fancy crossed L's within a palm wreath, etc. The last monarch to strike the louis d'or was Louis XVI (ruled 1774–1792); one of his early coins, minted in 1775, is shown in the illustration. The crown and shields reverse was inherited from the time of Louis XV; later issues used a bare head and a slightly different arrangement of the shields.

The last louis d'ors show the influence of the French Revolution. Louis XVI ruled as a constitutional monarch from 1791 until his overthrow in late 1792. A hybrid issue of louis d'or dated 1792 and 1793 display the monarch's head (in a highly unflattering portrait) on the obverse, a standing angel inscribing a tablet labelled CONSTITUTION on the reverse. The last of these coins were actually struck after the king's execution early in 1793, and were followed by a small issue of twenty-four-livre pieces (the old louis d'or, whose official name had been changed), which replaced the royal portrait with a design featuring the value within a wreath. The designs parallel those on the silver écu in the same period. A few years later, France adopted a decimal system, and neither the louis d'or nor the écu was represented.

The louis d'or served as a trade coin, and was well known among merchants from the Levant to colonial America.

See also ÉCU; ÉCU D'OR; TRADE COINS.

Love token. *A love token, probably engraved on a United States 10-cent piece, nineteenth century.*

LOVE TOKEN   A coin, with one or both sides planed smooth, then engraved with initials, scenes, or symbols.

The practice was largely confined to the nineteenth century, and most frequently embraced small- to medium-sized gold and silver coins. In essence, the love token was a relatively easy, inexpensive way to commemorate someone or something. A coin could simply be taken from circulation and fashioned into a love token. The donor did not have to pay for the manufacture of a round piece of precious metal suitable for engraving; his government provided it for him. And in the days of engraved tea services, gold watches, and a tradition of the sentimental inscription, there was a multitude of engravers. Indeed, the prospective donor could even try his own hand, if he was so inclined.

The pieces were dubbed love tokens because many bear inscriptions that indicate they were given as tokens of esteem. Yet not all are completely straightforward; most bear merely one or more initials, at times with a date. Nevertheless, the term "love token" embraces these doubtful pieces too, if only because they are more closely related to this branch of exonumia than to any other.

The piece in the illustration is a particularly well-engraved love token. The coin which served as its basis is probably an American ten-cent piece, and the general style suggests the late nineteenth century. One side bears the twined, ornate initials SSI, those of the person for whom the piece was intended. The other side shows a harbor scene, rendered in astonishing detail. It must be mentioned that the coin which served as the source of this token measured only 17.9 millimeters in diameter; obviously whoever engraved it was a master of the craft.

The preparation of love tokens in the United States and Canada seems to have ended about 1900. In Mexico, however, prisoners passed their time in jail by creating something very similar to love tokens for gifts or for sale. The practice ended when silver was removed from Mexican coinage. The love token was never popular in Europe or other parts of the world, and remained a distinctly North American form of exonumia.

See also EXONUMIA.

M

MACHINE-STRUCK COINAGE Money struck by mechanical means, as an addition to or substitute for simple human force.

The first phase in the mechanization of coinage began in the sixteenth century, when inventors wished to realize several aims: to accelerate the coining process; to accommodate it to the production of the heavier silver coins made possible by recent minting discoveries; to standardize coins, thus protecting them from counterfeiting and making it more difficult to tamper with them.

Planchet cutters, collars, and edge-marking machines were invented, to standardize and protect planchets. And the screw, rocker, and roller presses were also devised. Used with skill, these machines could strike more and larger coins than could be made by hand.

The second phase began at the end of the eighteenth century and continued through the nineteenth. During this period, increased production was most important, and this also involved the mass production of dies. New, quicker processes were invented to take advantage of the almost inexhaustible power sources—steam, and then electricity—that had been discovered.

The invention of mechanized coining devices was encouraged by the discovery of new sources of gold and silver in Europe, the Americas, and elsewhere. The metal was useless unless it could freely enter trade as coins. While coining machinery could do several things, two were paramount: it could strike larger coins and more of them.

The new machines were not adopted overnight, and in some areas (for example, Potosí) large numbers of coins continued to be struck by hand until well into modern times. But there was a decided shift to machine-struck money over the years, and the expanding money supply it helped to ensure has left its mark on the last four hundred and fifty years.

The new coins meant a greater accumulation of wealth in certain areas; reinvested, this wealth became the foundation of modern capitalism. As the wealth (and the capitalistic enterprises it founded) was usually found in places that were already trading crossroads (i.e., cities), emigration

Machine-struck coinage. *A steam-powered coining press, 1861.*
(From *Harper's New Monthly Magazine,* December 1861. Courtesy of the Library of the American Numismatic Society, New York)

look. Coinage, through the first two thousand years of its life, was not that common. Many transactions for which we now use coins could be and were carried on by other means—by barter, assumed obligations in goods and services, etc. The universal use of machine-struck coins changed this. Buying and selling were simplified, as goods and services now had defined prices. But for the individual the complexities of life magnified: the ties of village and family were weakened, and the sense of isolation sharpened.

To say that the course of history was determined by the invention of machines to produce coins is an obvious overstatement. But such machinery and the coins it struck were significant, not only in numismatic history, but in the history of mankind.

See also COLLAR; EDGE-MARKING MACHINERY; HUB; MILLED COINAGE; PLANCHET; ROCKER PRESS; ROLLER PRESS; SCREW PRESS.

to these areas grew rapidly, and with it, a spectacular rise in urbanization.

The new money was frequently invested in inventions which were designed to increase the output of wares other than coinage. The concepts of mass production, interchangeable parts, and the assembly line, were woven into the fabric of our daily lives. The factory system was born, drawing workers from city and farm into its orbit. No longer were workers paid in kind, as they had once been; now they received wages, payment in cash. The relationship between man and his work changed, becoming less intimate and this, in turn, contributed to the labor unrest attending the development of manufacturing.

In all this, there existed a new phenomenon, the significance of which has yet to be fully examined. More and more people were using coins for daily transactions than ever before, a fact we are apt to over-

MAMEITA GIN A thick, bean-shaped Japanese silver or billon coin, produced by the Tokugawa Shogunate (1599–1868).

The piece illustrated weighs 16.26 grams, is over 6 millimeters thick, and its oval shape measures 23 millimeters by 21.5 The obverse and reverse both show Daikokusama, the Japanese god of plenty. The character in the center of the figure indicates the era in which the coin was struck—in this case the Tempo period: this coin could have been minted at any time between 1837 and 1858.

The mameita gin resulted from weight deficiencies in the chogin, a bullion piece which originated about 1600. The chogin was cast, and as the casting was apt to be irregular, some pieces were distinctly underweight. Mameita gin were used to make up for the weight differences: a globule of the weight needed was pressed against a plate with carved characters or the figure of Daikokusama. These designs

Mameita gin. *Japan, 1837–1858.*

were thus transferred to the highest points of the globule. Two plates could also be used, and the globule pressed out between them. The distinctive shapes of the mameita gin derive from these practices.

Although the weight of mameita gin varied widely, the illustrated piece is extraordinarily heavy at 16.26 grams: the average is between 5 and 8 grams. Silver content paralleled that of the chogin, and was usually only 13.5 percent by the 1860s. Both mameita gin and chogin passed from the scene when mechanized coinage was introduced in Japan.

See also BILLON; CHOGIN.

MARAVEDÍ A Spanish coin, originally patterned after the Moorish gold dinar of the eleventh-century Murabit dynasty, from which the maravedí took its name.

Gold was an important element in Muslim coinage when it was nonexistent in the coinages of Christian Europe. During the period when Spain was largely controlled by the Moors, some of this gold was taken across the border into Christian territories, where gold dinars were eagerly

accepted. In the eleventh and twelfth centuries the Christian reconquest of the Iberian Peninsula accelerated, and important Muslim cities—and their wealth—fell into Spanish hands. Trade grew, as did general prosperity, and the Spanish kings began to strike gold coins. It was natural that their products should be influenced by the dinar: the new coins were flat and thin, and while the Christian coin weighed slightly less than its prototype (3.8 versus 4.1 grams), it was a perfectly acceptable trading piece. Following Islamic usage, the Spanish coins emphasized legends and inscriptions, rather than images. These new coins were first known as marabotins, the name the Spanish had previously applied to Murabit dinars; the name soon became maravedí, and remained so for the rest of the coin's career.

The illustration shows the obverse of an early gold maravedí, struck in 1185 under Alfonso VIII (ruled 1158–1214). The piece measures 26 millimeters in diameter, and has a Christian cross and ALF in its central circle. The surrounding legend and inscription are in Arabic and are a statement of the Christian faith, replacing the *Kalima* found on Muslim dinars. The gold maravedí was struck sparingly, and was not minted at all after the early thirteenth century, as the dobla and other coins gradually replaced it.

It was revived as a small copper coin by the first rulers of a united Spain, Ferdinand and Isabella (ruled 1479–1504). A law of June 13, 1497 made the maravedí the basic Spanish unit of account, with thirty-four equalling one silver real. The coin was struck intermittently until 1843. Multiples of the piece were in fact usually minted in its stead: coins worth two, four, or eight maravedís. The coin became obsolete with the monetary reforms of April 15, 1848, when Spain adopted a decimal monetary system.

Maravedí. *Castile, 1185.*

See also DINAR; DINERO; DOBLA; REAL; TRADE COINS.

MARK Originally, a middle European term for a specified amount of silver: later, a name applied to several different coins.

As a unit of measure, the mark varied from place to place; the Viennese mark contained 280.668 grams of pure silver, while the other two units in general use, those of Prague and Cologne, equalled 255.760 and 233.812 grams, respectively.

By the early sixteenth century, the word began to embrace coins. The Swedes struck silver marks as early as 1536, and coins bearing that name also appeared in various parts of northern Germany. But another three and a half centuries were to pass before the mark received universal acceptance in Germany as a coin.

The first step in that direction took place in 1753, when a convention of German states addressed the confusion—stemming from a multitude of coins, weights, and standards—that had been the bane of German commerce since the late Middle Ages. The states agreed to accept the fine mark of Cologne as the basic weight unit for silver; henceforth, all major German silver coins tended to bear legends or inscriptions giving their value in relation to that standard. Another monetary convention in 1838 raised the mark's silver content to 233.856 grams. The final step was taken by the German Empire: laws of 1871 and 1873 established a national decimal system based on a new silver coin, the mark. It measured 24 millimeters in diameter, weighed 5.556 grams, contained 90 percent silver, and equalled one hundred pfennig. One of the first of these coins is illustrated in the photograph. Note the extreme simplicity of its design, a fea-ture common to most of the empire's circulating coinage.

The mark's later career was somewhat checkered. It was struck in 90 percent silver until 1916, discarded, resurrected in 1924 at 50 percent silver, and struck at that content until 1927; then it was not minted again until 1933, when it was struck from nickel. Again abandoned at the outbreak of World War II, it was reinstated by East and West Germany in 1956 and 1950, respectively. The East German mark is aluminum, its West German counterpart, copper-nickel. In the tradition of the old imperial mark, both countries stress plain, almost spartan designs.

See also PFENNIG.

MARK (MINTMASTER'S OR ASSAYER'S) One or more initials, monograms, or symbols on a coin, identifying the person responsible for its production or in charge of its metallic content.

In a sense, coinage began through the use of such marks: one can interpret the obverse designs on the first Lydian coins (which were adaptations of the royal seal) as assigning responsibility for the coins' weight and purity. But when numismatists use the term today, they most often mean a small, subordinate device, either in a coin's field or as part of its legends.

Marks appeared as monograms or symbols on many ancient Greek silver tetradrachms and other coins. Frequently located in the field on the reverse, they are a clue as to who was responsible for the coin, and hence are of great aid to the modern numismatist establishing a relative chronology for undated coinage. Monogram "B" cut over monogram "A," for instance, indicates a change in mint personnel; a "B" coin would thus come after an "A" coin. The Greeks used such marks to identify the person liable for the issue of a coin, as there was a tacit assumption that whoever issued the piece also guaranteed its purity.

Mark. Germany, 1874.

Like the Greeks, the Romans favored monograms and symbols for many early coins, and mintmasters' names are seen in full or abbreviated form on silver denarii, a practice which continued throughout the republican period. The *officina* marks of the Roman Empire were related, but not identical, in purpose: although the intention was the same (to enable a coin to be traced to the workshop in which it was struck), the method used was not. *Officina* marks identified mint *branches*, not mintmasters.

While Byzantine coiners followed the example of their predecessors, and placed *officina* marks on many of their coins, in the medieval West there was a return to earlier Roman practice. Most English pennies up to the late thirteenth century, for example, carried—as reverse inscriptions or as legends—the names of the men responsible for them.

The importance of mintmasters' marks abated in the late Middle Ages, with names more often abbreviated or replaced by a symbol. This symbol, sometimes known as a différent, was either in the legend or in the field, and remains popular in the coinage of France, the Netherlands, and several other countries.

Although mintmasters' marks are far more common than assayers' marks, the latter are found on the coins of Spain and its New World dominions. The practice seems to have initiated in Spain in the late fifteenth century, and in later years was adopted in America, where it was applied to almost all precious-metal coins until the end of the Spanish rule. The Latin American successor states continued to affix assayers' marks on coins to about 1900; these marks usually took the form of one or more initials.

The illustration shows a Russian twenty-kopek silver piece of 1916. We see the obverse with the mintmaster's initials, BC—standing, in the Cyrillic alphabet, for VS: Victor Smirnov, chief moneyer at the St. Petersburg mint from 1913 to 1917. Smirnov was dismissed when the Russian

Mark (mintmaster's or assayer's). Russia, 20 kopeks, 1916.

Revolution overthrew the Tsarist government. Under the new Soviet regime, mintmasters' marks were discontinued. Their use has also declined elsewhere in the twentieth century, in part because precious metal has been eliminated from circulating coinage. Designed as guarantees of metallic worth or workmanship, marks have little to guarantee on today's coins.

See also ABBREVIATION; ASSAY; FINENESS; MINT MARK; MONOGRAM; *OFFICINA* MARK.

MATTE PROOF A proof coin or medal which has undergone a special step during the minting process, lending it a dull, finely granulated surface.

These proofs are created by a process conceived in the 1890s. Belgium is reported to have issued a few pieces with matte surfaces in 1896, although it has proven impossible to trace these coins. The matte proof was definitely in existence by 1902, however: England introduced the surface for the proof sets it minted that year. The United States struck matte proofs of its redesigned coinage of 1907–1921; and until 1935 it occasionally struck matte proof commemorative half-dollars, all of which are avidly sought by collectors. At the same time, other nations too were experimenting with the new surfaces.

The matte proof disappeared from coinage after 1935. The process that fashioned these coins is somewhat obscure, as mints jealously guarded their methods. Apparently, the surface was applied after

Matte proof. Italy, 100 lire, 1925.

the coin was struck, in contradistinction to the frosted proof, which acquires its cameo surface during striking. The coins chosen to be matte proofs were probably carefully struck several times, much like ordinary proofs, then "pickled"—etched in diluted acid. Why was the matte proof introduced in the first place? A possible explanation might be that the increasingly curved fields popular on early twentieth-century coins were difficult to polish uniformly on those dies designed for proofs, and matte and sandblast finishes were introduced to solve the problem.

The illustration shows a rare Italian gold matte proof of 1925, commemorating the twenty-fifth year of the reign of Victor Emmanuel III (ruled 1900–1946). As can be noted, the surfaces do not reflect light as an ordinary coin—let alone a proof—would. The sandblast proof has a similar appearance, but its granulated surface is a bit more obvious, and somewhat coarser, than that of the matte.

See also Frosted proof; Proof; Sandblast proof.

MAUNDY MONEY A British presentation coin, given on Maundy Thursday (the day before Good Friday) as part of a religious rite dating back to the early Middle Ages.

In the Maundy ceremony as presently conducted, the monarch bestows several gifts upon certain elderly townspeople, chosen for their services to the community. The number of recipients varies, al-

though it tends to be roughly twice the monarch's age. Among the gifts are Maundy coins—four silver pieces worth one, two, three, and four pence, respectively; every person receives a coin for each year of the ruler's life. The coins are currently struck with proof surfaces, and are presented in a leather purse.

The genesis of the ceremony—and its name—lies in the *mandatum* or "commandment" Christ gave His disciples: after the Last Supper, He washed their feet, an act of humility He commended to them (see John 13: 1–16). The practice was adopted by the early Christian Church, and was known in fifth-century Britain.

Money played no part in the ritual in those days, nor did the monarch. King John (ruled 1199–1216) seems to be the first ruler to have distributed money in a Maundy ceremony; in time, the monetary aspect overwhelmed the original act and the tenets it was meant to reflect. The last king to observe the washing of feet to demonstrate a monarch's humility toward his subjects was probably James II (ruled 1685–1688).

There is some controversy about when Maundy money ceased to be struck simply as a coin identical to circulating coins and became, instead, a special presentation piece, created solely for the ceremony. One widely accepted time for the first striking of coins specifically for Maundy Thursday is early in the reign of Charles

Maundy money. An English Maundy set, 1670.

II (ruled 1660–1685). The first full, dated sets of four coins appeared in 1670, and one of these sets is seen in the photograph. Maundy coins are still struck in silver; indeed, they are the only British pieces currently minted in that metal.

See also GROAT; PRESENTATION PIECE.

MEDAL A large, usually round object, produced by machinery similar to that used for minting coins, but struck for different reasons: coins are customarily minted to circulate as money, while medals are struck for award, celebration, or commemoration.

The term medal is often used indiscriminately to refer to decorations as well as those pieces which are actually medals. In correct usage, a decoration is an award designed to be worn by its recipient. A medal is not so intended.

Another problem of usage is related to two similar terms, medalet and medallion. These words refer to special *types* of medals, as we shall see, but are frequently applied to all medals; conversely, those special types are often described as "medals," a misleading practice and technically incorrect, as a "medal" is a *large* object.

The medal as we know it originated in fifteenth-century Italy, where a prospering economy was generating a change in man's view of art and himself. The heightened commercial tempo gave birth to a leisure class, with the time and money to patronize the arts and rediscover the classics. And rediscovery led to the recreation of classical forms in areas ranging from architecture to coinage and medals. The Romans had struck large, showy medallions, celebrating their emperors. Renaissance Italy would do much the same, using new medals—larger than the medallions—to celebrate its notables.

Hence, the modern medal evolved. Early pieces were cast, the easiest method of production then available. By the early sixteenth century, a mechanical contrivance known as a screw press was gaining popularity. Although we identify this machine with coins, it was first used to strike medals, and only later for coins.

More than any other area of numismatics, medals reflect the artistic tastes and sensibilities of the period in which they are produced. In part, their very size makes this so—greater space affords a designer greater freedom. In addition, the medal —not intended for general circulation, as is the coin—is a more suitable background for modern artistic concepts, while the coin must bear "safe" designs, which too often means bland or conservative ones.

We can see the art of the German Renaissance on the silver medal on the left, which dates from 1535; the piece on the

Medal.
Left: Saxony, 1535.
Right: France, 1972.

right, minted in France in 1972, expresses the tortured self-examination of contemporary art. Medals afford us something of a history of art, as they reflect all the currents of the past five centuries.

See also DECORATION; MEDALET; MEDALLION; PRESENTATION PIECE; SCHAUTHALER; SCREW PRESS.

Medalet. Bolivia, gold medalet, 1869.

MEDALET A small medal, with a diameter of 35 millimeters or less, and a descendant in part of the old jeton.

Jetons, originally used as counting devices, ceased to serve as such with the advent of modern times, and thereafter developed in several dissimilar ways. In some cases, they metamorphosed into gaming counters, fashioned of metal until about 1900, and subsequently of other materials. Another role for the jeton was as a medalet—a souvenir distributed upon the celebration of important events. Originally struck by hand, by 1600 such medalets were machine-produced by those same firms that had once struck jetons.

These "poor man's medals" were usually minted in base metals, such as copper or brass, and depicted allegorical scenes, incidents from Scripture, etc. The number of surviving medalets with holes indicates they were frequently pierced by their owners and worn for luck. They were especially popular in France and the Low Countries, which produced them in large numbers up to the nineteenth century.

Numbers of medalets were simply small medals, not redesigned jetons, and while base metals were most often used, this was not always the case, as the illustration shows. This medalet is from Bolivia, and celebrates the establishment of the country's first steam-powered coining press in 1869. It measures 24.5 millimeters, weighs 13.3 grams, and is made of solid gold. A blob of solder on the reverse may indicate that someone wore this medalet, perhaps as a button.

Medalets are still with us, and many have a political or commemorative purpose, as was true of their earlier counterparts.

See also JETON; MEDAL.

MEDALLION A large Roman presentation piece, struck in bronze, silver, and gold from the second to the fifth centuries A.D.

The earliest Roman medallions probably date from the reign of the emperor Hadrian (ruled A.D. 117–138), and were generally struck in bronze. The planchets used for these pieces were thick and broad, weighing some 50 grams—twice the weight of the heaviest Roman coin. It is not definitively known if these bronze medallions had an economic function; but we can say with certainty that many are among the finest achievements of Roman numismatic art. With additional space in which to work, engravers produced magnificent obverse portraits, and reverses rich in symbolism and allegorical representations.

Such medallions had virtually disappeared by the end of the third century A.D., victims of the economic collapse and military anarchy of the years from 235 to 284. By the 290s, however, medallions reappeared, but now in gold and silver. While still primarily ceremonial, and struck for presentation to domestic or foreign notables, these new medallions had an additional characteristic. They were *monetary* medallions, representing multiples of established coins, but while they

Medallion. *Roman Empire, Honorius, silver medallion,* A.D. *395–423.*

could be used in that capacity, presumably they seldom were. However, they were hoarded, and most surviving Roman gold and silver medallions are from hoards scattered from France to Yugoslavia.

What the medallions of the fourth and fifth centuries gained in intrinsic worth, they lost in artistic value. Their art grew stiff and formal—at one with the coinage of the time. Then too, Christian symbolism appeared in the fourth century, and circumscribed artists' possibilities. Still, Christian motifs did not predominate on medallions quite as much as on coins: pagan elements are seen on medallions as late as the mid-fifth century, when the art form itself died out.

The photograph shows a medallion of the emperor Honorius (ruled A.D. 395–423). It is of silver, weighing 13.09 grams and measuring 38 millimeters in diameter: it was the equivalent of five siliquae. The portrait is elongated in the fifth-century style, while the reverse is a reworking of pagan types, with Christian elements added. The reverse legend proclaims Honorius as conquerer of the barbarians —showing a splendid disregard for historical fact.

The term medallion is also used to describe something having nothing to do with medals: paper money collectors refer to the round or oval fancywork found at the corners of many older bank notes as medallions. These intricate engravings were created by hand and, later by a geometrical lathe, with the bill's denomination in the center of the medallion.

See also GUILLOCHE; HOARD; MEDAL; PRE-SENTATION PIECE; PORTRAIT; SESTERTIUS; SILIQUA.

MILIARENSIS A silver coin of the Roman and Byzantine empires.

An alternate spelling for the Roman version of this piece is miliarense (plural miliarensia), while its Byzantine counterpart is usually designated a miliaresion (plural miliaresia). All these names imply the coin was struck as the thousandth part of something; unfortunately, no one has been able to determine what that something was.

The miliarensis was introduced in the 320s by Constantine the Great (ruled A.D. 306–337). First struck at seventy-two to a Roman pound, each coin weighed about 4.5 grams. Shortly after Constantine's death, a "heavy" miliarensis of 5.4 grams entered circulation. Both "heavy" and "light" coins seem to have circulated side by side, but the heavier one was struck less frequently. The coin illustrated is of the "light" variety, and dates from the reign of Constantine's son Constantius II (ruled A.D. 337–361). It measures about 23 millimeters in diameter. The latest Roman miliarensis seems to have been struck under Theodosius I (ruled A.D. 379–395).

But the coin was reintroduced in the Byzantine Empire. Employed as a unit of account in the sixth century, it was struck as an actual coin from the seventh through the eleventh centuries and remained as a unit of account for many years after that. Early miliaresia were relatively small and thick. In their later form they were thin, weighing between 2 and 3 grams, with di-

Miliarensis. *Roman Empire, Constantius II,* A.D *355–360.*

ameters usually in the neighborhood of 27 millimeters.

The thinness of the miliaresion of the eighth and later centuries is evidence of a strong Islamic influence. The peoples of the new faith fancied a flat, thin coin, 30 millimeters in diameter and weighing 3 grams, which they called a dirhem. This particular coin was first struck shortly before 700. The new, thin miliaresion was introduced by Leo III (ruled 717–741), when trade between the Byzantine and Islamic worlds was at a high point, and it seems obvious that the miliaresion was designed in part to look familiar to Islamic businessmen.

The dirhem and miliaresion are alike in other respects also. Dirhems did not bear portraits, strictly forbidden by the Koran, and neither did the new miliaresion during the first two centuries of its existence. However, this is not evidence of Islamic influence, but rather the ascendance of the Iconoclasts, a Christian sect which frowned on imagery. On miliaresia coined between 717 and 912, the obverse type is a cross, usually raised on steps, while the reverse is a simple inscription in several lines, giving the emperor's name. The inscriptions are in Greek; by this time, the use of Latin on Byzantine coins had all but disappeared. Alexander (ruled 912–913) made a tentative move to break with tradition by placing a small full-face portrait of himself at the junction of the angles of the obverse cross. However, it was another twenty years before such heresy was accepted as general practice.

The miliaresion was struck in fair numbers during the eighth through tenth centuries, at which point its production fell drastically, perhaps a result of the "silver famine" affecting the Muslim world at the same time. The last miliaresion dates from the early part of the reign of Alexius I (ruled 1081–1118).

See also CROSS ON COINAGE; DIRHEM; HEXAGRAM; MONEY OF ACCOUNT; SCYPHATE COINAGE.

MILITARY PAYMENT CERTIFICATE A special form of United States paper currency, printed for use by American military and civilian personnel overseas.

First issued in 1946, in the aftermath of World War II, military payment certificates circulated in Japan, Germany, Korea, Vietnam, and other areas until late in 1973.

At the end of World War II, with the United States occupying large areas whose economies had been devastated by the conflict, the American army paid its servicemen in local currency with the understanding that it could be converted to dollars on demand. For their part, soldiers supplemented their earnings of mark, yen, or francs with the fruits of a flourishing black market. Thus, in addition to exchanging soldiers' pay for dollars, the Army suddenly found itself obligated to redeem vast amounts of foreign currency obtained through clandestine operations. The deficit grew until, at its peak, the army owed its servicemen over half a billion dollars.

The military payment certificate (or MPC, as it is known) was conceived as a way to pay servicemen, while at the same time preventing them from taking advantage of the government. Printing was strictly controlled. MPCs bore values in dollars, and legally local currency could not be exchanged for them. They were also non-negotiable within the United States. Furthermore, to make certain there was no attempt to stockpile the new money, the government periodically called in all old MPCs and very quietly and quickly—within twenty-four hours—replaced them with a new series. As no one knew when a change would take place, only the true gambler was moved to hoard.

MPCs were privately printed at first, and they were lithographed, as they continued to be after the government undertook their printing early in 1964. The frequent design changes on MPCs, and their use of colors other than black and

Military payment certificate. United States, 5 dollars, series 692 (issued 1970–1973).

green, also set them apart from ordinary United States paper.

MPCs are dated by series rather than year. The series, and the period during which they circulated, are as follows:

Series	Circulation Dates
461	Sept. 16, 1946–March 10, 1947
471	March 10, 1947–March 22, 1948
472	March 22, 1948–June 20, 1951
481	June 20, 1951–May 25, 1954
521	May 25, 1954–May 27, 1958
541	May 27, 1958–May 26, 1961
591	May 26, 1961–Jan. 6, 1964
611	Jan. 6, 1964–April 28, 1969
641	Aug. 31, 1965–Oct. 21, 1968
651	April 28, 1969–Nov. 19, 1973
661	Oct. 21, 1968–August 11, 1969
681	Aug. 11, 1969–Oct. 7, 1970
692	Oct. 7, 1970–March 15, 1973

The illustration is from the 1970–1973 series. MPCs were printed in denominations ranging from five cents to twenty

dollars. MPCs are no longer printed, nor are any in use.

See also OCCUPATION NOTES.

MILLED COIN A coin struck by machine rather than by hand; the term most frequently refers to early machine-struck coinage, minted before the advent of steam power in the late eighteenth century.

Milled coin derives from "mill," of course, which originally implied machinery used for grinding and crushing grain. By the sixteenth century the word was being used to designate any kind of machinery. The numismatic term milled coin is from this usage, as well as from the fact that some of the earliest machine-struck coins, minted in France in the early 1550s, were created by machines powered by a water mill. The machines in question were primitive, but the results nevertheless dramatically improved the appearance of coins, as the pieces in the photograph can attest. The coin on the left was made in the old hammered fashion, the one on the right by machinery.

A similar term—milling—often refers to the appearance of a coin's edge, which has been altered by any of several machine processes. It is more precise to use such descriptive phrases as reeded edge, upset edge, and so forth.

See also COLLAR; EDGE-MARKING MACHINERY; GRAINING; MACHINE-STRUCK COINAGE; ORNAMENTED EDGE; REEDED EDGE; UPSET EDGE.

Milled coin. Milled versus hammered coins. The French teston on the left was struck by hand, that on the right by machinery. Both date from 1552.

Milreis. Brazil, c. 1855.

MILREIS An old Portuguese and Brazilian money of account.

The word means "one thousand reis." The original Portuguese real (plural reis), was first struck as a silver coin in the time of Ferdinand (ruled 1367–1383). Its silver content soon diminished, as did its value.

By the reign of Manuel I (ruled 1495–1521), multiples of the real were entering circulation, and the real itself was no longer produced after the disastrous reign of Sebastian (ruled 1557–1578). However, the practice of reckoning by so many thousands of them—milreis—had taken root. The Portuguese were a trading people, and they chose to retain a coin of very little value as their monetary unit; thus, computations were in hundreds or thousands of reis.

The first appearance of the milreis as a distinct coin came with a rare gold issue from the Azores in 1582, but it was not until the late seventeenth century that the denomination won popularity in Portugal itself. It was struck sporadically until 1910, when the modern monetary system was established, based on a new coin, the escudo.

The milreis was also minted in Brazil; the first issues date from 1699, and the coin was struck in fair quantity until 1939. The Brazilian government also issued paper milreis. The piece pictured was printed by an English firm about 1855. The vignette on the left depicts Peter II, Emperor of Brazil from 1831 to 1889.

See also MONEY OF ACCOUNT; REAL.

MINT ACT OF 1792 The law which established a decimal system for United States coinage and set up a national Mint.

The Mint Act of 1792—passed on April 2nd—provided for a national Mint at Philadelphia, the nation's capital at the time. It also called for assayers, coiners, and others necessary to maintain the Mint, and enumerated their duties. It set salaries for the more important officers, and authorized the Mint's construction, expenses for which were to be defrayed from the seigniorage (profit) from coining and available treasury funds. The seigniorage, incidentally, was to come from copper coinage, pieces minted with less than their full intrinsic value in that metal.

The ninth section of the Mint Act authorized the issue of coins as shown on the top of page 213.

The tenth section was of almost equal importance, for it affected the basic look of American coins for well over a century. It required that one side of the coin be devoted to "an impression emblematic of liberty," with an inscription to that effect. Gold and silver coins were to bear an eagle on their reverses. Not until the early twentieth century did the United States break from this rigid mold which had fashioned dozens of Liberties of varying degrees of artistry, and a like number of eagles of varying degrees of credibility.

Section fourteen allowed people to bring gold and silver to the Mint, where it would be coined for them free of charge. This provision was absolutely necessary

Metal	Denomination	Value ($)	Weight	Fineness
Gold	Eagle	10	270 grains (17.496 grams)	.917
"	Half eagle	5	135 grains (8.748 grams)	"
"	Quarter eagle	2½	67.5 grains (4.374 grams)	"
Silver	Dollar or unit	1	416 grains (26.956 grams)	.892
"	Half dollar	.50	208 grains (13.478 grams)	"
"	Quarter dollar	.25	104 grains (6.739 grams)	"
"	Disme	.10	41.6 grains (2.696 grams)	"
"	Half disme	.05	20.8 grains (1.348 grams)	"
Copper	Cent	.01	264 grains (17.107 grams)	1.000
"	Half cent	.005	132 grains (8.553 grams)	"

for the Mint to become viable, but it also meant it would actually lose money. Employees had to be paid, and the seigniorage from copper coinage was not likely to offset these expenses. Final provisions of the Mint Act made United States gold and silver coins legal tender for all debts, pledged the Mint to preserve the legal weights and standards of the coinage, and established the death penalty for any mint worker who debased the coinage for profit.

Two asides: the word "disme" was pronounced "dime," and it soon yielded to the latter spelling. And the Mint never struck cents and half cents for circulation at their full weights—obviously it was more profitable to mint lighter coins for those denominations.

The Mint Act was implemented quite rapidly. Construction of the Mint began in 1792, and a few patterns were struck the same year. Regular coinage of cents and half cents began in 1793; by 1796 the Mint was coining all the denominations stipulated in the law, although none in large numbers. Expansion was slow, but a firm basis for it had been laid.

See also DECIMAL COINAGE; DOLLAR; LARGE CENT; PIECE OF EIGHT.

MINT LUSTER The sheen, or "bloom," on the surfaces of a coin or medal, caused by minute imperfections or rough spots on the dies and by the centrifugal flow of metal when struck by those dies.

Mint luster has a somewhat frosty or hazy appearance, which wears off very quickly once a piece enters circulation. The last places on a coin to lose their mint luster are usually the inner spaces of letters in legends.

Mint luster is important in grading coins. A coin in mint state with full mint luster is far more desirable than one without it, even when neither saw circulation. And any coin with even a hint of its original sheen commands a higher price than a similar piece whose mint luster has completely disappeared.

See also GRADING SYSTEMS.

Mint luster. Mexico City, Mexico, 8 reales, 1824.

Mint mark. *Chile, quarter real, 1816.*

MINT MARK An abbreviation, monogram, or symbol, placed on a coin to designate the mint responsible for its manufacture.

The mint mark tends to appear on the reverse of a coin, and the exergue is a traditional place for it. But it may also be found on the obverse and in the field, as it is on the coin in our illustration (the mint mark, an *so* monogram, stands for Santiago, Chile; the coin is a quarter-real of the late Spanish colonial period); and it can occur within a coin's legend, or even as a tiny, inconspicuous element of the actual type. Wherever its location, the mint mark serves a simple purpose: it identifies the mint responsible for a particular coin, thereby allowing a central authority to monitor its operations. Is the coin of the proper fineness? Is it well struck? Is it the correct weight? Governments must know, for money circulates in direct relationship to the confidence people have in it. With only one mint, there is no problem: we *know* who struck the coin. But when two or more mints operate concurrently, the mint mark becomes a necessity. Societies have realized this since the days of the ancient Greeks, and, while the problem of underweight precious-metal coinage is nonexistent in this century (due to the disappearance of precious-metal coinage itself), governments retain mint marks on coins, as both a respect for tradition, and an attempt to control quality. National pride, too, plays its part. A developing nation that forsakes imported coinage for that struck by its national mint may record the fact on its coins with mint marks.

See also ABBREVIATION; EXERGUE; FIELD; MARK (MINTMASTER'S OR ASSAYER'S); MONETA; MONOGRAM.

MINT SET A set of coins comprising one example of each denomination struck by a given mint in a given year for a particular country. The term is related to a method of coin collecting, and not necessarily to the condition of the coins collected.

The photograph shows a complete mint set from the Yemen Arab Republic, struck for that country by the Cairo mint in 1963. Two specimens of each denomination were included in this set, allowing its owner to view both obverse and reverse without touching the coins. This set may have been intended for presentation purposes, as witnessed by its fancy case. While the term presentation piece usually refers to a coin struck by special processes, thus setting it apart from regular issues, it is not necessarily the case. "Business strikes" such as the ones you see here can become presentation pieces, if a government wishes to use them for that purpose.

See also PRESENTATION PIECE.

Mint set. *Yemen Arab Republic, A.H. 1382 (A.D. 1963).*

Misaligned dies. Nepal, 5 paisa, Samvat 1997 (A.D. 1940).

MISALIGNED DIES Upper and lower dies which are either vertically or horizontally out of line with each other.

If dies are mismatched vertically, they will not strike the planchet in exactly the same position; consequently one side of the coin may be perfectly centered, while the other is slightly off-center. If the dies are not horizontally aligned, they tend to strike up one part of the coin sharply, the other weakly. The area of weakness will usually occupy the same relative position on each side of the coin.

The piece in the illustration resulted from horizontally misaligned dies. It is a five-paisa copper coin from Nepal, issued in Samvat 1997 (A.D. 1940), and it shows a very weak impression between 4:30 and 6:30 on obverse and reverse.

Misaligned dies are most often the result of old minting equipment and carelessness. Dies can work loose in an old press while it is operating, or they can be set in the press inaccurately. Carelessness, too, may explain another error, one which superficially resembles the error caused by horizontally misaligned dies, but in fact is not. If a metal strip for coining varies in thickness, a planchet stamped from it will be thinner in one spot than another. When this planchet is struck, the thin areas receive a weaker strike than the thicker part —and these feebly struck areas are directly opposite one another, on either side of the coin. Such coins actually diminish in thickness across their diameter, and are thus distinct from the products of misa-

ligned dies, whose thickness will be uniform.

See also ERROR; OFF-CENTER; PLANCHET.

MISMATCHED SERIAL NUMBERS Numbers on a note which do not exactly correspond to each other.

Serial numbers are used on a piece of paper money to record its ordinal position within a particular run, as a quality check, etc. At present, they are most commonly placed to the left and right of the central design on the note's face, and they usually have six, seven, or eight digits, which should be exact duplicates.

Mismatched serial numbers can be caused by human or mechanical error. The key to the modern serial number is the automatic numbering machine. For most notes, two such machines are employed. When a run of new notes is to be printed, these two number-stamps must be set manually to the correct number for the beginning of the series. It is at this juncture that many serial numbers are mismatched. The most famous example of such an error is an entire run of ten thousand United States one-dollar silver certificates of the 1957 series, with a left-hand number beginning with G55, and a right-hand number beginning with G54. The error was never detected during printing, and the bills were eventually released in 1963.

Still other mismatched serial numbers result from mechanical accident. The numbering stamps are a series of wheels, which can clog and cause sticking or skipping. Serial numbers mismatched in any other than the first two digits usually occur this way.

The mismatched serial number is essentially a product of modern mechanical printing. Prior to about 1850, most notes were numbered by hand, a process laborious enough to automatically eliminate most misnumbered bills. However, some did occur, for we know of bills on which

Mismatched serial numbers. Mexico, contemporary counterfeit of State of Chihuahua note, 1915.

someone has carefully written in the correct digit over the incorrect one; but a hand-numbered note with incorrect numbers remains a distinct rarity.

The note illustrated is a counterfeit from the Mexican Revolution. The original of this 1915-dated specimen was printed by order of Doroteo Aranga, better known to history as Pancho Villa. Villa lithographed quantities of this type of note, which was also extensively counterfeited. The left-hand serial number of our piece is 52937, while that on the right is 25937. Evidently, the counterfeiters had access to two numbering machines, and they were set incorrectly before printing began. The note is so crudely lithographed that one wonders how it ever circulated: but evidently it did, as it shows signs of wear. By the time this fake appeared, genuine Villa notes were virtually worthless, probably making people more tolerant of counterfeits.

See also COUNTERFEIT; ERROR.

MISPRINT An error in printing, usually referring to paper money.

For two reasons, this term is being used less and less. First, it is amorphous, incorporating everything from gutter folds to mismatched serial numbers—in short, anything that goes awry during the printing process. Then too, it is misleading. The generally accepted non-numismatic definition of "misprint" is a typographical error, and these rarely occur on paper money.

The illustration shows a spectacular double misprint. The note is a $4.50 bill, printed for secessionist authorities in Missouri about the beginning of 1863. The state was slipping from Confederate control at the time, and none of these notes ever circulated. Like most of the period's bills, this one was created in two steps. The main design was printed in one process (lithography, in this instance), while an undertype, usually of a more simple design and in a bright color, was added as a second element. The undertype on our note was orange, and is technically an overtype as it was added after the black printing was completed, distinctly unusual in those days. The note has only one printed face, common practice at the time.

Notes of the $4.50 denomination were two of the elements on a sheet, two $4.00 bills were the others. The two fours were at the top, and the two $4.50's at the bottom, an arrangement that held for both printing stages.

Evidently, the sheet was first printed in black, and set aside to dry. It was then fed into the second-stage printing press *upside-down*, explaining both the inverted orange

Misprint. Missouri, $4.50, c. 1863.

printing and the denomination error. The two $4.00 notes carried $4.50 undertypes, while the $4.50 notes had $4.00 undertypes. Of the sheet's original four notes, the specimen illustrated is apparently the only one to have survived.

See also ERROR; GUTTER FOLD; LITHOGRAPHY; MISMATCHED SERIAL NUMBERS; TRANSFER PRINTING.

MISSTRIKE Any error in the striking of a coin, medal, or related numismatic object.

The term misstrike is yielding its place to error, which embraces mistakes made during *all* phases of the coining process, not just during striking.

The illustration shows one variety of misstruck coin, the off-center strike. This United States cent of 1798 was badly centered in a screw press, and while part of it received an impression, most of it did not. Like other off-center coins, this one is not completely round, and its diameter is greater than it should be.

Misstrike. United States, cent, 1798.

See also BROADSTRUCK; BROCKAGE; CLASHED DIES; CRACKED DIES; CUD; CUPPED COIN; DIE BREAK; DIE CHIP; DOUBLE-STRUCK COIN; ERROR; FILLED DIES; FREAK; GHOSTING; MISALIGNED DIES; OFF-CENTER; OFF-METAL; RAILROAD RIM; ROTATED DIES.

MODULE The diameter of a coin or medal; also a word used for a coin's appearance, much as the word "fabric" is used.

If we talk about an early series of a "large module," and a later series of a "smaller module," we mean more than the coins' comparative diameters; their visual characteristics, thicknesses, etc., may also be implied. Today, the word is infrequently used in numismatics, perhaps because it is too vague for an age requiring precise terminology.

See also FABRIC.

MONETA The Roman personification of money.

Moneta was one of the aspects of the goddess Juno, and originally meant "adviser." A temple built to Juno Moneta at Rome became the site of the first Roman mint, in the third century B.C.

The use of the personification of Moneta on Roman coinage dates to the late Roman Republic. Denarii minted around 75 B.C. occasionally have Moneta's head as an obverse type, and an identifying inscription in the field. The personification was also used on a series of Roman medallions, minted by the imperial government during the third century A.D. In this case, there are three standing figures, presumably representing gold, silver, and *aes*, respectively—the metallic bases of Roman coinage.

The most widespread appearance of Moneta was on a series of large folles, struck by the emperor Diocletian (ruled

Moneta. Roman Empire, Galerius, follis, c. A.D. 302.

284–305) and his colleagues at the beginning of the fourth century. The reverse of one of these is seen here. It bears a standing figure of Moneta, holding a cornucopia and a scale. The accompanying legend refers to the sanctity of money, and has been interpreted as an allusion to Diocletian's Edict on Maximum Prices, promulgated in 301. This law doubled the value of the follis, and the Moneta type may have meant to underscore the inviolability of the new system. If so, it was a failure: the follis soon declined in size and value, and Moneta herself was summarily dropped as a type.

See also FOLLIS; MEDALLION.

MONEY Anything which, by common agreement, serves as a medium of exchange and as a measure of value within or between communities.

The word money immediately suggests coins and paper currency. But money as such is not restricted to bits of metal and pieces of paper. Indeed, it denotes anything that measures wealth and circulates, as long as it does so by the agreement of the people it serves.

Gold and silver have served as money, in part because they are beautiful and durable. So have feathers, also beautiful but not durable. And certain shells—neither beautiful nor durable. Essentially, objects used for money must have a quality that makes them attractive for that purpose, and it must be generally agreed that they *are* attractive in that way.

This is what separates money from barter. If I live in a society using copper coins as units of exchange, I know I can trade any coin I receive within that society. But should I live in a community where barter is the rule, I can only trade a small, round piece of copper to someone who wants it for itself—not because he can then use it to buy goods. My economic possibilities are curtailed, as are his.

In short, a system based on money is far more flexible and sensible than one based on barter: it facilitates trade; it makes possible the amassing of universally recognized wealth; and it is a necessary first step toward the development of civilized life. History supports these observations. Wherever people gathered to form communities, trade developed; and if it grew in importance, money developed. While the coin came to predominate, it was a relatively late step, and by no means a universal one. Actually, in the chronicle of the world's economies, it is the invention of the monetary *concept* that looms large; the emergence of the coin is an afterthought.

See also BARTER.

MONEY OF ACCOUNT A denominator of value or basis of exchange, used in keeping accounts; there may be an actual coin corresponding to the unit, but most often there is not.

The use of money of account began with the ancients. The Hebrews used the talent for such purposes—a denomination that never existed as a coin, but which was employed in bookkeeping for hundreds of years. It represented a very large amount of precious metal, as most monies of account do.

Money of account was also a common feature of medieval and early Renaissance commerce. Pounds and lire, for example, were reckoning units long before they became coins; while each unit represented a certain weight of precious metal, there was also a relationship between the unit of account and an actual coin. One pound equalled two hundred forty pence, while one lira was the equivalent of two hundred forty denari. Not all monies of account were represented by a real coin; the Portuguese conto de reis, equal to one million reis or a thousand milreis, remained a money of account throughout its long career.

In some instances, monies of account

represent extremely small sums, which governments find inconvenient to mint as coins, but which bookkeepers traditionally use for rendering accounts. The United States mill is one such unit. Although never struck, governments have used it for tax computation for many years, and to some extent businesses use it also. If it were a coin, it would take one thousand mills to equal one dollar.

The English guinea is yet another, but dissimilar, money of account. The guinea was an actual coin, in use from 1662 to 1816; however it remained as a money of account for another hundred and fifty years, with English prices regularly stated in terms of guineas.

See also DENARO; GUINEA; LIRA; MILREIS; PENNY; TALENT.

MONOGRAM A character or cipher composed of two or more letters which are interwoven or connected, and which commonly form the name of a person or a place, either in full or abbreviated.

The illustration shows a detail of a 1921 United States dollar. The coin's designer, Anthony de Francisci, used his initials as a monogram, placing the device below Liberty's head and immediately above the date on the obverse. This gives us certain facts about the monogram: in the modern age, it is usually a subordinate element, located in the field, and it frequently reveals who designed a coin, not who struck it.

Monogram. United States, dollar, 1921 (detail).

The ancient Greeks fancied monograms, and numbers of tetradrachms and other coins bore them on their reverses from the fourth century B.C. on. Greek monograms gave information as to minters, as did those on Roman coins.

With time, the monogram became increasingly significant. It was the central design element on obverses or reverses of many early deniers, struck by Charlemagne (ruled 768–814) and several of his successors. Charlemagne's monogram spelled his name in full: surrounded by a beaded circle, it made an ideal design for the small silver denier. Monograms were used in this fashion for many years during the early Middle Ages, adapting themselves well to the limitations the period's small coins placed on design.

Monograms were also pressed into service as mint marks, one of their primary functions in modern times. The coinage of Spanish America used monograms to designate mints during the colonial period, and continued to do so after independence. These marks were either in the legends or in a subordinate part of the field, an indication that the monogram was beginning to acquire its modern, secondary role. Although monograms will undoubtedly continue as a design element, they are unlikely to recapture the eminent position they had on medieval coinage.

See also ABBREVIATION; DENIER; MARK (MINTMASTER'S OR ASSAYER'S); MINT MARK; TETRADRACHM.

MORGAN DOLLAR The best-known United States silver dollar, taking its name from George T. Morgan (1845–1925), who, when he designed it, was assistant engraver at the Philadelphia Mint.

The Morgan dollar was struck without interruption from 1878 to 1904, and again in 1921. A total of nearly 660 million Morgan dollars were minted, outdistancing all other American coinage denominations of the period. At times it is also called the

Morgan dollar. *United States, 1878 CC.*

Bland dollar, from Representative Richard P. Bland, who introduced the bill authorizing the coin.

Until 1873 the United States had a bimetallic monetary system; that is, it used two metals—silver and gold—as units of value. From the 1830s to the early 1870s, the official ratio was sixteen ounces of silver to one of gold. The convertibility of one metal into the other was guaranteed, and there were no restrictions on the amount of either metal coined.

Increased silver production in the west, and its glut on the world market caused by German dumping in the early 1870s, concerned Dr. Henry Linderman, then Director of the United States Mint. An overabundance of silver could drive gold from circulation, inflating the economy with cheap money. The Coinage Act of February 12, 1873 was passed to avoid such an effect. Free coinage of silver was suspended, and the silver dollar was no longer struck. (A new coin, the trade dollar, took its place, but it was designed for Far Eastern commerce.) Coinage of the half dime was also suspended, but dimes, quarters, and half dollars continued to be coined.

Complaints from western miners were few—at least at first. With silver worth $1.30 an ounce, they could still make a profit. But when its value began to descend later in 1873, their voices became more vociferous. They demanded the repeal of the Coinage Act—dubbed the "Crime of '73"—and the resumption of "free and unlimited coinage of silver." Their ranks were swollen by impoverished farmers and debtors in general, who argued that inflating the money supply with "free silver" would make them able to meet their financial obligations.

The upshot was "Silver Dick" Bland's bill in the House of Representatives. Introduced several times in the mid-seventies and amended by Senator William B. Allison, the bill passed as the Bland-Allison Act on February 28, 1878 (over President Hayes's veto). The Act restored legal tender status to silver money, and committed the Treasury to buying between $2,000,000 and $4,000,000 in silver each month, at current market prices. This, in turn, was to be turned into silver dollars at the old (and by now artificial) ratio of sixteen to one. Each coin was to weigh 412.5 grains (26.76 grams), struck in 90 percent silver. The Bland-Allison Act was a compromise and alienated fiscal liberals because it failed to mandate a free and unlimited silver coinage. But it did permit a large coinage of cheap silver at inflated values, in turn alienating fiscal conservatives.

While Bland was steering his bill through Congress, George T. Morgan was preparing designs for the new silver dollar, directly competing with William Barber, chief engraver at the Philadelphia Mint. Morgan's design was the one adopted. We see it here, on an 1878 silver dollar from the Carson City facility (indicated by the two tiny C's below the eagle on the reverse; when Morgan dollars have mint marks this is where they appear). To modern eyes, the design is rather pedestrian; but then all of the period's American coins suffer from a lack of daring and artistry. Morgan's design was "safe," one of the reasons it was accepted.

Under the Bland-Allison Act, 378 million silver dollars were struck. It should be noted that the Act also provided for a new form of paper money, the silver certificate —issued at par with other forms, and exchangeable for Morgan dollars. Purchases of silver under the Bland-Allison Act continued until the Sherman Act was passed on July 14, 1890, repealing its provisions and providing for government purchase of even more silver—up to 4.5 million ounces each month. Eventually this yielded another 187 million Morgan dollars. President Grover Cleveland, a fiscal conservative, induced Congress to repeal the Sherman Silver Purchase Act in late 1893. His opposition to silver coinage meant there were fewer silver dollar issues during his term in office: most of the great rarities in the Morgan dollar series are from the mid-1890s.

The nation was then in the grip of a horrendous economic depression, with millions unemployed. During the presidential campaign of 1896, the Democrats endorsed the free and unlimited coinage of silver, while Republicans were opposed. The Morgan dollar thus commanded a central place in American politics of the time. The Republicans, better organized and better financed, won the election, and their emphasis on fiscal orthodoxy was to doom the Morgan dollar.

But not immediately. The nation's economy gradually recovered, and a business surge encouraged the production of more silver dollars. Metal for them had been purchased in the early 1890s, under the Sherman Act, and an additional five million or so were struck from silver originally earmarked for trade dollars. But no further purchases were authorized, and when supplies were depleted in 1904, minting of the Morgan dollar came to a halt.

By then, 570 million had been struck. Not all have survived, of course. The Pittman Act of 1918 directed that not more than 350 million silver dollars be converted into bullion, and either sold or used for subsidiary coinage. It also authorized purchase of domestic silver for recoinage of a like number of dollars. Under the Pittman Act, some 270 million silver dollars were melted down for sale to the British, who diverted the metal to India, in an effort to repress the influence of that country's silver speculators.

The Pittman Act permitted the coining of silver dollars as required, and in 1921 86 million were struck. While they retained Morgan's basic design elements, they differed slightly in types and lettering. At the end of 1921, the Morgan dollar gave ground to the Peace dollar.

See also BIMETALLIC CURRENCY; CARTWHEEL; DOLLAR; MINT MARK; PEACE DOLLAR; SILVER CERTIFICATE.

MOTTO A brief, epigrammatic statement on a coin or note, often of a religious cast.

Mottoes may appear on a nation's money over a long period of time without change. The mottoes E PLURIBUS UNUM ("Out of Many, One"), and IN GOD WE TRUST, for instance, have graced America's coins and bills for many years. A motto may also be of a more personal, transitory nature, as our illustration shows. It constitutes the reverse legend of a 1707 Swedish riksdaler, and was the personal motto of Charles XII (ruled 1697–1718). It reads MED GUDZ HIELP ("With God's Help")—an appropriate selection for the warlike Charles, who did battle with the Russians and needed help from all sources. The adoption of personal mottoes by successive monarchs has been common on Scandinavian coins from the sixteenth century to the present.

The roots of the motto lie with the Ro-

Motto. Sweden, riksdaler, 1707.

mans, who used a variety of political slogans as prominent reverse legends on their late issues. In time the motto assumed a subordinate position, and became a frequent element in heraldic designs. While earlier issues relegated it to the reverse, modern issues show no signs of a preferred position.

See also INSCRIPTION; LEGEND.

Mule. Alamos, Mexico, 5 centavos, 1878.

MULE A coin, token, or medal struck from two dies not meant to be used with one another, the conjunction of which can be accidental or deliberate.

Since dies of the same size are apt to be highly polished and hard to differentiate, it is quite possible that an inexperienced coiner will match a correct die with an incorrect one, and fashion a hybrid with traits of two separate coins. If the dies' dissimilarities are minor, the mule might not be detected before it is circulated. Today's careful minting procedures have made such accidental mules very rare.

They were more common in earlier days, and, like those deliberately manufactured, were usually created by small, provincial mints. The word *deliberate,* by the way, does not necessarily mean the intention to defraud. Rather, let us assume such a mint was ordered to furnish a particular coin, but lacked a necessary die. Perhaps the nation used similar coins struck in a different metal, and the provincial mint had both dies for these coins. Should one of the dies resemble the missing one, it might well be pressed into service. A mule was the result.

This is what took place with the coin in the illustration. It is a Mexican five-centavo silver piece, struck at the small northern mint of Alamos in 1878. The mint, having exhausted its supply of the necessary obverse (eagle side) dies, substituted one used for the obverses of gold pesos, which were about the same size; the marriage of the obverse die with an ordinary

reverse one yielded an 1878 mule. It was not unique. Mules emerged with some frequency from the Alamos mint in the 1870s and 1880s.

While the Alamos mule was deliberately coined to circulate, others have been created for sale to collectors. An outstanding instance of the practice occurred in England in the 1790s. A desperate scarcity of low-denomination copper coins led numbers of people to strike copper tokens, usually valued at a halfpenny but occasionally circulated as a penny or a farthing. Many were rather handsome; some were quite patriotic, and they were soon coveted by collectors. They formed the topic of some of the earliest numismatic books written in England.

As the early tokens were meant for trade, they contained quite a bit of copper. Their coiners soon discovered that, by selling their wares to collectors, they could reduce the tokens' weight while increasing their own profits. Not surprisingly, tokens grew lighter, and even more attractive. To hold collectors' interest, mules were produced, materially adding to the collectible varieties. Similar events took place in the United States during the Civil War, where muled varieties of Civil War cents are known. Muling for collectors has never been common for genuine coinage, but some examples emerged from the United States Mint in the middle of the last century, a corrupt period in that institution's history.

See also CIVIL WAR TOKENS; ERROR; TOKEN.

N

NAMI SEN A Japanese base-metal cast coin, minted from 1626 to 1867.

The nami sen had a stylized wave design as its reverse type; hence its name nami, "wave" in Japanese. The waves may have expressed the coiners' fantasy that the coins would be known on all the world's shores.

Certainly, great effort was made to ensure the nami sen's success. The numbers produced are not known, but one source estimates over 150 million were cast between 1787 and 1860 alone, and we know millions more had been manufactured before 1787. They were produced in several places—including Nagasaki, Osaka, and Edo (the future Tokyo)—most commonly in brass or copper.

The nami sen in the illustration was cast between 1769 and 1772—late in the Meiwa period (1764–1772)—and is typical of this type of coin, with a diameter of 29 millimeters and a weight of 5.66 grams. Like other coins of the Tokugawa Shogunate, nami sen disappeared after the restoration of the imperial government in 1868.

See also BRASS COINAGE; CAST COINAGE; TEMPO TSUHO.

Nami sen. Japan, 1769–1772.

NATIONAL BANK NOTE An obsolete form of United States currency—partly federal and partly local, partly public and partly private—issued between 1863 and 1935, the hybrid nature of which is one of the main reasons for its popularity among collectors.

Akin to other obsolete federal paper money, the national bank note sprang from the demands imposed on the government during the American Civil War. The Lincoln administration needed increasing sums of money to wage its war: to create funds, it issued demand notes in 1861–1862 and began printing legal tender notes in the latter year. The demand note was a limited issue, while the legal tender note was essentially fiat money, the value of which rose and fell with the fortunes of Union arms. The federal war effort was further hampered by the lack of a centralized banking authority with the power to print money. Instead, the nation relied largely on private banks, whose financial credibility varied greatly.

The National Banking Act of February 25, 1863, was intended to create more money with which to fight the war, but it also represented a half-hearted attempt to regulate the country's chaotic currency system. Under its provisions, private banks were encouraged to apply for federal charters, thereby becoming "national banks." These banks were then permitted to issue national bank notes. They used their funds to buy Union bonds (thus raising money for the war), deposited them with the Treasurer at Washington, and were then allowed to issue national bank notes to 90 percent of the value of the bonds on deposit. Each bank's charter ran for a renewable period of twenty years.

The advantages for the government were obvious. It received cash, and also had the start of a federal banking system capable of regulating banking activity. For their part, the national banks also benefited: a bank with the word "national" in its name could command more local trust and respect than a private bank. Then too, the administration passed laws to encourage private banks to join the national system. Strictly private banks soon found their paper heavily taxed, and those that opted not to join the new system closed their doors, or at least stopped printing money. During the Act's first year, 179 banks joined the system: by the end of 1865, the number had grown tenfold. When the last national bank notes came off the presses in 1935, 14,348 banks were members, although not all had actually issued notes. Most did, however, and note-

National bank note. United States, City National Bank of Tipton, Iowa, 20 dollars, 1903.

issuing national banks were found in all the states and territories, and in Puerto Rico and the Virgin Islands. The sheer extent of national bank note issues, the myriad banks taking part, the localism revealed (each national bank note bore real or facsimile signatures of local bank officials, and each had the bank's name and the town where it was located clearly spelled out), are the appealing elements for collectors of the national bank note.

While the notes were issued by local national banks, they were printed by central authorities. The federal government contracted for private printing of the first national bank notes, but by 1875, it chose to print them itself. Notes were sent to the national banks in sheets. When they arrived, they were signed by bank officers, either by hand or, as in the case of the Iowa note illustrated, by facsimile signatures applied by rubber stamps. They were then cut apart and circulated. Such a procedure was customary for small- and medium-sized banks; larger ones might have facsimile signatures applied by the printer, with the cutting done at the same time.

Let us examine the Iowa note more closely. Note the two dates on the bill, one the year the series was authorized, the other representing the date the bank was founded. Note the 6760 in the center and the margins of the note's obverse. This is the bank's charter number, and indicates that, shortly after its organization, the bank joined the system in 1903. The capital M's by the two large charter numbers were put there to simplify sorting when it was necessary to redeem the note. M stood for "Midwest." An N meant "New England," a P "Pacific," and so forth.

The large format adopted for this note was used for United States paper money until 1929, when the notes' size was reduced to cut printing costs. Collectors commonly speak of "large" and "small-sized" national bank notes, and in most cases, the first are more coveted than the second.

The year 1929 also saw the onset of the Depression which was to render the national bank note obsolete. Banks began to fail shortly after the new notes were introduced, and as they did, people withdrew their holdings from other banks, including national ones, thus weakening the banking system even further. The public's lack of confidence reached a crisis in 1933, and on March 6 the newly inaugurated Franklin D. Roosevelt ordered that all United States banks be closed. While they were the government examined them, and the entire banking and currency system, and found many banks to be so fiscally unsound they should remain shuttered. Others could reopen. It was also determined that the national bank note system was inflexible, antiquated, and not equipped to manage the monies of a nation in depression; the federal government needed a flexible, expandable money supply, and the National Banking Act of 1863 did not provide it. Roosevelt's government placed its faith in a banking tool it considered flexible, the Federal Reserve System. With the final issue of national bank notes in 1935, the note—and the system that created it—passed into history. Curiously, the legislation that established the system was never replaced. The government simply called in all federal bonds used to secure national bank notes, leaving the banks unable to issue paper money against them.

See also Broken bank notes; Demand note; Federal Reserve note; Legal tender note.

NECESSITY MONEY A term largely synonymous with emergency money: it thus describes any currency issued under extraordinary conditions, by other than ordinary authorities.

In an earlier age, the term was restricted to siege pieces. While its usage has expanded to embrace notgeld, provisional coinage, and paper money, vestiges of its military emphasis remain.

Our photograph shows a most peculiar piece of necessity money, illustrative of the term's non-military possibilities. Clearly this is nothing but a clamshell taken from the beach, but it was adopted as local money by the Chamber of Commerce of Crescent City, California. It is signed by the organization's secretary, and was redeemable for twenty-five cents. The piece was hand-lettered in the early spring of 1933, when the Depression had driven ordinary currency from circulation. Companion ten-cent pieces were also issued; predictably, smaller shells were used. While such necessity money was highly impractical in the long run, it was no more

Necessity money. Crescent City, California, 25 cents, 1933.

so than several other West Coast issues, printed on wood, leather, etc.; and, while clamshells were undoubtedly contrived as souvenirs to raise money for the town, eyewitness accounts indicate they did indeed circulate as money.

See also EMERGENCY MONEY; NOTGELD; SCRIP; SIEGE PIECE.

NICKEL COINAGE   Money struck from an extremely hard, durable, white metal of limited value.

Nickel is most commonly alloyed with copper and/or other metals when coinage is contemplated, as its hardness wears out coin dies at a prodigious rate. Its high melting point is also a drawback, as is the fact that in its pure state it is attracted to magnetic force. Nevertheless, many nations have chosen to use it in an unalloyed form for coinage. It is relatively cheap, not unattractive, and, of course, wears extremely well. The Swiss were the first to strike a purely nickel coin. Their twenty-centime denomination, originally struck in a bizarre mixture of copper, nickel, zinc, and silver, was minted entirely in nickel in 1881; pure nickel twenty-centime pieces were produced until 1938, by which time numbers of other countries were also striking nickel coinage.

Foremost among them was Canada, a leading producer of the metal. Canada introduced a pure nickel five-cent piece in 1922, and the coin has been struck in that metal through most of the ensuing years. The Canadians even issued a pure nickel five-cent commemorative in 1951, celebrating the bicentennial of the metal's discovery. In the late 1960s, Canada began using nickel for other denominations; currently, the only circulating Canadian coin not made of nickel is the cent, which is still minted from bronze.

While Canadian coinage is atypical in this respect, it indicates the growing popularity of nickel as a numismatic metal. Although it may never be as widely accepted as its copper-nickel alloy, it remains a viable if somewhat difficult material for coinage.

See also ALLOY; COPPER-NICKEL COINAGE; LAMINATION.

NIEN-HAO   A Chinese term referring to the title of an imperial reign; of great importance to numismatists, as it enables them to assign approximate dates to otherwise undatable Chinese ch'ien or cash.

A *nien-hao* was created every time a new emperor ascended the imperial throne. He had a personal name, of course, but it was considered sacred after his accession, and its use was precluded. Instead, the new ruler chose a name by which he wished his reign to be distinguished. He was then known by that reign-title, or *nien-hao*.

The *nien-hao* was in use for many centuries before it was thought to place it on a coin. The exact date of its introduction as a numismatic element is moot. J. H. S. Lockhart, an eminent Chinese specialist of the early twentieth century, placed it at 32–29 B.C., while other sources fix it in the early third century A.D. Whatever its date, it was not regularly added to coins until the birth of the T'ang dynasty (618–907) in the seventh century A.D. It remained a consistent feature of Chinese imperial coinage into the twentieth century. In the days of cast coinage, the *nien-hao* occupied the two vertical characters on the obverse, a position it retained on machine-struck issues of the late nineteenth and early twentieth centuries.

At first glance, the *nien-hao* seems to be ideal for dating Chinese coinage. Simply match the characters on a coin with those of an illustration in a reference book, and the chronology is accomplished. Unfortunately, it is not so simple. There were a great many emperors, but there was a finite number of appropriately impressive *nien-hao*, leading to duplication. Careful study of a coin's fabric is usually helpful.

Nien-hao. *China: Three ch'ien from the reign of the emperor Chen Tsung, bearing* nien-hao *used:*
Left: 998–1003
Center: 1004–1007
Right: 1008–1016.

A second problem with the *nien-hao* can be seen in the illustration. Here are three coins, all from the period of the Northern Sung emperor Chen Tsung (ruled 998–1022). However, the *nien-hao*, formed by the top and right-hand characters, are completely different from one another: this emperor, like many others, used one *nien-hao* for several years, then abandoned it in favor of a new one.

Despite such confusions, reign-titles on coins are a blessing to numismatists. The Japanese, Annamese, and Koreans also used them, and they, too, are of immeasurable aid to Far Eastern numismatists.

See also CASH; DATING SYSTEMS; FABRIC.

NOBLE The most notable English gold coin of the late Middle Ages, introduced in 1344 during the time of Edward III (ruled 1327–1377).

The original noble was tariffed at 80 pence, or 6 shillings 8 pence, weighed slightly under 9 grams, and was virtually pure gold—995 fine. The coin soon underwent slight weight reductions, as originally it had been undervalued in relation to silver. It stood at 120 grains (about 7.8 grams) until 1412, when its weight was again reduced—to 108 grains (almost exactly 7 grams), where it remained. Its fineness, too, continued unchanged throughout the entire period.

The illustration shows one of the earlier nobles, minted between 1356 and 1361. It measures 34 millimeters in diameter, and weighs 7.8 grams. While the piece was of major importance as a trading coin, its designs are what concern us here, for they are among the finest in English medieval numismatic art. And they are also more.

We see the king aboard ship, holding a sword aloft, and defending himself with a shield, upon which the quartered arms of England and France are emblazoned—both a display of national pride, and an announcement of royal ambitions. The obverse legend spells out his claims: king of England and France, master of Ireland —all by the grace of God. While the ship on which Edward stands symbolizes England's pride in its naval power, it has also been suggested that it could refer to the nation's overwhelming victory at Sluys in 1340, which won it control of the English Channel for many years.

The reverse of the noble bears a cross, a familiar image on medieval coins. Notice that the cross is smaller than it was on earlier coins, and at this juncture is merely

Noble. England, 1356–1361.

one rather ornate element of the design, along with crowns, lions, and fleurs-de-lis. The reverse legend, however, is ostensibly religious, although its wording, an adaption of the Vulgate version of Luke 4:30 ("But He [Jesus], passing through the midst of them, went His way"), is curious, and seems to have no immediate significance.

In brief, this piece is something new in English coinage. It celebrates nation and king, and is the numismatic equivalent of a declaration of war. (One authority sees the coin's design as signalling Edward's readiness to disembark and invade French territory.) Religious themes are muted, the nation's dreams of glory are not. When we reflect that this was also the first English gold coin to gain success in the economy (and gold coinage generally means increased business of one kind or another), it is clear it was an eventful period in England which would in time prod the nation into the modern age.

The noble was minted in large numbers during Edward's reign, at the end of which its production declined, although it was struck into the first reign of Edward IV (ruled 1461–1470, 1471–1483). By then, nobles were undervalued in relation to silver, and many were sent abroad for melting. This led to monetary changes in 1464–1465, which replaced the noble with two new denominations—the ryal or rose-noble, valued at 10 shillings, and the angel, tariffed at 6 shillings 8 pence, the original value of the noble.

See also CROSS ON COINAGE; FLEUR-DE-LIS; PORTRAIT; TRADE COINS.

NONCIRCULATING LEGAL TENDER
A term embracing a large series of contemporary, usually commemorative coins, minted by or for a country, for sale to collectors rather than for use as money.

The term is confusing, for while noncirculating legal tender (or NCLT) coins can be struck in the same manner as proofs, not all proofs are NCLTs. The proof could circulate as an ordinary coin; it is highly unlikely the NCLT would do so.

But noncirculating legal tender coins do have certain characteristics which, taken together, distinguish them from other coins. The number of NCLTs in any given series is small; they are often struck in precious metal, unlike ordinary coins; and they are not designed to be circulated. Furthermore, they are apt to be minted in uncommonly large denominations. The Panamanian five-hundred-balboa gold piece is a good example: the balboa is on a par with the dollar, and a five-hundred-dollar gold piece is a numismatic absurdity.

NCLTs are more frequently of a commemorative or medallic nature than ordinary coins, due in part to their generous module, which encourages designs impossible to execute on smaller coins. Finally, circulating coins are "sold" at face. NCLTs, on the other hand, cost more than their face value, as the government or private agency strikes them to be sold at a profit.

The piece illustrated, a quarter hau from Tonga, typifies the NCLT coin. Its total mintage was 1,700: the hau and its subdivisions do not serve as normal parts of Tonga's currency. The coin is a commemorative, celebrating the coronation of a new king, while its lettered edge (not seen here) tells us it was "historically the first palladium coinage." Palladium is a rare, heavy, white metal, not especially

Noncirculating legal tender. *Tonga, quarter hau, 1967.*

suitable for coinage, and the inscription is quite correct; palladium coins had never been struck (largely because it had never occurred to anyone to do so).

See also COMMEMORATIVE; FANTASY; INGOT; PROOF.

NOTAPHILY A recently devised expression for the study and collection of paper money.

The word may be awkward, but as paper money draws the interest of more and more collectors, it is a useful addition to the lexicon.

See also PAPER MONEY.

NOTGELD Literally, "emergency money": a word widely used to describe a series of emergency paper money, issued by states, towns, and cities, banks, businesses, and even private individuals during the first half of the twentieth century.

Notgeld has been issued throughout the world, but most numismatists restrict the term to German and Austrian emergency paper currency issued in the World War I period. We shall concentrate on the German variety: the word is German, and the greatest use of this type of money took place in Germany.

We can divide the history of this currency into six distinct periods. The first covered late 1914 and early 1915, when, at the start of World War I, notgeld appeared in border areas along the two German fronts. People in these regions had removed their gold and silver from circulation, impelling municipal governments to print notgeld to fill the void. Most of these early notes were quite crude—typeset or even printed with rubber stamps, as is the piece illustrated. This note is from the tiny village of Felleringen, and its

Notgeld.
Top left: Felleringen, 18 mark, 1914.
Top right: Hamburg, 50 pfennig, 1921.
Bottom: Bielefeld, 3 million mark, 1923.

value was inked in by hand, as was its signature. To the left, we can see part of the town seal; the other half was retained in a notebook, in the fashion of the modern check-stub. Authorities knew the crudity of their notes invited counterfeiting, hence the system of stubs, which allowed a comparison of a suspect bill with its corresponding stub to make certain the seal and perforations were in line. The notes were printed on only one side; the legal forms used here already had printing on the other side. Felleringen fell to the French later in 1914; local issues continued, however, with a French town seal substituted for the German one. The first issues of German notgeld are fairly rare; the towns issuing them were often quite small, and the bills' coarseness did not induce collecting them. In addition, many were eventually redeemed and destroyed.

The second type of German notgeld dates mainly from early 1917 to late 1918, although a few pieces are known from 1916. Virtually all this notgeld was issued in denominations of less than one mark, and it and the metallic kriegsgeld were Germany's basic small change during the last stages of World War I. During this period, notgeld was nation-wide, created in cities and villages near the fronts as well as those hundreds of miles distant. Having hoarded gold and silver coins in the face of an uncertain future, Germans were now also removing official small change from circulation.

At the end of 1918, which brought the collapse of the Western Front, the Armistice, and the proclamation of a German republic, notgeld entered its third phase. The notes of 1917–1918 had been in small denominations, but in the last months of 1918 and the beginning of 1919 another issue circulated too: bills in much larger denominations, ranging up to fifty marks and beyond. They were a direct result of a society in which coins were hoarded and government paper held suspect.

Many of these notes (as well as some of the small-denomination ones) were attrac-

tively printed. People started collecting the more artistic specimens in the small-denomination series, which, in the years 1919 to 1922, led to a boom in the production of notgeld of modest denominations, very often in series. Most pieces of surviving German notgeld are from this period, the fourth in the chronicle of this emergency money. Notgeld-for-collectors was ideal from everyone's perspective. The collector had a pleasing, inexpensive memento of a town through which he had passed. The town in turn made money, for it never had to redeem it for its face value. And the host of manufacturers of notgeld holders, the authors of articles and books on the subject, the printers of the bills themselves, all turned a handsome profit.

The second illustration shows a bill from this fourth stage. It comes from Hamburg, with an issue-date of July 1, 1921. It is intensely patriotic, printed in red, white, and black (the colors of the old imperial flag), with an ode to the nation's honor occupying the note's center.

When this note was issued Germany was beset by inflation, which was to grow worse until 1924. It ruined thousands, fanned political demagoguery, and fatally weakened the Weimar Republic. It also generated two additional forms of German notgeld. The first consisted of inflation issues of 1922 and 1923. These notes were a hybrid group. They were colorful, like the "collector" notgeld. On the other hand, they were also of high denomination, and in this sense akin to the issues of 1914–1915 and 1918–1919. The last bill in the illustration is typical of notgeld from this inflationary phase. It is blue and black, a product of authorities at Bielefeld, who printed it in 1923. The small marginal print reveals sardonic asides about Germany's monetary system, and the collapse of purchasing power since 1914. The denomination (three million mark) is by no means excessive; by late 1923, bills for billions of mark were common.

This notgeld kept pace with official German currency; as the latter depreciated, so did the former. Inflationary chaos led to a second kind of notgeld. Issued from late 1923 into early 1924, this group was of fixed value—its notes bore denominations in gold mark, dollars, even British pounds. A smaller number had denominations linked to commodities—so many kilograms of sugar, for example. Fixed value issues form our sixth and last category of notgeld. It is a rarer variety than several others, and not widely known outside of Germany. Allied loans in 1924 once again put the German mark on a sound footing. New notes, expressed in mark valued at the pre-1914 level and backed by gold, soon appeared; as they did so, notgeld disappeared.

Germany offers a textbook example of notgeld's operation. Although other countries saw its use—France, Austria, Russia, and Mexico among them—it is wisest to limit the term to German and Austrian issues, and to preface it with a qualifier (e.g., "Russian Civil War notgeld") when it is used for others.

See also EMERGENCY MONEY; GUTSCHEIN; INFLATION; KRIEGSGELD; LITHOGRAPHY; PHOTOLITHOGRAPHY; SCRIP; TYPESET.

NOVODEL A special Russian coin, struck from officially prepared dies; the term's meaning is indistinct, and is used for coins in at least three categories.

The first includes pieces struck in imitation of rare coins not readily available to the collector; new dies were prepared for this purpose. A second category embraces coins struck with dates not used on ordinary issues, intended to fill in missing dates in collections; here too, new dies had to be prepared. Novodels of this type are most frequently seen with dates between 1780 and 1810. The third category includes coins originally minted in extremely small numbers, the dies for which issues were retained and later used to mint specimens for collectors. (This third category is actually a restrike.)

Novodel. Russia, 5 kopeks, 1726 (probably nineteenth century).

The novodel in the illustration belongs in the first category, and is a copy of a rare Russian variety of platmynt, or copper plate money. This particular piece measures 45 millimeters on each side, and weighs 80 grams.

The rationale for this special coinage is hardly complex. The aristocrats of the Russian Empire were numerous, powerful, and quite accustomed to special favors from their government. As many of the nobility were avid collectors of Russian coins by date, the mints were more than willing to strike whatever novodels they needed to complete their collections. The practice, which modern numismatists find somewhat reprehensible, came to an end under Tsar Alexander III (ruled 1881–1894). Still, novodels are often the only clues we have to the look of early Russian coins, and hobbyists do seek them.

See also COPPER PLATE MONEY; FANTASY; RESTRIKE.

NUMISMATICS The study, science, and collecting of coins, medals, paper money, tokens, and related objects, all of which are linked to one another by economic function or physical appearance.

NUMMUS   Originally, a generic term for "money" in the Latin language; it also describes a small Roman and Byzantine coin of the fifth and sixth centuries, and a money of account based on that coin.

Initially the Romans applied the term to the most important coin at a particular time. Thus, nummus could be and was used for didrachm, denarius, sestertius, etc. By the fifth century A.D., however, it designated a single coin—an extremely small and light copper piece with a high lead content. Fifth-century nummi weighed less than a gram, and measured scarcely 10 millimeters in diameter. Their designs were usually simple—plain monograms and crosses being popular types. Their execution was wretched—in part because their size was so limiting, but also reflecting the period's sorry numismatic art. There was another factor too: the nummus was all but valueless.

Even so, the fifth-century nummus was an important coin, and virtually the only denomination then struck except for the gold solidus and the tremissis. Unfortunately, the solidus was tariffed at anywhere from 7,200 to 16,800 nummi, which must have made trade an arduous exercise. More likely than not, nummi used in large transactions were weighed rather than counted. They were also counterfeited: while worth very little, nummi were so crude they presented an easy target.

By the late fifth century, the monetary situation was nearing a crisis. The erstwhile classical world then consisted of the Eastern Roman or Byzantine empire, and a number of barbarian states in the West. About A.D. 475, authorities in Rome revived a large, fourth-century copper coin, the follis, and declared it equal in value to forty nummi; in 498, the Byzantine em-

Nummus. Italy, Ostrogoths, 40 nummi, A.D. 534–536.

peror Anastasius I (ruled A.D. 491–518) adopted the idea and issued the forty-nummi piece.

The follis drove smaller coins, including the nummus, out of circulation. The Byzantines would continue to mint nummi until the reign of Maurice (ruled 582–602), but never in large numbers. These coins, usually from provincial mints, carried the same elements as their predecessors—crosses, monograms, etc., and were tariffed at 7,200 to a gold solidus in 539, a ratio they retained. While no nummi were struck after approximately 600, the coin was a Byzantine accounting unit for another two centuries.

The illustration shows an outstanding Western forty-nummi piece, struck by Theodahad, king of the Ostrogoths between 534 and 536. Unlike its Byzantine counterparts, it bore no mark of value. It is ironic that in design the barbarian coin adheres more strictly to the classical Roman tradition than do folles minted by the Byzantines, self-styled inheritors of Roman culture.

See also CROSS ON COINAGE; DENARIUS; DIDRACHM; FOLLIS; MONEY OF ACCOUNT; MONOGRAM; SESTERTIUS; SOLIDUS; TREMISSIS.

O

OBAN The largest gold coin in feudal Japan.

The oban seems to have originated late in the Ashikaga era (A.D. 1392–1568), but the earliest surviving specimens date from the Tensho period (1572–1592), and set the style for all later oban. They were fashioned in an oval shape, then stamped near the edges with the *kiri* flower crest of the government, and inscribed with their value (nominally ten ryo) in India ink.

Oban were produced during the Tokugawa Shogunate (1599–1868), and were never meant to circulate as coins, because of their excessively high value compared to ordinary currency. Rather, they were reserved for court transactions, and occasionally used by the nobility as presentation pieces. They also served as a gold backing to the shogunate's financial system. In time, they did have a limited circulation, being used in large domestic transactions and as payment for imports. As they circulated, their ink rubbed off; the oban could be re-inked by paying a set fee to the government.

The oban illustrated is from the Manen era, and dates from between 1860 and 1862. The piece is huge, measuring 135 by 80 millimeters, weighing nearly 113 grams. Its gold fineness is only .344, however, a serious decline from its original purity. It is also smaller and lighter than earlier oban, indicating severe economic problems in late pre-modern Japan. Economic unrest was one of the bases for

Oban. *Japan, 1860–1862.*

the Meiji Restoration of 1868, which concentrated power in the emperor's hands and brought new gold coinage to the country. As the emperor was a reformer, the coins were struck on a Western pattern.

See also KOBAN.

OBOL   A small Greek silver coin, valued at one-sixth of a drachm.

Its name derives from *obelos* (a spit), just as drachm comes from *drax* (a handful of spits), evidence that both coins superseded a monetary system that used iron cooking-spits as the medium of exchange. Although it is not known for certain when the obol was introduced, we assume it was sometime in the sixth century B.C.

The piece in the illustration is an Athenian obol, minted in the following century. It weighs less than .7 gram and has a diameter of only 10 millimeters. Its designs —the goddess Athena for the obverse, the owl sacred to the goddess for the reverse —are also found on contemporary tetradrachms; in appearance this obol is essentially a miniature of the tetradrachm. Tiny though it was, there were several even smaller denominations, all struck in silver. Base-metal coinage came late to the Grecian world: while the obol and its subsidiaries were easily lost, the

Greeks preferred them to larger and perhaps more sensible issues of copper or bronze. So the obol circulated and was struck in numerous areas of the Greek world over several centuries. By the third century B.C., the silver obol was being replaced by the bronze obol; both issues disappeared with Rome's domination of the classical world.

The name, however, has lingered. At times, the medieval denier had a companion coin, worth half as much, and frequently called an obol, obole, etc. It was of some importance in the Crusader kingdoms of the Levant and in medieval Hungary and France. A copper coin known as an obol served the semi-independent Ionian Islands as late as 1863.

See also DENIER; DRACHM; TETRADRACHM.

OBVERSE   The side of the coin bearing the more important legends or types; its opposite side is the reverse.

Generally this definition applies to any given coin, but there are coins that carry important legends or types on both sides, while on still other coins, the side we would consider the obverse is officially the reverse.

The illustrations underscore these contradictions. The first coin is a United States five-dollar gold piece of 1804. American numismatists would agree that the side shown is the obverse. But where, then, is the name of the country, or any heraldic portrayal of it? They are on the *reverse*. The United States Mint Act of 1792 legally established which side of an American coin was its obverse and which its reverse. Thus, we see an entire series of coins whose obverse and reverse positions are exactly opposite the customary ones.

The second coin is an English penny of 1936, and an example of a "normal" distribution of obverse and reverse elements. In the tradition of royal portrait coinage, the king's head is on the obverse. Its Latin legends obliquely describe the country in

Obol. Athens, 480–406 B.C.

Obverse.
Left: United States, 5 dollars, 1804.
Center: United Kingdom, penny, 1936.
Right: Mexico, 25 pesos, 1972.

abbreviated form, naming the king's possessions; this, too, is traditional practice. The coin's reverse has a seated figure symbolizing the country; it also bears the denomination and date—all less important elements.

The last coin is a Mexican twenty-five-peso silver commemorative of 1972, marking the hundredth anniversary of the death of Benito Juárez. Juárez's portrait appears on the reverse; the obverse bears a stylized Mexican eagle and serpent, accompanied by the name of the country. In Mexico, as in several Latin American countries, the side of a coin with the national arms is considered the obverse, regardless of the elements on the other side.

Three coins, three different concepts of an obverse. But there are some basic rules which may be helpful. As mentioned, the more important legends or types are on the obverse. In the case of medieval (and later monarchical) coins, the side with the legend referring to the ruler is the obverse, regardless of type. If that legend continues from one side of the coin to the other, the side where it begins is considered the obverse, the one where it concludes the reverse. Further confusion is presented by the coinage of free cities and provinces, many of which have what might be described as *two* obverses: one with legends and types referring to an entire na-

tion or overlord, the other with the name and arms of the city or state where the coin was struck. In such instances, it is probably wise to call the "local" side the true obverse, as its information is the more essential. For cast Far Eastern coins, the obverse is usually the side with the greater number of characters; for early Islamic issues, it is the one on which the *Kalima* begins.

See also REVERSE.

OCCUPATION NOTES Paper currency issued, either during or immediately after a war, by a country that is occupying another.

The notes are usually issued in the language of the subject people, and denominations are those of its traditional currency.

The occupation note is essentially a phenomenon of the twentieth century, and its two world wars. In World War I, Germany and Austria printed occupation notes for use in areas of Romania, Italy, and Poland. The practice was broadened during and after World War II, with German, Italian, Japanese, American, French, English, and Russian issues for occupied lands.

Our two occupation notes are from this second global conflict. While neither bears

Occupation notes.

Top: Japanese occupation note for Malaya, 50 cents, 1942.

Bottom: American occupation note for Japan, 5 yen, 1942.

OCTADRACHM A large Greek silver coin—also spelled octodrachm—equal to eight drachms.

These coins were first minted about 500 B.C., and were produced at various times in Thrace, Macedon, and a few other places. The piece illustrated is an early product of the kingdom of Macedon, and was struck during the reign of Alexander I (ruled 498–454 B.C.). It has a diameter of about 30 millimeters, a weight of 29 grams. It is a splendid example of the archaic style in Greek numismatics: we see a nude horseman standing by a horse on the obverse, an incuse reverse punch with the king's name in a square border. Its silver is from the rich mining district of the Bisaltai, a tribe that had issued octadrachms before they were conquered by Alexander in the early fifth century. When he acquired their mines, he adopted their coin.

a date, both were authorized in 1942, at the height of the war. The piece carrying the name of the Japanese government was printed for use in Malaya, and is one in a series of notes ranging from one cent to one thousand dollars. The letter M of MP means the note was meant to circulate in Malaya; an O would have signified Oceania, a P the Philippines, etc. Japan printed occupation notes for a number of areas in Southeast Asia and the islands; collectively, they are known as JIMs— short for "Japanese invasion money."

The second note was issued by the United States for use in Okinawa, scene of furious fighting during the war. It too is part of a series of bills, ranging from ten sen to one thousand yen. A similar series was printed to serve the rest of Japan. These notes were privately printed in the United States, later in Japan, and eventually were replaced by ordinary Japanese currency. Both notes, by the way, were lithographed, a common practice for such issues.

See also LITHOGRAPHY; OVERPRINT.

Octadrachm. Macedon, 480–454 B.C.

The term octadrachm also refers to a large gold coin, issued by several of the successor-states to Alexander the Great. Egypt's Ptolemaic dynasty produced the best-known of such pieces, which often featured jugate portraits of the reigning king and queen.

See also ARCHAIC COINAGE; DRACHM; JUGATE.

OFF-CENTER Improperly struck, so that part of a coin's design runs off its edge or is absent. There will be a more-

or-less broad, unstruck area directly opposite the missing elements.

The off-center coin is an error created by improper positioning of the dies in relation to the planchet or to one another. In ancient times, they were the rule rather than the exception. A planchet was placed atop the lower die, and the upper die was driven into it by main force. Ordinarily the two dies were not connected to each other, and there was no way to make certain the planchet remained centered as it was struck, or, even if centered, that the top die would strike the exact center of the planchet. Morever, a planchet might well be carelessly placed on the lower, obverse die in the first place.

With ancient coins, one side—it tended to be the reverse—was usually more off-center than the other, a result of the freely moving upper die. Unless a mint's standards were extremely relaxed, the obverse was fairly well centered, as the coiner had greater control over that die, which was embedded in an anvil. If hinged dies were used (and they were, on occasion, in the period of hammered coinage), an off-center coin showed the same degree of imperfection on both sides, in directly opposite positions.

This is also generally true of the off-center coin in the age of machinery. Although misaligned dies can produce coins with one side well-centered and the other not, most modern off-center strikes duplicate the error on each side: coining machines are equipped with devices to keep their upper and lower dies in perfect alignment.

For mechanically struck off-center coins, we think of those struck in a screw press or its steam- or electrically powered descendants. The illustration shows an off-center error fashioned by a completely dissimilar press—the roller press, used in some sections of Europe during the sixteenth through eighteenth centuries, and then rejected for the screw press. This coin, a Swedish öre of 1627, tells us why.

The roller press consisted literally of

Off-center. *Sweden, öre, 1627.*

two rollers, each with several obverse or reverse dies. A strip of metal was run between the two: assuming the rollers were perfectly synchronized and each obverse matched the position of each reverse, a strip of well-struck coins emerged, which were then punched out and placed in circulation.

Unfortunately, keeping the rollers aligned was very difficult, while fixing them incorrectly in the first place was all too easy. Our specimen, the reverse of which is seen, makes the point. At the top, note the traces of the lower design: the rollers had their dies close enough to each other so the coin, if struck vertically off-center, incorporated some of the design meant for the next coin. Note too the series of dots around the top. These represented holes in the rollers, into which metal was forced to keep the rollers moving in alignment with each other. The straight edge at the right indicates the strip was too far over to one side. As the top roller struck obverses and the bottom one reverses, we can assume the strip was improperly positioned to the left.

Today the off-center coin is far less common than it was in earlier days. It is coveted by collectors of errors, and specimens that are severely off-center command high premiums. A synonym for off-center is off-flan.

See also ERROR; MISALIGNED DIES; ROLLER PRESS.

OFF-METAL   Struck in a metal not stipulated for the coin; a term most accurately applied to errors.

The *deliberate* striking of a coin in a non-standard composition is a trial strike, a pattern, or an outright fantasy, depending on what motivated it.

Under modern minting conditions, the off-metal error originates in the planchet stage; usually when a planchet of a particular metal, for a particular denomination, is mistakenly mixed with a different group of planchets. If it is the same size as, or smaller than, the other planchets, it may well be struck into a coin. In theory, it should be fairly easy to spot before this happens; but planchets are polished and washed before they are struck, and one shiny disc of metal can closely resemble another. Furthermore, if post-minting inspection is not stringent, the off-metal strike may be bagged and eventually distributed.

As mints *do* check their products with care, the error is infrequent and prized by collectors. Among all off-metal strikes, the most famous, and probably the most valuable, are the 1943 bronze cents of the United States. These coins (less than a dozen are known) were struck on planchets intended for cent pieces of a normal bronze composition. The cents of 1943, however, were to be struck in zinc-coated steel, presumably to save copper for the war effort. By accident, a few bronze planchets remained in the hoppers of coin presses at the end of 1942. On the first working day of 1943, the steel planchets mandated for cents of that year were put in the hoppers, and the entire mass then struck into coins. At the beginning of 1944 the steel cent was abandoned, when mint officials found that defective shell cases could be fashioned into bronze planchets. But a few 1944 steel cents are known, evidently created by the same process that yielded the bronze cents of 1943 (these are at least as rare as the 1943 errors, if not as well known).

The 1943 bronze cent proved to be one of the most valuable mint errors when one sold for over ten thousand dollars in the mid-1970s. Collectors should be wary of copper-plated steel 1943 cents, often touted as the 1943 bronze one. Steel, of course, reacts to a magnet, while bronze does not.

See also ERROR; FANTASY; PATTERN; PLANCHET; TRIAL STRIKE.

OFFICINA MARK   A Latin or Greek letter placed on many Roman and Byzantine coins to indicate the particular *officina*, or workshop, of the mint that produced them. Like the mint mark, the *officina* mark appears to have been added as a form of quality control, making it possible to trace a bad coin to the agency responsible for it. *Officina* marks will be found on coins from moderate- to large-sized mints (that is, ones composed of two or more *officinae*). Smaller facilities most often omitted the mark, but not always.

The genesis of the *officina* mark is in Rome during the time of Philip I (ruled A.D. 244–249). Initially its use was sporadic, but by the 270s it was a general practice. We can probably assume the mark was adopted to reassure the public of the value and purity of its coins, particularly in the third century, when inflation and debasement had left much currency distinctly impure. Coinage was stabilized at the end of the century, but the *officina* mark became a tradition of the Roman Empire and was maintained through many years of the Byzantine Empire.

The illustration shows the reverse of a large copper coin of Constantius II (ruled A.D. 337–361). Its central type depicts a warrior spearing a fallen figure which has been identified with the ruler of Rome's hereditary enemy, the Sassanians. The mint mark in the exergue indicates the coin was created in Antioch. Next to it is the *officina* mark—the Greek letter beta, standing for the second workshop of the Antioch mint. Greek letters were used to

Officina *mark. Roman Empire, Constantius II, AE 3, c. A.D. 348–350.*

designate Eastern *officinae*, and began with alpha and continued through the alphabet as far as necessary. In the Latin-speaking West, on the other hand, P, S, T, etc. (standing for *prima* [first], *secunda* [second], *tertia* [third], and so on), were often used. *Officina* marks were always on a coin's reverse and often in the exergue, as seen in the illustration, but they could also appear at the end of legends.

Following Roman practice, the Byzantines displayed the *officina* mark below the large M on the reverse of the follis. *Officina* marks appeared on Byzantine coins until the early eighth century.

See also ABBREVIATION; EXERGUE; FOLLIS; MINT MARK.

ORDER An exclusive, traditionally chivalric organization; membership is awarded in recognition of services to the nation.

Members are given the right to use the order's name with their own names, and to wear its decorations. These can include badges, sashes, collars, and stars, and are among the most eagerly sought of all decorations. Although the word is sometimes used to refer to the decorations themselves, it should be restricted to the organization bestowing them.

Chivalric orders began in the Middle Ages, when rulers wooed the rich and influential with gifts to make them beholden. Membership in a highly restricted group—an order—was especially seduc-

tive. To be a member was to be a favorite at court; to ensure the constancy of the elite meant safety for the king.

The bestowal of decorations to signify membership was a comparatively late development, and the full panoply of decorations associated with chivalric orders dates from the sixteenth century and after.

When they were introduced, it was with a vengeance. As orders had to be restricted in membership to attract people, more were created, and those already in existence were often divided into ascending classes, with ever more elaborate decorations.

Orders are not solely the creation of monarchies. In practice, any government wishing to curry favor with its people awards decorations, and what better way than through an order and its appropriate insignia? Hence republican orders ranging from the French Legion of Honor to the Order of the Grand Star of Yugoslavia.

The illustration shows the star of one of Europe's most distinguished orders, the Most Honourable Order of the Bath. Founded in 1399 and revived in 1725, it

Order. *England, Order of the Bath (star).*

was a military order until 1847, when Queen Victoria decreed that civilians could be members as well. It is bestowed in three classes, and membership is, of course, strictly limited.

See also BADGE; CAMPAIGN AWARD; DECO-RATION; GALLANTRY AWARD; RIBBON; SASH; STAR.

ORNAMENTED EDGE A fancy edge placed on coins by mechanical means, and like the reeded edge and lettered edge, originally intended to enhance a coin's design while protecting it from clipping, filing, and counterfeiting.

The ornamented edge repeats such small elements as squares, stars, ovals, etc. around a coin's circumference, and occasionally intermingles them with brief inscriptions, as can be seen on many older German coins. These elements may also be larger; a once-popular design showed two intertwined cords looping around the edge.

The same machinery used to create the lettered edge has produced the ornamented one. Since the design on an ornamented edge is not in a simple, vertical position, coins with relief-ornamented edges cannot be struck in a simple collar, as can plain or reeded edge coins. With the sixteenth century came the invention of the segmented collar, and with the seventeenth, the edge-marking machine. These two devices and their descendants have produced all coins with fancy edges.

It was during the eighteenth and nineteenth centuries that the ornamented edge flourished—on German thalers as well as on thaler-size issues from Russia, Italy, Spain and Latin America. Often, the ornamentation was coupled with edge lettering, as on French écus of the eighteenth century. This was also the time that virtually all ornamented edges were applied while the coins were still in the planchet stage, by edge-marking machinery on the Castaing model. The segmented collar was

Ornamented edge. *Colombia, 8 reales, 1835.*

rarely used, as the difficulty in controlling it retarded the coining process.

The coin in the photograph is an eight-real issue of the new republic of Colombia. The area had been under Spanish domination for nearly four centuries; when Bogotá's colonial mint was seized by insurgents, they struck Pieces of Eight with new obverse and reverse designs, but retained the royalist edge ornamentation of late Spanish issues until 1837.

In the nineteenth century, the ornamented edge fell into disfavor with the introduction of fully mechanized coinage. It was easier and faster to stamp coins with plain or reeded edges, and trust that uniformity of size and design would deter counterfeiters and clippers. The ornamented edge is still used today, but when it is, it is applied by a segmented collar or more often by a mechanized edge-marking device in the planchet stage, in which case the marked planchet, with *incuse* ornamentation, fits inside a one-piece collar and can be struck as an ordinary coin.

See also COLLAR; EDGE-MARKING MA-CHINERY; GRAINING; LETTERED EDGE; REEDED EDGE.

OVERDATE A date that has been altered; also, a coin bearing such an altered date.

The overdate is rarely seen on twentieth century coins, in part because of the greater ease of die production offered by hubbing and other mechanical techniques. When dies were totally or largely manufactured by hand, however, the overdate was common. Such dies required time and

Overdate.
Left: Zacatecas, Mexico, 50 centavos, 1884/3 (detail).
Right: United States, dime, 1942/1 (detail).

good steel, usually in short supply. Thus, if a mint worker inadvertently punched an incorrect digit on a die, or if a perfectly good die existed from a previous year, the tendency was to correct the date by cutting or punching in new digits, tidying up the result, and using the die to strike coins. Labor was saved, and more coins were created.

The first overdates on Western coinage appeared in the 1470s. Their growing incidence depended on several factors, of which mint control was the most important. If a mint's administration was lax, the overdate was seen as a matter of small concern. If it was a small facility, it might not strike coins of all denominations every year; dates were repunched as needed. Conversely, if the mint was sizable and had to strike a vast number of coins in a short time, it too might use all available dies, correcting dates as it did so.

Bearing this in mind, where are overdates found? Not on most English coinage. We do find them on many French coins until about 1800, and on American coins, particularly those struck during the Republic's first few years. Some Spanish-American colonial coins display them, as do numerous issues of Spain's successor states in Latin America. One of these, Honduras, reused dies so frequently that the last digits on some of its coins are mere blobs, and virtually unidentifiable.

Our first illustration shows a detail of an overdated coin from Mexico. This silver fifty-centavo piece, a product of the Zacatecas mint, was struck with an obverse die originally dated 1883, later corrected to 1884. Traces of the 3 can still be seen under the 4. In numismatic parlance, this coin would be known as an "1884 over 3," or "1884/3."

By the time it was struck, the mass production of dies was well under way; by 1900, the new technology, which centered on the Janvier lathe and complete hubbing of designs, had appreciably reduced the manual effort required to make dies—and the need for overdating. Overdated coins are rare in this century, but there have been a few, and our second illustration shows a detail of one of them, a 1942/1 United States dime. This coin presents problems. By the time it was made, the only element to be added to American coin dies was the mint mark, the rest of the design, including the date, having been set on the dies by hubbing. Why, then, do we have an overdate? Perhaps because the die was first struck—correctly—with a 1941 hub, then struck—incorrectly—with one dated 1942. Logic tells us this would have taken place toward the end of 1941, when 1942 dies were being created at the same time 1941 dies were still in use; the die for this coin might have been accidentally struck with two hubs. Hubbing takes several strikes, and someone making 1942 dies could have inadvertently placed a partially completed 1941 die in the hubbing machine during the process.

The twentieth century overdate is in the nature of an error, and exacts a greater price than perfectly dated coins, which is not generally the case for earlier overdates.

See also DATE LOGOTYPE; ERROR; HUB; PUNCH; RECUT DIE.

OVERPRINT Printing which is officially added to a note to change its basic nature —to alter its denomination or indicate a shift in the name or nature of the authority issuing the note.

When overprints are used to change denominations, it is customarily for an *upward* revision. Should an issuer need a new denomination, it might well overprint a note already extant. The overprinted note circulates at the new value, the non-overprinted one at the old. In time, fresh notes printed for the new denomination are acquired, and the overprinted ones are retired.

This use of overprinting most often reflects inflation. Let us suppose a central bank places an order for new currency, but by the time it receives the shipment the denomination's value has sunk alarmingly. An overprint is then locally applied to raise the note's value to a more reasonable level.

This is what occurred with the note pictured. This thousand-drachma Bank of Greece note began as a hundred-drachma piece; when the issuing authority received it, it was necessary to increase its stated value. This was done with several overprints in dark green and black, applied to either side of the bill.

When we talk about overprints to change the issuing authority, we mean two dissimilar things. Certain other Bank of Greece notes exemplify the first—an overprint to alter the name of a fiscal authority. Until the late 1920s, the Bank of Greece was known as the National Bank of Greece; when the bank changed its name, a series of overprints resulted.

The overprint is also used to indicate a change in the nature of the governmental issuing authority, a practice widely employed during World War I and World War II when nations occupied part or all of one another's territory. In many instances, early issues of the occupying nations were simple overprints on notes of the vanquished—Austrian issues in Montenegro in 1916–1918, which were merely circular rubber stamps applied to national issues of this Balkan state, are an example. Overprinted notes, then, can be a type of occupation currency, to be replaced, in time, by more orthodox money.

See also EMERGENCY MONEY; INFLATION; OCCUPATION NOTES.

OVERSTRIKE A coin manufactured with a previously struck coin used as a planchet.

Ordinarily, the planchet begins as a blank piece of metal, and is struck with obverse and reverse dies to make a coin. When the planchet is blank, the highlights of the coin's designs are crisp, its fields flat and clear.

Upon occasion, coiners have reason to strike coins in a different fashion. They may lack the tools needed to produce planchets, or the time to do so. In either

Overprint. Greece, Bank of Greece, 1,000 drachmai, 1939.

case, they may use other coins, be they domestic or foreign, to strike their own. When they do, they create an overstrike. The new designs are known as overtypes; should traces of the original designs remain, they are called undertypes.

Overstrikes are rare in contemporary coinage. Very infrequently, a foreign or domestic coin can be accidentally run through a coining press for a second—and unintended—strike; such an overstrike is considered an error. But at one time overstrikes were common, encouraged by a lack of centralization and control, frequent emergencies, the primitive nature of the coining process, and the smaller number of coins required. These overstrikes were deliberate, and have a pedigree dating to antiquity.

The Romans, for instance, first practiced overstriking during a period of acute political tension, the civil war following Julius Caesar's assassination in 44 B.C. The Byzantine Empire overstruck copper folles in quantity early in the seventh century A.D., when it was beset by wars and invasions. Indeed, some were so hastily executed that neither overtype nor undertype can be fully deciphered; we know what they are and when they were made in part because of their crudity.

Among more modern overstrikes, the two pieces illustrated are especially interesting. The first is the "Bank of England dollar." A product of the financial crisis generated by the Napoleonic Wars, the Bank of England dollar (or, more properly, five-shilling piece), is nothing more or less than a Spanish-American Piece of Eight overstruck with new dies by the British Royal Mint. All these coins are dated 1804 in the overtype, as is a companion piece struck in the same fashion to be used in Ireland. These particular overstrikes were done with care, the original designs having been largely removed by planing, to make the undertypes invisible.

By 1815 a far more spectacular overstrike was circulating. In the Portuguese colony of Brazil between the years 1810

Overstrike.
Left: United Kingdom, 5 shillings, 1804.
Right: Brazil, 960 reis, 1813.

and 1822, minting authorities struck an inordinate number of nine-hundred-sixty-reis pieces, again with Pieces of Eight as planchets. Independent Brazil continued the practice until 1825. While British authorities made a determined effort to erase the undertypes before they struck their coins, the Brazilians apparently overstruck the coins exactly as they found them, with the result that issues exist where the undertypes almost obscure the overtypes. The Brazilians, then enjoying a rapid expansion of trade, collected imported coins, and after a cursory inspection, overstruck them for immediate dispersal. They are still quite plentiful, and collectors can often decipher the undertype, even the mint mark and date.

See also COUNTERSTAMP; EMERGENCY MONEY; ERROR; FOLLIS; PIECE OF EIGHT; PLANCHET.

OWL A popular name for the Athenian tetradrachm, adopted because the coin's reverse type was an owl.

Owl. *Athens, tetradrachm, c. 500 B.C.*

Use of the term dates to ancient times and is first mentioned in the comedy *The Frogs* (produced in 405 B.C.) by the great playwright Aristophanes (c. 450–c. 385 B.C.). Many authorities believe the owl was the first biface coin (one struck with true obverse *and* reverse dies). The earliest specimens would date from about 515 B.C.

See also ARCHAIC COINAGE; TETRA-DRACHM.

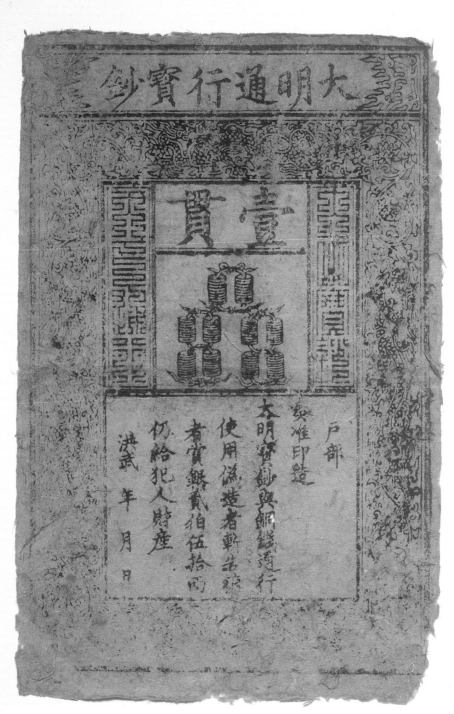

Pioneer in Paper

China, Ming Dynasty, 1,000 ch'ien, c. 1400.

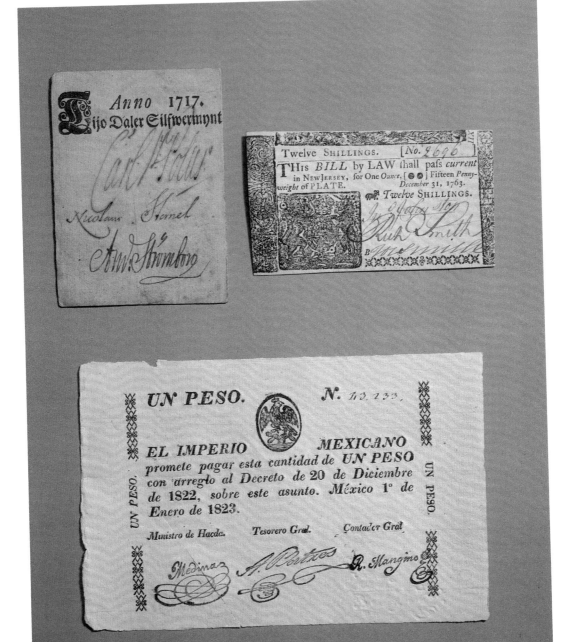

The Spread of an Idea
Top left: *Sweden, 10 daler, 1717.*
Top right: *New Jersey, 12 shillings, 1763.*
Bottom: *Mexico, peso, 1823.*

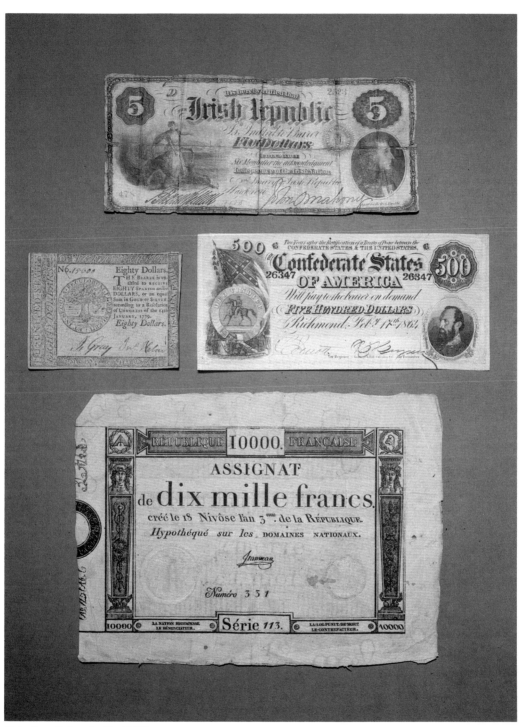

Printing Paper to Fight Wars
Top: *"Irish Republic" (Fenians), 5 dollars, 1866.*
Center left: *United States, 80 dollars, 1779.*
Center right: *Confederate States of America, 500 dollars, 1864.*
Bottom: *France, 10,000 francs, 1795.*

The "Broken Bank" Note in the United States, 1800-1865
Top to Bottom: *Boston Bank, 2 dollars, 1825; Bank of Augusta, 10 dollars, 1826; Bank of the Republic, 5 dollars, 1852; Chemical Bank, dollar, 1858.*

European Paper Money, 1800-1900
Top: *France, 50 francs, 1894.*
Center left: *Russia, 10 rubles, 1855.*
Center right: *Austria, gulden, 1858.*
Bottom: *Denmark, rigsdaler, 1804.*

European Paper Money, 1900-1945
Left, top to bottom: *Germany, 50 mark, 1920; Finland, 50 markkaa, 1918; France, 50 francs, 1938.*
Right, top to bottom: *Hungary, 100 pengo, 1930; Iceland, 50 kronur, 1928; Estonia, 10 krooni, 1928.*

Paper Money of the Third World, to 1945
Top to bottom: *China, Bank of Communications, 10 yuan, 1914; Mexico, Banco Mercantil de Yucātan, 1,000 pesos, c. 1890 (essay); Afghanistan, 5 afganis, 1926; India, 5 rupees, 1918.*

Paper Money Since 1945
Top to bottom: *Libya, 5 piastres, A.H. 1371 (A.D. 1952); Brazil, 100 cruzeiros, 1970 (specimen); Netherlands, 10 gulden, 1968; Bermuda, 10 dollars, 1970.*

Above: The Problem with Paper Money—Inflation
Germany, 5 billion (=5 trillion) mark, 1924.

The Medal to 1700
Top: France, portrait of Louis XIV by Jean Mauger, 1662. Bottom, left to right: Roman Empire, medallion of Probus, A.D. 276-282; portrait of Pisano by Antonio Marescotti, fifteenth century; portrait of Johann Wilhelm of Saxe-Weimar, school of Tobias Wolff, c. 1570.

Medals of the Eighteenth and Nineteenth Centuries
Top left: *Bohemia, entrance of royal family to Prague, by Joseph Lerch, 1833.*
Top right: *France, "Libertas Americana" medal by Augustin Dupré, 1783.*
Bottom left: *Prussia, founding of Königsberg, by Jakob Abraham, 1755.*
Bottom right: *Bolivia, prize medal by E. Molon, 1850.*

The Medal in the Twentieth Century
Top left: *United States, Winston Churchill, by Ralph J. Menconi, 1965.*
Top right: *United States, inaugural medal for Theodore Roosevelt by Augustus Saint-Gaudens, 1905.*
Bottom: *Germany, satirical medal by Karl Goetz, 1918.*

The Great Chivalric Orders
Left: *Scotland, Order of the Thistle.*
Center: *Austria and Spain, Order of the Golden Fleece.*
Right: *Denmark, Order of the Elephant.*

The Gallantry Award
Top: *Prussia, Pour le Mérite.*
Bottom, left to right: *United Kingdom,*
Victoria Cross; United States, Army Medal
of Honor; Russia, Order of St. George.

The Campaign Award
Top left: *Germany, campaign medal for China.*
Top right: *United Kingdom, Waterloo Medal.*
Bottom left: *United States, Philippine Campaign medal.*
Bottom right: *Romania, Victory Medal, First World War.*

A Collection of United States Scrip from New York, All Dated 1862

Tokens

First row, left: *Roman Empire, contorniate, c. A.D. 400;* right: *England, halfpenny token, 1667.*
Second row, left: *Scotland, halfpenny token, 1797;* right: *Russia, 3 ruble bank token, 1918.*
Third row, left: *United States, New York, Civil War token, 1863;* right: *Canada, penny token, 1857.*
Fourth row, left: *Italy, telephone token, 1968,* right: *United States, Missouri, tax token, c. 1935.*

Emergency Money: The Siege Piece

Right: *Cattaro, Yugoslavia, 5 francs, 1813.*
Bottom, left to right: *Limerick, Ireland, halfpenny, 1691; Newark, England, halfcrown, 1646; Mainz, Germany, 5 sols, 1793.*

Notgeld

Top, left: *Schalkau, Germany, 10 pfennig, 1918;* right: *Grenoble, France, 50 centimes, 1915.*
Center, left: *Philippine Islands, Philippine National Bank, 10 centavos, 1918;* right: *Liepaja, Latvia, 25 kopeks, 1915.*
Bottom, left: *Erivan, Armenia, kopek, c. 1918;* center: *Liechtenstein, 20 heller, 1920;* right: *Schildorn, Austria, 10 heller, 1920.*

P

PACKSADDLE MONEY A distinctive Thai form of silver currency, produced between the late thirteenth and the mid-sixteenth centuries.

The Thai word for this money is chieng, which also means "city," and is an element in the names of several towns in northern Thailand. Packsaddle money is known by a variety of names—Chieng Mai, Chieng Nan, etc.—depending on the city in which it was made.

Each piece of packsaddle money was created from a silver bar whose ends curved inward. The bar was then partially split, and opened outward in the center. The chieng was stamped with the name of the issuing authority, after which it could enter commerce.

The piece illustrated is typical. It weighs about 61.4 grams, and initially it measured about 50 millimeters by 20. The piece equalled four baht, the standard weight for chieng money.

Packsaddle money was essentially a product of the northern Thai kingdom of Lannat'ai, overthrown by the Burmese in 1558. The official manufacture of chieng ceased at that point, although it continued in use for a number of years. Other indigenous forms of Thai money, most notably the bullet pieces discussed elsewhere, eventually replaced it.

See also BOAT MONEY; BULLET MONEY; PUNCH-MARKED COINS.

Packsaddle money. *Thailand, packsaddle money or chieng, 1296–1558.*

PAN LIANG The first round coin to see universal usage within China; of cast bronze, bearing two characters, and having a square center hole, the pan liang was a model for Chinese coinage for two thousand years.

The pan liang was introduced during

Pan liang. *China, 221–210* B.C.

the period of the first Ch'in emperor, Shih Huang-ti (ruled 221–210 B.C.), who was also responsible for the Great Wall of China. He unified the country for the first time in its history; to symbolize and aid this feat he unified the country's coinage. The old spade and knife money were replaced by the pan liang—so called because the inscription on each coin informed its owner that it weighed one-half (*pan*) of a Chinese ounce (*liang*). The inscription formed the two characters on the obverse; the reverse was blank. Pan liang weighed about 10 grams at first, and measured some 33 millimeters in diameter.

Ch'in rule was overthrown by the Han dynasty in 206 B.C., but it did not occasion any immediate change in Chinese coinage. Pan liang were cast in large numbers under the early Han emperors, their weight and size the same as those of their Ch'in predecessors. In time, however, they suffered a reduction in weight and metallic quality—inflation was a problem in China, just as in the West. By 187 B.C. the coin's actual weight was reduced to one-third of a Chinese ounce. Ten years later it had fallen to a sixth of an ounce; by 140 B.C. to an eighth.

In 118 B.C. the emperor Wu-Ti recalled the pan liang, replacing it with a piece that weighed five *shu*, rather less than half the weight of the original pan liang. This wu shu coinage met with great success, and the pan liang was never revived.

See also CAST COINAGE; KNIFE MONEY; SPADE MONEY; WU SHU.

PAPER MONEY Official issues of currency manufactured from paper.

Paper money began in China as early as the seventh century; it was reinvented and used in the West in the late seventeenth century. Its employment has steadily increased over the years, and it would be safe to say that it now serves as the medium of exchange in all normal, large-scale transactions, as well as many small ones.

Paper money has advantages and disadvantages for issuer and consumer alike. It is inexpensive to produce, and the relatively large size of most notes allows the incorporation of self-serving or patriotic designs, slogans, and inscriptions. Further, a monetary system based on paper is easy to expand and contract as needed— at least in theory. For the public, the medium offers greater convenience, and somewhat greater safety, than coinage. In nineteenth-century America, it would have been difficult to carry five thousand dollars in gold from one place to another. But a like amount in paper was different. It could consist of a few high-denomination notes only, easily carried on the person. In themselves, these notes had no value, but they *represented* wealth, and were a promise that five thousand dollars in gold was awaiting the traveller at the end of his journey. The convenience of paper is obvious, and this factor is probably the most important one in the public's acceptance of the medium. That and the conviction that the paper is worth whatever the government or bank says it is worth in "real" money.

This is where paper money can prove disadvantageous, even disastrous, to issuer and user. As paper has no real value in and of itself, should people equate its stated value with its intrinsic one, trouble is likely to result.

We are talking about inflation, of course. For the issuer, public distrust of paper money may mean its production in larger and larger quantities and in higher and higher denominations. This leads to a continuing erosion of faith in the currency, with the issuing agency faced with only one recourse—to print still more, hoping public acceptance will return, bills will be paid, and all will turn out well.

Paper's disadvantages for the issuer do not stop with the risk of inflation. Paper money has tempted counterfeiters for decades, and this risk must also be attended to: if people suspect one particular note is counterfeit, they may suspect *all* notes. In the history of paper money, it is the chronic threat of counterfeiting that has led to virtually every development in the technology it involves.

For the public, too, paper's inflationary aspect presents problems, ranging from minor inconveniences in daily trade to complete eradication of the value of savings. Traditionally, the middle class is often the most severely affected by inflation, for its members are the depositors of savings banks. The poor rarely have money to save, while the rich invest theirs in stocks, lands, and businesses, which are less vulnerable to the entire inflation process. In any event, as the middle class comprises a plurality or absolute majority in industrialized countries (the ones most subject to inflation), monetary depreciation in paper causes widespread misery and anger wherever it occurs.

Regardless of the arguments for or against the medium, there is little doubt that it will continue to be the prevailing form of money.

See also BANK NOTE; COUNTERFEIT; INFLATION.

PATINA The natural coloring acquired over the years by a coin, token, or medal with a pure or high copper content.

Such coloring can take various forms. If the piece has toned naturally through time, it is apt to take on a rich, reddish- or yellowish-brown cast, which is actually a thin film of oxidation. But if the object has been buried in the soil or deposited under-

water, its patina is apt to be far thicker, and its colors range from reddish-brown to gray to light or deep green or blue. The color it assumes depends very much on the metallic composition of the object, in addition to the nature of the soil or water in which it was immersed.

Regardless of its color or nature, this patina is an integral part of the item which bears it, and it is wise not to remove it. Cleaning a coin or medal decreases its saleability, and, in the case of pieces made from copper or copper alloys, it is also perilously difficult. If bronze disease is present, some cleaning may be needed, but even here it should only be done with extreme caution.

Thus far, we have discussed natural patinas: they can also be created artificially. One process, applied to new medals and such to enhance their appeal to collectors, uses acids to achieve an artistic finish. The other "patina" is often simply paint, applied to a forgery to lend it credibility. (Acids are sometimes used for the same purpose.) Such practices are prevalent on forgeries of ancient Chinese money, which collectors are advised to examine carefully. In most cases, the faked patina will be a bit too regular, and a bit too uniform in color.

See also BRONZE DISEASE; COUNTERFEIT AND FORGERY DETECTION; PITTING.

PATTERN A proposed coin of a new design, metal, or denomination, which is not adopted during the year that it is submitted.

A pattern can be officially prepared by a mint or its authorized agent, or prepared unofficially by someone choosing to do so. The pattern can be struck in a variety of metals, minted on a normal or thick planchet, and bear some indication of its purpose. This may be expressed on one or both of the dies (the words ESSAI, PROVA, etc., are frequently used in this way, appearing in small letters in an inconspicuous part of the field), or it may take the form of a counterstamp, a common practice for Far Eastern patterns.

Patterns belong to the age of machine-struck coinage—from about 1500 to the present. Some of the earliest reflected the change from hammered to machine-made coinage. In England, for example, the seventeenth-century patterns of Thomas Simon fall into this category, as do a few similar issues from France. The eighteenth century saw the production of additional patterns, but the nineteenth and twentieth centuries have witnessed a spate of them, generated, in part, by political conditions. These two centuries have seen considerable upheavals among nations—shifts affecting their governments, their boundaries, and their very existence. With every change, the designs to be adopted for coinage are of some consequence; hence the numbers of patterns. A second reason for the rising tempo of pattern production comes from growth in the technology of coinage: the new, mechanized presses, the new devices used to prepare dies; new, previously overlooked metals and alloys; improvements in die production; new concepts in coinage design—all have quite naturally meant the production of more patterns.

Yet a third consideration is economic. In an age in which everyone's money seems to decline in value, old coins are often retired or hoarded, and fresh ones must be created. Different metals may be used, or the size of coins may be altered. Such modifications also encourage patterns.

Finally, there is the influence of collectors. Patterns are usually minted in small quantities, and have always been fancied by numismatists. There is little doubt that some United States patterns of the mid-nineteenth century, and many contemporary ones from other nations, have been struck with the collector in mind. In these cases, the pattern is primarily meant to be profitable as a collectible; its future as a circulating coin is secondary.

Pattern. *England, pattern halfpenny, 1788.*

The pattern in our illustration was a proposed design for an English halfpenny. It was prepared by Jean-Pierre Droz, a celebrated Swiss engraver and inventor, and it dates from 1788, when Droz was in England working for the firm of Boulton and Watt. Matthew Boulton had been trying to win a contract from the Royal Mint for several years—and eventually he succeeded, producing the cartwheel coinage of 1797. Droz's halfpenny pattern of 1788 was an earlier effort.

The pattern is a demonstration of the potential of Boulton's steam-powered coining machine, and the artistry of Jean-Pierre Droz. His obverse and reverse designs were far superior to anything seen on earlier English halfpennies. His ingenuity was proven by an edge inscription reading RENDER TO CESAR [sic] THE THINGS WHICH ARE CESARS [sic]—applied by a six-piece segmented collar which Droz had invented himself a few years before.

See also PIEFORT; TRIAL STRIKE.

PEACE DOLLAR The popular and official name for United States silver dollars minted between 1921 and 1935.

The name reminds us that this coin was originally proposed as a commemorative issue, to celebrate the end of World War I. Later it was authorized as a general issue under the provisions of the Pittman Act of April 23, 1918.

In late 1921 a design contest was held for the new coin. The winner was a young

Peace dollar. United States, 1927.

New York sculptor, Anthony de Francisci, who used his wife as a model for the Liberty head on the reverse. The first Peace dollars—slightly more than a million of them, all in fairly high relief—were struck during the last five days of 1921, and distributed at the onset of the following year. In 1922 the relief was lowered: Peace dollars of this second type were struck between that year and 1928, inclusive. No dollars were produced between 1929 and 1933, due in part to the economic depression. Coinage was resumed in 1934 and continued into 1935. The last Peace silver dollars show some minor design differences from earlier issues, but these are primarily of concern only to the specialist.

The coin in our illustration is a typical Peace dollar. On the obverse, a modern portrait of Liberty—obviously to some degree inspired by the work of Saint-Gaudens—faces left. Her hair blows freely in the wind, a design characteristic which caused some adverse comment from traditionalists when the coin was introduced. On the reverse is a standing American eagle, facing the dawn. The rock upon which the bird perches bears the inscription PEACE—the artist's interpretation of the commemorative intent of the coin. The designs are soft, rounded, almost fluid, a radical departure from the Morgan dollar, but in harmony with America's improved early twentieth-century coins.

The Peace dollar was a stunning coin, but it did not circulate widely (partly because of its size), and in 1935 it vanished. In 1965, Lyndon Johnson ordered a resumption of its production, in accordance with Congressional legislation passed the previous year. A total of 316,076 Peace dollars were struck at the Denver mint in 1965, all dated 1964. They were the result of pressure from Western silver mining interests. On the other hand, pressure from the idea's opponents induced the Treasury Department to cancel production on May 24, 1965. None was released to the public, and all were ordered melted down. However, it is rumored that a few escaped the melting pot. If so, they would bring an astronomical price in today's market—except for the nettlesome fact that it is illegal to buy and sell them.

See also COMMEMORATIVE; DOLLAR; MORGAN DOLLAR.

PENNY The dominant English coin from the late eighth to the late thirteenth century, and virtually the only one.

The penny was minted in silver, imitated widely, and eventually lent its name to numerous coins of small denomination, some linked directly to it, others not.

Events in France gave birth to the English penny. Pepin the Short (ruled 751–768) of the Carolingian dynasty had introduced the silver denier of about 1.3 grams. The influence of this soon made its way across the Channel, where it seems to have been imitated in Britain by two minor kings of Kent, perhaps about 765. The first substantial coinage of the penny dates from the reign of Offa, king of Mercia (ruled 757–796), who conquered Kent in 783–784, and adopted the transplanted denier for his own ends. Like Pepin, Offa was an ambitious prince, and he placed his portrait and name on the obverses of many of his pennies. A central cross was a frequent reverse design, along with the coiner's name. These basic design elements were repeated on most English pennies for hundreds of years. Offa's coins were similar in size and weight to Pepin's. Both were somewhat thicker and smaller than later issues, in essence a hybrid be-

Penny. *England, 1066–1087.*

tween the fabric of the sub-Roman coin and its medieval successor. By the reign of Coenwulf of Mercia (ruled 796–822), the coins were wider, measuring some 21 millimeters. They were also thinner, as their weight had not been increased, making them typical medieval silver coins.

The penny's importance grew during the remaining years of the Anglo-Saxon period. When William, duke of Normandy, conquered England in 1066 (ruling it as king until his death in 1087), he retained the penny, for the wretched Norman monetary system was hardly worth importing. However, he increased the coin's weight, and for the next two hundred years pennies were struck at a weight of 22.5 grains—slightly under 1.5 grams.

The penny illustrated dates from the reign of William the Conqueror. It measures just under 20 millimeters, and weighs slightly more than 1.4 grams—indications that it may have been clipped or filed. On the obverse is a full-face portrait of the king, complete with crown and scepter, with a legend giving his name. Full-face portraiture was an innovation on English coinage, and is perhaps attributable to indirect Byzantine influences. The reverse bears a cross, in the angles of which are seen the four letters P, A, X, and S, each in a roundel or circle. They spell PAXS, a variance on *pax,* peace. The reverse legend reveals the name of the moneyer, a custom to be continued through the first two centuries of Norman rule.

The penny was an admirable coin at this point. Its silver content and weight were strictly controlled through a central-

ized minting organization, making it a most useful trade coin. It had had many imitators during the Anglo-Saxon period, and their ranks swelled at the beginning of Norman control—the Low Countries, Scandinavia, Bohemia, and Poland all copied it. The extraordinary influence of Offa's coin is attested to by the existence of a "penni" coin in nineteenth-century Finland.

Unravelling the origin of the word penny prove troublesome. The Frankish denier, the penny's prototype, was originally known as a novus denarius ("new denarius") or denarius. The word was used in England, too, where its abbreviated form (d.) symbolized a penny until 1971. But the derivation of penny remains unclear; it has been traced to *pennigr,* an Old Norse word meaning pan-shaped—but not too convincingly. Perhaps it began as a mispronunciation of denier. We simply do not know. Nor do we know when penny, or something like it, superseded denarius in everyday conversation.

In England the coin's design showed a remarkable conservatism for many years. Henry II (ruled 1154–1189) introduced a slight modification to the penny's reverse design around 1180. This was the so-called Short Cross variant, and until the 1240s, Henry's successors retained the design—as well as Henry II's portrait and titles on the obverse. The tradition's rationale has been much debated, but it seems that by issuing coins of an unchanging type, England's kings hoped to shore up faith in their currency, both at home and abroad.

The Short Cross type encouraged clipping, and Henry III (ruled 1216–1272) discarded it. His Long Cross pennies, probably introduced in 1247–1248, had a reverse cross intercepting the legend and extending the design to the coin's edge, thus making clipping easier to detect. Henry III also began to omit the moneyer's name from the reverse, and it was entirely abandoned under his successor, Edward I (ruled 1272–1307).

During Edward's reign the penny began to lose its absolute dominance of English coinage. Edward introduced a new, larger silver coin, the groat, useful for the country's burgeoning trade. Although it was shortly discontinued, it reappeared in the middle of the following century, and this time to stay. Edward also introduced subdivisions of the penny, the halfpenny and the farthing.

The penny's weight gradually diminished. In 1346 it was still 20 grains (almost 1.3 grams); by the early sixteenth century, it was about half that. The English silver penny was not produced for general circulation after the latter part of the seventeenth century, having lost much of its importance long before, but it was still struck as part of a special type of presentation coinage known as Maundy money.

The penny did survive, however, as a copper or bronze issue. English copper pennies were struck sporadically from 1797 to 1807, and fairly regularly between 1825 and 1860, when their composition was changed to bronze. Between 1860 and 1967, they were produced annually for general circulation. With the adoption of the decimal system, the place of the English penny was assumed by the new penny, which is currently issued. The later, base-metal pennies bore the monarch's head on the obverse, and a seated allegorical figure representing Britain on the reverse.

See also CROSS ON COINAGE; DENIER; IMITATION; MAUNDY MONEY; PFENNIG; PORTRAIT; TRADE COINS.

PESO The official or popular name for a number of different coins from areas formerly ruled by Spain.

The genesis of all pesos is the Piece of Eight, the Spanish equivalent of the thaler. The Spanish Piece of Eight was a multiple of another coin, the silver real (eight reales equalled one Piece of Eight). While peso was used in popular parlance for the Piece of Eight minted in Spain and its colonies, the Spanish and their early national successors in Latin America did not usually put the word on their coins, although it does appear in official documents of the period.

The introduction of peso as an actual, official designation on a coin owed something to another colonial successor state, the United States of America. That nation based its coinage on the Piece of Eight, but its value was expressed as a unit—a dollar —rather than as a multiple of another unit. And it was part of a system based on tens. This was far more comprehensible than the old arrangement of multiplying and dividing by eights, and in the mid-nineteenth century Latin America—and Spain itself—began to move toward a decimal system. In Spain the new coinage unit was called a peseta; in Latin America it was a peso. And while a hybrid arrangement of ten reales to the peso saw some use, it was dropped for a simple peso unit, made up of one hundred centavos, céntimos, etc., and so it has remained. The name peso has often surrendered to ones of a more local, patriotic appeal—the bolívar in Venezuela, the córdoba in Nicaragua— but the decimal idea has endured.

Our illustration is a reminder that the Spanish Empire extended beyond the Americas: it is a Philippine peso, struck during the area's last days as a Spanish colony. Spain's administration of the Philippines ended less than two years after this

Peso. *Philippines, 1897.*

coin was struck, but the succeeding United States administration also struck pesos in and for the Philippines. The current Philippine monetary unit is called a piso, making its ancestry clear.

See also DECIMAL COINAGE; PIECE OF EIGHT; REAL.

Pfennig.
Left: Regensburg, 1002–1024.
Right: German Federal Republic, 1971.

PFENNIG The German version of the French denier and the English penny: a term referring to a bewildering number of small silver coins, important in Germany and adjacent lands from the tenth century until approximately the beginning of the fourteenth.

As with its English counterpart, the derivation of the word pfennig (plural pfennig or pfennige) remains somewhat mysterious. We know it appears in many medieval documents of the time, as the accepted translation of denarius.

The pfennig was an imitative coin, drawn largely from French sources. Under the vigorous early rulers of the Carolingian dynasty, the Franks extended their borders east and south, occupying much future German territory. They created mints in several towns, and these struck deniers of the type minted elsewhere in the Frankish realm. As the ineptitude of Charlemagne's successors in the ninth and tenth centuries cost them control of the Germanic areas, the mints started striking coins closely based on the denier in type and weight, but issued under the authority of Germanic rulers. These were the first pfennig; many originated in southern Germany and the Rhineland, whose particular issues represented the beginnings of the eastward push of German coinage.

The first piece illustrated is a silver pfennig from the Regensburg mint, struck under the Holy Roman Emperor Henry II (ruled 1002–1024). It reveals a portrait of some sophistication for its day, perhaps because this mint had been an important coining center under the Franks, who also favored profile portraiture. The reverse bears a cross and a legend with the moneyer's name. The piece measures 20 millimeters in diameter, and weighs over 1.6 grams, which was heavy for the period.

The pfennig was one among vast numbers of more or less interchangeable trading coins, produced from Britain through central and southern Europe. Much like its counterparts in other regions, its significance receded later in the Middle Ages, as the grosso and its copies—larger silver coins that proved more useful in commerce—drew merchants' favor. The pfennig's production continued for hundreds of years, and in many places, however; indeed, today it is part of the monetary system of both Germanies, with one hundred pfennig equalling one mark. Our second illustration shows the West German version of this modern pfennig; unlike its ancestor, it is a clad coin, made of copper and steel.

See also BRACTEATE; DENIER; GROSCHEN; GROSSO; PENNY; TRADE COINS.

PHOTOLITHOGRAPHY A printing process in which an impression from printer's type—or a design or picture, often with a halftone screen interposed—is first photographically transferred to a sensitized sheet of zinc, aluminum, or paper, then developed, made receptive to printer's ink by a greasy chemical, and used finally as a printing plate.

Although the method has been used in this century for the printing of scrip and

Photolithography. *A typical photolithographed copy of a bill (Bank of the United States, 1,000 dollars, 1840).*

notgeld, it is of interest to present-day numismatists primarily because it is used to create copies of old currency for sale to collectors.

In the last twenty years the market has been deluged with such pieces, of the general type seen in the illustration. They are frequently simple to detect, and should not confound the hobbyist. Since an original note must be used to produce the photolithographic plate, all the replicas will bear identical serial numbers, and signatures. Were a maker of replicas to use a *remainder note* for his products—a bill with no signatures or numbers—he could fashion a far more convincing reproduction, with each note signed and numbered in a slightly different way. But this would entail more labor than the replica's selling price warrants.

A second way to determine whether a particular note is a copy produced by photolithography is to examine the color of the signatures and serial numbers. With the passage of years, the black ink most often used on original notes fades to yellowish-brown. But printer's ink has a different chemical composition, and does not fade. If you have a note on which the handwritten portions are of the same hue and intensity as the printed parts, it is almost certainly a copy.

At present, nearly a hundred such reproductions are known, and most are products of photolithography. Their manufacturers seem to have concentrated ex-clusively on early American notes, Continental Currency, broken bank notes, and the like, but we have no assurance they will continue to restrict their efforts. If their products remain as obvious as they now are, they will present no problem to numismatists. Sadly, that is not as true for non-numismatists, who may easily be duped.

See also COPY; ENGRAVING; LITHOGRAPHY; NOTGELD; SCRIP.

PIECE OF EIGHT A common term for the Spanish and Latin American eight-real silver coin, produced from around 1500 to 1900, which due to its size, high silver content, and huge production, was probably the world's most successful trade coin.

The majority of Pieces of Eight (and most of those circulated in international trade) were minted in Latin America, a result of the exploitation of the region's rich silver deposits. The first Pieces of Eight were actually minted in Spain, however, as its equivalent of a central European coin, soon to be called the thaler.

The trade potential of the new thaler impressed Ferdinand and Isabella, joint rulers of Spain from 1479 until her death in 1504. They introduced a large silver coin of their own, the equivalent of eight silver reales. The exact date of its appearance is not known, but is likely to have followed soon after the coinage reform of 1497, which heightened the importance of the real. These first Pieces of Eight weighed around 27 grams, and measured some 38 millimeters in diameter. They carried a crowned coat of arms on their obverses, along with the denomination and a mint mark. The obverse legend gave the names and titles of the monarchs; this legend was continued on the reverse, whose central types were a yoke and a bundle of arrows, symbol of the unity of the new Spain. The coins were struck by hand, with mediocre results, and most were created in Seville, a city active in overseas trade.

For reasons unknown, coinage of the Piece of Eight was soon suspended. It resumed under Philip II (ruled 1556–1598), when mints in the Americas (Mexico City, Lima, Potosí) issued them, as well as Spanish facilities. The Mexico City mint was authorized in 1535, and the other two in 1565 and 1575 respectively; the earliest Pieces of Eight struck in the Americas are probably Peruvian, and date from about 1568. Coinage of the Spanish Piece of Eight was resumed, with many of the coins coming from the mint at Segovia, equipped with new roller presses. Other Spanish mints, like their colonial counterparts, continued to strike Pieces of Eight by hand. The obverses of coins from this reign still featured the crowned royal arms, but the yoke-and-arrows device was discarded for a large cross, with castles and lions (for Castile and Leon) in its angles.

By now, we can speak of two distinct versions of the Piece of Eight: The machine-struck issues, initially made at Segovia and later at other Spanish mints; and the cobs, very crude, hand-hammered coins mostly from the Americas. Initially, both types held similar designs, in obedience to a royal proclamation of 1570. But dissimilarities were soon apparent, and, by the time of Philip IV (ruled 1621–1665), the Lima and Potosí facilities were using a completely different reverse design, featuring the Pillars of Hercules and ocean waves, which had appeared on some of the earliest Mexican coinage, and would be important on Pieces of Eight and their subdivisions in the next century.

In Spain, designs for the Piece of Eight remained unchanged until the reign of Charles III (ruled 1759–1788). In 1772, he radically altered the coin's design, displaying his portrait on the obverse, and the Spanish arms on the reverse. He also slightly reduced the coin's silver fineness, from 91 percent to 90.27 percent. These basic changes remained in effect until 1820, when the coin was discontinued in Spain.

Piece of Eight. Mexico, 8 reales, 1746.

For the Americas, machine-struck coinage of Pieces of Eight began in the 1730s at Mexico City and spread south in succeeding decades. As it did so, it brought new designs of the type illustrated. This Mexican Piece of Eight of 1746 bears a fancy obverse coat of arms, and a striking reverse design with two globes atop ocean waves, the whole flanked by the Pillars of Hercules. The reverse Latin motto VTRAQUE VNUM refers to the unity of the Old and New Worlds, and to the dominant role Spain played in each. This coin measures 39 millimeters in diameter, and weighs slightly more than 27.1 grams. It boasts an ornate, floreated edge (placed on the coin by a marking machine in the planchet stage).

The Spanish-American Piece of Eight in this style was struck in quantity from the 1730s to the early 1770s, at which point its designs were modified to bring it more into harmony with its Spanish companion. Again, Charles III placed his image on the obverse, relegating the coat of arms to the reverse. It was now flanked by the Pillars of Hercules, however, to indicate this was a coin from the New World. Charles struck such pieces until his death in 1788. His successors, Charles IV (ruled 1788–1808) and Ferdinand VII (ruled 1808–1833) continued the series. The last regular Spanish-American Piece of Eight was minted at Potosí in 1825.

But the story does not end here, for the coin was adopted by Spain's successor states in Latin America, which obviously needed a form of money, and whose people were familiar with the Piece of Eight. It might be officially renamed, as it was in

Bolivia, or referred to popularly as a peso or a duro, but in terms of fineness and size, it was faithful to its predecessors. In time, the area adopted decimal coinage, and the Piece of Eight vanished. But its tenacity was remarkable: although Mexicans called their coin a peso, the government stamped it 8R (for 8 reales) until 1897, after which it became a peso in official name also.

The coin's influence was extensive, both in the places that issued it and the lands to which it travelled. For the Piece of Eight was never designed solely for local consumption: it was intended for trading abroad, and such disparate examples as the Australian Holey Dollar, the Bank of England dollar, chop-marked coins, and even the New York Stock Exchange (which still lists stocks in eighths of a point, a throwback to the days of the eight-real piece) indicate the Piece of Eight fulfilled its obligations nobly.

See also BIT; COB; HOLEY DOLLAR; OVER-STRIKE; PESO; PISTAREEN; REAL; THALER; TRADE COINS.

PIEFORT: A coin struck with ordinary dies on an unusually thick planchet. It is not intended for circulation, and is therefore distinct from the dump, a thick coin struck for commercial use.

Pieforts have been minted since the late thirteenth century; France, Germany, Bohemia, and to a lesser degree England have been the centers of their production. Their original purpose is unclear. While some may have circulated, they do not seem to have been primarily designed to do so. Their weights bear no logical relationship to other coins. For example, if we were to find a penny-sized English piefort of the reign of Edward I (ruled 1272–1307), struck with dies identical or similar to those used for ordinary pennies, but with a weight three times greater, we could argue that it was meant to circulate as a threepence. But while pieforts are known

Piefort.
Left: France, piefort of a double tournois, 1607.
Right: An ordinary coin of the same denomination and date.

from Edward's reign, none fits into such a rational pattern.

It seems, then, pieforts were not originally intended as circulating multiples of regular coins. Were they minted as trial pieces or die proofs, struck to see how the finished work would look? Again, probably not. A trial strike can be effected in any thickness, and a thinner planchet would probably give a truer impression of the dies.

What was their purpose? L. A. Lawrence, the noted numismatist, convincingly argued that English pieforts at least were designed as *models* for circulating coins: a master engraver would create two dies as prototypes, and use them to strike pieforts. They would satisfy the master engraver that his work was as he wished it to be, then they would be shipped to workshops for engravers to see just what their master wanted them to duplicate. Lawrence's theory is a sound explanation for the coins' thickness: no one at a mint could confuse them with ordinary coins, and they would be readily available when new dies were needed, as thick prototypes would be less easily lost than thin ones.

The pieces in our illustration confirm this explanation. Both are French copper coins of the double tournois denomination, minted in Paris in 1607. The actual denomination is on the reverse of each coin, effectively destroying any notion that a thicker multiple of the double tournois was contemplated. The piece on the left is a piefort; it weighs almost 13.7 grams and measures 21.5 millimeters in diameter, with a thickness of nearly 5 millimeters. It has been given a reeded edge, probably to distinguish it further from ordinary coinage. The coin on the right is a regular double tournois, struck for circulation. Its diameter is 21 millimeters, but its thickness is only 1.3 millimeters, and it has a plain edge. It weighs slightly under 3 grams; the weight ratio alone should convince us that the piefort was not meant to circulate, for 3 grams bears no discernible relationship to 13.7. In brief, the piefort seems to have been a model, intended to help die-sinkers accomplish their task with more precision. The reason pieforts and ordinary coins emanated from the same dies, as we know some did, might be that once prototypes had been struck from the model dies, it was judicious to use those dies for ordinary coinage.

In modern times the piefort has taken on other characteristics and meanings. Its modern uses emphasize its role as a pattern, with medallic overtones. An extreme example of this is a pattern twenty-dollar American gold piece of 1907, which was struck on a planchet the size of those used for ten-dollar pieces, but twice as thick. The French actively continue the piefort-as-pattern tradition; but many of theirs are actually closer to noncirculating legal tender coins, directed at the collector, than they are to patterns.

See also DUMP; NONCIRCULATING LEGAL TENDER; PATTERN; TRIAL STRIKE.

PILE One of the terms designating the lower of the two dies used to produce hammered coinage (anvil die, staple, and standard also refer to this lower die).

The term *pile* is French, and derives from the Latin *pila*, one definition of which is "pillar." The obverse die employed for ancient and medieval coins resembles a pillar in its general outlines—but then, so does the upper die. In any event, we encounter the term frequently in coining treatises of the late medieval and early modern periods.

The typical pile was 175 to 200 millimeters long. One end was engraved with the design for one side of a coin. The other end was splayed outward halfway up, and then tapered to a point. The pile could be fitted into a block of wood and held fast, rather than being forced downward from repeated blows of the hammer. This design was adopted early, and continued to be used as long as hammered coinage itself.

See also DIE; HAMMERED COINAGE; TRUSSELL.

PINE TREE SHILLING A famous colonial American silver coin of the late seventeenth century: minted between 1667 and 1682, it lent its name to an entire series of silver coins struck in Massachusetts from the 1650s to the 1680s.

The genesis of the Pine Tree shilling lay in the rapid growth of Boston, capital of the colony of Massachusetts Bay. It was founded in 1630, and within twenty years its trade was well developed. To further its business growth, the new entrepôt needed an abundant, circulating currency medium. Unfortunately, the Atlantic seaboard of North America lacked the precious metals for such coinage—at least as far as anyone knew at the time, and Massachusetts's English overlords were not inclined to provide the colonials with coins.

Some of their reluctance stemmed from the theory of mercantilism, then fashionable in England and on the Continent. It held that colonies were useful tools, suppliers of raw materials and precious metals to the homeland, and in return, were to receive those manufactured goods which they could not (or would not be allowed to) produce for themselves. Colonies were to trade only with the mother country.

If England adhered faithfully to mercantilism, it was clear Massachusetts colonials could not look to that country as a source of coinage—the whole theory stressed that precious metals should come from the colonies not go to them. There was yet another aspect. Despite the restrictions on trade, the colonists—finding that their timber, fish, and other products could fetch good prices in the Caribbean, then controlled by Spain—developed a flourishing exchange. Colonial authorities in the Caribbean and Massachusetts both looked the other way, and Massachusetts cod went south while Mexican cobs went north.

At this juncture, mercantilism reentered the picture. Most foreign coins reaching Massachusetts continued on to London to pay for English goods; relatively few remained in the colony. By 1650 the situation was critical. Massachusetts desperately needed coinage if it was to continue to expand, and some way to keep money in the colony had to be fashioned. Yet by English law only the king enjoyed the right to coin money. In the next few years these stumbling blocks were removed, and Massachusetts produced its sorely needed coins.

The Massachusetts General Court ordered the production of the first metallic currency in English North America in 1652. That it was able to do so hinged on political events in the mother country. Charles I had been beheaded three years earlier, leaving the control of England to republican forces, led by Oliver Cromwell. As only the throne possessed coining rights, and the throne was vacant, the law no longer applied—or so the colonists reasoned. Furthermore, Cromwell and the reformed Parliament might be more sympathetic to the idea of an American coinage than the late king had been.

Of course, it was still necessary to find precious metal, and to devise some plan to keep the coins in the colony. Mercantilism had not died with the king, and coins would inevitably tend to flow to England.

The resourceful colonials solved the first problem by using imported silver, in the form of underweight Pieces of Eight and subsidiary coins from Spanish America. And they met the second problem by intentionally making their coins underweight. The new Massachusetts shilling would weigh 22.5 percent less than its English counterpart—almost guaranteeing its rejection by English merchants. Hence it would stay in Massachusetts.

The idea seemed feasible, and was put into effect in May of 1652 when John Hull, a local silversmith, was appointed mintmaster; he chose Robert Sanderson as his partner. A modest mint was founded, and the first Massachusetts coins—shillings, sixpences, and threepences—were struck that summer, and are known as the NE variety. It must be remembered that Hull and Sanderson were novice coiners. Consequently, the NE coins were essentially blank planchets, with a simple NE (for New England) on their obverses, XII, VI, or III (for twelve, six, or three pence) on their reverses, all elements contained in rectangles stamped near the coins' edges. Needless to say, the crudity of this early coinage was a boon for clippers, and the General Court soon ordered that designs cover the entire surface of each side of the coin. Hull and Sanderson complied, producing a new obverse design which featured a crude tree and the legend MASATHVSETS (the Indian spelling of the colony's name) IN. The new reverse design revealed the value and a date (1652), with the surrounding legend NEW ENGLAND AN DOM. This reverse legend was used on shillings; it was shortened on the smaller coins. Numismatists call this coinage the Willow Tree series, as its central tree resembles a willow slightly more than other trees.

Willow Tree coinage seems to have been struck intermittently from 1653 to 1660. Its success was not outstanding, in part because it was made with a freely rotating lower die, leading to extensive double-striking. Most surviving specimens are virtually illegible, particularly on the reverse. The engraving of the dies was also too shallow, and impressions were weak.

By 1660, authorities chose yet another design, and seem to have used a screw press to produce it. The reverse continued unchanged, but the "willow" tree was replaced with an oak. Coins of this Oak Tree series were produced until about 1667, in a fair quantity, and are, as a rule, quite well struck. The denominations produced were still shillings, sixpences, and three-pences—and in 1662, a fourth denomination, a twopence, was added, bearing the actual date of issue. All other dated Massachusetts coins use the year 1652, perhaps to commemorate the founding of the mint, but more likely to avoid the Crown's disfavor. By 1660, a king was again on the English throne and he might well take a dim view of his royal prerogative being flouted by colonials. If all coins were dated 1652, however, how could he prove which were legal and which were not? They need not have bothered, for Charles II (ruled 1660–1685) simply let the matter pass—at least for the moment.

Meanwhile, a fourth and final design change produced the real Pine Tree shilling. In 1667, Hull and Sanderson signed a contract with the General Court, and subsequently produced shillings, six-pences, and threepences with the familiar pine tree design on the obverse. The tree symbolized Massachusetts's wealth in timber—and was also easy to reproduce on a die. Pine Tree shillings and their subsidiaries were coined on large, thin planchets until 1674. Smaller and thicker ones were used from 1675 until the end of the entire coinage in 1682, as they extended the life of the dies. This was an important consideration: Hull and Sanderson produced thousands of coins during the fifteen years of the Pine Tree design, and die life had to be prolonged as much as possible.

The piece in our illustration is from the 1667–1674 period, and measures between 28 and 29 millimeters in diameter, with a weight of 4.7 grams. The planchet is wavy and significantly out of round, but

Pine Tree shilling. Massachusetts, dated 1652, struck 1667–1674.

the coin is no more primitive than numbers of contemporary European issues, and it is a good deal more sophisticated than most seventeenth-century South American attempts.

At King Charles's bidding, the coining of Massachusetts silver was halted in 1682. A proposal to renew it in 1686 was rejected by the General Court, perhaps from fear of royal displeasure. Within four years, the Massachusetts colonists were to happen upon a new medium of exchange, however, which would see them and their fellow colonials through the remaining years of British rule. It was paper money. In the use of this currency, as in the earlier minting of silver coins in a land where silver was not yet mined, Massachusetts showed a daring and an ingenuity which were rapidly becoming marked traits of the colonial American.

See also CLIPPING; EMERGENCY MONEY; EVASION; PIECE OF EIGHT.

PISTAREEN A lightweight Spanish silver two-real piece circulated widely in colonial America and the early United States.

The derivation of the word is unclear; one source indicates it was a corruption of peseta, the Spanish diminutive of peso.

The pistareen was introduced about 1686. Prior to that, the Spanish dollar consisted of eight reales, with intermediate denominations of two and four reales. All these coins were fashioned of good silver, well over 900 fine. The Piece of Eight weighed nearly 27 grams, while the two-real coin weighed in proportion. In 1686 a new, lighter Piece of Eight was introduced, weighing only about 21 grams, and the weight of the two-real piece was reduced accordingly. The Piece of Eight was soon restored to its old weight, but the two-real piece continued to be struck at the lighter weight. As a result, it took five of them to equal one Piece of Eight, rather than four. There were now two kinds of two-real coin: the American variety, four of which made up one peso, and the Spanish type, or pistareen, with five to the peso. So it remained for well over a century.

Spanish mints struck large numbers of pistareens during the eighteenth century; the piece shown is typical. Its design duplicates that used on Pieces of Eight of the period. The obverse bears a crowned shield, the mint mark (in this case a crowned M for Madrid), an assayer's initial, the denomination (R II—two reales); and a legend naming the king. The reverse continues the legend in Latin, which encircles a castle and lion device. The date appears near the top. This particular specimen weighs 5.5 grams, and measures 28 millimeters. The coin's designs were altered in 1772 to include a bust of the king on the obverse, with the crowned shield moved to the reverse. These designs were retained until the coin's demise in the early part of the next century.

Through the years, the silver fineness of the pistareen declined. Issues of Philip V (ruled 1700–1746) were 833 fine, while those of his son Charles III (ruled 1759–1788) were initially 826 fine, and later 813 fine. The last pistareens, coined during the time of Ferdinand VII (ruled 1808–1833), maintained this fineness.

The pistareen was interesting for a number of reasons. Unlike most coins of the period, many pistareens were created by roller press rather than by screw press. The roller had been introduced to Spain in the 1580s, and was used to strike various coins, including the pistareen, until well into the eighteenth century. More important, the pistareen was a highly popular trading coin in America during the eighteenth and early nineteenth centuries. It was regularly included in exchange tables of the period, and initially passed at twenty cents in the money of the new United States of America. An adverse report by the Director of the United States Mint in 1827 lowered its exchange value to seventeen cents, and by the early 1840s it had disappeared from North American circulation.

See also FINENESS; PIECE OF EIGHT; REAL; ROLLER PRESS; TRADE COINS.

PITTING Minute holes or pits on the surface of a coin or coin die, caused by oxidation.

Pitting is very common on ancient copper or bronze coins, and may be expected on modern ones also, providing they have been exposed to the elements or buried for extended periods. The pitting is frequently below a protective film or surface —a patina—and is exposed once that surface is removed.

Pitting can also be present on coin dies, which are made of iron or steel and therefore susceptible to rust. Should the surface oxidation be removed, revealing the pitting, and the dies then be used to strike coins, the surfaces of those coins will show *reverse* pitting—numerous tiny raised dots or irregular configurations. Pitted dies can result from careless mint practices. Then

Pistareen. *Spain, 2 reales, 1719.*

Pitting. United States, "1804" cent (actually an unofficial restrike made around 1860).

too, they can occur with the simple passage of time at a small mint that tries to take care of its dies but uses them only sporadically. These are legitimate, if regrettable, reasons for the existence and use of pitted dies. But there is another, illegitimate and highly regrettable reason for their use: the restriking of rare coins for private gain.

The illustration shows what is often called an "unofficial" restrike, a fake 1804 American cent, minted about 1860. The 1804 cent is a rare coin, and even as early as 1860 collectors coveted it. Such being the case, someone unearthed a badly cracked and rusted obverse die for an 1803 cent, altered the 3 to a 4, and combined it with a reverse die of 1820. The result was so coarse it can have fooled no one. The granular surfaces of the obverse gave it away, as did the marked difference between the reverse of a genuine 1804 cent and this fake. Whoever was responsible for this monstrosity remains anonymous. It was formerly assumed the piece was struck inside the United States Mint, an extremely corrupt institution at that time. The consensus now is that the cent was made outside the Mint.

The word pitting may also be applied to more modern forged coins, produced by the centrifugal casting method. Such forgeries use plaster of Paris molds which tend to leave them with a slightly gritty surface, especially in the intricate areas of the coin, such as those between the denticles. There may also be numbers of tiny globules on the coin's surfaces, created when molten metal penetrates broken air

bubbles in the plaster. Such drawbacks, frequently obvious under even low magnification, are a major reason for the increasing rejection of cast forgery for die-struck forgery.

See also BRONZE DISEASE; CAST COUNTERFEIT; COUNTERFEIT AND FORGERY DETECTION; FORGERY; PATINA; RESTRIKE.

PLANCHET A disc of metal used to strike a coin or medal.

Ordinarily we think of the planchet as a blank piece of metal (and in fact the word blank is sometimes used as a synonym; flan is another), but a previously struck coin can also serve as a planchet, resulting in an overstrike.

The great majority of planchets, however, begin as "fresh" pieces of metal. Over the years, a number of methods have been employed in their production. In ancient days, planchets for heavy coins were usually cast. Those for Greek issues of the classical period were cast in a globular form, explaining the thickness and rounded edges of coins of that period. Planchets for later Greek coins (and presumably for Roman ones as well) were cast in terra cotta or sand molds, either individually or in groups. Another method was to cast a long strip of metal, and then cut it with a chisel into pieces of the appropriate size. These were struck in that form (as in the case of some Byzantine copper

Planchet. United States, planchet for a silver dollar, 1935 or earlier.

coins), or the pieces were heated and hammered into discs. Another way to manufacture planchets in the pre-machine age was to hammer metal into a thin strip and cut it into planchets with shears.

The sixteenth century saw the mechanization of planchet production. Two machines were needed: one to roll the metal into a uniform thin sheet, the other to cut it into shape. Both were invented in the sixteenth century: a planchet-cutting machine was being used in Venice as early as 1528. It simply stamped the planchets from a metallic strip, functioning much as a cookie-cutter does. Various refinements have been added since, but the basic process remains the same.

The illustration shows a typical planchet—in this instance one intended for a United States silver dollar of 1935 or earlier. The piece measures 38.3 millimeters in diameter, whereas the finished coin would measure 38.1 millimeters. The difference arises from the fact that this planchet never received its upset edge, which would have slightly reduced its diameter and at the same time thickened its edge.

See also COLLAR; HAMMERED COINAGE; MACHINE-STRUCK COINAGE; OVERSTRIKE; UPSET EDGE.

PLAQUE   A rectangular medal, usually of a commemorative nature.

Plaques are very often uniface, yet are struck in the same fashion as round medals. They were much in vogue in the late nineteenth and early twentieth centuries, but are no longer widely produced. The piece in the illustration is the work of Victor D. Brenner (1871–1925), one of America's most gifted sculptors, and commemorates Abraham Lincoln. It measures 89 millimeters by 66.5, typical for a medal of its kind. It was executed in 1908, and the design was carried over to the one-cent piece Brenner produced for the United States the following year. This portrait is still used on the cent.

Plaque. *United States, plaque commemorating Abraham Lincoln by V. D. Brenner, 1908.*

The term plaque also refers to a particular type of award intended for display, and not to be worn; such plaques were fairly common in imperial Russia. They are also known as table medals.

See also DECORATION; MEDAL.

PLATED COINAGE   Coinage struck with precious-metal outer surfaces and base-metal cores.

We must distinguish between counterfeit and genuine coins; the practice of creating plated counterfeits has been a common one through the years, but officially minted plated pieces have been rare.

The best-known example of official plated coins is a series of Athenian tetradrachms, minted after that city's final defeat in the Peloponnesian War (431–404 B.C.). This was an emergency coinage, as the city's economy was in ruins, and its silver supplies were severely limited. The

Plated coinage. *Athens, tetradrachm, c. 390 B.C.*

coiners did what they could to stretch their slender reserves: they produced a copper core, encased it in silver, and struck it as a tetradrachm. One of these pieces is illustrated here. It measures 24 millimeters (the correct size for a tetradrachm), but is distinctly light, weighing only 14.6 grams. The hole accounts for part of the discrepancy, but unholed specimens weigh only a gram or so more. Note that the plating has worn off in several places. Tetradrachms of this type were produced until 393 B.C., by which time the Athenian economy had revived, and the production of good silver tetradrachms was resumed.

As mentioned, ancient and modern plated *counterfeit* coins are very common. They were certainly thorns in the sides of the Greeks and the Romans. In the case of the latter, the introduction of the serrated coinage has sometimes been ascribed to the quantity of counterfeit denarii entering circulation in the second and first centuries B.C., although majority opinion no longer accepts this theory.

A list of plated counterfeits could go on indefinitely. The medieval florin was counterfeited and plated; so were the Piece of Eight, the English sovereign, and the American half eagle. For these last two plated counterfeits platinum was frequently used as the core; it was then cheaper than gold, but could pass most of the tests for gold coins.

The age of the plated counterfeit ended in this century, as the intrinsic value of official coins diminished.

See also CAST COUNTERFEIT; DIE-STRUCK COUNTERFEIT; EMERGENCY MONEY; TETRADRACHM.

PLUGGED Pierced and refilled: specifically, any coin or medal which has had a hole drilled in it after leaving the mint, with the hole in question later filled with metal.

The metal most often used to fill the hole is lead or pewter; there may then be some effort to plate the plug, plane it to the level of the coin's surfaces, and even to continue the legends or designs of the coin by engraving them on it.

If performed by an expert, plugging can be extremely difficult to detect. There will usually be a slight difference in color between the plug and its surrounding surfaces, however; and if the coin's designs are continued on the plug, they are apt to vary slightly from those on the rest of the piece. Finally, even a perfectly plugged coin rings at a different pitch from an unplugged one.

Plugging was once a regular numismatic practice; hobbyists recognized that a holed coin was better than no coin at all, and that plugging improved the mien of a holed coin. The custom reached its high point of skill on rare coins. Much the same rationale yielded the electrotype, a mere copy which could be used as a place-holder in a collector's cabinet. The plugging of rare coins has waned considerably in our century; the consensus of collectors now seems to be that a pierced coin should be left as it is, if only for honesty's sake.

Plugging of coins was never confined to rare specimens. Businessmen who received holed coins in trade plugged them so they could be passed. This plugging was far less elaborate, as the money involved was usually not as large as it was in the case of a rare coin. Governments too have occasionally countenanced the release of plugged coins. In the British Caribbean colony of Grenada, which had no coinage of its own and depended on that of other countries, lightweight and counterfeit Brazilian gold johannes were holed and plugged by local goldsmiths under official direction, to raise their weight to a prescribed standard. This also occurred on the islands of Martinique and St. Vincent; all three places issued plugged gold coins in 1798.

See also COUNTERSTAMP; ELECTROTYPE; FILLER.

PORTRAIT A pictorial representation of a human, particularly of the head.

Technically, the term should be applied only to depictions of an actual person, not to imaginary or divine beings, personifications, and such. Numismatists frequently use the term to refer to any depiction of a human being, real or imaginary, as no other word is available. We shall do the same in examining the development of coin portraiture over the years.

The ancient Greeks were the first coiners to attempt to depict people on coins. Their early efforts belong to the archaic period, in the sixth and fifth centuries B.C. The Athenians were pioneers, and their tetradrachm of the late sixth century and later set the tone of much early portraiture. The head of the goddess Athena, rendered in a stiff, unnatural style, appeared on the tetradrachm. She is shown with the "archaic smile" common to Greek sculpture of the period, while her eye is seen full-face, not in profile as it would be in reality.

This was an imaginary portrait, rather than one of a living being. The Greeks excelled in this form of portraiture over the next two centuries. The archaic aspect of their design repertoire was soon abandoned, and in the fifth and fourth centuries they produced some of the most masterful numismatic portraits in history. They cannot be called "realistic," but then they were not meant to be. Concerned with the Ideal, the Greeks concentrated on producing only beautiful faces, especially those of deities and heroes, reasoning perhaps that, while no *human* face was perfect, that of a god might well be. Their goal was to capture perfection on one side of a small piece of metal, the coin; and some of them were remarkably successful.

At this point, a few words should be added about the various types of portraits. To begin, the majority concentrate on either a head or a bust (the head, shoulders, and a portion of the chest). Full-figure portraits are possible, but have not been widely used for living people, as the style means the subject's head must be quite small, and most rulers portraying themselves on coinage insist their faces be identifiable. Hence, full-length portraits are more often used for allegorical representation or personification.

There are several styles among portraits featuring heads or busts. The most popular has been the profile, in which a head is rendered at a 90-degree angle from the viewer. The facing or full-face portrait is far less common, and is often done so poorly that the person portrayed is hard to recognize. Another possibility is usually called a three-quarter portrait, and shows the head slightly turned away from the viewer. It often portrays the neck, shoulders, and upper part of the torso as well; if so, it is known as a three-quarter bust, just as a full-face portrait in the same genre is called a facing bust. Other portrait styles are the jugate and the vis-à-vis types.

The ancient Greeks experimented with many possibilities, but tended to use the profile most often. By 300 B.C. their attentions shifted to the portrayal of living people, and in the process they demonstrated they could create "realistic" art if they chose. The depiction of real people was a logical outgrowth of conditions after the conquests of Philip of Macedon (ruled 359–336 B.C.) and his son and successor, Alexander the Great (ruled 336–323 B.C.) At Alexander's death his generals hastily divided up his vast empire, creating several large successor states. The new kings were eager to impress their subjects with their power, majesty, and divinity: coins displaying their profiles were an excellent way to do so. True portrait coinage is thus familiar from 300 B.C. on, although it never completely displaced idealized personification during ancient times.

There are numerous parallels between Greek and Roman portraiture, which also began with simple, even crude, depictions of divinities. The quality of these portraits (all done in profile) gradually improved, reaching its height in the first century A.D. The Romans excelled at realistic portraiture, and many of their coins evoke the shock of recognition we experience when encountering a modern face in a very old photograph. But the quality of their art waned in the second century, and by the third, Roman portraits had sadly degenerated, with all emperors looking very much alike.

Artistry and accuracy continued to decline in the fourth and fifth centuries. A rather odd, attenuated profile portrait came into vogue; perhaps it was an effort to emphasize the spirituality of the newly Christian princes. At the same time, other styles became popular—full-face, and particularly three-quarter renditions. After the fall of the Roman Empire in the West, the Byzantine East and most of the barbarous West eventually chose the full-face portrait as the customary design.

After the mid-sixth century it was all but universal in the East: emperors and their consorts were always seen directly facing the viewer. It was less widely accepted in the West, however, and while most of the medieval world adopted the facing portrait, there were persistent holdouts—in parts of Spain and a few other areas—who still favored the profile. Still, the facing portrait was simple to execute, as long as the mintmaster did not strive for accuracy. That would have retarded die production, at the very time coiners were discovering they could create all of a coin's elements very quickly by using small punches. A profile portrait would have been difficult to create with this method. In addition, the average medieval coin was small, and hence realism in its portrait was restricted. The full-face portrait served well enough.

The last centuries of the Middle Ages saw many changes. As economies revived, new, larger coins were needed. Strong rulers emerged, and nation-states arose. Fortified with more money and virtually limitless ambition, the new rulers sought ways to enhance their majesty and proclaim their divine right to govern. The rediscovery of classical works and artifacts —including coins and medallions—proceeded apace. Almost inevitably, the kings' aims met and mingled with the skills of artists, who increasingly turned to the classical world for inspiration, and again changed the nature of coin portraiture.

Differences between old and new are apparent on the two coins illustrated, English groats of Henry VII (ruled 1485–1509). Henry VII had overthrown his predecessor in 1485. To many, he was a mere usurper, ruling by the caprice of military fortune, not by divine right. Somehow the new king had to persuade Englishmen that he was indeed entitled to the throne; he saw portraiture on coinage as one way to do so. Abandoning the full-face portrait, seen on the left, in favor of the profile interpretation on the right, he hoped to intensify the aura of majesty he needed to create. (Note that the crown on the profile groat is more prominent than on the full-face one.) But he also wanted his subjects to have an accurate notion of his appearance, which would distinguish him from the long line of kings seen in full-face on English coinage since the days of William the Conqueror. It is interesting that Henry only used this technique on

Portrait. England, groats, 1485–1509.

medium- to low-value coins, those designed to reach the greatest number of people.

The great age of modern portraiture lasted from about 1500 to 1800. During this period of absolute monarchy in Europe, numismatic portraiture attained a level of artistry rarely found in earlier years, and never in ensuing ones. Die engravers shunned full-face techniques, and concentrated instead on perfecting the profile portrait. They were assisted by new coining technology, which generated the enormous force needed to strike in high relief.

Regrettably, the art of the numismatic portrait has languished since 1800. There are several reasons: the use of low-value and brittle alloys that do not strike particularly well; the exigencies of modern commerce, which is unappreciative of coinage in high relief; the disappearance of precious metals from coining; and the use of new die- and coin-making machines that place a premium on shallow relief and "safe" designs. Most coin portraiture is still rendered in profile, although there has been a resurgence of the full-face portrait in recent years, largely for commemorative and noncirculating legal tender pieces. But to find excellence in contemporary numismatic portraiture, however it is rendered, we must look to the modern note, where a modicum of artistry survives.

See also ARCHAIC COINAGE; COMMEMORATIVE; JUGATE; NONCIRCULATING LEGAL TENDER; PUNCH; TESTONE; VIS-À-VIS TYPE.

POSTAGE STAMP MONEY Postage stamps which are temporarily used, either in a modified or unmodified state, in lieu of small-denomination coins.

The use of stamps as coins is quite recent. (The postage stamp itself was not seen in its modern form until 1840.) But it springs from the same basic circumstances responsible for other kinds of modern emergency money. An uncertain future encourages the hoarding of coins, even those of small denominations, and makes it necessary to fill the void. In a sense, postage stamps are an eminently sensible solution. Issued by a government, they may well appear to have a greater value than private scrip or local notgeld. But they also have drawbacks. They are fragile, and deteriorate quickly with use. Their gummed backs can make them irksome to handle, and they are easily lost or mislaid.

It was during the American Civil War (1861–1865), when postage stamps were first widely used as money, that these disadvantages became obvious. The government and its people conceived a variety of solutions. Private citizens devised ways to encase and protect the stamps, which worked, but also added to the unit-cost per stamp without increasing its value. The government, for its part, fashioned small notes that resembled stamps and could be redeemed in stamps—postage currency, the direct ancestor of the more famous fractional currency. This new money replaced higher-value postage stamps.

The next noted period of postage stamp money occurred during and after World War I (1914–1918). Again, economic and political fears sent coins into hiding, and substitutes were sought. The postage stamp was one. Our illustration shows the obverse and reverse of a piece of Russian postage stamp money, printed between 1915 and 1917. In this case, we have something printed with the same plates used to make ordinary stamps, on

Postage stamp money. Russia, 10 kopeks, 1915–1917.

the same module (24 by 30 millimeters), but ungummed, made on a thicker than average paper, and with reverse printing stating, in effect, that the stamp's value was that of a ten-kopek coin. The gentleman on the front is Nicholas II (ruled 1894–1917), last Tsar of All the Russias. At the same time other countries were also using stamps as money. In Germany and Austria, many of the stamps were encased in cheap, transparent holders. The denomination could be seen on one side, while the reverse was often used for advertising purposes: here, as in many areas, the practice of using stamps as coins was a private rather than a governmental concern. Still other places, such as Madagascar, glued the stamps to cardboard backings before circulating them.

Postage stamp money was also employed during the Spanish Civil War (1936–1939) and in numbers of countries during and after World War II (1939–1945). Occasionally the practice is still encountered: the United States cent shortage of the early 1970s saw a brief revival of postage stamp money, although in this instance, the stamps were encased or otherwise protected.

See also CIVIL WAR TOKENS; EMERGENCY MONEY; ENCASED POSTAGE STAMP; FRACTIONAL CURRENCY; NOTGELD.

POTIN A type of billon: a base metal alloy containing varying amounts of lead, copper, tin, zinc, and silver, and used to strike debased coinage in ancient times.

Egyptian tetradrachms of the Roman period were struck in this metal, as were Roman antoniniani of the mid-third century A.D. Some of the Gallic imitations of the Macedonian stater were also struck in potin. The word is more specific than billon: billon refers to any base alloy containing less than fifty percent silver, while potin makes some distinction as to the exact composition of a particular billon alloy.

Since the relative proportions used to make potin varied, so did the alloy's appearance. In general, coins struck from potin have a grayish to whitish cast, with red undertones. Many potin pieces show split or cracked surfaces, the result of attempting to strike coins from a very brittle alloy.

See also ANTONINIANUS; BARBAROUS IMITATIONS; BILLON; GREEK IMPERIALS.

PRAGER GROSCHEN An important Bohemian silver coin of the fourteenth through sixteenth centuries: a central European development of the Italian grosso, whose production was made possible by the discovery of silver at Kuttenberg (today Kutná Hora) during the second half of the thirteenth century.

Bohemia's King Wenceslas II (ruled 1278–1305) decided in 1298 that a mint should be opened at Kutná Hora to allow for maximum exploitation of the silver deposit. Wenceslas abandoned the traditional Bohemian bracteate for a new coin modelled on the Italian grosso, which soon became known as a Prager groschen, due to its reverse inscription GROSSI PRAGENSES. No mention was made of where it was minted; it may be assumed the reference to Prague indicates this was the new, standard coin of the capital and therefore of the entire kingdom. The central type on the Prager groschen's reverse was a splendid lion of Bohemia, symbol of the country, while the obverse type was a crown, surrounded by legends referring to the

Prager groschen. Bohemia, 1278–1305.

king. The specimen illustrated measures slightly over 27 millimeters, and weighs 3.58 grams.

Prager groschen were struck in large numbers by Wenceslas II and his successors. They may have played a role in the flowering of Czech culture in the late Middle Ages, which left Prague with such architectural masterpieces as the Charles Bridge and the Cathedral of St. Vitus. Circulating extensively in European commerce, Prager groschen were soon imitated in those parts of eastern Germany with access to silver. They were also copied in Poland, where the crown device was retained, but the Bohemian lion replaced by the Polish eagle.

Bohemia lost its independence in 1526, becoming a hereditary possession of the Hapsburg archdukes of Austria. The Prager groschen was abandoned in 1547 for the larger silver coins then in fashion. Late issues of Prager groschen were still struck at Kutná Hora, and some also at Joachimsthal and Prague itself.

See also BRACTEATE; GROSCHEN; GROSSO; TRADE COINS.

PRESENTATION PIECE

PRESENTATION PIECE A coin intended for bestowal or award rather than general circulation.

Such a coin may have designs radically different from those on other issues of the same denomination, as is the case with Turkish gold presentation pieces of the nineteenth and twentieth centuries. On the other hand, designs on the presentation piece may be identical with those on circulating coins, as is so with the early English Maundy money. At all times, the important factor is intent—the desire to award someone on a special occasion.

See also MAUNDY MONEY; PROOF.

PRIVATE GOLD COINS

PRIVATE GOLD COINS A term describing a series of emergency United States gold coins, struck privately from 1830 to the early 1860s; the phrase is largely synonymous with another, territorial gold.

Gold was accidentally discovered in North Carolina in 1799, and a good deal more was unearthed a few years later. A modest gold rush ensued in the Charlotte area; another took place near the northern Georgia hamlet of Dahlonega. The gold was at once a boon and a problem. It was one thing to extract a precious commodity from the earth, quite another to obtain its full benefit. The metal would have to be converted to coins to achieve its maximum value, but the only federal coining facility at the time was in Philadelphia, and transporting the gold to the Mint was troublesome.

Hence miners and other citizens agitated for branch mints near the sources of the gold. Congress eventually enacted a law mandating three branch mints (at Charlotte, Dahlonega, and New Orleans), but not until March 1835; and it was another three years before the new facilities were ready to strike coins. Dilatory governmental response to a local problem prompted the private gold coin: if the government would not coin their bullion, the people would do so themselves.

Two firms were established to mint private gold. One was owned by Templeton Reid, who set up shop in Milledgeville, Georgia, in July 1830. Not long after, he moved to Gainesville to be nearer the mines, and most of his coins were struck there. They were uncomplicated (as were many private gold coins), with Reid's name as assayer, the value and provenance of the gold, and usually the date. Reid's coins were minted in $2.50, $5.00 and $10.00 denominations, and all are extremely rare today.

The coinage of the other firm, operated by several members of the Bechtler family, is more common. The Bechtlers' mint operated in Rutherford County, North Carolina, from 1830 to 1852. Their coins too were simple in design, most often undated, with the gold content of each piece carefully indicated on the coin. The

Bechtlers were the first minters to strike a gold dollar; the United States government did not adopt the idea until 1849.

The same year saw the beginning of a more extensive issue of private gold coins, this one from California. Early in 1848, gold was discovered in the Sacramento Valley, some seventy miles inland from San Francisco—the Gold Rush was on, and thousands of miners thronged from all corners of the globe, seeking a quick fortune. The influx cost Californa its pastoral way of life, and abruptly thrust it into the modern era.

If the problems in Georgia and North Carolina were thorny, those in California were even more so. The federal government could hardly supply thousands of new settlers with circulating coinage overnight, especially as no transcontinental railroad existed, nor was there a Panama Canal. In any event the government was quite logically more interested in transporting gold to the East, where it would benefit far more people.

History repeated itself in California. Local agitation for a federal mint eventually yielded one, established in San Francisco in 1854. However, by the time it opened its doors, people had been striking private gold coins in California for five years.

The first to do so were Norris, Grieg & Norris, who began operations near San Francisco in the spring of 1849. One of their pieces, a half eagle, is illustrated here. The art work leaves much to be desired: a rather woebegone eagle on one side, the denomination, the firm's initials, and the date on the other. Yet the coin was struck in pure gold, while its official counterpart was alloyed with ten percent copper; the private piece actually weighed more than the official one.

The pattern was set. Over the next few years, private gold coins were struck by dozens of firms in and around San Francisco. They ranged from Lilliputian twenty-five-cent pieces to huge fifty-dollar "slugs." While most coins were round, some were octagonal, and a few companies even settled for rectangular ingots, which apparently circulated along with everything else. It seems the last of the larger coins were struck late in 1855, although the tiny "fractional" pieces, quarter- and half-dollars, continued to be minted until the early 1880s. These pieces are frequently seen by collectors, as are replicas of them; but the latter do not bear the words CENTS, DOLLAR, or their abbreviations, making detection simple.

Two other groups used California gold to mint their own coins. One was the Oregon Exchange Company, a purely private firm. In 1849, it created a makeshift mint in Oregon City, whose population of 1,000 gave it the distinction of being the metropolis of the Oregon Territory. The other group was an official one, an arm of the Utah theocracy established by the Mormon leader Brigham Young. A mint was erected in Salt Lake City, and a number of coins struck there with the dates 1849 and 1850. Gold for the coins emanated from California, and was exchanged in Utah by Mormon miners returning home. A later issue of Mormon five-dollar pieces, dated 1860, used gold from yet another source, Colorado, where the metal had been discovered the previous year.

The first Colorado coins were struck in 1860, and minting continued well into the summer of 1861. With the exception of "fractional" pieces, these were the last private gold coins struck, the federal government declaring such activity illegal in 1864. Fractional pieces minted subse-

Private gold coins. California, Norris, Grieg & Norris, 5 dollars, 1849.

quently are illegal issues, but by then, more often than not, they were treated as souvenirs rather than coins. In essence, the government declared private coinage illegal because it was at last willing and able to provide its citizens with enough official coins to meet their needs.

See also COPY; EMERGENCY MONEY; INGOT; SLUG.

PROCLAMATION PIECE A medal struck to "proclaim" something of national importance, such as the onset of a new administration.

The term is most often used to describe a long series of Spanish and Latin American medals, sometimes struck as mementos, other times minted as commemorative coins meant to be circulated.

The roots of these proclamation pieces are found in sixteenth-century Spain, when, during the period of Philip II (ruled 1556–1598), silver medals were fashioned to celebrate various important events. By the following century, many such pieces were struck by or for various cities to proclaim a new reign. Some also began to assume a quasi-monetary aspect: a cast medal of Seville of 1621 pays homage to King Philip IV (ruled 1621–1665), but also shows evidence of circulatory wear, while its weight (slightly over 13.4 grams) is that of the current four-real coin.

In the seventeenth century, the vogue for the proclamation piece spread throughout Spain, and with the start of the eighteenth century it had crossed the Atlantic to Spanish America, where it became very popular. Pieces commemorating the beginnings of the reigns of Charles IV (ruled 1788–1808) and his son, Ferdinand VII (ruled 1808–1833), are particularly common, and many were struck in a fashion and module identical with those of circulating coins.

With Ferdinand's reign came the liberation of most of Spanish America by insurgent forces, and the formation of separate republics. As there were no longer kings to proclaim, it might be assumed the Latin American proclamation piece would vanish (as its Spanish counterpart was doing). Not so. Indeed, the output of proclamation pieces actually rose in many cases after Latin American independence, and in one nation, Bolivia, their production assumed the characteristics of a national industry.

In part this was because they were a form of advertising for the new republican regimes. The removal of royal authority from Latin America was traumatic, displacing, as it did, the traditional, universally acknowledged source of legitimate governmental power. If new nations were to be created and governed, their new leaders must acquire some legitimacy. Self-advertising was one way to do so. In an era without radio, television, decent roads, or a literate population, the proclamation medal was one of the few available options.

Hence it evolved into a uniquely Latin American piece. While medals were still struck to commemorate or announce new "reigns" or presidencies, many concentrated on presidential activities during administrations. Constitutions were commemorated, as were military victories and presidential visits. So too were events of a more personal nature: several presidents of Bolivia celebrated their birthdays by giving themselves and their constituents proclamation pieces.

Two other changes in the nature of these medals deserve mention, both especially applicable to Bolivia. First, many of the original royal proclamation pieces had actually been struck by cities and towns, but their republican counterparts usually issued from a national mint. While there was a semblance of spontaneity, many of these pieces used regular coinage punches, were edge-marked at the mint, etc., and were in truth advertising for the government, prepared by the government.

Proclamation piece. *Bolivia, proclamation piece of the same size and weight as an 8-sol coin, 1852.*

Second, while royal proclamation pieces were sometimes minted in the same size and weight as circulating coins, it was common practice for republican issues, especially in the case of Bolivia, where there seems to have been a concerted effort to strike medals on a coin module. While it could be argued that it was simply easier to mint them in this fashion, the degree of wear many of them exhibit suggests the government knew they would be used as coins, and indeed encouraged it.

And so they were. Mexico, Guatemala, Peru, Chile, and several other nations issued proclamation medals, but all were overshadowed by Bolivia, where the communications system was more rudimentary than that of any other country in the region. Our illustration shows a large Bolivian medal of 1852. Its size (36.5 millimeters) and weight (26.4 grams) are exactly those we expect on the current peso or eight-sol coin. It was a product of the presidency of Manuel Ysidoro Belzú, who governed the country between 1847 and 1855. Belzú's dictatorial regime incited a revolt in 1850, during which he was wounded in Potosí on September 6. He recovered, and exercised his power to commemorate this. September 6 was proclaimed a national holiday. A round chapel was ordered built on the very spot where Belzú had been attacked, and invitations were issued to all the republic's bishops, asking their attendance at a gala dedication ceremony, to be held on September 6, 1852. The chapel was com-

pleted, the ceremony was held—and this proclamation piece was struck, for general consumption. The obverse shows an angel, blowing a trumpet. The banner hanging from her trumpet declares VIVA BOLIVIA, and the plaque she holds in her other hand reads **XX** (VIVA) EL JRAL BELZU—"Long Live General Belzú." The reverse renders homage AL SER SUPREMO QUE SALVO A BOLIVIA ("To the Supreme Being [i.e., God] Who Saved Bolivia"). The reverse type is the chapel the grateful *caudillo* had had constructed.

The proclamation piece began to lose favor in Bolivia and the rest of Latin America after the 1850s. In Bolivia's case, the last president to issue such pieces was General Hilarión Daza, who released one in 1879 honoring his birthday.

See also COMMEMORATIVE; MEDAL.

PROOF   A coin struck on a special planchet, from specially prepared dies, in a different process from that used for ordinary coins or business strikes.

Proofs are minted for presentation or for sale to collectors, and are generally considered examples of the finest work of which a mint is capable. Proofs ordinarily employ brilliant mirror-like fields, while their types and legends may be shiny or dull, depending on the desire of the mint. Whatever their appearance, the details of the types are very sharp, clearer than those on a business strike; the legends too, are clear and precise. The edge of the proof is sharp, and forms a perfect 90-degree angle with the upper and lower surfaces or faces of the coin, whereas the edge of the business strike is usually somewhat rounded where it joins the coin's rims. If a reeded edge is utilized for the proof, it is sharp to the touch; should an ornamented or lettered edge be preferred, the elements are also distinct.

It is important to note that the term proof has nothing to do with the condition of a coin. And it should never be used to describe a coin in a superior mint state. The word refers to the procedures used to mint a particular coin, practices not followed for other coins. In other words, proof describes processes, not a state of preservation.

An essential attribute of the proof coin is that it has been struck in place more than once. This is what emphasizes the types' details. The first proofs seem to have been struck in England, although the exact date of their introduction is unclear. There are coins which may or may not be proofs dating from the 1650s, but the first certain proof specimens must be placed in the following decade. These are extremely rare, as is generally the case for proofs struck up to the early years of the present century. Our illustration shows an eighteenth-century proof English halfpenny, coupled with an ordinary coin of the same date. Note the detail on the proof, and its glossy surfaces, common on toned copper proofs. Note also the slightly different treatment of the denticles on the proof coin: early English proofs almost always incorporated details not found on ordinary coins, perhaps to underscore their "special" quality.

Proof.
Top: England, proof halfpenny, 1770.
Bottom: England, ordinary halfpenny, 1770.

When Matthew Boulton harnessed James Watt's steam engine to a coining press, it meant the availability of an almost unbelievable force for striking. Proofs could be minted more perfectly, with greater detail than ever before. Its production facilitated, the vogue for the proof coin grew during the nineteenth century. The United States Mint struck presentation coins between 1792 and 1816, but it is not entirely clear whether these pieces were proofs or not. Beginning in 1817, however, proofs are definitely known, although until about 1850 all are extremely rare. By the 1830s there was a tendency to mint a complete set of proof coins, representing each denomination then in circulation. This has been the rule since, for American coins at least.

Gradually, the notion of issuing proofs for presentation began to yield to minting them for sale to collectors, and the United States and several other nations were doing so by the later nineteenth century. But it is the present century that has seen an explosion of proof issues of this type, and most proofs are now struck for coin collectors.

Through the decades, a variety of types of proofs have been minted. The first, and probably best known, could be called the classic proof. The completed die for such a proof was carefully checked for imperfections, then painstakingly polished on its high points until they resembled a mirror. The lower points (which would create the coin's designs) were left unpolished. A proof struck from such a die shows a brilliant, reflective surface on its fields, a duller one on its types and legends. Virtually all proofs minted before 1900 are of this type. A logical step was to increase the contrast between field and device by etching the die in dilute acid, then polishing the fields. This technique produces the frosted proof, the most common type in current production.

In yet another type, the brilliant proof, *all* the dies' surfaces are highly polished. While the results are dramatic, the polishing may lead to a loss of detail. This type of proof was fashionable in the United States from the 1930s to the early 1970s, but has since been replaced by the frosted proof. Several other countries, among them England and Canada, have also issued brilliant proofs in this century, and the technique is still popular elsewhere.

Two other proof techniques have fallen into disuse, however—the matte proof and the sandblast proof. Developed about 1900, each treated the coin with a special, dull to grainy finish after it was struck. Matte and sandblast proofs are in favor with modern collectors, but were not well received when they were actually struck. For coinage, these types of proofs disappeared about 1935, although one still encounters them in the field of medals.

See also FROSTED PROOF; GRADING SYSTEMS; MATTE PROOF; NONCIRCULATING LEGAL TENDER; PRESENTATION PIECE; PROOF-LIKE; SANDBLAST PROOF.

Proof-like. *Guadalajara, Mexico, 4 reales, 1844/3.*

PROOF-LIKE Having a surface that is unusually brilliant or flawless.

The term is applied to uncirculated production coins that manifest some of the outward characteristics of a proof. Such pieces, which represent the best coins that can be produced under ordinary minting circumstances, almost always command a higher price than normal uncirculated specimens. The term may be somewhat misleading, as the word proof properly refers to a coining process that is completely different from that used for striking regular coins, even proof-like ones. *Proof-like* is used rather indiscriminately by dealers to encourage interest in their wares, and collectors should be aware of it.

The term can describe a variety of types of coins, among which are first strikes—the first coins to be struck with fresh, new dies. The highly polished fields of the dies, the somewhat frosty appearance of their lettering and types, have not

yet had time to become worn, and the coins they strike may superficially resemble proofs. Other proof-like coins have been struck from dies originally intended for proofs, then converted to ordinary coinage once the desired number of proofs had been struck.

The phrase also describes a coin deliberately struck to resemble a proof, albeit struck once like any ordinary coin. If such is the case, highly polished blanks are struck with highly polished dies. Great care is taken to make certain the new coins are not nicked or otherwise blemished, and eventually they are sold by mints to collectors, either in sets representing the denominations made at the facility or as special commemorative issues. This practice began in Canada in 1953, and the term *proof-like* was actually first used in that country, as a descriptive one for the new coins.

The coin illustrated, a Mexican four-real piece of 1844, is a good example of the appearance of a proof-like business strike. If you look closely you can see mirror surfaces near the rays, within and beneath the legend, etc., contrasting dramatically with the type and legend. These are hallmarks of the proof-like coin.

See also COMMEMORATIVE; FIRST STRIKE; GRADING SYSTEMS; PROOF.

PUNCH A tool, usually a cylindrical rod of steel, shaped at one end to impart designs to dies or coins.

In the argot of numismatics, punch is often used for tools that produce such minor designs as mint marks, while puncheon is occasionally used for tools producing such major elements as portraits or other types. However, punch *can* be used for both kinds of tools.

For information on punches used directly on coins or planchets, see the entry for Counterstamp and its cross-references. Here, we shall examine the punch in relationship to a coin die.

There is evidence that some ancient coin dies were prepared in part with a punch, but ancient minting practices are still not wholly understood. It is not until the Middle Ages that we can definitely ascertain the use of punches; from then on it is seen with increasing frequency.

An early example is the English penny and its Continental equivalents. By about 1000, trade was undergoing a modest revival in the West. More coins were needed, and the punch entered medieval numismatics. It was discovered that, if the basic components of a design were determined and a simple punch created for each—a dot, a crescent, a straight line—coin dies could be made more rapidly; hence coins could be produced more rapidly. To some extent this explains the abysmal portraiture on many medieval coins: designers sacrificed artistry for speed.

With the growing importance of portraiture and other large types, the use of punches changed. They were still employed to produce a legend's letters, and would be soon to give dates, but their role in portraiture and other central designs declined. Furthermore, the punches used for letters and numbers were now carved in the exact form desired, not created from a number of punches as before.

In time, the punch was rediscovered for large elements, and gradually evolved into the hub, described elsewhere. But before that could occur, and larger, more

Punch.
Left: Bolivia, an obverse punch used for peso Melgarejo dies, 1865.
Right: Bolivia, peso Melgarejo, 1865.

elaborate punches could find their proper niche in die production, a machine would have to be devised to do the work.

It was soon learned that a screw press could drive a large punch, or puncheon, into a die more efficiently than could simple manual force. The design could then be refined by hand, and the legends, denominations, date, and other elements could be added by individual, smaller punches.

The photograph shows an elaborate obverse punch used to prepare dies for the Bolivian peso Melgarejo in 1865, along with one of the coins it produced. This particular punch was driven into die blanks by a screw press. The elaborateness of the punch, and the limited motive force available to the Bolivian mint at the time, meant each die had to be extensively reworked before it was ready to strike coins. The reworking differed, of course, from die to die, and the peso Melgarejo is known in a number of die varieties.

See also ARCHAIC COINAGE; COUNTERSTAMP; DIE VARIETY; HUB; PORTRAIT; PUNCH-MARKED COINS.

PUNCH-CANCELLED A note or other form of paper money which has been invalidated by having a hole or holes punched out of it.

The punch cancellation illustrated appears on a three-dollar note issued by the state of Mississippi in 1870. The Reconstruction government issued five hundred thousand dollars in these notes, which were actually certificates of indebtedness, exchangeable for interest-bearing bonds. A special tax was levied to redeem such bonds, and the notes were punch-cancelled as they were submitted, thus retiring them from circulation.

Punch-marked coins. India, purana, c. 500 B.C.

Punch cancelled. A punch cancelled note (State of Mississippi, 3 dollars, 1870).

The punch-cancelled note is primarily a phenomenon of the early days of paper currency. Although a few issues are known from this century, they are usually found on emergency money, not on official notes.

Slash cancelling and cut cancelling are terms for similar processes, performed with a knife or other device for the same purpose.

PUNCH-MARKED COINS Silver and copper coins of ancient India, struck with numbers of punches rather than with ordinary obverse and reverse dies.

The date punch-marked coinage was introduced to India is widely disputed.

Some place it as early as 1000 B.C., although a date of 500 B.C. is more likely. The date of the last punch-marked coins is also debatable but A.D. 500 is probable. A common name for coins in this series is purana.

Our specimen measures about 15 millimeters on each side, and weighs slightly less than 3.1 grams. It is fashioned of silver, as are the majority of punch-marked coins. Such coins were apt to have a set number of symbols or punches on the obverse (often five), and a variable number on the reverse. The exact meaning of these punches has not been fully deciphered. It is assumed they allude to ruling dynasties, and they have been used to establish a chronology for early Indian history, a practice that is not universally accepted. One thing is certain: puranas were coins, rather than mere ingots. They adhered to definite weight standards, and were guaranteed by someone, although we do not know by whom. In later years, the purana's popularity waned, and Indian coinage adopted the trends then seen in the West and Middle East. Yet an original Indian coinage did exist, and coinage itself seems to have begun there spontaneously.

See also COUNTERSTAMP; SQUARE COINAGE.

R

RADAR NOTE A bill on which the serial number reads the same both forward and backward, forming a palindrome.

An example of a radar serial number on a United States bill is 40977904. With American printing and numbering practice what it is, such a note appears roughly once every ten thousand times. The ratio of radar notes to ordinary notes varies throughout the world, but they always command a premium among collectors.

Contrary to the opinion of some hobbyists, they are not errors, but perfectly printed notes whose numbers happen to read in an unusual way. A note numbered 40977904 is no rarer than one numbered 40977905, merely more interesting to the general collector. Radar is itself a palindrome—hence the term.

RAILROAD RIM A coinage error created by striking a planchet when it is partially out of the collar into which it should fit during striking, resulting in an edge of two distinct yet parallel steps around the coin's circumference.

The term comes from the edge's resemblance to a railroad wheel. The wide portion was struck outside the collar, expanding at the moment of impact, while the narrower portion was struck inside the collar, making expansion impossible.

Our photograph illustrates a typical railraod rim on a United States dime of 1897. As dimes are struck in a reeded, closed collar, the lower, narrower half of this railroad rim is reeded. In the case of this dime, the lower die, which was to occupy the lower position in the collar, had evidently not retracted far enough after the previous strike, and was too high. When the planchet was automatically laid on top of it, the reeded collar encircled the lower half of the blank, but not its upper half. Striking it in this fashion produced the error.

The railroad rim is a consequence of

Railroad rim. United States, dime, 1897. (Courtesy COINHUNTER, Philadelphia) modern coining machinery, which stresses automatic devices and closed collars. Also known as a flanged edge, it is a coveted error among collectors, particularly on older coins from United States mints.

See also COLLAR; ERROR.

RARITY A term indicating the number of surviving specimens of a particular coin or other numismatic object.

The word is usually employed in a relative sense: we may speak of the rarity of an 1804 United States cent relative to that of an 1803 cent. And it must be emphasized that rarity is not necessarily determined from published mint figures, which may be inaccurate; even if not, they merely record the number of coins of a certain type originally struck, without reference to how many were later melted down, lost, or otherwise disposed of. An excellent example of a divergence between mint figures and known specimens occurs with United States twenty-dollar gold pieces struck in Denver in 1927. While the official report lists 180,000 as having been coined that year, less than a dozen are currently known, the rest presumably having been melted down in the early 1930s.

Assuming we trust the figures of the United States Mint, 1804 cents were once rarer than 1803s. But how much rarer are they *now*, given loss and attrition over the years? And could the present number of surviving 1804s actually be *greater* than that of 1803s, a reflection perhaps of widespread melting of 1803 cents? Finally, what happens when mint figures do not exist? How do we establish the rarity of a particular Roman coin, for instance?

The answer involves prodigious research and a bit of inspired guesswork. But once it is established which coins are common and which are not, we might devise a rarity scale based on as accurate a count as possible, to denote relative scarcities of coins within or between series. Unfortunately, there is no universally agreed-upon formula for such a scale. Most often, Europeans use one with symbols, ranging from C (common) through R^1 (rare) to R^8 (extremely rare—only two or three known). Americans, on the other hand, use a variety of scales; one of the best-known combines symbols and numbers. Thus, R-1 means more than five thousand specimens exist, R-5 indicates a population of seventy-five to two hundred, while R-10 means the piece is unique.

The marriage of rarity and price is a complex one. Rarity plays a part in the sense that a rare coin is apt to be worth more than a familiar one in the same condition and in the same series. But a series may have many rarities within it and be thousands of years old, and yet, its rarities may be of less value than common, much later coins. Supply and demand are the arbiters. If Roman coins hold no interest for collectors, rare Roman coins may sell more cheaply than common American ones. For rarity to assume its potential role in numismatic pricing, there must be a keen interest in the field in which the rarities are found.

See also HOARD.

REAL An important Spanish and Spanish-American silver coin from the late Middle Ages well into modern times.

The real was introduced by Peter the Cruel, king of Castile and Leon (ruled 1350–1369). It was struck at an official fineness of eleven dineros, four granos—slightly over 93 percent pure silver—weighed about 3.5 grams, and measured approximately 27 millimeters in diameter. The obverse bore a crowned P accompanied by religious slogans arranged in two circular legends. The reverse had a central device of castles and lions (for Castile and Leon), and a surrounding legend with the king's title. Our specimen shows a tiny B beneath the central reverse type, indicating it was minted in Burgos. A similar half-real piece was released at about the same time. Together, these coins suggest

Real. *Castile and Leon, 1350–1369.*

Spain's prosperity during these years, despite the alleged ferocity and cruelty of its ruler.

The real circulated widely and was regularly minted by Peter's successors through the remainder of the Middle Ages. In time, a profile portrait became a popular obverse type, while the reverse tended to follow Peter's original designs. Introduced first for Castile and Leon, the coin soon spread to neighboring states, including Valencia, Majorca, and Aragon. Shortly before 1500, issue of the real became general throughout Spain: the Pragmatic of Medina del Campo (June 13, 1497) abolished all previous monetary systems, establishing in their place a unit of account called a maravedí. Thirty-four copper maravedís equalled one silver real, and multiples and subdivisions of the real were devised. Valencia alone retained its own coinage system, but this was regarded as provincial and downgraded accordingly.

The significance of the real in Spain was magnified when Spain explored and conquered much of the Americas, unearthing vast deposits of precious metals as it did so. This led to Spanish-American reales, and mints in or near the mining areas of Mexico, Peru, and Bolivia. The first of these opened its doors in Mexico City, in the spring of 1536. Among its first coins were silver reales, minted to the same fineness as the Spanish real.

While finenesses of American and Spanish reales were identical, their designs differed. Issues from both realms bore crowned shields on their obverses, but Spanish coins had reverses with a yoke and arrows design, and their American counterparts carried the Pillars of Hercules, waves, and an abbreviated form of the motto PLUS ULTRA as reverse devices. This American design was meant to reveal that new lands existed beyond the confines of Europe and Africa—the Americas—and were the preserve of Spain.

In 1570 a uniform pattern for Spanish and American reales and other coins was decreed. The obverse continued to display a crowned shield, the reverse a large cross with castles and lions in its angles. However, the uniformity was only temporary: by the following century, colonial mints were again experimenting with various designs.

By this time, reales bore types identical to those on the Piece of Eight. The fancy crowned shield and globes and pillar designs began on American reales in the 1730s, while in the 1770s a portrait bust of the king replaced previous obverse designs. Spanish issues now bore crowned arms on the reverse, as did American ones, which added flanking columns to their designs, again referring to the Pillars of Hercules and the coins' transatlantic origins.

The last Spanish coin to bear the name real was struck in 1864. It was different from previous coins bearing the name, however, and was tied in with the new Spanish decimal monetary system adopted in 1848.

Initially, the new nations of Latin America retained the colonial monetary denominations, including the real, as people were familiar with them. But with the growth of decimalizaton by the mid-nineteenth century, the real gradually vanished. The last country to strike it was Guatemala, whose final reales were minted in 1912 (of copper-nickel rather than silver).

See also DECIMAL COINAGE; DINERO; MARAVEDÍ; PIECE OF EIGHT.

RECUT DIE A die with one or more of its elements deliberately, officially altered to change the date on the die, the mint mark, the denomination, etc., or to strengthen certain elements of the type, reduce or eliminate others.

The term implies that someone set about with an engraving tool to retouch the areas to be changed. Indeed at times this has been the case, but the term more often refers to a repunched die—one element is removed and another placed on the die with a punch. The die may have been used previously or it may be unused, but with something on it necessitating an alteration. An overdate, at least in modern times, is often the creation of a die which has been used previously, and then repunched with a new date. If so, the result can be coins of two different years, made by the same die. Or the die may never have been used, in which case, nothing but overdates will emerge from that particular die.

The illustration shows a detail from an unusual coin, a Mexican eight-real of 1896 struck from a repunched die, originally designed to serve in the small northern mint of Alamos. The date, assayer's initials, and mint mark were all carefully punched in. Whether the die was actually used at the Alamos mint is moot; what is not is that when the mint closed in 1895, the die was transported several hundred miles to a larger mint at Guanajuato, where it was "recut"—given a new mint mark, date, and assayer's initials—and used to coin Guanajuato eight-real coins

Recut die. Guanajuato, Mexico, 8 reales, 1896 (detail). The die was originally made for the Alamos mint, dated 1891, and the assayer's initials were M.L.

of 1896. Mexican overdates are common, as are recuts of assayer's initials. But recutting a mint mark is distinctly unusual, and this is the one known example of the practice in Mexico. It can also be seen on a few late eighteenth-century French décimes.

See also ALTERATION; DÉCIME; MARK (MINTMASTER'S OR ASSAYER'S); MINT MARK; OVERDATE.

REEDED EDGE An edge design with vertical, measured striations, applied to a coin by a closed collar at the same time the coin is struck.

Essentially the reeded edge is the fruit of the semi- and fully automatic coining machines developed in the late eighteenth century, and perfected in the nineteenth and twentieth. Speed was the most important factor and artistry was sacrificed for uniformity. Fancy edges slowed production, and at least initially there was no way they could be executed with a closed collar. (Eventually Germany invented an incuse ornamented edge to fit inside a closed collar, but its design possibilities were limited.) To achieve uniformity, the closed collar was essential, and uniformity was necessary to make it harder to clip, file, or counterfeit coins.

In the early days of the closed collar, there were only two design options: no design at all, or a vertical reeding—small striations around the coin's entire edge. The marks were placed on the inside of the collar, and the coin took the design as pressure from the upper and lower dies forced the metal outward from its center, against the collar's inner circumference. The marks were vertical, to enable the finished coin to be pushed through the collar and ejected from the press. The plain collar would allow for the ejection of the coin, of course, but the reeded one had the advantage of imparting a simple design, another deterrent against clipping and counterfeiting. This was particularly important in the case of precious-metal coins.

Reeded edge. United States, dollar, 1845.

Traditionally, the reeded closed collar has been used for coins of higher denominations originally minted in gold or silver, while the plain closed collar has served for lower denominations.

The photograph shows a typical reeded edge—simple, and not particularly attractive—on a United States silver dollar of 1845. As anyone knows who has examined numbers of counterfeits, it is exceedingly difficult to reproduce a true reeded edge. Those given to clipping and filing, on the other hand, discovered that only an infinitesimal amount of metal could be removed from a reeded edge and go undetected.

See also Collar; Edge-marking machinery; Graining; Ornamented edge.

REMAINDER NOTE   A note printed for issue but never placed in circulation; such notes are usually found in new condition, unsigned, and unnumbered.

A variety of circumstances spawn remainder notes. During the period of private, unregulated banks, many went bankrupt, leaving a supply of unissued new notes on hand. Banks that remained solvent might have decided to change the designs of their notes, and issued new ones while retaining their predecessors. In either case, the discards are remainder notes, and can be found as uncut sheets or as individual notes ready for circulation.

In still other instances, the issuing authority was semi-official. Remainder notes exist for the Missouri Defense Fund, a fiscal creation of the state's Confederate authorities. No notes from this series are known to have circulated, and all could be considered remainder notes. By the time the notes were printed, Missouri was essentially beyond the Confederacy's jurisdiction, and any hope of circulating the notes had vanished.

Remainder notes are found primarily in eighteenth and nineteenth century issues. Our illustration shows a typical nineteenth-century note, printed for the Bank of Augusta, Georgia, around 1843. The bank created new designs for the two-dollar denomination, and some bills with the older design were never issued. The bank continued to release notes well into the Civil War years.

See also Broken bank notes.

RESTRIKE   A coin or medal produced from the original dies but at a later date.

A restrike may be created by an official agency, such as a government mint, for numerous reasons. Gold restrikes may be coined to dispose of excess bullion in small lots which the public can afford and which

Remainder note. Georgia, Bank of Augusta, 2 dollars, c. 1843.

Restrike. *Austria, 4 ducats, 1915 (a restrike made in the 1960s).*

earns money for the government. If so, the denomination stated on the restrike bears little or no relation to present circulating denominations. Thus, a Mexican restrike of the fifty-peso gold piece would cost some three thousand pesos, regardless of the denomination of the coin. And the piece illustrated, a 1960s restrike of the Austrian four-ducat coin of 1915, has no connection with current Austrian coinage—indeed, the ducat no longer exists in Austria. Governments may also specifically fashion restrikes for sale to collectors, a common practice with popular medals.

A mint can also make restrikes in an unofficial capacity, to enrich the personal coffers of its overseers—even to fulfill a personal whim—but seldom to benefit the mint. In the mid-nineteenth century, many rare early American coins were restruck for just such reasons at the corrupt United States Mint in Philadelphia.

Profit motivates private restrikes as well. Joseph Mickley, a noted American collector, secured a number of mint dies as scrap metal, and in 1859 put two to use to create a restrike of the rare 1811 half cent.

Increasingly stringent regulations have eliminated private restriking, and unofficial restriking within a mint. However, official restrikes are still minted, usually to dispose of bullion.

See also BULLION; FANTASY; INGOT; NOVODEL; TRADE COINS.

REVERSE The opposite side of a coin from the obverse; the term is also used in conjunction with medals, tokens, decorations, and paper money.

Generally it can be said that the reverse holds a coin's subordinate designs, but the statement must be qualified: the designs are deemed subordinate by the people who struck the coin. Thus, to most non-Mexicans, the side of a Mexican coin depicting an eagle and serpent is the reverse, but to the Mexican government and its people, it is the obverse. In fact, the Mexican coinage law of 1823, establishing coin designs, specified the eagle side as the obverse.

What is to be found on coin reverses? For ancient Greek and Roman coins, seated or standing figures are common. For Far Eastern issues of the same period, blank reverses are the rule, with inscriptions limited to the obverse. Byzantine reverses may relate the value, mint, and date of manufacture (this is so for early issues: crosses dominate on many later copper reverses and are also prominent on gold and silver ones through much of the Byzantine era). On Western medieval coins, crosses in various guises are to be seen until the thirteenth century or so, with some heraldic elements added subsequently. In the case of more modern coins, heraldic elements appeared on obverses and reverses for a number of years, but in time were confined to the reverse. The contemporary reverse may feature wreaths with denominations, elements of heraldry, local scenes—indeed, the list of designs is almost endless.

This is not so for tokens, which are usually simpler than coins, with a primary emphasis on the legend, inscription, or value. The reverse designs of early tokens are frequently allegorical, while the reverses of more recent ones merely contain statements of value. Many medals use the obverse for detailed portraiture, the reverse for allegorical figures or lengthy inscriptions. Should they carry dates, these can be expected to appear on the reverse. For decorations, the reverse may be an important element or have no significance whatsoever. For example, the crosses of chivalric orders have fancy reverses, but stars for the same orders normally have blank reverses, except for a maker's mark. The gallantry award also shows a blank or nearly blank reverse, upon which the recipient's name can be engraved. The reverses of campaign medals, on the other hand, may be more involved, displaying symbolic figures or the names of the campaigns for which the medals are awarded.

With paper money, the reverse was generally blank until after 1850, when designs were added. Initially they concentrated on an indication—often very ornately done—of the note's denomination, and any portraits or vignettes were printed on the obverse. On issues after 1880 or thereabouts (slightly earlier in the United States and Canada)—pictorial elements began to appear on reverses, and on most modern notes they have as much imagery as their opposite sides. Today many reverses are used for commemorative purposes, a trend likely to continue in the future.

See also DIE; OBVERSE.

RIBBON A distinctive loop of cloth, from which a decoration is suspended; a common feature of campaign and gallantry awards and chivalric decorations.

Each gallantry award, campaign medal (except for those in the general service category), and chivalric decoration has a ribbon in a particular color or colors and of a distinctive design, meant to reveal at a glance the nature of the award. This is particularly necessary, as the ribbon is often the only element worn by the recipient. When such is the case, it usually takes the form of a small bar, fashioned from ribbon or enameled to resemble it.

Early ribbons were customarily of a single color, and blue—the color of the sky and the symbol of royal honor and virtue —was the one most often used. The English Order of the Garter adopted it, as did many other chivalric orders. Red—

Ribbon. *United States, World War II Victory Medal with ribbon.*

symbolizing blood, courage, and love— was also popular, and is found with the British Order of the Bath, the French Legion of Honor, and the Victoria Cross, England's most eminent gallantry award.

The Prussian Order of the Black Eagle, on the other hand, chose orange for its ribbon, while the Scottish Order of the Thistle opted for green.

By the eighteenth century, bicolored ribbons began to appear, and their use spread as the number of decorations proliferated. With yet more colors added, ribbons were composed of vertical, horizontal, or diagonal stripes of varying widths. The multicolored ribbon illustrated was issued by the United States at the conclusion of World War II, and is one of the most common and attractive of modern campaign ribbons. Its scarlet central stripe is flanked by two narrow white bands. In turn, these white bands border on complex left and right outer stripes displaying all the colors of the rainbow.

See also CAMPAIGN AWARD; DECORATION; GALLANTRY AWARD; ORDER; SASH.

Rim. *United States, 20 dollars, 1907.*

RIM The thin line on a coin or medal where the face joins the edge.

On modern proof coins, the rim will be entirely squared, with the point where the face meets the edge forming a perfect right angle. For other modern coins—business strikes, produced for circulation—the rim will normally be slightly rounded. For ancient coins, a rounded rim was the rule, as there was no machinery to prevent it—nor any particular inclination to do so.

The knife rim or wire edge is a special rim, given to a coin either by accident or by design. During striking, metal is forced between the coin dies and their collar, resulting in a rim that is sharp to the touch.

A coin's rim is an acutely vulnerable area. Should the coin be dropped or otherwise mishandled, the rim is apt to have nicks or "edge dings." If blemishes detract from a coin's appearance, catalogs from reputable auction houses will usually make note of them, for they can seriously affect a coin's value.

See also RAILROAD RIM; WIRE EDGE.

ROCKER PRESS A variant on the roller press, which was extensively used for the production of coinage in the seventeenth century.

Both roller and rocker press forced metal between the upper and lower dies, in a mechanical process that was not dependent on a screw device to strike the coins. But there the similarity ends. The roller press had multiple dies engraved on cylinders, between which a strip of metal

passed; coins were then punched out of this impressed strip. The roller press did not allow for proper adjustment of the weight of coin blanks before striking, and any adjustment needed after striking marred the coins' surfaces.

The rocker press, on the other hand, did permit such adjustment, as it struck coins from planchets, not strips. It consisted of upper and lower "rockers"—curved coin dies of the type illustrated. The rockers were pivoted together and operated by a seesaw bar attached to the upper rocker. A planchet placed between the two dies was forced through and struck once the bar was depressed.

Rocker press. *An obverse rocker press die used to mint 3-kreuzer coins of Anhalt, c. 1624.*

The rocker press was not ideal. It was apt to produce imperfect impressions and misshapen coins, as the pressure was not equally distributed over the surfaces of the planchet. It seems the rocker press was primarily used for low-denomination coins, partly because of these very deficiencies. While it did have some advantages over the roller press, the screw press worked better than either, and rocker and roller press alike fell out of favor in the eighteenth century.

See also MACHINE-STRUCK COINAGE; ROLLER PRESS; SCREW PRESS.

ROLLER PRESS A coining machine that impressed obverse and reverse designs on a strip of metal drawn between two rollers.

The device arose logically from the improvement in methods of producing metal strips of a uniform thickness. In prior coining procedures, the strips were cut into planchets, then stamped. With the roller press, the strips were stamped and then cut into coins.

To achieve this, two rollers were needed: they were steel cylinders, with varying numbers of obverse dies engraved on one, and reverse dies engraved on the other. For the largest coins, each cylinder would contain only one or two dies; for smaller coins, as many as a dozen might be present. Whatever the number of dies on each roller (and rollers for any given coin obviously used the same number of obverse and reverse dies), two things were necessary. First, the dies on each cylinder had to be in perfect alignment, equally spaced around the roller's circumference. Next, the dies had to be engraved as broad ovals, not as perfect circles. This was because the pressure of the rollers on the metallic strip caused it to expand longitudinally; the ovoid shape compensated for this, and round coins emerged. In addition to a coin's engravings, each roller held several square impressions, which acted as cogs in the coining process. Parts of the strip forced themselves into these holes, which pulled the strip of metal through the device with upper and lower dies—and their impressions—in correct alignment.

The roller press was invented in the mid-sixteenth century, and seems to have been first used in the city of Hall, Austria. It was quickly adopted in adjacent Germany, and in Spain in the 1580s. The illustration shows an early Spanish product, a 1586 Piece of Eight struck by the Segovia mint. England, too, used the roller press, but only to manufacture copper farthings.

The roller press had several distinct drawbacks. As coins were struck in strips before they were punched out, there was no way to guarantee proper weight in the planchet stage. Any filing to correct an overweight piece had to wait until the coin was struck, which meant adjustment marks marred the coin's surface or edge. Furthermore, achieving and retaining the proper alignment between the upper and lower rollers was tricky at best. Should one roller move slightly faster than another, it could result in an entire strip of misstruck coins. And the same would occur if the rollers were not correctly set in the first place.

There was a final disadvantage. If any one of a roller's dies suffered a major chip, crack, etc., the entire roller, with all the other dies, would have to be scrapped. Eventually, detachable dies were invented, but even so, coining money with the roller press remained an arduous and risky task; the machine was gradually abandoned in the eighteenth century, although in a few places it was used for small change until after 1800. The roller and the rocker press both yielded to the screw press, which, in turn, yielded to the steam-powered contrivances spawned by the Industrial Revolution.

See also ADJUSTMENT MARKS; MACHINE-STRUCK COINAGE; ROCKER PRESS; SCREW PRESS.

Roller press. Spain, 8 reales, 1586.

ROSA AMERICANA COINAGE

ROSA AMERICANA COINAGE   A lightweight, contract coinage struck for use in England's American colonies in the early 1720s.

William Wood (1671–1730), was responsible for Rosa Americana coins. The owner of a large copper and iron works in western Britain, Wood was an innovator, and seems to have been the first ironmaster to attempt to manufacture iron with pit coal, a process that was an essential first step in the Industrial Revolution. Wood was prosperous, and took on contract coinage as yet another money-making venture. He was to be sadly disappointed, however, for his Rosa Americana coins and a parallel issue for Ireland (the Hibernia series) were generally spurned—primarily because they were lightweight. The coins for Ireland were only some two-thirds the weight of their English counterparts, while his issues for the "Plantations" (the English colonies on the Atlantic seaboard) weighed less than half. In effect, Wood debased his own coinage to increase his profits, but also to meet the sizable sum he would have to invest to buy two coining contracts, one for issues for Ireland, the other for the colonies.

Both contracts were granted by George I (ruled 1714–1727) in the summer of 1722. Under them, Wood received the exclusive privilege of striking Irish halfpennies and farthings, and American twopenny pieces, pennies, and halfpennies, over a fourteen-year period. The Irish issues were to be struck from copper, those for America from Bath metal—an alloy of 75 percent copper, 24.7 percent zinc, and 0.3 percent silver. Wood was allowed to coin up to three hundred sixty tons of money for Ireland, three hundred for the colonies.

In turn, Wood was obliged to render several hundred pounds a year to the king's comptroller and to the king himself. Then, too, there was the king's mistress, the Duchess of Kendal, to whom George had granted the right to sell the coinage contracts to the highest bidder. She did, and Wood found himself owing the duchess ten thousand pounds for the contracts.

His coins would have to be lightweight if he was to realize any profit from his labors. Never doubting the coins' acceptance in Ireland and America, they were summarily shipped, without their recipients' knowledge—and without their approval. The reaction was worst in Ireland. To

a proud people, such disregard of their opinion was but the latest outrage perpetrated on Catholic Ireland by Protestant England. Goaded in part by a series of brilliant satirical articles by Jonathan Swift, they angrily rejected the Hibernia coinage, and riots ensued. In August 1725 the Crown cancelled Wood's contract to make coppers for Ireland, in recompense for which he was to be awarded an annual pension of three thousand pounds for the next eight years.

But there was still America. The first Rosa Americana coins reached the colonies late in 1722, and met with varied reactions. This was particularly adverse in Boston: an emergency issue of penny, twopenny, and threepenny notes was printed on parchment, to prevent the circulation of Wood's hated lightweight coins in Massachusetts. While other areas were more accepting of the Rosa Americana pieces, the overall reception was unfavorable. The Crown did not revoke Wood's American contract, but he seems not to have exercised his rights under it after 1723. The production of the Rosa Americana coins had come to an end.

In retrospect, it is a shame Wood's American issues had so short a life. The coins were well struck at a private London mint with the latest equipment. Because their alloy was soft, the coins took sharp impressions from the dies, which were themselves carefully and artistically rendered. The piece illustrated is a twopenny coin, with designs typical of those seen on

Rosa Americana coinage. Twopence, 1723.

other coins in the series. George I's portrait graces the obverse, while the reverse has a crowned rose with the legend ROSA AMERICANA (which gave the series its name, and may also have been an attempt to flatter the colonists). The Latin motto at the bottom can be translated, "The useful with the pleasant"—referring to a coin that is both attractive and serviceable, a sad misjudgement as it so happened.

See also BATH METAL.

ROTATED DIES Dies which do not possess the obverse/reverse relationship or die axis intended by a mint.

The term has relevance only for machine-struck coinage, in which the dies are supposed to function in a precisely set, undeviating relationship to one another. Rotated dies can be the result of sloppy mint practice, in which dies are carelessly set in a coining press. Or the dies may have been correctly set, working their way loose—rotating—during the striking process. Coins struck from rotated dies were fairly common in the days of the screw press; they are less frequently encountered today. They qualify as a minor mint error, and are of some interest among specialists in that field.

See also DIE AXIS; ERROR.

RUBLE A basic Russian coin and unit of account since the Middle Ages.

The ruble began as an oblong block of silver, weighing approximately 200 grams. Such pieces were first cast at Novgorod, perhaps as early as the thirteenth century, and their production continued there and in other trading centers into the fifteenth century. By then, more orthodox forms of money were entering commerce, and the ruble became a unit of account. Two hundred dengi—small silver coins—equalled one ruble; with the introduction of the kopek in the sixteenth century, one hundred kopeks equalled one ruble. In

time the system expanded; the kopek became the lower unit in a Russian system of decimal coinage, and the ruble its upper one.

The first attempt to strike the ruble as a coin was in 1654, under Tsar Alexei Mikhailovich (ruled 1645–1676). Lacking previous experience with a large-sized coin, the Russians simply engraved new dies—the mounted figure of the tsar for an obverse, the imperial eagle for a reverse—and overstruck whatever foreign thalers they happened upon. These were the first Russian rubles that were coins, rather than ingots.

They were not a success. The thaler contained less than a ruble's worth of silver, and its value was downgraded accordingly. The value of the first ruble struck was established at sixty-four kopeks in 1655, and in 1659 the coin was demonetized and recalled. Until the early eighteenth century, the only coins in active circulation were the smaller kopeks and dengi. Peter the Great (ruled 1682–1725), however, effected dramatic changes. In 1700 he decreed a decimal coinage system: one hundred kopeks would equal one ruble, as before, but the ruble would henceforth be issued as a coin, with an essential and enduring place in the country's money system. And to ensure standardization of size and weight, and a pleasing design, the revived ruble and other coins would be struck by machinery, not by hand.

The new kopek (now fashioned of copper rather than silver) was introduced in

Ruble. *Russia, 1721.*

1704, as was the silver ruble. Many of the earliest rubles struck during Peter's reign were overstrikes. It was a way to simplify the coining process, and save time and money in the initial stages of the change.

The photograph shows one of Peter's later rubles, minted in 1721, the designs of which were copied until the Russian Empire's end. The coin is large, with a diameter of 41.5 millimeters, and heavy, weighing 27.1 grams. Later rubles diminished in size and weight, and the last issues, those of Nicholas II (ruled 1894–1917), measured about 34 millimeters and weighed 20 grams. The ruble's fineness, however, actually increased through the years, from 750 fine in the late eighteenth century to 900 fine at the beginning of the twentieth.

The ruble survived the Russian Revolution, even if the system that spawned it did not. Sporadically produced in silver in the early 1920s, it was reintroduced in an alloy of copper, nickel, and zinc in the early 1960s. One of its functions today is as a commemorative coin.

See also DECIMAL COINAGE; KOPEK; OVERSTRIKE; WIRE MONEY.

RUPEE An important silver coin of the Indian Subcontinent, first struck in Bengal during the tenure of the Mughal ruler Sher Shah (ruled A.H. 946–952; A.D. 1539–1545). His coins weighed about 11.7 grams, and measured approximately 30 millimeters. The rupee soon appeared elsewhere in India, as well as Ceylon, Mombasa, and other places, and in time dozens of states produced it.

Rupees fall into two major categories. In the first are those of purely native in-

Rupee.
Left: India (Mughals), A.H. 977 (A.D. 1569–1570).
Right: Portuguese India (Goa), 1839.

spiration. The coin on the left is such a piece, dated A.H. 977 (A.D. 1569–1570), and struck by another Mughal ruler, Jalal al din Akbar. It is probably from the city of Lahore. The specimen on the right is illustrative of rupees in the second category—those struck under European domination or inspired by Western models. This piece is from Goa, a Portuguese colony.

The British were for a time the rulers of the entire subcontinent. They too produced rupees, initially adhering to traditional Indian design elements, later adopting more Western ones. While the last century of British India saw rupees struck at Madras, Calcutta, Bombay, and Lahore, the coins were Western in their basic appearance.

When India regained independence in 1947 it retained the rupee as its monetary unit. National issues have been made from nickel or copper-nickel, however: here, as elsewhere, silver has disappeared as a coinage medium. The rupee is also the monetary unit of Pakistan, Ceylon (today Sri Lanka), and several of the region's smaller states.

See also BILINGUAL MONEY.

S

SANDBLAST PROOF A proof coin with a uniform, granular sheen.

Although the sandblast proof closely resembles the matte proof, its surfaces are somewhat rougher. The hazy surface is created after the coin is struck, and involves spraying the piece with a stream of fine sand in compressed air. The exact surfaces achieved vary with the fineness of the sand and the velocity of the spray.

The sandblast proof appeared around the turn of the twentieth century, and enjoyed a certain vogue in the United States and elsewhere until the mid-1930s. Walter

Sandblast proof. United States, Hawaiian Sesquicentennial half dollars, 1928. The coin on the left is an ordinary strike, while that on the right is a sandblast proof.

Breen, an outstanding specialist on proof coins, suggests the sandblast proof, like the matte proof, may have emanated from the difficulty of uniformly polishing those dies with the increasingly curved fields that were favored by early twentieth-century coin designers. The sandblast proof was not particularly popular with collectors of the day, and the technique is used now only for some medals.

The photograph shows two United States commemorative coins of 1928, celebrating the sesquicentennial of Hawaii's discovery by Captain James Cook. The issue was small, with barely ten thousand coins minted. The piece on the left is a normal or "business" strike, of which 9,958 were made. The coin on the right is one of fifty sandblast proofs that were struck. The difference between the coins' surfaces are obvious.

See also FROSTED PROOF; MATTE PROOF; PROOF.

SASH Part of a decoration, and a variant of the ribbon.

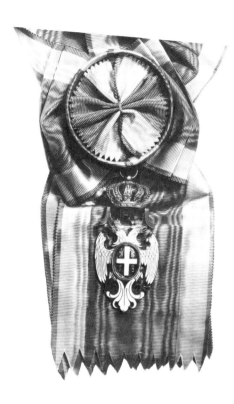

Sash. *Serbia, Order of the White Eagle (civil), sash and badge.*

The sash is far broader than the ribbon, and is made to be worn over one shoulder, with its two ends joining at the waist, from which a badge is customarily suspended. (The sash may or may not have a rosette of the same material.) Chivalric and civil orders use the sash, and essentially its development parallels that of the ordinary ribbon. Its colors, or combinations of colors, are distinctive, enabling a ready identification of the order.

The illustration shows a typical sash with an attached badge. This one has a rosette, with alternate stripes of red and light blue. Its order is that of the White Eagle, one of the highest awards of the former kingdom of Serbia.

See also BADGE; DECORATION; ORDER; RIBBON.

SCEAT An Anglo-Saxon silver coin, predecessor of the penny, that was most probably introduced sometime between 680 and 700, serving as the basic English coin for the next century.

The sceat (plural sceattas) grew from a modest increase in trade in the seventh and eighth centuries, and its development was clearly influenced by Merovingian France. The Merovingians had retained an old Roman coin, the tremissis, and the concept of this small gold coin crossed the Channel to England in the early seventh century. This English gold coinage was never produced in quantity, and ended about 675. Some of the English tremisses had been struck in an alloy of gold and silver in which silver came to dominate, and it appears it was decided to remove gold from the coinage and to strike a purely silver coin—the sceat. This change paralleled events in France, where the Merovingians had shifted to the production of small silver coins, ancestors of the Frankish denier, to be seen in the next century.

We tend to associate sceattas with England, but they were struck in several other places as well, particularly on the Frisian coast. Hoard evidence indicates English sceattas served well as trade coins, and were widely imitated by others in northwestern Europe. The typical sceat weighed about 20 grains or 1.3 grams, and measured about 12 millimeters in diame-

Sceat.
Left: England, late seventh–late eighth century.
Right: Continent, late seventh–late eighth century.

ter. Initially its silver content was good, and its weight of 1.3 grams was eventually adopted for the English penny and the Frankish denier.

The repertoire of designs for sceattas was borrowed from the Romans and barbarians alike. The sceat on the left, based on a fourth-century Roman prototype, reveals a crude head on the obverse and a standard, or altar, on the reverse. This sceat is English. The piece on the right originated on the Continent, and shows strong Teutonic qualities. It portrays a mythical animal on one side, a bird on the other.

In time, the sceat declined in weight and fineness, and in southern England was replaced by the new penny late in the eighth century. In northern England, however, it was more tenacious; a variant composed of debased silver—later of pure copper or brass—was struck in York until that city's capture by the Vikings in 867. This coin is referred to as a styca.

See also BARBAROUS IMITATIONS; DENIER; PENNY; STYCA; TREMISSIS.

SCHAUTHALER An early thaler which had a semi-medallic quality.

The coin was struck for commemorative purposes rather than general circulation; a center for its production was Austria during the sixteenth century.

Both the artistry and physical characteristics of the schauthaler distinguished it from ordinary coins. The piece illustrated, for example, measures a full 53 millime-

ters in diameter and weighs nearly 40 grams; a circulating thaler of the same period measured only 42 millimeters and weighed about 31 grams. This particular schauthaler dates from 1541, during the time of Austria's Ferdinand I (ruled 1521–1564). The obverse bears an equestrian portrait of the monarch, while the reverse features a splendid heraldic eagle with a coat of arms. The obverse and reverse legends enumerate the lands over which Ferdinand ruled.

The schauthaler presents numismatists with something of a dilemma. A coin this size would have to have been struck by machinery. Yet at the time, the screw press had not been introduced in Austria. Nor was the roller press used: coins struck with that device "feel" different than this piece, and, furthermore, the roller press was not used in Austria until the 1560s. How, then, was the coin struck? One possibility is a gravity or drop press, which worked something like a guillotine—a heavy weight was dropped from the top of a tall, narrow frame, forcing the upper die downward. Such a press would have subjected dies to excessive punishment, but it would have exerted sufficient force to impress a coin of this size. It is known that such presses did see limited use in the sixteenth century, and one of their products might well have been the schauthaler.

See also COMMEMORATIVE; MEDAL; THALER.

Schauthaler. Austria, 1541.

SCHEIDEMÜNZEN Coins with an actual value considerably less than the stated one, due to their mixed metallic composition.

Scheidemünzen (German for "small change") are usually fashioned from a mixture of silver and base metals, such as copper and tin. Hence scheidemünzen can be roughly categorized as billon coinage. It is probably wisest, however, to restrict the term to those German issues of the eighteenth and nineteenth centuries which

Scheidemünzen. Prussia, 2½ silber groschen, 1842.

often carry the word itself on their reverses.

The piece illustrated is a Prussian 2½ silber groschen of 1842. Outwardly, the coin looks silver, but in fact, its legal silver content was only 37.5 percent, the remainder being base metal. A companion silber groschen contained only 22 percent silver. This type of coinage was particularly common in the early and middle years of the nineteenth century. With the establishment of the German Empire in 1871, and the introduction of silver coins struck at a fineness of 900, the manufacture of scheidemünzen ended.

See also BILLON.

SCHILLING A northern German silver coin popular from the fifteenth through nineteenth centuries.

The schilling was introduced in 1432 by six member cities of the Hanseatic League. As the product of a trading confederation, the schilling represented an attempt to produce an easily traded coin

Schilling. Lübeck, 1430s.

having a consistent weight and fineness wherever it was issued.

Its usefulness was quickly proven, and it was soon copied by other German states. Rulers in Swabia issued schilling, as did those in Saxony, Pomerania, and a number of other places. These early schilling were often issued by the member states of a monetary convention, in which case designs were very similar. The schilling in the illustration is from Lübeck, one of the Hanseatic cities that introduced the denomination in the 1430s. Here we see the obverse; the legend gives the town's name, and the local badge—a double-headed eagle—forms the coin's central obverse type. The reverse shows a cross. Hamburg, also a member of the Hanseatic League, introduced a schilling of its own about the same time, retaining the cross design for the reverse, but placing its own name and arms on the obverse. These coins make it clear their minters wished to accomplish two things at once—to strike interchangeable trading coins, and at the same time satisfy local pride. The Lübeck schilling is about 26 millimeters in diameter and weighs 2.34 grams, statistics common to many of the period's schilling.

The schilling was later superseded by larger silver coins, notably the thaler. Its silver content declined, and the last schilling, struck in 1851 in the free city of Hamburg, were of billon. In a few years, the schilling, groschen, thaler, and kreuzer alike would be replaced by a single coin, the mark.

See also TRADE COINS.

SCREW PRESS The pre-eminent coining machine of early modern times.

Although the screw press was originally designed to create medals and other large objects, its most significant application was in the creation of money, where it held sway for well over two hundred years.

Credit for its invention is given to Donato Bramante (1444–1514), an architect who worked in Rome about 1500 and played a major role in the design of St. Peter's. He also served as seal-master to the Pope, and in that role devised a machine to strike the heavy lead papal bulls. Later used to strike medals, the machine had upper and lower dies in a fixed relationship to one another, which impressed a planchet by a downward, squeezing motion applied by a screw—and not by the familiar hand-hammering motion. Bramante's machine was, in fact, the first screw press, but while of considerable consequence, it was not as innovative as it might seem: both the wine press and early printing press worked on the same principle. All the same, it was a welcome addition to the array of coining tools.

For its original users it was an excellent way to produce medals in high relief; for the governments and their coiners who were to use it later, it was a means to strike more coins of a larger size and higher value than could be struck with the old, hand-hammering method. And eventually it was discovered that many elements of the coin dies could also be produced with a screw press, thereby ensuring standardization of dies (a protection against counterfeiting) and faster die production. Hence more coins: hence more wealth.

By all that is logical, Europe's nations

should have welcomed and adopted the screw press forthwith. In practice, they did not. Coiners were convinced the new machine would displace them, and they did not fancy the prospect of being without work. France under Henry II (ruled 1547–1559) is illustrative. In 1550, it was learned that a goldsmith of Augsburg, Germany had devised a coin-making machine—actually an improved screw press —together with a rolling mill and a device to stamp blanks. They were ordered and installed at the Paris mint, where they immediately met with vociferous opposition from the coiners. Used only briefly to strike silver coins, the screw press was then relegated to the minting of medals, jetons, and copper coins, objects the coiners thought unworthy of their attention.

A decade later history repeated itself. In 1561, machines on the French model were installed at the London mint by Eloi Mestrell, a former employee of the Paris mint. Again, they encountered stiff opposition; not only did the machines threaten moneyers' employment, they were inefficient and costly—or so it was said. In 1572, England abandoned them, and Mestrell himself passed from the scene soon after, being hanged for counterfeiting in 1578. Despite persistent attempts to reinstall the screw press and other machines in both

Screw press. A screw press at work, late eighteenth century. (From Diderot's *L'Encyclopédie*, 1776. Courtesy of the Library of the American Numismatic Society, New York)

countries, hammered coinage continued in France until the 1640s, and was not abolished in England until 1662.

Elsewhere, the screw press was more welcome. It was used in scattered sections of Scandinavia, Italy, and Germany (where it competed with the rocker and roller presses) prior to 1600, and by 1700 was paramount throughout most of Europe; by 1750 it was displacing hammered coinage in the Americas.

The screw press in our illustration is from the 1776 edition of Diderot's *Encyclopédie*. Let us examine this machine more closely. It took five men to operate it—two on each end of a weighted iron bar, a fifth sitting in a recess in front of the press. This man's task was to insert planchets and remove the finished coins; the other four tugged on leather straps attached to the weighted bar. The bar was attached to a heavy iron screw, which drove the upper die down toward the lower one. The upper die was not an integral part of the screw; rather, it was attached to a sleeve so it could be raised or depressed in a particular position relative to the lower die. The lower die was fixed to an anvil.

Coining began. The man in charge of the planchets placed one on the lower die: the two men on one end of the bar pulled it toward them, causing the planchet to receive a simultaneous impression of the obverse and reverse dies. The two men on the other end of the arm then pulled it, thus raising the screw and upper die. The coin was then removed, and another planchet inserted. Primitive though it was, this method was fairly rapid: a good team of coiners could produce several dozen small pieces per minute. It was also hard labor, and perilous, at least for the layer-on, who could easily lose a finger if he was not adept.

The heyday of the screw press was between 1750 and 1790. By 1750 it had essentially eliminated it rivals; by 1790, steam-powered machinery was being conceived, and in time eliminated the screw press. The United States abandoned the machine in 1836 in favor of steam, as had Europe before it; Latin America did so later in the century.

See also MACHINE-STRUCK COINAGE; ROCKER PRESS; ROLLER PRESS.

SCRIP Paper currency in the United States and Canada, issued as a substitute for ordinary money by individuals, businesses, and towns.

Scrip is usually printed in denominations of one dollar or less, and is redeemable for a dollar-amount of goods rather than actual currency. Scrip and notgeld share many traits, enough to make it safe to describe scrip as a North American paper version of notgeld.

It is printed and issued when money is scarce, for whatever reason. In the case of the piece illustrated, a Canadian issue of 1837, the panic and depression then gripping the United States affected Cananda as well. People took their money from circulation, and merchants produced scrip, redeemable in real currency, as they were also doing in the United States. This note is of particular interest as it bears several denominations—sixty sous, one écu, two shillings sixpence, and half a dollar. Canada eventually adopted the dollar as the unit of exchange, but in the 1830s its currency system was obviously still in flux.

Scrip can also be the consequence of war. In the United States, both North and

Scrip. *Canada, Distillerie de St. Denis, 60 sous, 1837.*

South issued an abundance of scrip during the Civil War, which saw the widespread hoarding of money. The year 1862 marked a high point in the North's printing of scrip, coinciding, not accidentally, with Northerners' doubt of emerging victorious.

In the twentieth century, scrip was most widely issued in the 1930s, particularly during 1933–1936. It was known as Depression scrip, born as it was of the economic paralysis of those years. Most of this scrip was printed in the United States, a good deal in cities and towns which took currency matters into their own hands in the absence of an effective national policy. Unlike its 1830s counterpart, this scrip was frequently issued in denominations of more than one dollar.

Scrip can also refer to tokens issued by coal mines and sutlers, a confusion that would not exist if the word was restricted to emergency paper money.

See also Emergency money; Notgeld; Shinplaster; Sutlers' checks.

SCYPHATE COINAGE

Coinage deliberately struck to resemble a shallow bowl, with convex obverses and concave reverses.

Its semblance is achieved by using a concave die for the obverse, a convex one for the reverse. A coin of the same general appearance may be *accidentally* produced using flat dies, in which case it is called a cupped coin, and is a spectacular mint error.

Scyphate coins may have existed as early as the second century B.C., and they are known to have been used in a number of places, including India, whose ramatankas fall into the category. But the most noted examples are from the Byzantine Empire, where the shape was adopted under Constantine IX (ruled 1042–1055), to distinguish heavy gold coins from lighter ones. The style was later extended to silver and base-metal issues as well, and

Scyphate coinage. Byzantine Empire, Constantine IX, scyphate histamenon, 1042–1055.

it remained a feature of Byzantine coinage for the next three and a half centuries. Scyphate coinage never completely displaced regular, flat coinage, and coins of both types were concurrently struck.

The coin portrayed is a scyphate histamenon of Constantine IX. The convex obverse depicts a seated figure of Christ, while the emperor is seen in full regalia on the concave reverse. These elements and their relative placement were common to much scyphate coinage of the Byzantines. The coin is broad and fairly thin, measuring about 29 millimeters in diameter but weighing less than 4.5 grams.

Several adjacent areas under Byzantine influence also struck scyphate coinage, among them Cyprus and Serbia. It should be noted that the term *scyphate* was not used by the Byzantines to describe these coins (histamena was), nor did they consider it synonymous with "concave." The word may have had Arabic origins, referring to a coin with a wide border; one could argue that it was used for histamena, which had such borders, to distinguish them from the lighter tetartera, which did not. It might be advisable to substitute the term cup-shaped for "scyphate."

See also Cupped coin; Solidus; Tetarteron.

SEAL

A device with a design that can be imparted in relief on a soft, tenacious substance such as clay or wax.

Seals proclaim ownership, official

Seal.
Left: A Sassanian agate seal.
Right: Its plaster of paris impression.

duced in 1940 on notes issued by the Bank of England, and has grown in popularity over the past two decades. The one illustrated appears as part of a Thai ten-baht note of 1969. The note also carries an elaborate watermark, another useful security measure.

See also COUNTERFEIT; WATERMARK.

guarantee, or protection, and are one of the oldest artifacts of civilized life. The Sumerians used them, as did the Egyptians, Greeks, Romans, and later peoples, and they are still with us.

For numismatics, seals have a particular significance. Many early ones were, in effect, governmental guarantees. When people first struck coins, what could be more natural than to use a seal to guarantee the purity and correct weight of the metal used in the coin? Hence, coining seals were carved from cylinders of hard metal, and these seals are known as dies.

See also ARCHAIC COINAGE; DIE; HAMMERED COINAGE.

SECURITY THREAD A colored thread running through the paper of a modern note from top to bottom, intended as an anti-counterfeiting device.

The security thread is the descendant of several earlier attempts to make the paper used for money immune to counterfeiting. Multicolor threads or bands were tried, as were small, variously colored paper dots. All were added *to* the paper— not printed on it—to give the material a "feel" or depth not found on ordinary paper. Of course, as bills become worn, these minor elements were harder to detect, and deterred forgery less effectively, which may be why governments adopted the security thread. It is obvious to sight and touch even after extensive circulation.

The security thread was first intro-

Security thread. *Thailand, 10 baht, 1969 (detail).*

SEDE VACANTE COINAGE Coins struck during a break in a ruling (usually ecclesiastical) succession; the term is most frequently used for coins minted in the period between one Pope's death and another's election.

The tradition harks back to 1521, and the death of Pope Leo X. The Treasurer of the Holy See, Cardinal Francesco Armellini, struck coins to commemorate the vacancy of the papal throne. Minted in gold and silver, they were struck through December and until early January, when

Sede Vacante coinage. *Papal States, scudo d'oro,* 1721.

the selection of a new Pope brought a halt to their production. Cardinal Armellini's coins had obverses which substituted his arms for that of the late Pope, while the legend SEDE VACANTE replaced the papal titles. The reverses bore religious figures, as did most papal coinage.

Sede Vacante coinage became a fixture of papal numismatics. Issued for most papal interregna since the 1520s, the latest examples of the coin are from the time following the death of John Paul I in 1978. The coin illustrated is a gold scudo of the 1721 interregnum. The obverse carries the Treasurer's arms as do all Sede Vacante coins, but the reverse bears a dove, symbol of the Holy Spirit. This was the design repeated on most later coins of the series.

Sede Vacante coinage was not restricted to Rome. Various bishoprics, archbishoprics, and other church bodies with temporal powers also struck them. A series of very large, ornate coins of this type, struck in Germany in the seventeenth and eighteenth centuries, and known as Vikariatsthalers, are among the most spectacular commemorative coins ever produced.

See also COMMEMORATIVE.

SENATORIAL COINS A term for Roman imperial coins struck under the nominal authority of the Roman Senate, and distinguished by the letters SC, the abbreviation for *Senatus Consulto* ("By Decree of the Senate"), seen either in the field or the exergue of the reverse.

Senatorial coins were those at the lower end of the imperial money spectrum and included the as and its subdivisions, the semis and quadrans, as well as its multiples, the dupondius and sestertius. All such coins had a base-metal composition, with copper used for some, *orichalcum* or brass for others. There was never an attempt to put precious metal coinage under the purview of the Senate, which, in fact, had little or no real control over the composition and designs of Senatorial coinage either.

Augustus achieved sole power in 31 B.C., and introduced the Senatorial pieces a few years later. While a monarch in fact, he was not one in name: he was forced to accommodate the fiction that Rome remained a republic, in which he was merely the first citizen among equals, and that his power was shared with others. Hence, some Roman provinces were under Augustus's control, while others were the concern of the Senate—some coins were demonstrably struck by the prince, others by the Senate. In reality, of course, the emperor decided on composition and design, but tradition was observed and a sense of continuity retained.

Augustus and his successors sanctioned Senatorial coinage for the next three hundred years. The SC mark was rarely as predominant as it is on our illustration, a copper quadrans struck around 9 B.C., but it was always present in large or small letters, depending on the require-

Senatorial coins. *Roman Empire, Augustus, quadrans, c.* 9 B.C.

ments of the denomination and its design. The mark's position on coins was linked to the fate of the coins themselves: when large, base-metal coins disappeared in the late third century A.D., so did the initials. When Diocletian reintroduced a large, base coin—the follis—his issues no longer bore the SC initials; by then, the emperor was a semi-divine monarch with no need to continue the sham of shared political control.

The term Senatorial coin is fading from usage; originally meant to distinguish copper and brass imperial coins from gold and silver ones, it could be used with equal justification for all republican issues. Today's scholars, however, tend to designate Roman coins by their real names (insofar as they are known), and avoid all-embracing terms.

See also ABBREVIATION; AS; DUPONDIUS; SESTERTIUS.

SERRATED COINS
Coins with edges indented like the teeth of a saw.

Serrated coins were occasionally minted by the later Greeks, but the most typical ones are Roman republican silver denarii of the second and first centuries B.C.

In Rome the first serrated coins were fashioned by the moneyer Caius Talna, who worked between about 165 and 150 B.C. His seem to have been an isolated attempt, for the next serrated denarii did not appear until about 118 B.C. This rather large issue was something of a com-

Serrated coins. Roman Republic, serrate denarius, c. 106 B.C.

memorative, celebrating the foundation of the colony of Narbo (the modern Narbonne) in southern Gaul. Serrated coins continued to be produced sporadically in the last decade of the second century (our specimen dates from that period, having been minted in or around 106 B.C) down to the 60s of the first, after which they fell from favor. Serrated coinage was never part of the imperial series.

Before striking, serrated coins were apparently chisel-notched at some twenty or more points around their circumference. The task was arduous, and slowed the entire coining process. If moneyers took the time and trouble, they must have had good reason. Perhaps the serrated edge was meant as an anti-counterfeiting device, in an age of plated counterfeits. If so, it failed, as counterfeiters had only to silver-plate serrated counterfeits. It has also been suggested that serrated coins were intended for non-Italian circulation (the pieces celebrating Narbo might lend some credence to this idea), but there is no proof that such was the case. Perhaps it is wiser to simply accept this coinage as one of the many early attempts to explore the boundaries and potentials of coinage itself.

See also DENARIUS; DIE-STRUCK COUNTERFEIT; PLATED COINAGE.

SESTERTIUS
A small silver coin of the Roman Republic; later, a large *orichalcum* coin of the early Roman Empire.

The silver sestertius, with a value of two-and-one-half asses, was introduced around 211 B.C. Like the denarius and quinarius, it bore an obverse head of the goddess Roma and a reverse depiction of the *Dioscuri* (divine patrons of the city of Rome) on horseback. The word ROMA appeared beneath the riders, while a mark of value, expressed in asses, occupied the obverse field behind Roma's head—IIS.

The silver sestertius was produced irregularly and in small quantity, never quite achieving the popularity of the other coins in the series. If the first issue of these coins was about 211 B.C., the second issue did not appear until about 90 B.C.; a third was released between 49 and 44 B.C., after which its production was suspended. These last silver sestertii were minted under the dictatorship of Gaius Julius Caesar. In time, his great-nephew, Octavian, would serve as Rome's first emperor and revive the denomination in a dramatic new form, ensuring its production and circulation for the next three centuries.

Octavian assumed mastery of the Roman world in 31 B.C., at the end of the republican civil wars. When he established one-man rule, the machinery of the state was in disarray. In no area were the problems greater than in Rome's monetary supply, where the scarcity of small change had reached a dangerous level. No official base-metal coins had been minted for over half a century, and new ones were desperately required for daily commerce. About 23 B.C., Octavian, now called Augustus, began providing a host of copper and brass coins, ranging in value from a fourth to a sixty-fourth of a denarius. This reform was designed as much for his benefit as that of his subjects: he would be esteemed in the business world.

Augustus's sestertius weighed about 25 grams, and measured some 39 millimeters in diameter. The coin's obverse featured an oak wreath between branches of laurel, with a legend referring to the honors bestowed on the emperor in 27 B.C. (the year he was voted the title "Augustus" by the Roman Senate). The reverse used a sizable SC as a central type, surrounded by the names of its coiners. These last soon disappeared, but the SC, for *Senatus Consulto* ("By Decree of the Senate")—the body theoretically responsible for the coin—was retained.

Most of Augustus's sestertii were struck close to the reform date of 23 B.C. The denomination would not be a continuing feature of Roman coinage until Augustus was succeeded by Tiberius (ruled

A.D. 14–37), at which time the coin's commemorative and celebratory possibilities were being realized. Several decades later they blossomed.

The sestertius is one of the most impressive coins in the Roman series; it is also the one most laden with propaganda. Regularly used to proclaim imperial virtues, triumphs, and accomplishments, sestertii serve as an important key to our understanding of the Roman mind.

It must be remembered that the emperor did not rule by divine right, but by the sufferance of his subjects. Therefore, they had to be convinced he was the best man for the position, and should be retained. Lacking our modern media with which to proselytize, emperors used what was at hand, including coinage. It cost no more to strike coins with propaganda than it did other types, and as they circulated, they carried their message over thousands of miles. The sestertius's impressive size made it an ideal propaganda vehicle, while its relatively low value made it accessible to multitudes. For modern numismatists, the sestertius offers the best and most artistic glimpse of the Roman past they are likely to find.

The sestertius in the photograph, dating from late in the reign of Nero (ruled 54–68), is a case in point. On the obverse is a splendid if unflattering portrait of the emperor, while on the reverse are two mounted horsemen flanked by the letters SC. The horseman on the left is Nero, and the inscription in the exergue reads DECVRSIO: Nero had participated in military maneuvers and wanted it known to

Sestertius. Roman Empire, Nero, A.D. 64–66.

his people. This coin weighs 24.7 grams, and measures 37 millimeters in diameter.

Art on the sestertius was at its finest during the late first and early second centuries A.D. The coins were well struck, almost medallic in nature, and their subject matter was virtually limitless. In time, the sestertius suffered the fate of the as and others in the Roman series—metallic content diminished, as did artistry and spontaneity. The last sestertii may have been struck under the emperor Postumus (ruled 260–268), but the coin had lost its importance in the Roman monetary system after 250.

See also As; DENARIUS; DUPONDIUS; SENATORIAL COINS.

SHEKEL Originally a Near Eastern weight for gold and silver; later, a coin.

The weight of the shekel varied: the coinages of Tyre and Sidon were postulated on a shekel weighing some 7 grams, while Hebrew issues, which were struck at a much later period, weighed about twice that.

When we think of the word shekel, we often imagine a Jewish coin. Yet the Jewish shekel was a late development, and was struck for only a short period of time—a few years in the first century A.D., a few more in the second.

In both instances, it sprang from the Jews' resistance to the power of Rome, which ruled Judea through a series of tyrannical procurators until the revolt in A.D. 66. A short-lived independent republic was established, and the Romans were temporarily ejected. The Roman emperor Nero (ruled A.D. 54–68) dispatched his general Vespasian to quell the rebellion, known to history as the First Revolt. This revolt produced a fair quantity of copper and silver coinage, including Judea's first coined shekel, one of which is shown. Its designs are simple, in part because of religious strictures, in part because the Jews were inexperienced in coining. The ob-

Shekel. *Judea, shekel of the First Revolt, Year Two* (A.D. 67).

verse depicts a sacred chalice with the legend "shekel Israel." The letters above the chalice reveal the coin's date, the second year of independence, or A.D. 67. The reverse carries a stem with three flowers, probably meant to represent pomegranates, and the legend "Jerusalem the Holy." This coin measures 24 millimeters and weighs 13.92 grams.

With the end of the First Revolt, the land settled into an uneasy peace. But in 132, Jewish discontent with Roman rule led to another full-scale revolt under Simon Bar-Kochba. In 135, Jerusalem was again captured by the Romans, who barred the Jews, forcing them to disperse throughout the world. This Second Revolt also spawned shekels, although in a smaller quantity. Their obverse types abounded with religious significance—a depiction of the Temple of Jerusalem with the screen of the Tabernacle and the Ark of the Covenant. The reverses had a bundle of twigs, called a *lulab*.

The shekels were struck over earlier silver coins, indicating the emergency conditions under which they were created; dated ones are known for the first two years of the Second Revolt.

When the modern State of Israel was established in 1948, its government tended to reproduce the coinage types of the First and Second Revolts. The pomegranate device seen on shekels has appeared on several modern Israeli coins, and in the spring of 1980 the denomination itself was revived: it is now the official monetary unit of the State of Israel.

See also OVERSTRIKE; TALENT.

Shinplaster. An advertisement for shinplasters, c. 1862.

SHINPLASTER A term of derision for a number of small United States or Canadian notes of limited or depreciated value.

Writing in 1859, John Bartlett observed that the term was born during the American Revolution when soldiers found that the small notes of the Continental Congress, while of little value as a medium of exchange, served spendidly to bandage leg wounds. Hence, smallness and limited values are characteristics of shinplasters in general. For a while the term disappeared from the vernacular, but it was revived about 1837 to describe notes for fractions of a dollar, issued by private bankers and others during the period's financial crisis. It was later applied to fractional currency of the Civil War, as well as to private scrip of the same years.

The illustration shows a curious lithographed note, probably dating from 1862. It is not a shinplaster, but rather an advertisement *for* shinplasters, conceived by an enterprising printer named Ferdinand Meyer. Meyer's firm was located in New York City, and, as advertised, he provided many of the city's small-denomination private notes during the war: in fact, his products were used throughout New York State and beyond.

Shinplaster also refers to Canadian scrip of the 1830s and later official fractional currency. The term's popularity has waned in both countries.

See also CONTINENTAL CURRENCY; FRACTIONAL CURRENCY; SCRIP.

SIEGE PIECE An emergency coin or bill, issued by authorities in a city or town surrounded by hostile forces, and thus cut off from the standard monetary supply.

The necessity for siege pieces (or obsidional money, as they are also known) sprang from the nature of early modern warfare. Much of it was static, with each side firmly entrenched. Defenders waited for attackers to lose their morale and retire; attackers, on the other hand, waited for the defenders to starve. Siege warfare was natural to an age in which forts and walled cities proved stronger than any firepower that could be used against them. The sixteenth and seventeenth centuries in particular were years of endemic wars, many with Catholics pitted against Protestants. These wars of religion influenced the geographical origin of siege pieces: numbers came from the Low Countries and Germany, battlegrounds between Christianity's contending factions.

Our first illustration shows one such siege piece. It is a twenty-eight-stuiver "coin" from the besieged Dutch city of Leyden, made in 1574. Similar to paper money, it was embossed on pigskin rather than stamped in metal. Its real value was far less than its stated one, a general rule for siege pieces.

Our second siege piece illustrates the fact that precious metal, if available for this kind of emergency money, can be used in almost any form. Dies can be cut and round coins struck; or the coins may simply start out as square or lozenge-shaped planchets, as with klippe pieces. In

Siege piece.
Left: Leyden, Netherlands, 28 stuiver, 1574.
Right: Scarborough, England, 2 shillings, 1645.

the case of our second illustration, however, the metal was used as it was found: this piece, a two-shilling coin from Scarborough, England, began as a silver spoon. It was separated from its handle, slightly flattened, struck with a royal hallmark, the value, and a castle device, and put into circulation. No attempt was made to fashion a round coin or to engrave decent dies, the royalist defenders of Scarborough having no time for such niceties.

The issue of siege pieces continued until after 1800. There were several such emissions, both of coins and paper money, during the Napoleonic Wars (1792–1815), but siege money declined rapidly after that, as the nature of warfare changed. Increased firepower made fortresses and walls more vulnerable to direct assault, and the siege became increasingly unnecessary. Nevertheless, the British defenders of the South African town of Mafeking found they had to issue siege money, in the form of promissory notes, as late as 1900.

See also EMERGENCY MONEY; KLIPPE; NECESSITY MONEY.

SIGLOS   The dominant silver coin of the Persian Empire, minted in quantity from the late sixth to the late fourth centuries B.C.; it seems to have existed in a fixed

relationship with the gold daric, in which twenty sigloi equalled one daric.

The siglos was noted for the extreme conservatism of its design and execution. The first sigloi seem to have been introduced about 515 B.C., and the style, module, execution, and relationship to gold all borrowed generously from Lydia, conquered by the Persians in 546; the imitation is most immediately noticed in the coin's fabric. In essence, it is a bean-shaped lump of silver, impressed with a crude figure on the obverse, while the reverse bears the mark of the punch used to drive the silver lump into the obverse die —common attributes on archaic coinage wherever it was produced. What is uncommon, and remarkable, is that the Persians retained this form for sigloi and darics several hundred years after it was discarded elsewhere. In short, once Persian imperial coinage had appropriated archaic styles and techniques, it progressed no further.

Not only were the designs on Persian sigloi static; their number was extremely limited. Their reverse "design" consisted of a rough punch mark. Their obverses always bore a portrayal of the monarch, in whole or part. Invariably he is seen in one of three poses: at half length, shooting with his bow, or running with a bow and spear. The obverse designs lack legends or inscriptions, making the coins of one monarch difficult to distinguish from those of another. Any dating of Persian sigloi and darics must be based on hoard evidence, which remains inconclusive.

Siglos. *Persian Empire, fifth century* B.C.

The siglos's conservatism simply mirrors the society's conservatism. The Persians conceived of coinage exclusively as a tool of trade. It mattered not at all whether coins were aesthetically pleasing, only that they circulated easily; for this reason, the weight and fineness of Persian coins were carefully controlled. The siglos illustrated measures 16 millimeters by 13, and weighs a bit over 5.6 grams. This is exactly what it should weigh, and what its counterparts weighed until the fourth century. The silver content of this coin is high: the siglos's silver purity would also be retained until the end of the series.

Sigloi were struck in the millions over a period of nearly two centuries. The old Lydian mint at Sardis may have produced most of them, and it has been suggested they were intended for use in the western provinces of the Persian Empire rather than in the central or eastern ones. The series ended in 331 B.C. with the conquest of the Persian Empire by Alexander the Great.

See also ARCHAIC COINAGE; DARIC; HOARD; TRADE COINS.

SILIQUA A term for a particular late Roman and early Byzantine silver coin.

The coin's origins can be traced to Diocletian's monetary reforms of the 290s (he ruled 284–305), which were designed to phase out bad coins and introduce good ones. For silver, this meant introducing a small coin with a theoretical weight of ¹⁄₉₆ of a Roman pound (about 3.4 grams). In practice, the weight was seldom attained, and most of the new coins weighed closer to 3.2 grams. Although in a sense these coins were a revival of the earlier denarius, their exact value and place in the new monetary system are not known. The coin may have been valued at about ¹⁄₂₄ of an aureus, and its popular, though not necessarily official, name *may* have been a siliqua; this is supported by certain contemporary evidence. We use the term

Siliqua. Roman Empire, Procopius, A.D. 365–366.

here for the sake of convenience, and conformity to numismatic practice.

Production of the siliqua temporarily ceased about 310, but the coin remained in circulation, and minting of it was revived about 325 under Constantine the Great (ruled 306–337). Its weight then was slightly over 3.1 grams, and it was struck in almost pure silver, standards that were retained for some twenty years. Types were limited: profile portraits of the rulers dominated the obverses, while reverse designs featured a limited number of allegorical figures, in common with other coins of the period. At some time in the late 350s, the siliqua's weight was reduced to 2.2 grams; this "light" siliqua is far more familiar than its "heavy" predecessor, and it played a vital role in the currency system of the late fourth century—at least according to evidence from hoards. Although its production later fell off drastically, it appeared occasionally until the early seventh century, outlasting the Western Roman Empire.

The coin illustrated is a "light" siliqua, a product of the Constantinople mint under the usurper Procopius (ruled 365–366). The head of the would-be emperor adorns the obverse, and is seen with the diadem and mantle befitting the semi-divine status claimed by the empire's leader. The reverse carries a simple wreath with the inscription VOT V, a reference to Procopius's having taken the *vota suscepta*, the imperial vows, to inaugurate his reign.

The issue of siliquae and other silver coins virtually ceased in the Roman West after 400. In the East the Byzantines continued to coin the siliqua with some regularity in the sixth and early seventh centuries, when it seems to have been valued at half a miliaresion.

See also CENTENIONALIS; MILIARENSIS.

SILVER CERTIFICATE Once a very popular form of United States paper money, redeemable in silver upon the bearer's demand.

The silver certificate originated with the Bland-Allison Act of February 28, 1878, which also introduced the Morgan dollar. Dollar coinage was resumed to satisfy western silver mine interests; the addition of a paper currency, redeemable in the new coins, would make it possible to replace some existing American certificates of indebtedness such as the national bank notes, and at the same time supply the monetary needs of a growing economy.

The first silver certificates were those of the 1878 and 1880 series. Printed in denominations ranging from ten to one thousand dollars, they had reverses printed in black to distinguish them from other paper currency. Legal tender and national bank notes still served for denominations under ten dollars; silver certificates did not appear in one-, two-, or five-dollar denominations until 1886, when an act passed on August 4 of that year permitted their issue.

The silver certificate was always a well-printed note. It displayed vignettes of famous Americans, patriotic scenes, and allegorical figures. The five-dollar note of the 1886 series actually depicts the five silver dollars for which it could be exchanged. The most artistic silver certificates—indeed, perhaps the most beautiful of all federal notes—are the "educational notes" of the 1896 series; the dollar member of the group is shown in our illustration. The bill has a curious "filled in" quality not ordinarily seen on United States paper: every square centimeter of the face is occupied by engraving of extraordinary depth and quality. The vignette is "History Instructing Youth," hence the term "educational note." The reverse, by then printed in dark green, bears vignettes of George and Martha Washington, fancy scrollwork, etc. No other American note has ever attained its beauty; indeed, few have even tried to.

Later issues of silver certificates were in accord with the nation's circulating paper money. Under the direction of President Hoover, the size of American paper money, including silver certificates, was reduced in 1929. In the same year designs were also standardized, and silver certificates were distinguishable from Federal Reserve and other notes chiefly by the color of their seals and serial numbers (dark blue). By this time, the number of silver certificate denominations had been drastically reduced, and would be further curtailed. After 1953 the only silver certificates printed were of the one-dollar denomination, and these, too, were discontinued in the 1960s for new Federal Reserve notes.

See also FEDERAL RESERVE NOTE; LEGAL TENDER NOTE; MORGAN DOLLAR; NATIONAL BANK NOTE.

Silver certificate. United States, dollar, series of 1896.

Slug. San Francisco, California, United States
Assay Office of Gold, 50 dollars, 1852.

SLUG Any of a number of round or octagonal fifty-dollar gold pieces issued in California in the early and middle 1850s.

The slug seen in the illustration is a behemoth which weighs almost 83.5 grams, and measures nearly 45 millimeters across at its widest point. It was produced by the United States Assay Office of Gold (a misleading name, for the organization was a private one) in San Francisco in 1852. Like other private or territorial gold coins, it was a local response to a local problem—a plethora of precious metal, and the lack of an official mint to fashion it into normal coinage. This huge slug might be somewhat inconvenient to use in trade, but it was clearly better than gold dust; round and eight-sided coins of the denomination were struck intermittently by several groups through 1855.

The term slug is also sometimes used for the two fifty-dollar gold commemoratives issued at the time of the Panama-Pacific International Exposition of 1915. These particular slugs were official United States coins, but their denominations and shapes (octagonal and round) were obviously inspired by the earlier private pieces.

The word has still another meaning, designating a token manufactured to serve in a coin-operated machine, such as a telephone or casino slot machine.

See also COMMEMORATIVE; PRIVATE GOLD COINS; TOKEN.

SMALL CENT The one-cent piece of reduced size, first adopted in the United States in 1857 and in Canada in 1920; a term that has meaning only in relation to its predecessor, the large cent.

The small module was adopted for one-cent pieces to save money. In the United States the price of copper rose through the early and middle 1850s; by 1857, copper cents cost nearly as much to manufacture as they were worth in trade. Furthermore, the large cent's size and weight (29 millimeters and some 10.9 grams, respectively), coupled with its low value, made it unfashionable; it circulated very little outside New York and a few other large cities.

Given these facts, the government opted for a smaller cent. Several reduced-size cent patterns were created in the mid-1850s, and one of them, featuring an obverse with an American eagle in flight, was adopted for coinage in 1857. The new cent departed from tradition in several ways. It was the first American base-metal coin not to carry the personification of Liberty, for which it was much criticized. Moreover, it introduced nickel to American coinage. The white metal constituted 12 percent of the coin, while copper made up the remaining 88 percent. The new coin measured 19 millimeters, and weighed only about 4.7 grams. Its designs may not have been appreciated, but its utility was.

This "flying eagle" cent was struck for circulation in 1857 and 1858. In 1859 the eagle was replaced by the portrait of an Indian princess and its reverse wreath was simplified. A shield was added above the wreath in 1860, and this "Indian head" cent, as it was known, was struck with no modifications of its design for nearly a half century. Its metallic content, however, did change: in 1864, nickel was removed from the coin, and a new composition of 95 percent copper, 5 percent tin and zinc was created. (The period's young state of technology made the coining of a nickel alloy particularly difficult.) The new cent was thinner and lighter than earlier ones, its weight standing at 3.11 grams. It has retained that weight up to the present, even though its metallic composition has undergone a few minor alterations (and one major one: in 1943, to save copper for the American war effort, cents were made of zinc-plated steel and weighed only 2.70 grams).

In 1909 the American small cent was completely redesigned. It was the centenary of Abraham Lincoln's birth, and the talented designer Victor Brenner honored Lincoln by placing his portrait on the cent's obverse. The reverse revealed the denomination and country of issue between two stylized ears of wheat. This simple and effective reverse was replaced in 1959 with a depiction of the Lincoln Memorial, an effort as unwise as it was ambitious, for it seriously damaged the coin's aesthetic impact.

The coin's history in Canada is more briefly told. The Canadians had had a large-sized bronze cent since 1858. By 1920 it was apparent the coin, which measured 25.4 millimeters and weighed 5.67 grams, was uneconomical to strike, and the Canadian government opted for a smaller cent. The new one featured an obverse portrait and a reverse with maple leaves, the country's name, denomination, and date, all of which had been on the

larger coin. However, the new cent measured only 19.05 millimeters and weighed 3.24 grams, representing an enormous saving for the mint. The rise in the price of copper in recent years has put the fate of the small cent in doubt in Canada and the United States.

See also COPPER-NICKEL COINAGE; LARGE CENT.

SO-CALLED DOLLARS Medals roughly the size of the American silver dollar (38.1 millimeters), originally struck for commemorative purposes, later for monetary ones as well.

The term is usually limited to the area of United States medals, and while some so-called dollars have actually been struck in silver, many more have been minted in bronze, brass, aluminum, and white metal. The pieces in the series have sometimes had the monetary nature of tokens, redeemable in specified goods or services within a stated time-frame.

The first so-called dollars appeared about 1825, and were clearly thought of as commemorative medals. Their production expanded with time, and they became popular items at fairs and expositions. Gradually some became political or satirical in nature as well.

The so-called dollar in the illustration is related to the silver controversy of the late nineteenth century. A product of Joseph Lesher, owner of a silver mine near Central, Colorado, it was one of a series generally known as "Lesher referendum dollars"—"referendum" in the sense that Lesher "referred" them to the people for acceptance or rejection as money.

Lesher, who had supported William Jennings Bryan for the presidency in 1896 and 1900, was convinced most people wanted an unlimited silver dollar coinage. Setting out to prove this theory, he issued silver dollars, which he called "referendum souvenirs." They were manufactured at exactly one troy ounce, and released at

Small cent.
Left: Canada, large cent, 1920.
Right: Canada, small cent, 1920.

So-called dollars. *Colorado, Lesher referendum "dollar," 1900.*

a face value of $1.25, almost double the accepted price of an ounce of silver at the time. Nonetheless, Lesher was certain his coins would circulate, for he believed the real value of silver was actually $1.29 per ounce. He proposed to redeem his coins at their issue price, $1.25.

The arrangement was hardly practical, and Lesher persuaded a grocer in his home town of Victor, Colorado, to redeem his coins in goods or cash. The obliging grocer was A. B. Bumstead, and most of the coins bear his name as well as Lesher's. All Lesher coins were privately struck in Denver. Those dated 1900 weighed one troy ounce (31.1035 grams) and measured 35 millimeters across their centers. Issues for 1901 were somewhat smaller (32 millimeters in diameter) and weighed the same as a genuine silver dollar (26.73 grams). Lesher valued his 1901 issues at a dollar each.

So sure was he of his idea that he obtained a government patent on it; but it was for nought. Federal agents seized his dies, and the public's response was less enthusiastic than Lesher had anticipated. Production of referendum coins ceased in 1901.

The piece illustrated is one of the rarest in the series. It is a die trial for a Lesher coin to be redeemed by banks; only six such pieces are known, as Lesher wisely abandoned the idea of having banks redeem his coins. Had he not, undoubtedly he would have encountered even more trouble from the federal government.

The referendum pieces are the best-known so-called dollars issued as money. More often, the term has referred to commemorative or celebratory items of a purely medallic nature, and most contemporary so-called dollars are in this latter category. Literally hundreds of so-called dollars have been issued through the years; their low initial price, which places them within the reach of most collectors, ensures their continued popularity and future production.

See also COMMEMORATIVE; MEDAL; TOKEN.

SOLIDUS A Roman and Byzantine gold coin which was a mainstay of late classical and early medieval commerce.

The solidus was introduced as a Roman coinage denomination by Constantine the Great (ruled A.D. 306–337), who meant it to replace the aureus. Constantine's new gold coin appeared around 310, and had an average weight of about 4.45 grams. Its early career was hardly spectacular, and it did not displace the aureus as the standard Roman gold coin until 324. But its subsequent career was brilliant: the Romans and later the Byzantines struck it for trade for the next seven centuries, and during most of those years it was virtually the only moderate-sized, circulating gold coin in Europe.

The early solidus is a typical late Roman coin. Emperors and others are shown in profile, and later in a three-quarter view, on the obverse, with their official regalia. A symbolic lance and shield may also be present. Reverses depict allegorical or real figures, often in martial poses. The artistic repertory of Roman coinage was limited by this time, and Christian symbolism was coming to the fore. A figure personifying Victory, fashionable on fourth- and fifth-century solidi, was being transformed into a Christian angel.

In 395 the Roman Empire was permanently divided into eastern and western halves. Shortly, the western half fell to barbarian tribes, while the eastern half survived, as the Greek-influenced Eastern Roman or Byzantine Empire.

Initially, these momentous events had little effect on the solidus. The coin was struck in both parts of the sundered empire in the fifth century, and the barbarian tribes in the West eventually struck solidi of their own in the name of the Byzantine emperor. Types and portraiture on the coin showed scant evidence of external events, and its weight and fineness were unchanged. After approximately 500 the solidus was rarely struck in the barbarian West. But the coin was well liked in the Byzantine East, where it was struck for centuries, its designs changing in the process.

An early sixth-century Byzantine solidus resembled a late Roman one, with a bust of the ruler on the obverse and a standing angel on the reverse. The mint might be indicated by a symbol in the reverse field; later, some indication of the mint might also appear in the exergue. The vast majority of Byzantine solidi were from a single mint, however—the central facility at Constantinople.

Under Justinian I (ruled 527–565), there was a minor change in the portraiture of the solidus, with the three-quarters facing style replaced with a full-face bust in 538. Two new reverses were also introduced during this reign, both showing an angel directly facing the viewer, and carrying a globe with cross in one hand. The illustration is of a solidus of the new type

from the Constantinople mint: it has a diameter of 20 millimeters, and weighs 4.4 grams. Although less than artistically executed, the coin was esteemed for its consistent weight and fineness.

The visual nature of the solidus underwent a slow change. A new reverse design, a simple cross on steps, was tentatively introduced in 578. This design, put aside after a few years, was reinstituted in 610, and prevailed through most of the seventh century. Late in the 600s however, the entire fabric of the coin altered. In 692, the emperor Justinian II (ruled 685–695 and 705–711) introduced a bust of Christ as the obverse type, relegating his own portrait to a small standing figure holding a cross on the reverse. His reasons for such modesty are not known, but the artistic quality of the solidus improved markedly, and remained so through its production. Henceforth, Byzantine solidi usually carried a facing portrait of Christ on the obverse; when they did not, the emperor's facing portrait was a frequent obverse type, with one or more members of the imperial family gracing the reverse. In time the cross-on-steps reverse motif was seldom used; while the older angel type vanished completely.

Although the solidus was struck until the eleventh century, its position had been undermined a century before. The emperor Nicephorus II (ruled 963–969) introduced a new gold coin, a tetarteron, similar to the solidus but somewhat lighter: the net effect was the circulation of two basic Byzantine gold coins. The solidus, struck at full weight, was henceforth called a histamenon, literally a "standard," as opposed to the substandard tetarteron. Its career as the solidus/histamenon was not happy: debasement began in the eleventh century, and with the coinage reforms of 1092, the coin disappeared.

The solidus served in a vital capacity as a trading coin when the West was unable to produce such pieces: all later ducats, florins, and genovinos owe much to this earlier coin.

Solidus. Byzantine Empire, Justinian I, A.D. 538–565.

See also CROSS ON COINAGE; PORTRAIT; SCYPHATE COINAGE; TETARTERON; TRADE COINS; TREMISSIS.

Sovereign. England, 1504–1507.

SOVEREIGN A British gold coin worth twenty shillings.

The sovereign was first issued in 1489 by Henry VII (ruled 1485–1509), and was born of the period's political and social upheaval. The new king was a usurper, gaining his throne after a successful revolt against his predecessor, Richard III (ruled 1483–1485). Richard's reign had been controversial, yet he was the legitimate king; it remained to be seen whether Henry VII could win the loyalty of his new subjects.

Henry chose to do as rulers for hundreds of years before him had done —to use coinage to proselytize. He employed silver coins for the purpose, but some of his best efforts are on gold coins. His sovereign was a large coin, measuring some 42 millimeters, with a stipulated weight of 240 grains—15.55 grams—and a fineness of 994.8. Its size provided the space needed for a propaganda statement, and there is little doubt this was the main reason for striking such a large piece.

The basic design elements of the coin were adopted from those of the large real d'or, a Dutch coin struck for the future Holy Roman Emperor Maximilian in 1487: the real d'or magnificently displayed the regal symbolism associated with the new absolute monarchies of the Continent. Henry selected the sovereign's designs, and also seems to have named it.

His wish to emphasize the grandeur of monarchy, ruler, and England itself inspired all that appears on the coin. On the obverse is the king enthroned, surrounded by heraldic symbols, the very embodiment of a legitimate monarch. The reverse, as rich in ornament and detail as the obverse, shows the royal arms impaled upon a great rose, the symbol of the new English ruling house of Tudor.

The coin's weight and fineness remained unaltered in the early years of Henry VIII (ruled 1509–1547), Henry VII's son and successor, and the father's portrait was carried on the son's coinage. By the mid-1520s, however, there were hints of change. English gold coins were undervalued in relation to silver, and many were exported to reap the benefit of higher exchange rates abroad. Henry VIII's rather freehanded approach to state finance was also a problem, the more so as he was organizing for a war with France; the situation could only degenerate. As a result of such pressures, the value of the sovereign was raised by 12 percent in 1526, to twenty-two shillings and six pence. Its gold fineness and weight stayed what they had been.

Henry's expropriation of Church estates, an outgrowth of the English Reformation, afforded him enough property and money to temporarily defray his increasingly expensive tastes and the rise in prices characteristic of sixteenth-century Europe. By 1540, however, he was again short of money, and soon turned to the time-honored remedy of debasing his coinage. In 1542, Henry secretly ordered a reduction in gold fineness from 994.8 to 958.3; he also reduced the weight of most of his coins, including the sovereign, leaving it with a theoretical weight of 200 grains (12.96 grams).

These changes were proclaimed in 1544. It was soon clear that further reductions and debasement were necessary; by 1546 the sovereign's legal weight was 192 grains (12.44 grams), and its fineness 833.3. This last sovereign of Henry VIII generated interesting design modifications. The figure on the coin's obverse is now recognizably Henry VIII rather than his father, while the royal shield on the reverse is supported by a lion and a dragon.

Henry VIII died in 1547, succeeded by his ten-year-old son, Edward VI (ruled 1547-1553). Edward's advisers left the debased coinage as it was for the reign's first three years, and sovereigns bearing the new monarch's name do not seem to have appeared until about 1549. In 1550 a sovereign valued at thirty shillings was introduced, duplicating the weight and "fine" gold content (994.8) of Henry VII's original coin as well as its designs. In addition, a new twenty-shilling sovereign was released in "crown" gold, fineness of which was only 916.6. This lesser sovereign weighed 174 grains (11.28 grams), and bore radically new designs. On its obverse was a half-length figure of the king, facing right, holding an orb and a sword; its reverse bore the royal arms, once again supported by a lion and a dragon.

By Edward's death, it was possible to discontinue the use of "crown" gold and to retain the larger, purer sovereign. This improvement was only temporary. By the time James I (ruled 1603–1625) had succeeded, the twenty-shilling piece in "crown" gold, called a pound and later a unite, had displaced the thirty-shilling sovereign. This coin, struck with a variety of designs, was minted occasionally until 1662, when it yielded to a new coin, the guinea, whose value was eventually settled at 21 shillings.

The sovereign was not minted again until 1817, and then in a very different guise. The new coin was much smaller and lighter, with a diameter of 23 millimeters and weight of 7.988 grams. Its fineness was 916.6—the same as several earlier issues. These sovereigns were struck by machine, and had been redesigned. The monarch's head now occupied the obverse, while the reverse revealed a spirited rendition of England's patron, St. George, slaying a dragon. These basic designs were retained for most sovereigns for the coin's remaining circulatory life.

Gold sovereigns are still minted upon occasion, but only to maintain a theoretical standard, to sell to collectors, or to bestow as presentation pieces.

See also GUINEA; NOBLE; PORTRAIT; PRESENTATION PIECE.

SPADE MONEY One of several early cast forms of currency used in ancient China.

Most specialists believe this money's shape derives from a real spade, presumably once used as a medium of exchange. It is a logical development in an agricultural country, where farming implements were necessary.

The first and larger of the two specimens illustrated is an early spade coin, whose date has been put at sometime in the ninth century B.C., and is a close approximation of a real spade, down to the hollow socket at the top, which could have accommodated a wooden handle had the space actually served as a tool. The points curving downward at either end of the blade precluded that, however, and may have been put there to indicate the piece was designed solely as money.

The specimen shown weighs 110.4 grams, has a maximum length of nearly 120 millimeters, and was cast in bronze, as were all Chinese coins of this and many future periods. With time, spade money diminished in size and weight. It was still cast with a hollow socket, but the socket no longer projected below the blade's shoulders, as it does on our specimen. Later spades often carried one or more characters, representing the name of a mint or the denomination of the piece.

By about 400 B.C., the hollow handle originally on spade money had disap-

Spade money.
Left: Chinese spade money from the ninth century
B.C.
Right: From the third century B.C.

peared, while the crescent-shaped blade had become a deep, trapezoidal gash, giving the spade two "feet." These feet may be square, as they are on the second coin seen, or rounded. The shoulders too can be square or rounded. Our specimen is also much smaller and lighter than earlier spades, measuring 51 millimeters in length, and weighing about 13.3 grams.

These late spade coins originated in northern China, as did their predecessors, and their production has been dated as between 400 and 250 B.C. The coin's obverse usually gives the place of mintage: the right-hand specimen comes from the facility at An-yang. Many of these pieces bear marks of value as well.

The spade, along with other early forms of Chinese currency, was cast aside with the reforms of the emperor Shih Huang-ti (221–210 B.C.), who made a round coin with a square hole (the pan liang) universal throughout China. Chinese specialists frequently use the term pu for spade money, just as they refer to knife money as tao.

See also CAST COINAGE; KNIFE MONEY; PAN LIANG.

SPECIFIC GRAVITY The ratio of a coin's weight to that of an equal volume of another substance used as a standard—usually water.

Specific gravity is useful in detecting counterfeits and forgeries, especially in cases where the coin, if genuine, is made of pure gold or silver. It is also useful for gold-copper and silver-copper alloys when the official proportions of the two metals are known.

The underlying principle of specific gravity is simple, and was known to the ancient Greeks. Archimedes found that the volume of an irregular mass of metal could be determined by weighing the volume of water which it displaced.

Let us say we have a precious-metal coin which could be counterfeit. If we weigh the coin once, in air, and then again, in distilled water, the difference between the coin's weight in air and its weight in water is the weight of the water is has displaced. This figure, divided into the weight of the coin in air, gives us the coin's specific gravity figure.

Assuming we know what the specific gravity of the coin's alloy *should* be (there are reference works on this subject), a significant difference between the figure we have found and the standard figure exposes our coin as counterfeit. It is wise to run the specific gravity test three times on any given coin, and average the three figures obtained, which are apt to vary slightly due to changes in temperature and atmospheric conditions. The coin being tested must be perfectly clean, and there must be no air bubbles adhering to it when it is being weighed in water. If distilled water is not available, carbon tetrachloride may be used as a substitute.

The denser the metal being tested, the higher its specific gravity. The test is quite accurate for metals at the upper end of the density spectrum, but less so as the spectrum is descended. The following table may be of use. It lists specific gravity quotients for various alloyed and unalloyed metals, and can be used as a reference point in testing suspect coins.

Specific Gravities of Unalloyed and Alloyed Metals

Unalloyed

Gold	19.32+
Silver	10.49+
Copper	8.96+
Nickel	8.90
Tin	7.298
Zinc	7.13

Alloyed

95% copper, 2½% zinc, 2½% tin	8.87270
95% copper, 5% zinc	8.8685
75% copper, 25% nickel	8.945
10% copper, 90% silver	10.337
10% copper, 90% gold	17.2

As chemical imbalances may well exist in alloys, a plus or minus variation of .5 in a reading is acceptable. It must be stressed that the specific gravity test will not offer definitive proof for all coins, and is essentially useless for very small ones, as it is particularly difficult to weigh them accurately in water. For specific gravity testing, an exact scale that provides readings down to one grain (about a sixth of a gram) is necessary: a number of fairly inexpensive ones are on the market. Specific gravity testing offers scant protection against modern die-struck forgeries, but it works well for earlier, cast varieties. This is because the density of metal in a cast forgery is always less than it is in a die-struck coin. The variation is of enough significance to show up as a lower-than-normal reading in the specific gravity test.

On the other hand, the struck forgery begins as a piece of solid metal and, assuming the forger adheres to the metallic standards of the original coin, any specific gravity test is likely to be inconclusive.

See also AUTHENTICATION; COUNTERFEIT AND FORGERY DETECTION.

SPECIMEN NOTE An actual bank note, bearing the overprinted or perforated word SPECIMEN or its equivalent, and ordinarily produced for distribution to banks, treasuries, and law enforcement agencies to familiarize them with a new currency design.

The word specimen is frequently used in both English-speaking and non-English-speaking countries. Other words indicating the nature of these notes are MÜSTER (used in Germany and Austria), MUESTRA (Spanish-speaking nations), SEM VALOR (Portugal and Brazil), and WZOR (Poland).

Not all specimen notes are rare, nor do all enjoy a premium over ordinary notes. The note shown is an example. It is an unissued fifty-korun bill from the German protectorate of Bohemia and Moravia, and was prepared for sale to collectors after World War II. Unissued notes from the first Czechoslovak republic and the German satellite of Slovakia were similarly perforated, and sold to raise much-needed foreign currency. In most cases, specimen issues from these regimes are actually

Specimen note. *Bohemia and Moravia, 50 korun, 1944.*

worth less than legitimate circulating notes.

The specimen note should not be confused with the essay, which represents a different stage in the production of paper money, and performs a different function.

See also ESSAY NOTE.

SPIELMARKE A metallic gambling counter or chip, developed in Germany from the earlier jeton.

The piece illustrated dates from around 1860, and is a deliberate imitation of the United States twenty-dollar gold piece (an especially popular model for these counters). It has the same diameter, 34 millimeters, but it is much lighter: like most of these pieces, it was fashioned of brass, not gold. The basic types are those of the real coin, and the edge is reeded; however, the legends are different, and the word spielmarke appears on both sides of the token, as no one wished to be prosecuted for counterfeiting.

The production of spielmarken seems to have continued until about 1900, after which they were replaced with the cheaper plastic gaming chip and the metallic or plastic casino token designed specifically for gaming houses in Nevada, Monte Carlo, and elsewhere. The latter usually indicate their value and origin; the former do not.

See also JETON; TOKEN.

Spielmarke. A German gambling token made to resemble a United States 20-dollar gold piece, c. 1860.

SPURIOUS Not genuine; counterfeit or false.

The adjective is often used to describe an original creation, rather than a copy of a known item. In this respect, its meaning is similar to the term fantasy: both words refer to objects deliberately fashioned to mislead the public. But "spurious" also can refer to an outright counterfeit or forgery of a known item, while "fantasy" cannot.

See also FANTASY; FORGERY.

SQUARE COINAGE A minor but persistent shape, found throughout the whole history of coinage.

Square coinage.
Left: India, Indo-Scythians, copper coin, c. 75 B.C.
Right: Netherlands, 5 cents, 1941.

Square coinage may come to exist for a number of reasons. It can be generated by emergencies or sieges; such specimens are discussed elsewhere. It can also serve as a commemorative or a pattern. Or governments and their people may simply prefer square coins; a government may find a square coin easier to manufacture than a round one; it might adopt the shape to eliminate confusion between two denominations of similar size and weight; or it may wish to satisfy the citizenry with a tradition of square coinage.

The Indian punch-marked silver coins were square, and seem to have been struck as early as 500 B.C. Our first illustration shows a later square coin, a copper issue of the Indo-Scythians from around 75 B.C. The Indian tradition has been retained, although the obverse legend is rendered in Greek. The coin measures 20–21 millimeters on each side and weighs 7.73 grams.

The persistence of the concept is shown by our second coin, a Dutch zinc five-cent piece issued in 1941, during the Nazi occupation. The coin's edges are rounded, as is the practice on modern square coins, and it measures 18 millimeters on each side, weighing 3.55 grams. This coin was not an emergency issue, as it happens: the Dutch had been using square coins for this denomination since 1913. Square coins are still regularly produced by several countries, including India and the Philippines.

See also KLIPPE; PUNCH-MARKED COINS; SIEGE PIECE.

STAR An order's decoration or emblem, not attached to a ribbon, sash, collar, or bar, but usually secured with a screw or pin and worn on the breast.

The star is most frequently associated with heraldic orders, which, as they evolved, granted membership in a number of ascending classes. By varying the size or design of the star, the exact grade of the recipient could be indicated.

Star. Bavaria, Order of Saint Hubert (star).

The first stars were actually embroidered and sewn onto a uniform. Later, as the number of orders increased, detachable metal stars were created. Not all orders award stars.

The star is usually eight-pointed, perhaps four-pointed for a lower grade. Its design may duplicate that of the badge, or be simpler and incorporate only part of the badge; this recalls the days when stars were embroidered, making it arduous to include fine detail.

The star in the illustration is one awarded by the Bavarian Order of Saint Hubert. The order was founded by Duke Gerhard V of Jülich-Berg (ruled 1437–1475) in 1444 to commemorate a victorious battle fought on Saint Hubert's Day (November 13), and was issued into the early twentieth century.

See also BADGE; DECORATION; ORDER.

STATE COINAGE A series of coppers minted by or for New York, New Jersey, Massachusetts, Vermont, and Connecticut during the middle and late 1780s.

The Articles of Confederation, in force from 1781 to 1788, reserved most powers to the individual states. While the federal government was responsible for such matters of common interest as the national defense, it was felt that the states were capable of coping with daily concerns. At that time, the states were seen as sovereign entities from which the national government derived its sovereignty, rather than the reverse.

This perception of sovereignty was to have interesting consequences. Coinage and the production of money have long been regarded as perquisites and proclamations of sovereign power. In practical terms it meant that, while the new federal government had the right to issue money, so did the states. By the middle 1780s, some were taking advantage of this right: partly to declare their own sovereignty, partly to alleviate a scarcity of small change. We tend to call their products "cents," but the term coppers is preferable. With the exception of the Massachusetts issues, the coins bore no marks of denomination, nor were they the size and weight of the federal cent, which was to be adopted by the Mint Act of 1792. Again with the exception of Massachusetts issues, the coins were not produced by the states, but contracted for by the states. (New York neither produced its own coins nor contracted for them; but several enterprising coiners struck them anyway.) In the case of New Jersey and Connecticut, output of "cents" was quite large, and these coins are by far the most common American issues struck prior to 1800.

By an act of June 1, 1786, New Jersey granted the exclusive right of coinage to Walter Mould, Thomas Goadsby, and Albion Cox, who were to coin three million coppers, each weighing 150 grains (about 9.72 grams), within two years. For this profitable privilege (the coins were lightweight, and intended to pass at a value far in excess of their intrinsic one) the coiners were to pay 10 percent of their coins into the state treasury. The three men leased the Rahway mills of Daniel Marsh, a member of the state legislature who had helped them secure their contract.

New Jersey coppers were struck until 1789, although the last date to appear on the coins is 1788. All the coins used the same basic designs. The obverse carried elements representing the state—a horse's head and plow from the state seal, and the state's name in Latin. The reverse emphasized federal motifs, with the United States shield as a central element, and the Latin legend E PLURIBUS UNUM ("Out of Many, One")—the first time this motto was used on a coin produced in the United States. The piece illustrated measures 28 millimeters and weighs 9.72 grams, as specified in the contract.

By the time this coin was minted, the contract's original signers had seriously quarreled. Walter Mould had done little or nothing to fulfill his end of the agree-

State coinage.
Top: New Jersey, copper, 1787.
Bottom: Massachusetts, cent, 1787.

ment, and later fled to Ohio. Meanwhile, Goadsby and Cox had parted ways, mint machinery was removed from Rahway, other figures entered the picture, and other sites were used to strike the coins. In addition to the original mint at Rahway, New Jersey, coppers were struck at Morristown, Elizabethtown, New York City, and Machin's Mills, near Newburgh, New York.

The history of Connecticut's coppers is somewhat similar to that of New Jersey's: a coining contract; disputes; reorganizations among the contractors; coinage in several places; and dozens of die varieties, all adhering to the same basic designs. The Connecticut coppers were deliberate imitations of the British halfpenny, a coin well-known to the newly independent Americans. The obverse bore an armored bust, facing either left or right, and the reverse a seated figure with a shield. The date appeared in the exergue of the reverse, and the four years from 1785 to 1788 are represented. These coins were cruder and a bit lighter than their New Jersey counterparts, but were produced in quantity: among the state coinages, Connecticut's stands out for its sheer bulk.

The idea of a contract coinage was debated in New York and eventually rejected. No matter: reasoning that coppers would be accepted by the people if not by the state government, two private coiners, in separate mints, struck most of New York's unauthorized coins. The first mint, located in New York City, was operated by John Bailey and Ephraim Brasher. They are credited with striking numerous coppers using the designs on the English halfpenny, and with the obverse legend NOVA EBORAC, Latin for "New York." All the coins are dated 1787.

The other private mint operated in clandestine fashion at Machin's Mills. Established in 1786 on the outskirts of Newburgh by Captain Thomas Machin, it began minting coppers for the state of New York the following year. In addition, Machin and his associates produced coppers for New Jersey and Vermont, as well as an entire series of imitation English halfpennies—the latter a quasi-legal activity at best. Although Machin's Mills coins for the state of New York are dated 1787, the establishment seems to have remained in high gear for several more years.

Among state coinages, those of Massachusetts and Vermont are special cases. Late in 1786, Massachusetts elected to organize its own mint rather than depend on contractors. The following May, the state appointed Captain Joshua Wetherle, a Boston goldsmith, as master of the mint, and authorized him to build it and its machinery, while the legislature detailed the coins' designs. The obverse, adapted from the state seal, would show an Indian with a bow and arrow and the legend COMMONWEALTH. The reverse would display a heraldic eagle with the national shield, the name of the state, and the date.

The Massachusetts coins were innovative. They were not copies of British designs, and the legends were in English, not Latin. Moreover, the coins bore a denomination: if you look closely at the eagle's breast on the reverse of the illustrated piece, you will see the incuse word CENT,

the coin's name. Massachusetts also struck half cents, with the denomination appearing in the same spot. These were the first United States issues to actually state these denominations on the coins themselves. Massachusetts struck cents and half cents in 1787 and 1788. The cent shown measures 29 millimeters and weighs 10.07 grams, making it larger and heavier than coins of other states. Dies for some of the 1788 coins were engraved by Jacob Perkins, who later had a brilliant career in the field of paper money.

Although Vermont contracted for its coinage, there is a difference: the state was an independent country and not part of the United States until 1791; its coins emphasized that fact. Early coppers, struck by Reuben Harmon, Jr., of the town of Rupert, carried a landscape on the obverse, with the legends VERMONTS. RES. PUBLICA, VERMONTIS. RES. PUBLICA., or VERMONTENSIUM. RES. PUBLICA.—the variations created by an uncertain knowledge of the Latin for "Vermont Republic." The reverse's central design was an Eye of Providence surrounded by thirteen stars and thirteen rays; its legend read STELLA. QUARTA. DECIMA. ("the fourteenth star"—a reference to the state's wish to join the new federal Union). These designs were used in 1785 and part of 1786, but coiners found their novelty made them unpopular. A more orthodox design closely resembling the contemporary English halfpenny was adopted, and the Vermont coppers of late 1786, 1787, and 1788 look much like those of Connecticut and New York. Indeed, some of the later issues were made in New York, by the enterprising people at Machin's Mills.

The year 1787 saw both the zenith of state coinage and the onset of its demise. A new federal Constitution was drafted then, giving the national government more power and withdrawing states' right to coin or print money. The requisite number of states had ratified the new charter by the middle of 1788, and a new federal government was inaugurated the following spring. Its move to a national coinage culminated in the Mint Act of 1792.

See also BRASHER DOUBLOON; FUGIO CENT; LARGE CENT; MINT ACT OF 1792.

STATER   The principal denomination of a coinage in the eastern Greek world, first struck in electrum, later in silver or gold.

Stater derives from the Greek for "weigher," which in turn relates to the eastern Mediterranean practice of establishing units of weight that were divided into subunits. Thus, a stater was divided into thirds, sixths, and so forth, down to a tiny coin worth one ninety-sixth of the basic unit. This was unlike the western Greek tradition, which tended to establish a unit, such as a drachm, and then speak in terms of multiples of that unit—didrachm, tetradrachm, etc.

The stater was based on a number of different weight standards. The original electrum stater of the Lydians weighed slightly over 14 grams. When pure gold coinage first appeared, in the middle of the sixth century, the gold stater's weight decreased to slightly above 8 grams, while the weight of the silver stater was placed at nearly 11 grams, yielding a silver to gold ratio of 13⅓ to 1. By the time coinage spread from Asia Minor to Greece, new weight standards were being established, creating a good deal of confusion until partial standardization was achieved during the Hellenistic age in the fourth century B.C. For those who actually used the coins, however, it was probably not too chaotic: silver and gold coins were frequently traded in ancient times as simple pieces of precious metal, making the nominal standard of a coin of only minor importance.

The stater was widely used as a trade coin. The gold stater of Philip of Macedon (ruled 359–336 B.C.), for example, was traded throughout the classical world and well beyond it. The coin in the illustration

Stater. Corinth, c. 450 B.C.

is another popular trading piece, a Corinthian silver stater minted around 450 B.C., struck to a standard of 8.6 grams. The coin's obverse shows Pegasus, the mythical winged horse emblematic of the city; the persistence of this type earned Corinthian staters the popular name of "colts." On its reverse is a small head of the goddess Athena, also identified with the city. Though other areas were experimenting with "modern" coinage designs, the style of this coin is archaic. Many Greek trade coins—and trade coins in general—reveal an immobilization of types and techniques, presumably to avoid risking people's innate suspicion of a "new" coin's legitimacy. Hence, the "colt's" essential design remained unchanged for the rest of its life —that is, down to 223 B.C.

See also ELECTRUM COINAGE; TRADE COINS.

STELLA   A pattern United States four-dollar gold coin, struck in 1879 and 1880.

The unusual denomination was the suggestion of John A. Kasson, then United States Minister to Austria-Hungary, and former Chairman of the Congressional Committee of Coinage, Weights, and Measures. Kasson's rationale was that the United States needed a gold coin whose value approximated that of those European coins based on the metric system— the French twenty francs, the Italian twenty lire, the Spanish twenty pesetas, and the eight-florin piece of Austria-Hungary.

The committee on coinage was receptive to the plan, and chose stella, Latin for

Stella. United States, pattern 4-dollar gold piece or "stella," 1879.

"star," as its name. Charles E. Barber fashioned the designs, featuring a Liberty head with flowing hair for the obverse, and a large, five-pointed star with the incuse inscription ONE STELLA 400 CENTS for the reverse. Fifteen patterns were struck in gold with Barber's designs, an additional number in copper and aluminum. The stella's gold was actually a peculiar "metric" alloy, consisting of 6 grams of gold, 0.3 of silver, and 0.7 of copper, the whole equalling 7 grams, the proposed weight of the new coin. In keeping with the period's less than rigorous standards, these "original" stellas were offered to the coinage committee's members at cost.

They proved so popular that, early in 1880, more were mandated: as there were no hubs to create new dies, the 1879 dies were used to mint four hundred additional pieces. Unlike the originals, these restrikes were minted in the ordinary 90 percent gold alloy. Barber produced a few more stellas actually dated 1880, and in this instance, they were struck in the metric gold alloy, as were the original 1879s. Yet other 1880-dated patterns in aluminum and copper were also struck with Barber's flowing hair design.

Meanwhile, another mint engraver, George T. Morgan, responsible for the revived silver dollar of 1878, had been at work on the stella. Morgan retained Barber's reverse design, but on his obverse Liberty's hair was coiled, in the fashion of the period. Morgan's stellas were struck in aluminum, metric gold, and copper, and on the whole, are rarer than stellas with the Barber design. Furthermore, they do not seem to have been restruck.

The stella never emerged from the pattern stage. Kasson's idea would have given the United States a gold coin nearly equal to foreign ones—but not quite, as the conversion could not have been exact. Congress and the Mint, having just abandoned the twenty-cent piece—a splendid idea in theory—were disinclined to risk another failure.

See also PATTERN; RESTRIKE; TRADE COINS.

STONE MONEY Large, circular discs of stone with center holes, formerly used as money in Yap, one of the Caroline Islands of the western Pacific (*fé* or *fei* in Yapese).

Stone money. Yap.
(Courtesy of The Chase Manhattan Bank, N.A.)

As the photograph indicates, the stones were too large to be actively used in daily trade. Rather, they *represented* wealth and status, because of the labor required to procure them. Fé were created from aragonite, a variety of calcite. The stone is not native to Yap, and had to be quarried on the islands of Palau and Guam, several hundred miles from Yap. Once quarried, they were transported across the open sea by outrigger canoe, at a tremendous risk to men and boats. In essence, scarcity, risk, and labor made stone money valuable, just as they made a metal such as gold valuable.

Once on Yap, the fé was displayed in front of a house to indicate the wealth and status of the owner. There was little danger of theft; everyone in a village knew exactly where every piece should be. Fé rarely entered into commerce; when it did, it was usually reserved for momentous transactions such as buying a group's neutrality in a tribal war. Smaller stone pieces do seem to have seen some circulation as ordinary money, but most trade was conducted by barter. Fé was the basis of the Yapese monetary system until the outbreak of World War II, after which it was supplanted by the currency of the United States, the United Nations administrator of the island.

See also BARTER; MONEY.

STORE CARD A token bearing the name and the location of a business, meant to serve both as a medium of exchange and an advertisement for the business.

The first widespread use of the store card took place in seventeenth-century England, where numbers of copper tokens in penny, halfpenny, and farthing denominations circulated as advertisements as well as trading pieces. Many English copper tokens of the late eighteenth and early nineteenth centuries are also categorized as store cards.

Store card. *A store card from Arbuckle, California, good for one drink at a local saloon, c. 1900.*

But their widest use was in the United States. Numerous Hard Times tokens of the 1830s and 1840s were store cards, as were many Civil War tokens of the 1860s. By far the majority of these early American store cards were designed to replace the official cent, which was being hoarded in quantity, and most were made of copper. Later the store card became a fixture in the American West, for which it was often struck in brass or aluminum. The store card could be had in a variety of denominations or, as is the case of the one shown, as a token directly exchangeable for a specific commodity, such as a drink at a local saloon. This store card is aluminum, and measures 25 millimeters in diameter. Its intrinsic value is essentially nil, but it and its fellows were accepted in regions chronically short of small change. Merchants benefitted, as did the audience their cards reached. Quantities of American store cards were produced well into the present century, and a few new ones are still issued from time to time, generally for use in small, isolated communities. Since the nineteenth century, store cards have also featured prominently in Canadian numismatics, their use also encouraged by a scarcity of official small change.

See also CIVIL WAR TOKENS; HARD TIMES TOKENS; TOKEN.

STYCA A name given to the Northumbrian sceatta of the eighth and ninth centuries.

Unlike sceattas produced in the south

of England and on the Continent, where they were initially struck in good silver and only later declined in metallic purity, the styca began as a debased coin with a high percentage of copper—a debasement which grew worse with time. This probably reflects a general shortage of silver in the north of England rather than a deliberate policy of adulteration.

Stycas were struck in two parallel series. The earlier of these was royal, minted by authority of the kings of Northumbria. The date of the introduction of this coinage is uncertain, but must have occurred early in the eighth century. Royal stycas were in more or less regular production from the time of Eadbehrt (ruled 737–758) to that of Osbert (ruled 844–867). The earlier issues in the royal series carried an obverse with the king's name surrounding a central cross or similar device, and a reverse depicting a four-legged, dragon-like animal, similar to the one on some of the sceattas. Later issues abandoned the reverse's animal design for a moneyer's name encircling a central cross or one or more pellets. These later coins were created entirely of brass or copper.

The other styca series was ecclesiastical, and produced by the archbishops of York. The earliest examples date from the tenure of Eadbehrt's brother, Ecgberht, archbishop from 734 to 766. Ecgberht took care to include his brother's name in addition to his own on the coins, which often had a standing figure bearing two crosses on the reverse. This design was akin to the one seen on some sceattas from London; it was also fitting for an archbishop. Subsequent archbishops simplified the designs, and omitted the king's name in favor of those of their moneyers'. Small crosses were familiar central devices for clerical coins, as they were for royal ones.

The piece illustrated is an ecclesiastical styca produced under Wigmund, archbishop of York between 837 and 854. The obverse gives Wigmund's name, the reverse the moneyer's, Coenred. The coin is tiny (only 13 millimeters in diameter),

Styca. *Archbishopric of York, 837–854.*

which explains the simplicity of its design. It is fairly thick, however, and weighs over 1.2 grams. This and other stycas depart from the general current of English coinage: the small, thick, base-metal coin had been abandoned elsewhere for the broader, thinner silver penny. When the kingdom of Northumbria was overthrown by the Vikings, who took York in 867, the coinage of stycas ceased.

See also PENNY; SCEAT.

SUTLERS' CHECKS Metallic, hard rubber, or paper tokens issued by Union sutlers (owners of military cànteens) during the American Civil War.

Sutlers' checks were spawned by the dearth of small change affecting soldiers and civilians alike. In the absence of official small change, the sutler devised an unofficial one, the sutler's check, which circulated freely within the sutler's unit. Quickly adopted as a medium of exchange between the soldiers themselves, the tokens probably constituted most of the small change actually in circulation among the western armies.

The first sutlers' checks were fashioned of cardboard or paper; these soon wore out, and a metallic check was devised. The metallic tokens were of various denominations from five to one hundred cents, and of an extremely simple design. Most were struck by a Cincinnati firm, and usually in brass, although a few were also made in copper and hard rubber, or vulcanite.

Sutler's checks. *A token good for 10 cents in trade, issued by J. A. Leggat, sutler to the Third Michigan Cavalry, c. 1863.*

The piece illustrated dates from about 1863, and was issued by J. A. Leggat, sutler to the Third Michigan Cavalry. Leggat's check is a bit more elaborate than most, and is in copper rather than brass. Its size and weight approximate those of the American small cent of the early 1860s.

Soldiers were not particularly taken with sutlers' tokens—or with the sutlers themselves. The latter were universally (and usually correctly) looked upon as shysters and charlatans, who habitually overcharged the troops, and accepted their own tokens at a deflated value. All the same, an overpriced blanket was better than no blanket, as an undervalued token was better than no money. The sutlers and their tokens thrived for the duration of the war.

See also CIVIL WAR TOKENS; SCRIP; TOKEN.

SWEATING The removal of minute amounts of precious metal from coins by placing numbers of them in a box or bag, and shaking them vigorously until bits of the metal worked off.

Much like clipping and filing, sweating was a way of "making money from money." Once the coin had been sweated, it was returned to circulation, and passed at its nominal value. Sweating was the popular antidote to the edge designs mints had added to coins to discourage filing and clipping. It had the advantage of removing metal from the entire coin, not just its edge, and was thus more difficult to detect.

But sweating was arduous work. Even for soft gold, a good deal of labor had to be expended. Some clever people conceived the notion of attaching a bag of coins to the rear axle of a wagon, and letting the roads do the work—a risky practice, as the bag could be stolen, and at worst its owner could be imprisoned or even executed.

Gold coins were the most frequently sweated, as their relative softness and high value made them attractive targets. When electrolysis was invented, it proved a boon for sweaters: an electric current could remove metal evenly from the coin's surface without causing the damage that came from shaking it in a bag. Even though the sweated coin appeared somewhat worn, its chances of successfully returning to circulation were enhanced. The electrolytic method also meant far less physical labor.

At first glance, the sweating of gold coins would seem more trouble than it was worth. But the minute quantity of gold removed from each coin did add up, an observation supported by an accidental sweating of gold coins by the United States Treasury. Charged with transporting a million dollars in gold from one place to another, officials opted to weigh the coins after they had reached their destination. They did, only to discover that the coins' total weight had been reduced by twenty-five pounds troy, or 9.33 kilograms. Sweating was a profitable and not too risky practice, and continued as long as did gold coins themselves.

See also CLIPPING; FILING.

SYCEE A pre-modern Chinese silver trading ingot.

The sycee's weight was expressed as a multiple or division of the *liang* or *tael*, the Chinese ounce of about 37 grams. The name seems to be a corruption of *hsi ssu*, Chinese for "fine silk," given to these in-

Sycee. *China, 50 taels, nineteenth century.*

gots because of the purity of the metal in which they were cast. Normally they took the shape of very thick oblong ovals of variable size. The most common variety is raised at both ends, because it was rocked back and forth while cooling.

The ingots were cast in molds, allowed to cool partially, and stamped with a maker's mark and that of a public assayer. Additional marks could be applied with pen and ink, or with merchants' chops. The cast pieces varied in weight from one tenth of a tael to fifty taels. The piece shown is a fifty-tael ingot, weighing some 1850 grams.

The concept of the sycee has been traced to the Han dynasty (206 B.C.–A.D. 220). The typical, boat-shaped sycee in the illustration seems to have been introduced much later, under the Mongol emperor Kublai Khan (ruled A.D. 1280–1295); almost all surviving specimens date from the last two centuries. It also seems the one-tael sycee was produced in larger quantities than any other denomination, but Western observers in the nineteenth century reported seeing laborers carrying entire trays of fifty-tael ingots around coastal cities as accounts were settled at the end of each working day.

Sycees were used until the mid-1930s. Early ingots were cast by silver firms and other private groups, although sporadically governments tried to monopolize their manufacture. Under the Manchu dynasty (1644–1911) such attempts were abandoned; later sycees were entirely the creations of private enterprise. They persisted into the early republic, which finally banned their use in 1935.

See also CHOP MARK; INGOT; TAEL.

T

TAEL A Chinese monetary unit of account—and later a silver coin—equal to one *liang* of silver, and theoretically equal to a thousand copper ch'ien or cash; although in practice the ratio between the tael and the ch'ien fluctuated, as did the weight of the tael itself.

The tael became a coin at an extremely late stage in its development. When ancient China used precious metal in trade, it usually was in the form of ingots of varying weight. The production of silver coins on a national scale did not begin until 1889. At that time, the Chinese dollar, which formed the unit of the new coinage, weighed slightly less than three-quarters of a tael. A few silver tael coins were also struck, though they did not fit readily into the new decimal monetary system. Many were patterns, as is the one in the illustration. It was not struck in China proper, but by a British mint in Hong Kong. It was a proposed trade coin, to be used on the Mainland, and revealed an interesting mixture of British and Chinese designs. Tariffed according to the Shanghai tael, with a weight of some 36.7 grams, it measured 39 millimeters in diameter.

This coin never progressed beyond the pattern stage. While recognizing that a tael coin might be useful, the Chinese objected strenuously to the designs chosen by the British. They particularly disliked the British coat of arms and the English legends, all of which were on the more important obverse side of the coin, with the Chinese elements relegated to the reverse. The designs were rejected, and the patterns were ordered destroyed. A few survived, probably retained as souvenirs by employees of the Hong Kong mint.

See also INGOT; PATTERN; TRADE COINS; YUAN.

Tael. Hong-Kong, pattern tael, 1867.

TALENT An ancient Greek reckoning unit, most commonly the equivalent of sixty *minae,* and thus of six thousand drachms.

The early Hebrews seem to have used the same figure for their silver talent, while a gold talent was equal to fifteen silver ones. It is important to note that in both cases we are speaking of *theoretical* units of measure: there was never a Greek or Jewish coin called a talent.

See also MONEY OF ACCOUNT.

TEMPO TSUHO An oval base-metal coin of nineteenth-century Japan, minted in Edo (Tokyo) and Osaka until 1870.

The production of tempo tsuho was huge: Jacobs and Vermuele (see Bibliography) estimate that close to five hundred million were created. They had a theoretical value of one hundred mon, making forty equal to one gold koban. This was patently absurd and the public knew it. All the same, the coin was widely circulated, due to a previous monetary shortage, and seems to have been well accepted.

The tempo tsuho's design was never altered, and its size and weight remained fairly constant. However, its metallic content did vary, as the proportion of copper used in the coin diminished over the years. This explains the coppery look of some examples and the brassy look of others. Our specimen, a typical tempo tsuho, mea-

Tempo tsuho. Japan, 1835–1870.

sures 49 millimeters by 32.5 and weighs 22.7 grams. Related pieces were cast for use in the Ryukyu Islands around 1863. Like other coinage of feudal Japan, the tempo tsuho ceased production shortly after the Meiji Restoration (1868). The coin continued to circulate until about 1900, with a new value of slightly less than a hundredth part of the new silver yen.

See also CAST COINAGE; KOBAN.

TESSERAE Roman cast lead and bronze tokens, whose exact purposes are not completely known.

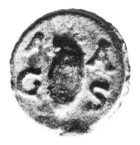

Tesserae. Roman Empire, lead tessera, fourth century A.D.

Tesserae often bear simple figures, numbers, or inscriptions, and are rather small. Although some of the bronze tokens seem to have been connected with government grain doles (the token entitling its holder to a specific amount of food), we can only guess the intentions behind others. They may have served as gaming counters, entrance tickets, receipts, etc. They may also have been used as small change late in the imperial period, when official coinage was in short supply. The tessera illustrated is made of lead, measures 21 millimeters, and weighs 7.75 grams. It carries an indecipherable obverse type, and its purpose will most probably remain a mystery.

See also CONTORNIATE; TOKEN.

TESTONE A medium-sized silver coin, introduced about 1475 by Galeazzo Maria Sforza, duke of Milan (ruled 1466–1476).

Inspired by an experiment with a silver lira by Nicolò Tron of Venice in 1472, Sforza decided to issue a lira carrying his portrait on it for use in Milan. He made his coin heavier than its Venetian counterpart, fixing it at 9.8 grams. Tron's lira had borne the doge's head on the obverse, and its use of a portrait upset republican sentiment in Venice, where the coin was rejected. The Milanese version, on the other hand, was instantly accepted. It was most useful for the duchy's busy commerce, and inhabitants were quite accustomed to seeing their rulers' portraits on coins. Sforza's lira was widely imitated, and due to its portraiture, its common name quickly became testone, from *testa*, meaning head.

Previously, Milanese artists had done excellent work on smaller coins. Now, with the creation of a fair-sized coin, they were to fashion some of the greatest masterpieces of Renaissance portraiture. Rulers are portrayed realistically, albeit with a grandeur elevating the renditions far above the merely representational. It was a level of artistry maintained through the remaining years of Milanese independence and well beyond. The city eventually fell to the Holy Roman Emperor Charles V in 1535, but some of the best portraits, including the one illustrated, actually date from Charles's reign in Milan, which lasted until 1556. The coin shown here measures 30 millimeters in diameter,

giving ample space for a masterful obverse portrait and a reverse design that refashioned figures from classical Roman art. This example weighs 11.6 grams, heavier than the earliest testones.

Milan was by no means the only city in which these coins were struck. Many came from Ferrara, Bologna, Mantua, and other cities, and they too revealed a high degree of artistry. The concept of the testone, if not its marvelous portraiture, was not confined to Italy. The French were soon striking a teston, the Portuguese a tostão, and the British a testoon. By 1600, the testone was obsolescent in Italy, with the exception of Rome, where it was minted until 1846. These last testoni were mere shadows of the earlier coins, the artistry that had given the coin its name and its place in numismatics having long since disappeared.

See also PORTRAIT; TESTOON.

TESTOON An English and Scottish coin patterned on the Italian testone.

The English version was first struck about 1504 and was valued at twelve pence or one shilling, formerly a simple monetary unit of account. The new coin weighed 144 grains (roughly 9.33 grams), twelve times the stipulated weight of the current penny.

The testoon was innovative. Like several other English silver issues introduced at the time, it carried a profile portrait of the current ruler, Henry VII (ruled 1485–1509). The portrait was not as artistically executed as those on Italian testoni of the same period, but it served a political purpose, by stressing Henry's position as monarch.

However, it was not an immediate success. From the number of surviving dies, we may surmise the projected issue was to be quite large, but the number of surviving coins indicates the coin was unpopular. The reasons are not known, and the next issue of testoons was not produced until

Testone. Milan, 1535–1556.

Testoon. *Scotland, 1561.*

late in the reign of Henry VIII (ruled 1509–1547). Henry debased his silver coinage, including the revived testoon, and by his death in 1547, the coin was only one-third silver. By returning to the full-face portraiture of old, and using this billon mixture—which meant the coin's high points soon turned coppery—Henry won the sobriquet "Old Coppernose."

The testoon's fineness was revived under Edward VI (ruled 1547–1553), by which time its name was being replaced by shilling.

In Scotland the testoon first appeared in 1553. Using their own monetary system, the Scots initially valued the testoon at four and later five shillings. The piece illustrated dates from 1561: it has a diameter of 29 millimeters, and weighs 7.82 grams. The portrait is of one of Scottish history's most romantic and tragic figures, Queen Mary (ruled 1542–1567), who was eventually imprisoned and beheaded by Queen Elizabeth of England. The last Scottish testoon was struck in 1565, late in Mary's reign.

See also BILLON; GROAT; PENNY; PORTRAIT; TESTONE.

TETARTERON A Byzantine gold coin of the tenth through the twelfth centuries.

Introduced by the emperor Nicephorus II (ruled 963–969), initially it bore designs identical with those on the solidus, but weighed somewhat less (around 4.1 grams), leading Byzantine chroniclers to accuse Nicephorus of greed and debasement of the coinage. The emperor's avarice, or at least his need for money (he was involved in costly wars during most of his reign), led to his scheme to pay government obligations with tetartera while requiring taxes be paid in solidi. However, the coin was also introduced for reasons of trade. Roughly on a par with the current Syrian dinar, Nicephorus may have intended to use the tetarteron in his Eastern conquests.

Nicephorus's issues featured a bust of Christ on the obverse, with busts of the emperor and his nominal colleague Basil II or the Virgin on the reverse. After the reign of John I (ruled 969–976), whose tetarteron is shown here, there would be an attempt to differentiate the coin from the full-weight solidus (or histamenon, as it was henceforth known). The histamenon would become broader and thinner, while the tetarteron would retain its original module.

During the late tenth and early eleventh centuries, the tetarteron was made in fair quantity. Obverse designs usually showed a facing Christ in elaborate regalia. Early reverse designs favored the depiction of two figures: on the tetarteron illustrated, the Virgin is in the act of crowning the emperor, an indication of the close relationship between church and state in the Byzantine world. By the time of Constantine VIII (ruled 1025–1028), the single figure of the emperor began to dominate the reverse, as that of Christ dominated the obverse. Still later, the Virgin became a popular obverse type, while

Tetarteron. *Byzantine Empire, John I, 969–976.*

the ruler (often in conjunction with a second figure) remained on the reverse. Throughout all these design changes, the types on the tetarteron are very similar to those on the histamenon. While the latter coin was larger, and was becoming scyphate (cup-shaped) by the middle of the eleventh century, there was a determined attempt at uniformity of design between the two series.

There were also parallels of another kind: with Michael IV (ruled 1034–1041), the histamenon was starting to be debased, and the tetarteron soon followed suit. The quality of Byzantine gold coinage deteriorated until 1092, when a coinage reform of Alexius I (ruled 1081–1118) created a new, relatively pure gold coin called a hyperpyron or hyperper. The histamenon was eliminated entirely, and the tetarteron existed in name only, as a small copper coin.

See also SOLIDUS.

TETRADRACHM The most famous ancient Greek silver coin, equal in value to four drachms.

Different cities used different weight standards for tetradrachms, but more often than not that of Athens was the one adopted. Under the Attic standard, the weight of the tetradrachm was about 17.2 grams. Its diameter hovered around 25 millimeters, but individual coins could deviate from this figure, and later tetradrachms were far broader and thinner than earlier ones.

Athens was the center of the early tetradrachm production, and the first coins probably date from the years between 575 and 550 B.C. Early issues are classified as wappenmünzen, or "heraldic coins," because they carry simple obverse types, interpreted as the family or personal badges of those in power (and in control of the mint). The reverse has only the imprint left by the punch. Later in the sixth century, probably about 515 B.C., this punch

was elaborated into a reverse die. It appears this new element was first used for the Athenian tetradrachm.

This later coin portrayed Athena's head on the obverse, with an owl (sacred to the goddess) on the reverse. The style of the coin was archaic, and remained so for years. The "owl" in fact was a well received trade coin, and its minters had no reason to make major alterations in its style and appearance.

Elsewhere, however, the tetradrachm underwent a rapid artistic evolution, as did other Greek coins. The tetradrachm was large enough to permit experimenting with new concepts and types, and artists —vying with one another to create exquisite designs—reached heights equalled only on the commemorative decadrachm.

Portraits in astounding relief were particularly fancied for obverses. Most depicted gods, goddesses, and heroes and were executed in profile, but the three-quarter portrait method was also tested— the ancient Greek designers were virtually the only artists to triumph over this difficult technique. For reverses, the early technique of placing designs within an incuse square disappeared, and gods, animals, and sometimes entire scenes could be shown, with or without a circular border.

By the fourth century B.C. major shifts were occurring. Philip of Macedon (ruled 359–336 B.C.) had added most of Greece to his kingdom by 338. His son, Alexander the Great (ruled 336–323 B.C.) went on to incorporate vast areas of Asia into the Macedonian realm. Such events could not

Tetradrachm. Macedon, 336–323 B.C.

help but affect the history of the tetradrachm: the coin spread far past its original confines in and around Greece. But it was to change as it did so. A world empire requires a standardization of coinage, and while Alexander's state did not survive his death, the standardized tetradrachm did. The illustrated coin was actually struck during Alexander's lifetime, but nearly identical specimens were minted many years after his death, differing only in minor stylistic details.

There were further developments. In the Hellenistic successor states, the depiction of gods and goddesses on obverses was yielding to portraits of living rulers—an essentially non-Greek idea, inspired by traditions of the Eastern lands annexed by Alexander. After about 300 B.C. they were very much in vogue, and remained so until the end of the tetradrachm. The third and second centuries saw some outstanding portraiture on the tetradrachm, much of it from the farthest reaches of Alexander's old empire, including the central Asian kingdom of Bactria. Many later portrait tetradrachms were executed on flans that were broader and thinner than those of early issues. While the early tetradrachms measured 25 millimeters or so, their third- and second-century descendants were frequently 30 millimeters or more. The coin's weight remained about 17 grams, however.

Together with the new portraiture, two other developments on the reverse are worthy of mention. Longer legends or inscriptions became the rule; and the number of reverse types diminished appreciably. Alexander's coin shows a seated figure of Zeus, a type adopted by a number of mints during and after his reign: later tetradrachms from the kingdoms established by his successors also retained a limited number of standard types, often through several reigns.

The importance of the tetradrachm diminished with the rise of Rome, which of course had its own monetary system to impose on conquered areas. Yet some coining of tetradrachms was allowed to continue due to special considerations. The best-known example occurred in Egypt, which was permitted to strike a series of increasingly debased tetradrachms until almost A.D. 300. The later representatives of this series were small, base-metal coins, devoid of any artistic merit.

See also ARCHAIC COINAGE; DECADRACHM; DIDRACHM; DRACHM; GREEK IMPERIALS; OCTADRACHM; OWL; PORTRAIT; TRADE COINS.

THALER A generic term for a broad, heavy silver coin of central Europe, minted from the late fifteenth through the late nineteenth centuries; also, an actual coinage denomination of that name.

The size and weight of the thaler varied throughout its career. Early issues were between 39 and 45 millimeters in diameter, and weighed between approximately 25 and 30 grams. Later issues were more standardized and became smaller and lighter.

The thaler's origins are in the exploitation of central European silver deposits in the late Middle Ages. The Austrian Tyrol was a center of such deposits, and its count Sigismund (ruled 1439–1490) elected to fashion coinage from the silver.

The coin in the illustration is one of Sigismund's, and measures about 41 millimeters in diameter with a weight of nearly 31.3 grams. On the obverse, the archduke

Thaler. *Tyrol, guldengroschen, 1486. This coin was the direct ancestor of the thaler.*

is seen in a standing position—an immediate advantage of the new coin was its size, which offered greater possibility for adventurous portraiture and designs than the older, smaller coins. The reverse shows a mounted armed figure, surrounded by heraldic shields, with the date (1486) beneath the horse. The use of a Christian date on coinage was a fairly new concept at the time.

Sigismund's innovation was well liked, and within a few years other states in mining areas were minting similar coins. The counts of Schlick, owners of the productive Joachimsthal mine in Bohemia, were especially active. In the 1520s their coins were struck in abundance, and in even greater quantities in the 1530s. Their name—Joachimsthaler—was soon used for other large silver coins of the day and, gradually it was shortened to thaler (also spelled taler).

It was as a thaler that the coin spread to other parts of central Europe and rapidly proved itself a valued trading piece. Indeed, in the myriad large and small states comprising the Holy Roman Empire, it became well-nigh universal, as princes found its space so useful to celebrate themselves and their accomplishments. (From early times, the thaler was also used as a commemorative coin.)

As both trade coin and commemorative, the thaler was struck for nearly four centuries. But it was in the eighteenth century that it reached its zenith in artistry and popularity. At the same time, attempts were made to standardize its weight and fineness. In 1753 a monetary convention was signed establishing a Conventionsthaler or Speciesthaler, which weighed 28.067 grams and was 833 fine. The agreement was enforced in Austria and its possessions, and some other Germanic states also adhered to it. Others did not, however, and among them was Prussia, without whose concordance a truly universal thaler could not be realized.

An 1857 monetary agreement helped reduce the confusion. A new Vereinsthaler was introduced, weighing 18.518 grams and composed of 90 percent silver, and was adopted by all the states of Germany, including Prussia. However, the new coin's value fluctuated: it was worth one-and-one-half Austrian gulden, one-and-three-quarters gulden of the southern German states, and thirty silber groschen if it happened to be a Prussian coin. In any case, its circulation was short-lived. In 1871, Prussia unified most of the German states into an empire, and based the imperial coinage on a new unit, the mark, while Austria ceased to produce the coin in 1867 for any but commemorative purposes.

The significance of the thaler can hardly be overstated. Although its size stimulated new mint technology and great artistic expression, its main role was always as a trade coin. It is interesting that restrikes of a 1780 Austrian thaler are still produced for use in North and East Africa and the Near East. Over the years, some eight hundred million of these restrikes have been minted.

See also COMMEMORATIVE; DOLLAR; GULDEN; JOACHIMSTHALER; MACHINE-STRUCK COINAGE; MARK; PIECE OF EIGHT; SCHAUTHALER; TRADE COINS.

TOKEN An object made of metal or another hard substance, which represents value or coin.

Tokens have been a feature of numismatics since ancient times, and fall into literally dozens of categories, making an exhaustive study troublesome. Most share certain basic qualities, however. They are usually made of metal, and almost always a base metal. Copper, bronze, brass, and lead were used for early tokens; aluminum, copper-nickel, white metal (mainly tin), and brass predominate in modern examples. If non-metallic substances are used, they tend to be hard rubber or plastic. Whatever the token's composition, its intrinsic value is always less than its stated one: to create an undervalued token would be an economic absurdity.

This leads us to another consideration. Tokens are manufactured for profit. Use a hundred dollars' worth of metal to create a thousand dollars' worth of tokens, and you are likely to make money. But the tokens will not circulate at their stated value unless they are forced into circulation (as with coal mine tokens, hacienda tokens, and several other types), or unless a shortage of real money forces them into circulation (as with Civil War tokens).

Let us examine the broad categories into which most tokens fall. Following the British numismatist Philip Grierson, we shall distinguish three basic types: monetary, semi-monetary, and non-monetary. Monetary tokens may be minted by private parties, companies, or city governments, which do not normally possess the right of coinage. They are frequently meant to remedy a shortage of small change. Our illustration shows such a token, minted by a facility in Birmingham, England, owned by the Parys Mines Company, which had extensive copper mines in Wales. The token was minted in 1787, when there was a dearth of small change in the British Isles, and it is one of the first in a vast series of English, Scottish, and Irish coppers minted from the late 1780s and through the 1790s. Its stated value is one penny; its lettered edge declares it is redeemable on demand in a number of places.

The monetary token may have existed in the Low Countries as early as the thirteenth century, and has been a recurrent feature of numismatics to the present. Some pieces exhibit a high degree of artistry: others are more modest.

The monetary token can be issued because of a lack of small change, or to provide a convenient monetary denomination for a specific end. In New York City, for example, a subway token valued at thirty-five cents had to be prepared when the fare rose to that level, as there was no official coin of that denomination. The thirty-five-cent token served in the transit system, and also in ordinary transactions as a thirty-five-cent *coin*.

The siege piece was a special kind of monetary token. It usually had an intrinsic value less than its stated one, but it also carried an implicit or explicit promise of full redemption once the siege was lifted.

The second category encompasses semi-monetary tokens, and includes such items as pickers' chits, issued to agricultural workers in places where payment is reckoned not by the hour but by the amount of work performed. Such a token is redeemable for cash, even though its value may be expressed in terms of another unit—so many baskets of fruit, etc. These tokens are usually very simple, incorporating only the name or initials of the farmer and the quantity of produce which they represent. Similar tokens have been used in the mining and manufacturing industries.

The gaming counter is also a semi-monetary token, for it replaces a coin while a game is being played, but is converted into money once play ends. The well-known brass imitation of the "spade" guinea of George III is one of the best-known in this genre; others include the German spielmarke of the past century.

The third group of tokens is non-monetary in nature. These pieces provide the right to goods or services, but are not redeemable in cash. They include communion tokens and tesserae, and some types of store cards. The line of demarcation between this token and the other

Token. Anglesey, Wales, penny token, 1787.

types is often hazy. A metallic pass to a theater would be included in the non-monetary category, whereas a subway token would be considered monetary. The difference between them is slight, and lies in the fact that the subway token has a fixed value, and can be sold to someone for that value, whereas the theater token *probably* could not be traded in such fashion. Therefore, one token is closer to "real" money than the other. The distinction remains vague, however, and should remind us that the categories we have mentioned should be treated only as general guidelines.

See also CIVIL WAR TOKENS; COMMUNION TOKEN; CONTORNIATE; EMERGENCY MONEY; HACIENDA TOKEN; HARD TIMES TOKENS; HIGLEY TOKENS; JETON; KRIEGSGELD; NOTGELD; SIEGE PIECE; SO-CALLED DOLLARS; SPIELMARKE; STORE CARD; SUTLERS' CHECKS; TESSERAE; VECTURE; WOODEN NICKELS.

TOLA An Indian weight, usually of gold or silver, which originally varied widely from place to place, but was established at a weight of 180 grains (11.664 grams) by British colonial authorities in the 1830s.

About 1900, many Indian banking houses began to issue tolas in gold. These pieces were essentially ingots, and bore only the name of the issuing authority and the fineness of the gold. They proved a popular way to handle relatively small amounts of precious metal, and were traded back and forth, amassed for dowries, etc.

Tola. India, gold tola, 1940.

In time, the British government in India issued its own tolas. The piece illustrated is undated, but was struck by the Bombay mint in 1940. The obverse reveals the name of the mint, while the reverse states the name and fineness of the piece. It measures 23 millimeters at its widest point. The scalloped edges are reminiscent of actual Indian coinage of the period.

See also INGOT; RUPEE.

TOMBAC The name given to a base-metal alloy of a brassy nature, consisting of 88 percent copper and 12 percent zinc.

Its most important numismatic use occurred in Canada, where five-cent pieces were fashioned from the alloy from late 1942 through 1943, while nickel was diverted to the war effort. The tombac coins were only moderately successful, as people did not like their looks and were unfamiliar with the alloy. When the Canadians found copper and zinc were also critical war metals, tombac was replaced by plated steel for the 1944 and 1945 issues. At the war's end, nickel coinage was reinstated.

See also ALLOY.

TOOLED Altered with a metalworking device, such as a graver or smoother.

The term is most commonly applied to coins treated in this way. Tooling may be done to "improve" a coin's appearance—to smooth the nicks in its fields, and to render letters or dates easier to read. It may also be done to create a rarity, most often designed for resale: a date may be changed, a mint mark added or subtracted. In the United States, thousands of "1804" dollars, "1815" cents, and other rarities have thus been created. Some of these alterations are quite expert, and many people have purchased the tooled pieces in good faith. But careful examination with a magnifying glass usually re-

Tooled. *Hamburg, 1½ thaler, c. 1620. Note the tooling in the field.*

veals the tooling, for it is very difficult to alter a coin this way without leaving some telltale scratches or other marks. In addition, the collecting public is now relatively aware of what a genuine rarity should look like. Hence, tooling to fashion a rarity is no longer an important weapon in the forger's arsenal.

Nor is tooling often used today to improve the surfaces or legends of coins. In earlier days, it was a familiar practice, sometimes executed by collectors who wanted a more comely coin for themselves, rather than for resale. The coin in our illustration was probably altered by such a collector, for its tooling is too obvious to fool anyone. It is a huge one-and-one-half-thaler commemorative coin from Hamburg, Germany, dating from around 1620. The tooling is most evident in the field, surrounding Christ and St. John the Baptist, although this collector seems to have made some effort to improve the legend as well. Such tooling is deplorable from the viewpoint of the modern collector, who holds to the belief that a coin is best left as is, and not "improved."

See also ALTERED; PLUGGED.

TRADE COINS Coins whose economic functions transcend the national boundaries of the states issuing them.

Numismatists are apt to forget that commerce is the underlying reason for producing coinage. Although coins may be minted to use for propaganda, or struck as artistic creations, if they do not succeed in the marketplace, they must be judged failures: the major purpose, the essential use of a coin, is for trade, and this has always been so.

Over the past twenty-five centuries, thousands of types of coins have been issued. Most have been of only local significance, and limited in life and circulation. But a substantial number of coins have transcended their original boundaries, to be traded hundreds or even thousands of miles from their places of mintage. Furthermore, many have been imitated. The list is long, and includes the tetradrachm, the stater, the penny, the grosso, the florin, the Piece of Eight, the thaler. What is it about these coins that won them such wide acceptance? Why did they become trade coins?

Convenience, standardization, and *purity* are primary reasons. Let us briefly examine each.

First, for a coin to be successful within or beyond its place of issue, it must be convenient to use, and contain a sufficient amount of gold or silver to make it useful in trade. (It should be noted that we always mean coins with at least some precious metal content when we speak of trade coins; ancient and modern issues made entirely of base metal are not taken with enough seriousness to be considered trade coins.) It cannot be too large, however, or the number of economic transactions into which it can enter will be too limited. Through much of the history of coinage, there was a tendency to move from smaller to larger coins, once ample supplies of metal had been unearthed. The earlier Middle Ages saw the penny, abandoned in time for the grosso, which in turn yielded to the testone and the thaler. This progression is by no means universal (the Attic tetradrachm, developed early in the story of numismatics, was large, while the basic Roman silver coin—introduced much later—was always rather small), and there is obviously a point beyond which a coin cannot grow if it is to remain convenient. The definition of excessive size varies: those who used the first thalers rarely complained about their inconvenience, while those who employed their descendant, the American silver dollar, did—and avoided the coin.

If convenience is one factor in the creation of a trade coin, standardization is of even more importance. We refer to two types of standardization here, weight and design, with weight the more significant. For a coin such as the tetradrachm to trade freely, there had to be agreement on the coin's weight. Ideally, a single standard should have existed, so any Greek tetradrachm contained as much silver as any other Greek tetradrachm. In practice, such uniformity was never achieved; yet numerous city-states did adhere to a particular weight standard, which encouraged the spread of the tetradrachm as a trade coin.

Design standardization is necessary, because people have traditionally distrusted money of an unfamiliar appearance. Hence a trade coin of broad use is likely to retain its original designs for long periods.

Examples of this immobilization of types and legends abound. Year after year, the Athenian tetradrachm was struck in a stiff, archaic style, which bore no relation to the artistic abilities of the Athenians, simply because the coin was accepted as it was. The first illustration shows a more modern, and even more rigid, application of this idea. This Austrian thaler, with a date and designs originally adopted in 1780, was actually struck in 1915 or 1916. The peoples in North and East Africa and the Near East, for whom it was minted, were extremely suspicious of innovation on money, and would have re-

Trade coins.
Left: Austria, thaler, dated 1780 but struck 1915–1916.
Right: United States, trade dollar, 1880.

jected any coin with a noticeable design change as false—as the Italian government discovered when it produced a coin closely fashioned after the Austrian thaler. To the merchants of the Red Sea area, it was not close enough, and it was summarily rejected.

The third determinant in the fortune of a trade coin is its metallic purity. Indeed, a rationale for standardizing design is to assure people a later coin is no different from the earlier one which they know to be pure. No trade coin can survive for long if the quality of its metal diminishes, and governments issuing trade coins have traditionally taken great pains to make certain their products adhere to an unchanging standard.

How does a government benefit from a trade coin's prosperity? By receiving worldwide prestige, for one thing. But the trade coin may also have a political significance. It can serve as a wedge for national expansion, driving other coins from circulation, encouraging businessmen, and perhaps the government of the issuing nation, to enter new areas and claim them for their own.

The appearance of the United States trade dollar, the second coin illustrated, is relevant here. It was first struck in 1873, when Americans were beginning to entertain the notion of a colonial empire in the Pacific and the Far East. The coin was meant to supplant the Mexican Piece of

Eight or peso, which for centuries had been the dominant trade coin in the Far East, and the Americans carefully recorded the coin's purity on the piece itself, as the Mexicans did. Even so, the trade dollar was not fancied, due partly to its unfamiliar designs, partly to the Mexican peso's entrenched position in the Chinese market. Coinage for circulation was halted in 1878 and never resumed. This brings us to one final point: a successful trade coin is accepted not only for the reasons discussed, but also because of tradition. In some instances, the tradition has enough flexibility to admit the addition of another trade coin; in others its rigidity is stifling.

The trade coin has joined history, a victim of the growing economic complexity, inflation, and dislocation of the twentieth century. Although a number of convertible coinages still exist, they do not feature trade coins in the true sense of the word. Commodities, not coins, are fast becoming the true international currencies of our present day.

See also BARBAROUS IMITATIONS; DENIER; DOUBLOON; DUCAT; FLORIN; GROSSO; IMITATION; OWL; PENNY; PESO; PIECE OF EIGHT; SOLIDUS; STATER; TETRADRACHM; THALER; TREMISSIS.

TRANSFER PRINTING   A printing error on paper money, in which part or all of the obverse of a bill appears in reverse on its back; also known as an offset print.

The mistake takes place in the following manner. In many cases, paper money reverses are printed and left to dry until the following day; then the obverses are added. At that point, an obverse press can be activated without a sheet of paper in it. The impression roller that would ordinarily force the paper against the inked plate instead touches the plate directly, picking up the inked design as it does so. An ordinary sheet is now fed into the press, with its reverse side uppermost. When the impression roller presses the paper onto the lower plate to print the obverse side, the inked impression the roller has accidentally picked up is transferred to the already printed reverse. The transferred image is, of course, in reverse. Subsequent sheets pick up less and less of the offset, and it disappears entirely after a few impressions. Transfer printing (usually near the top margin of the reverse) is a common error on recent United States paper money.

See also ERROR.

TREMISSIS   A small gold coin of the late classical and early medieval period; also known as a triens.

The gold tremissis as we know it dates from the 380s, the product of Theodosius I (ruled A.D. 379–395). Weighing 1.5 grams, and about 15 millimeters in diameter, three tremisses equalled one solidus —the main circulating gold coin of the time.

The tremissis was struck regularly throughout the fifth century. By far the majority were minted in the eastern half of the Roman Empire, primarily at Constantinople, while Western issues were coined by Roman mints and, later, by the barbarian successor-states which inherited those mints. East or West, the small size of the coin discouraged artistic experimentation and excellence of design—as did the lamentable numismatic taste of the period, with its stiff, unnatural portraiture, and its limited arsenal of reverse types. A crude profile portrait of the ruler, often an unintentional caricature, graced the obverse; Victory, holding a wreath and palm, or a cross circled by a wreath, were standard reverse designs. One can surmise that the profile portrait remained in vogue on the tremissis long after it had been abandoned on other coins because the coin's small size discouraged full-face portraiture.

Later tremisses developed along two paths, which diverged as time passed. In the East, the Byzantine state minted tremisses until the middle of the reign of Basil I (ruled 867–886), and large numbers were struck through much of the sixth and seventh centuries. During the first reign of Justinian II (ruled 685–695, 705–711), the full-face portrait finally came into favor, as that emperor adopted a facing bust of Christ as the obverse type, and a standing figure of himself as the reverse image. The tremissis was keeping pace with design changes seen on solidi and other coins. These later designs vied with earlier ones for much of the remaining life of the Byzantine tremissis, while sometimes, during shared reigns, the senior emperor's full-face portrait adorned the obverse, with that of the junior partner on the reverse.

In the West, the barbarian inheritors of the former Roman realm initially struck tremisses that imitated early Byzantine issues, and their rulers were content to copy designs and legends in toto. Tremisses of Anastasius I (ruled 491–518) and Justinian I (ruled 527–565) were the most frequently imitated coins.

In time, the barbarians added the initials or monograms of local rulers to the reverses of the imitations, often in the left field. Still later, they issued coins with their own names and portraits, and an identifiable Western tremissis gradually emerged. However, many of these coins remained heavily dependent on Byzantine coinage for inspiration, as the illustration shows.

Tremissis.
Left: Byzantine Empire, 491–518.
Right: France, 613–629.

The coin on the left is a tremissis of Anastasius I, while that on the right is a Merovingian issue of Clotaire II (ruled 613–629). Clotaire's name is on his coin, and the portrait is meant to represent him, but the coin is still clearly imitative of its Byzantine predecessor. Other areas spawned a more individual Western tremissis. The best example is Visigothic Spain, where an imitative coinage evolved which, despite some wretched full-face portraits, is of native inspiration and shows a certain degree of sophistication.

By the middle of the eighth century, the Western tremissis had all but vanished. In Spain, its issue ceased abruptly with the Moslem conquest of the early eighth century. In France and Britain, its production had stopped some years before. The minting of tremisses persisted in the Lombard state in Italy until approximately 750. The coin's disappearance occurred in part because of a shortage of gold in the early medieval West (this scarcity was one reason why the barbarians had copied the tremissis and not the larger solidus in the first place). Silver, a somewhat more plentiful precious metal, replaced gold, and such silver coins as the denier replaced the tremissis.

See also CROSS ON COINAGE; DENIER; IMITATION; PENNY; PORTRAIT; SOLIDUS.

TRIAL STRIKE A piece struck at any point in the preparation of coin or medal dies, allowing the engraver or designer to gauge the work's appearance, and determine what must be done to complete the designs to his or his employer's satisfaction.

The trial strike gives the artist an accurate, three-dimensional representation of his work as it stands. Is the relief too high or too low? Is the placement of the types and legends as pleasing in metal as it was on paper? Should the designs be modified; if so, how? The trial strike points the way.

Trial strikes are usually executed with

Trial strike. United States, trial strike in copper for a pattern quarter dollar, 1869.

a single die, which can be in any stage of preparation. White metal has requently been used for this purpose, as have copper discs and even other coins. A nineteenth-century variant on the trial strike was the *splasher*. Here, the artisan poured some fusible alloy onto a piece of paper, then struck it with his die before it had had a chance to harden.

The trial strike is a rarity, as it is never meant to leave the mint, and is made solely for the use of its employees. This distinguishes it from the proof and, to a degree, from the pattern as well. The photograph shows the obverse of an early American trial strike, an incuse copper impression of a punch to be used in preparing dies for an 1869 pattern quarter-dollar. The artist has not yet added the obligatory word LIBERTY to the figure's headband, indicating the piece was prepared early in the elaboration of the punch. A pattern coin with this head was eventually created, but never adopted for regular coinage. Several dozen patterns were struck, but this trial strike is apparently unique.

The paper money equivalent of the trial strike is the essay note.

See also DIE; ESSAY NOTE; PATTERN; PROOF; WHITE METAL.

TRUSSELL The upper of the two dies used to create hammered coinage.

It appears the term derives from the Old French *troussel* (a bundle). Another name for the trussell is punch die. As it evolved, the typical trussell was an iron bar, as long as 300 millimeters, and slightly larger in diameter than the coin it was designed to strike. The coin's design (the trussell was ordinarily used for a coin's reverse) was cut into the trussell's lower face. The upper face received the hammer's blows; its sides bent outward and down from this repeated pressure, eventually forming what was known as a "beard."

When speaking of hammered coinage, the terms anvil die and punch die are preferable to pile and trussell, as they communicate a notion of the actual appearance and purpose of the objects being described.

See also DIE; HAMMERED COINAGE; PILE.

TUGHRA A decorative calligraphic element found on numerous coins of the Ottoman Empire and related states.

As the Koran forbids the depiction of living objects, artists very early turned to calligraphy as a mode of expression, and from this the tughra was conceived.

The graceful, upsweeping script on the Turkish coin in our illustration incorporates the name of the reigning sultan, 'Abd al-'Aziz, who ruled the Ottoman state from A.H. 1277 to 1293 (A.D. 1861–1876). It also includes the name of his father and predecessor, 'Abd al-Majid I, customary practice on the tughra.

Tughra. Turkey, 40 para, 1864–1865.

Used initially on seals and documents, by the early fourteenth century the tughra began to appear on coins of the Sarukhan dynasty of southern Anatolia. The Ottoman Turks used it for the first time on a coin of the emir Suleyman (ruled A.H. 806–813; A.D. 1403–1410). It was seen on coins only sporadically until the seventeenth century, after which it was in general use on Ottoman coinage until the dynasty's end in 1922.

As an obverse design, the tughra was most consistently employed in Turkey, the center of the Ottoman Empire. However, it was adopted in Egypt—nominally a province of the empire until it became a British protectorate late in 1914—and in such areas totally independent of Turkish control as Hyderabad, in India; Mogadishu, on the East African coast; and Pakistan, where a tughra with the country's name in Urdu (rather than the ruler's name in Arabic) was used regularly until 1974.

See also SEAL.

TYPE   The dominant design on each side of a coin or related object.

The term also refers to a class or group of coins united or related to one another by their design. Thus, numismatists commonly describe a series of Mexican pesos minted from 1824 to 1897 as the "cap and rays" type, because of their central reverse design. Then, too, the word can allude to the central reverse design found on a particular peso within that series.

See also OBVERSE; REVERSE.

TYPE SET   A collection composed of one of every coin in a given series.

The rules for what does and does not constitute a type set are unclear: we can only say that the collection must have a unifying idea. Thus, in the United States, type sets may be made up of one coin from every major design or metallic change in a

given denomination from its inception to the present. A type set might also concentrate on the work of a particular artist, with one example of each coin he designed. As currently used, the term can even denote a set of coins by various designers, in a variety of denominations, provided there is a concept consolidating them—for example, odd denominations.

TYPESET   Printed from movable type as opposed to an engraved plate.

Ordinarily, the typeset note is printed on a press very similar to, if not identical with, that used for printing books—although hand-stamped, typeset notes are also known. (These have usually been of an emergency nature; the bush notes of German East Africa are a well-known example.)

The printing press was introduced about 1450, the first Western paper money some two centuries later. From the beginning, two avenues were open to printers of bank notes: they could borrow from the earlier technique of printing from movable type, or they could print from engraved plates. In the dawn of paper currency, most adopted the first method, as it had several advantages over the second. It was relatively quick, and needed little further development, as the basic processes already existed. Moreover, it could be done in establishments already existing (Benjamin Franklin's firm began as a newspaper and book printer, and later expanded into paper money).

Printing from an engraved plate, on the other hand, was both costly and slow. The plate had to be absolutely flat, or printing was virtually impossible; and it was difficult to make a decent flat plate at that time. Moreover, the copper used for the plate was fairly soft, and the engraving had to be touched up occasionally. The use of a hard steel plate would have been preferable, but a way to do it was not discovered until the nineteenth century. Finally, the degree of artistry needed to produce a handsome engraved note far exceeded that required for a typeset one. The engraved note did have one signal advantage over its typeset counterpart, however: it was harder to counterfeit, a consideration which eventually turned printers away from movable type. As that occurred, engravers found ways to prepare and use steel plates, to transfer vignettes, and so forth. The modern paper note would be born: it would be engraved, while the typeset note would be relegated to only occasional use, most often in a time of emergency when the rapidity of its production still outweighed the risks of its falsification.

All this lay in the future. Between 1650 and 1800, the majority of paper money was printed from movable type. Printers were perfectly aware of the danger of counterfeiting, and took what measures they could to counteract it. The watermark was commonly used for this purpose. Franklin devised the "nature print," a vignette taken from an impression of a real object (usually a leaf), which he used on the reverses of his notes. Other printers used fancy cast borders, any odd bits of type which they had in their shops, etc.— all in an effort to create a typeset bill too complex to counterfeit. Still others printed notes with a mixture of engraving and movable type. The expedients were numerous, but none was successful for more than a brief period: what one man could invent, another could reconstruct.

The note in the illustration was printed from moveable type in 1883 for a small provincial bank in Colombia. This is quite

Typeset. *Colombia, Banco Popular de Bolívar, peso, 1883.*

late for a typeset product, and we can only speculate that it was an interim printing, created while the bank awaited delivery of imported engraved notes. Its production was entrusted to a local printer, Antonio Araújo, who seems to have made use of every last piece of type in his shop to print it. The background of the side seen here was printed in light green, the borders and central fancywork in magenta, while the actual lettering was in black. Araújo built up his plate bit by bit, combining many small simple elements into one large and intricate one. He did the same for the reverse, although that side was printed only in gray.

It is not known how long this bill circulated. It appears the issuer, the Banco Popular de Bolívar, received a shipment of peso notes from a United States printer in or about 1886, after which the homemade product was presumably retired.

See also BANK NOTE; BUSH NOTES; ENGRAVING; PAPER MONEY; WATERMARK.

U

UNPUBLISHED Not previously documented or catalogued in the numismatic literature.

It is important to note that this term is not consistently wedded to the rarity or value of a piece. Some series, such as Greek and Roman coinages, have been painstakingly catalogued: an unpublished coin of this type could be a major event. Yet in other fields, such as Latin American coinage, notgeld, and paper money, little has been published. Interest in these areas is recent, and our knowledge is relatively incomplete. The discovery of an unpublished broken bank note therefore, would be more or less taken in stride, as it may be unpublished only because no one had thought to look for it, or to record its existence.

See also RARITY.

UPSET EDGE The edge of a planchet that has been thickened by compressing it between two rollers.

Such thickening is done to raise the planchet's borders so they fit more closely into the peripheries of the upper and lower dies. Once upsetting has taken place, less metal has to be displaced at the borders during striking to produce the desired raised, protective areas. And less force has to be applied to the dies, ensuring their longer wear. Coins with raised protective borders have a longer life, as the borders receive most of the abrasion suffered by a coin. The principle of upsetting planchet edges seems to have originated with Matthew Boulton in the 1790s, and is universally used today. The illustration shows part of an upset planchet, intended for an American quarter dollar.

See also BROADSTRUCK; ERROR; PLANCHET.

Upset edge. *United States, detail of a quarter-dollar planchet showing upset edge, 1965 or later.*

V

VECTURE A transportation token.

The word most likely derives from the Latin *vehere,* to carry, and is an obsolete term for a conveyance or carriage. Collectors of transportation tokens are known as vecturists, and the accumulation of vectures is a rapidly growing branch of numismatics.

The vecture may be used for two kinds of transactions: to pay tolls on roads, bridges, etc., or to pay a fare on public or private conveyances. It appears that tokens started to be used in such fashion in sixteenth-century Germany, at a time when cities were often walled and their gates were closed at night for the town's protection. A way had to be devised to identify late-returning citizens. "Gate tokens" were the answer: sold to those who had to pass through the gates after nightfall, they served as identification and helped to pay the gatekeepers' salaries.

Although in time the walls were no longer seen as defenses, the practice of issuing gate tokens continued as a form of tax, levied on everyone who entered a town after dark, and in some cases during the day as well. And should someone have

to cross a moat or stream to enter the city, there were bridge toll tokens made for this purpose. The earliest surviving one is dated 1549, and is from Regensburg, Germany.

The Germans who emigrated to America took the idea with them: the earliest use of transportation tokens in America was in the 1790s, in Lancaster County, Pennsylvania, where the "Pennsylvania Dutch" (actually Germans) used them on an elaborate system of toll roads.

Within a short time, vectures were employed to pay fares. In America, there were several advantages to using vectures instead of actual coinage in this way. Small change was always scarce in the country, and the purchase of several tokens for an even sum was helpful to the consumer. So was the competition between transportation companies, which often led them to sell tokens at a discount. Later, vectures were used to permit certain people—schoolchildren or employees—to ride at a reduced rate.

Thousands of different types of fare vectures have been issued in the nineteenth and twentieth centuries. First used

Vecture. Davenport, Iowa, Tri-City Railway Company fare token.

on omnibuses, they soon paid fares on elevated railroads, trolleys, subways, and motor buses, and still do. The United States and Canada are the major producers of fare tokens.

The vecture illustrated is a typical fare token. Note that part of the piece has been punched out: this was both a convenience for conductors, who could simplify their work by stringing the vectures on wires, and a protection against counterfeiting. Such cut-outs are common on vectures. These tokens are made from a number of metals, with brass, copper, white metal, and zinc the most important. This piece measures 21 millimeters in diameter, and is made of white metal. Vectures have also been fashioned of celluloid, fiber, plastic, and hard rubber.

See also TOKEN.

VIGNETTE The pictorial part of a paper note, as distinguished from the frame and lettering.

The vignette has always had two functions. It embellishes a note, but is also meant to protect it from counterfeiters. Largely because of the latter, the vignette has existed almost as long as paper money itself.

Vignettes are found on the first paper money of the Massachusetts Bay Colony, produced at the beginning of the 1690s. A few years later we see them on notes of the Bank of England, and during the eighteenth century the practice spread further. Early vignettes were small, and occupied a distinctly subordinate position on notes, as they were only one of several anti-counterfeiting devices used at the time.

By the nineteenth century, however, their real value, as a deterrent to counterfeiting and as decoration, was quite clear. The size of the vignette grew, as did its complexity and beauty, and the importance of its position on the note. A twentieth-century development is the printing of multicolored vignettes; some countries now manufacture notes with vignettes closely resembling color photographs.

The vignette in the illustration appears on a note issued by a bank in Pontiac,

Vignette. Michigan, Bank of Oakland at Pontiac, dollar, 1837 (detail).

Michigan, in 1837 and indicates the state of vignette art at the time. It is heavy with symbolism, and is also a masterpiece of miniaturization—note the tiny locomotive and cars on the left.

See also BROKEN BANK NOTES; ENGRAVING.

VIS-À-VIS TYPE   A coin or medal design with two portraits in profile facing each other; a method of portraiture occasionally employed on coins from ancient times until the early modern period.

The technique was never especially popular, as it presented a number of design problems. First, the vis-à-vis portrait was not the best use of the circular area of the coin's face. If busts rather than heads were rendered, as was frequently the case, the result was often a noticeably empty space in the center of the coin. If heads were depicted instead, it was easy to make them look crammed together; several Roman issues have vis-à-vis heads whose noses nearly touch, and the effect is ridiculous.

Unlike the jugate portrait, the vis-à-vis portrait reproduced each head or bust in its entirety, which created a second difficulty: it was almost impossible to achieve admirable portraiture in the limited space available. The Austrian thaler in our illus-

Vis-à-vis type. Austria, thaler, 1518.

tration is one of the more successful uses of the technique.

The Holy Roman Emperor Maximilian I (ruled 1493–1519), whose coin this is, had his reasons for demanding the unusual vis-à-vis treatment. He appears on the left; the boy on the right is his grandson Charles, whom the emperor hoped would be chosen as his successor. Placing his portrait opposite that of Maximilian (with an accompanying legend underscoring the relationship) was a logical campaign tactic, and an effective one. In 1519 the boy was elected emperor, ruling, as Charles V, until 1558.

See also COMMEMORATIVE; JUGATE; PORTRAIT.

W

WA DO KAIHO The earliest Japanese coin to be produced on a major scale.

The discovery of large copper deposits in the province of Musashi made wa do kaiho (which translates "Japanese copper initial treasure") possible. First cast in A.D. 708 during the reign of the empress Genmyo (ruled 708–714), they were accompanied by a similar cast issue in silver. The silver coinage ceased the following year, but the wa do kaiho was produced for another half century.

The coin owed much to contemporary Chinese issues, and clearly reflected the fact that the Japanese had previously imported Chinese coins. Indeed, the model for the wa do kaiho was a ch'ien of the early T'ang dynasty (618–907).

Wa do kaiho. Japan, 708–714.

Wa do kaiho are in one of two series, distinguished from each other by their workmanship. From 708 to 720, the Japanese cast the coins themselves, resulting in pieces that were slightly rough in execution. In 720, Chinese craftsmen were hired to work in the facility at Nara, then Japan's capital. Immediately the quality and workmanship of the coins improved, and this second class of wa do kaiho was cast until the country's coinage was reformed in 760. The illustrated specimen measures 25 millimeters and weighs 2.2 grams.

See also CASH; CAST COINAGE.

WAMPUM Beads made from clam, conch, or similar shells, and used as money by North American Indians.

Wampum was also used to send messages, and for personal adornment. The name derives from the Algonquian *wampumpeage,* meaning "a string of white beads." Although the Indians had another term for the rarer beads fashioned of black or purple shell—*suckauhock*—the

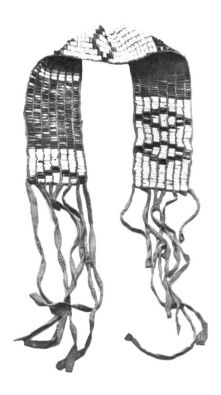

Wampum. *Wampum trade belt, Nova Scotia.*
(Courtesy of the Museum of the American Indian—
Heye Foundation, New York)

first European settlers used the word wampum to describe both colors, and it has persisted.

It is not known precisely when wampum originated. The French explorer Jacques Cartier encountered it in 1535, and the Iroquois speak of using wampum beads earlier than 1570. It seems clear various tribes had adopted it as money before the white settlers appeared, but it was probably only used for large transactions, with smaller ones conducted by barter.

According to Don Taxay, an expert on primitive money, wampum was introduced to New England in 1627 by Isaac De Razier, the Secretary of New Netherland, and rapidly spread among the struggling coastal English colonies, with eastern Long Island becoming a center for its production. Both colonists and Indians prized wampum, the former because of a chronic shortage of circulating coin, the latter

partly because their new white neighbors took it so seriously.

Wampum belongs in the general category of commodity money, and like all the group's currency, it varied in quality and value. Most beads were purple or white, with purple ones double the worth of white ones. In short order, some enterprising settlers discovered white beads could be dyed purple, or otherwise falsified—the introduction of counterfeiting to North America. Their untutored fellow-colonists were ready targets; the Indians were not.

The unit of wampum money was a *fathom,* and consisted of three hundred sixty strung beads; the actual value of each bead varied from colony to colony. In 1637 the authorities of Massachusetts Bay declared six white beads the equal of one English penny, while the Connecticut rate was four to the penny.

By the late 1650s, so much wampum was circulating that the medium began to depreciate in value. Massachusetts revoked its legal tender status in 1661, and other colonies followed suit. The last official use of wampum among Europeans seems to have taken place in the early 1690s. Unofficially, it circulated for many years in remote areas, and the Indians used it for money until the middle of the nineteenth century. This later wampum was made for the Indians by white men, and a good part was created from porcelain and materials other than shells. The Campbell family of New Jersey produced wampum for Indians—and, at the end, for museums—until 1905.

See also BARTER; COMMODITY MONEY.

WATERMARK A design impressed into paper during its manufacture, visible when the paper is held up to the light, long employed for paper money as a counterfeit deterrent.

The watermark represents a slight thinning of the paper at a particular point, and results from the use of special wires or metallic strips fixed to the dandy roll, which presses their designs into the moist paper. When the paper is dried, the watermark is retained.

Watermarks seem to be an Italian invention: the earliest watermarked paper appeared there about 1270. (The Chinese, who had invented paper itself hundreds of years before, did not use watermarks for any of their paper products, including paper money.)

The use of the watermark to curb paper money counterfeiting was started by the Bank of England in 1697. The practice spread with the development of paper money, and has become almost universal in this century, with the exception of the Americas, where it has usually found less favor.

Watermarks can be divided into three categories. On early notes, a large, simple design was favored, and it often occupied the entire area of the note. It could be the national arms, the name of the bank, and the note's denomination, or merely a collection of parallel lines. This type of watermark has been abandoned today for two others, the first of which might be called a border watermark—a design appearing in an otherwise unadorned area on one end of the bill. Germany has faithfully followed this practice, and most German notes made in this century reveal it. The border watermark's subject has varied from a relatively simple statement of value to a more complex shaded portrait. This shaded, dimensional watermark—a vast improvement over the simple lettering or outline executed by earlier means—was invented in the middle of the last century, and later used on paper money. Now it is the prevailing watermark technique for creating the border watermark and the vignette watermark, the third category.

The vignette watermark is found inside the bill's printed border, rather than on its outside. Early vignette watermarks tended to be allegorical or symbolic, while modern ones frequently reproduce the

Watermark. *Israel, 5 lirot, 1968 (detail).*

central figure on the obverse of the note. Thus, the detail of the Israeli five-lirot note in the photograph shows a watermark of Dr. Albert Einstein, whose portrait also occupies the right-hand side of the note (not seen here). If you look closely, you may see a security thread to the right of the watermark; many countries use both devices. The vignette watermark, very much in vogue in this century, is now the predominant form.

See also ENGRAVING; PAPER MONEY; SECURITY THREAD; VIGNETTE.

WHITE METAL   Any of several white alloys, consisting of lead, tin, zinc, and other metals with low melting points. White metal has found a certain use in the manufacture of tokens, inexpensive medals, and trial strikes, but its softness and lack of intrinsic value have discouraged its use for coinage.

See also BRITANNIA METAL; TOKEN; VECTURE.

WILDCAT NOTES A popular name for the unsupported issues of certain private banks in nineteenth-century America.

Many of these banks were deliberately established in areas remote from civilization, to make the redemption of their notes in specie as arduous as possible. More often than not, wildcats outnumbered the lands' people, and some see this as the term's genesis. Another theory, and one espoused by John Russell Bartlett, the nineteenth-century American lexicographer, holds that the name, which originated in Michigan, derived from a vignette of a wildcat seen on one of the notes. Bartlett's is likely to be the correct explanation.

It is not surprising that the wildcat note was born in Michigan. The Michigan General Banking Law of 1837 made it an absurdly simple task to organize a bank and issue money. Over fifty banks were immediately founded, most for the sole purpose of issuing paper money. The result was a rapid expansion of the money supply and an equally rapid collapse. In 1838, with the state's economy in ruins, the law was suspended. All the new banks, and many older ones, had broken. This could have been averted had the state written strict supervisory provisions into the 1837 law. But it did not; given the *laissez-faire* attitude of the time, no one had thought they would be necessary.

The Michigan bank crash, and other disasters, made "broken bank" and "wildcat note" part of the American argot, and also prepared the ground for a national currency system.

See also BANK NOTE; BROKEN BANK NOTES.

WIRE EDGE A sharply raised area on a coin's rim where the metal has been forced between the die and the collar during striking.

In British numismatics, the term knife rim is standard, and could win favor elsewhere, as it is a more accurate description than wire edge.

Wire edge. United States, 20 dollars, 1907 (detail).

The wire edge may be deliberate or accidental. A small issue of United States ten-dollar gold pieces was given wire edges in 1907 as part of an experiment conducted during that year by the Mint. Other wire edges are accidental, the product of excessive pressure used in striking, of bad design, or of the normal wear and tear to be expected on collars. Many double eagles of the Saint-Gaudens design show wire edges on the high relief issues of 1907. The dies prepared for these coins had indeterminate borders. At the same time, their depth required that each planchet be struck several times to bring up the full relief. This multiple striking forced metal between the collar and the dies, creating the wire edge. The problem was noticed, the dies were retooled, and double eagles were then struck in high relief with flat rims. The relief itself was eventually lowered, permitting the coins to be struck in a single blow.

Unless they are very obvious, accidental wire edges are not considered mint errors.

See also COLLAR; RIM.

WIRE MONEY Small Russian coins which used lengths of wire as planchets.

Apparently the practice started in the fourteenth century, and it continued until the beginning of the eighteenth. A silver coin, the denga, was the first coin produced in this fashion; it was joined by the copper puls or pulos in the fifteenth century, and by the silver kopek in the sixteenth.

Wire money. Russia, kopek, 1547–1584.

Although it is uncertain whether or not wire money was invented in Russia, it is known a variant of the idea evolved far to the south and east (in the lands bordering the Persian Gulf and Indian Ocean), and generated the larin. This would seem to be a later invention than Russian wire money, but the series is still not fully documented. In any case, while both the larin and the Russian coin stressed the use of wire as a planchet, they elaborated it in dissimilar ways.

The Russians rolled silver into wire, then sliced it into equal sections of the proper weight. Next, the Russian minter hammered the length of wire into a small, flat plate, generally in an oval shape (although the top and bottom of the oval might come to a point where the original wire had been cut). This method had a signal advantage over those procedures used farther west. The coiner began with pieces of silver of identical length, thickness, and hence weight, which did not have to be remelted or reworked before striking could take place.

After flattening, the ovals were heated to soften them, and then struck between an upper and a lower die. The obverse or lower die commonly bore a mounted horseman or a heraldic device, with the occasional addition of a mint mark and (after about 1600) a date beneath the figure. The reverse or upper die gave the title of the ruler responsible for the coin.

The specimen of wire money in the illustration is a silver kopek of Tsar Ivan IV (ruled 1547–1584). A mint mark for Moscow appears beneath the horse. The coin measures 17 millimeters by 11.5, and weighs seven-tenths of a gram. As can be seen, its designs are incomplete, parts of them running off the flan. This was caused by round dies being used on an oval planchet: inevitably, something was lost.

The last wire money was coined under Peter the Great (ruled 1682–1725), who decreed a more modern Russian coinage in 1700. All the same, Peter allowed silver wire kopeks to be issued until the beginning of 1718, in part because many found his new, machine-struck copper kopek suspect.

See also DECIMAL COINAGE; KOPEK; LARIN.

WOODEN NICKELS A collective term for coin-like objects made of wood.

Initially these were actually intended, at least in part, for commerce, as they were produced during a period of emergency and an accompanying shortage of small change. Their first recorded use in the United States occurred in Tenino, Washington, in 1931–1932, at the height of the Great Depression, but very similar pieces were made in Austria in 1920, part of the flood of notgeld printed there after the end of World War I.

The Tenino pieces, and their Austrian counterparts, were rectangular rather than round, and were designed both for local circulation and for sale as souvenirs. Within a few years, however, they served only as souvenirs; most wooden nickels from then on were "struck" to celebrate local events, as advertisements, and so forth. Until the middle 1950s, most were rectangular; while five cents was the traditional denomination, wooden "dimes" and "quarters" are also known. At present, they are usually printed with rubber dies, and are circulated as advertisements or mementos, with no values expressed. While Canada and other countries have created such wooden pieces from time to time, they are considered a distinctly American contribution to exonumia.

See also EMERGENCY MONEY; EXONUMIA; NOTGELD.

Wu shu. *China, 118* B.C.–A.D. *619.*

WU SHU A long-lived Chinese bronze coin, the direct ancestor of the ch'ien or cash, and introduced by the emperor Wu-Ti in 118 B.C., to replace the pan liang.

Wu-Ti's new coin weighed five *shu* (twenty-four *shu* made up the *tael,* or Chinese ounce). Like the pan liang, the wu shu was cast; it bore two characters on the obverse, giving the coin's weight, and no characters on the reverse. It also had a square hole, as did the pan liang. But Wu-Ti added new elements: a raised obverse and reverse rim, designed to prevent filing; and, as decoration, a raised rim around the square hole on the reverse. These would be retained for the subsequent ch'ien.

Wu-Ti's coin was a great success, and was cast in astronomical quantities over the next few centuries. No complete mintage records exist, but one authority has estimated some two hundred eighty million wu shu coins were cast down to the onset of the Christian era alone. Many millions more were manufactured during the remaining six centuries of the coin's production. Undeniably, the wu shu is the most common ancient Chinese coin available to collectors.

It is impossible to date, however. It was issued by nine regular and twenty-three irregular dynasties, ruling over all or part of China, successively or contemporaneously, for a period of more than seven hundred years—with virtually no change in inscription or design. A study of changes in calligraphy is of some use here, but at best dating remains approximate. The wu shu illustrated, with a diameter of 26 millimeters and a weight of 3.85 grams, may be considered typical of the entire series.

It is obvious the wu shu was one of the most popular Chinese coins ever to circulate. As long as it was cast at its stated weight, it satisfied people's daily monetary needs, and since it bore no *nien-hao,* it could be used by each successive dynasty.

Its weight declined with time, however, and its metallic content had always varied. A new dynasty, the T'ang, rose to power in the early seventh century A.D., and its first emperor, Kao Tsu, introduced a new coin, similar to but somewhat larger than the wu shu, with four obverse characters rather than two. Two of these characters gave the new ruler's *nien-hao;* the other two informed the public the coin was current. Furthermore, the coinage would now be cast of six parts copper and four of other elements, an attempt to reach some metallic standardization. Each coin was to weigh a tenth of a tael. The new piece is generally known as a ch'ien or cash, and the proclamation which created it (and displaced the wu shu) dates from 620.

See also CASH; CAST COINAGE; HOLED COINAGE; *NIEN-HAO;* PAN LIANG.

Y

YUAN The current monetary unit of Taiwan and the People's Republic of China.

In Chinese, the word means "circular," and it eventually designated the large, foreign silver coins entering China through trade. By 1889 the Chinese were relinquishing their traditional coinage and striking their own large silver coins. Based on the United States silver dollar, these new coins were generally known as yuan, although most bore a different designation, based on their silver weight in relation to the *tael,* or Chinese ounce. During the last fifteen years of the empire, however, a few yuan were actually struck with that name.

With the overthrow of the emperor in October 1911, and the creation of a republic soon after, the yuan's position as the Chinese monetary unit became permanent. Henceforth, the name appeared on Chinese coins and notes, often with the English word dollar. Production of the silver yuan was sporadic until 1936: today it is represented by a paper note in the People's Republic of China, and by a small, base-metal coin in Taiwan.

The piece shown was struck in 1932, and features the portrait of the Chinese republic's founder, Dr. Sun Yat-sen, on the obverse. The reverse design was controversial, some interpreting it as a reminder of Japanese encroachments on the country during this period. The scene's rising sun is, of course, the emblem of Japan, and the three birds bear an uncomfortable resemblance to Japanese warplanes. Both sun and birds were excised from later issues.

See also DOLLAR; TAEL.

Yuan. *China, 1932.*

Z

ZECCHINO A synonym for the Venetian gold ducat and some of its imitators.

Zecchino presumably derives from the Italian word for mint, *zecca*. In several places it was corrupted to sequin, and in late medieval and early modern sources the Venetian ducat is frequently referred to by the latter name.

See also DUCAT; TRADE COINS.

ZINC COINAGE Coinage made from a silver-gray metal with a relatively low melting point.

In its pure state, zinc is fairly soft; this and its low intrinsic value have hindered its popularity as a coinage medium. However, it has had a limited use for tokens and metallic notgeld, as well as occupation and regular issues struck by Germany, Austria, and Hungary during and after the world wars. The piece shown is a zinc twenty-five centime coin struck in Belgium in 1916 by German forces. Note how the metal has tarnished to a uniform, rather unpleasant gray, another factor inhibiting its use for coins. Zinc is common in coinage alloys, however; a mixture of copper and zinc yields brass, a popular coining material for many centuries. At present, the only major use of the unalloyed metal is in the Austrian five-groschen piece.

See also ALLOY; BRASS COINAGE; KRIEGS-GELD; TOKEN; VECTURE.

Zinc coinage. Belgium, 25 centimes, 1916.

Bibliography

GENERAL

American Numismatic Society. *Numismatic Literature.* Vol. 1–. New York: American Numismatic Society, 1947–.

Babelon, Jean. *Great Coins and Medals.* Translated by Stuart Hood. London: Thames and Hudson, 1959.

Bachtell, Lee M. *World Dollars, 1477–1877. Pictorial Guide.* Ludowici, Georgia: The Author, 1974.

Bartlett, John Russell. *A Dictionary of Americanisms. A Glossary of Words and Phrases Usually Regarded as Peculiar to the United States.* 2nd ed., rev. Boston: Little, Brown and Company, 1859.

Bloom, Murray Teigh. *Money of Their Own: The Great Counterfeiters.* New York: Charles Scribner's Sons, 1957.

Carson, R. A. G. *Coins: Ancient, Mediaeval & Modern.* London: Hutchinson, 1962.

Clain-Stefanelli, Elvira Eliza. *Select Numismatic Bibliography.* New York: Stack's, 1965.

Coin World Almanac. 3rd ed. Sidney, Ohio: Amos Press, 1977.

Doty, Richard G. *Coins of the World.* New York: The Ridge Press, Inc., and Bantam Books, Inc., 1976.

———. *Money of the World.* New York: The Ridge Press, Inc., and Grosset & Dunlap, Inc., 1978.

Eckfeldt, Jacob R., and Du Bois, William E. *A Manual of Gold and Silver Coins of All Nations, Struck Within the Past Century.* Philadelphia: Assay Office of the Mint, 1842.

Einzig, Paul. *Primitive Money.* London: Eyre & Spottiswoode, 1949.

Frey, Albert R. *Dictionary of Numismatic Names.* New York: American Numismatic Society, 1917; reprint edition, with addenda and glossary by Mark M. Salton, London: Spink & Son Ltd. and Organization of International Numismatists, 1973.

Grierson, Philip. *Bibliographie numismatique.* 2e édition revue et augmentée. Cercle d'Etudes Numismatiques, travaux 9. Brussels: Cercle d'Etudes Numismatiques, 1979.

———. *Numismatics.* London: Oxford University Press, 1975.

Hobson, Burton. *Coin Identifier.* New York: Sterling Publishing Co., Inc., and London: Oak Tree Press, Ltd., 1966.

Kroha, Tyll. *Lexikon der Numismatik.* Gütersloh, W. Ger.: Bertelsmann Lexikon-Verlag, 1977.

Linecar, Howard. *Coins and Coin Collecting.* London: The Hamlyn Publishing Group, Ltd., 1971.

Martini, Angelo. *Manuale di metrologia.* Turin: Ermanno Loescher, 1883.

Narbeth, Colin. *The Coin Collector's Encyclopaedia.* London: Stanley Paul & Co., Ltd., 1968.

Newton, Joseph. *An Introduction to Metallurgy.*

2nd ed. New York: John Wiley & Sons, Inc., 1947.

Porteous, John. *Coins in History.* New York: G. P. Putnam's Sons, 1969.

Quiggin, A. Hingston. *A Survey of Primitive Money: The Beginnings of Currency.* Rev. ed. London: Methuen & Co. Ltd., 1963.

Reinfeld, Fred. *Treasury of the World's Coins.* New York: Sterling Publishing Co., Inc., 1953.

Schrötter, Friedrich Frhr. v. *Wörterbuch der Münzkunde.* Berlin: Verlag von Walter de Gruyter & Co., 1930.

ANCIENT AND MEDIEVAL

Banks, Florence Aiken. *Coins of Bible Days.* New York: Macmillan Publishing Co., Inc., 1955.

Bellinger, Alfred R., and Grierson, Philip, eds. *Catalogue of the Byzantine Coins in the Dumbarton Oaks Collection and in the Whittemore Collection.* 3 vols. in 5 pts. Washington: Dumbarton Oaks Center for Byzantine Studies, 1966–1973.

Brett, Agnes Baldwin. *Catalogue of Greek Coins.* Boston: Museum of Fine Arts, 1955.

Casey, John, and Reece, Richard, eds. *Coins and the Archaeologist.* British Archaeological Reports, no. 4. London: Institute of Archaeology, 1974.

Catalogue of Greek Coins in the British Museum. 29 vols. London: British Museum, Department of Coins and Medals, 1873–1927.

Cochran-Patrick, R. W. *Records of the Coinage of Scotland.* 2 vols. Edinburgh: Edmonston and Douglas, 1876.

Grant, Michael. *Roman History from Coins.* Cambridge, Eng.: University Press, 1958.

Grierson, Philip. *Monnaies du Moyen Age.* Translated by Hélène Huvelin. Fribourg, Switz.: Office du Livre, 1976.

———. "Nummi scyphati. The Story of a Misunderstanding." *Numismatic Chronicle,* Seventh Series, 11 (1971), pp. 253–60.

Grueber, H. A. *Coins of the Roman Republic.* 3 vols. London: British Museum, Department of Coins and Medals, 1910; reprinted 1970.

Head, Barclay V. *Historia Numorum: A Manual of Greek Numismatics.* New and enlarged edition. Oxford, Eng.: Clarendon Press, 1911.

Hendy, Michael F. *Coinage and Money in the Byzantine Empire, 1081–1261.* Dumbarton Oaks

Studies, no. 12. Washington: Dumbarton Oaks Center for Byzantine Studies, 1969.

Jenkins, G. K. *Ancient Greek Coins.* New York: G. P. Putnam's Sons, 1972.

Kent, J. P. C. *Roman Coins.* Rev. ed. New York: Harry N. Abrams, Inc., Publishers, 1978.

Klawans, Zander H. *Reading and Dating Roman Imperial Coins.* 4th ed. Racine, Wisc.: Western Publishing Co., Inc., 1977.

Kowalski, H. "Die Augustalen Kaiser Friedrichs II." *Schweizerische Numismatische Rundschau* 55 (1976), pp. 77–150.

Kraay, Colin M. *Archaic and Classical Greek Coins.* Berkeley and Los Angeles: University of California Press, 1976.

Lawrence, L. A. *The Coinage of Edward III from 1351.* Oxford, Eng.: University Press, 1937.

———. "English Piedforts and their Purposes." *British Numismatic Journal* 16 (Second Series, Vol. 6), 1921–1922 [1924], pp. 113–17.

Mattingly, Harold. *Roman Coins.* 2nd ed. London: Methuen & Co. Ltd., 1960.

Mattingly, Harold, *et al.*, eds. *The Roman Imperial Coinage.* Vol. 1–. London: Spink & Son Ltd., 1923–.

Meshorer, Ya'akov. *Jewish Coins of the Second Temple Period.* Translated by I. H. Levine. Tel Aviv: Am Hassefer, 1967.

Metcalf, D. M. *The Origins of the Anastasian Currency Reform.* Amsterdam: Adolf M. Hakkert, 1969.

Price, Martin, and Waggoner, Nancy. *Archaic Greek Coinage: The Asyut Hoard.* London: V. C. Vecchi and Sons, 1975.

Reece, Richard. *Roman Coins.* London: Ernest Benn Limited, 1970.

Rogers, Edgar. *A Handy Guide to Jewish Coins.* London: Spink & Son Ltd., 1914; reprint ed., New York: Sanford P. Durst, 1977.

Seaby, H. A. *Roman Silver Coins. Vol. 1: The Republic to Augustus.* 3rd ed. revised [by] David R. Sear and Robert Loosley. London: Seaby Publications Ltd., 1978.

Sear, David R. *Byzantine Coins and their Values.* London: Seaby Publications Ltd., 1974.

———. *Greek Coins and their Values. Vol. 1: Europe.* London: Seaby Publications Ltd., 1978.

———. *Roman Coins and their Values.* 2nd rev. ed. London: Seaby's Numismatic Publications Ltd., 1974.

Seltman, Charles. *Greek Coins.* London: Methuen & Co. Ltd., 1933.

Sutherland, C. H. V. *Roman Coins.* New York: G. P. Putnam's Sons, 1974.

Whitting, P. D. *Byzantine Coins.* New York: G. P. Putnam's Sons, 1973.

Yeoman, R. S. *Moneys of the Bible.* Racine, Wisc.: Whitman Publishing Co., 1961.

MODERN

Anderson, P. K. "The Ephemeral Coinage of Spain." *The Numismatist* 65, 9 (September 1952), pp 866–69.

Asbun-Karmy, Luis Alberto. *Monedas, medallas, billetes, acciones, y documentos bancarios de Bolivia.* Oruro, Bolivia: Banco de Crédito Oruro, 1977.

Batalha Reis, Pedro. *Preçário das moedas portuguesas de 1140 a 1640. Preçário das moedas portuguesas de 1640 a 1940.* Lisbon: The Author, 1956.

Brekke, B. F. *The Copper Coinage of Imperial Russia.* Malmö, Sweden: Förlagshuset Norden AB; New York: Galerie des Monnaies of Geneva Ltd., 1977.

Castán, Carlos, and Cayón, Juan R. *Las monedas españolas desde Don Pelayo a Juan Carlos I, años 718 a 1979.* [Madrid: The Authors, 1979].

Castelin, Karel. *Grossus Pragensis. Der Prager Groschen und seine Teilstücke, 1300–1547.* 2. vermehrte Auflage. Brunswick, W. Ger.: Klinkhardt & Biermann, 1973.

Charlton, J. E. *1978 Standard Catalogue of Canadian Coins, Tokens, and Paper Money.* 26th ed. Toronto: Charlton International Publishing, Inc., 1977.

Cipolla, Carlo M. *Le avventure della lira.* Milan: Edizioni di Comunitá, 1958.

Craig, William D. *Coins of the World, 1750–1850.* 3rd ed. Edited by Holland Wallace, Racine, Wisc.: Western Publishing Company, Inc., 1976.

———. *Germanic Coinages (Charlemagne through Wilhelm II).* [Mountain View, Calif.:] The Author, 1954.

Davenport, John S. *European Crowns, 1600–1700.* Galesburg, Ill.: The Author, 1974.

[Fonrobert, Jules.] *Die Jules Fonrobert'sche Sammlung überseeischer Münzen und Medaillen.* Bearbeitet von Adolph Weyl. Berlin: Verlag von J. A. Stargardt, 1878; reprint ed., Sepulveda, Calif.: Organization of International Numismatists, 1970.

Gadoury, Victor. *Monnaies françaises, 1789–1977.* Troisième édition, révisée et corrigée. Baden-Baden, W. Ger.: Franz W. Wesel Druckerei und Verlag. 1977.

Gadoury, Victor, and Droulers, Frédéric. *Les monnaies royales françaises de Louis XIII à Louis XVI, 1610–1792.* Monte Carlo: The Authors, 1978.

Gil Farrés, Octavio. *Historia de la moneda española.* 2a edición, ampliada. Madrid: The Author, 1976.

Grunthal, Henry. *The Coinage of Peru.* With the collaboration of Dr. Ernesto A. Sellschopp. Frankfurt am Main, W. Ger.: Numismatischer Verlag P. N. Schulten, 1978.

Hanley, Tom, and James, Bill. *Collecting Australian Coins.* Sydney: K. G. Murray Publishing Company Pty. Ltd., n.d.

Harris, Robert P. *Guidebook of Russian Coins, 1725 to 1970.* Santa Cruz, Calif.: Bonanza Press, 1971.

Hobson, Burton. *Catalogue of Scandinavian Coins.* New York: Sterling Publishing Co., Inc., 1970.

Krause, Chester L., and Mishler, Clifford. *Standard Catalog of World Coins.* 6th ed. Iola, Wisc.: Krause Publications, 1979.

Minners, Howard A. "The Origin of the Silver Taler," in *Actes de 8ème Congrès Internationale de Numismatique.* Paris: Association Internationale de Numismates Professionneles, 1976, pp. 605–29.

Muntoni, Francesco. *Le monete dei Papi e degli Stati Pontifici.* 4 vols. Rome: P. & P. Santamaria, 1972–1973.

Pradeau, Alberto Francisco. *Historia numismática de México, de 1823 a 1950.* 3 vols. Mexico City: Sociedad Numismática de México, 1957–1961.

———. *Historia numismática de México. Desde la época precortesiana hasta 1823.* Traducida, corregida y aumentada por Román Beltrán Martínez. Mexico City: Banco de México, S.A., 1950.

Pridmore, F. *The Coins of the British Commonwealth of Nations.* Vol. 1–. London: Spink & Son Ltd., 1960–.

Remick, Jerome, *et al. The Guide Book and Catalogue of British Commonwealth Coins, 1649–1971.* 3rd ed. Winnepeg, Can.: Regency Coin and Stamp Co. Ltd., 1971.

Robinson, Brian. *The Royal Maundy.* London: Kaye & Ward, 1977.

Rulau, Russell, and Hook, Mary Jane. *Modern*

World Mint Marks. 2nd ed. Sidney, Ohio: The
Sidney Printing & Publishing Company,
1970.

Seaby, Peter, and Purvey, Frank, eds. *Standard
Catalogue of British Coins. Vol. 1: Coins of En-
gland and the United Kingdom.* 16th ed., rev.
London: Seaby Publications Ltd., 1978.

Skinner, Dion H. *Rennicks Australian Coin and
Banknote Guide.* 9th ed. North Adelaide, Australia: Owl Pty. Ltd., 1975.

Sobrino, José Manuel. *La moneda mexicana: su historia.* Mexico City: Banco de México, S.A.
1972.

Spassky, I. G. *The Russian Monetary System.* Translated by Z. I. Goroshina. Revised by L. S. Forrer. Revised and enlarged edition. Amsterdam: Jacques Schulman N. V., 1967.

Sutherland, C. H. V. *English Coinage, 600–1900.*
London: B. T. Batsford Ltd., 1973.

Went, Arthur E. J. "King James II's Money of
Necessity." *Numismatic Scrapbook Magazine* 36,
418 (December 1970), pp. 1548–50.

UNITED STATES OF AMERICA

Adams, Edgar H. *Private Gold Coinage of California.* Brooklyn, N.Y.: The Author, 1913.

Bowers, Q. David. *The History of United States
Coinage as Illustrated by the Garrett Collection.*
Los Angeles: Bowers & Ruddy Galleries,
Inc., 1979.

Breen, Walter. *Walter Breen's Encyclopedia of
United States and Colonial Proof Coins, 1722–
1977.* New York: F.C.I. Press, Inc., 1977.

Bressett, Ken, and Kosoff, A., eds. and comps.
*The Official American Numismatic Association
Grading Standards for United States Coins.* Colorado Springs: American Numismatic Association, 1977.

Crosby, Sylvester S. *The Early Coins of America.*
Boston: The Author, 1875; reprint ed., Lawrence, Mass.: Quarterman Publications, Inc.,
1974.

Judd. J. Hewitt. *United States Pattern, Experimental
and Trial Pieces.* 6th ed. Racine, Wisc.: Western Publishing Company, Inc., 1977.

Kessler, Alan. *The Fugio Coppers.* Newtonville,
Mass.: Colony Coin Co., 1976.

Massey, J. Earl. *America's Money.* New York:
Thomas Y. Crowell Company, 1968.

Newman, Eric P., and Bressett, Kenneth E. *The
Fantastic 1804 Dollar.* Racine, Wisc.: Whitman
Publishing Company, 1962.

Newman, Eric P., and Doty, Richard G., eds.
Studies on Money in Early America. New York:
American Numismatic Society, 1976.

Noe, Sydney P. *The Silver Coinage of Massachusetts.*
Lawrence, Mass.: Quarterman Publications,
Inc., 1973.

Reed, Mort. *Cowles Complete Encyclopedia of U.S.
Coins.* New York: Cowles Book Company,
Inc., 1969.

Ruddy, James F. *New Photograde: A Photographic
Grading Guide for United States Coins.* Los Angeles: Bowers & Ruddy Galleries, Inc., 1979.

Schilke, Oscar G., and Solomon, Raphael E.
America's Foreign Coins. New York: The Coin
and Currency Institute, 1964.

Sheldon, William H. *Early American Cents, 1793–
1814.* New York: Harper & Brothers, 1949.

[Taxay, Don.] *The Comprehensive Catalogue and
Encyclopedia of United States Coins.* 2nd ed. Revised by Joseph H. Rose and Howard Hazle-
corn. New York: Scott Publishing Co., 1976.

———. *An Illustrated History of U.S. Commemorative Coinage.* New York: Arco Publishing
Company, Inc., 1967.

———. *Money of the American Indians.* New York:
Nummus Press, 1970.

———. *The U.S. Mint and Coinage.* New York:
Arco Publishing Company, Inc., 1966.

Van Allen, Leroy C., and Mallis, A. George. *The
Comprehensive Catalogue and Encyclopedia of
U.S. Morgan and Peace Silver Dollars.* Revised
edition of *Guide to Morgan and Peace Dollars.*
New York: FCI Press and ARCO, 1976.

Yeoman, R. S. *A Guide Book of United States Coins.*
Edited by Kenneth Bressett. 34th rev. ed.,
Racine, Wisc.: Western Publishing Company,
Inc., 1980.

INDIA—ISLAMIC

Bates, Michael L. "Islamic Numismatics." *Middle
East Studies Association Bulletin* 12, 2 (May
1978), pp. 1–16; 12, 3 (December 1978), pp.
2–18; 13, 1 (July 1979), pp. 3–21; 13, 2 (December 1979), pp. 1–9.

Catalogue of Oriental Coins in the British Museum.
10 vols. London: British Museum, Department of Coins and Medals, 1875–1890.

Gupta, Parmeshwari Lal. *Coins.* New Delhi: National Book Trust, India, 1969.

———. *Punch-Marked Coins in the Andhra Pradesh Government Museum.* Andhra Pradesh

Government Museum Series, no. 1. [Hyderabad:] The Government of Andhra Pradesh, 1960.

Hull, Donald B. *Collectors' Guide to Muhammedan Coins of India, 1200 A.D. to 1860 A.D.* [Alhambra, Calif.:] The Author, 1972.

MacKenzie, Kenneth M. "A Tughra Review for Coin Collectors." *World Coins* 9, 105 (September 1972), pp. 1238 ff.; 9, 107 (November 1972), pp. 1438 ff.

——. "Tughras on the Coins of Islamic States." *World Coins* 11, 129 (September 1974), pp. 1654 ff.

Mitchiner, William. *Oriental Coins and their Values: The Ancient and Classical World, 600 B.C.–A.D. 650.* London: Hawkins Publications, 1978.

——. *Oriental Coins and their Values: The World of Islam.* London: Hawkins Publications, 1977.

Plant, Richard J. *Arabic Coins and How to Read Them.* London: B.A. Seaby Ltd., 1973.

Sircar, D.C. *Studies in Indian Coins.* Delhi: Motilal Banarsidass, 1968.

THE FAR EAST

Coole, Arthur Braddan. *Encyclopedia of Chinese Coins.* 6 vols. Vol. 1, Denver, Colo.: The Author, 1967; vols. 2–6, Lawrence, Mass.: Quarterman Publications, Inc., 1972–1976.

Jacobs, Norman, and Vermeule, Cornelius C., III. *Japanese Coinage.* New York: Numismatic Review, 1972.

Kann, E. *Illustrated Catalog of Chinese Coins.* New York: Mint Productions, Inc., 1966.

King, Frank H. H. *Money and Monetary Policy in China, 1845–1895.* Cambridge, Mass.: Harvard University Press, 1965.

Le May, Reginald. *The Coinage of Siam.* Bangkok: The Siam Society, 1932.

Lockhart, James H. Stewart. *The Stewart Lockhart Collection of Chinese Copper Coins.* Royal Asiatic Society, North China Branch; Extra Volume No. 1. Shanghai: Kelly & Walsh, Ltd., 1915.

Mandel, Edgar J. *Cast Coinage of Korea.* Racine, Wisc.: Western Publishing Co., Inc., 1972.

Munro, Neil Gordon. *Coins of Japan.* Yokohama: The Author, 1904.

Polder, Léon van de. "Abridged History of the Copper Coins of Japan." *Transactions of the Asiatic Society of Japan* 19, pt. 2 (May 1891), pp. 419–500.

Schjöth, Fredrik. *Chinese Currency.* Revised and edited by Virgil Hancock. Iola, Wisc.: Krause Publications, Inc., 1965.

Wang, Yü-Ch'üan. *Early Chinese Coinage.* Numismatic Notes and Monographs, no. 122. New York: American Numismatic Society, 1951.

PAPER MONEY

Andersen, Gunnar. *Banknotes.* Copenhagen: Danmarks Nationalbank Banknote Printing Department, 1975.

Angus, Ian. *Paper Money.* New York: St. Martin's Press, 1974.

Barrett, Don C. *The Greenbacks and Resumption of Specie Payments, 1862–1879.* Harvard Economic Studies, vol. 36. Cambridge, Mass.: Harvard University Press, 1931.

Chase, Philip H. *Confederate Treasury Notes.* Philadelphia: The Author, 1947.

Doty, Richard G. *Paper Money of the World.* New York: The Ridge Press and Bantam Books, Inc., 1977.

Friedberg, Robert. *Paper Money of the United States.* 9th ed. Revised by Arthur L. Friedberg and Ira S. Friedberg. New York: The Coin and Currency Institute, Inc., 1978.

Galetovic M., José, and Benavides T., Hector R. *Billetes de Chile: catálogo ilustrado.* Santiago, Chile: José Galetovic M., Editor, 1973.

Hessler, Gene. *The Comprehensive Catalogue of U.S. Paper Money.* Rev. ed. Chicago: Henry Regnery Company, 1977.

——. *U.S. Essay, Proof and Specimen Notes.* Portage, Ohio: BNR Press, 1979.

Jaksch, Karl, and Pick, Albert. *Katalog des Österreichischen Notgeldes, 1916–1921.* 2. Auflage. Berlin: Verlag Pröh, 1977.

Keller, Arnold. *Das deutsche Notgeld von 1914.* 2 vols. 2. Auflage. Berlin/Wittenau: The Author, 1956; reprint ed., Munich, W. Ger.: Battenberg Verlag, 1976. (Keller published catalogues on most aspects of German notgeld in the 1950s; Battenberg Verlag has reprinted these works, with illustrations.)

Newman, Eric P. *The Early Paper Money of America.* Bicentennial edition. Racine, Wisc.: Western Publishing Company, Inc., 1976.

O'Donnell, Chuck. *The Standard Handbook of Modern U.S. Paper Money.* 6th ed. Philadelphia: Harry J. Forman, Inc., 1977.

Pick, Albert. *Standard Catalog of World Paper Money.* 3rd ed. Iola, Wisc.: Krause Publications; Munich, W. Ger.: Battenberg Verlag, 1980.

Schwan, C. Frederick, and Boling, Joseph E. *World War II Military Currency*. Portage, Ohio: BNR Press, 1978.

Shafer, Neil, *A Guide Book of Modern United States Currency*. 8th ed. Racine, Wisc.: Western Publishing Co., Inc., 1979.

——. *Let's Collect Paper Money!* Racine, Wisc.: Western Publishing Co., Inc., 1976.

Vort-Ronald, Michael P. *Australian Banknotes*. Whyalla Norrie, Australia: The Author, 1979.

Warns, M. Owen, ed. *The National Bank Note Issues of 1929–1935*. [N.P.]: The Society of Paper Money Collectors, 1970.

TOKENS

[Atwood, Roland C.] *Atwood's Catalogue of United States and Canadian Transportation Tokens*. 3rd ed. Boston: American Vecturist Association, 1970.

[——.] *Atwood's Catalogue of United States and Canadian Transportation Tokens*. 3rd ed. 1977 supplement. Boston: American Vecturist Association, 1977.

Bailey, Clement F. "Dr. Samuel Higley and his Coppers." *The Numismatist* 89, 9 (September 1976), pp. 1955–66.

Bell, R. C. *Commercial Coins, 1787–1804*. Newcastle upon Tyne, Eng.: Corbitt & Hunter Ltd., 1963.

——. *Copper Commercial Coins, 1811–1819*. Newcastle upon Tyne, Eng.: Corbitt & Hunter Ltd., 1964.

Dalton R., and Hamer, S. H. *The Provincial Token-Coinage of the 18th Century, Illustrated*. [Bristol, Eng.: The Authors, 1910–1918]; reprint ed., Stow, Mass.: A. D. Hoch, 1967.

Davis, W. J. *The Nineteenth Century Token Coinage of Great Britain, Ireland, the Channel Islands and the Isle of Man*. London: Spink and Son, 1904.

Fisher, Alan S. "Hard Times Tokens: The Legacy of Jackson and Van Buren." *The Numismatist* 91, 8 (August 1978), pp. 1573–83.

Fuld, George, and Fuld, Melvin. *Patriotic Civil War Tokens*. 3rd ed., rev. Racine, Wisc.: Whitman Publishing Company, 1965.

——. *U.S. Civil War Store Cards*. 2nd ed. Lawrence, Mass.: Quarterman Publications, Inc., 1975.

Hudson, Thomas. *Guide Book of Wooden Money*.

6th ed. Gardena, Calif.: Payne Publishing Company, 1966.

Lamb, Robert A. *Catalogue of German War Tokens. The Municipal Issues, 1914–1921*. Rev. ed. Tucson, Ariz.: The Author, 1966.

Low, Lyman Haynes. *Hard Times Tokens*. 2nd ed., revised and enlarged. New York: The Author, 1899.

Smith, Kenneth E. *Catalogue of World Transportation Tokens and Passes, except North America*. Redondo Beach, Calif.: The Author, 1967.

Trowbridge, C. O., and Wood, Howland. "Sutlers' Checks Used in the Federal Army During the Civil War." *American Journal of Numismatics* 38, 1 (July 1903), pp. 23–26; 38, 2 (October 1903), pp. 56–59; 38, 3 (January 1904), pp. 82–85.

Upton, Richard, ed. *Emergency Coins of Germany. Metal and Porcelain, 1914–1923*. [Pimento, Ind.:] Emergency Money Society, 1970.

Whiting, J. R. S. *Trade Tokens: A Social and Economic History*. Newton Abbot, Eng.: David & Charles, 1971.

Wood, Howland. "Paper Money Issued by Sutlers in the Federal Armies During the Civil War." *American Journal of Numismatics* 47 (1913), pp. 164–66.

MEDALS

Forrer, L. *Biographical Dictionary of Medallists*. 8 vols. London: Spink & Son Ltd., 1902–1930.

Goldscheider, Ludwig, ed. *Unknown Renaissance Portraits*. London: Phaidon Press Ltd., 1952.

Hibler, Harold E., and Kappen, Charles V. *So-called Dollars*. New York: The Coin and Currency Institute, 1963.

Hill, George. *Medals of the Renaissance*. Revised and enlarged by Graham Pollard. London: British Museum Publications Ltd., 1978.

Metcalf, William E. *Roman Medallions*. New York: American Numismatic Society, 1979.

Toynbee, Jocelyn M. C. *Roman Medallions*. Numismatic Studies, no. 5. New York: American Numismatic Society, 1944.

Whiting, J. R. S. *Commemorative Medals*. Newton Abbot, Eng.: David & Charles, 1972.

DECORATIONS

Angus, Ian. *Medals and Decorations*. New York: St. Martin's Press, 1973.

Dorling, H. Taprell, and Guille, L. F. *Ribbons and Medals*. Rev. ed. London: George Philip & Son Ltd., 1960.

Hieronymussen, Paul. *Orders and Decorations of Europe in Color*. Translated by Christine Crowley. New York: Macmillan Publishing Co., Inc., 1967.

Měřička, Václav. *Orders and Decorations*. Translated by Berta Golová. Edited by Dermot Morrah. London: Paul Hamlyn Ltd., 1967.

Risk, James Charles. *British Orders and Decorations*. London: J. B. Hayward & Son, 1973.

Werlich, Robert. *Orders and Decorations of All Nations*. 2nd ed. Washington: Quaker Press, 1974.

MINT TECHNOLOGY AND ERRORS

Bausher, Jess, and Dolan, Charles. *It's Only Money! (A Comedy of Errors)*. Birdsboro, Penn.: Numismatic Enterprises, Inc., 1966.

Becker, Thomas W. *The Coin Makers*. Garden City, N.Y.: Doubleday & Company, Inc. 1969.

Breen, Walter. *The Minting Process. How Coins Are Made and Mismade*. Beverly Hills, Calif.: American Institute of Professional Numismatists, 1970.

Dickinson, H. W. *Matthew Boulton*. Cambridge, Eng.: University Press, 1937.

Durán, Rafael. "La acuñación en el molino de la ceca de Segovia." *Numisma* 5, 14 (January–March 1955), pp. 119–58.

Marvin, Paul, and Margolis, Arnold. *The Design Cud*. [VanWert, Ohio:] The Authors, 1979.

Moser, Heinz, and Tursky, Heinz. *Die Münzstätte Hall in Tirol, 1477–1665*. Innsbruck, Austria: Verlag Dr. Rudolf Erhard, 1977.

Spadone, F. G. *Major Variety—Oddity Guide of United States Coins*. 7th ed. Florence, Ala.: ANCO, 1977.

Taxay, Don. *Counterfeit, Mis-Struck, and Unofficial U.S. Coins*. New York: Arco Publishing Company, Inc., 1963.

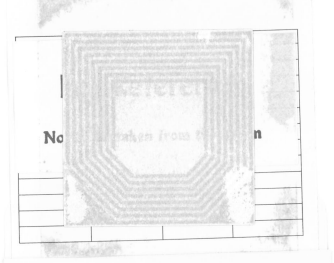